Classical World Literatures

Sino-Japanese and Greco-Roman Comparisons

WIEBKE DENECKE

OXFORD
UNIVERSITY PRESS

OXFORD
UNIVERSITY PRESS

Oxford University Press is a department of the University of Oxford.
It furthers the University's objective of excellence in research, scholarship,
and education by publishing worldwide.

Oxford   New York
Auckland   Cape Town   Dar es Salaam   Hong Kong   Karachi
Kuala Lumpur   Madrid   Melbourne   Mexico City   Nairobi
New Delhi   Shanghai   Taipei   Toronto

With offices in
Argentina   Austria   Brazil   Chile   Czech Republic   France   Greece
Guatemala   Hungary   Italy   Japan   Poland   Portugal   Singapore
South Korea   Switzerland   Thailand   Turkey   Ukraine   Vietnam

Oxford is a registered trademark of Oxford University Press
in the UK and certain other countries.

Published in the United States of America by
Oxford University Press
198 Madison Avenue, New York, NY 10016

Library of Congress Cataloging-in-Publication Data
Denecke, Wiebke.
Classical world literatures : Sino-Japanese and Greco-Roman comparisons / Wiebke Denecke.
pages. cm.
ISBN 978-0-19-997184-8
1. Classical literature—History and criticism.   2. East Asian literature—History
and criticism.   I. Title.
PA3010.D46 2013
809—dc23
2012046082

9 8 7 6 5 4 3 2 1
Printed in the United States of America
on acid-free paper

Für Z
fortunati amoris divinatione
denn er hat seinen Engeln befohlen
daß sie dich behüten
auf allen deinen Wegen

CONTENTS

Acknowledgments   ix

Introduction   1

CHAPTER 1   Setting the Stage: Sino-Japanese and Greco-Roman Constellations   20

CHAPTER 2   Starting *avant la lettre*: An Essay on How to Tell the Beginnings of Literature and Eloquence   62

CHAPTER 3   Latecomers: Of Ornament, Simplicity, and Decline   81

CHAPTER 4   City-Building or Writing? How Aeneas and Prince Shōtoku Made Rome and Japan   120

CHAPTER 5   Rome and Kyoto: Capitals, Genres, Gender   154

CHAPTER 6   Poetry in Exile: Sugawara no Michizane and Ovid   203

CHAPTER 7   Satire in Foreign Attire: The Ambivalences of Learning in Late Antiquity and Medieval Japan   234

CHAPTER 8   The Synoptic Machine: Sino-Japanese and Greco-Roman Juxtapositions   265

EPILOGUE   Beyond the Comforts of Influence: Deep Comparisons   289

Bibliography   301

Index   327

ACKNOWLEDGMENTS

This book has taken time and courage. I have been blessed with people around me who made sure that neither was in short supply. Without them I could have never embarked on this ambitious project. I had some fairly circumscribed China- and Japan-related book projects lined up, when suddenly opportunity struck in 2004: a long-awaited and eye-opening trip to Greece with my husband Zolti and my parents, and a conference on "transcultural literary history" hosted by a Swedish research group at Villa Brevik outside of Stockholm, where I presented *faute de mieux* on early Japanese and Latin attempts at writing literary history, made me realize that this book needed to be written. I found myself wanting to make it up to my formidable teachers of Latin and Greek at the humanistic "Max-Planck Gymnasium" in my hometown of Göttingen who taught me the love of grammar and Greek and Latin literature from childhood, before I could even utter a word in a foreign language other than my native German: the late Fritz Tamm, Helga Ströhlein, Oscar Mattner, Wolfgang Fauth, and Otta Wenskus. I felt I had let them down, having drifted to studies of classical China and Japan instead of staying with my passionate interests in Classical Antiquity.

But the idea was not enough. I needed encouragement to work on the com- parison of the Sino-Japanese and Greco-Roman cultural constellations for which I could not look to any previous pioneering scholarship. Throughout, Zolti was the most vigorous fan of the project; David Damrosch an enthusiastic supporter when the road was bumpy; Michael Puett an ever-inspiring advocate of bold com- parative work; and the positive response to the earliest seed chapters from Wai-yee Li, Katharina Volk, and Stephen Owen gave me further confidence that this could work. A conference on "*Translatio:* Translation and Cultural Appropriation in the Ancient World," which David and I organized at Columbia University in 2006, confirmed the impression that scholars of Greco-Roman, Near Eastern and Indian antiquities were all too eager to ask a new set of compelling comparative ques- tions. An emerging wave seemed under way.

Graced with support on so many fronts, I was lucky to spend time in stimulat- ing communities that allowed me to devote myself to the project. The period at the Society of Fellows at Columbia University, under the directorship of David Johnston, proved crucial to the initial phase of hunting and gathering. My time as a fellow at the Princeton Institute for Advanced Study thanks to the Mellon Foundation pushed the project to a new level. Thanks go to Provost Liz Boylan and my department chair Rachel McDermott for allowing me that time away from Barnard College. Conversations with Nicola di Cosmo, Heinrich von Staden, Caroline Bynum, Dan Potts, Denis Feeney, and Ben Elman led the way. I can only apologize to Patricia Crone for not following her urgent prodding to introduce a Persian-Arabic perspective into my epilogue; but the instructive resonances and divergences with the Sino-Japanese and Greco-Roman constellations remain within my collateral vision. Satō Michio's continuous support through a four-year long "Center of Excellence" project at Keiō University in Tokyo gave me the opportunity to dive into a number of challenging *kanbun* texts. Suzuki Sadami's hosting at the International Research Center of Japanese Studies (Nichibunken) in Kyoto under the auspices of a Japan foundation fellowship allowed a previous Tokyo-ite immersion in the old capital and its research communities. And a stay at the American Academy in Rome, thanks to Carmela Vircillo Franklin, let me change roles and gaze back from Rome to Kyoto.

This book has benefited from the inspiration of a few projects that unfolded in parallel: the work with Pete Simon, Martin Puchner, and our small group of editors on the *Norton Anthology of World Literature* (3rd edition, 2012) was a memorable journey of comparably daunting scope. Albert Hoffstädt's inspired support at Brill Publishers for the new *East Asian Comparative Literature and Culture* book series, which Zhang Longxi and myself are editing, helped establish a new venue for cross-cultural comparative studies with an East Asian component, which will hopefully invite further conversations that I try to start in this book. Discussions and workshops with my colleague Sunil Sharma and the core group of our " Boston University Comparative Studies of the Premodern World Initiative" have been a great foyer for enterprising comparative thinking and collaboration. I am pleased to be part of the lively crowd of the young Modern Languages & Comparative Literature Department at BU: William Waters, Pat Johnson, and Gina Sapiro gave me a warmest welcome when I joined the faculty in 2010; the collegial ambiance and day-to-day collaboration with my colleagues Cathy Yeh, Sarah Frederick, Keith Vincent, Yoon Sun Yang, Huang Weijia, Anna Elliott, Sunil Sharma, Margaret Litvin, William Waters, Peter Schwartz, Gisela Hoecherl-Alden, Abigail Gillman, and Robert Richardson has been a pleasure.

I am greatly indebted to those who volunteered to read draft chapters and offered ample wise advice and welcome correction: Lewis Cook, Kathryn Gutzwiller, Peter Kornicki, Wai-yee Li, Stephen Owen, and James Uden. David Damrosch and Denis Feeney were infinitely generous with their time, reading and thinking through incarnations of the entire manuscript. I have equally benefited from valuable discussions about specific points in the manuscript with Haruo Shirane, Satō Michio, Kōno Kimiko, Kannotō Akio, Yoshihara Hiroto, Uchida Mioko, Hatooka Akira, Yamamoto Tokurō, Shinma Kazuyoshi, and Wang Yong.

The hosts and audiences on the occasion of lectures at Columbia University, Zhejiang Gongshang University (Hangzhou), University of Venice, Keiō

University, Meisei University (Tokyo), Princeton University, Harvard University, Yale University, University of Hong Kong, Nichibunken (Kyoto), Kansai University (Osaka), and Boston University have provided great food for thought. And conferences and panels at various AAS and ACLA Annual Meetings and EAJS conventions, at Harvard University, Fudan University (Shanghai), Boston University, and Tsinghua University (Beijing) have helped me place my project into ever-new frames and stimulating conversations.

I could have accomplished nothing without the lifeline of this project: the various libraries at Harvard, Columbia, Princeton, Keiō, Nichibunken, and Waseda University (Tokyo). I am most grateful for the great assistance I received from patient librarians in these various places. They helped with books, materials, smiles, and everyday good humor.

The publication of this book would have been considerably delayed without the tireless and clever help of Sumiyoshi Tomohiko (Shidō bunko, Keiō Institute of Oriental Classics) and Iwasaki Yuko in gathering some tough permissions for visuals. Jeff Henderson, Paul Taylor (Warburg Institute), Sandy Paul (Trinity College Library, Cambridge), and Peter Green have also greatly facilitated the permissions process. Thanks go to Daniel Poch and Dustin Dixon for their meticulous help with proofreading. I am also truly grateful to Bonnie Costello and the Boston University Center for the Humanities who most generously supported this project with a publication production grant.

This book does not fit any clear disciplinary or thematic categories in the publishing world. I was all the more impressed with Stefan Vranka's careful initial probing into the manuscript and enthusiastic support for its publication with Oxford University Press. His broad vision, keen judgment, creative mind, and exemplary efficiency never fail to surprise me. Working with his expert assistant, Sarah Pirovitz, has been a joy. And I am grateful for the indefatigable efforts Stacey Victor and Molly Morrison devoted to the careful production of this book.

Lastly, I would like to thank two more unpredictable forces for their gracious support: the anonymous reviewers for their strong advocacy of this project and their offering of immensely helpful and extensive comments; and our son Simon for patiently waiting for mommy to finish her manuscript before taking his resolute dive out into this wondrous world.

Boston, May 2013

Classical World Literatures

1. The Relative Age of Cultures

Like people in a community, cultures in contact have relative ages. A community might respect older people's life experience and wisdom or consider them a reactionary burden to society. In turn, youth can be the blessed phase of bold courage and innovation or the period of life when everything that is dubious about human beings—blind ignorance, unbridled libido, oblivious disdain for the voice of reason and wisdom of experience—bursts out and threatens a community's cherished values. Regardless of particular images of youth or old age, the relative age of people and cultures plays out on the grounds of seniority and inferiority, cultural and political capital, expectations of rise and decline, novelty and tradition. The youth of the United States of America is the closest site in today's world that allows us to experience the drama of the relative age of cultures. And in the decades to come the economic and political *tête-à-tête* between the young America and the newly-young age-old China will not just prove decisive for our daily lives, but also provide a monumental spectacle for the study of the relative age of cultures and the purposes it can serve.

This seems to be an apt moment to turn our gaze back by a few millennia and reflect on some particular ways in which the drama of relative age played out in early East Asia and the Ancient Mediterranean, in particular in Early Japan and in Ancient Rome. This book explores how writers of younger cultures were affected by the presence of what we will call an older "reference culture." How did Latin and Early Japanese authors write their own literature through and against their cultural models of Greece and China? How did authors of the younger cultures respond to the challenge of appropriating foreign precedents of genres and literary forms, rhetorical sophistication and poetological reflection, conceptual vocabulary and lexical imagination for their writing in a different language and within new political and cultural contexts? How did they navigate between the attractions of cultural self-colonization, which promised access to a realm of venerable refinement and sophistication of the reference culture, and the desire for self-assertion fueled by cultural pride and anxious competition for recognition?

Unlike with individual people's minds in a community, there is of course no such thing as an Ancient Japanese or Roman collective consciousness vis-à-vis the older Chinese or Greek civilizations. Perspectives on the reference cultures were manifold and contradictory; and the political and cultural constellation between China and Japan and between Greece and Rome underwent significant changes throughout the periods considered in this book, namely Ancient Japan during the Nara (710–784) and Heian Periods (794–1185), and Ancient Rome from the Middle Republic of the third century BCE to the Late Roman empire of the fifth century CE. In particular, the Greco-Roman constellation changed drastically during the first centuries of Roman literary production. A number of Roman writers of the third and second centuries BCE were Greek or Greek-speaking, while living on the Italic peninsula that was rapidly becoming the master of the Mediterranean; by the first century BCE the Greek motherland and many Hellenized areas of the Mediterranean were under Roman rule and Greece had to deal with its sudden political submission to what had once only been a primitive polity in the Italic area of Latium, negligible in the greater scheme of powerful Hellenistic states dominating the Eastern and Western Mediterranean.

The Greeks had not always been older. In Plato's dialogue *Timaeus* they seemed like innocent infants to Egyptian priests:

> Then one of the priests, a very old man, said: "Solon, Solon, you Greeks never grow up. There isn't an old man among you." "What do you mean?" Solon replied. "None of you have mature minds," the priest replied. "You have no ancient tradition to imbue your minds with old beliefs and with understanding aged by time."[1]

This is how an aged Egyptian priest scolds Solon, one of the Greek Seven Sages, when Solon visits the city of Sais in Egypt and has little to offer when asked to tell his Egyptian hosts about the Greek past. What the Greek Solon cannot deliver, the Egyptian priest does: he divulges to Solon the glorious past of the city of Athens, saying that Athens fought back the powerful dynasty of the sunken island of Atlantis. In so doing, it saved not just itself, but most of the Mediterranean, even up to Egypt, from being enslaved by the Atlantides. Thus, according to the Egyptian priest, Athens has a glorious past, even if Greeks cannot remember it. This is because, unlike Egypt, where historical records survive intact, Greece and the rest of the world were regularly conflagrated by fires and deluges that destroyed all previous records of civilization. In the *Timaeus* the old Critias, possibly modeled on Plato's great-grandfather, relates how the "hieroglyphic record" saved Athens' unknown past from oblivion.

The main subject of discussion in the *Timaeus* is the origin of the cosmos; and Critias's account of Solon's experiences in Egypt is only a prelude to the philosopher Timaeus's long exposition of the generation of the world and humankind.[2]

---

[1] *Timaeus* 22b. Translation from Waterfield 2008, 9. καί τινα εἰπεῖν τῶν ἱερέων εὖ μάλα παλαιόν· 'ὦ Σόλων, Σόλων, Ἕλληνες ἀεὶ παῖδές ἐστε, γέρων δὲ Ἕλλην οὐκ ἔστιν.' ἀκούσας οὖν, 'πῶς τί τοῦτο λέγεις;' φάναι. 'νέοι ἐστέ,' εἰπεῖν, 'τὰς ψυχὰς πάντες· οὐδεμίαν γὰρ ἐν αὐταῖς ἔχετε δι' ἀρχαίαν ἀκοὴν παλαιὰν δόξαν οὐδὲ μάθημα χρόνῳ πολιὸν οὐδέν.
[2] For the complex play with beginnings in the dialogue, see Sallis 1999.

But the two accounts are connected by the vertiginous trompe l'oeil of relative time scales through which Plato manages to give Greece and Athens old pedigree, despite the Egyptian priest's lament over their childish ignorance. Consider the telescopic (or should we say, teletemporal?) setup of Solon's account of his experiences in Egypt: On the day of the festival for the Egyptian goddess Neith, identified with the Greek Athena, a very old Egyptian priest tells young Solon a tale about the pre-history of Athens, which Solon later in life tells Critias, the young son of a friend of his; the very same Critias at the age of ninety tells this to his ten-year-old grandson Critias during a festival that features competitions in poetry recitation. It is this child Critias who in old age relates the incident to Socrates as a speaker in Plato's *Timaeus*. With generous counting, Solon's tale about the all-too-youthful Greeks is about half a dozen generations old by the time it is imparted to its listeners. Thus, Plato's lengthy explication of the transmission of the story becomes structural evidence of Greece's deep historical memory, which competes with the literal grain of the story and seems to confer the prize of wisdom and old age on Egypt.

Replacement or subtle transposition is one of the key procedures in *Timaeus*. There is a dynamic of transposition between Egypt and Greece, Athena's city of Sais, and Athena's Athens, an Egyptian priest and a Greek sage. Then there is the transposition of a Socratic tale into one told by Critias: we learn in the *Timaeus* that Socrates had sketched his ideal state just a day before (in what is known as Plato's *Republic*) and that Socrates expected to be paid back for his efforts, asking his interlocutors to apply his outlines of an ideal state to a concrete city; it is no coincidence that the *Timaeus* is set during the Panathenaic Games, an annual festival celebrating the goddess Athena, and that Critias complies with something like a praise hymn to Athena and Athens, the hitherto unknown savior of the world from Atlantic military aggression.

Lastly, there is a seemingly ingenuous replacement of bad imitative with good philosophical Platonic poetry: Plato replaces his attack on Homer and on poetry as an "imitative," deceptive art, which Socrates had advanced in the last book of the *Republic,* with a praise of Solon as a poet in the *Timaeus*. Critias's grandfather claims that Solon would have been more famous than Homer or Hesiod had he only had the time to frame his experiences in Egypt in poetry. Although the myth of Atlantis has captured the imagination of generations of readers, since the first commentaries on it were written in the Early Academy, and persists in our mapping of the world, Plato is our single source for the tale of Solon and Atlantis. That he relates it in a philosophical dialogue, filling in for the poetry Solon did not get to write, shows that the *Timaeus* is not just a time-tale about the relative age of cultures, Egyptian and Greek, but also about the relative age of forms of wisdom, older poetry and younger philosophy.

Plato's *Timaeus* and Critias's hymn to pre-deluge Athens, as recovered from Egypt, is a relentlessly suggestive tale and a virtuosic exercise in trying to "out-past" its rival, as Eviatar Zerubavel has called the attempt to make one tradition or culture look older than the others. In *Caesar's Calendar: Ancient Time and the Beginnings of History* Denis Feeney masterfully traces the politics of time and "out-pasting" in the Ancient Mediterranean.[3] At first sight Critias has Egypt "out-past" Athens, but Plato has Athens also "out-past" Egypt. "Out-pasting" is a reaction to the perception of "historical flatness," the experience through cultural contact that one's own culture lacks the historical depth available to the members of an older reference culture.

2. Reference Cultures

I will use the term "reference culture" to describe the roles that the older cultures of China and Greece played in the literary cultures of early Japan and ancient Rome. Unfortunately, our current conceptual vocabulary for describing cross-cultural processes often fails to render important characteristics in the Sino-Japanese and Greco-Roman cultural constellations. The metaphorical talk of "mother" and "daughter" cultures, probably inspired by the life sciences, leaves us wondering about the absence of the *patria*, while also reducing the process of active cultural appropriation to a process of biological replication. It encourages old and pervasive prejudices against Rome and Japan as cultures lacking creative independence and originality. The curse of the imitative has haunted studies of Japanese and Roman culture in equal measure, though to different effect. Latinists are scholars of a long-lost empire that existed on distant territory (at least for American Latinists) and are part of a global community of scholars in various countries of Europe and North America, each with more or less legitimate national traditions of Classical and Latin studies. Arguments about the originality of Roman culture or lack thereof seem to be part of the teasing between Hellenists and Latinists and a function of professional pride, but they can only step on long-rotten toes.

Japan, in contrast, is a living nation state still headed by an imperial family that administers the heritage of a continuous imperial tradition, presumably stretching back more than two-and-a-half millennia. Claims to "Japanese uniqueness," an intellectual club against the prejudice of a lack of originality, have survived from the imperialist period into the postwar era.[4] Japanese scholars growing up in the fabric of Japanese society and researching their own national literary tradition are indirectly affected by this cultural framework and produce undoubtedly the largest part of research on Japanese literature in the world. Scholars outside Japan can contribute to the rich field of "national literary studies" (*kokubungaku* 国文学), but the center of authority in the field of Japanese literature is unmistakably Japan, not a transnational set of claimants that accepts each other on quite equal terms, as is the case with the field of Classics in Europe and the West. Thus, the curse of the imitative has haunted Latinists more than Japanese literature scholars, who

---

[3] Feeney describes in particular how the synoptic time-tables in works by the church fathers Eusebius and Jerome showed graphically that Hebrew and Asiatic history reached much further back than pagan Greek and Roman history. Feeney 2007, 29. Feeney's inspired study of how the process of synchronizing—matching important events in one locale with those in another—created shared history, and shared cultural identity (as well as competition over both) in the Hellenistic Mediterranean and in Rome has much to say about the question of relative age in general.
[4] For an analysis of the symptoms and implications of the debates around Japanese uniqueness, see Dale 1986.

can naturally rely on their national cultural confidence. But for both fields the terms "mother" and "daughter" cultures, though they sound cozy, direct our view on the Sino-Japanese and Greco-Roman constellation in an unproductive direction, suggesting a passive and imitative reception rather than active and creative appropriation of the reference culture.

Many studies of intercultural communication and acculturation processes rely on the concepts of "source culture" and "host/target culture," borrowed from linguistics and translation studies. If applied to the translation of a text from a "source language" (SL) into a "target language" (TL) the terms are useful, because they refer to two concrete linguistic and physical objects and to the one specific moment in time when somebody consciously transfers, in whatever slavishly literal or creatively imagined way, an extant original set of sentences into a new language, producing a new set of sentences. However, once the linguistic transposition process is applied metaphorically to cultural *translatio* the terms fail to describe what is most fascinating about the process of cultural appropriation and acculturation. There is no one source or origin, in double ways: There was no essential "source China," when rulers and elites from the Japanese archipelago started to model their state more closely on Chinese and Korean precedents from the seventh and eighth centuries onward. What they gathered about "China" was a coincidental mix of traditions picked up from various locales, books, and people during a period of disunion, the Six Dynasties Period (220–589), and the new, ethnically diverse cosmopolitan Tang Empire (618–906). Yet more importantly, what early Japanese extracted from the influx of Chinese books into the archipelago and the direct experience of the very few Japanese who had visited China, and what they then chose to adapt for their own purposes, is yet farther away from any imaginary "source China." There was no singular "source text" for "translators" to work from.

Nor was the "host culture" necessarily a hospitable "host": when a new wave of Hellenistic culture reached Rome due to its conquest in the Eastern Mediterranean in the second century BCE, many Romans, such as Cato the Elder, made vehement arguments against "hosting" it. They were conscientious objectors against the host role in their public poise, but they were themselves already heavily Hellenized and had little control over the messy and overwhelming influx of Greek luxury goods, philosophical ideas and technical terms, religious cults, Greek rhetoricians and doctors that changed the face of Roman culture and Roman self-understanding within a few generations. Thus the "host" metaphor vastly downplays two of the most intriguing and tantalizing aspects of cultural contact: the degree of initial resistance to the foreign and the uncannily rapid adoption of the foreign that is soon no longer consciously "hosted," but considered as own. And there was no "target culture" either: Greek immigrants into the Italic peninsula did not "target" Latium and Rome with their cultural influence. Neither did Chinese emperors "target" Japan with a conscious *mission civilisatrice* that would have gone beyond firm conviction that barbarians who were lucky enough to be exposed to the transformative power of Chinese civilization could become cultivated and morally superior individuals and would greatly benefit from cultural contact with China.

Curiously, despite the fact that human relations are at the heart of processes of cultural contact, metaphors drawn from the language of human relations fail to capture crucial aspects of the dynamics of cultural exchange between early Japan and China, and of Greece and Rome, respectively. What then about the concept of "reference culture"? How can it draw out those aspects and allow us to get a more palpable sense of the abstract notion of a "Sino-Japanese constellation" and a comparable "Greco-Roman cultural constellation"? First, there is the legal meaning of "reference," the referral of a matter to a higher legal authority for ultimate decision. Both China and Greece loomed as cultures that not just served as the basis of Japanese and Roman legal culture, but also, metaphorically, had the status of a higher authority, a cultural superego that could be drawn on for one's own justification.

Second, in ethical terms, the association with an older "reference culture" granted a certificate of civilized conduct, much like a "reference letter." Younger cultures would be elevated by their association with an older reference culture and show themselves to be on the side of civilization, not barbarity. When, for example, the Chinese Emperor Xuanzong (685–762) closes a farewell poem addressed to a Japanese ambassador about to return to Japan with, "thanks to this astonishing Confucian gentleman, our royal transformative power will shine brightly abroad,"[5] he makes the Japanese ambassador a flattering compliment, placing him on equal moral ground with Chinese subjects because he has received the benefits of "royal transformative power." In the case of Japan, we can pinpoint when Chinese stopped considering the Japanese simply as one out of the many barbarian states surrounding China. Chinese had associated the Japanese archipelago with *Wo* 倭 (pronounced *Wa* in Japanese), possibly meaning the land of the "dwarf people" for almost half a millennium, but started to use a much more flattering epithet in the early eighth century: *Nihon* 日本, "Root of the Sun." Although *Wa* continued to be used, the new nomenclature signified that the Chinese no longer lumped Japanese together with the dozens of "barbarian" polities that regularly sent ambassadors and paid tribute to the Chinese court, but were now elevating Japan to a Confucian state with Confucian subjects like the ambassador Emperor Xuanzong addressed, who had acquired the values of Chinese civilization.

Third, the concept of a "reference culture" also brings out the material dimension of how Chinese and Greek civilization shaped Japanese and Roman communities and social space. In a social science context, a "reference group" is a control group of individuals with certain behavioral patterns considered normal against which behavioral scientists measure the aberration of social behavior. Of course, neither Japan nor Rome was "aberrant," China or Greece were no absolute golden standard, and there is no figure of a demiurge, the social scientist comparing two groups, who is undertaking his experiments with early Japanese and Ancient Romans. Rather, individuals living in Japanese and Roman society were part of social practices that originated in part in their older "reference cultures" and that profoundly shaped the material landscape they inhabited. The Athenian

---

[5] *Yin jing bi junzi / wanghua yuan zhaozhao* 因驚彼君子・王化遠昭昭 *Quan Tang shiyi* 1, 10241. See also Zhang Buyun 1984, 1–2.

institution of annual ritual events featuring theatrical performances was eventually adopted in Rome and resulted in the construction of Greek-style theaters by the mid-first century BCE.[6] Chinese centralized rule had resulted in a highly compartmentalized, checkerboard structure of Chinese urban centers, and when early Japanese rulers tried to enhance their grip over larger parts of territory through centralization measures, they came to construct capitals based on the model of Chinese capitals such as Chang'an. The checkerboard structure of modern-day Xi'an in China and of Nara and Kyoto can still be enjoyed by the leisurely strolling visitor. Thus, political measures and social practices in the "reference cultures" produced material culture such as cities and theaters, visible "frames of reference," which Japanese and Romans adopted and adapted to their own purposes.

In a fourth, linguistic, sense "reference" means the thing to which a word refers. The word and "signifier" "Rome" refers to the city and "signified" "Rome" in the visible world. The linguistic meaning of "reference" is particularly useful in thinking about younger cultures that develop in close symbiosis with older ones. Beyond the references that authors of the younger culture could make to specific books and texts of the older culture, to which we will turn momentarily, they also developed images of the older culture as an "object reference," an icon often designed to closely converge with or diverge from their own image. In the early modern world of European Rococo a chinoiserie was a decorative element that introduced European reimaginations of Chinese style elements into interior design, furniture, pottery, or garden architecture. The orientalizing wall paintings and porcelains in the Chinese Teahouse that Johann Gottfried Büring constructed for Frederick the Great in the Potsdam palace of Sanssouci were made to please Prussian eyes. Similarly, though called "Pekings," the decorative silken wall screens were produced in Prussian silk factories that had adopted East Asian techniques of silk production to satisfy their domestic demands. The concept of chinoiserie originated in the visual culture of seventeenth- and eighteenth-century Europe, where reports about Chinese arts, philosophy, and politics publicized by missionaries working in China fuelled the emergence of China as a domestic icon. But we could also apply the term to early Japan and speak of chinoiseries in Japan. Early Japanese texts variously show China as an exotic foreign country, as unsurpassed in its authority, or, quite to the contrary, either not comparable to Japan or simply, *as* Japan. When the "reference culture" becomes an "object reference," an icon of sorts, the older culture is not engaged on its own grounds, but staged in a play whose rules the younger cultures determine. In this sense the "reference culture" could become a large-scale iconic signifier in the eyes of the younger cultures' beholders that signified more than any of its actual historical incarnations.[7]

---

[6] There was, of course, a reversal of this process in Rome, after it conquered Greece: Romans introduced features characteristic of the Roman forum and, later, of the Roman imperial cult into the Greek cityscape. See Walker 1997.

[7] For a collection of essays analyzing ways in which certain texts and genres have constructed "China" as an iconic object of knowledge, see Hayot, Saussy, and Yao 2008. The editors of the volume coin the suggestive term "Sinography" for a proposed history of the distinctive constructions of the iconic object "China" in sinology.

Two further connotations of "reference" bring us to this study's specific focus on Japanese and Roman literary cultures. There is the bibliographical dimension of the word "reference," meaning the use of a reference work for study and scholarly verification. Japanese and Roman literary culture relied heavily on the thesaurus of Chinese and Greek literary learning. Young Japanese aristocrats studied the canon of Confucian Classics to derive values of moral behavior and acquire polished eloquence just as adolescent Romans read Homer and the tragic poets to reflect on human conduct and enhance their rhetorical training. Yet more importantly, the canon of the reference culture was not studied as naked text, but read alongside a great variety of scholarly reference works from China and Hellenistic centers of learning.

Lastly, the concept "reference culture" points eloquently to the most microscopic symptoms of cultural intertwinement: allusive "references" that authors of the younger culture make to texts produced by authors of the older reference culture. This more strictly textual aspect of the Sino-Japanese and Greco-Roman relation, which we can capture with terms such as creative emulation, parody, allusion, or, in more recent parlance, intertextuality, has engendered a scholarly field and methodology of its own. Tracking down presumable allusions in Japanese and Roman texts to their Chinese and Greek source of origin has been one of the most fundamental paradigms for textual criticism of Japanese and Latin literature. This scholarly instinct has produced meticulous, impressive commentarial apparatuses and editions. It has added depth to our reading of the Japanese and Roman texts by excavating the layers of echoes from Chinese or Greek texts that a Japanese or Roman author might have intended to underlay his words. At the same time, when focusing on tracking down allusions to their presumed origins in the reference culture without exploring their significance, it can encourage lingering prejudices against Japanese and Roman literatures as mere imitative shadows of their Chinese and Greek sources, a mere locus passivus of their reference culture's locus classicus. Yet, in the past twenty some years allusion as a form of literary inventiveness and creative self-assertion has received much attention, in particular in Latin studies and, to a limited degree, in Japanese literary studies. Literary reception studies are a lion's share of what Japanologists and Latinists have done and do with their texts. Therefore, the concept of a "reference culture," a culture that Japanese and Latin authors point to through an infinite number of allusive vectors, seems especially apt to capture the characteristic nature of the Sino-Japanese and Greco-Roman cultural constellations and their comparability.

It is in particular the bibliographical and literary aspect of "reference" in "reference culture" that distinguishes the Greco-Roman constellation from the engagement between Egypt and Greece, which we touched upon with the *Timaeus*. In Greek writings on Egypt there is much admiration of its ancient civilization and we can see a great scientific and ethnographic curiosity in authors like Herodotus and Diodorus Siculus, Strabo, Plutarch and Iamblichus. Also, after the conquest of Greece by Alexander the Great, Alexandria in Lower Egypt became the scholarly center of the Hellenistic world and its librarians and scholars lived in contemporary Ptolemaic Egypt while working on Greek grammar and producing the foundational editions and commentaries for classical Greek literature. There were even members of the Egyptian priestly elite such as Manetho, Apion, and Horapollon Nilotes, who wrote in Greek while mastering the hieroglyphic, hieratic, and demotic sources of their own tradition. But the Greeks' curiosity was not matched by Egyptian interest in Greek culture. The Egyptians did not even have a precise term for the Greeks, but hieroglyphic texts call them "those who squat in the swamp holes," which was an epithet used for people imagined to live in the extreme North (much as the Greeks would call people living in unknown northern realms "Hyperboreans," "those beyond the North Wind").[8]

It is extraordinary that, as Jan Assmann puts it, "whereas the Greeks showed an eager interest in the culture and the land of Egypt without, however, making the effort to study the language, the Egyptians learned Greek without getting interested in Greek culture and geography."[9] Late texts like the *Corpus Hermeticum,* a collection of apocryphal treatises written in the first three centuries of the Common Era, explain the absence of textual engagement between Egypt and Greece with secrecy commandments:

> Leave this text untranslated, so that these secrets remain hidden from the Greeks and their irreverent, feeble, and orotund speech does not undermine the dignity and vigor of our language and the energy of the names. For the discourse of the Greeks, though outwardly impressive, is empty, and their philosophy is nothing but verbose noise. We by contrast, we employ not words but sounds full of energy.[10]

Attributed to Thoth, the Egyptian god of scribes, and his Greek embodiment Hermes Trismegistus, the *Corpus Hermeticum* sounds at times like a Greek collection with Oriental religious coloration, but at other times like an Egyptian text filled with Neoplatonic thought. This corpus shows probably the most intimate mutual engagement between Greece and Egypt and is so ambivalent that the reader constantly wonders which is the "tenor," and which the "vehicle" of this comparative allegory of Egypt and Greece. The argument against translation in this passage, ironically written in Greek, is an argument about the loss of the magical power of original Egyptian words and names, a prominent concern in cultures with a written tradition and in particular of mystery cults in multilingual contexts. Thus, the passage tells us more about the logic of secrecy in mystery cults and in the milieu of hermetism in Egypt that produced this corpus of texts.[11] It can hardly explain the puzzling disjunction between Greeks' enthusiasm about Egyptian culture and customs, but lack of interest in learning to read Egyptian texts. For the Greeks, Egypt was fascinating and challenging because it was old and venerable but it always remained the distant exotic other. This remarkable feature of the Egypto-Hellenic cultural constellation and the lack of textual engagement with the other culture explains why Egypt never became a "reference culture" in all the

---

[8] Assmann 2005, 41.
[9] Ibid., 41.
[10] Quoted from Assmann 2002, 396.
[11] On the milieu of hermeticism in Egypt and the *Corpus Hermeticum*, see Fowden 1986.

connotations of the term noted above, but always remained on the level of the linguistic "object reference," an Orientalized icon. Traces of this iconization persist to this day in scholarship, museum culture, and fashion.

3. The Comparative Imperative

In Chapter 1 we will examine in more detail the similarities and complicating divergences that justify the comparison between Japanese and Roman literary cultures, which is the focus of this book. We will see that both developed late against the backdrop of the highly sophisticated literature of their reference cultures and reflect on its implications. We will also see that they both started from a scholarly world in their reference cultures that had already produced a canon of literature and learning, when the younger literary cultures emerged, which then came to serve as the basis for elite education in both younger cultures. That the Sino-Japanese and Greco-Roman constellations were radically different in their geopolitical and linguistic dynamic, and that their literary cultures had their distinctive spectrum and hierarchy of genres, complicates our comparison. But it also gives it further depth, because these three dissimilitudes will allow us in the chapters to come to more easily distinguish choices and preferences of particular Japanese and Latin authors from more systematic differences between their texts that are rooted in the fundamental divergences of the Sino-Japanese and Greco-Roman constellations.

The first chapter will provide justification for the comparative project of this book, but the justification of a particular comparison says hardly anything about the motivation for undertaking it. Why plunge into an enterprise covering so many grounds and texts that, on top of being vast, have been so well trodden and scrutinized by such a variety of unrelated specialists that need to be engaged, let alone satisfied? This book tries to open a new field of study, hoping that others will follow. There is an increasing number of inspiring studies comparing the intellectual, cultural, and scientific history of early China and Greece. Karl Jaspers's Axial Age paradigm, which locates the emergence of the world's most important philosophical and religious traditions in India, China, Europe, and the Middle East in the last half of the first millennium BCE, has certainly encouraged such comparative approaches.[12] More recently, historians have started to pursue comparisons of China and Rome in the context of global studies of empire and bureaucratic formations.[13] Yet to my knowledge nobody has so far undertaken an extended study involving literatures of multiple early East Asian and Mediterranean cultures, as this book does in comparatively exploring the Sino-Japanese and Greco-Roman literary constellations.

---

[12] Important edited volumes and monographs on comparisons of Greece and China include Reding 1985, Raphals 1992, Lu 1998, Shankman 2000, and Shankman and Durrant 2002. For comparisons in history of science, see the extensive work of G. E. R. Lloyd, including Lloyd 2005. For a graceful comparative study of Greek and Chinese medicine, see Kuriyama 1999. Beecroft 2010 is an inspiring study comparing early Greek and Chinese poetry through the lens of concepts of authorship.
[13] See for example Scheidel 2009, and Mutschler and Mittag 2008.

My project has been driven by a restless, inevitable urgency, the sense of a comparative imperative that has been imposing itself as the only means to keep intellectually sane in our ever more intertwined global world. It is not simply the product of a liberating intellectual flaneurism that more casual comparative enterprises of previous generations, so I like to imagine, could indulge to freely engage in. But the nostalgia for such comparative flaneurism is much less sweet than today's formidable challenge to conceptualize the tremendous cultural and historical gaps of our economically and physically interconnected world. To understand the urgency of the project a few words about its author's trajectory are in place. As a German citizen I was trained as a Sinologist and Japanologist in Germany, several European countries and the United States, accompanied by periods of study and work in China and Japan. But the first foreign languages I learned when growing up were Latin and Greek. I was about to embark on university studies of Mediterranean antiquity, when a stay in China—in the context of medical studies I pursued in parallel to my degrees in East Asian languages and Greek and Roman philosophy—put me on a path toward premodern China and Japan, and led eventually to PhD studies and teaching posts in East Asian studies in the United States. Many readers of these lines will probably have trajectories that are similarly brimming with exposure to life and work on different continents, and reading, thinking, and arguing in a host of different languages and through the lens of various academic traditions. This holds also true for many of my students, whose family histories, emigration and immigration experiences, and unusual combination of disciplines and languages produce a vertiginously rich "world." Exposure, perhaps one of the most iconic words for the current globalization process, imposes as well. We cannot choose whether our reading of a Japanese Noh play will affect our long-standing cherished readings of Greek drama; whether a sudden passion for Sanskrit poetics might warp our previous convictions about Chinese literary thought; or whether our knowledge of Hungarian grammar, which allows for the inflection of an infinitive depending on the agent or implied personal pronoun, will make all languages that do not allow for it (most, I guess) suddenly look sorely imprecise. We cannot choose—our exposure will impose. Keeping track of this continuous and salubrious intellectual contamination is both a biographical enterprise for many of us and the urgent call of our present moment, which makes the comparative unprecedentedly imperative in our scholarly pursuits. In the end, my students' anxious desire to tame the confusion of loose ends, make revelatory connections and inscribe them into the mental map of their dreams and goals in life has been the strongest motivation for me to take the comparative imperative seriously and write this book. Their curiosity and persistent questions deserve answers, or at least strategies for answers.

While trying to better understand the cultural dynamics between Chinese and Japanese literary cultures, I came to see the Greco-Roman case as an excellent vantage point from which to better grasp the Sino-Japanese constellation. As I went along, my motivations for the project exceeded the simple utilitarian calculus of gaining a better glimpse of Japan through Rome. I discovered that I was drawn to a comparison focused on antiquity, because comparative work on the formative early stages of cultures would be particularly important to notice and question old habits. Comparisons might be equally valuable, but they matter differently: Greco-Roman antiquity sets the stage for virtually all grand narratives of Western cultural history, and so does Chinese antiquity for East Asian cultural history. By working on the most overdetermined, classical periods on both sides, my study hopes to shift well-known ground to greatest effect for our contemporary self-understanding.

This decision also guided me away from other grand comparative projects that are often evoked by Japanologists, but largely still await pioneering treatment: for example comparisons involving early Japanese and medieval European literatures that examine the dynamic between classical and vernacular languages and literatures, the rhetoric of courtly love, or the emergence of romance and tale literature. To accommodate the Greco-Roman comparison, I also decided to focus exclusively on the Sino-Japanese constellation in Japan and to stay away from the triangular Indo-Sino-Japanese mindmap that, naturally, informs much of popular Buddhist literature in early Japan. For the questions and Latin authors I am treating, Judaism or Christianity was simply not relevant, just as for early Japanese elite literature the Sino-Japanese constellation was the dominant cultural paradigm until the medieval period, when the triangular constellation including India came to deeply penetrate literary culture. For a comparison of two triangular cultural constellations I would have needed to move into both Europe's and Japan's medieval period and would have treated completely different questions and authors. As the chronologically and conceptually more fundamental comparison, focusing on ancient Rome and early Japan and the related Greco-Roman and Sino-Japanese constellations appeared more attractive to me. Needless to say, this is also the comparative project that seemed in tune with my expertise and interests.

Also, I framed my study in this particular way because I wished to revisit our repertoire of common comparative tools. The logic of comparison is inherently binary and ontologizing, which leaves us with disarmingly few choices for description, *same/similar/different*, and even fewer choices for judging historical developments, *extant/absent*. This ontologically tinged vocabulary, which claims that cultures *are* in a certain way, plagues most binary East-West comparisons, whether they propagate dichotomies and difference or argue against them. The binary model creates ontological ellipsis, the sense that, in comparison to Greece, X did not exist in China (with X = experimental science, epic, democracy, individualism, etc.). Formulated in this brute way such comparison might simply sound ridiculous and harmless, but the lingering prevalence of arguments based on cultural binaries, which inevitably produces the failure of one tradition on another's ground, should make us concerned. Zhang Longxi has boldly fought against this conceptual prejudice in much of his work, most notably in *Mighty Opposites: From Dichotomies to Differences in the Comparative Study of China.*[14] I have framed my comparison as a quadruple constellation, which, although it still consist of two binaries, avoids essentializing dichotomy and the creation

---

[14] Zhang 1998. Zhang goes even a step further, moving away from both dichotomy and difference, toward a new emphasis on cultural similarities and affinities in Zhang 2007.

of false ellipses. China and Japan, and Greece and Rome, are not conceived as cultural binaries, but as long-standing constellations of cultural reception processes, of cultural *translatio*. Thus, when we come to compare the four literary cultures of the Ancient Mediterranean and East Asia, we are not in fact comparing cultures, but reception processes. This constitutes a double move. First, we shift from an ontological to a dialectical comparative approach—from asking, for example, "how do Japanese and Latin literature compare?" to asking "how did Japanese and Latin authors deal with the historical flatness of their own tradition vis-à-vis their reference culture's?" Also, we move from a comparative approach that results in detecting ellipsis—the absence of something that makes one of the cultures look deficient—to an approach that profits from catachresis—the temporary application of an existing name to something that does not have one. We can get stuck in unproductive ellipsis by saying, for example, "In Japanese literary culture the earliest literature was highly valued, so that a rich textual record dating back to the earliest period survives today; in contrast, Roman literary culture lacked that respect for its origins, which led to the loss of most of early Latin literature." Only once we apply the Japanese case to the Roman one through productive cross-application, catachresis, can we make unexpected discoveries and ask intriguing questions: as we will see, the Japanese case shows that Rome's loss of its early literature is not necessarily the norm and cannot be explained away by the assumption that early stages of literary production are awkward and simply propaedeutic for a greater future and thus "deserve" their loss. Which aspects in Roman literary culture facilitated the loss of early works? And, in catachrestic turn, which features of Japanese literary culture, if applied to the Roman case, would have prevented the loss of early Latin literature? (For the curious reader, I address these questions in Chapter 3.) Indeed, comparison should be a two-way catachrestic laboratory rather than a trial court imposing on one party the guillotine of ellipsis and cultural deficiency.

Catachresis might also be the term to describe how the East Asianists and Classicists can learn from each other if they choose to engage more closely. For the scholar of early China and Japan, there is so much in the field of Classics to admire and aspire to—first and foremost, a nearly ambidextrous training in Greek and Latin that constitutes a rare exception in East Asian studies. China scholars, unlike Hellenists, have little incentive to seriously study premodern Japan. In contrast, Japan scholars would have every reason to also be China specialists, but with the demise of the Chinese and Sino-Japanese canon in Japanese education in the latter half of the twentieth century and the nationalist focus on vernacular Japanese literature, the mainstream of Japanese literary studies has not encouraged parallel in-depth study of Chinese literature. However, I consider myself part of a heartening new wave of Sino-Japanese literary studies that has been gaining steam over the past decade in the United States and in East Asia. As the reader will notice, I have consciously put a spotlight on Sino-Japanese literature in this book in an attempt to restore it to the central position—now hardly recognizable—that it had well into the twentieth century in Japanese literary culture. At this point it is hard to imagine how there could ever be a field of "classics" (East Asian, that is, and with a lowercase *c* to distinguish it from its well-established venerable Western sibling), because national rhetoric has now become the constitutive master-narrative of literary historiography and criticism in China, Japan, Korea, and Vietnam. That is precisely where we could and should learn from the field of Classics and take our cues from the liberating momentum of this Catholic, denationalized field, which might have distinctive national schools—British, German, Italian, and so forth—but can boast a cosmopolitan, egalitarian academic ethic. That neither Greece nor Italy can easily lay claim to an unbroken legacy going back to Ancient Greece and Rome helps this transnational spirit. In contrast, the political, linguistic, and cultural continuity of the different modern East Asian nations, and the legacy both of China's traditional hegemony and of Japan's modern imperialism in the area, has made such transnational spirit little attractive.

Another enviable characteristic of the field of Classics is the in-depth mastery of the relatively limited corpus of Greek and Latin literatures. This is not the case for East Asian studies, where subgroups of scholars working on certain periods (such as "Early China") or genres (such as "vernacular fiction") certainly share a grounding in their corpus of materials. But the mastery of a body of texts is not defining for the identity of East Asian Studies as a whole and does not constitute the central assumption and arena for scholarly debate. We are reminded of this when we see an *index locorum* at the end of books published in Classics indicating the pages where passages from certain Greek or Latin authors are discussed; such an index is not part of the template for books published on East Asian literatures. There are many reasons why a well-defined textual corpus is not the defining platform for China or Japan studies: first and foremost it has to do with the sheer volume of texts produced over many more centuries in a much larger geographical area. But ideological reasons have also played a central role: though Sino-Japanese literature had enjoyed a place at the top of the genre hierarchy of Japanese literature until the early twentieth century, a nationalistic emphasis on Japanese vernacular literature has lobotomized the most authoritative half of Japanese literature. Today most middle-aged Japanese are unable to even decipher and understand Sino-Japanese texts, which their grandparents might still have jotted down with quotidian ease. This has another effect. Thanks to the in-depth mastery of the Greco-Roman textual corpus, Classics as a field has created much more, and thus also much more subtle, thinking about literary reception and intertextual processes both within and across languages. This asymmetry will surface time and again throughout this book.

The most fundamental difference between Classics and East Asian Studies is, of course, their respective standing in today's academic landscape. If Classics is often called the oldest of "area studies," East Asian studies is one of its youngest specimen in the West. Currently, class enrollments, funds, and publicly perceived relevance strongly favor modern over premodern subfields. Quite to the contrary, the sense of centrality of Classics within the traditional spectrum of humanistic study in European cultural history gives the field an incomparable *gravitas*.

Yet, Classics' gravitas has suffered corrosion in the last decades, a fact that one might lament but also see as a terrific chance. Here is Charles Martindale's prophetic advice for its restoration, drawn from an article that muses on the future of the emerging field of "reception studies," devoted to the exploration of the legacy of Greco-Roman antiquity in Western cultural history:

> What's in a name? In the years to come people may, or they may not, find "reception" a useful label for certain scholarly activities.... Two things above all I would have classics embrace: a relaxed, not to say imperialist, attitude towards what we may study as part of the subject, and a subtle and supple conception of the relationship between past and present, modern and ancient. Then classics could again have a leading role among the humanities, a classics neither merely antiquarian nor crudely presentist, a classics of the present certainly, but also, truly, of the future.[15]

This is an exciting vision for the future of Classical Studies. All I can add is that it would be yet more exciting if classicists added to the proposed "subtle and supple conception of the relationship between past and present, modern and ancient" a similarly "subtle and supple conception of the relationship between Greco-Roman and other antiquities." It may seem that this would only add one more comparative angle to the relations between "past and present, modern and ancient," which are comparative projects of sorts. However, this angle would have a yet more thought-provoking effect and allow for a leading role of Classics with a much more global gravitas. It is most pleasant to imagine how a fuller engagement with other antiquities—in particular Near Eastern, Indian, East Asian—with their distinctive shapes of historical, intellectual, religious and literary traditions, could create new questions, even new answers, and certainly a new conceptual vocabulary for the traditional field of Classics.

Now that I have sketched what East Asianists such as myself might admire in the field of Classics, it would be appropriate to give Classicists an incentive to look beyond their traditional geographical and linguistic boundaries and elaborate on what the study of China and Japan can offer them. Among other things this book tries to make a seductive case for dialogue. Because we first need to make our way through its chapters before reflecting on what attractions young fields like East Asian Studies in the West might hold for more mature ones like Classics, we postpone this task to the Epilogue. Thus we end our introduction close to where we had begun, with the drama of relative age—of disciplines.

***

Let us start on our course. Chapter 1 lays the foundations for our comparison of Japanese and Roman literary cultures. It discusses three fundamental similarities between them and three divergences that complicate our comparison. Both literary cultures were latecomers vis-à-vis their reference culture's; due to their belatedness they started against the backdrop of highly sophisticated stages of literary production—Chinese Six Dynasties and Early Tang literature for Japan, and Hellenistic literature for Rome; and their education systems were based on the adoption and adaption of the literary canon developed by scholars of their

---

[15] Martindale and Thomas 2006, 13.

reference culture. However, the geopolitical constellation of China and Japan, and Greece and Rome, respectively, were radically different. Because Rome, unlike Japan, conquered its reference culture early in its history, there was a disjunction between cultural (Greek) and political (Roman) capital. Also, the linguistic constellation of Japanese and Roman literary cultures was radically different. While Japanese developed a reading technique that allowed them to read Chinese texts without the need for translation, Latin literature started with the translation and adaptation of Greek texts. The third divergence between Japanese and Latin literary cultures was their different spectrum and hierarchy of core genres: Forms of short lyrical poetry headed the hierarchy of literary genres in Japan. In contrast, epic poetry—which did not exist in China and Japan—and drama—which did not develop until the early modern period in East Asia—were prominent genres in early Latin literature.

The remaining chapters are designed as case studies devoted to particular questions and themes and explored through a highly selective set of examples from Japanese and Latin works. Chapter 2 and 3 are devoted to one of the fundamental similarities of the Sino-Japanese and Greco-Roman constellation, their position as latecomers. Chapter 2 explores what kind of strategies Japanese and Latin authors designed to tell the beginnings of their own literature and eloquence in a way that allowed their own tradition, despite its historical flatness, to compete with Chinese and Greek precedents. It showcases four texts from four different historical moments, on the Japanese side the *Florilegium of Cherished Airs* (*Kaifūsō* 懐風藻, 751)—the first Japanese anthology of Sino-Japanese poetry (*kanshi* 漢詩)—and the *Collection of Ancient and Modern Poems* (*Kokinwakashū* 古今和歌集, 905), the first imperial anthology of vernacular verse. We will show how Cicero's account of the development of Greek and Roman eloquence in his dialogue *Brutus* bears striking resemblance to the strategy of the *Kaifūsō*'s compiler and that the interpretation of Roman reception of Greek literature of the early imperial historian Velleius Paterculus shows interesting resonances with the strategies in the *Kokinshū* Prefaces.

Chapter 3 explores how notions about simplicity, ornateness, and cultural (or literary) decline, which could be blamed on foreign influence, became one of the arenas in which the ambiguous psychology of the younger literary cultures unfolded. The claims to natural and self-sufficient beginnings of indigenous literature and eloquence stood in stark contrast to the fact that both Japanese and Latin Literature emerged in dialogue with a highly refined stage of literary development in their reference cultures. By examining texts from the first two Japanese poetry anthologies *Florilegium of Cherished Airs,* the *Collection of Myriad Leaves* (*Man'yōshū* 万葉集), and the earliest *waka* poetics, Fujiwara no Hamanari's *Code of Poetry* (*Uta no shiki* 歌式, 772) alongside with Cicero's *Brutus* and *On the Orator* (*De oratore*) and Horace's *Satires*, this chapter argues that Latin writers had good reasons to be more aggressive, more diplomatic, and more embarrassed vis-à-vis Greek precedent than their Japanese colleagues vis-à-vis the Chinese tradition.

The next three chapters revolve around the symbolic centers of the Roman and Japanese Empires, first comparing founding figures of state formation, such as Aeneas and Prince Shōtoku, and then moving to images of the capitals, Rome and Kyoto, as sites of literary production. A chapter comparing Japanese and Latin exile poetry closes the sequence on the symbolic centers of two very different empires. Chapter 4 compares how the legendary figure of Prince Shōtoku and of Aeneas were both founding figures of the new Roman and Japanese state, but also empowered by their connection with their respective reference culture. Aeneas was sometimes depicted as Greek, while Prince Shōtoku was recognized as the incarnation of the Chinese Buddhist patriarch Huisi. Why does Virgil's Aeneas appear as a dutiful and domestically minded city-builder, giving laws and ensuring the worship of the domestic gods he brought from Troy, whereas Prince Shōtoku is depicted most of all as a consummate writer and interpreter of texts? This chapter argues that there was little advantage in making Aeneas into a hero of literacy, whereas it was highly profitable in the East Asian context to make a Japanese symbol of state foundation into a brilliant writer.

Chapter 5 compares the capitals of Rome and Kyoto as literary spaces, first reminding us how very unlike Kyoto and Ancient Rome were as capital cities and then exploring how these differences informed literary production along two vectors: the vector of time and the vector of romance. How did Heian authors and how did Augustan authors locate the capitals they inhabited in time? With what kind of teleologies, vectors of destiny, did they endow their cities and how did the genres they chose inflect their capital visions? We examine Virgil's *Aeneid* and the eleventh-century poetry anthology *Wakan rōeishū* 和漢朗詠集 (Collection of Japanese and Chinese-style Poems for Recitation). We then explore how Augustan Rome and tenth- and eleventh-century Kyoto were the sites of literary revolutions that were intricately connected with the urban fabric and capital culture: a new literature of romance. What were the rules and assumptions of this new game of love? To explore these questions we compare some of Propertius's (ca. 49–16 BCE) *Elegies* with moments from Sei Shōnagon's (ca. 966–1017) *Pillow Book* (*Makura no sōshi* 枕草子).

Chapter 6 concludes the cycle of chapters on the symbolic centers of the Japanese and Roman empires by examining texts written by poets exiled from the capital. In 901 Sugawara no Michizane, a prominent statesman and poet, was degraded to the office of governor of Dazaifu in Kyushu, far away from the capital, but close to developments in Korea and China. In 8 CE Augustus sent Ovid into exile at Tomi, previously a colony of Miletus mostly inhabited by descendants of Greek merchants and Getes. Some themes are strikingly similar in Michizane's exile poetry and Ovid's *Tristia* and *Letters from Pontus*: the sorrows of being misunderstood by barbarians or uncongenial people, memories of the glorious times had in the capital, and the hopes of a return, which neither in Michizane's nor in Ovid's case came true. Yet the chapter argues that there are significant differences in their exile experience and poetry that are rooted in the different position of poets in Rome's and Early Japan's society, their respective poetic decorum, and their different relationship to the reference cultures Greece and China.

The last two chapters explore prominent strategies of self-definition through and against the image of the older reference cultures: satire and what I will call "synoptic texts." If exiles praised the ultimate grandeur of the capital as symbolic cultural center, there was one area of cultural achievement that both Rome and Japan self-consciously lacked: indigenous philosophical traditions. Precisely that lack made philosophers in Rome and Confucian scholars in Japan into much coveted exemplars of authority and erudition. At the same time, it made them into ready targets for satirical attack. Chapter 7 explores the role of the satirical in the relationship of Japanese and Latin authors to the older thought traditions of China and Greece, by comparing the hitherto neglected *Genji Poems* (*Fu Hikaru Genji monogatari shi* 賦光源氏物語詩, thirteenth century), a medieval recreation of Murasaki Shikibu's *Tale of Genji* in Sino-Japanese verse, to Martianus Capella's *Marriage of Philology and Mercury* (fifth century AD), an influential compendium of the Seven Liberal Arts framed as an allegorical marriage tale. The chapter argues that the *Genji Poems* and Martianus's *Marriage* both show how serious aesthetic and philosophical critique joins hands with parody and satire that serves as a tool of canonization, of cultural reconciliation, and empowering self-deprecation toward the cultural hierarchies rooted in the reference cultures.

Satirizing those aspects of the reference culture that the younger cultures perceived as lacking in their own traditions was one way of relating to the reference culture. Another strategy was to directly juxtapose the reference culture with one's own culture in the form of "synoptic texts," a rather exceptional form of texts that juxtapose Greek with Roman elements and Chinese (or Sino-Japanese) with Japanese. From the small number of synoptic texts Chapter 8 selects the *Newly Selected Anthology of Myriad Leaves* (*Shinsen Man'yōshū* 新撰万葉集, 893), a poetry anthology that juxtaposes vernacular waka with Sino-Japanese quatrains, and compares it to Plutarch's *Parallel Lives* (*Bioi parallêloi*, after 96 CE), which juxtapose biographies of famous Greek mythical figures, politicians, and military commanders with carefully chosen Roman correlates. Because Plutarch was a Greek living in the Roman Empire, this chapter thematizes again the disjunction between political and cultural capital that Rome's conquest of Greece brought about and that did not occur in premodern Japan. The chapter argues that the very act of juxtaposition influenced the representation of cultures on both sides, resulting in iconized vignettes of cultural competition and complementarity for the purpose of aesthetic or moral education.

In a book of this scope it would have been impossible to represent all periods, genres, and authors evenly. It is ultimately also undesirable. I have instead focused on particular themes and issues and selected the Japanese and Latin texts that appeared most interesting and illuminating as such, and most resonant as a comparative pair. The reader will see that I have placed enormous emphasis on certain works by Cicero, on Virgil's *Aeneid*, and, more generally, on works from the Late Republican and Augustan Periods. From the rich post-Augustan imperial literature I only include three outsiders: a lesser historian (Velleius Paterculus), an imperial Greek author (Plutarch), and a Latin writer from Late Antiquity that basically only medievalists care about (Martianus Capella). On the Japanese side I have given strategic attention to Sino-Japanese texts, some of which are canonical and representative (such as Michizane's poetry), while others are exceptional or even obscure (the poetic exchange between Yakamochi and Ikenushi in the *Man'yōshū* or the *Genji Poems*). Because the comparison between Aeneas and Prince Shōtoku was too attractive and productive to leave out, I have even included a Buddhist hagiographical biography for comparison with the *Aeneid*. Although it might sound counterintuitive, the reader will see in each of the case study chapters how the asymmetries in text selection serve a heuristic purpose and, surprisingly, sometimes precisely enable us to gain representative insights through bold comparison of very particular texts.

Now it is time to lay the foundations for the more specific case studies and to take a closer look at fundamental similarities and dissimilitudes of the two cultural constellations that are the focus of this book.

| Setting the Stage
Sino-Japanese and Greco-Roman Constellations

1. *Foreground: Approximations*

Starting Late

At least three fundamental similarities between the literary cultures of early Japan and Rome encourage their comparison. First, both Japanese and Roman literatures were jumpstarted based on Chinese and Greek literary precedents, which served as sophisticated models for script, lexical borrowings, rhetorical sophistication, and a great variety of literary genres and verse meters. Both Japanese and Roman literatures were self-conscious "latecomers," with a strong sense both of themselves and of their belatedness vis-à-vis their reference cultures.

Starting Refined

The second fundamental similarity was an indirect consequence of the first: because they were latecomers, Japanese and Roman literary cultures developed against the backdrop of highly sophisticated stages of literary development in China and Greece. If we count back to the earliest parts of the Confucian Classics dating to the Western Zhou Dynasty (1045–771 BCE), Japan's earliest historical annals and poetry anthologies from the eighth century faced the voluminous outpour of more than one-and-a-half millennia of textual record in China. In the last five hundred years preceding the rise of literature in Japan, Chinese writers of the Six Dynasties Period (220–589) and the early Tang Dynasty (seventh century) experimented with ever more ornate forms of poetry and prose: they developed the highly polished genre of "regulated poetry" that demanded attention to tonal patterns and parallel structures and wrote in a variety of prose genres that prescribed the use of parallel lines. The latest Chinese literature to reach Japan at the beginning of its literary culture in the late seventh and eighth centuries was a far cry from the oldest parts of the *Classic of Poetry* (詩經 *Shijing*, compiled ca. 600 BCE), but both temporal book ends and much that happened in-between (and that reached Japan in book form) become the basis for the fledgling Japanese literary culture. Consequently, simplicity and sophistication mingled in ways that would have been unthinkable in its reference culture China, which took centuries and millennia to develop the densely allusive literature available to the very first known Japanese authors.[1]

The first authors writing in Latin in the third century BCE had only about half a millennium of previous Greek literary record to shoulder, if we count back to the first records of the Homeric epics around the eighth century BCE. The considerably shorter temporal *écart* between the beginning of Greek and Latin literatures resulted in a more synchronous unfolding of Hellenistic and early Roman literatures. In contrast to the half millennium of more ornate literary experiments in China that preceded the earliest Japanese literary works, Hellenistic literature, with its poised exuberance and refined postures, took off in the late fourth and third centuries BCE. To put a symbolic date on this phenomenon: Callimachus, poet, critic, and scholar employed at the Library of Alexandria by Pharaoh Ptolemy II Philadelphus and a defining figure of Hellenistic taste for Roman poets, died around 240 BCE. Livius Andronicus wrote Latin versions of two Greek plays during this very same year, a date which Romans at least since Cicero fixed as the beginning of their literary tradition. To grasp it through an imaginary crosscultural *chiasmus*, the Six Dynasties Period that early Roman authors had to grapple with was much shorter than China's Hellenistic Period, against the backdrop of which Japanese authors set out to write their own literature. But the self-conscious awareness of their latecomer status was so crucial for both Japanese and Latin writers that the next two chapters, "Starting *avant la lettre*: Ways to Tell the Beginnings of Literature and Eloquence," and "Latecomers: Of Simplicity, Ornament, and Decline" are entirely devoted to exploring the literary psychology of traditions that developed late in symbiosis with an older reference culture. We will then return to the question of how Japanese and Latin authors were affected by the fact that their literatures developed in the face of an arguably joyfully—or turgidly—exuberant "Hellenistic Six Dynasties" Period in their reference cultures. Let us now move to the third fundamental similarity between Japanese and Latin literary cultures.

Starting Canonical: Early Japanese and Roman Education

Again, the (Japanese) ruler asked the (Korean) land of Paekche to present worthy men if they had any. When they had received the command, they thus presented one named Wani-kishi. They also presented the Confucian *Analects*, in ten volumes, and the *Thousand-Character Classic*, in one volume, all together eleven volumes. (This Wani-kishi is the ancestor of the Fumi no Obito lineage of scribes).

又、科賜百済国、若有賢人者、貢上。故、受命以貢上人、名和爾吉師。即
論語十巻、千字文一巻、并十一巻、付是人即貢進。＜此和爾吉師者、文
首等祖。＞[2]

RECORD OF ANCIENT MATTERS (KOJIKI 古事記, PRESENTED TO THE THRONE IN 712 CE)

The study of language and literature (or grammar) was once not even known at Rome, much less respected, since the community, being then uncultured and

---

[1] To get a taste of the refined literary culture of the latter part of the Six Dynasties see Tian 2007. For an inspiring introduction to Hellenistic literature see Gutzwiller 2007.
[2] *Kojiki* 266–68. (Reference is to page numbers unless otherwise noted).

devoted to warfare, did not yet have much free time for liberal learning. The first stages of this study, too, were undistinguished, inasmuch as the earliest teachers, who were at the same time poets and half Greek—I mean Livius and Ennius, who are on record as having taught both languages privately and publicly—merely clarified the meaning of Greek authors or gave exemplary readings from their own Latin compositions [...] In my view, therefore, the first person to introduce the study of grammar to the city was Crates of Mallos, a contemporary of Aristarchus. Sent to the senate by King Attalus between the Second and Third Punic Wars, at just about the time of Ennius's death, Crates fell down and broke his leg in a sewer-hole in the neighborhood of the Palatine and spent the whole time of the embassy and of his recuperation constantly giving a host of lectures and holding frequent discussions, thereby providing an example for our countrymen to imitate. Still, they imitate him only to the extent that they carefully reviewed poems that had as yet not been widely circulated—the works of dead friends, or of any others they approved—and by reading and commenting on them made them known to the rest of the population as well.[3]

Grammatica Romae ne in usu quidem olim, nedum in honore ullo erat, rudi scilicet ac bellicosa etiamtum civitate necdum magnopere liberalibus disciplinis vacante. initium quoque eius mediocre extitit, siquidem antiquissimi doctorum, qui idem et poetae et semigraeci erant—Livium et Ennium dico, quos utraque lingua domi forisque docuisse adnotatum est—nihil amplius quam Graecos interpretabantur aut si quid ipsi Latine composuissent praelegebant. [...] Primus igitur, quantum opinamur, studium grammaticae in urbem intulit Crates Mallotes, Aristarchi aequalis: qui missus ad senatum ab Attalo rege inter secundum ac tertium Punicum bellum sub ipsam Enni mortem, cum regione Palati prolapsus in cloacae foramen crus fregisset, per omne legationis simul et valetudinis tempus plurimas acroasis subinde fecit assidueque disseruit ac nostris exemplo fuit ad imitandum. hactenus tamen imitati, ut carmina parum adhuc divulgata vel defunctorum amicorum vel si quorum aliorum probassent diligentius retractarent ac legendo commentandoque etiam ceteris nota facerent.

SUETONIUS (C. 69–122 CE): *ON GRAMMARIANS AND RHETORICIANS*

The third fundamental similarity between Japanese and Latin literary cultures was that literary production was rooted in the adoption and adaptation of the educational canon of their reference cultures. Children of elite families studied the Confucian Classics and canonical Chinese histories and poetry at a state academy set up based on Chinese precedent in the late seventh century and, increasingly since the ninth century in schools run by hereditary scholarly family lineages.[4] At least since the second century BCE children of Roman elite families received training in Greek poetry, drama, and rhetoric, often from private tutors.[5]

---

[3] *De grammaticis et rhetoribus* 1–2. Translation from Kaster 1995, 5.
[4] The date and surrounding conditions for the foundation of the Academy is disputed. See Hisaki 1990, 22–49. On education in early Japan see also Momo 1994, Borgen 1986, 69–112, Ury 1999, Shirane 2000b, and Ceugniet 2000.
[5] Fundamental works on Hellenistic and Roman education include Marrou 1971, Bonner 1977, Cribiore 2001 and Morgan 1998.

Although the memorable anecdotes from the *Record of Ancient Matters* and Suetonius's *On Grammarians and Rhetors*, which encapsulate the earliest introduction of education and learning into early Japan and Rome, respectively, are both probably apocryphal and anachronistic, they illustrate crucial points about the similarities and differences of education in both cultures. Certainly, the earliest Japanese chronicle, presented to the court in 712, represents conditions at the early eighth century court: by that time the *Analects*, a collection recording Confucius's (551–479 BCE) words in conversation with disciples and rulers, and the *Thousand Character Classic*, a Six Dynasties collection of four character phrases, were widely used as writing primers. This situation was projected back to events during the late fourth and early fifth centuries, when Japan requested "worthy men" from the Korean state of Paekche and one Wani arrived at the Japanese court. Wani's arrival as depicted in the chronicle marks the earliest introduction of books, and indeed introduction of the technology of writing into Japan is consciously framed by eighth-century interests to relate writing to power and scribes to the fledgling Japanese court.[6] The Korean state of Paekche is represented as in a tributary relationship to Japan; and the authors of the chronicle are eager to connect contemporary scribal kinship groups to their continental origins on the Korean peninsula.[7]

A similar anachronism can be detected in the writings of C. Suetonius Tranquillus (c. 69–122), a highly educated scholar of the equestrian order who served as literary advisor and supervisor of the public libraries of Rome for some time during the reigns of Emperors Trajan and Hadrian. Suetonius has his own agenda, when he surveys the history of the study of grammar and rhetoric in Rome through the roughly three centuries from their beginnings to his own time in the part of his biographies on famous men that treats grammarians and rhetors. That Suetonius wrote biographies of emperors as well as of learned men such as poets, historians, philosophers, and teachers says more about his identity as a scholar and as an imperial functionary—in a court culture, where education, patronage, and public service were closely intertwined—than about the place of learning in the preceding three centuries he covers. Also, the *Record of Ancient Matters* plays the Korean state of Paekche up as transmitter of the technology of writing and of books (though playing it down as a tribute state to Japan); similarly, Suetonius— confident of Roman accomplishments in a mature Roman empire—downplays the influence of Greek grammar and rhetoric on Roman literary culture.

Both moves show the Japanese and Roman cultural pride that our authors project back onto the periods in which the anecdotes are set—possibly the late fourth century CE for Wani's arrival in Japan and the third century BCE for Livius Andronicus's and Ennius in Rome. But despite the obvious traces of our authors' own interests in the depiction of events that predate them by roughly three hundred years in both cases, both vignettes of the origin of learning and education

---

[6] On Japanese book imports from China until the end of the Heian Period see Kornicki 1998, 278–88.
[7] On more scenes of literacy and the presence of scribes at court from the first to sixth centuries see Lurie 2011, Chapter 2.

still capture significant realities of early Japanese and Roman education systems. In both cultures education was based on the precedents of their reference cultures: Writing, books, and learning arrived in Japan through the mediation of the Korean peninsula from China, in a context that implies later elite court culture and central political control. Similarly, the study of grammar and poetry did start in Rome under Greek influence. But in contrast to the court setting sketched in the vignette in the *Record of Ancient Matters,* where the previously Korean transmitter stays on in Japan and becomes the founder of a lineage of professional scribes, grammar education was introduced by a traveling Greek, Crates of Mallos, when he was briefly stranded in Rome. Although Crates moved on, "half Greeks" like Livius Andronicus and Ennius from the Greek-speaking Italian South, were among the first permanent teachers of grammar in Rome.

The different degree of state involvement in both vignettes is remarkable: On the one hand there is a Korean emissary to the Japanese court. On the other, there is Crates, who comes from Asia Minor on a diplomatic mission to Rome, but his introduction of grammar teaching to Rome is unrelated to his official mission. The people of Rome were lucky that he broke his leg in a sewer hole—plumbing being one of the glories of Roman material culture—and used his time of recovery for private lectures to the Roman public. That Suetonius describes the teaching of the semi-Greeks as negligible and ascribes the introduction of grammar to the trivial, absurdly coincidental breaking of a Greek leg underlines his agenda of showing the triumphant self-sufficient evolution of Roman civilization from crude beginnings to the refinements of his day and keeping Greek influence down to a minimum.[8]

Still, that none of the propagators of education in Suetonius's account are state-employed points to one fundamental difference between the Roman and early Japanese education systems. Undoubtedly, the degree of state involvement in education was considerably higher in early Japan. Not only was there a State Academy (*daigakuryō* 大学寮) in the capital—and for some time also in the provinces—that was sponsored by the state; until the ninth century the imperial court even sponsored a select amount of students and monks for their studying abroad in China. Some of them studied in China for many years and were a costly burden for the Japanese court. It is true that after the ninth century, when the Fujiwara clan came to dominate government posts at court, studying at the State Academy became less attractive, because it ceased to be a venue for obtaining high office. Therefore, private tutoring at home or in the schools sponsored by the hereditary scholarly families such as the Sugawara and the Ōe became the norm. However, throughout the Heian Period the Academy retained its symbolic significance as the locus of the commitment of the Japanese imperial court to Confucian learning and its foundational importance to Japanese society: the semiannual ritual observances to Confucius (*sekiten* 釈奠) were held in the Academy, its professors gave lectures on Chinese texts for the emperor at court, and together with their

---

[8] The topos of the contempt for elementary writing teachers and grammarians might also play into Suetonius's judgment of Livius Andronicus and Ennius. See Harris 1989, 237 ff.

students, they were regularly called into imperial presence to compose poetry on official court occasions.

In contrast, education was a more private affair in Rome. There was hardly any centralized educational effort from the government, unless we regard the repeated expulsions of Greek grammarians, rhetoricians, and philosophers considered dangerous to public morals as an educational effort. Personal tutors hired for home instruction played a crucial role in Roman education. Some Greeks actually criticized the lack of state involvement in Roman education.[9] The status and ethnic background of these tutors is another major difference of education in Japan and Rome captured in our two vignettes. Wani might count as something of a "tribute gift" to the Japanese court, but he was no slave and became the ancestor of a lineage of scribes that had the privilege of providing service to the emperor. Livius Andronicus was allegedly captured when Rome sacked his hometown Tarentum in Southern Italy and came to Rome as a slave, later taking on the name of the man who freed him.[10]

Education in Rome would have been unthinkable without the great number of Greek-speaking slaves or freedmen, who taught grammar and poetry to the children of the Roman elite.[11] These were for the most part bilingual individuals who could read, write, and speak both Greek and Latin. Although eighth century Japanese chronicles claimed immigrants from the Korean peninsula like Wani as ancestors of scribal lineages and a large number of both students and teachers at the State Academy in the seventh and eighth centuries were of peninsular descent,[12] there was no instruction in conversational Chinese (only, for some time, specialized training in Chinese-style pronunciation of words) and native speakers of Chinese played no role in Japanese education.

It would have been unthinkable in early Japan to encounter somebody like the philosopher and orator Favorinus (ca. 80–160), who came from the city of Arles in Latin-speaking Gaul and, when delivering lectures in Greek in Rome, presumably enthralled even those few in his audience who did not understand Greek but relished the melody of his voice and the rhythms of his speech. Even if those few monks and scholars who had studied in China and must have learnt Chinese for conversation had decided to deliver a public address in Chinese, there would hardly have been any audience at all who would have understood them. And the dramatic point about the ability of those in Favorinus's audience who did not understand but could at least enjoy Greek would not make sense in an anecdote about a public lecture delivered in any Chinese dialect in early Japan: no speaker desiring to make himself understood would have made that language choice and no spectators would have found joy in listening to mumblings in a language foreign to virtually everybody in the audience.[13]

---

[9] As Cicero relates in *De re publica* 4.3.3.

[10] For arguments that speak against this theory see Suerbaum 2002, 95.

[11] For biographies of grammarians see prosopography of Christes 1979. For a fascinating cultural and sociological portrait of the profession of grammarians in Late Antiquity see Kaster 1988.

[12] See table in Hisaki 1990, 40.

[13] Philostratus *Vitae sophistarum* ("Lives of the Sophists"), 491.

One implication of this contrast between a Japanese centralized education system and a lack thereof in Rome is that, while we know the Japanese examination
system in detail, we hardly know anything about how students' performance was
measured in Rome. The State Academy was modeled on the Chinese education
system. Since the foundation of a State academy under Emperor Wu of the Han
Dynasty in 136 BCE, a variety of state-sponsored educational institutions developed. By the Tang Dynasty there were six state institutions in the capital and regular civil service exams, which became the main mechanism in the recruitment of
government officials and political elites until the early twentieth century, when the
civil service exam system was abolished during the last chaotic years of the Qing
Dynasty, the end of imperial China.[14] China's "exam culture" not only shaped the
ruling elites who governed China through the centuries, but it also drove many
areas of intellectual and cultural production: many of the most productive intellectuals of the Song Dynasty contributed to fierce debates over the exam curriculum,
and their stances on learning, self-cultivation, and the relevance of schooling to
life were shaped by the development and exigencies of the examination system.
Exam culture also found expression in a whole subgenre of novels devoted to
poor but talented young men who finally triumph in the face of adversity through
success in the exams, handily matched by success in romantic affairs. Whereas
a centralized examination system fostering social mobility, intense competition,
endless disputes over the curriculum between participants in the system, and the
lore of spectacular success or failure shaped the social fabric and imagination of
Chinese society, there is no indication that there were any formal exams administered by teachers or the government in Greco-Roman education.[15]

The State Academy in Japan never had its Chinese model's scale or importance
as a road to government office, especially with the rise of the Fujiwara clan in the
ninth century, but its curriculum focused exclusively on Chinese canonical texts.
Until the early twentieth century Chinese and Chinese-style literature had the
highest status in the hierarchy of three major textual canons: the Chinese, the
Buddhist, and the vernacular Japanese canon, which took shape as a subject for
formal education only in the Late Heian and early Medieval Periods, beyond the
temporal limits of this study.[16]

There were several tracks of study, including the track focusing on the Confucian
Classics (Myōgyōdō 明経道), a Law track devoted to legal codes (Myōbōdō 明法道),
a mathematical track (Sandō 算道), and a track focusing on Chinese literary and
historical works (Monjōdō 文章道, Kidendō 紀伝道). This last track was first considered of lesser status and only added in 730, and included the study of the foremost
Chinese anthology of poetry and literary prose, the Literary Selections (Wenxuan
文選, early sixth century) and the three earliest Chinese official histories (Records
of the Grand Historian (ca. 91 BCE), Book of the Han Dynasty (92 CE), Book of the
Later Han Dynasty (445 CE)). But it became the most prominent one through the

[14] On Chinese education and the exam system see Lee 2000, Miyazaki 1976, and Elman 2000.
[15] Morgan 1998, 79 f.
[16] For an overview of the development of these three canons into the modern period see
Shirane 2000b.

eighth and ninth centuries. In the mature form of the curriculum, the student in the popular "Literature and History" track would first have to study the Confucian Classics and then take an entrance exam administered by the State Academy, the "bureau exam" (*ryōshi* 寮試), which would make him a "Provisional Scholar of Letters." He would then have to pass an exam administered by the Ministry of Ceremonial, the "ministry exam" (*shōshi* 省試), which upon passing would make him a "Scholar of Letters." The two best candidates of this exam would receive a government stipend and the title of "Distinguished Scholars of Letters." They were qualified to try taking the highest level of exam in the examination system, which was administered under imperial auspices and included the composition of examination essays on policy issues based on Chinese canonical texts.[17] Although only a small fraction of students passed the highest level in the examination system, the study of the *Wenxuan* and the Chinese official histories in this popular track provided all students with an intimate familiarity with Chinese historical events and protagonists, with the stylistic variety of various prose genres used in official correspondence, and with precious literary vocabulary. The popularity of this track, which was a Japanese modification of the Chinese curriculum, can at least partly explain why Heian scholar poets were so prone to larding their texts with Chinese historical anecdotes and *recherché* allusions to Chinese texts.

The elaborate Japanese examination ladder contrasts dramatically with what little we know for sure about the Hellenistic and Roman curriculum. While we have several early Japanese law codes that contain regulations of personnel, curriculum, and exam procedures and we only need to problematize the relation between the codes and their execution, it is hard to grasp a generalized Hellenistic or Roman curriculum in our sources. We can imagine that because of a lack of central control and of an examination system, the teaching curriculum was probably much looser and more varied. There is the notion of an *enkyklios paideia*, a "comprehensive education," which dates as far back as Aristotle but takes on various meanings depending on the text. Quintilian (ca.35–100), a scholar and rhetorician from Hispania who is our most extensive source on education and rhetorical training in Rome, defines it as learning how to read and write, and as studying grammar and literature, geometry, astronomy, and principles of music and logic; and, obviously, rhetoric and philosophy, the ultimate goals of such a comprehensive education, which he describes in his large pedagogical treatise on rhetoric.[18]

This program approaches the late antique and medieval curriculum of the Liberal Arts, the *Trivium* of Grammar, Logic, and Rhetoric, and the Quadrivium of Arithmetic, Geometry, Music, and Astronomy. But how it was studied and how much of it was studied in a rigorous curriculum even during Quintilian's time is unclear. Scholars of Greco-Roman education are increasingly moving away from their previous assumption of a clear-cut curriculum where students would have proceeded from learning with a reading and writing teacher, followed by successive training in grammar, poetry, and rhetoric. Because this "curricular model"

---

[17] Between 704 and 931 apparently only sixty-five men passed this level. Ury 1999, 371.

[18] *Institutio Oratoria* 1.10. For various definitions of *enkyklios paideia* see Morgan 1998, 33–39.

does not fit the contradictory statements in received sources and is also not backed up by recent archeological evidence from papyri excavated in Egypt, Teresa Morgan has argued to replace the curricular template with a "core/periphery" model of education.[19] The "core" that most people learned and practiced longest was learning how to read and write through the copying of alphabets, syllabaries, gnomic moral sayings, and, on a more advanced level, word lists containing names of protagonists from Homeric epic, Greek drama, and Virgil in the Latin-speaking West. The "periphery" would include a much more varied set of materials, like Euripides and Menander, or the more advanced study of rhetoric.

Thus the image of the curriculum that authors like Quintilian give us is an image of education of the highest echelons of society, who would indeed become orators or political players. They would be trained in the various types of rhetorical propedeutical exercises, *progymnasmata*, that Quintilian describes in Book Two and Three of his *Institutio*. They range from simpler exercises like the paraphrase of a saying (*chreia*) or a maxim (*sententia*), the paraphrase of a fable (*fabula, apologus*), or a mythological scene (*narratio*) to more elaborate exercises like the developing of rhetorical commonplaces, the elaboration and description of a given topic, praise speeches—*encomia*—or denunciations of legendary and historical figures, and the impersonation of famous heroes in the *prosopopoeia*. The most demanding exercises were *controversiae* and *suasoriae*, mock speeches arguing a legal case or deliberating on a question of general importance, which prepared the aspiring orator for court litigation and public speaking.[20] Whether trained in oratory on Quintilian's model or drilled in the composition of examination essays on Chinese canonical texts (and of poetry on assigned topics), the ultimate goal of this kind of education was to master various registers of language, to have a command of canonical classical texts, and to hone one's ability to write articulately and speak eloquently, relying on the creative use of the store of knowledge and experience with those texts that the diligent student had amassed through years of study and practice. Although the political system of the Nara and Heian courts and the Roman Republic and the Roman Empire were vastly different and required different sets of skills from their respective participants, the ability to write and speak well was coveted in both political and literary cultures.

Japan's and Rome's late start had also significant implications for their education systems. Unlike Chinese and Greek literary culture, Japanese and Roman education developed on the basis of previous canonization efforts and scholarly literature of their reference cultures. In China scholarly culture took off with the Han Dynasty, when scholars assembled a Confucian canon, wrote extensive commentaries, and began to be employed at a State Academy founded by Emperor Wu. By the time of the earliest Japanese literature, Chinese scholars from the Han through the Tang Dynasties had written commentaries (even officially sanctioned subcommentaries to commentaries) that were used alongside a great variety of dictionaries, containing explanations on meaning and pronunciation of

---

[19] Morgan 1998, 67–89.
[20] On rhetorical exercises see Bonner 1977, 250–76 and, against the background of relevant excavated Egyptian papyri, Morgan 1998, 190–239.

characters, and encyclopedias that brought synonymical expressions, *loci classici*, and associations of poetic topics to the fingertips of the aspiring student working on his literary compositions.[21] In turn, Hellenistic scholars had produced standardized texts, added punctuation and accentuation, developed theories of literary genres and grammar, and commentaries that become the basis for literary studies in Rome.[22] Put simply, learning for a Nara or Heian Japanese and for a Roman was a radically different process from that of a Chinese before the Han Dynasty or a Greek in classical fifth-century Athens.

Our two vignettes contain, again, suggestive indications of this point. Not coincidentally, Suetonius gives us an intriguing synchronism: the mission of Crates of Mallos to Rome and the beginning of grammar studies in Rome coincided with the lifetime of Aristarchus of Alexandria, key figure in the development of a system of critical marks facilitating the reading of Homer and the poets. Although the foundation of the library and museum at Alexandria around 285 BCE lay much closer to the beginnings of literary production in Latin in the latter half of the third century BCE, the prolific studies of grammar, lexicography, and textual criticism that the Alexandrian head librarians produced spread quickly in the Greek-speaking world and had profound impact on Roman students and writers. Among the recently excavated papyri there are more copies of the *Iliad* and *Odyssey* than of all other texts combined, and the first two books of the *Iliad* were apparently particularly popular for grammar training. A papyrus fragment dating to around 145 BC from the Egyptian city of Tebtunis features lines from the second book of the *Iliad*. With some luck it was preserved because the papyrus on which it is written was later reused as casing for a crocodile mummy. (see Figure 1.1)

Although we cannot be sure how many school texts did indeed include critical marks, this one is a good example of those that did feature them: The horizontal stroke in the upper right corner is an *obelos,* which indicates lines that are considered inauthentic. The oblique stroke next to the second line and on the bottom of the column marks the beginning of a new section. These signs taught students notions of textual authenticity and invited them to narrative and prosodic analysis and it was based on this educational experience that Romans came to write their own literature.

The *Analects* and the *Thousand Character Classic* mentioned in the anecdote about Wani had as prominent a role in Japanese education as Homer had in Hellenistic and Roman education. Note that our vignette of the beginnings of learning in Japan expressly mentions an edition of the *Analects* in "ten books," a clear indication that this copy of the *Analects* was not a naked version of the text, but probably an edition that included the commentary of the prominent Chinese scholars Zheng Xuan (127–200) or He Yan (190–249). Thus even the very first book that reached Japan, if we believe the *Record of Ancient Matters,* was the product of Chinese scholarly efforts that in turn shaped the experience of its Japanese students. The discovery of Egyptian papyri has made it possible to study literacy

---

[21] On writing primers and educational aids prevalent in the formative period of the seventh and eighth centuries see Tōkyō daigaku kyōyō gakubu 2007, 3–32.
[22] On genres of Greek scholarship see Dickey 2007.

FIGURE 1.1 *The Homeric Epic as Hellenistic Schoolbook Text*
Homer's Iliad, Book 2, lines 172–210. Tebtunis Papyrus 4, Egypt. © Bancroft Library,
University of California, Berkeley.

and education based on writing samples and documents produced directly by students rather than based on the views of education propagated by philosophers of education like Quintilian. In comparable fashion, the discovery of several hundred thousand of inscribed wooden tablets (*mokkan* 木簡) since the 1960s has revolutionized our view of the emergence of multiple literacies in seventh- and eighth-century Japan and the acquisition of writing skills.[23]

Although the *Analects* seems to have been more important as a text for practicing one's calligraphy and writing skills, reproducing the original text rather than accompanying commentaries, the samples of passages from the *Analects* surviving on excavated wooden tablets show intriguing traces of another type of scholarly notation: If Roman students read Greek canonical texts in Greek inscribed with critical marks developed by Hellenistic scholars from Alexandria, Japanese students came to read Chinese canonical texts in accordance with Japanese, not Chinese, syntactical order and developed their own set of critical marks to facilitate the reading of Chinese texts. This reading technique was called *kundoku* 訓読, or "reading through glossing" and Japanese scholars still use it today, even to read

[23] For an overview of the discovery of the wooden tablets and its implications for our view of early Japanese literacies see Lurie 2007. On wooden tablets inscribed with passages from the *Analects* and *Thousand Character Classic* see Tōno 1977.

FIGURE 1.2 *The* Analects *as Japanese Schoolbook Text*
This wooden tablet shows the opening of the Confucian *Analects* in garbled word
order. Instead of 子曰 學而時習之 ("The Master said: To learn and sometimes review
what one has learnt, (is that not pleasure)?"), it reads 子曰 學而習時. Scholars have
argued that the inversion of "sometimes" 時 and "review" 習 and the omission
of the object marker 之 ("what one has learnt") indicates that the scribe produced
the *Analects* passage based on assumptions of Japanese gloss-reading (*kundoku*) of
Chinese texts. © Tokushima kenritsu maizō bunkazai sōgō sentā. Shikoku, Japan.

Classical Chinese texts. We will discuss this complex reading technique further
below, but let it suffice here to say that the Japanese from early on added to the
layers of Chinese scholarship inscribed into the Chinese canonical texts they studied, their own system of reading marks that allowed them to vocalize the Chinese
texts in Japanese.

Thus, Chinese canonical texts like the *Analects* were used by Japanese students to acquire familiarity with Japanese scholarly reading practices such as
gloss-reading. Although the earliest extant manuscripts containing critical marks
for gloss-reading date only to the late eighth century, the practice of transposing
Chinese texts into Japanese word order, a crucial operation of gloss-reading, is
clearly much older: a wooden tablet from the second half of the seventh century
features the opening lines of the *Analects*, with character inversions of the original
text in accordance with Japanese word order.[24]

---

[24] For further discussion of this tablet and its implications for our understanding of the development
of writing in Japan see Lurie 2011, Chapter 4.

We have identified several significant points of difference in the education systems of early Japan and Rome such as the different degree of central government involvement in education, the divergent social status and cultural background of educators, the formative presence of the examination system for the elite culture of China and Japan and the lack of indications for exams in the Greco-Roman world. But all these differences do not seem to have much affected the similar ways in which Japanese and Roman students wrote the canon of their reference cultures into the works they came to produce as writers and scholars during their lives. The extensive copying, memorization, and study of canonical Chinese and Greek texts, including the scholarly cultures inscribed in their editions, became the basis for Japanese and Roman literary production. Without them, there would not have been a comparable Sino-Japanese and Greco-Roman constellation and no book about them.

Let us turn now, however, to the differences in these constellations that complicate our comparison.

2. Depth: Dissimilitudes

Geopolitics

How carefully the magistrates of old regulated their conduct to keep intact the majesty of the Roman people and their own can be seen from the fact that among other indications of their duty to preserve dignity they steadfastly kept to the rule never to make replies to Greeks except in Latin. Indeed, they obliged the Greeks themselves to discard the volubility which is their greatest asset and speak through an interpreter, not only in Rome but in Greece and Asia also, intending no doubt that the dignity of Latin speech be the more widely venerated throughout all nations. Not that they were deficient in attention to polite studies, but they held that in all matters whatsoever the Greek cloak should be subordinate to the Roman gown, thinking it unmeet that the weight and authority of empire be sacrificed to the seductive charm of letters.[25]

Magistratus vero prisci quantopere suam populique Romani maiestatem retinentes se gesserint hinc cognosci potest, quod inter cetera obtinendae gravitatis indicia illud quoque magna cum perseverantia custodiebant, ne Graecis umquam nisi Latine responsa darent. quin etiam ipsos linguae volubilitate, qua plurimum valent, excussa per interpretem loqui cogebant non in urbe tantum nostra sed etiam in Graecia et Asia, quo scilicet Latinae vocis honos per omnes gentes venerabilior diffunderetur. nec illis deerant studia doctrinae, sed nulla non in re pallium togae subici debere arbitrabantur, indignum esse existimantes illecebris et suavitati litterarum imperii pondus et auctoritatem donari.

VALERIUS MAXIMUS (EARLY FIRST CENTURY CE): *MEMORABLE DOINGS AND SAYINGS*

---

[25] Valerius Maximus, *Factorum et dictorum memorabilium* II.2.2. Shackleton Bailey 2000, 139.

Chinese chief administrator of the city of Zhengzhou to Japanese monk Ennin on the ninth day of the sixth month of 845 ce, when Ennin had to leave China during the Buddhist persecutions under Emperor Wuzong:

"Buddhism no longer exists in this land. But it has been said since ancient times that Buddhism will flow toward the East. I want you to do your best to reach your homeland soon and propagate the Buddhist Law there. Your disciple has been very fortunate to have seen you many times. Today we part and we are not likely to meet again in this life. When you have attained Buddhahood, I hope that you will not abandon your disciple."

「此國佛法即無也, 佛法東流, 自古所言. 願和上努力, 早達本國, 弘傳佛法.
弟子多幸, 頂謁多時. 今日已別, 今生中應難得相見. 和上成佛之時,
願不捨弟子.」[26]

ENNIN, *RECORD OF A PILGRIMAGE TO TANG CHINA IN SEARCH OF THE LAW* (*NITTŌ GUHŌ JUNREI KŌKI* 入唐求法巡礼行記)

Comparisons are not inconvenienced, but enabled by controlled dissimilitude. Below I focus on three points of substantial dissimilitude between literary cultures of Early Japan and Rome that complicate our comparison and give it depth. The most formative difference was geopolitical: The Roman Empire conquered the Greek mainland by 146 BCE, during what still counts as the "archaic" period of Latin literature, and became the agent that spread Hellenistic culture in its Roman inflections throughout the Mediterranean and later Europe. In contrast, premodern Japan had no history of conquest that would have bound it politically to its reference culture. It was never conquered by China, nor did it defeat China until the first Sino-Japanese War in 1895, about a millennium after the Heian Period, the classical period for Japanese literature to which later ages would look back with nostalgia. The unexpected and completely unprecedented reversal of cultural hierarchies in East Asia, which happened in the late nineteenth century and culminated in the Japanese imperialist colonization of parts of China, Korea, and Southeast Asia between 1895 and 1945, was indeed a phenomenon of great improbability.[27] If current frictions between the Chinese and Japanese governments focus on economic hegemony, historical atrocities, and expected apologies, they are only a tip of the real iceberg: the still undigested shock on the part of the Chinese that a belated, insular culture like Japan could have reversed the millennia-old dynamics of the East Asian cultural hierarchy. Up to that point China, despite shifting dynasties, governments, and territorial shapes, had always been the hegemonic reference culture in East Asia, uninterruptedly, without a "conquest of Greece," a "fall of Rome," a "rise of Europe" and recent American world hegemony. If we apply the Sino-Japanese War of 1895 CE, the symbolic date of cultural reversal in East Asia, to the Roman timescale (equating it with 146 BCE, the Roman conquest of Greece), we are now, with 2013 CE, in 28 BCE, three years after the fateful battle of Actium, when Augustus, still Octavian at that point, routed

---

[26] Text based on Ono 1992, 472.

[27] For the radical change of Japanese perspectives on China and Japanese travelers' experiences in China see Fogel 1996. For the change of Chinese perspectives on Japan see Lu 2004.

the fleet of Mark Antony and cleared the way for becoming emperor of a great empire to come. Indulging this virtual historical calculus can give us a taste of how very novel, seen à longue durée, the shift of cultural hierarchies in East Asia has been. And it leaves us to wonder what kind of exciting new cultural, political, and economical balances will emerge in the future, particularly because, unlike with Rome of 28 BCE, the Japanese empire in East Asia was short-lived, not lasting beyond half a century.

Because of the fundamentally different geopolitical situation, Greece and Greek-speaking people became physically and psychologically integrated into Roman affairs in ways that China never became in premodern Japan. If we arrange the ways cultures can relate to each other in order of political and psychological proximity, conquest is the closest and most coercive type of relation, followed by colonization, migration, and self-colonization or, as the anthropologist Michael Herzfeld has called it, "crypto-colonialism," the most voluntary form of submission to powerful foreign cultural influence without any direct political or military imposition.[28]

To put it simply, Greece and Rome had a shared history of earlier Greek colonization of the Western Mediterranean, including the Italic Peninsula, and of later Roman conquest of the Eastern Mediterranean, including the Greek mainland and the Hellenistic states that had followed in the wake of the dissolution of Alexander the Great's conquest empire. In contrast, premodern China and Japan had no documented shared history of mass migration to speak of, but a history of unilateral large-scale self-colonization on Japan's part. In other words, while people and territories were physically integrated in the Greco-Roman constellation, they were distant and remote in the Sino-Japanese constellation, where imported Chinese texts rather than native Chinese teachers with their texts and textual expertise transmitted continental culture to Japan. The implications of this radically different mode of cultural translatio—one through slave-teachers and texts, the other almost exclusively textual—are hard to exaggerate, as they profoundly shaped just about any aspect of the Sino-Japanese and Greco-Roman cultural relation. I will not sketch them here, but leave it to the chapters of this book to tease out how the different modes of cultural translatio led to incommensurable, yet still comparable, positions and concerns in Japanese and Latin authors.

Rome's demographic and geopolitical difference from Japan started with the waves of Greek colonization in the Western Mediterranean and on the Italic peninsula.[29] The "Great Greek Colonization" that created the Greek cultural sphere of Magna Graecia in Southern Italy and Sicily peaked between 750–500 BCE, when Greek-speaking people of about twenty Greek municipalities on the Greek mainland, Aegean islands, and the West coast of Asia minor, modern-day Turkey, created a couple of hundred trading ports on the coasts of Southern Italy, the Black Sea, and Gaul. The Greeks were not the only trade colonizers, but at the same time the Phoenicians, in search for precious metals, set up their trade ports

---

[28] Herzfeld 2002.
[29] Boardman 1980, Chapter 5. Snodgrass 1994, 1–10.

throughout the Western Mediterranean. The Greeks also competed with simultaneous Etruscan colonization in northern and central Italy. Overpopulation at home, political crises, or the lure of trade profits all might have contributed to these large-scale migration movements, and the effect was spectacular: southern Italy became a major stage of Greek cultural developments such as Pythagorean philosophy, vase painting, and even Greek drama. Thanks to his successive visits to Sicily, Aeschylus was very popular in Italy and he even devoted a play to a Sicilian topic, the *Women of Aetna*, which celebrated the founding of the city of Aetna. His play *Persians* was reproduced there right before or after its presentation in Athens in 472 and a flood of vases in the fourth century with theater scenes from Aeschylus and Euripides attests the close connection between the Italian Greek cities and the Greek motherland.

Although the direction of demographic and cultural flows had initially been from Greece to Southern Italy, it is crucial to note, in contrast to Japan—which lacked comparable Chinese "colonies"—that already in the fourth century BCE, before the Roman conquest of the Eastern Mediterranean, the cultural flow went both ways, to Italy and back to Greece. An illustration of this two-way flow is that Italic Greeks competed, literally, on the Athenian stage: the Sicilian tyrant Dionysius I of Syracuse (r. 405-) fought the competing Carthaginians and Phoenicians and brutally conquered territories for Syracuse with an iron fist, but distinguished himself more nobly when his play *Ransom of Hector* won first prize in the drama competition in Athens in 376 BCE.[30]

When Dionysius I's play won first prize in Athens, the small city of Rome was threatened by Celtic invasions—the Gauls had taken Rome in 390—and was just about to enter a new phase, moving toward mastering the peninsula and getting involved in maritime commitments. Only the third century BCE saw Rome's direct involvement in the affairs of the southern Italian Greek-speaking cities. After a decade of struggle over Tarentum, a prominent Dorian colony on the heel of the Italian boot, which called on King Pyrrhus of Epirus (nowadays the border region between Greece and Albania) to fight pro-Roman factions, Rome captured the city in 272 BCE, making it pay heavy compensation. This was an important date in the conquest of Graecia Magna, for Rome the Greek-speaking territories closest to home, and it led to Rome's first extensive exposure to Greeks and Greek culture. Only the second century brought Rome in direct interaction with Hellenistic states outside of Italy and led eventually to the conquest of the Greek mainland, with the defeat of the Achaean League at Corinth in 146 BCE.

This phase, when Rome expanded its power beyond the Italic peninsula into the Eastern Mediterranean, seems to hold the key to long-standing scholarly debates about the nature and motives of Roman imperialism. To counter opinions that see Rome as an always already bellicose predator set to conquer the world from early on, Arthur Eckstein offers an alternative reading of Roman military and diplomatic engagement in the Eastern Mediterranean during the decisive period from 230 to 170 BCE. In his view Rome's role changed from being one of many players in a

---

[30] For Greek drama in Sicily see Dearden 1990, 231–42, in particular p. 234.

long-prevailing "Hellenistic multipolar anarchy" to being the hegemonic power in a now Rome-centered unipolar hierarchy, which eventually enabled the rise of the Roman Empire.[31] These developments were not predictable—there are repeated signs that Rome was not keen on conquering and keeping territories in the East during this period—but rather induced through a "power transition crisis." The Ptolemaic dynasty in Egypt faltered after ca. 207 BCE and threw the Hellenistic multi-polar system off-balance, leading to a hotly debated pact between Philip V of Macedon and Antiochus III of the Seleucid empire, another Hellenistic successor state to Alexander's conquests, which covered large stretches of land from Syria to Bactria and modern-day Afghanistan. According to Eckstein, this set off a "diplomatic revolution," and Rome eventually decided to intervene.[32] At least since 280 BCE the Hellenistic state-system power balance had been tripolar, a balance among Macedon, the Seleucid Empire, and Ptolemaic Egypt. In long and costly wars, Rome curbed two major players in the Hellenistic multistate system: it foiled Antiochus's ambitions to bring Greece to its knees in 188 BCE and abolished the Macedonian royal dynasty in a third Macedonian War (171–168 BCE). Eckstein's compelling analysis of Rome's gradual emergence as a hegemonic power in the Eastern Mediterranean effectively undoes the common teleology of Rome's rise and triumph and instead recaptures the period preceding Rome's hegemony as a period of political maneuvering in a multistate Hellenistic world whose rules broke down with the crisis in Egypt, not simply because of Rome's aggressive imperial ambitions.

Eckstein's analysis of the power balance in the Mediterranean during the third and second centuries BCE resonates with recent scholarship on the Chinese influence sphere in East Asia, which moves away from a priori assumptions of Chinese hegemonic dominance and shows instead mutual stimulation and consolidation in an ever fluid East Asian multistate system, emphasizing the political agency of Japan, Korea, and Vietnam, to name just the very few of those states that survived in some form into the modern period and still have a voice to remind the world of their national histories.[33] It also underscores the surprise effect that Rome's gradual conquests in the East must have had on its contemporaries: they were perhaps not as surprising as Japan's defeat of China in 1894, but marked the beginning of a cultural reversal of world-historical scope.

It is no exaggeration to say that Rome's conquest of the Greek mainland was one of the single most influential moments for Western cultural history, as we know it unfolded. It is also one of the single most important differences from the Sino-Japanese, and overall East Asian, cultural constellation. True, in contrast to China during the Tang Dynasty (and even during the more segregated Six Dynasties Period) "Greece" was not a single state, but consisted of multiple Hellenistic States that shared the Greek language, or dialects thereof, and Greek culture. Still, Rome's defeat of the Achaean League at Corinth in 146 BCE was not one of many isolated Roman victories in the Eastern Mediterranean, but came

---

[31] Eckstein 2008, 381.
[32] Ibid., 181–270.
[33] See in particular Wang 2005, and Holcombe 2001.

to represent the endpoint of a longer process of the submission of Greece and the Greek world to Rome. As Michael Herzfeld remarks on the status of Greece in Western cultural history, "Greece may be unique in the degree to which the country as a whole has been forced to play the contrasted roles of *Ur-Europa* and humiliated oriental vassal at one and the same time."[34] Although Valerius Maximus, the author of *Memorable Doings and Sayings* quoted above, has a dubitable reputation for being superstitious, unreliable, and chatty, his anecdote about the old Roman magistrates captures the significance of this event in a symbolic tableau: "but they held that in all matters whatsoever the Greek cloak should be subordinate to the Roman gown, thinking it unmeet that the weight and authority of empire be sacrificed to the seductive charm of letters *(sed nulla non in re pallium togae subici debere arbitrabantur, indignum esse existimantes illecebris et suavitati litterarum imperii pondus et auctoritatem donari)."* The submission of the Greek cloak to the Roman toga meant a disjunction between political and cultural capital, the "weight and authority" of the empire that faced the "sweetness" *(suavitas)* of letters and cultural sophistication associated with Greeks. Although Valerius's formulation gives culture a lightweight role in contrast to *imperii pondus et auctoritas,* the Roman anxiety of being perceived as lacking "learning" *(studia doctrinae)* lurks in Valerius's defense of the magistrate's linguistic violence, their imposition on Greek-speaking people to communicate in Latin not *faute de mieux,* but paradoxically *malgré mieux.* This anxiety motivated Roman clichéd invectives against the defeated "little" Greeks, the *Graeculi,* who were cast as voluble, inept, lighthearted, and effeminate, against the self-aggrandizing gravity, dignity, piety, and military valor of the Romans.[35]

Debates about what "Romanization" of Greece meant on a political, administrative, cultural, religious, artistic, and literary level, how "Romanization" under Roman rule in general differed from "Hellenization" in the wake of the successor states of Alexander the Great's empire, and how to divide agency between the "Romanizers" and their "Romanized subjects" have produced a voluminous literature in the last decades.[36] What is crucial for our comparison with the early Japanese situation is the physical integration of Greek and Latin-speaking populations that was a direct result of Rome's conquest of Greece. Studying rhetoric and philosophy in Athens or Asia Minor became a common element of Roman elite education, a great number of Roman businessmen and traders resided in the Greek-speaking world, and tens of thousands of Roman veterans inhabited almost fifty settlements in the Eastern Mediterranean under Augustus alone.[37] In turn, each conquest of Greek-speaking territory led to an influx of Greek slaves to Italy,

---

[34] Herzfeld 1987, 19.
[35] For further prejudices see Alcock 1993, 1–32, in particular p. 28.
[36] To name just a few central titles: first, on Romanization: the groundbreaking studies in Gruen 1984 draw our attention to the Hellenistic premises on which Rome expanded its domination over the Mediterranean; see also Woolf 1998, Macmullen 2000, and Wallace-Hadrill 2008. On Greece under Roman rule: Woolf 1994, Alcock 1993, Alcock 1997, and Swain 1996. On literary and intellectual developments in Rome and Roman Greece, in particular the "Second Sophistic" revival during the first centuries of the Common Era: Anderson 1993, Whitmarsh 2005, and Goldhill 2001.
[37] Macmullen 2000, Chapter 1 and the map on p. 8–9.

where they would often work as teachers and tutors in Roman households. The history of spectacular expulsions of educated Greeks from Rome, something that to my knowledge is not attested for Chinese from early Japan, is only thinkable in a world where actual people and not just cultures embodied in imported texts collide and coexist.

Greek-speaking philosophers, sometimes also rhetors, were expelled repeatedly in the earlier phase of Greek and Roman cultural rapprochement. This was certainly a symptom of ambivalence toward increasing Greek cultural influence during the second century BCE.[38] The most famous drama of expulsion unfolded in 155 BCE when an embassy from Athens that included representatives of the Stoic, Peripatetic, and Academic schools was sent to ask for a reduction of a fine Athens had incurred for attacking a neighboring city in Attica, came to Rome. Its leader Carneades of Cyrene, head of the Platonic Academy, spoke one day in favor and the next day against the value of justice, making sure to mention Rome as example of how to become powerful through injustice. Cato the Elder was so incensed by this insult and the perfidious logic of the sophistical argument that he asked the Senate to throw the philosophers out of the city. Equally interestingly, "Latin rhetors" were expelled in 92 BCE by a decree stating that "we have been informed that there are persons who have established a novel sort of instruction and that the youth gather at their school; that these persons have styled themselves 'Latin rhetoricians,' and that young persons idle away whole days there (*renuntiatum est nobis esse homines qui novum genus disciplinae instituerunt, ad quos iuventus in ludum conveniat; eos sibi nomen imposuisse Latinos rhetoras, ibi hominess adulescentulos dies totos desidere*)."[39] Though clothed in a Latin name and probably indeed Romans in flesh, these people were clearly the Roman equivalent of Greek rhetoricians or philosophers, dangerous because of their proverbial seduction of the young. This decree was issued by the prominent orator Crassus, censor at the time, whom we will encounter in later chapters as the charismatic speaker in Cicero's dialogue *On the Orator*. The dissolution of the school has been interpreted as an attempt of the Roman aristocracy to monopolize access to the training in the civic tool of oratory. However, the precedent of expulsions of Greek rhetoricians and philosophers facilitated the argument for it and made it possible to adduce the well-worn cliché of the corruption of youth.

The expulsions are a fascinating phenomenon, especially given that the Roman political establishment was so little interested in getting involved in education otherwise. It is important to point out that they were signs of Greco-Roman proximity rather than distance. Only because Greek speakers had such a pervasive presence in Rome and became the brain trust of the Roman education system could they come under suspicion.

The massive migration movements caused by the "Great Greek colonization" of southern Italy and the Roman conquest of Greece contrast sharply with the probably extremely limited movement of actual people between the continent and

---

[38] For an overview of expulsions of foreigners and certain professional groups such as religious cult leaders and actors from Rome see Noy 2000, 37–47.
[39] Suetonius, *De Grammaticis et Rhetoribus* 25.2. Kaster 1995, 30–31.

the Japanese archipelago after the seventh century and the large-scale process of self-colonization the Japanese engaged in.

There are at least three major differences in the early Sino-Japanese geopolitical constellation compared to the Greco-Roman case. First, nowadays questions of ethnicity and linguistics, often tinged by nationalist undertones, dominate the discussion over the early period before centralized state formation in the late seventh and eighth centuries. Second, there was an intermediary third player, the states on the Korean peninsula, which played a major role in transmitting new technologies from China or of their own.[40] Third, the "Chinese world order" was not based on conquest and direct rule, but on a cultural influence sphere and tribute system enacted through an investiture system in which the Chinese court gave titles and gifts to chiefs of surrounding polities and expected regular tribute missions to the Chinese capital as symbolic return.

Let us begin with the first aspect, the national veil that hovers over questions of ethnicity and linguistics in discussions of Japan's origins. The origins of Rome and the enthusiastic search for archeological and textual clues about Rome's early development are certainly an urgent topic of inquiry for historians, opera lovers, and tourists alike. Yet, I dare say its urgency is incomparable to the feverish public search for historical identity pursued in today's Japan. The question of where the inhabitants of the Japanese archipelago came from, how they relate to their continental neighbors on the Korean peninsula and China, to which language family they belong, how the various Japanese, Korean, and Chinese sources relating to early events on the Japanese archipelago compare with each other, and how they relate to the wealth of recently excavated archeological materials is of premier national importance in Japan.[41] The assumption that Japan and the Japanese have always possessed a distinctive cultural essence that makes them unique and exceptional— whether in their origins, in their peculiarly creative reception of Chinese culture, or in their paradoxically successful way of Westernization through which they preserved their traditional national character—has been so pervasive in Japan that it would be wrong to call it a nationalistic ideology. Rather, it is an ingrained culturalism that is blind to its nationalistic bias. According to one estimate, more than a thousand books on *Nihonjinron* 日本人論, "theory on the nature of the

---

[40] This is of course a complex situation in the case of Rome: there are the various Italic people such as the Etruscans, Oscans, Umbrians, Messapians, and so on who had long-standing relations with the Greek cities in Italy and certainly had a mediator function. Further afield, there were large empires in close contact with Hellenistic culture, such as the Seleucid and Macedonian kingdoms, the Ptolemaic kingdom, or the Carthaginians. But our sources do not suggest that any of these minorities or empires developed a rich national literature as the Romans did. Thus, for Latin literature, Greek and Greeks were the only reference culture in the full sense explained above. Feeney reminds us how exceptional and surprising the emergence of Latin literature truly was: "After 240 BCE the preservation of vernacular poetic (and eventually not only poetic) texts became a distinguishing mark of Rome as well—and of nowhere else in the non-Greek Western Mediterranean." Feeney 2005, 231. Emma Dench's work is crucial for understanding the complex psychology of Rome's multiethnic state. For an overview see Dench 2010.
[41] An account of the thorny issues around the origins of the Japanese, combining biological anthropology, linguistics, archaeology, genetics, and ethnography is Hudson 1999. On archaeology and identity issues see also Denoon, Hudson, McCormack, and Morris-Suzuki 1996, Part I "Archaeology and Identity."

Japanese," were published between 1945 and 1990, arguing each in more or less similar ways for the uniqueness of Japan, its people and its history.[42] This type of inquiry flourishes both in public and academic circles. Against this background it is interesting that the theory about the ethnic origins of Japanese culture that has gained the strongest scholarly consensus since the 1990s emphasizes Japan's major indebtedness to the continent. In the "dual-structure hypothesis" proposed by the Japanese anthropologist Kazurō Hanihara in 1991, immigrants from what today is Northeast China and Korea are the ancestors of most Japanese. He proposed that, in a first step during the Pleistocene, immigrants from Southeast Asia and Southern China settled the Japanese islands; these were the ancestors of the *Jōmon* 縄文 people, whose "corded-ware pottery" scholars use to define the "Jōmon Period" (ca. 10, 000–300 BCE). In this society of hunters and gatherers intruded immigrants from the Northeast Asian continent during the Yayoi Period (ca. 300 BC-300 CE), introducing wet-rice cultivation and bronze and iron metallurgy into the Japanese islands. They settled all islands of the archipelago except for the northern island of Hokkaido and the southern chain of the Ryukyu Islands, so that the indigenous Ainu people in Hokkaido and the Okinawans should be considered remnants of the earlier Jōmon population.[43] Although the Jōmon people were not completely replaced, genetic data does indicate that the massive immigration from northeastern China and Korea during the Yayoi Period contributed the lion's share of today's Japanese genetic pool.

Thus, unlike with Ancient Greeks and Romans, who shared Indo-European ethnic, linguistic, and religious roots, and unlike modern Greeks and Italians, who might care about their role as cultural cradle and catalyst in Western cultural history but much less about any unique "national essence" rooted in ethnic attributes, modern Japanese care deeply about their origins and about the question of how immigration from China and Korea shaped their prehistory, which could potentially threaten their claim to "uniqueness." Until the first mention of a polity called *Wa* 倭 on the Japanese islands in Chinese sources of the third century CE, there is no textual evidence to support our reading of the prehistoric archaeological record. Chinese official histories, which discuss tribute missions and polities in the Chinese influence sphere, and later Japanese and Korean annals, which record their own emerging state formation, give a spotty picture of sustained contact zones. But they fail to give us a sense of how much of the significant technology transfer during that period from the continent to the Japanese Islands happened through diffusion of ideas or how much of it happened through migration of actual people and artisans.

This is the period when the mediation of Chinese influence through the state formation on the Korean peninsula was decisive. To return to Eckstein's hypothesis, the emergent Roman state was part of an anarchic multipolar Hellenistic state system, kept in some kind of balance through the three main powers of Ptolemaic Egypt, Macedonia, and the Seleucid Empire, before Rome emerged

---

[42] Hudson 1999, 234.
[43] Ibid. 60–81.

as a unipolar hegemonic power in the Mediterranean in the late third century BCE. Rome, both before and during the empire, functioned in a world of manifold ethnicities and cultures, but, except for the Etruscans in the archaic period, there was no prominent singular intermediary of different linguistic and cultural background through whose transmission and transformation Rome would have gained access to Greek culture. The Greeks in Greece and in the colonized world of Magna Graecia were basically Greeks, in contrast to the states on the Korean peninsula that were linguistically and culturally distinct both from China and Japan. Although China had established four commanderies on the Korean peninsula during the Han Dynasty in 108 BCE, the state of Koguryo was established in the North by the first century CE, followed by the foundation of the states of Silla in southeastern Korea and Paekche in southwestern Korea around the fourth century CE. Until 668, when Silla destroyed the two other kingdoms of the so-called early Three Kingdom Period and unified the peninsula under its rule, the hostilities between these states and their rivalries over Chinese attention was a driving force both for state formation in early Japan and for the transmission—and sometimes Korean transformation—of Chinese technologies.[44] State formation of Silla and Paekche in the fourth century seems to have run parallel to the emergence of a state with some form of centralized government, as can be seen from the uniform distribution of labor-intensive keyhole-shaped tombs from southern Kyushu to northern Honshu that archeologists have used to designate the "Tomb Period" (ca.300–552 CE). Archeological evidence for this period indicates a large-scale influx of Korean-borne technology: ironworking, gold, silver metallurgy, stoneware manufacture, and the use of horses and horse equipment. They also included writing, Buddhism, Buddhist architecture and sculpture, and Chinese-style law and bureaucratic accouterments such as surnames, titles, and ranks that helped build a central government.[45] Some of these technologies required the presence of expert artisans and cannot have reached Japan only as ideas without the experts to execute them. William Wayne Farris has proposed four mechanisms by which technologies spread from the Korean peninsula to Japan: trade, immigration, plundering of Japanese troops involved in battles on the peninsula, and fourth, an official exchange between Japan-friendly states such as Paekche, who granted critical goods and services to the Japanese in return for their military support.[46] But again, the proportions of the actual demographics behind these exchanges, which could give us a better sense of the type of cultural translatio taking place in prehistoric Japan, remain hard to grasp.

Japanese earliest annals, the *Record of Ancient Matters* and the *Chronicles of Japan* (*Nihon shoki* 日本書紀) from the eighth century, do give us some glimpse of the influx of people and technologies from the Korean peninsula and family

---

[44] Important studies of Japanese state formation include Barnes 1993, Chapters 13 and 14, Barnes 2007 and Piggott 1997. For a history of Japanese state formation from an East Asian perspective see Holcombe 2001.

[45] For an overview of the relations between early Japan and the Korean peninsula see Farris 1998, Chapter 2 and Holcombe 2001, 165–214.

[46] Farris 1998, 121.

registers of aristocrats indicate that as much as a third of the eight-century bureaucracy could trace their origins to Korea since 300 CE.[47] However, the archeological record suggests a much greater Korean immigration than the annals indicate for the period between 300 and 700. And there are clear biases in the way the eighth-century Japanese court wanted to have their history represented. First, there is a persistent bias against Silla. The Yamato regime in Japan was a traditional ally of Paekche, which even sent their princes to Japan for protection during tensions with Koguryo and Silla, and kept Japanese troops and interests involved on the peninsula. After all, it was the lifeline to advanced Chinese technology and culture. When Silla destroyed Paekche in 663 in the process of the unification of the peninsula, there was a last great wave of highly skilled immigrants that brought continental know-how to the Japanese archipelago. On the eve of the emergence of fuller literacy and the beginning of literary production in the eighth century, immigration from the Korean peninsula came to a decisive, historically influential halt. Thereafter, Japan was to be bound to the continent mainly by embassies and imports, not by migration and ethnic integration like in the early period leading up to the seventh century.

The third important difference of the Sino-Japanese from the Greco-Roman geopolitical constellation was the political texture of Chinese cultural hegemony in East Asia. Since the Han Dynasty (206 BCE–220 CE), China started to connect surrounding polities to its empire in a multistate system of investiture. Chieftains of surrounding polities would receive titles and prestige goods such as inscribed seals and mirrors from the Chinese court in return for tribute gifts and political allegiance to the Chinese emperor shown through regular—costly—tribute missions. Polities on the Japanese islands participated in this system since at least 57 CE, when Emperor Guangwu of the Han entrusted a seal to a messenger from Wa.[48] State formation on the Korean peninsula and the Japanese islands was in large part an outcome of securing access to Chinese titles and technologies and the local chieftains on the archipelago thus enhanced their domestic influence, particularly before the unification of Japan in the hands of the Yamato monarchs in the Kinai area around Nara and Kyoto in the fifth through seventh centuries.[49]

Although Japan had sent numerous missions to several Chinese dynasties since the first attested mission in 57 CE, the embassies to the Sui (581–618) and Tang courts (618–906) ushered in a new phase of cultural interaction with the continent and China. From the seventh to the late ninth century the Japanese court appointed about twenty missions to China. From a Chinese perspective, the Japanese missions were conveying tribute to the court of the Son of Heaven in the capital Chang'an, as dozens of other states and polities did. From a Japanese perspective the missions were costly and complex diplomatic maneuvers, especially during the stormy period of the Silla unification of the Korean peninsula in the late seventh century. Later missions functioned increasingly as channels

---

[47] Ibid. 121.
[48] For an overview of the history of Sino-Japanese relations see Fogel 2009, Chapter 1 "Sino-Japanese Relations: The Long View," and Kimiya 1965.
[49] See Wang 2005, 17–32.

for cultural exchange, transporting Japanese monks and students to China or, very occasionally, Chinese envoys and monks to Japan, and enabling the importation into Japan of books, Buddhist scriptures, and devotional objects. To a limited degree, the missions provided trade opportunities, and gave the Japanese envoys the chance to gain high rank or other coveted rewards both before their departure and after the successful completion of the mission to compensate them for the great dangers.[50] Japan's Tang missions paradoxically foreignized China for the Japanese while at the same time providing the very channels to familiarize them more thoroughly with contemporary Chinese culture. The standard narrative about the Tang missions, which emphasizes the familiarization aspect of the process of cultural exchange, overlooks the fact that China became foreign to the Japanese envoys only in the moment they stepped on Chinese soil. Thoroughly familiar with the Chinese world in the Chinese canonical texts they were raised on in Japan, the cultivated envoys must have experienced nothing less than a culture shock when they reached the actual China after their perilous trip. So much was unfamiliar: The foreign-sounding language; the dealings with the Tang bureaucracy, which paid for their stay but monitored them on every step; the sudden encounter, during the pompous tribute ceremony, with envoys from the Korean Peninsula, Cambodia, or Tibet and with the mixed urban populations of the Tang Empire that included Arab merchants, Persian doctors, and people of Nestorian or Jewish faith; the monumental scale of the imperial court compared to its modest incarnation of Nara and Kyoto; the exotic products that the growing monetary economy of the markets of Tang cities had to offer.

This form of cultural translatio was also very peculiar in another respect: we might almost call the Japanese embassies a *synecdoche* of cultural exchange between China and Japan, rather than an extensive and regular ongoing process of exchange. During the twenty embassies—often merely one every few decades— only a minimal number of highly educated Japanese individuals actually went to China and interacted with Chinese officials and literati, monks, merchants, and clerks; each embassy had at most a hundred or a few hundred members, most of whom were seamen handling the ships. When carrying out their mission and attending the tribute ceremony in the Chinese capital Chang'an, the envoys engaged in very brief diplomatic interactions of symbolic value—only a few days of ceremony after many months of travel by ship and on horseback. But these fleeting moments of symbolic value were given utmost attention and lavish financial support from the Japanese court for almost three centuries until the late ninth century, when they were somewhat inexplicably abandoned as too costly, too dangerous, or perhaps less pressing after the fall of the Tang in 907 and the ensuing chaotic Five Dynasties Period. Yet, and here comes the power of the synecdoche, those few fleeting encounters of the embassy members and the longer study periods of a very small number of Japanese students and monks in China who accompanied the missions had a disproportionately formative impact on Japanese society: on

---

[50] For a history of the Tang missions see Charlotte von Verschuer 1985, Wang 2005, Tōno 1999, Wang 1998, and Furuse 2003. For the Tang context of foreigners, visitors, and ethnic identity see Abramson 2008.

how cities and temples looked and which devotional objects they contained, on its ritual observances and law codes, on fashion in poetry, music, and painting, herbs, medicine, divination; in short, on just about anything.

All factors that distinguish the Sino-Japanese from the Greco-Roman constellation—geopolitical distance from the reference culture versus its physical integration and conquest; modern nationalist involvement in historical debates in East Asia versus symbolic dissolution into a shared Latin heritage in the West; the presence of a prominent third player, the Korean peninsula, versus its lack in the Roman world; and, lastly, the strange type of cultural translatio effected in the Japanese tribute missions within the framework of the Chinese investiture system versus a cultural translatio that involved a demographics of migration and exchange of populations—all these factors made China into a somehow distant and malleable phenomenon for early Japanese.

In premodern Japan there was no disjunction between cultural and political capital, which Rome's conquest of the Greek-speaking world brought about in the ancient Mediterranean. Japan remained marginal to the Chinese world order, in line with its role of a younger culture vis-à-vis its reference culture. This marginality gave Japanese authors great freedom to imagine themselves in relation to a "third space," a China shaped by Japanese exigencies and desires. This "third space" had nothing very conscious and nothing necessarily fictional about it, although it could take extreme forms of wishful thinking in literary accounts of imaginary voyages to China that play out fantasies of inverting the cultural hierarchy between China and Japan.[51]

Is the Japanese monk Ennin 円仁 (793–864), who accompanied the penultimate embassy to the Tang in 838 and was forced out of China in 847 because of Emperor Wuzong's persecution of Buddhism, dreaming a dream of prophetic Japanese importance in a world where it was lacking? As we learn from the diary quoted above, which Ennin wrote during his stay in China, a Chinese official of the city of Zhengzhou, who had always looked out for Ennin, dashes on horseback after the Japanese monks who are anxiously fleeing China, expelled due to the persecutions. In the moment of cultural crisis, when a Chinese emperor was eager to please Daoist quacks and fill the empty state coffers by forcing tens of thousands of tax-exempt monks and nuns into taxable laity and sacking the wealth of their monasteries, the Chinese official from Zhengzhou subjects himself as a "disciple" to a Japanese monk and prophetically declares Japan into the place of the future, a haven for Buddhism on the verge of extinction at home. "Buddhism no longer exists in this land. But it has been said since ancient times that Buddhism will flow toward the East. I want you to do your best to reach your homeland soon and propagate the Buddhist Law there."[52]

For Japanese monks, India and China were the countries of the origin of Buddhism. The monks went to China "in search of the Law," to study the newest developments in Buddhist doctrine, practice with Chinese and Indian masters,

---

[51] For an intriguing analysis of a few such tales and plays see Sakaki 2007, Chapter 1.
[52] For a translation and study of Ennin's diary see Reischauer 1955b and its companion volume Reischauer 1955a.

and bring home Buddhist texts, paintings, and devotional objects. Ennin's diary is rather factual and sober and it is thus not impossible that the official of Zhengzhou did indeed grace the Japanese monk with these flattering words of adieu. But they are only imaginable in a context of Chinese cultural cataclysm. The infamous burning of books by the First Emperor of the Qin in 213 BCE or the Buddhist persecutions under Wuzong were the type of moments for which Chinese did imagine a role of importance for Japan, the role of an "outsourced" receptacle for precious cultural goods about to perish in China. In the early modern period Chinese intellectuals recovered—and imagined—all those Chinese books preserved only in Japan; to this day exciting finds in hidden-away Japanese imperial, private, or temple libraries of Chinese materials lost in China are important events in the field. But we should not forget: whereas Rome became the receptacle that assimilated and propagated Hellenistic culture through its empire, subjecting the "Greek cloak" to the "Roman toga," Japan was marginal to China. Only in moments of Chinese cultural cataclysm could it rise to its own imagined historic role in East Asia; and even then only, from the Chinese perspective, as a conscientious receptacle of Chinese belongings that should be claimed back by their true owners at some point in a better future.

Language

Linguistic configuration of the Sino-Japanese and Greco-Roman constellations is another site of complex divergence that gives depth to our comparison. In both premodern Japan and Rome, writers, most often members of the educated elite, would have intimate knowledge of both their reference culture's and their own literary tradition. It was not enough to understand Chinese and Greek, but for cultural literacy one needed to know and inhabit the genres, authors, myths, themes, associations, and metaphors distinctive of each literary tradition. Yet Japan was a monolingual empire—forms of vernacular Japanese were the basis of oral communication—while Rome's Republic and Empire grew multilingual in proportion to its conquests. As Rome's territory expanded beyond Latium and local relevance, Rome became ever more multilingual. Latin coexisted in the early period on the peninsula with a host of Italic languages and dialects such as Umbrian and Oscan, or even non-Indo-European languages like Etruscan, but no substantial corpus of high literature was produced in these other languages that would have entered the canon of Roman education.[53] Although Ennius (239–170 BCE), whom we encountered in Suetonius's biographies of grammarians above, was trilingual and had reputedly the "three hearts" of Greek, Oscan, and Latin, he wrote his *Annals,* an epic history of Rome where he introduced the Greek hexameter into the Latin epic tradition to come, in Latin, not in Oscan.[54] Thus, although the Roman world was multilingual, its literary culture was largely confined to the mastery of two languages, namely Latin and Greek.

---

[53] For an overview of spoken and written languages of the Roman world see Harris 1989, 175–90. The first handbook to provide detailed overview of the various languages and literatures of the Roman empire will be Selden and Vasunia (in preparation).

[54] For early Italic languages and their relation to the diffusion of writing see Mauro Cristofani 1999.

To clearly formulate the crucial differences between the pattern of literacy in Rome and Japan at the outset: At least since the second century BCE, the Roman elite was *bilingual*—they spoke both Greek and Latin; their education was *bicanonical*—they were trained in both the Greek and growing Latin literary canon; and their literary production was predominantly *monoliterate*—they wrote their works in Latin. True, early Latin historians like Fabius Pictor had written works in Greek to present the history of the rise of Rome in favorable light to a Hellenistic audience, and obviously Greeks living under Roman domination would write in their Greek mother tongue.[55] But none of the great Latin authors produced a work in Greek that became the foundation of his fame. The Japanese scheme of literacy was radically different. The early Japanese elite was *monolingual*—with the exception of very few individuals who came from the continent or studied in China for a long time, Japanese could not speak Chinese; their education was *tricanonical*—including the Chinese canon, and the growing Sino-Japanese and vernacular Japanese canons; and their literary production was *biliterate*—they produced texts in both Sino-Japanese and the vernacular, and many genre-dependent hybrid idioms in between.

It was both easier and more difficult for Romans to acquire Greek language skills than it was for Japanese to read Chinese. Learning Greek was easier for a speaker of Latin, because both languages are Indo-European, inflecting languages that share lexical roots and syntactical patterns. Latin has more cases than Greek, while Greek has inflections for a "middle voice" between active and passive voice or an "Aorist" inflection to express particular aspects of the past tense, but they are both highly inflected languages. In contrast, Chinese and Japanese belong to two unrelated large language families, the Sino-Tibetan and, arguably, the Altaic languages, respectively. Once Japanese started to write their own language with the help of Chinese characters and the uses of writing expanded with the emergence of a more centralized state in the seventh century, much of the Chinese lexicon was imported and still constitutes the shared lexical pool between modern varieties of Chinese and Japanese. Yet in terms of syntax, Chinese and Japanese belong to opposite ends of the linguistic spectrum: Chinese is an uninflected, so-called "isolating" language, lacking cases, tenses, and inflections. Japanese, in contrast, is an "agglutinative" language, inflecting words through "glued-on" suffixes and auxiliary verbs or particles. Moreover, it is an "SOP" language (subject-object-predicate) as opposed to Chinese, which like English is an "SPO" language, where the object follows the predicate of a sentence. Thus, learning to read Chinese was more difficult for the Japanese, because the languages are syntactically so different that the Japanese needed to switch word order and add a host of suffixes and inflections to a naked Chinese sentence in order to make sense of it in Japanese.

However, in another way it was much more difficult for a Roman to learn Greek than it was for a Japanese to learn Chinese. Alphabetic languages—languages that are recorded based on the sound produced in pronouncing the words—have the

---

[55] For the first two generations after Livius Andronicus we had, as Denis Feeney notes, a "striking chiasmus: the 'Greeks' [such as Andronicus and Ennius] are writing drama and epic in Latin, and the Romans [such as Fabius Pictor] are writing ethnographic history in Greek." Feeney 2005, 237.

disadvantage of requiring translation.[56] Hungarian uses the Latin alphabet, but one has to learn lexicon and grammar to be able to understand a text in Latin letters written in Hungarian. Similarly, Latin speakers would not be able to understand a Greek sentence, even if it were written in Latin, not Greek, letters. They would have to learn lexicon and grammar to make sense of a Greek sentence. Not so for highly logographic languages such as the East Asian ones, that use characters for writing words, which might be pronounced differently depending on whether a Chinese, Korean, Japanese, or Vietnamese person voices it in their vernacular language. The Japanese developed a reading technique, which, as mentioned above, was called *kundoku*, or "reading through glossing," which allowed the reader to read out Chinese sentences in accordance with Japanese syntax. The famous opening of the Confucian *Analects*, which in modern Mandarin reads *xue er shi* xi zhi, *bu yi yue hu* 學而時習之、不亦説乎 ("to learn and sometimes review what one has learnt, is that not pleasure?)" (*Analects* 1.1) could be vocalized by a Japanese reader as *manabite toki ni* kore o narafu, *mata yorokobashikarazu ya.*[57] The Japanese vocalization of a Chinese sentence through the *kundoku* reading method involves three procedures: first, the association of logographs of Chinese origin with Japanese words (e.g., the logograph 習 ("review"), pronounced xi in Mandarin with the Japanese word narafu with the same meaning); second, the transposition of the resulting words into Japanese word order (e.g., by placing the object before the verb: inverting the Chinese xi ("reviewing") zhi ("that which (one has learned")) into the Japanese kore ("that which (one has learned") narafu ("review"); third, the addition of grammatical suffixes and particles (e.g., the Japanese object marker o in kore o narafu ("review what one has learnt").[58]

   Although one could technically call this transposition an instant "translation" on the go—and there is much debate about this issue—it was a reading technique that students would learn from childhood on as the natural way of reading Chinese texts, and it did not involve the learning of a foreign language, as the Chinese text was voiced in Japanese vernacular.[59] Not only did the Japanese the *kundoku* reading method that enabled them to read Chinese texts directly, without the need for translation. More importantly, from the seventh throughout the early twentieth century, Japanese authors produced texts in "reverse *kundoku*": they wrote texts in Chinese word order and without Japanese grammatical markers, which, if written in a genre that favored pure Sinitic style over a hybrid of Chinese and Japanese vernacular, were perfectly readable for Chinese (and premodern Korean and Vietnamese, for that matter). This literature has been called "Sino-Japanese"

---

[56] For further reflections on the impact of phonographic versus logographic scripts on literary cultures see Denecke (forthcoming).

[57] As with glossing or translating, there are many other ways in which this phrase could be vocalized and was vocalized throughout history. For a few different readings of this sentence through history see Kin 2010, 72 f.

[58] For further explanation of the nature and development of *kundoku* see Lurie 2011, Chapter 4.

[59] There was also an alternative way of reading called *ondoku* 音読 (reading by (original) sound), which involved reading each Chinese character with approximating Chinese pronunciation in Chinese word order. However, this reading technique was probably limited to very special genres and occasions, such as the recitation of rhymed Chinese-style poetry, the memorization of primers, or the ritual chanting of Buddhist texts.

or "Japanese *kanbun* 漢文," ("Japanese Chinese").[60] The ingenuous method of *kundoku* for reading, which eliminated the necessity of translating Chinese, and its reverse application by Japanese authors in writing, which created a whole independent literary canon of Japanese *kanbun* produced by Japanese authors, led to an intriguing linguistic constellation of premodern Japanese literary culture. As mentioned above, Japanese literary culture was largely monolingual, biliterate, and tricanonical; or, put differently, a literary culture whose participants used Japanese in oral communication were familiar with the Chinese and Japanese literary corpus, and mastered the three canons that made up the Chinese and Japanese literary corpus: the Chinese canon on the one hand, and the indigenous Japanese canon—which consisted of literary works divided into Japanese *kanbun* and vernacular Japanese—on the other. Japanese *kanbun* was the written language associated with the court bureaucracy, scholarship, and Buddhism. While aristocratic women also received ample education in Chinese and Japanese *kanbun* literature, the authors producing Japanese *kanbun* were almost exclusively male during the Heian Period. Vernacular Japanese, or *wabun*, literature 和文 had its own set of genres, some of which were strongly associated with female subjectivity, private sentiment, and romantic emotions.

Japan's monolingual, biliterate literary culture with a triple canon is a particularly interesting case even within East Asia, because the literary cultures of Korea and Vietnam functioned for a long time virtually only in the Chinese-style idiom and did not develop vernacular literatures until much later, whereas Japanese authors produced a rich literature in the vernacular and in Japanese *kanbun,* Chinese-style, or Sino-Japanese literature, from the outset. It is also distinctive because it is strongly gender-inflected and highly genre-bound. As one can expect with a long and multifaceted literary tradition, the association of the female gender with vernacular and of male court culture with Sino-Japanese writing is much more complex and also varies depending on historical period, but gender stays always a relevant category when it comes to the choice of language and genre in literary production. Also, unlike Latin's functioning as a spoken *lingua franca* among the educated elites of medieval and early modern Europe, Japanese *kanbun* was only a "grapholect,"[61] an idiom that was produced when a Japanese reader needed to vocalize texts written by Chinese or by Japanese in Chinese-style *kanbun*. Japanese spoke only Japanese, but could communicate within the "sphere of Chinese writing" with Chinese, and people in Vietnam and on the Korean Peninsula through their Chinese-style writing in the form of so-called "brush talk," conversation carried out with brush and ink in written Chinese for lack of a common vernacular language.

Chinese characters have shaped East Asia, understood as the "Sinographic sphere," over the last two millennia. Chinese-style writing has gradually disappeared from East Asia over the last hundred years, when vernacularization movements, in unison with modern nationalisms, called for vernacular writing styles;

---

[60] The nomenclature is hotly debated. For an incisive overview of the complex issues at stake see Kornicki 2010 and Wixted 1998.
[61] See Lurie 2011, Chapter 4.

in China itself, literary Chinese, the lingua franca of East Asia, has itself been displaced by vernacular Chinese in the radical reform movements of the early twentieth century. Although this process of "vernacularization" started already in the early modern period, new power constellations and modern language nationalisms have eradicated the written language that had shaped East Asia for so long and allowed sophisticated (if silent, nonvocalized) communication across borders.[62] Today, in the aftermath of the demise of the "Sinographic sphere," the people of East Asia ironically need to rely on English to understand each other.

That the Greco-Roman linguistic constellation was bilingual and monoliterate, while the Sino-Japanese constellation was monolingual and biliterate, had profound consequences for their respective literary cultures. These differences are evident from their earliest beginnings. The most important implication was that Latin literature started with the *translation* of Greek models, whereas Japanese literature began as a *continuation* of Chinese literary production, supplemented by literary production in vernacular genres that had no Chinese precedent.

Let us consider this contrast between the need for translation from Greek into Latin literary culture and the blurred boundaries of Japanese literary culture vis-à-vis Chinese literature by looking at some of the earliest products of Latin and Japanese literary culture. Livius Andronicus—one of the "semi-Greeks" in Suetonius's vignette of the beginnings of grammar instruction in Rome—possibly came as a prisoner of war to Rome when his hometown of Tarentum in the heel of Italy was sacked by Rome in 272 BCE. He worked as a grammar teacher and probably also actor, while writing his own plays. The date of 240 BCE, when he translated into Latin two Greek plays on the occasion of the Roman games, came to be seen as the beginning of Latin literature by Cicero's times. He received high public honors when composing a hymn in honor of Juno in 207 BCE, whereafter his guild of scribes received a public building for use.[63] Today only about sixty fragments, preserved in the works of authors or grammarians of the Republican and Imperial periods, survive of Livius Andronicus's writings, mostly from plays with Greek-sounding titles and from his translation of Homer's *Odyssey* into old Latin Saturnian verse. As a grammar teacher, Livius must have frequently taught this central text of the Hellenistic curriculum. That he was familiar with scholarship on the *Odyssey* is evident from a fragment where he inserts a Hellenistic commentary rather than translating the original Homeric text.[64] But his *Odusia* was not a pedestrian paraphrase of the Greek original for those of Livius's Roman students who did not know their Greek. The surviving fragments of his translation show traces of literary ambition, of an attempt to produce an artistic translation and registers in Latin that could express this ambition. Except for the "popular literature" of drama, translation of Greek literature into Latin was mostly of aesthetic and literary interest, not necessarily of practical value, since Roman elites were bilingual.

---

[62] For a compelling comparative perspective on vernacularization in Japan, Korea, and Vietnam see Kornicki 2008.
[63] For a brief portrayal of Livius Andronicus see Conte 1994b, 39–42 and Fuhrmann 2005, 99–101.
[64] Feeney 1991, 100.

Luckily, the opening lines of Livius's *Odusia* survive and we can witness how he rendered the famous opening praise of Ulysses: "Andra moi ennepe, Mousa, polutropon!" ("Of a man tell me, Muse, of many turns" Homer, *Odyssey*, I, 1). This is how Livius says it, making large steps toward adapting Greek meter, rhetoric, and meaning to the Latin language as a new medium for literary pretensions:

> *Virum mihi, Camena, insece versutum*[65] ("Of a man tell me, Camena, a
> turned one")

What a bold vision Livius's adaptation of the Greek phrase reveals: There is Livius's sensitivity to rendering the archaic dignity of the Greek *ennepe* ("tell") into the—already by Livius's time—solemnly archaic Latin *insece*. There is the great leap of cultural adaptation and approximation: rather than sticking with the resonant Greek "Muse"—origin of all literary inspiration, to which Ennius shortly afterward would strategically revert—Livius gives the Muse a Latin name. *Camena*, one of the ancient Italic water divinities associated with a spring outside of Rome's Porta Capena, was a name that echoed Roman "song" (*Casmena/Carmena-carmen*) for Livius's reader. And third, there is the sly self-referential evocation of Livius's translation project in the epithet *versutum* ("a turned one") that literally refers to far-roaming Ulysses of "many turns" (*polútropos* in the Homeric text). It also refers to Ulysses as *pars pro toto*, who stands in for the *Odyssey* and Homeric epic that Livius here "turns," "translates" (*vertere*) for the first time into Latin.[66] *Vertere* is the technical term for translation. When the early Latin playwright Plautus makes fun of himself in the explanatory prologue of one of his plays by saying "*Vertit barbare*" ("[Plautus] translated [the play] into the barbarian language of [Latin]") the reference to translation from Greek into Latin seems like a pose of comic self-detachment. Might Plautus be mocking those Greeks who mock Latin by calling it a "barbarian" language? There is nothing comical in Livius, but we have a similar degree of self-consciousness in translating the opening line of the *Odyssey*: There is Ulysses, whose adventures Livius intends to present with the help of the Greek Muse transferred to Latium just before the gates of Rome. But there is also the joyously celebrated "gain in translation" that Roman song, *Carmen,* is heralded by the new muse, *Camena*, and that the transposition of Ulysses—whose adventures had long been associated with Italic shores—to Rome and into the Latin language is a new theme, a meta-theme of the epic in translation.

How do texts from Japan's literary beginnings deal with the transposition of literature from China to Japan? We will see that the Roman "drama of translation" contrasts with a Japanese "drama of continuity." Although Japanese chronicles and early poetry anthologies contain songs that are associated with legendary emperors of high antiquity, we only get a glimpse of an emerging literary culture in the late seventh century with the court of Emperor Tenji (r. 668–671). Tenji gets

---

[65] *Livius Andronicus* I, 1. Latin text from Warmington 1982, 24. For brief commentary on Livius's fragments see Verrusio 1977.
[66] On all three points see Hinds 1998, 58–62. For further thoughts on possible signs for Livius's self-perception and self-representation see Suerbaum 1968, 1–12.

associated with the foundation of the State Academy and with the hosting of court banquets, during which he would call on courtiers with literary learning to compose poetry on the occasion. Let us look at two poems from Emperor Tenji's era as a way to think through the different beginnings of Japanese and Latin literatures.

The very first poem in the earliest preserved Japanese poetry anthology, *Florilegium of Cherished Airs* (*Kaifūsō* 懷風藻) compiled in 751, is by Emperor Tenji's son Prince Ōtomo. The unfortunate prince was later killed by Tenji's brother Tenmu, who assumed the throne after a brief war of succession in 672; but here he is in the peaceful period before the civil war, celebrating his father's rule at one of the literary banquets that was recently introduced to court life:

侍宴	In service at a banquet
皇明光日月	His August Radiance sparkles like sun and moon
帝德載天地	His Imperial Virtue covers Heaven and Earth
三才並泰昌	The Three Talents (Heaven, Earth, Mankind) line up in grand prosperity
萬國表臣義	And myriads of states show their obedience as loyal subjects.[67]

This praise poem in honor of Emperor Tenji resorts to cosmic proportions and Chinese solemn vocabulary to praise a ruler of a fledgling state without even a stable capital yet. All metaphors projecting cosmic grandeur, such as "Heaven and Earth," the "Three Talents," and the "myriad states" of faithful loyal subjects, are resonant expressions from the Confucian Classics and lend their radiance in this somewhat elementary poem to a Japanese ruler. In accord with Chinese political cosmology, cosmological imagery creates political resonance: Tenji's radiance is equal to sun and moon, his virtue is made greater than Heaven and Earth, and the alignment of the triad of Heaven, Earth, and Mankind ensures prosperity. The cosmo-political resonance is also expressed in the numerous parallelisms that keep numbers and cosmic elements in strict order. This is a Chinese-style poem (*kanshi* 漢詩), a quatrain consisting of four lines with five characters each; although from the perspective of Chinese imperial panegyrics nothing is particularly new about this poem, it is a new poem, written in the vein of Chinese panegyric poetry by a Japanese prince of a fledgling polity on the periphery of the Chinese empire.

How did vernacular poetry (*uta* 歌) from the same period, which was without Chinese linguistic and genre precedent and could not rely on the continuation of established Chinese practice, look like? In a poem from the earliest anthology of vernacular poetry, the *Collection of Myriad Leaves* (*Man'yōshū* 万葉集, ca. 759), Princess Nukata (ca. 638–690s), whom Emperor Tenji had presumably snatched away from his brother Tenmu while they were still princes, composed the following poem in response to an unusual request Emperor Tenji made of his palace minister:

When the Emperor [Tenji] commanded the Palace Minister, Fujiwara no Asomi [Kamatari], to match the radiance of the myriad blossoms of the spring mountains

[67] *Kaifūsō* no.1.

against the colors of the thousand leaves of the autumn mountains, Princess Nukata decided the question with this poem:

天皇、内大臣藤原朝臣に詔して、春山万花の艶と秋山千葉の彩とを競ひ憐れびしめたまふ時に、額田王、歌を以て判る歌

冬ごもり	When spring comes forth
春さり来れば	That lay in hiding all the winter through,
鳴かざりし	The birds that did not sing
鳥も来鳴きぬ	Come back and sing to us once more;
咲かざりし	The flowers that did not bloom
花も咲けれど	Have blossomed everywhere again.
山をしみ	Yet so rife the hills
入りても取らず	We cannot make our way to pick,
草深み	And so deep the grass
取りても見ず	We cannot pluck the flowers to see.
秋山の	But when on autumn hills
木の葉を見ては	We gaze upon the leaves of trees,
黄葉をば	It is the yellow ones
取りてそしのふ	We pluck and marvel for sheer joy,
青きをば	And the ones still green,
置きてそ嘆く	Sighing, leave upon the boughs—
そこし恨めし	Those are the ones I hate to lose.
秋山そ我は	For me, it is the autumn hills.[68]

Though the palace minister, not Nukata, is asked to answer the call of a courtly pastime, Nukata jumps in with her poem and decides to deliver her choice. As a poem celebrating the aesthetics of choice, where not the decision but the poetic explanation for it counts, it resonates strongly with the literary culture of the Chinese Six Dynasties. Raising her voice in the last phrase to announce her decision with *are wa*, "as for me" adds bold charm to the game. The perfectly balanced parallelisms—birds and flowers, hills and grass, yellow and green leaves—have benefited from the Chinese poetic habit of parallelism, but also replicate the underlying theme, the choice between binaries. Nukata's decision is based on two beautiful moves. First, to choose the best, one needs to see all options. That disqualifies the spring blossoms, because they are so abundant that one cannot even get into the overgrown hills to pick them. An aesthetics of scarcity, the ever thinning leaves of autumn, make choice possible, intuitively a more mature solution. Second, the sad joy of grasping the workings of time, rather than enjoying the freshness of the immediate moment, is an equally mature aesthetic stance: we pluck the yellow ones in the joy of the moment, but sigh preemptively about the green ones not yet ripe to go, whom we anticipate to turn yellow soon.

How should we pinpoint the intriguing contrasts between literary beginnings with Livius Andronicus's *Odusia* in Rome and the literary beginnings at Emperor Tenji's courtly poetry banquets in Japan? There is the obvious: Livius's text is a

---

[68] *Man'yōshū* 1.16. Translation from Cranston 1993, 175.

translation of an extant Greek text, while Prince Ōtomo's and Princess Nukata's poems are newly created poems. They either continue the subgenre of Chinese imperial panegyrics or are written in the distinctively Japanese vernacular verse form, but tinged by the dynamic of Chinese poetic pastimes and the rhetoric of Chinese literary tropes. By implication, Livius's text is less directly tied to the political scene: he does not need to lavish praise on the powerful or show off his poetic eloquence and mature aesthetic judgment. Yet he manages to introduce into the opening of his translation the Latin drama of translation, of "transposing the Greek muse" to Latium, and allows it to gain in the process.

And there is the less obvious difference: Livius's lines only survive because Aulus Gellius (130–180 CE), a polymath living during the reigns of Hadrian, Antoninus Pius, and Marc Aurel, quoted the line to illustrate the curious archaic spelling of *insece* ("tell!") without the usual *u* in *insecue*. In his *Attic Nights* he remarks:

> I found in the library at Patrae a book of true antiquity by Livius Andronicus with the title *Odyssey*. It contained the first line with the word "inseque" spelled without the letter u: "Of a man tell me, Camena, a turned one."[69]

> *Offendi enim in bibliotheca Patrensi librum verae vetustatis Livii Andronici, qui inscriptus est Ὀδύσσεια in quo erat versus primus cum hoc verbo (inseque) sine u littera: Virum mihi, Camena, insece versutum.*

Even in the Late Republic somebody like Cicero said Livius Andronicus was not worth a second reading and two centuries later, by the time of Aulus Gellius, Livius's *Odusia* wasted away on remote library shelves and attracted only the attention of those interested in orthographic idiosyncrasies. Aulus Gellius was keenly interested in questions of translations from Greek into Latin of literary and philosophical texts as well as of didactic prose.[70] Even somebody like Aulus Gellius who was tuned into questions of the value and means of translation could apparently only look at Livius's translation as a fossilized repository of archaic spelling habits instead of grasping its significance as a courageous and witty beginning of literary culture in Rome.

Latin literature from Livius Andronicus's time into the first century BCE only survives in fragments, except for the corpus of Plautus's and Terence's plays and Cato's treatise *On Agriculture*. Aulus Gellius is a vivid illustration that early writers like Livius Andronicus fell out of favor after the Late Republic and ceased to be transmitted whole, except for serving as a quarry for treasure seekers of grammatical and lexical curiosa.

In contrast, not only were Prince Ōtomo's and Prince Nukata's poems transmitted intact until today; they survived inside entire poetry collections. The first anthology of Chinese-style poetry, the *Florilegium,* is a modest collection of 120 poems. But the first anthology of vernacular poetry, the *Man'yōshū,* survived practically intact in twenty volumes with more than 4,500 poems and was graced with a commentarial tradition at least since the medieval period. *Man'yōshū* studies are

---

[69] *Noctes Atticae* XVIII. 9. 5. Text from Rolfe 1967, 329.
[70] For Aulus Gellius and his remarks on translation and the comparative contrast of Greek and Latin see Foegen 2000, 190–220.

a vast field in modern Japanology, with its own journals, specialists, and a voluminous annual output of scholarship. And the *Man'yōshū* is only one of the many large texts that survived from the eighth century, the first century of full-fledged literary production in Japan. I am not spelling out these facts to incite the envy of Latinists, for whom the early Japanese textual cornucopia evokes ever more melancholy feelings over the scarce and inherently biased shards of early Latin literary production that survived the times. Rather, the radically different preservation pattern of early Japanese and Latin literatures gives us a new vantage point to reflect on how and why Japanese treasured and transmitted much of their earliest literature and why, in contrast, so much of early Latin literature is lost.

I would argue that the different preservation pattern is not unrelated to the fact that Roman literature started with translation, while Japanese literature did not need it and was rather rooted in the continuation, variation, and adaptation of Chinese practices. Let us think for a moment about the implications of this difference. First, the need to translate and the very possibility (and everyday practice) of putting a Greek original side by side with a Latin translation enhanced a pervasive perception among Latin authors that the Latin language was deficient and poor in contrast to Greek. This linguistic inferiority complex of the "poverty of our forefathers' language (*patrii sermonis egestas*)" was commonplace, discussed extensively and repeatedly by authors as varied as Lucretius, Cicero, Quintilian, Aulus Gellius, and later various church fathers.[71]

Whether Cicero points to the need to "enrich the Latin language" (*augere linguam Latinam*)[72] or Quintilian fantasizes about the attractiveness of the Greek sounds of *ypsilon* and *zeta* and deplores some of the "sad and horrid" sounds of Latin that Greek avoids,[73] the poverty of the Latin language (*egestas, paupertas, inopia*) was a given that most Latin authors simply took for granted. Cicero, probably the strongest supporter of the virtues of the Latin language, tries at times to argue forcefully against the common prejudice that surrounded Latin. At one moment in *On the Ends of Good and Evil* he goes as far as stating stubbornly that Latin is richer (*locupletior*) than Greek.[74] But even he has to admit that the default assumption is the opposite and he acknowledges elsewhere that Latin lacks technical vocabulary in many disciplines, a gap that throughout his life he tried to mend with his own translations of Greek into Latin and the introduction of Greek technical vocabulary into the Latin language. Cicero believed that a text gains in

---

[71] Joseph Farrell puts it forcefully: "Again and again, when Latin culture confronts itself and inquires into its nature, it sees Greek. The conclusion that often follows is that Latin is derivative and inferior—that in trying to be Greek Latin dooms itself to epigonal status. For the Latin speaker an authentic and unmediated connection between nature and culture is unattainable. But such a relationship is imagined to exist for Greek, and this belief becomes a source of envy, perceived inferiority, and self-deprecation.... The theme under discussion runs through Latin literature and through the reception of Latin literature in all periods. So common a theme deserves a name: call it 'the poverty topos.'" Joseph Farrell 2001, 28. Farrell's second chapter "The poverty of our ancestral speech" discusses this language complex in more detail. For a monograph treating this important topic see Thorsten Fögen 2000

[72] Cicero *De fato* 1.

[73] Quintilian. *Institutio oratoria* XII.10.27.

[74] Cicero *De finibus bonorum et malorum* 1.10.

translation, as we would put it today, and his confidence in the Latin language seemed partly motivated by a vision of its future and his own role in creating the technical preciseness it still lacked in contrast to the Greek scholarly vocabulary.

Though the connection between translation and linguistic self-esteem is a complex one, a passage from Aulus Gellius about his reading experiences of Latin comedies and their Greek originals shows strikingly how the prominence of translation from the Greek in Roman literary culture and the very existence of two texts—an original and a translation—could make Latin suddenly, inexplicably look bad:

> I often read the comedies of our Latin poets, in which they used and translated Greek...comedy writers. And each time I read them nothing in the least actually displeases me, they seem indeed to be elegantly and beautifully written, so that you think there could not possibly be anything better. But if then you put the Greek text, from which they are taken, next to it and you compare them, and you subject single passages to careful and meticulous juxtaposed and alternating reading, then the Latin starts to look suddenly weak and poor. Thus the Latin passages lack the wit and sparkle of the Greek original, which they fail to emulate.

> *Comoedias lectitamus nostrorum poetarum sumptas ac versas de Graecis...comicis. Neque, cum legimus eas, nimium sane displicent, quin lepide quoque et venuste scriptae videantur, prorsus ut melius posse fieri nihil censeas. Sed enim si conferas et componas Graeca ipsa, unde illa venerunt, ac singular considerate atque apte iunctis et alternis lectionibus commitas, oppido quam iacere atque sordere incipiunt, quae Latina sunt; ita Graecarum, quas aemulari nequiverunt, facetiis atque luminibus obsolescunt.*[75]

Even if considered poor, Latin became the principal literary language in the Roman world used by non-Greek authors. Libyac, Phrygian, or Gaulish, to name but a few of the languages of the Roman empire, were only local in-group languages for which we have more or less of an epigraphic record, but no substantial literary tradition. People might have called Latin "barbarian" in the early period, based on the model of Greek dialects that were contrasted with the non-Greek outside world of barbarian languages, but Plautus's joke about his translation of a Greek play into barbaric Latin is evidence for Greek prejudice against Latin rather than of the way Romans saw their mother tongue. By the first century CE even Greek authors moved to a tripartite model of the languages in the world, consisting of Greeks, Romans, and Barbarians. Declaring Latin into a version of an Aeolic Greek dialect as Greek grammarians such as Dionysius of Halicarnassus or Latin grammarians such as Philoxenos did was of advantage for both Greeks and Romans: Greek subjects of Rome could be proud to have given one of their dialect to their conqueror, while the Roman conquerors could feel civilized about their Hellenic language.[76]

---

[75] *Noctes Atticae* II.23.1–3. In chapter 11.16 Aulus Gellius treats the problem that it is often impossible to translate an elegant Greek expression into a single Latin word. Here again, it is the process of word-by-word translation, the search for equivalence, that lets Latin appear in unfavorable light. On this chapter see Foegen 2000, 210–11.

[76] Foegen 2000, 47–50.

We can now sum up the differences in the linguistic constellations between Japan and China and Greece and Rome in the following approximated paradoxes: Latin literary culture was bilingual, monoliterate, and bicanonical; it began with translation and existed with the consciousness of a double textuality, a Greek original and a Latin adaptation. Early Japanese literary culture was monolingual, biliterate, and built on a triple literary canon. The continuity between Chinese and Japanese literary production was assumed, there was no drama of translation, and the literate elite was trained to naturally read Chinese texts in Japanese word order. Thus there was a continuous spectrum of more sinitic and more vernacular stylistic registers instead of a clear-cut contrast between two languages. Although the distinction between Chinese and Sino-Japanese was particularly blurred and at times imperceptible, it could be exploited for aesthetic effect as in the case of the eleventh century anthology *Collections of Japanese and Chinese Poems for Recitation* (*Wakan rōeishū* 和漢朗詠集). The anthology arranged short excerpts from Chinese, Sino-Japanese, and Japanese poems or prose texts under thematic categories, featuring first Chinese, then Sino-Japanese, verse and prose excerpts, and lastly, vernacular Japanese poems illustrative of the theme. The aesthetic of juxtaposition of this format dramatized difference and gave the audience the pleasure of experiencing how "summer," "gibbons," or "singing girls" could look so different when clothed in the Chinese, Sino-Japanese, or Japanese poetic logic. But the pleasure lay in the experience of a different poetics, not in the assumption that the excerpts arranged under a topic heading would be reducible to each other through a notion of "original" and "adaptation." Thus, what I call the "drama of translation" played an important role in the relationship Latin authors had to Greek literary precedents,[77] while the "pretense of continuity" and the "pleasure of variation and juxtaposition" allowed Japanese authors to creatively play with Chinese, Sinicized, and vernacular registers as they pleased.

Genres

Japanese and Latin literature developed such different genres and genre hierarchies that in particular their early stages seem to lack easy points of meaningful comparison. Epic and drama, the genres that had the highest standing in the hierarchy of genres in Greece and Rome, had no even vaguely related counterpart in early Japan. Much has been made of the question of China's lack of epic poetry; as China, Japan had no epic; and dramatic literature such as Noh developed only much later, in the fourteenth century. Instead, Chinese-style poetry, *kanshi*, and, since the mid-Heian Period, Japanese waka poetry commanded the genre hierarchy of Japan's double literary canon. Comparing *kanshi* and waka with Greek and

---

[77] Hinds 1998, Chapter 3 "Diachrony: literary history and its narratives" discusses the pervasive phenomenon of Latin authors' claim to first translation or transposition of certain Greek practices or genres.

Roman poetic genres is a complex enterprise in its own right.[78] But suffice it to say here that brief genres such as the elegy, satire, or the epigram, although they became popular and respected by the Late Republic in Rome, were construed as the "lesser genres" against the backdrop of the authority of epic and drama established in Aristotle's *Poetics*. In Japanese literary culture, in turn, the brief genres of mostly four- to eight-line *kanshi* and the short thirty-one-syllable waka was the pivot of authority that shaped the patterns of the genre hierarchy.

If we look at the hierarchy of prose genres in Rome, we can find a bit of common ground with Japan in the genre of historiography. Works on history and rhetoric, genres of didactic literature, *Fachprosa,* were the domain of aristocratic writers of the Roman ruling class who used the genres as a platform to formulate and affirm political and moral values of the Roman state. Although writing in Greek was at odds with the tradition of pontifical annals written in Latin on which early Roman writers of history relied, the high-brow nature of historiography can be seen from the fact that Roman historiography before Cato was written in Greek. Fabius Pictor (fl. 200 BCE), of the patrician family of the Fabii, presumably introduced the custom of writing Roman history in Greek. As Rome's influence in the Eastern Mediterranean increased, Roman nobles apparently wanted to reach the Greek-speaking world with a favorable picture of Rome and its history. Cato (234–149 BCE) created the tradition of historiography in the Latin language, which set the stage for the Roman historiographical tradition and the works of Caesar, Livy, Sallust, and Tacitus. Historiography had a comparable high standing in early Japan, as the Japanese court adopted for some time the Chinese practice of entrusting state-employed scholars with the production of official histories.

The earliest longer Japanese texts date to the eighth century and include two large historical annals, the *Record of Ancient Matters* (712) and the *Chronicles of Japan* (720), both covering the legendary history from the age of the gods up to the seventh century. The high standing of historiography in Japan is also evident from the fact that these two histories were written in different linguistic idioms, one in a form of vernacular Japanese and the other in Sino-Japanese, closer to the language of Chinese official histories.

The discipline of rhetoric is more difficult to relate to Japan's literary culture and its genres. The social practices that produced reflections on and handbooks of rhetoric in Rome had no correlate in Japan: the various civic assemblies and legal practices, and—increasingly since the empire that put an end to the political functions of those assemblies—public declamation of epideictic speeches. Some case could be made, however, that lyrical poetry in China and Japan served some of the functions rhetoric had in the Greco-Roman world. Poetry, like rhetoric, was a crucial genre in educating members of the elites in the highest registers of literacy, which would be needed in service to the state; that is the reason why poetry during the Tang Dynasty was an assignment in the civil service examinations. Also, poetry in Japan, like rhetoric in Rome, was performance. There was hardly a court event

---

[78] For an approach from the perspective of poetic form, language, and social occasion see the two roundtable discussions between Japanese scholars of Japanese and Greco-Roman poetry in *Bungaku* 2010. For an approach from the perspective of genre hierarchies see Denecke 2012.

in Nara and Heian Japan that would not have included the composition and recitation of poetry, since the mid-Heian period composed increasingly on set topics. Although there was little semblance in content, form, and recitation styles, poetry functioned a bit like epideictic rhetoric in imperial Rome, certainly a more comparable setting to early Japan than political oratory during the Roman Republic.

There is also a slight similarity between the two in that they catalyzed foundational meta-discourses: poetry in East Asia, like rhetoric in the Greco-Roman world, became the locus for reflection on the political role of literary expression and for strong beliefs in its capacity for moral education. Thus, in some way poetics in China and Japan was to poetry's role in Chinese and Japanese societies what the rhetorical treatise was to rhetorical practice in the Greco-Roman world.

Without stretching the comparison between poetry in East Asia and rhetoric in Japan, which will be the basis for exploring Japanese and Roman accounts of their own literary history in Chapter 2, let us now move to the more difficult terrain, epic and drama. With the medieval *Tales of the Heike,* the accounts of the bloody wars between two aristocratic clans at the end of the Heian Period, and the genre of War Tales (*gunki monogatari* 軍記物語), we do get epic "songs of weapons and heroes" and a comparably complex vocabulary of warfare and honor, and of war's tools and casualties. Versions of the *Tales of the Heike* were passed down orally and performed by itinerant minstrels (*biwa hōshi* 琵琶法師) on the *biwa,* a pear-shaped lute. But this is where the similarity to the Homeric epics ends. The genre of war tales only took off in the medieval period, it was a prose genre, and it never stood at the top of the genre hierarchy and informed the entire literary field as the Homeric epics did.

Although we like them for their protagonists, for Achilles and Hector, Ulysses and Circe, Greek epic was not just epic for telling heroic tales in hexameter. It was poetry of divine, musical inspiration, prefaced by the mandatory invocation to the Muse; and together with tragedy, it came to command the hierarchy of classical Greek literary genres. The competition among early Roman writers about the "introduction" of the Greek Muse to Rome and its literature is the best indication of the supreme standing of the genre of epic and its Muse. Who could lay claim to having first brought the Greek Muse to Rome? Livius Andronicus? But, well, as we saw above, he said "Camena," not "Muse." Ennius? His credentials are hard to beat, because in his *Annals* Ennius has Homer appear to him in a dream and declare the Roman poet into his own reincarnation. Or actually, as Stephen Hinds has slyly asked, Fulvius Nobilior, Ennius's patron, who pillaged Greek statues of the Muses from the Greek city of Ambracia and brought them as war spoils to Rome for a new shrine and cult of "Hercules of the Muses"?[79] Although the competition was particularly fierce for the genre of epic because of its overwhelming authority, smaller versions of it unfolded for other Greek genres: the "inventor" figure, which Greek scholars ascribed to their genres and arts, had as equivalent a new inventor figure in Rome, the first translator and transmitter of a given Greek genre or discipline. The inventor trope was at the center of the "drama of translation" that occurred between Greek texts and Roman authors and unfolded both on the level of linguistic translation and on the level of the cultural and literary translatio of

---

[79] Hinds 1998, Chapter 3.

genres to Rome. Neither the drama of linguistic translation nor the drama of genre translation played any role in the Japanese reception of Chinese literature (or, obviously, in Japanese vernacular literature that lacked Chinese precedents).

Thus, it is important to note that epic was not just one genre among others to be missing from Chinese and Japanese literatures. It was the ultimate centerpiece of the Greco-Roman literary world and implied a notion of dramatized transmission that profoundly shaped the entire literary field: transmission from divine beings to humans, from humans of one to humans of another language, or even, as perhaps with Livius Andronicus's *Camena*, from divine beings directly to those humans of another language.

The trope of *recusatio* is another example of how epic (and tragedy) aligned the entire literary field: for Hellenistic and Roman poets it became fashionable to "recusate," to ostentatiously refuse to write in the higher genres of epic and tragedy and affirmatively indulge "lower genres" in the genre spectrum such as pastoral poetry, love elegy, and erotic lyric poetry. This recusatio was not a word figure, or a figure of thought, but was nothing less than a figure of cultural reception designed by Hellenistic authors to relate to their Greek classical past and Roman authors to relate to another culture (and, yet more complicated, both its reference culture's classical past, and its own past). There are interesting resonances between Greco-Roman recusatio and gestures of empowering self-deprecation that one can find in vernacular genres vis-à-vis Sino-Japanese literature; we will see an example of this with the *Genji Poems* in the chapter on satire. But it has nothing of the subtle enervation with which it plays out in Latin authors, nothing of the centrality it had in Latin literary culture.

Although authors claimed to keep genres strictly apart through recusatio by refusing to write in one genre and ostentatiously switching to a lower genre, Roman literature is pervaded with the "mixing of genres," the play with their genres' imaginary limits and their reader's expectations. How, to which degree, and to which effects Latin authors mixed genres has been the topic of extensive debates.[80] But the complex genres of "signatures" Latin authors put on their works, including the play with marking genre boundaries and with breaking them in word or practice, is distinctive of Latin literary culture. Although genre hybridization plays an important role in Japanese literature, authors seemed much less interested in making the discourse about the mixing of genres into a mouthpiece of their aesthetic program.

Like the absence of epic, the absence of dramatic literature in early Japan constitutes a fundamental difference in Japanese and Latin literary culture. And like epic, theater was not just a literary genre. It was a popular spectacle open to all social classes, a public display mounted to express the prestige of the patron or financier of the particular event. Theater plays or *ludi scenici* were part of the official state cult, which included annual sacrifices, processions, and other ceremonies. It was for the Roman Games, *Ludi Romani*, celebrated in honor of Jupiter Optimus

---

[80] Fundamental for the debate on the "mixing of genres" is Kroll 1924, 202ff. See also Conte 1994a, 120. Conte is a particularly fine thinker on genre issues in Latin literature.

Maximus that Livius Andronicus wrote his plays in 240 BCE. Other prominent games that included theater performances were games devoted to Flora, Roman goddess of fecundity, and to Apollo, Ceres, and Cybele. Although by Augustus's time Latin tragedy had lost popularity and had gradually been replaced by mimes, theater played a crucial role in Roman society and early Latin literature, as we can see from the fact that only the comedies by Plautus and Terence survived as a genre corpus from the early period. That the only documented genre of early Latin literature did not have a functional correlate in early Japan is particularly unfortunate and adds a temporal asymmetry to our comparisons in some chapters of this book. When the scarcity of the early Latin literary record forces me to compare the earliest Japanese texts from the eighth century to Late Republican authors, I will embrace this asymmetry for additional insight rather than considering it only as a disadvantage. However, the accessibility of theater for all classes of Roman society, its institutional presence in Rome in the form of a guild of authors and actors (*collegium scribarum histrionumque*) since 207, and the close relation of Roman scripts to the plays of Greek New Comedy make theater, next to epic, into the most vital part of early Roman literary culture that cannot be reduced or approximated to any part of the early Japanese literary world. For the illiterate lower classes, theater was possibly the only entertainment that gave them access to a literary learning of sorts. Plautus's and Terence's *palliatae* or "comedies in Greek cloak" were not just set in Greece and used Greek protagonists, but were modeled on specific Greek plays by New Comedy writers like Menander. Thus, for the educated classes, theater was the kind of entertainment that allowed them to enjoy the fruits of their education. Even if their grammar teacher had to beat Greek tragedies and comedies into their brains with physical force, here they could chuckle over a witty deviation from the Greek original or ruminate on the charming effects of *contaminatio,* the popular practice of Roman playwrights to stitch the plot of several different Greek scripts together into one play.

Although I would hardly ever feel compelled to make strong generalizing statements about two literary cultures that are as rich as the early Japanese and Roman ones, which never fail to surprise, I will make one here: there was simply no phenomenon comparable to Latin comedy in early Japanese society. The broad scope of theater in early Roman society, the pervasive status of epic, with tropes such as recusatio that it conditioned are absent from early Japan. In turn, Japan had a much richer spectrum of genres. We do not need to believe Quintilian, who singles out satire (*"satura quidem tota nostra est"* "Satire at least is all ours") as the only truly "Roman" genre. We will see in Chapter 3 that Horace related Roman satire to Greek Old Comedy and thus—at least at a particular moment of his text—claims a Greek precedent for satire. But it is true that the Roman spectrum of genres was largely coextensive with the spectrum of Greek literature. Similarly, Japanese *kanbun* literature adopted the Chinese spectrum of genres; some genres never became quite popular in Japan like the eminent Chinese rhapsody genre (*fu* 賦); others developed differently, like the genre of prefaces (Ch. *xu*, J. *jo* 序) that went its own ways in Japan, because it became the companion genre for so-called Topic

Poetry (*kudaishi* 句題詩), a distinctively Japanese genre of poetry written at social occasions on set topics based on a highly codified set of poetical rules.[81]

However, the vernacular half of the Japanese literary canon had no precedent in Chinese genres—what a joy it would have been for Quintilian to list vernacular *waka* poetry, tale literature (*monogatari* 物語), diaries (*nikki* 日記), and anecdotal literature (*setsuwa* 説話), to name just a few extremely productive vernacular Japanese genres. The works of classical Japanese literature in translation that have made it into the canon of today's "world literature" anthologies —the *Man'yōshū*, the *Collection of Ancient and Modern Poetry*, and, most of all, Murasaki Shikibu's *Tale of Genji*—are all part of the vernacular canon.

With this brief overview of the spectrum and hierarchy of genres we have reached the limits of our comparison of Japanese and Roman literary cultures. We have explored three fundamental similarities between Japanese and Roman literary cultures—their late start, their beginning against the backdrop of highly sophisticated stages of literary developments in their reference culture, and the adoption and adaptation of their reference culture's textual and educational canon. And we have explored and qualified three complicating divergences between them—the geopolitical and linguistic constellations and their spectrum and hierarchies of literary genres.

We have thus set the stage for tackling the comparison of particular issues and authors in the following chapters. In the next chapter we will showcase how early Japanese and Roman authors dealt with the "historical flatness" of their literary traditions and devised strategies to acknowledge their debt to their reference culture, while carving out space for their own literature and asserting their independence.

---

[81] On the history, practice, and significance of this genre see Satō 2007 and Denecke 2007.

| Starting *avant la lettre*

An Essay on How to Tell the Beginnings of Literature and Eloquence

BEGINNINGS ARE ALWAYS A different affair from retrospective narratives of beginnings developed to sanction current practice. The gap between beginnings and narratives of beginnings is particularly blatant in younger cultures that cannot easily lay claim to independent development. This essay highlights how at four different historical moments, four Japanese and Latin authors developed clever strategies to tell the beginnings of their own literature and eloquence in a way that allowed the indigenous tradition to compete with Chinese and Greek precedents.

***

Ōe no Masafusa 大江匡房 (1041–1111) is arguably the first Japanese author to have envisioned a "World Republic of Letters." He was a scholar-official at the Heian court with predilections for Chinese literature and scholarship. The title of his elegant Sino-Japanese prose composition is "A Record on the Realm of Poetry" (*shikyōki* 詩境記). Masafusa had a bent for the quirky and liminal realms—he also wrote records on courtesans, itinerant puppeteers, and fox-magic—and his whirly creativity comes to the fore in this unique piece, too. As the emblematic genre of literary composition Masafusa has "poetry" stand quite simply for "Letters;" and although his "realm" does not cater to our enlightenment associations of a "Republic" of Letters, Masafusa unmistakably sketches a space distinct from either the political or the natural world. This space has an enchanted logic of its own:

> As for the Realm of Poetry: it lacks water or soil, mountains or rivers and has no inhabitants or settlements. Even its whereabouts are unknown. One gets there in the blink of an eye just to be suddenly gone again. Reaching this fair realm is one of the most difficult things to achieve. Brush and ink are its expanse, sentiment and suffering its customs. Taxes are collected in units of blossoms and moon, and salary is exchanged with smoke and mist.

Peaches and pears effect unspeakable moral transformation, while orchids and chrysanthemums satiate with their fragrant virtue.[1] Never would you hear of dust-stirring military upheavals or see cold dew and fog attack your body.

夫詩境者。無水土山川。無人民戶邑。又不知在何方面。瞥然而至。倐忽而往。至其佳境。難中之難也。以翰墨為場。以感傷為俗。花月輪租稅。煙霞代封禄。桃李施不言之化。蘭菊飽惟馨之德。不聞風塵之變。不看露霧之侵。[2]

Masafusa probably knew texts like "A Record on the Land of Drunkenness" (Ch. *Zuixiangji* 醉鄉記) by the Chinese poet Wang Ji (590–644).[3] Grafting his "Realm of Poetry" onto a "Land of Drunkenness" seems perfectly sensible from the perspective of a literary tradition in which composing poetry and getting drunk are metonymical endeavors and commitments. More importantly, Masafusa sketches his literary realm along two diametrically opposed vectors: on the one hand it is spaceless, empty and hard to get to, but then he takes pains to flesh out the imaginary realm with its definite expanse, customs, taxes, ranks and salary, moral authority and virtuous government. In this way he sparks the reader's hope that one can visit that realm as nimbly as one's mind moves back and forth. Empty illusion or allegorical incarnation, epitome of inaccessibility or armchair travel destination, Masafusa builds his realm on highly ambivalent ground.

In a further step Masafusa confirms that his Realm of Poetry is indeed universal and for everybody. Masafusa serves us a digest of poetics that any educated Heian Japanese would have been familiar with, because it belonged to the exegetical tradition of the canonical *Classic of Poetry* (ca. 600 BCE):

As the heart is moved within, words form outside. If singing it out loud is not enough, then you sigh; and if sighing isn't enough, then you will unknowingly dance it with your hands and tap it with your feet.

心動於中、言形於外。詠歌不足、故嗟嘆。嗟嘆不足、故不知手之舞足之蹈。[4]

The "Great Preface" to the Confucian *Classic of Poetry* proposes a universal psychology of composition, which posits ever-advancing levels of expressive intensity in case

---

[1] *Classic of Poetry*, Mao 247: "Making us drunk" (*jizui* 既醉). *Maoshi zhengyi* 17.2, 1089–97: "You make us drunk on wine and satiate us with virtue. May you enjoy, o our lord, myriads of years! May your bright happiness be increased forever."

[2] *Chōya gunsai*, 64. My translation is based on the *Shintei zōho Kokushi taikei* edition and on Gotō 1986–87.

[3] Wang Ji's "Record" is preserved in the "Parables" section of the *Wenyuan yinghua*, 833 (Li 2006). See also Zhang 1995, 134–35. Although Wang Ji's piece dates to the Early Tang Dynasty, the image of a "Land of Drunkenness" became very popular in the mid- and late Tang and is also eagerly used by Japanese *kanshi* poets such as Sugawara no Michizane, Ki no Haseo, and Masafusa's grandfather Ōe no Masahira. Wang Ji's "Record" was highly popular and also applied to other alternative realms: The monk Ennin (794–864) who wrote a diary of his stay in China from 838 to 847 used Wang Ji's "Record" as a blueprint for his "Record on the Land of Stillness and Enlightenment" (*Jakōdoki* 寂光土記) to depict the promised land of Tiantai Buddhism. See *Dainihon bukkyō zensho, Tendai shōbushū shaku*. (Gotō 1986–87, 326, n. 6).

[4] *Chōya gunsai*, 64.

words do not suffice. Quite handily for Masafusa, the Preface to the *Classic of Poetry* also relies on a spatial metaphor: poetry is the outer manifestation of the poet's inner heart. It translates out of the heart into the world as words, song, or dance.

There is a nice pas de deux between the spatial metaphor of Masafusa's "Realm of Poetry" and the *Classic of Poetry*'s spatial conceptualization of the process of poetic composition, for Masafusa undertakes a double translation: natural landscape gets translated into poetic currency in the first section and, in the process, the internal landscape of the poet is translated into the outer world taking shape in words. The universal poetics of the *Classic of Poetry* is the emblematic beginning of Masafusa's detailed account of Chinese literary history, in which he stays strictly true to his allegorizing impulse. Poets are the aristocrats and leaders of the realm, where emperors are led by poets. In one case, poets respond to the execution of poets by emperors—euphemistically referred to as "expulsion from the Realm"—by instituting new "laws" and "rules"—namely the tonal rules underlying Chinese "Recent-Style Poetry." So far, so good. The "Realm of Poetry" is a seemingly universal interior psychological space, but it is also fleshed out in the "translation" of Chinese literary history into a true "Republic of Letters." Yet the loving care with which Masafusa produces this allegorical "translation" of Chinese literary history is choked off once he moves to matters in Japan:

> At our Japanese court [poetry] arose between the Kōnin (810–824, Emperor Saga) and Jōwa (834–48, Emperor Ninmyō) eras, flourished between Jōgan (859–77, Emperor Seiwa) and Engi (901–23, Emperor Daigo) reached an intermediary peak in the Jōhei (931–38, Emperor Suzaku) and Tenryaku (947–957, Emperor Murakami) eras and flourished again during Chōhō (999–1004) and Kankō (1004–1012, both Emperor Ichijō). Broadly speaking three-dozen poets, and if we limit ourselves to the outstanding ones we hardly get beyond six or seven.

> 我朝起於弘仁承和。盛於貞觀延喜。中興於承平天曆 。再昌於長保寬弘。廣謂則卅餘人略其英。莫不過六七許輩。[5]

It comes as a severe disappointment that the transmitted text breaks abruptly off after this sobering statement and the reader is left to wonder what Masafusa would have said further about Japan. Poetry in Japan lacks everything that had made the Chinese realm so attractive and convincing: whereas in China poets and their materials rule supreme, Japanese literary history unfolds as a mechanical teleology of imperial eras. The rich Chinese pantheon of poetic geniuses that Masafusa had just paraded in front of our eyes meets unfavorably with the paucity of the Japanese record: only three dozen poets and hardly six or seven good ones. And, most divisive of all, Masafusa literally excludes Japan from the "Realm of Poetry" by denying it his allegorical translation. We are dropping out of the allegorical travel account into plain historical narrative.

Since we are dealing with an unfinished or fragmentary text there is no way to know, but there is a slight chance that everything might have ended

---

[5] *Chōya gunsai*, 65.

happily after all. At the end of his "Record of the Land of Drunkenness"—the above-mentioned blueprint for Masafusa's piece—the Chinese poet Wang Ji declares that he wrote his "Record" because he was about to visit that land himself. Along these lines we could imagine Masafusa declaring himself the apogee of a tradition that started admittedly poorly, but by his time—and perhaps even with him—had become a rightful region of the "Realm of Poetry," where he comes and goes as a regular. In other writings Masafusa often boasts his precocious literary talents and exploits, and he would certainly be capable of ending his vision of the "Realm of Poetry" with a telescopic close-up of his own flattering literary profile.

***

I have outlined Masafusa's vision as a foil to help us appreciate the earliest Japanese attempts at writing literary history. Masafusa's account differs greatly from earlier attempts. First, because it tells the truth—after all, the Chinese *Classic of Poetry*, compiled around 600 BC, predated the Kōnin Period, Masafusa's supposed "rise" of poetry in Japan, by 1,400 years of prolific literary production. Second, because he seems to all too willingly accept inequality between China and Japan in the realm of letters. The twelfth century, the Late Heian Period, is a particularly strange moment for pitiful laments over the absence of a domestic tradition, because by Masafusa's time the Japanese could parade a prolific production in all major Sino-Japanese genres and had developed a sense of historical depth toward their own literary tradition and an indigenous Sino-Japanese canon that coexisted with the Heian curriculum of Chinese texts.

Earlier accounts of literary history did not propagate inequality vis-à-vis the Chinese literary tradition. They tended to design highly sophisticated scenarios that attenuated and diffused inequality, or even declared superiority. Most often such accounts did so ironically by using the rhetorical power of Chinese intertexts. To opt for a narrative of homology rather than for a story of inequality like Masafusa's was not just a manipulative device to assert one's cultural ego, although my constructivist vocabulary here seems to suggest that. Instead, it was a learning strategy of a fledgling literary tradition: homology served to imagine practices of writing literary history in the first place. That is certainly a powerful reason why the earliest Japanese accounts of literary history tend to be fictions of similarity, rather than acknowledgments of difference.

Masafusa's piece is a powerful tool to formulate fundamental questions about the writing of literary history in cultures that grow in symbiosis with a canonical reference culture. How can one write literary history in the face of the historiographical models and prolific literary production of the older, possibly much older, reference culture? How should one deal with what we might call "historical flatness," as one writes from a place in which both literature and reflection on literature are jumpstarted through models of the reference culture? These were models, which in turn were developed over a much longer time period in the reference culture and in response to its distinctive logic of cultural development. Below I will show how ingeniously four key texts from the Japanese and Roman traditions responded to these challenges.

1. Making Sense of the Regime of "Letters" in Eighth-Century Japan: The Kaifūsō

The *Kaifūsō* 懐風藻 (Florilegium of Cherished Airs), which we already introduced in the previous chapter, is a collection of 120 Sino-Japanese poems arranged by chronology and rank. Compiled in 751, it is the earliest extant poetry collection of Japan. It has a preface by an anonymous compiler that recounts the development of civilization, learning, and literature from the beginnings up to the times of the compilation. The *Kaifūsō* is a product of the explosion of textual production and literacy that gripped Japan in the seventh and eighth centuries: a centralized state based on Chinese precedent was being built, and as it gradually extended its administrative control over the provinces, the state needed an ever growing number of scribes adept in the various genres of bureaucratic correspondence. Besides, the phenomenal expansion of state power was established and justified through imperially commissioned compilation projects that bolstered imperial ideology and the budding authority of the centralized state. *Records of Wind and Earth* (*Fūdoki* 風土記) of 713 enhanced the state's symbolical grip on the provinces by recording their local legends and customs and exploring their potential for exploitation of resources and tribute products. The *Record of Ancient Matters* (*Kojiki* 古事記) of 712 legitimated the imperial lineage by distilling the gradual and complex emergence of Yamato rule into a straight line reaching back to one imperial ancestor, the sun goddess Amaterasu. The *Chronicles of Japan* (*Nihon shoki* 日本書紀) of 720, closer to Chinese traditions of historiography, voraciously assembled various versions of events into a history of Japan from its beginnings to the recent past.

The composition of Sino-Japanese poetry was not just a side effect of this explosion of literacy and the state's instrumentalization of textual production, but was part and parcel of establishing imperial power. Much of the poetry in the *Kaifūsō* was composed at court banquets and eulogized the splendors of the current regime. Against this background it comes as no surprise that the *Kaifūsō* is preoccupied with making sense of the explosion and diversification of "Letters" 文 (Ch. *wen*, J. *bun*) in the seventh and eighth centuries. *Wen* is the pivotal concept at the heart of the collection, and both the preface and the poetry itself show traces of thinking and playing through wen in all its meanings, connotations, and implications.

Wen—a resonant multifaceted key concept of the Chinese tradition—referred originally to the patterning of animal fur or the tattooing of the human body, and thus to "ornament." By further extension, it came to mean "civilization" and "cultural refinement" as well as "writing" and "literature." It is also the name of King Wen, one of the founders of the Chinese Zhou Dynasty (ca. 1045–256 BCE). A pun in the Confucian *Analects* first equated King Wen with the "cultural heritage" (Ch. *si wen* 斯文) of the Zhou dynasty and, in a next step, Confucius declared himself custodian of this heritage. In this way the regime of wen was also intimately linked to the Confucian tradition.[6]

---

[6] For an exploration of the significance and rich meaning of the concept of *bun* in Japanese literary culture from the beginnings into the 20th century see Denecke and Kōno 2013.

By choosing wen as the guiding concept, the *Kaifūsō* could do several things at once, namely simultaneously tell the beginning of civilization, the advent of writing, the beginning of Confucian learning in Japan, the beginning of literature, and, last but not least, Japan's homage to King Wen as the ideal Confucian king and a model of Japanese imperial power.

The *Kaifūsō* Preface gradually projects the multilayered power of wen onto a historical timeline in precisely this fashion. As a result, literature proper, belles lettres and poetry, appear in the preface as the rather late outcome of a long process of civilization (or wen-ization, as we might say). This was certainly a double-edged strategy: "literature" or "Letters" came to encompass all of civilization and its history. Yet, by the same token the preface had to concede a rather late beginning of literature in Japan, exposing a vulnerable spot that was going to be exploited by the compilers of the next text we will discuss, the *Collection of Ancient and Modern Poetry* (*Kokinwakashū* 古今和歌集).

The compiler of the *Kaifūsō* had no qualms about admitting to a late beginning of Sino-Japanese poetry in Japan, especially because this move enabled a powerful conceptual absorption of the history of civilization into the special history of Sino-Japanese poetry. As a countermove to a story of late arrival, the preface cleverly downplays the importation of the writing system from China through Korea. Instead, it posits writing symbolically as a natural presence in Japan from times immemorial. It taps into the Chinese ideology of writing that declares writing a natural phenomenon rather than a human invention. True, mythical sages of Chinese high antiquity were regarded as figures of invention and human creation, as in the case of Fu Xi, who allegedly devised the symbols of the hexagrams in the *Classic of Change* by watching natural patterns, or Cang Jie, who presumably invented written characters by imitating bird tracks in the sand. Yet their acts of inventions were described as mimicry of the natural world, not as the creation of human artifice. In China this ideology of writing had enabled forceful claims of textuality over reality: textuality became a correlative to the cosmos to the extent that textuality could not just influence the cosmos, but take precedence over it.[7]

The *Kaifūsō* Preface relies on the ideology of the "naturalization" of writing in order to disguise the trauma of the importation of foreign writing into a local oral culture. Here is how the preface accomplishes this:

逖聽前修	I have heard of sages from the remote past
遐觀載籍	and surveyed the written records of yore.
襲山降蹕之世	In the age when the Heavenly Grandchild's[8] chariot descended upon the Peak of So
橿原建邦之時	and our state was founded in Kashiwara,[9]
天造草創	the workings of Heaven had barely begun

---

[7] On the ideology of writing in early China and various historical figures associated with it see Lewis 1999, 195–240.
[8] Referring to the descent to earth of the grandson of the sun goddess Amaterasu on Mount Takachiho recorded in the two early chronicles mentioned above.
[9] Palace of the mythical Emperor Jinmu (trad. ca. 600 BC), the first emperor of the "Age of Humans" following the "Age of the Gods" in the chronicles.

人文未作	and human civilization/writing/letters (*wen*) was not yet created.
至於神后征坎	Then, Empress Jingū (r. 201–69) campaigned in the direction of the "Hole" hexagram[10] (against Korea)
品帝乘乾	and Emperor Ōjin (r. 270–310) rode the powers of the "Heaven" hexagram[11] (and came to the throne).
百濟入朝	The Korean state of Paekche did obeisance at our court
啓龍編於馬厩	unravelling dragon texts in the horse stables.[12]
高麗上表	And the state of Koguryo submitted memorials to our throne,
圖烏冊於鳥文	drawing up their crow documents with bird-track patterns.[13]
王仁始導蒙於輕島	First Wani introduced study and learning to Karushima
辰爾終敷教於譯田	and Shinni completed this by spreading the doctrines in Osada.[14]
遂使俗漸洙泗之風	Thus (our) customs gradually absorbed the influence of the Zhu and Si Rivers
人趨齊魯之學[15]	and people tended towards the teachings from Qi and Lu.[16]

This passage makes two clever moves. First, it claims for Japan what I would call a "hexagrammatic literacy," the existence of writing literally *avant la lettre*. Although writing is "not yet created" and the Korean envoys have yet to bring their diplomatic documents and Chinese characters to Japan, Empress Jingū and Emperor Ōjin align their actions with the hexagrams from the *Classic of Changes*, symbols consisting of a combination of six strokes that are either continuous (yang strokes) or broken (yin strokes). According to the "Appended Phrases," a commentary to the *Classic of Changes,* the mythical hero Fu Xi allegedly invented them as a type of proto-writing. "Hexagrammatic literacy" deleted the trauma of the advent of writing from the outside.

Second, the preface downplays the importation of Chinese writing through Korea by tapping into the Chinese discourses of the "naturalization" of writing. The official documents are "dragon texts," possibly echoing the story of texts on a turtle's back that appeared from the Yellow River. The "bird-track patterns" allude to Cang Jie's invention of writing. The novelty the Korean envoys have to offer is

---

[10] 29th hexagram of *Classic of Changes.* Associated with water and the north, thus referring to the crossing of the ocean northwards, when Empress Jingū launched an attack on the Korean state of Silla.

[11] 1st hexagram of the Classic of Changes. Associated with *yang* forces and imperial power.

[12] Perhaps reference to the legendary appearance of a dragon or tortoise from the Yellow River, carrying an inscribed tablet on its back. The Korean envoy Akichi is said to have presented horses to the Japanese court and instructed a Japanese prince in the Chinese Classics.

[13] Reference to the legendary invention of writing by the mythical hero Cang Jie.

[14] Wani and Shinni are both Korean envoys who visited Emperor Ōjin's (r. 270–310) and Emperor Bidatsu's (r. 572–85) capital, respectively.

[15] *Kaifūsō* preface. Kojima 1964, 58–62.

[16] Both states were associated with Confucian learning. Zhu and Si are rivers in the ancient state of Lu, Confucius's home state.

presented as a diplomatic tribute to an imagined superior Japanese court—a court that already possessed the technology of writing. Instead, the Koreans bring the teachings contained in the Confucian Classics.

As the first extant attempt of narrating literary history in Japan, the *Kaifūsō* Preface draws up a powerful history of literature as a history of wen in all its manifestations and connotations. And by suggesting a "hexagrammatic literacy" of early Japanese emperors and tapping into Chinese discourses of the naturalization of writing as mimicry of the cosmos, it also succeeds in downplaying the advent of a foreign writing system in Japan.

2. Competing with the Sino-Japanese Tradition: the Universal "Way" in the Kokinshū

The *Kokinshū* (*Collection of Ancient and Modern Poems*) is the first imperially sponsored anthology of vernacular poetry. Compiled in 905 under the auspices of Emperor Daigo after a century of imperial support for Sino-Japanese poetry, the collection was under enormous pressure to make a convincing argument for Japanese poetry that lacked the public stature of its Sino-Japanese twin and rival. One sign of the seriousness of this competition is that the *Kokinshū* has two prefaces: one written in Classical Japanese and a second one, in Sino-Japanese, in closer dialogue with Sino-Japanese and Chinese precedents. In a landmark article John Timothy Wixted has shown how the *Kokinshū* Prefaces tapped into Chinese poetics to affirm the public stature of waka (Wixted 1983). In the next two chapters I complement his perspective by also looking at how the *Kokinshū* Prefaces positioned themselves vis-à-vis the Sino-Japanese anthologies produced in Japan that had preceded the first imperial waka collection, most notably the *Kaifūsō*. This approach resonates with Thomas LaMarre's more recent attempt to argue against the lingering assumption of an ethnolinguistic dichotomy between "Chinese" and "Japanese" modes in Heian culture and for the idea that many Heian practices juxtaposed "Chinese-style" and "Japanese-style" aesthetic sensibilities that mapped on indigenous distinctions such as the notion of formal (*hare*) and more informal (*ke*) modes with respect to anything from poetry to clothing, architecture, and calligraphy styles.[17]

Bolstering Japanese waka poetry as public discourse meant to devise a storyline for its development that outsmarted the narratives used to justify Sino-Japanese practice. The *Kokinshū* Prefaces did so, first, by evoking the psychology from the "Great Preface" to the Confucian *Classic of Poetry* (partly restated by Masafusa above). The *Kokinshū* Prefaces constructed a timeless and universal "Way" (道Ch. *dao*, J. *michi*) of poetic composition that transcended the historical narrative of wen of the *Kaifūsō* Preface.

Second, having polemicized against wen through the universality of the "Way," the authors of the prefaces proceeded to capture cosmogony as literary history. Although they gave up on the broad semantic spectrum to which the Sino-Japanese anthologies had laid claim in using wen as civilization, literature, and Confucian

---

17 See LaMarre 2000 and in particular Chapter 7 on the *Kokinshū* Prefaces.

governance, they made poetry into an even more powerful entity by implanting it into a cosmological discourse emerging from the beginning of heaven and earth.

The radical novelty of the *Kokinshū* Prefaces in comparison to the prefaces of the previous Sino-Japanese anthologies did not depend on new Chinese texts that would have reached Japan in the meantime or on a forceful assertion of complete independence of the indigenous tradition from Chinese precedent. Instead, the crucial difference was a clever shift in the choice of canonical Chinese subtexts— in particular the "Great Preface" to the *Classic of Poetry*. The most effective step in this scheme was to capitalize on a niche left by the Sino-Japanese anthologies' focus on wen: Wen failed to give a psychological account of poetic creativity. Wen was a great way to talk about the invention of writing, the establishment of Confucian-style governance and literary production. But why write in the first place? The *Kokinshū* compilers found their best choice to exploit that blind spot in the Preface to the *Classic of Poetry*, with its psychological explanation of the unfolding of poetry from the latency in the heart into words manifest in the world. It allowed them to sketch a vision of the nature and history of Japanese waka poetry not only on a par with Sino-Japanese poetry, but psychologically and historically surpassing it.

The Sino-Japanese Preface to the *Kokinshū* opens:

夫和歌者	Japanese waka poetry
託其根於心地	takes root in the soil of one's heart
発其華於詞林者也	and spreads its flowers into a Forest of Words.
人之在世	While in this world
不能無為	mankind cannot be idle.
思慮易遷	Thoughts and concerns easily shift,
哀樂相変	sorrow and pleasure alternate.
感生於志	As feelings in the intent mind,
詠形於言	…song takes shape in words…
若夫春鶯之囀花中	It is just like the warbler in spring singing among blossoms
秋蟬之吟樹上	or the cricket in fall humming in the treetops:
雖無曲折	though nothing forces them to do so,
各發歌謠	each puts forth its song.
物皆有之	All creatures do it,
自然之理也[18]	it's a natural principle."

It is significant that the image of vegetable growth is chosen to convey the process of how a poem becomes manifest, or "grows," because it facilitates a convenient figural flow between nature and the mind, and enables the "interiorization" of nature into psychological processes—"every creature has its song."

The preface describes Japanese poetry as an inborn response to scenes in nature and a "forest of words" shared by all living creatures. This naturalistic

---

[18] *Kokin wakashū*, Sino-Japanese Preface. Kojima and Arai 1989, 338–41, and Katagiri 1998 vol. 1, 279–82. For a complete English translation of the *Mana* Preface see Leonard Grzanka's in Rodd 1984, 379–85.

account was a powerful counter-vision to the Sino-Japanese anthologies' support of wen. It replaced culture and history with nature and psychology, wen "Letters" with dao "the Way."

The last section of the Sino-Japanese preface vividly shows this powerful replacement of wen with "the Way" and of the previous hegemony of Sino-Japanese poetry with a future flourishing of vernacular poetry. After lamenting the decline of waka poetry and describing the Emperor's desire to "resurrect the long-deserted Way" the preface closes on this powerful gesture, a majestic leap to secure waka poetry eternity in the face of Sino-Japanese wen:

適遇和歌之中興	If Japanese poetry should meet with a new revival
以樂吾道之再昌	we will delight in the resurrection of Our Way.
嗚呼 人丸既沒	Alas, with Hitomaro long dead,
和歌不在斯哉[19]	is not [the art of] Japanese poetry contained in this/here with us!

This is a brilliant appropriation of a pun in *Analects* 9.5, in which Confucius, when surrounded by enemies in Kuang, exclaims, "With King Wen long dead, is not this our cultural heritage (*si wen*) residing here in me?" (文王既沒、文不在茲乎). The *Kokinshū* Preface implies the following bold pattern of replacement: Hitomaro, the unrivalled poet-saint from the mid-eighth century *Man'yōshū* replaces King Wen; "this Way of waka poetry" replaces the "Zhou cultural heritage (*wen*)," and "Confucius" as the curator of this tradition is replaced with both the contemporary Japanese poets at Emperor Daigo's court and the *Kokinshū* itself. The "Way of waka poetry"—a notion that was brought to its full consequences only later in the medieval period—resides both in the collection offered to the throne and in the poet-compilers who compiled it.[20]

A second strategy that both prefaces of the *Kokinshū* use to lay claim to the higher status of Sino-Japanese poetry is to employ the rhetoric of cosmogony borrowed from the earlier chronicles, in particular the above-mentioned *Chronicles of Japan* (*Nihon shoki*) that tell the beginning of Japanese poetry. The Sino-Japanese preface goes farther in translating cosmogony into what we might call "poetogony." The preface says:

然而神世七代	But in the Seven Generations of the Age of the Gods
時質人淳	the times were unsophisticated and people simple.
情欲無分	Emotions and desires were not distinguished
和歌未作	and Japanese poetry had yet to arise.

---

[19] Kojima and Arai 1989, 348–51.

[20] This clever assertion of the Japanese Way of poetry over the Sino-Japanese culture of wen bears an uncanny relationship to the way the *Laozi* and early Daoist traditions attempted to dislodge their Confucian rivals—the *Laozi*'s claims of precedence over the Confucian tradition by asserting a timeless natural "Way" against the Confucian historical consciousness of civilization and the importance of ritual and ethical values. The concept of "the Way"—a term that plays only a minor role in the *Analects*—was an attractive niche to exploit and this move was obviously effective enough to result in a thought school called "Daoism." To pursue this issue in the context of early Chinese Masters Literature see Denecke 2010 Chapter 6.

| 逮於素盞烏尊到出雲国 | Later when the god Susano-o arrived at Izumo, |
| 始有三十一字之詠[21] | the thirty-one syllable song (i.e. waka poetry) first appeared. |

Where the cosmogony of the *Nihon shoki* states that "Yin and Yang forces were not yet divided," the poetogony of the Sino-Japanese Preface proudly translates Yin and Yang into poetic currency: "Emotions and desires were not yet distinguished." In the same way as Masafusa had translated Chinese literary history into an allegorical "Realm of Poetry," the *Kokinshū* Preface established a realm of poetogony that could not fail to be both temporally and psychologically superior to Sino-Japanese literature.

3. The Assertion of a "Natural History" of Roman Oratory in Cicero's Brutus

Cicero was certainly not the first to reflect on the development of polished speech and writing in Rome.[22] We have a number of fragments by Accius, Porcius Licinius, Volcacius Sedigitus, and Valerius Soranus on the development of the theater, biographies of poets, or lists of comedy writers. Varro Reatinus (116–27 BC) was a philologist and librarian who was briefly charged with the supervision of the Roman public library by Caesar, lost his property during the proscriptions of Mark Antony following Caesar's death, and finally gained Augustus's confidence and support. He wrote lost or partially preserved treatises on various topics such as poetry, theater, famous authors, the Latin language, and libraries among others, but only his treatise on agriculture (*Rerum rusticarum libri tres*), a successor treatise to Cato's popular *On Agriculture* survives in full. Cicero had the highest respect for Varro, crediting him with starting philosophy in Rome, providing poets with proper Latin diction, and giving a home (*domus*) to the formerly "vagrant" Latin literature.[23] In short, Varro is a figure who reflected and inspired Cicero's own aspirations and accomplishments.

The image of "home-coming" is significant: Latin literature became a Roman affair and not only a Greek variant. In *Brutus,* an account of the history of eloquence and oratory in Greece and Rome, Cicero also attempts a "home-coming," though on quite contradictory levels as we will see.

The *Brutus* is a pedagogical dialogue—not by coincidence staged under a statue of Plato at Cicero's residence in Rome. It takes place between Cicero, in the instructor role, his friend Atticus (110–32 BC), and the young Brutus (the later murderer of Caesar), on whom Cicero pins his hopes for the future of the Republic and of Latin rhetoric. The dialogue traces the development of Greek and Latin rhetoric by dwelling in more or less detail on the abilities of more than 270 orators, most of whom we know nothing about. Cicero emphatically uses the term "rhetoric" (*eloquentia*) both in the technical sense of "public oratory," the cardinal virtue of Republican spirit, as well as in a broader sense of "proper and refined use of language" in general.

---

[21] Kojima and Arai 1989, 340–41.
[22] On the ways authors of the Late Republic and early Empire constructed a history for Latin literature see Goldberg 2005.
[23] *Academica* I 3.9

Cicero's treatment of the relationship between Greek and Roman cultural history in the *Brutus* is remarkably different from the views in his earlier masterpieces, such as *On the Orator* (*De oratore*, 55 BCE), to which we will turn in the next chapter, and *The Republic* (*De re publica*, 51 BCE). In the 50s Cicero looked for similarities across cultures and even assumed that Greek and Roman culture unfolded almost contemporaneously. By the time of the *Brutus*, a mere five years later in 46 BCE, Cicero suddenly seems aware of Rome's belatedness vis-à-vis Greek oratory and literature and is struggling to find a model to account for that difference. Denis Feeney has attributed this dramatic change of mind to Cicero's reading of his friend Atticus's *Liber Annalis*, an annalistic history that probably included synoptic tables, which inevitably showed that Greece had a literature from its early beginnings, while Latin literature only emerged a short couple of centuries before Cicero's own *Brutus*.[24] Cicero's startling discovery is palpable in the complex and at times paradoxical set of timelines he devises for the history of Roman oratory. There are at least three histories of oratory in *Brutus*. First, there is what we might call a "natural history" of oratory: oratory as a characteristically Roman virtue, a political practice of venerable, independent, and unquestionable domestic standing. Cicero grafts the apogee of this natural history of Roman oratory onto the figure of Cato (234–149 BCE), famous for his proverbial, though complex, hostility toward Carthage and Hellenic influence. Cicero proceeds with utter caution, according Cato a surprisingly high place, but immediately also acknowledging that his interlocutors—and indeed his readers—might laugh at his eulogy of Cato:

> As for Cato, who of our orators nowadays reads him or is familiar with him at all? And yet, good gods, what a man! I pass over him as a citizen, a senator and commander—here we only seek out the orator.[...] Select from [his speeches] the remarkable and praiseworthy passages: you will find all oratorical virtues in them. [...] The Greeks consider it an embellishment of speech, if they use substitutions of single words, which they call 'tropes' [τρόπους] and figures of sentences and speech to which they give the name of 'schemata' [σχήματα]; it is hardly believable how versatile and distinguished Cato is in the use of both devices. Of course, I am not unaware that he is not yet sufficiently polished as an orator and that one has to seek something more perfect; and that is not strange, since according to the reason of our times he is so antiquated that no older text before him exists that would be worth reading.[25]

Cato's eloquence is intuitive and unschooled in Greek precedent; he is an exception to the principle emphasized by Cicero earlier in the dialogue that every art needs time to mature and reach perfection. It is ironic that Cato, untouched by

---

[24] Feeney, 2007, 26–28.
[25] *Brutus* 65–69. *Catonem vero quis nostrorum oratorum, qui quidem nunc sunt, legit? aut quis novit omnino? At quem virum, di boni! mitto civem aut senatorem aut imperatorem—oratorem enim hoc loco quaerimus [...] Licet ex his eligant ea quae notatione et laude digna sint; omnes oratoriae virtutes in eis reperientur. [...] Ornari orationem Graeci putant, si verborum immutationibus utantur, quos appellant τρόπους, et sententiarum orationisque formis, quae vocant σχήματα; non veri simile est quam sit in utroque genere et creber et distinctus Cato. Nec vero ignoro nondum esse satis politum hunc oratorem et quaerendum esse aliquid perfectius, quippe cum ita sit ad nostrorum temporum rationem vetus, ut nullius scriptum exstet dignum quidem lectione quod sit antiquius.* All translations from *Brutus* are my own.

rhetorical artifice, intuitively applies rhetorical "tropes" and "schemata," words that Cicero's text spells out in the Greek alphabet and treats with deliberate naïveté.[26] Cicero's quick concession that Cato is "not yet sufficiently polished" tries to forestall his interlocutor's doubts, in particular the protest of his friend Atticus who was thoroughly Hellenized since he had left Rome during the Sullan proscriptions and had lived several decades in Athens. Atticus's judgment operates on a second model for the development of Roman oratory. This second model is a "reception history" of Roman oratory: the discipline of oratory developed under Greek influence and based on Greek precedent. For this storyline, *politum*, "the refined and sophisticated" constitutes the yardstick, which Cicero replaces boldly with intuitive talent in the case of Cato. Third, there is an autobiographical history of oratory, probably outpacing the other two and installing Cicero in a proud position of dominance: the discipline in which Cicero considered himself most adept and which, in the climate of the civil wars of the Late Republic, was at risk of losing its traditional function.[27] From the point of view of the third storyline the *Brutus* is Cicero's last will, a testament that entrusts the history of rhetoric on the verge of its extinction to the hands of his designated successor, Brutus.

The chronotopes of these three storylines are at times inverse and at times intersecting. The "natural history" culminates in the figure of Cato and recedes into decline by Cicero's times. The "reception history" works slowly from Greek Hellenistic precedent to a corresponding high level of sophistication in Rome which only Cicero himself presumes, not without self-congratulatory tones, to have reached. In this respect it overlaps with the zenith of the "autobiographical history" that inevitably focuses on Cicero alone. The clashing chronotopes of these three storylines give the reader the unsettling impression of reading both a tale of promising new beginnings (or a first real "home-coming" of oratory in Rome) and a disheartening swansong for a threatened discipline.

Cicero immodestly performs a barely veiled self-enthronement as the champion of both the "reception history" and the "autobiographical history." Even while parading his naïve belief in a "natural history" of oratory with Cato as its champion, he self-consciously pulls back to escape Atticus's superior derision. Atticus takes ample opportunity to chide Cicero for completely overrating earlier Roman orators. He cannot believe that Cicero dares to put Cato on the same level as the Atticist master Lysias

---

[26] On Cato himself as the founder of a nativist ideology of Romanness (*latinitas*) see Bloomer 1997, 18–37. It is important to distinguish Cicero's nativist portrayal of Cato in the *Brutus* from the actual historical figure. Erich Gruen has shown that Cato, rather than being the hostile anti-Hellene he is usually portrayed to be, had deep knowledge of Greek language and culture from early on, emphasized the historical connections between Greece and the Italic peninsula, and even employed a Greek tutor in his household, although he tutored his own sons himself. Gruen convincingly shows how seemingly anti-Greek statements should be seen as an advocacy of Rome's superiority rather than a form of vitriolic anti-Hellenism. Gruen also reminds us that Cicero portrayed Cato as thoroughly familiar with Greek literature in other works, such as *On Old Age* (*Cato maior de senectute*). Gruen 1992a, 52–83.
[27] Jürgen Paul Schwindt acknowledges this storyline: "Cicero sprach, so wissen wir jetzt, von Anfang an von sich selbst, Roms Rhetorikgeschichte ist seine Geschichte, Roms rednerische Anfänge sind seine Anfänge, Roms rednerische Entwicklung ist seine Entwicklung, ihr τέλος [telos] war er selbst, doch hat er die Bahn noch nicht einmal ganz durchschritten." See Schwindt 2000, 120.

and he rants that Cicero would call everybody who just opened his mouth in Rome an "orator." Atticus is not just a critical opponent, but the model of the thoroughly Hellenized Roman aristocrat—almost a naturalized Greek—who laughs at Cicero's Roman fantasizing about the independent roots of a "natural" oratory in Rome.

Here we see a crucial difference from the strategies of the *Kaifūsō*: the *Kaifūsō* compiler could insouciantly claim equality with China, a civilization of primary script invention, by imaging a "hexagrammatic literacy" of Japanese emperors before the introduction of the Chinese writing system that actually enabled the written fixation of Japanese. Only few Chinese could have talked back to him. Cicero, in contrast, has to deal with a Roman Greek of sorts, his friend and opponent Atticus. Cicero braves this challenge in the end by vaguely suspending his entire dialogue in a web of Socratic irony. Of course, Cicero, the author, does not do it himself. He wants to be credible with his story of a "natural history," but also does not want to be *too* credible. He has Atticus do it to Cicero, the fictional character, in the dialogue:

> "Now that your speech seems to look towards its end, I will say, if you will, what I think." "By all means, Titus [Atticus]" [said I]. "I think," said Atticus, "that that 'irony' which Socrates is said to have possessed and which he uses in the dialogues of Plato, Xenophon, and Aeschines is indeed a witty and elegant thing. It reveals a man as anything but foolish and at the same time witty if, when discussing wisdom, he denies it to *himself*, but attributes it playfully to those who arrogate it to *themselves*, like when in Plato Socrates heaps praise to the heavens on Protagoras, Hippias, Prodicus, Gorgias and all those others, while pretending to know nothing about anything and playing the fool. I don't know, this somehow fits his style and I don't agree with Epicurus who reprehends him for it. But in an historical account such as you have provided throughout in your speech when dwelling on the qualities of each orator, I ask you whether irony should not be as reprehensible as it would be in a witness stand in court." I replied, "What are you getting at with this? I don't really understand." [Atticus] retorted, "That's why: First, you have praised some orators to such degree that you possibly mislead people who don't know anything about them. To tell you the truth, I could hardly keep myself from laughing out loud, like when you compared the Athenian Lysias to our good Cato: a great—even unsurpassed and unique—man, by Hercules! Nobody would say otherwise. But an orator? And, on top of it, on par with Lysias, with the latter's unsurpassable refinement? Nice irony, if we're playing around. But if, however, we give an honest account we should, you see, be as conscientious as if we were giving testimony on oath.[28]

Atticus does not spare Cicero his harshest criticism: Socratic irony, the only motivation that in Atticus's eyes could explain Cicero's ludicrous stylization of Cato into a Roman Lysias, is a sublime art but has no place in a historical account, and

---

[28] *Brutus* 292–93. *Nunc quoniam iam ad perorandum spectare videtur sermo tuus, dicam, opinor, quod sentior. Tu vero, inquam, Tite. Tum ille: Ego, inquit, ironiam illam quam in Socrate dicunt fuisse, qua ille in Platonis et Xenophontis et Aeschini libris utitur, facetam et elegantem puto. Est enim et minime inepti hominis et eiusdem etiam faceti, cum de sapientia discepteur, hanc sibi ipsum detrahere, eis tribuere illudentem, qui eam sibi arrogant, ut apud Platonem Socrates in caelum effert laudibus Protagoram Hippiam Prodicum Gorgiam ceteros, se autem omnium rerum inscium fingit et rudem. Decet hoc nescio quo modo illum, nec Epicuro, qui id reprehendit, assentior. Sed in historia, qua tu es usus in omni sermone,*

particularly not in an account of oratory. A history of oratory should mimic the norms of the profession; it should abide by the rules of the court and be delivered like a testimony under oath. As one of the great moments in the whole *Brutus*, the fictional Cicero plays dumb, claiming he "does not understand" what Atticus is "getting at" with his invective.[29] This allows Cicero the author to embrace both Atticus's criticism as well as the fictional Cicero's bold argument at the same time. Cicero the author brilliantly suspends his judgment between his fictional alter ego's bold argument for a "natural history" of Roman oratory and the voice of Greek refined reason arguing for a "reception history" that is channeled through his friend Atticus.

He also gains from his fictional self's denial of Socratic irony and Atticus's ascription of precisely that irony to at least Cicero the author, if not the fictional character. Cicero's subtle play with irony and the fictionality of the characters of his dialogue lends him a credibility of sorts: at least, it enables the articulation of the "natural history" of Roman oratory in the first place. It should make us suspicious that Cicero fashions Cato into a hero of a primordial archaic Roman oral culture in a text that also relied on a reception model and on an autobiographical narrative to tell the history of early Roman oratory. Although scholars like Thomas Habinek have recently revived the idea of a vibrant Roman song culture on the Archaic Greek model, Cicero, a central testimony for archaic Roman literary culture, had clearly his very own, and ever shifting, agendas and can certainly not be read at face value.[30] His Cato in the *Brutus* allowed him to proudly assert Roman independence from Greek historical contingency, which he had to otherwise accept in the very same text.

4. *Velleius Paterculus's Vision of Creativity Through Envy*

In 30 CE Paterculus published a two-volume *Compendium of Roman History* (*Historiae Romanae*) from the city's beginnings to the times of Tiberius. For most of the time Velleius has been considered a minor writer and part of the reason for his lack of reputation is that he lived in the shadow of the post-Augustan age and chose to praise the wrong monarch, namely Tiberius, the lusterless successor of Augustus.[31] He did have some fervent admirers in the eighteenth and nineteenth centuries: the Prussian classicist Barthold Georg Niebuhr (1776–1831) deemed his intellectual subtleness far superior to his contemporaries, and the French literary historian Charles Augustin Sainte-Beuve (1804–69) considered him a "true modern

---

cum qualis quisque orator fuisset exponeres, vide quaeso, inquit, ne tam reprehendenda sit ironia quam in testimonio. Quorsus, inquam, istuc? Non enim intellego. Quia primum, inquit, ita laudavisti quosdam oratores ut imperitos posses in errorem inducere. Equidem in quibusdam risum vix tenebam, cum Attico Lysiae Catonem nostrum comparabas, magnum mehercule hominem vel potius summum et singularem virum! nemo dicet secus; sed oratorem? sed etiam Lysiae similem, quo nihil potest esse pictius? Bella ironia, si iocaremur; sin asseveramus, vide ne religio nobis tam adhibenda sit quam si testimonium diceremus.
[29] After Cicero affirms again that he spoke in good faith without any intention of irony, Atticus flatters him by claiming that Cicero has something in common with great Socrates.
[30] For incisive skepticism toward the oral song culture model see Feeney 2005, 233–36.
[31] Lamenting the neglect and misrecognition of his work is a commonplace in the scholarship devoted to him. See A. J. Woodman 1975, 1 and footnote 2. See also the first chapter of Schmitzer 2000, which is defensively entitled „Velleius Paterculus: Urteile und Vorurteile der Wissenschaft."

thinker among the ancients." Last but not least, Johann Wolfgang Goethe—probably in connection with his ideas about "Weltliteratur"—was enthusiastic about Velleius's universal theory of artistic creativity, which is precisely what interests us in this chapter.[32]

Velleius's *History* is unique and something of an orphan in the tradition of Latin historiography. First, it is extremely short, covering all of Roman history in two books. It values brevity over copiousness—a programmatic statement against most earlier Roman historians, in particular Livy, who had just recently accomplished the same task in the daunting course of 142 books. Also, Velleius presents an intriguingly interwoven synoptic history of various Asian empires, Greece, and Rome. And lastly, despite his history's brevity, Velleius chooses to intersperse his political chronology with long digressions about literary history, producing something closer to a cultural history that also gives him the occasion to speculate about the nature of artistic and literary production.[33]

In these digressions Velleius is particularly interested in the question of why great ages produce clusters of great minds. He gives a psychological explanation of the phenomenon, evoking the key terms of "envy" (*invidia*) and "competitive imitation" (*aemulatio*):

> I am almost obliged to omit matters of essential importance rather than to embrace unessential details, yet I cannot keep myself from noting down a subject which has often occupied my thoughts but has never been clearly reasoned out. For who can marvel sufficiently that the most distinguished minds in each branch of human achievement have happened to adopt the same form of effort, and to have fallen within the same narrow space of time? Just as animals of different species when shut in the same pen or other enclosure still segregate themselves from those which are not of their kind, and gather together each in its own group, so the minds that have the capacity for distinguished achievement of each kind have set themselves apart from the rest by doing like things in the same period of time. A single epoch, and that only of a few years' duration, gave luster to tragedy through three men of divine inspiration, Aeschylus, Sophocles, and Euripides. So, with Comedy, a single age brought to perfection that early form, through the agency of Cratinus, Aristophanes, and Eupolis; while Menander, and Philemon and Diphilus, his equals in age rather than in performance, within the space of a very few years invented the New Comedy and left it to defy imitation.[34]

---

[32] Not by coincidence does Goethe call Velleius a "Weltmann" in *Winckelmann und sein Jahrhundert* (1805). The very existence and subtitle of a recent Danish translation—"a concise Roman world history"—indicates that Velleius's fortune might be on the rise thanks to the currently expanding fields of world history/global history and world literature. Persson and Rasmussen 2010.
[33] Schmitzer acknowledges the uniqueness of Velleius's literary excursus and believes that they represent the historian's own original ideas and do not simply rely on a Hellenistic precedent. Schmitzer 2000, 100.
[34] *Historiae Romanae* Book I, 16. 1–3. Translation from Shipley 1979, 40–43. *paene magis necessaria praetereunda quam supervacua amplectenda, nequeo tamen temperare mihi, quin rem saepe agitatam animo meo neque ad liquidum ratione perductam signem stilo. Quis enim abunde mirari potest, quod*

Velleius also lists philosophy and oratory as other examples that support his observation that great minds cluster in small spans of time. Then he goes on to make the same argument for Rome:

> This phenomenon occurred among the Romans as well as among the Greeks. For, unless one goes back to the rough and crude beginnings, and to men whose sole claim to praise is that they were the pioneers, Roman tragedy centres in and about Accius; and the sweet pleasantry of Latin humour reached its zenith in practically the same age under Caecilius, Terentius and Afranius.[35]

After marshaling some more evidence from historiography, poetry, oratory, grammar, painting, and sculpture, Velleius reflects on the reasons for this. Apart from giving a reason for the accumulation of greatness, he also finds reasons for failure and imperfection:

> Though I frequently search for the reasons why men of similar talents occur exclusively in certain epochs and not only flock to one pursuit but also attain like success, I can never find any of whose truth I am certain, though I do find some which perhaps seem likely, and particularly the following. Genius is fostered by emulation, and it is now envy, now admiration, which enkindles imitation, and, in the nature of things, that which is cultivated with the highest zeal advances to the highest perfection; but it is difficult to continue at the point of perfection, and naturally that which cannot advance will recede. And as in the beginning we are fired with the ambition to overtake those whom we regard as leaders, so when we have despaired of being able either to surpass or even to equal them, our zeal wanes with our hope; it ceases to follow what it cannot overtake, and abandoning the old field though pre-empted, it seeks a new one. Passing over that in which we cannot be pre-eminent, we seek for some new object of our effort. It follows that the greatest obstacle in the way of perfection in any work is our fickle way of passing on at frequent intervals to something else.[36]

---

eminentissima cuiusque professionis ingenia in eandem formam et in idem artati temporis congruere spatium, et quemadmodum clausa capso aliove saepto diversi generis animalia nihilo minus separata alienis in umum quodque corpus congregantur, ita cuiusque clari operis capacia ingenia in similitudine et temporum et profectuum semet ipsa ab aliis separaverunt. Una neque multorum annorum spatio divisa aetas per divini spiritus viros, Aeschylum Sophoclen Euripiden, inlustravit tragoediam; una priscam illam et veterem sub Cratino Aristophaneque et Eupolide comoediam; ac novam comicam Menander aequalesque eius aetatis magis quam operis Philemo ac Diphilus et invenere intra paucissimos annos neque imitandam relinquere.

[35] Historiae Romanae Book I, 17.1. Shipley 1979, 42–43. Neque hoc in Graecis quam in Romanis evenit magis. Nam nisi aspera ac rudia repetas et inventi laudanda nomine, in Accio circaque eum, Romana tragoedia est; dulcesque Latini leporis facetiae per Caecilium Terentiumque et Afranium subpari aetate nituerunt.

[36] Historiae Romanae Book I, 17.5–7. Huius ergo recedentis in suum quodque saeculum ingeniorum similitudinies congregantisque se et in stadium par et in emolumentum causas cum saepe requiro, numquam reperio, quas esse versa confidam, sed fortasse veri similes, inter quas has maxime. Alit aemulatio ingenia, et nunc invidia, nunc admiration imitationem accendit, naturaque quod summo studio petitum est, ascendit in summum difficilisque in perfecto mora est, naturaliterque quod procedere non potest, recedit. Et ut primo ad consequendos quos priores ducimus accendimur, ita ubi aut praeteriri aut aequari eos posse desperavimus, studium cum spe senescit, et quod adsequi non potest, sequi desinit et velut occupatam relinquens materiam quaerit novam, praeteritoque eo, in quo eminere non possumus, aliquid, in quo nitamur, conquirimus, sequiturque ut frequens ac mobilis transitus maximum perfecti operis impedimentum sit.

Velleius accomplishes several things at once: He puts Roman and Greek literature on the same footing by universalizing human—even animal—genius. Also, he justifies this universalization with the concepts of "envy" and "competitive emulation." Jürgen Paul Schwindt has noted that he is unique in Roman literary history in this transposition of the concept of fruitful competition between the Greek city-states.[37] And third, Velleius explains the decline of excellence not through the commonsensical logic of decadence, but through the toxic effect of an anxiety of influence: if one cannot live up to the greatness of one's predecessors, one turns to other fields in which challenges seem doable. Velleius shifts here from the intercultural emulation between Greek and Rome to intracultural competition within the same tradition. Blurring the line between inter- and intracultural emulation helps once more blur the distinctions between Greek and Roman cultural history.

Velleius's psychologization of the development of the arts is unprecedented and erratic in Roman tradition but it makes perfect sense once we understand it as a strategy to cope with the burden of living not just in Rome, but in the post-Augustan age. Velleius sets up a complex system of intercultural webs: He clearly plays various Asian empires against Greece's importance in his synoptic history. But when focusing on the history of literature and the arts, Asia drops out completely and the sole focus is on the competition between Greece and Rome. In the same way as the *Kokinshū* Prefaces replaced the historical teleology of wen with the ahistorical circularity of "the Way," Velleius gets rid of a teleology of rise and decline in favor of the synergistic incentive of excellence, ultimately implying that excellence is always and everywhere possible, if you just have the courage to face the shadows of your predecessors. "The Way" of Velleius is a universal psychology of creativity that should encourage his contemporaries to bring about a new period of cultural flourishing that resembles the "renewal of our Way of Japanese poetry" the *Kokinshū* Preface calls for.

***

We analyzed four accounts of the beginnings of literature and eloquence from different periods and places: The *Kaifūsō*, the first Sino-Japanese poetry collection, tried to come to grips with the explosion of textual production in seventh- and eighth-century Japan and sketched a history of literature along the multifaceted paths of the Chinese concept of wen, downplaying the advent of writing in Japan through the notion of "hexagrammatic literacy" and relying on Chinese claims to the naturalization of the human technology of writing. The early tenth-century *Kokinshū*, the first imperially sponsored collection of Japanese vernacular poetry, pitted vernacular poetry against the rival Sino-Japanese tradition and challenged the regime of wen through a universal "Way," a dao, of poetic composition, empowering the waka tradition in a grand narrative of a "poetogony" going back to the Age of the Gods. Third, Cicero's *Brutus* from the Late Republic brought Socratic irony into play to make a bold argument for a "natural history" of Roman oratory with Cato the Elder as its champion. And, lastly, Velleius Paterculus, during the Early

---

[37] See Schwindt 2000, 139–52.

Empire, imagined ways to overcome a sense of postclassical belatedness in his vision of a universal psychology of creative competition through productive envy.

The *Kokinshū* Prefaces, positioning themselves against previous Sino-Japanese poetry anthologies, sketched a universal psychology of poetic composition, a universal "Way," to make a case for Japanese poetry. Velleius Paterculus proposed a universal psychology of artistic production for a post-Augustan age. The similarity in strategy seems to point to a common teleology of narratives of literary history in periods of belatedness that could be fruitfully explored within and across many other traditions.

We also encountered a case of instructive difference: Cicero, living in a state that had conquered its reference culture, had to carefully maneuver between domestic self-assertion and modesty toward the reference culture, whereas the *Kaifūsō* compilers did not have to worry about an ironic backlash from Chinese readers, the appearance of an imaginary eponymous "Sinicus" who, like "Atticus," would speak with authority as a sophisticated connoisseur of things Chinese in general and in Japan in particular. Still, the relative similarity of the strategies shows that writers in both early Japan and Rome were facing the same challenge and developed comparable solutions to their desire to relegate their belatedness out of sight for brief moments.

CHAPTER 3 | Latecomers
Of Ornament, Simplicity, and Decline

From the time when Prince Ōtsu first composed Chinese-style poems and poetic expositions, poets and talented men admired this custom and followed in his wake. They imported those Chinese characters and transformed customs in our Japanese land. All at once the ways of the people were changed, and Japanese poetry gradually declined. Yet we still had the noble master Kakinomoto [no Hitomaro] who loftily stirred thoughts of divine marvels and who alone straddled the past and the present. And there was Yamabe no Akahito; he, too, is an immortal of Japanese poetry.

自大津皇子之。初作詩賦。詞人才子。慕風継塵。移彼漢家之字。化我日域之俗
。民業一改。和歌漸衰。然猶有先師柿本大夫者。高振神妙之思。獨歩古今之間
。有山辺赤人者。並和歌仙也。[1]

KI NO YOSHIMOCHI (-919 CE): "SINO-JAPANESE PREFACE" TO THE *COLLECTION OF ANCIENT AND MODERN POEMS* (*KOKINSHŪ* 古今和歌集)

I shall speak about those Greek fellows in their proper place, son Marcus, and point out the result of my enquiries at Athens, and convince you what benefit comes from dipping into their literature, and not making a close study of it. They are a quite worthless people, and an intractable one, and you must consider my words prophetic. When that race gives us its literature it will corrupt all things, and even all the more if it sends hither its physicians. They have conspired together to murder all foreigners with their physic, but this very thing they do for a fee, to gain credit and to destroy us easily. They are also always dubbing us foreigners, and to fling more filth on us than on others they give us the foul nickname of Opici. I have forbidden you to have dealings with physicians.

Dicam de istis Graecis suo loco, M. fili. quid Athenis exquisitum habeam et quod bonum sit illorum litteras inspicere, non perdiscere, vincam. nequissimum et indocile

---

[1] *Kokin (wa)shū*, 342 f.

genus illorum, et hoc puta vatem dixisse: quandoque ista gens suas litteras dabit, omnia corrumpet, tum etiam magis, si medicos suos hoc mittet. iurarunt inter se barbaros necare omnes medicina, et hoc ipsum mercede faciunt ut fides is sit et facile disperdant. nos quoque dictitant barbaros et spurcius nos quam alios opicon appellatione foedant. interdixi tibi de medicis.[2]

CATO THE ELDER (234–149 BC) AS REPORTED BY PLINY (CA. 23–79 CE)

ONCE UPON A TIME people's customs were undisturbed and pristine, simple and uncorrupted. Native poetry and populations flourished in an age of divine marvels. Then came intruders who destroyed the paradise of blissful simplicity: Chinese writing and literature, Greek letters and physicians. They were set on obliterating local customs, whereupon native poetry declined. They applied names of barbarian Italic tribes like the "Opici" to humiliate the Roman people, and their doctors profited from killing them with their evil quackery.

Neither Japan nor Rome ever got rid of this curse of foreign intrusion and influence. It was a question of an author's period and character whether this was seen as blessing, bane, or both. Narratives of decline are certainly not unique to Japan and Rome, or China and Greece for that matter. They have been a staple of the writing of literary and other histories from antiquity to the present. In the most fundamental sense they depict change with the help of natural metaphors of waxing and waning, continuity and disruption, and make narratives of literary history possible. Only a curve, not a horizontal zero line, can have a narrative. Platonic imagery of the ages of men was applied to the arch of Latin literary history as rising to "Golden Latinity" and declining since "Silver Latinity."[3] Confucian concepts of decline from the age of the "Classics" (*jing* 經), which Confucius was believed to have compiled, to the later Age of the Masters (*zi* 子) after Confucius's death in 479 BCE, when true meaning supposedly waned, was inscribed into the literary history sketched in the imperial bibliography of the *Han History* (first century CE). Narratives of decline became the weapon for various literary reformers during the Tang Dynasty (618–907) in China, who claimed that overindulgence in literary ornament during the fragmented Six Dynasties Period (220–581) had led to a loss not just of moral substance but also of political control. These were the earlier "returning to antiquity" (*fugu* 復古) movements that have rippled up and down the timeline of China's cultural history up to the present.[4] The persuasiveness of such reform movements often depended on how cleverly they designed narratives of decline as launching boards for their new visions. Narratives of decline have been a powerful means for writers to

---

[2] *Naturalis historia* 29.14. Translation from Jones 1968, vol.8, 190–93.
[3] Though once the most prominent scheme of decline ever developed for the periodization of Latin literature, surprisingly little thought has been given to its origin and implications. Wolfram Ax traces it back to Renaissance or Early Baroque writers who applied Hesiod's and Ovid's model of four ages of the world—golden, silver, bronze, iron—to the development of literature. Ax 2006.
[4] On "return to antiquity" movements during the Tang see Bol 1992, Owen 1975, 8–23, Sun 1984 and DeBlasi 2002, 115–45.

gain support for a revival movement and gesture toward a visionary future, and also for scholars to capture a "graphic" narrative of literary history in retrospect. Because scholars depend on the narratives of the authors they study, there is always a danger of taking at face value what writers of decline narratives wanted posterity to believe about them and their visions.

This is the charm and danger of reading narratives of decline. Ancient Rome and Japan were particular cases in this broader picture, because their writers could blame decline on the onslaught of foreign influence more easily than other traditions, such as Greece and China.

Yet, Ki no Yoshimochi and Cato wrote their narratives of decline from very different vantage points. Cato lived right through the high point of Roman confrontation with Hellenistic states during its conquest of the Eastern Mediterranean; he died a few years before the decisive 146 BCE defeat of the Achaean League at Corinth, which meant the Roman submission of the Greek motherland. Although Greek cities had colonized southern Italy since the eighth century BCE and the growing Roman state was increasingly exposed to Greek influence through its conquest of southern Italy in the third century BCE, it was in Cato's later life that the blessings of Greek culture became ever more acutely felt and feared. This period saw the beginning of an education system that relied on Greek freedmen and slaves as Greek and Latin grammar teachers and meant that Romans, unlike Japanese, learned the canon of their older reference culture from actual natives, not just from books. In contrast to Cato, Yoshimochi wrote at a time when more immediate Chinese impact had waned: Waves of immigrants from the Korean Three Kingdoms of Silla, Paekche, and Koguryo brought Chinese culture such as written characters, literature, and Buddhism and its material culture to Japan. This process peaked particularly in the late seventh century, when Silla put an end to the Three Kingdoms Period and unified the peninsula. By Yoshimochi's time, the early tenth century, it was predominantly books, not people, who transmitted the knowledge of Chinese culture to and within Japan.

This fundamental difference in political and physical proximity is palpable in the different anxiety level of Yoshimochi's and Cato's respective narratives of decline. Chinese characters and literature, Yoshimochi's intruders, seem less overtly harmful than the murderous designs of Cato's Greek doctors and the prophecy of wholesale corruption by Greek literature. Yoshimochi's intruders are not real people, but pernicious signs and texts, which are introduced by a Japanese prince, not an ill-intentioned Chinese doctor. For Romans, Greeks were much more threatening and ambiguous: Greeks were the people of Homer, science, and some religious cults, they could hold prestigious positions as tutors and doctors, but there were many who came to Italy as prisoners of war and lived their lives as menials or members of slave gangs.

In Chapter 2 I explored how some Japanese and Latin texts, when devising accounts of their literary beginnings, dealt with the "historical flatness" of their fledgling literary tradition vis-à-vis their older reference cultures. In this chapter I will investigate the flipside of the coin: the "literary density" with which early Japanese and Latin writers saw themselves confronted when they looked back and up to Chinese and Greek models.

First, there was the temporal weight of the textual record. Although we do not exactly know what proportion of the Chinese corpus in circulation had reached Japan, it is safe to say that when Japanese started to record poetry in the late seventh and eighth centuries they were facing about two millennia of textual tradition in China. In this time, to put it breathlessly briefly, the earliest corpus of historical and poetic writings had received the blessings of Confucius in the fifth century BCE and were canonized in the Han Dynasty (206 BCE-220 CE) as "Confucian Classics," which led to a rise of a culture of commentary and scholarship, alongside with the emergence of more properly literary genres like the rhapsody and "classical poetry" in five- and seven-character lines. Poetry, in turn, developed highly regulated forms in the Six Dynasties Period and the Tang Dynasty, accompanied by a prolific production of works on literary history, technical poetics, anecdotal biography and shaken since the mid-eighty-century High Tang by calls to refrain from the ever more ornate court style common until the Early Tang. This only sketches the broader development of poetic forms and leaves out the vast corpus of prose genres.

In contrast, the symbolic beginning date of Latin literature came only about half a millennium after the first recording of Homeric epic, with Livius Andronicus's translation of two Greek plays into Latin for performance at the Roman Games in 240 BCE and his Latin adaptation of the *Odyssey*. But this time span was enough to see the development of epic, elegy, iambic, comedy, and tragedy (all ruled by a complex system of verse meters) in Asia Minor and mainland Greece, alongside with philosophical literature, historiography, oratory, and poetics. Greek literary production reached a highpoint in fifth century BCE Athens and the rhetorical culture its democracy nourished, which was followed by the massive expansion of Greek language and literature thanks to Alexander the Great's empire and its successor states throughout the Near East and the Mediterranean. Centers of scholarship canonized Greek literary and rhetorical learning and fostered the development of a sophisticated "Hellenistic literature," which was exemplified by the third-century scholar-writer Callimachus, was marked both by copious erudition and by elliptic brevity, rhetorical, restraint and deliberate pathos, and had a strong impact on Roman writers.

With the temporal weight of the textual record came stylistic density. That neither the earliest literature in Japan nor what we have of the earliest literature in Latin has the fresh candor of poems from the Chinese *Classic of Poetry* (ca. 600 BCE) or an archaic Greek poem by Sappho has to do with the radically different growth curve of the younger literary traditions. Many of the writers of early Latin and Japanese literature were either directly related to the older reference culture— Greeks or Chinese-trained Koreans—or thoroughly educated in the Greek and Chinese curriculum of their times. As discussed in Chapter 1, they "jumpstarted" Japanese and Latin literature from a highly refined and ornate stage of literary development, namely the ornate literature of the Six Dynasties and Early Tang in the Japanese case and the exuberant and erudite Hellenistic literature in the Latin case. In this sense both Japanese and Latin literary traditions were latecomers. In writing and reflecting on literature they had the exquisite advantage of having at their disposition a sophisticated repertoire of genres and diction, without going through the long literary development that had gradually refined these tools. Launching on the path of this "shortcut" cost these latecomers, on the other hand, the unambiguous entitlement to it. It spurred early writers to eagerly embrace this sophistication as their own while sensing it was not quite theirs, but also inspired them to assert their independent identity. The latecomer's literary and psychological ambiguity came to play out in notions of ornate sophistication and pristine simplicity of literary expression, and in curiously self-serving narratives of decline.

What is the relation between ornamentation and simplicity in early Japanese and Latin literary texts? Why do claims to a supposedly characteristic "simplicity" of Japanese and Latin literary beginnings only start a couple of centuries after the onset of these younger traditions? Why was ornate style sometimes perceived as an aesthetic, civic, and moral threat in both Japanese and Latin literary cultures? How do ornate style, and debates on style, play out differently in Japanese from Latin literary cultures?

This chapter explores some of these questions on the example of texts that address these issues in particularly interesting or influential ways. For Japan, we will trace them in passages from the earliest extant poetry anthologies already discussed in the previous chapters, the *Florilegium of Cherished Airs* (*Kaifūsō* 懐風藻, 751) and the *Collection of Myriad Leaves* (*Man'yōshū* 万葉集) (ca. 759), as well as in the earliest treatise on waka poetry, the *Code of Waka Poetry* (*Uta no Shiki* 歌式) of 772. We know that neither the *Kaifūsō* nor the *Man'yōshū* were the first poetry anthologies of their kinds, although we can be fairly sure that the earliest anthologies belong after the turn of the eighth century. Thus, looking at the first repository of Sino-Japanese poetry (*Kaifūsō*) and vernacular Japanese poetry (*Man'yōshū*) does allow us to examine attitudes toward ornateness and simplicity from the very first century of the Japanese literary tradition. I hope to show that the narrative of a pristine simplicity destroyed by the influx of Chinese literature sketched in the Sino-Japanese Preface to the *Kokinshū* discussed above, is a late construction and that, quite to the contrary, eighth-century texts revel in the opportunities that ornate expression based on Chinese precedent afforded them.

Due to the dearth and fragmentary transmission of early Latin literature, we are forced to leap to the late Republic to explore notions of simplicity, ornateness, and related narratives of decline. Because the surviving corpus of Latin literature in the Late Republican Period represents a later stage in development than what we see in the subsequent early Japanese texts, we will start in Rome at the moment in literary history where we left off in Japan. We will see how in his dialogue *On the Orator* (*De oratore*) Cicero boldly proposes a properly Roman philosophy that mends the intellectual decline brought about by the indisputable Greek master Socrates and returns to a presumably pristine unity between rhetoric and philosophy. Although we have a villain from the older reference culture rather than a native like Prince Ōtsu, this vision is arguably something of a *Kokinshū* moment in Latin literary culture. In his *Dialogue on Orators* (*Dialogus de oratoribus*, ca. 102 CE), a debate with Ciceronian flair, Tacitus articulates a grand theory of decline, which is much better known than Cicero's intervention in *On the Orator* and has dominated visions of Latin culture until today: namely, that Roman oratory went into a steep decline with the advent of the empire and the disappearance of the institutional foundations and the political challenges that the volatile climate of the Late Republic had provided. First, Marcus Aper, a spokesman for the superiority of modern oratory, makes his case, followed by a counterstatement from Vipstanus Messalla, a member of a venerable Republican family who argues for the superiority of past oratory. He detects the causes for the decline of oratory in bad education (for example, by "worthless Greek maids" rather than Roman mothers), exposure to vice (on stage and in gladiator games), and the loss of solid moral, legal, and historical knowledge (replaced with meaningless fictitious debates staged in the school of rhetoricians). But it is the fulminant statement of Maternus—a retired orator who has turned to writing poetry and plays—that enshrines the influential claim that only political strife births brilliant orators, because they are not needed in a peaceful and well-governed empire. In this book we will not deal with the much more famous decline narrative from Tacitus's *Dialogue*. For our purposes, the lesser known decline narrative from Cicero's *On the Orator* is more interesting, because it is earlier, which is important for our attempt to trace the emergence of narratives of decline and arguments for simplicity versus ornateness. Also, because Cicero is undoubtedly the most important mediator of any concept of Latin literature before 45 BCE, it is more consequential to understand his strategies of construing literary history in the comparative fold between Greek and Roman precedents.[5]

After exploring Cicero's use of a narrative of decline to sketch a national Roman project, we move to his involvement in the complex debates about plain and ornate styles that unfolded in the context of a new classicism: "Atticism." These debates, which originated possibly in Greece itself but became first palpable in Late Republican Rome, looked back to "Attic" writers of classical Athens as rhetorical models and denigrated Hellenistic exuberance and ornateness as bad "Asiatic" taste. We will return to the *Brutus*, discussed in the previous chapter, and read it this time as the key text in which Cicero defends himself against accusations that he indulges in Asiatic bombast.

Harkening back to older Greek literature for rhetorical models, this new classicism encouraged, among other things, a rejection of earlier Latin literature, which had relied more on the Hellenistic exuberance of then-contemporary Greek writers. We will look at Horace's confusing play in his *Satires* with the image of the earlier satire writer Lucilius to show how the historical self-consciousness of Latin authors led them to a complex engagement with different stages of both Greek and Latin literary developments that did not occur in early Japanese literature. Combining our insights of early Japanese views leading up to the *Kokinshū* and of Late Republican texts leading away from the Ciceronian "*Kokinshū* moment," we will see that Latin authors were, and had to be, much more aggressive, much more diplomatic, and more embarrassed about their relation to Greek precedent and their own earlier tradition. How and why this was so will be this chapter's larger concern.

---

[5] On this point see Feeney 2005, 227.

1. The Elusiveness of Ornament

Before starting our exploration of actual texts, a few words may be in order on "ornament" and "ornateness." Whereas the concept of a "narrative of decline" should be obvious from Yoshimochi's and Cato's statements above and needs little further clarification, "ornateness" is too elusive to be clearly definable. How much needs to be said on the overdetermined concept of "ornament" for our purpose? This chapter looks both at critical debates about concepts of ornateness, as well as ornate style as practiced in literary texts, and so we need both a critical and a functional description of ornateness.

For our purposes I will confine myself to mentioning one key term for "ornament" in each tradition that has been particularly central to its development. For capturing the use of "ornateness" as a critical concept I want to focus on the Chinese term of *wen* 文 (J. *bun*) and on the Latin *ornatus*. They have different locations in their respective literary cultures. Wen functions in the space of literary cosmology: it establishes a relation between natural pattern in the cosmos and human writing and civilization. In contrast, the Latin term ornatus is one of the traditional five parts of Greco-Roman rhetoric and functions as mediator between a public speaker or writer and his audience. As explained in the previous chapter, wen in the Chinese and East Asian context can mean anything from the pattern of animal fur or tattooing of the human body, to script, literature, culture, and civilization. Wen is the center of a complex web of associations and antonyms.[6] The antonym most relevant for its meaning of "ornament" is "substance" (*zhi* 質). Wen and zhi were understood as a polar pair at least since Confucius's remark that "only once ornament (wen) and substance (zhi) are in balance, do we have a superior person 文質彬彬, 然后君子 *wen zhi binbin, ranhou junzi*" (*Analects* 6.18). Although Confucius's followers prized refinement and ritual over simplicity and raw nature, writers since the Six Dynasties Period developed a much stronger anxiety over a too-much of ornament, rather than a too-much of substance, so that some voices by the Tang Dynasty were convinced that the over-ornamented poetry of the Six Dynasties had led not just to bad taste, but even to the fall of dynasties.[7]

---

[6] Texts discussing these concepts are too numerous to list. In the Chinese context Liu Xie's *The Literary Mind and the Carving of Dragons* (*Wenxin diaolong* 文心雕龍) is a key text to grasp the vocabularies, influential arguments, and ambivalences around the issue of "ornament" and "ornateness." For a bilingual translation see Yang 2003. For a stimulating exploration of the significance and notion of wen in Chinese culture and in Western perceptions of it see Saussy 1997. Cai 2001 contains several articles relating to the notion of wen. See in particular Li Waiyee on the rich ambiguities of wen in "Between 'Literary Mind' and 'Carving Dragons': Order and Excess in *Wenxin diaolong*": "In *Wenxin diaolong*, Liu Xie tries to build a comprehensive system of literary creation, signification, and communication. In the process, the word *wen* is used in various contexts to mean pattern, words, language, writing, literature, refinement, aesthetic surface, culture, or civilization, with the idea of pattern as the apparent common denominator facilitating logical transitions. But even as patterning can be both sedate balance and arabesque effervescence, *wen* embodies immanent order as well as excesses that undermine order in *Wenxin diaolong*." Li 2001, 193.

[7] Fusheng Wu has argued against prejudices of "decadence" toward ornate poetry that pervade Chinese cultural history. His study of the literary heritage of "Palace Style Poetry" tries not just to salvage this genre's reputation, but also to throw light on how its rhetoric and denigration informed poetic production beyond Palace Style Poetry. Wu 1998. To get a taste of Six Dynasties courtly literature and the literary cultures that produced it see Birrell 2004 and Xiaofei Tian's masterful study *Beacon Fire and Shooting Star: the Literary Culture of the Liang* (502–557).

The Latin concept of ornatus, a translation of the Greek *kosmos* or *kataskeue*, was a central concept in rhetorical theory and practice. According to the conventional five parts involved in crafting a persuasive speech, the orator needed good ideas ("invention," *inventio*), which had to be adroitly arranged ("arrangement," *dispositio*). But to articulate them in words one needed "ornament" ("style," *elocutio*) to reach the audience, which needed to be memorized ("memory," *memoria*) and then, in the final step, performed before the target audience ("delivery," *actio*). Though all five parts of rhetoric received attention in rhetorical treatises into the early modern period, it is fair to say that part 3, the "rhetorical colors" of elocution, were expanded most drastically as time went on. They included "figures of speech" and "figures of thought," and the ever-expanding list of such tropes came to be the part of ancient rhetorical theory that had most effect on the development of oratory and literature.[8] In addition to its place in the "style" category of the five parts involved in the preparation of speeches, ornatus was one of the "virtues of speech" (*virtutes dicendi*) that Aristotle's disciple Theophrastus had first formulated, which also included linguistic correctness (*hellenismos*/in Rome: *latinitas*), clarity (*perspicuitas*), and appropriateness (*aptum*). More broadly, ornatus was associated with "ornate" rather than "plain" speech, emotional exuberance rather than cool restraint, and figures of amplification such as "copious diction (*copia*)," rather than ellipsis and brevity.

Wen and ornatus operated in slightly different spheres: although in both cultures it belonged to the sphere of education and literary training, it had a stronger cosmological connection in East Asia. However, debates about wen and ornatus shared one fundamental concern: namely, the question whether ornament was simply applied to, or truly constitutive of, substance. Should it be thought of as mere decoration or integral part of an utterance?

Moving from "ornament" as critical concept to its operation in actual writing, it is hard to give anything other than a minimalist working definition. We can use the helpful linguistic terminology of Roman Jakobson to define "ornate" writing as a writing style that has "vertical/paradigmatic" thickness and "horizontal/syntagmatic" pattern. In other words, lexically, ornate style relies heavily on paradigmatic substitution of vocabulary: instead of "white" the poet says "like snow," "like crane feathers," or "like the temples of the medieval Chinese poet Pan Yue who lamented that his hair began to turn gray at the age of thirty-two." There were poetic encyclopedias, which helped poets to play the game of substitution with synonyms and search out ever more arcane literary allusions that could function as synonyms. Syntactically, ornate style is patterned and relies heavily on the use of repetition and repetition with difference. Parallelism in poetry and prose was brought to excruciating perfection during the Six Dynasties and Tang Period and was equally central to literary production in Nara and Heian Japan. *Isokola*,

---

[8] For a concise introduction to Greco-Roman rhetoric and its historical context see Pernot 2005. For an extensive treatment of the typology of tropes see Lausberg 1960. Book III of Cicero's *On the Orator* and Book VIII of Quintilian's *The Orator's Education* are central among the many texts that treat ornatus.

parallelism of cadences with equal number of words and syllables, was seen as a feature of ornate speech in Greco-Roman rhetoric.

"Ornateness" as critical concept and literary function is a highly ambiguous and paradoxical phenomenon. First, more so than with other notions, its use as a critical concept and its operation in actual texts are typically at odds. Liu Xie's (ca. 465–521) treatise *The Literary Mind and the Carving of Dragons* expounds on the history and power of literature using an ever more dazzling brocade of ornate verbiage, while at the same time forcefully castigating the evil of over-ornamentation. This is a typical example of the fascinating cognitive disjunction between the critical use of the concept of ornament and the production of ornate text.

Part of this disjunction can be blamed on cognitive habituation: the more ornately Six Dynasties poets came to write, the more natural the patterns of this world of artifice appeared to them. On the other hand, and this is the second paradox of "ornateness," the disjunction is rooted in a bias against "ornament" that haunted debates about a desirable balance between "ornament" and "substance" in East Asia as well as Greece and Rome: Unlike "substance," "ornament" could more easily be seen as a vice rather than a virtue. If one said of the writings of one's opponent that they were "ornate," it most often meant that their style was *unduly* ornamented and excessive. Literary reform movements rarely called for more ornament; ornament and stylistic density increased naturally over time. Instead, reform movements more often called for a return to "substance," an imagined simplicity that needed to be uncovered from the soil presumably spoiled by excessive ornament. As we will see in the debates about the virtues of classical "Attic" style in Late Republican Rome nobody wanted to look "Asiatic" and ornate; those accused of "Asiatic" excesses defended themselves by showing how very "Attic" they believed themselves to be. Thus, "ornateness," unlike its antonym of "pristine substance," was more often considered an aesthetic vice with potentially damaging moral and political consequences.

Let us now take a closer look at the Japanese and Latin texts and see how, despite the irreconcilable differences in genre, form, chronology, and cultural context, we can discern a common cluster of aesthetic and moral concerns centered around the issues of simplicity and ornateness, and trace where and how they played out differently in Early Japan and Rome.

2. Embracing Ornament: From the Kaifūsō to the Kokinshū

2a. The Kaifūsō and Ornateness in Sino-Japanese Poetry

The eighth century saw an explosion of textual production in Japan, resulting in the compilation of the earliest historical annals, gazetteers, and poetry collections. Much of the poetry in the *Kaifūsō* was composed at court banquets and sang the praises of the current regime. In the previous chapter I argued that wen (J. bun) was the pivotal concept at the heart of this earliest extant poetry collection, and that both preface and poetry itself strive to think through wen in all its meanings, connotations, and implications for a nascent culture. Wen as the "civil" appears also as contrast to *wu* 武, the "martial," in the biographies of the first two princes and poets of the anthology, Prince Ōtomo, the son of Emperor Tenji who failed to succeed him, and Prince Ōtsu, the son of Tenji's brother Tenmu, who was executed on charges of rebellion. It shows that balancing the "civil" and the "martial" is laudable, while leaning toward the "martial" leads to hubris and ultimate execution. Wen as in "literary production" becomes also a topic for reflection in poetry by monks, who admit dallying in the petty "insect carving" that is literary composition, which should not befit their status as monks.[9] In the previous chapter I focused on wen as a convenient super-concept in the *Kaifūsō* to tell the early cultural and literary history of Japan. In this chapter I show how wen also underlies the *Kaifūsō* Preface as a concept for literary "flourish" and sophistication.

We saw how the preface tells of the beginning of wen, literature proper and poetry, at Emperor Tenji's court banquets. Following this iconic beginning, the preface shifts narrative gears and tells the history of poetry after Tenji's death through two pairs of poets and their poems in the anthology:

自茲以降	Since those times
詞人間出	poets have emerged now and then:
龍潛王子	A crown prince—a hidden dragon
翔雲鶴於風筆	made cloud-dwelling cranes soar with his elegant wind-brush (in poem no. 6).
鳳翥天皇	An emperor—a raising phoenix
泛月舟於霧渚	had the moon boat float by misty islands (in poem no. 15).
神納言之悲白鬢	Counselor Ōmiwa [Takechimaro] lamented his white temples (in poem no. 18)
藤太政之詠玄造	and Chancellor Fujiwara [no Fuhito] sang of mysterious creation (in poem no. 29).[10]
騰茂實於前朝	They elevated the lush fruits of previous reigns
飛英聲於後代	and let their grandiose voices fly on to later generations.[11]

The passage forces very different individuals into a parallel structure: Prince Ōtsu, an overambitious prince dreaming of becoming emperor, is treated favorably when put on a par with the short-lived but successful Emperor Monmu (r. 697–707), under whose behest the famous Taihō legal code of 701 was promulgated; then there are the two high officials Ōmiwa no Takechimaro and Fujiwara no Fuhito. The line-up of these two pairs of political figures and their poems reveals a preference for literary sophistication. Clearly the most ornate rather than the most morally instructive poems are chosen to represent their authors. This choice is particularly pertinent in the case of Prince Ōtsu. Out of the four poems by the prince, it is not the prince's famous deathbed quatrain that is selected, although it would have alluded to his rebellion and forced suicide, and thus added force to a condemnation of the prince's behavior on moral and political grounds suggested

---

[9] For further elaboration on how the *Kaifūsō* plays on wen see Denecke 2006, in particular pp. 76–93.
[10] Fujiwara no Fuhito, the most powerful courtier after Monmu's death, was Monmu's father-in-law. Fujiwara no Fuhito's poetry is the least ornate out of the four poets mentioned and one wonders why he was chosen by the compiler to stand in this double pairing. Fuhito's political and familial relation with Monmu made a good match between a ruler and a high official.
[11] *Kaifūsō* Preface. Kojima 1964, 60–61.

in his biography in the *Kaifūsō*. Instead, the preface evokes this beautifully crafted couplet:

天紙風筆畫雲鶴　　On heaven's paper the elegant wind-brush paints
　　　　　　　　　cloud-dwelling cranes—
山機霜杼織葉錦[12]　Mountain loom and frosty shuttle weave leafy brocade.

Nature is made into her own craftsman, painting with an "elegant" "wind" brush (*fūhitsu* 風筆) and weaving a brocade of foliage over the mountain ridges. Nature adorns herself with artifice designed to reveal natural beauty. The couplet is a decorative reverie, weaving nature and art into one landscape and affirming that the nature of poetry is to have wen, clever ornament.

The choice of the ornate over the instructive is even clearer in Emperor Monmu's case. Out of his three poems included in the anthology, "Stating my Feelings" (no. 16) shows the emperor's earnest attempts at Confucian self-cultivation. Yet the author of the *Kaifūsō* Preface chooses the most delicate poem to match Prince Ōtsu's elegant couplet:

詠月　　　　　　　Composing on "Moon"

月舟移霧渚　　The moon boat advances by misty islands,
楓楫泛霞濱　　cassia oars float along the hazy shore.
臺上澄流耀　　[The moon's] liquid luster shines on the terrace
酒中沈去輪　　as its departing wheel sinks into the wine cup.
水下斜陰碎　　Slanting shadows scatter on the flowing water.
樹除秋光新　　Its autumn light shines fresh through sparse trees.
獨以星間鏡　　Alone like a mirror among stars
還浮雲漢津[13]　it once more floats through the Milky Way's ford.

Emperor Monmu lives up to the decorum of the genre of "poetry on things," as he unfolds layer upon layer of moonlight when composing on the topic of "Moon." There is the reflection of the moon, which is like a boat floating next to the poet's boat; the moon's glow on the vast expanse of the terrace, its almost tactile caressing of the trees, like a mirror among the stars. This multiplication of layers of translucence is played off against multiple layers of concealment: misty islands and hazy shores, the shrinking reflection in the small wine cup, which in turn is particularly striking in contrast to the vast expanse of the terrace, and the scattering shadows. The most luminous layer of concealment is the Milky Way, whose own brightness dims the brightness of the moon, when it "floats" through its "ford." The tension between translucent and concealed brightness is delicately accentuated in the beautiful closure of the poem: the image of the moon as one and alone contrasts with the surrounding stars, which it infinitely reflects as a mirror. The multiplicity of stars produced by the moon-mirror reminds the reader of the repeated self-multiplication within the landscape of luminous reflective surfaces that the moon underwent in the poem when traveling through lake waters, wine cups, terraces, trees, and the Milky Way. A poem like this would have been unthinkable in an

---

[12] *Kaifūsō* no. 6.
[13] *Kaifūsō* no. 15.

early Chinese collection like the *Classic of Poetry*; it needed many centuries of Chinese literary developments to become possible.

The *Kaifūsō* Preface describes two phases of literary history: the iconic beginning of literature at the banquets of Emperor Tenji's court and a second phase, from the Jinshin War until the Wadō era (708–715). The anthology includes a substantial body of poetry from a third phase (715–729), which was composed at the Estate of the great literary patron Prince Nagaya, grandson of Emperor Temmu, and from a fourth phase (729–751), which was partly created under the patronage of Fujiwara no Muchimaro (680–737), who took over Prince Nagaya's role as literary patron after the latter's forced suicide in 729. While the preface elaborates on the first two phases, the third and fourth phases go unaccounted for. And only for the second phase does the preface discuss poets and their poems. For Prince Ōtsu and Emperor Monmu it clearly selects the most ornate poems from among their handful of poems to represent this phase of literary production. This proud line-up of poets and their sophisticated poems suggest that the compiler of the *Kaifūsō* embraced ornateness, not simplicity and plain-worded moral instruction, as a key value of the aesthetics of Sino-Japanese poetry in the mid-eighth century.

2b. Elegance and Literary Knowledge in Early *Waka* Poetics

Although it claims to be a history of Japanese civilization in general and literature in particular, the *Kaifūsō* Preface introduces a collection of Sino-Japanese poetry, *kanshi*. It is therefore crucial to show that ornate elegance was not just a value claimed for kanshi, but also for vernacular poetry, waka. The *Code of Waka Poetry* (*Uta no shiki* 歌式) or *Model Forms for the Canon of Waka Poetry* (*Kakyō hyōshiki* 歌経標式) of 772 is the earliest extant poetic manual for waka composition. Written at Emperor Kōnin's behest by Fujiwara no Hamanari (724–790), the great-grandson of the Fujiwara-ancestor Nakatomi no Kamatari (614–669), it contains about three dozen poems used to illustrate seven poetic "faults" (*yamai* 病) and proposes a typology of three poetry "types" (*katai* 歌体).[14]

The text is fascinating because it would make for a wonderful study of how concepts can survive in separation from actual content. Although later waka treatises would routinely refer to it as a precedent, its poetics remained almost completely without influence. In his treatise, Hamanari does nothing less than claim that a superior feature of waka poetry is that it rhymes (which it actually does not, unlike Chinese poetry) and that, based on this presumption, certain rules of euphony need to be observed, prohibiting sound repetition in certain places of the poem. Chinese poetry rhymes, and during the Six Dynasties Period an elaborate set of rules for tonal euphony and variation was developed that led to the birth of "regulated poetry" (*lüshi* 律詩). These Chinese rules of "four tones and eight faults" (*sisheng babing* 四聲八病) were a staple of Tang technical poetics, and Hamanari apparently felt he could not do without them in his discussion of waka. I will not

---

[14] For a study of the manual's various titles, its author, content, and transmission history see Rabinovitch 1991. Pages 524–60 contain a translation of the manual, which I have consulted for my own translation below.

explore further how Hamanari attempted to accomplish the feat of transposing the "faults" of Chinese poetics into "faults" of waka poetry, but I will limit my discussion to what Hamanari says on the place of ornate and plain speech in waka. Hamanari reveals his partiality to elegance, first, in his praise of sophisticated diction and figurative speech, and second, in his preference for complex poetic form. In the opening of his manual he claims that waka differs from common speech by virtue of its "elegant and subtle" use of rhyme:

> Since its beginning waka poetry is what stirs the deep feelings of spirits and gods, and consoles heavenly and human hearts filled with love. Rhyme is what distinguishes (waka) from customary language and makes it suitable to the spirit of pleasure excursions. Thus, the Heavenly Grandchild[15] presented a love poem to his wife the Dragon Princess when she returned to the sea, and the assembled mourners of Ame-no-waka-hiko composed a poem praising his awesome power.[16] These two poems were the first to give full play to the elegant and subtle use of rhyme.

> 原夫歌者所以感鬼神之幽情、慰天人之恋心者也。韻者所以異於風俗之言語、長於遊楽之精神者也。故有龍女帰海天孫贈於恋婦歌、味耜昇天会者作称威之詠。並尽雅妙之音韻之始也。[17]

Like the *Kokinshū* Prefaces later on, Hamanari ascribes a numinous force to waka poetry. It is striking that Hamanari considers poetic language as "elegant" and distinct from everyday speech and that he claims that it uses elegant and subtle rhyme. Obviously, the early divine beings Hamanari adduces from the chronicles to show the beginning of elegant waka poetry must have had quite some literary training in poetic rules. Thus, Hamanari's earliest stage of waka poetry boasts elegance and literary knowledge, not plain speech and innate ability. This is the tenor of Hamanari's beginning of the history of waka, which prepares us for a very different kind of decline narrative:

> Poets of the recent age, though good at producing poetic phrases, know nothing of the use of rhyme. While they give their readers elation, they still have no understanding of "poetic defects." When measured against the poetry of high antiquity, (recent poetry) lacks the grace of spring flowers; when transmitted to future generations, there is no flavor of autumn fruits. Without the Six Poetic Modes how can it stir the feelings and soothe the hearts of gods and humans? I have thus drawn up a volume on the (proper composition) of rhymed verse, supported by new examples, and titled it *Code of Waka Poetry*. Surely those who recite it will avoid giving offense, and those who hear it receive sufficient admonishment.

---

[15] Great-grandson of the Sun Goddess Amaterasu and grandfather of Emperor Jinmu, the first human emperor of Japan. He tried to appease his wife Lady Toyotama with a love poem, when she was furious that he had witnessed her change into a crocodile or dragon when giving birth (*Kojiki* no.8).
[16] The deity Aji-suki ascended to heaven to mourn the passing of his friend Ame-no-waka-hiko ("Heavenly Young Lad") and flew in a rage when he was mistaken for his corpse. The assembly of mourners tried to appease him with a poem when they discovered the mistake (*Kojiki* no.6; *Nihon shoki* no.2).
[17] Okimori 1993, 113–14. Punctuation added by author.

近代歌人、雖長歌句、未知音韻。令他悦懌、猶無知病。准之上古、既無春
花之儀、伝之来葉、不見秋実之味。無六体何能感慰天人之際者乎。故建新
例、則抄韻曲合為一巻。名曰歌式。蓋亦詠之者無罪、聞之者足以戒矣。[18]

Hamanari attributes a recent decline of the art of waka to the ignorance about poetic defects such as the faulty repetition of sounds within and between lines.[19] Only if one knows the "Six Modes" described in the "Great Preface" to the Chinese *Classic of Poetry* can one write waka. Only if one masters the three rhetorical techniques of *fu* 賦 "enumeration," *bi* 比 "comparison," *xing* 興 "evocative image" and has training in the three parts of the *Classic of Poetry* the *feng* 風 "Airs," *ya* 雅 "Odes," and *song* 頌 "Hymns," can one hope to miraculously stir the hearts of Japanese humans and gods with Japanese poetry. If according to the Sino-Japanese Preface of the *Kokinshū* recent poets have lost the innocence of their art because of too much knowledge of Chinese writing and literature, Hamanari's recent poets have lost the knowledge of their art and have too *little* knowledge of Chinese writing and literature.

With a diametrically opposed notion of the causes for decline comes a different vision of the good old poetry of high antiquity. It is not innocent and untouched against the threatening backdrop of the sophistication intruding with Chinese influence, but already from its very beginnings does waka poetry balance the Chinese-style parallelism of the taste of the autumn fruit's "substance" with the looks of the spring flower's "flourish." Accordingly, Hamanari is not a prophet calling for a return to a golden age of innocent simplicity, but a poetic priest calling on his community to follow his holy book of precepts. Although the phrase "those who recite it will avoid giving offense, and those who hear it receive sufficient admonishment" is adapted almost literally from the "Great Preface" to the Chinese *Classic of Poetry*, the notion of avoiding "offenses/sins" (*tsumi* 罪) and "receiving admonishment" (*imashimuru* 戒むる) had by Hamanari's time gained Buddhist undertones and came from the mouth of somebody who was an expert in Yin-Yang Learning (*onmyōdō* 陰陽道). Knowledge of the "Faults" and "Six Modes" contained in his holy book would ensure a proper balance between substance and flourish, as it prevailed in high antiquity.

A second way in which Hamanari espouses the ornate over the plain is his preference for oblique types of poetry. Poetry using "elegant and beautiful" diction (*garei* 雅麗) and creating novel literary expression is preferable to poetry using "plain diction" (*jikigo* 直語) that is faulty, because it is too close to everyday

---

[18] Ibid., 113–14. Punctuation added by author.
[19] The seven defects of a thirty-one-syllable waka (5-7-5-7-7) and their fanciful typological labels are: (1) "Head-Tail" defect: same sound at the end of the first two lines; (2) "Chest-Tail" defect: same sound at the end of the first line and the third and/or sixth syllable of the second line; (3) "Waist-Tail" defect: same sound at the end of lines 1, 2, or 4 with the basic "rhyme syllable" at the end of line 3; (4) "Mole" defect: sound of basic "rhyme syllable" used in any line of the poem; (5) "Roaming Wind" defect: sound of second syllable of any line identical to sound at the end of the same line; (6) "Homophone Rhyme" defect: the two "rhyme syllables" at the end of lines 3 and 5 are identical; (7) "Entire Body" defect: more than two identical sounds anywhere in the poem, except for the basic "rhyme syllable." For euphony in early Japanese poetry and Hamanari's relation to Chinese models see Rabinovitch 1991, 488–506.

speech. Hamanari's preference for poetic sophistication reaches its eccentric peak when he declares that the highest form of poetry is the "riddle" (kenkei 譴謷), in which the poet expresses feelings through veiled words.[20] Our expectations are set high, given that this is the only extant poem composed by Hamanari and that it exemplifies the type of poetry he praises most. Be prepared for an instructive disappointment:

ねずみのいへ	A mouse's house:
よねつきふるひ	Sift the rice
きをきりて	Cut the wood
ひききりいだす	Ready the flint
よつといふかそれ[21]	Is it the number four?

If this does not make a lot of sense at first reading, here is the recipe that allows us to savor the puzzle: Reduce each line into one word: a "hole" for "mouse's house," "flour" for "sift the rice," "fire" for "cut the wood, ready the flint" and "four" for "is it the number four." Reassemble the words into "Hole-Flour-Fire-Four" as "ana-ko-hi-shi" 穴粉火四. Now transpose the sounds "ana-ko-hi-shi" into meaningful characters as あな恋し "Oh, how I love you!" With this poem the mountain gives, literally, birth to a mouse. Ironically, linear meaningfulness is replaced with cumbersome cleverness encoded in three transposition processes—from phrase to word, from senseless word to sound, and from sound into, finally, meaningful phrase. The resulting phrase yields a trivial statement: "Ana koishi" is certainly the most blatant "plain speech," which Hamanari would elsewhere probably shun as lacking elegance.

Though highly praised by Hamanari, the "riddle" type of poetry luckily was and remained rare in the waka tradition. But even if these thirty-one syllables fail as a poem, they succeed and convince as a product of an educated eighth-century Japanese, who revels in the possibilities of play with recherché expression made possible by the use of Chinese characters in writing Japanese and inspired by a Chinese poetic tradition of the Six Dynasties that enjoyed puns and double play.[22]

Hamanari's treatise shows an eccentric veneration for sophistication in the writing of waka and thus manages to come up with a rather unusual narrative of decline. In contrast to the more common narrative of decline through a "too much" of ornament (wen), Hamanari blames decline not on excessive over-ornamentation, but, quite to the contrary, on the lack of education of recent waka poets, and thus on the "under-ornamentation" of their poems. Hamanari's treatise is a reverie obsessed with the desire for typology rather than a treatise descriptive of past poetic practice or prescriptive for future poetry. Let us therefore turn to actual poetry written about a generation before Hamanari's treatise. We

---

[20] This obscure word is probably a misreading for meiyu 謎譬 "hidden comparison, allegory" or meikei 謎警 "hidden alert, riddle."

[21] Okimori, Kakyō hyōshiki: chūshaku to kenkyū, 179.

[22] Although I will not explore this here, a third level on which Hamanari shows his taste for the complex and recherché is his use of graphs. He tends to use rare and complex characters for phonographic inscription, which differ clearly from the phonograms used in writing for everyday purpose.

will not judge this poetry by Hamanari's standards, but his sense that "recent poets" were too little educated in Chinese poetics is proven wrong by Ōtomo no Yakamochi 大伴家持 (ca.717–785) poetic exchange with his kinsman Ōtomo no Ikenushi 大伴池主. They indulged the expressive possibilities that Chinese characters and literary precedents afforded them in ways different from Hamanari's, yet with equal enthusiasm. Although this exchange is exceptional it does show us what some eighth century poets were capable of.

2c. The Beginnings of the *Wa-Kan* Game: Yakamochi and Ikenushi on the Pleasures of Sickness, Spring, and Simplicity

Half a year after being appointed governor of Etchū Province, Yakamochi, prominent poet of his generation and compiler of the *Man'yōshū*, fell ill in the second month of 747. The second lunar month was a bad time to be sick, because one missed out on the beginning of spring and its various celebrations. We can sense how much Yakamochi missed spring on his sickbed from an extraordinary poetic exchange between him and his kinsman Ikenushi, who served as provincial secretary at the time. Instead of wasting away on his sickbed, Yakamochi seemed to be in possession of his full powers when he launched onto an unprecedented poetic experiment. The resulting correspondence was written in two literary idioms: vernacular Japanese and Sino-Japanese. It was conducted in four literary genres: vernacular *tanka*, ("short poems," later called waka), *chōka* ("long poems"), and Chinese-style prose (kanbun) and poetry (kanshi). And it took the form of a poetic gift exchange with precise matches in kind: For the three rounds of gift giving, Yakamochi's first two tanka are matched in kind by Ikenushi. Next, Yakamochi's chōka with three tanka envois are matched by Ikenushi's chōka with two envois. Third, Ikenushi interjects into the correspondence initiated by Yakamochi a kanshi that he composed at the "Winding Stream Banquet" on the third day of the third month, to which Yakamochi responds in kind. As a weak coda to the three rounds of exchange, the correspondence ends on two tanka by Yakamochi in response to the two envois of Ikenushi's previous chōka. All poems are prefaced by Chinese-style prose letters. The precise gift exchange in poetic genre is followed through in the careful matching of the compositions in theme, structure, and even single expressions. This poetic exchange, experimenting with the juxtaposition of Japanese vernacular (wa) and Sino-Japanese (kan) words, genres, and themes, is exceptional in the otherwise vernacular poetry collection of the *Man'yōshū*; it is even unique in early Japanese literature and certainly not representative. Still, it can show us how debates over ornamentation and simplicity could play out when fought at the intersection of vernacular and Sino-Japanese poetic worlds.

The correspondence dwells only on a few circumscribed key topics that are paraded with all registers of tone and variety. There is the tension between Yakamochi's illness and the vernal vigor; there are spring splendors suggested by a few plants, such as cherry blossoms, peach blossoms, willows, and mountain roses; by a few animals such as warblers, butterflies, swallows and departing geese; and by a few spring pleasures such as wine, music, and young women picking violets in the fields. There is the topos of mutual yearning: Yakamochi and Ikenushi transpose their feelings from a male realm of companionship in kanshi into the heterosexual romantic realm of waka to strange effects. Lastly, there are matters of most trivial and most weighty concern: we never hear why Yakamochi and Ikenushi cannot meet up, but obviously they need distance to engage in the thrill of letter writing. It helps them to pass the time and also affords them the opportunity to discuss weighty questions such as whether poetic talent is inborn or can be learned.[23] The precise matching of genre with genre, theme with theme in variation, wording with synonym or antonym makes the correspondence more reduced in content but also infinitely richer by virtue of form. The functional definition of "ornateness" above, which includes "vertical/paradigmatic thickness" and "horizontal/syntactic pattern," describes perfectly the nature of the correspondence between Yakamochi and Ikenushi. When holding an imaginary "seismograph of ornateness" to the prose of both authors, we will get the most violent amplitude close to Ikenushi's lines. He is without question the Alexandrian at heart, eager to show off his store of Chinese learning in every way and moment. In riposte, Yakamochi feigns literary ignorance and introduces a self-conscious discourse about sophistication and simplicity in poetic composition in the second round of exchanges:

> Your magnanimous virtue has condescended to give thought to this wormwood body; your incalculable favor has extended comfort to this petty mind. I am overwhelmed by your attentions, for which there is no possible comparison. However, when young I did not frequent the garden of arts, and consequently the products of my flowing brush are naturally deficient in the "insect carving" that is literary composition. In my tender years I never betook myself to the gates of Yama(be no Akahito or Yamanoue no Okura) or Kaki(nomoto no Hitomaro),[24] so that now when it comes to fashioning a poem I lose my words amidst thickets of grass and trees. And in this connection I am abashed at your reference to joining wisteria to brocade; rather, I have gone on to indite a composition that is tantamount to mixing stones with gems. It is my old habit, vulgar and stupid, of being unable to remain silent. And so I present you a few lines, whereby I shall repay your kindness with a laugh.[25]

> 含弘之徳、垂思蓬体、不貲之恩、報慰陋心。　載荷来眷、無堪所喩也。但以稚時不渉遊芸之庭、横翰之藻、自乏乎彫虫焉。幼年未逕山柿之門、裁歌之趣、詞失乎蓁林矣。爰辱以藤続錦之言、更題将石間瓊之詠。固是俗愚懐癖、不能黙已。仍捧数行、式酬嗤咲。[26]

Yakamochi responds to Ikenushi's ornate verbiage with a carefully crafted sermon on his own lack of education. "When young" he presumably lost out on Confucian

---

[23] For a detailed discussion of the exchange from the perspective of tropes of friendship and love in Chinese and Japanese poetry see Tatsumi 1997, 107–58. For a discussion of the impact of Six Dynasty poetics on the exchange see Hu Zhǐang (J. Ko Shikō) 1998, 333–54.

[24] There is much debate whether "the gates of Yama or Kaki 山柿之門" refers to Yamabe no Akahito and Hitomaro or Yamanoue no Okura and Hitomaro. For insight into the debate and related literature see Kōnoshi and Sakamoto 1999, vol. 8, 164–75. Yet the relevance of the debate for the interpretation of this passage is rather limited. Yakamochi simply gestures at famous poets on whom he would have modeled himself in his youth.

[25] Translation by Edwin Cranston with modifications. Cranston 1993, 605–606.

[26] Man'yōshū XVII. 3969. Kojima et al. 1994–96, 181.

education, but knows of the "Garden" of traditional "Arts." He laments his poor performance in the writing of elegant Chinese-style poetry and prose, but eruditely calls this practice by the metaphor of "insect carving." In strict parallel, in his youth he claims not to have studied waka poetry, but knows of the grand old poets Akahito (or Okura?) and Hitomaro. He pretends to get lost in a forest of words, but describes his versifying with the unusually voluntary craftsman-like expression of "fashioning poetry" (*saika* 裁歌).

Beneath Yakamochi's erudite claim to a lack of education in Chinese-style and Japanese literary matters lurks a playful and liberating renunciation of sophistication with Daoist undertones. Yakamochi seems to tease Ikenushi for his Alexandrian zeal. This renunciation happens as a result of—not due to—a lack of education, which is clear from the double negation implied in Yakamochi's "deficiency" at the despicable practice of "insect carving." The association of "insect carving" with youthfulness calls to mind the confession of the Han scholar-poet Yang Xiong 楊雄 (ca. 53 BCE-18 CE) who in adulthood decided to stay away from the writing of rhapsodies (fu 賦), the most ornate and exuberant of Chinese literary genres:

> Somebody asked: "When you, Master, were young you liked to compose rhapsodies." [Yang Xiong] replied: "Yes, as a child I engaged in 'insect carving and character cutting.'" After a moment he added, "As an adult I didn't do it any more." Somebody asked: "Can you voice criticism with the help of rhapsodies?" He replied: "Criticism?! If your criticism puts a stop to it, yes, if not, I'm afraid you will inevitably provide encouragement!"
>
> 或問：吾子少而好賦。曰：然。童子雕蟲篆刻。俄而，曰：壯夫不為也。或曰：賦可以諷乎？曰：諷乎！諷則已，不已，吾恐不免於勸也。[27]

Against the backdrop of this famous anecdote, Yakamochi transforms Yang Xiong's youthful faux pas of rhapsody writing into his own triumph of adult success. If unlike Yang Xiong you fail to acquire an ineffective, possibly counterproductive tool for moral instruction in youth, you can securely celebrate your success of renunciation in adulthood. On Ikenushi, who believes in the transparent power of cultural capital and does not understand Yakamochi's wise pose in support of a secondary simplicity, the counterintuitive gain of Yakamochi's game seems lost. He feels obliged to save Yakamochi from the negative associations of petty "insect carving." He therefore praises Yakamochi's intellect beyond the sky and transforms the ignominious "insect carving" into grandiose "dragon carving":

> Yours is a master spirit, a stellar phenomenon. Your outstanding meters surpass those of other men. Your nature, which being wise loves the water, and being benevolent loves the mountains, contains within it the shining of a lovely jewel; your talent, which like Pan Yue's is a river, and like Lu Ji's is a sea, of itself qualifies you for a place in the palace of letters. Your conceptions are extraordinary, your feelings governed in accordance with reason. You finish a composition in

---

[27] *Fayan yishu*, 45.

seven paces, and the numerous poems fill your paper to overflowing. Skillfully you drive away the heavy distress of the grieved one; capably you dispel the accumulated longings of the lovesick one. Compared with this, the fountain of poetry of Yama(be no Akahito or Yamanoue no Okura) and Kaki(nomoto no Hitomaro) was as nothing. I have been afforded a brilliant glimpse of a sea of letters where genius carves dragons. Your servant is fully aware of his good fortune.

英霊星気、逸調過人。智水仁山、既韞琳瑯之光彩、潘江陸海、自坐詩書之廊廟。騁思非常、託情有理。七歩成章、数篇満紙。巧遭愁人之重患、能除恋者之積思。山柿歌泉、比此如蔑、彫竜筆海、粲然得看矣。方知僕之有幸也。[28]

Does Ikenushi grasp Yakamochi's Daoist game of appearing higher by proclaiming to be lower and therefore pull all stops to save Yakamochi from the grip of his self-deprecation? Or does he indulge his friend tongue-in-cheek by waxing rhapsodic as if he wanted to set himself as a youthful Yang Xiong against Yakamochi's conceit of being a better Yang Xiong who avoids the pitfalls of ornate writing? Though hard to resolve, the ambiguity adds to the charm of the exchange. What is clear is that Ikenushi spreads an expansive canvas before our eyes dotted with Chinese references: Out of the brushwood where Yakamochi got lost, Ikenushi leads him to the waters and mountains, the love of which Confucius ascribes to the wise and benevolent in *Analects* 6.23, and escorts him to his proper place in the "palace of letters" along the river that is Pan Yue's forceful writing and across the ocean that is Lu Ji's power of composition, both sophisticated Six Dynasties poets of the third century. Ikenushi says that concepts and feelings, rule and reason are in balance, and that Yakamochi's skill reaches the heights and rapidity of Cao Zhi, who composed a poem in seven paces under the death threat from his invidious brother Cao Pi, Emperor of the Wei Dynasty (220–265). Even more, Ikenushi compliments Yakamochi on his poetic powers that drive away worry and cure lovesickness, so that Akahito and Hitomaro's "source" of poetry appear as nothing in comparison.

The vast aquatic dimension with which Ikenushi sweeps aside Yakamochi's confusing brushwood unfolds in all its glory when Ikenushi at last exclaims "I have been afforded a brilliant glimpse of a sea of letters where genius carves dragons." According to Ikenushi, Yakamochi misnamed as "insect carving" his unsurpassed literary skill of "dragon carving." Certainly, Ikenushi's praise is so overblown that its message shimmers between therapeutic eulogy and therapeutic satire. In his next response Yakamochi plays along with this ambivalence and presents us with yet more understatement:

[Y]our lowly servant has a nature difficult to carve, a dark spirit impossible to burnish. I take my brush in hand and rot the tip; I face the inkstone and forget it is dry; all day I watch the water flowing, but am unable to compose. Writing is an innate gift, not something to be learned. By searching for characters and choosing rhymes, how should I be able to harmonize with your elegant compositions?

---

[28] *Man'yōshū* XVII. 3973. Translation by Cranston with modifications. Cranston 1993, 610–11.

但惟下僕、稟性難彫、闇神靡瑩。握翰腐毫、対研忘渇、終日目流、綴之不能。所謂文章天骨、習之不得也。豈堪探字勒韻、叶和雅篇哉。[29]

Yakamochi rejects Ikenushi's compliment on his craft and applies "carving" to his own nature based on Confucius's lament upon finding his disciple Zai Yu asleep in broad daylight: "Rotten wood is difficult to carve." (*Analects* 5.10). Yakamochi says his nature is "difficult to carve" and his brush's tip "rots" under his efforts to write. He seasons his confession of writers' block with the bold claim that writing is an innate gift, "heavenly bone" (*tenkotsu* 天骨), that can not be acquired through practice. Searching out characters and rhyme-words, the usual catalysts that set well-trained poets like Ikenushi on the path to produce "elegant compositions" (*gahen* 雅篇), can not propel Yakamochi's humble nature into creating poetry.

Thus ends the exchange between Yakamochi and Ikenushi about poetry, human nature, and the carving of insects and dragons.[30] Their joyful freedom of moving between sophisticated diction and the sophisticated denial of sophistication is palpable in every phrase, but they take strikingly different poses. Ikenushi indulges in what we could call a "primary ornateness." When he loses himself in allusions and figurative language, we get a sense of the primal excitement about the repertoire of literary sophistication that was at the disposition of early Japanese poets in the eighth century, but that took many centuries to develop in the hands of Chinese poets. Yakamochi's introduction of the crafts metaphor of "carving" is more subtle and brings into play a notion of "secondary simplicity," of an ostentatious renunciation of sophistication.

Yakamochi's gain is at least triple. He gets a most enthusiastic compliment on his poetic craft of "dragon carving." He appears humble when he denies both his education and talent in poetry. And he has the chance to sketch a poetics that gives the poet much creative freedom, because it accommodates the inspiration by learned precedent, both Chinese and Japanese, but also carves out space for the pursuit of untutored novelty.

2d. Reverse View: Looking From the *Kokinshū* Back to the Eighth Century

> When times shifted towards superficiality and people treasured excess and wantonness, superfluous words arose like clouds, flashy new currents bubbled forth like a spring, and the kernel [of poetry] declined completely and only its flower thrived. It thus happened that those love-hungry courtiers used [poetry] as a go-between of "flowers and birds," and those food-begging monks took it as a ruse to make their living. Therefore it partly became the handmaid of women and was not suitable to present before noblemen.

---

[29] *Man'yōshū* XVII. 3975a. Cranston 1993, 613.

[30] In addition to Yang Xiong's confession of "insect carving" and Liu Xie's claim for literature to "dragon carving" Pei Ziye's *Discussion of Insect Carving* (*Diaochonglun* 雕蟲論) was an important text for the "carving" discourse. It castigates "florid" writing by providing a hefty decline narrative that sees the poetry of ancient sages evaporate into contemporary superficiality. If it was part of Pei Ziye's *Essential History of the Song Dynasty* (*Song lüe* 宋略), completed in the late fifth century, so Yakamochi might have known it. For its place in the Liang literary scene see Tian 2007, 139–41. For a translation see Wu 1998, 30–32.

及彼時変澆漓。人貴奢淫。浮詞雲興。艶流泉涌。其実皆落。其華孤栄。至有好色之家。以此為花鳥之使。乞食之客、以此為活計之謀。故半為婦人之右、難進大夫之前。[31]

FROM THE "SINO-JAPANESE PREFACE" BY KI NO YOSHIMOCHI (-919)

This is how the "Sino-Japanese Preface" to the *Kokinshū* bemoans the embarrassing decline of vernacular poetry that presumably came in the wake of Prince Ōtsu's introduction of Chinese writing and literature. Note how loaded this short passage is with judgmental vocabulary related to surface flourish: "superficiality," "excess and wantonness," "superfluous words like clouds," "flashy new currents bubbling force like a spring," and "flower" versus "kernel." Moral decline is also related to social decline: poetry is abused for vile love affairs and monopolized by greedy monks and women. Yoshimochi is clearly opposed to anything associated with surface flourish: he castigates the decline of "kernel/substance" (*mi* 実), of which only the shadow of superficial "flower/flourish" (*hana* 華) survives.

Interestingly, only the "Sino-Japanese Preface" associates ornament with poetic and moral decline. Ki no Tsurayuki's "Japanese Preface" to the same collection was one of the fledgling attempts to write prose in the vernacular, which up to the ninth century used to be written in Sino-Japanese. Therefore, it had less conceptual baggage to handle than the "Sino-Japanese Preface" that is in closer dialogue with established Chinese rhetorical patterns and allusions.[32] Not only is the evocation of surfaces and flourish as stimuli for poetic composition more common in the Japanese preface, but Tsurayuki even uses the language of "flourish" as a positive quality at the very moment when he laments a penchant toward the superficial:

> Nowadays because people are attracted to appearances and their hearts have become like flowers, only "fruitless" poems and trivial words appeared. Poetry has become unknown in public, buried like a wooden log in the houses of pleasure-lovers, and is not something that could be brought out like buds of flowering pampas grass in "true" public places.

> 今の世中、色に付き、人の心、花に成りにけるより、不実なる歌、儚き言のみ出来れば、好色みの家に、埋もれ木の、人知れぬ事と成りて、実なる所には、花薄、穂に出すべき事にも有らず成りにたり。[33]

Tsurayuki clearly picks up on the resonant Chinese concept of "fruit/substance" and "flower/flourish": people's hearts are flowers, but only produce "poetry without fruit/**substance**" (*adanaru uta*不実なる歌); monopolized for private love affairs, poetry is hidden like buried wood and too trivial to recite in "**substantive**/true places" (*mamenaru tokoro* 実なる所). Yet he wants a poetry that can assert itself in public like "buds of flowering pampas grass" (*hanasusuki ho* 花薄穂), a beautiful image of substance inserting itself in the form of colorful flourish. In this

---

[31] *Kokin wakashū*, 342–45.
[32] See, again, Wixted 1983.
[33] *Kokin wakashū*, 9.

passage Tsurayuki plays masterfully with the Chinese-style conceptual pair of "substance" versus "flourish," at times in agreement with Yoshimochi's diatribe against flourish and at times able to appreciate substance in flourish. Choosing elegant play with concepts over Yoshimochi's clear-cut moralizing, he also has no use for a villain on whom to blame the decline: Prince Ōtsu does not appear at all in Tsurayuki's "Japanese Preface" to the anthology, nor is there anybody else who took Prince Ōtsu's dubitable role as the peddler of Ancient Japan's cultural innocence. Although there is no space here to show it through actual poetry from the anthology as I did with the *Kaifūsō*, suffice it to say that the bulk of poetry in the *Kokinshū* is clever and ornate. It inspired the praise and canonization by the following generations as well as the bile of early modern and modern detractors who missed true transparent national spirit in what they considered to be its too oblique and Sinicized style.

Unlike with the *Kaifūsō*'s overall embracing of "ornament," the poetics in particular of the Sino-Japanese Preface to the *Kokinshū* is at suggestive odds with the poetry in the anthology. The detraction of ornament and assertion of a presumably genuine old simplicity is an early tenth-century vision of Japanese literary beginnings, one that, as we saw, stands in contrast to eighth-century poetic thought and practice. For the authors of the Prefaces to the *Kokinshū* this was an acceptable price to pay for propelling waka to public importance and have it stand on a par with Sino-Japanese poetry, which had received strong imperial support in the preceding century.

3. Simplicity and Hellenism in Late Republican Rome

As discussed in the first chapter, the dearth of surviving early Latin literature before the first century BCE is striking in contrast to the wealth of complete compendia of poetry and history that survive from Japan's literary beginnings in the eight century. From the staging of Livius Andronicus's plays in 240 BCE, we have to move into the first century BCE to get beyond textual fragments to entire texts, with the exception of Cato, Plautus, and Terence. This radically different textual record for early Japanese and early Latin literature forces our comparison to be asymmetrical, and we will have to move to the Late Republic to explore how debates about ornateness and simplicity play out in some of Cicero's and Horace's work.

Relative temporal symmetry certainly makes for easier comparability. As we already saw, the earlier absorption of the reference culture's literary sophistication and the later construction of notions of a lost simplicity by writers of the younger culture is a very time-sensitive process, and debates about ornament and simplicity will look fundamentally different depending on when they occur in the relative development of a literary culture. However, the asymmetry is not without advantage methodologically, because it obliges us to develop a more imaginative approach and expand our repertoire of methodological "figures of thought" for comparative work. Lacking better sources, I undertake in the following what I will call a "mutual virtual history."[34]

---

[34] Virtual history has been a sentiment rather than a methodology. One appeal of asking "what would have happened if not X" has been to use the counterfactual to better grasp the significance and broader implications of what actually happened. In that sense virtual history serves as a tool to filter out the "white noise" of the limitlessly tumultuous soundscape of history. For such an approach see Hawthorne 1991. There is also a more sensationalist type of virtual history that appears in many

Claims of a lost simplicity and corruption by foreign sophistication in the "Sino-Japanese Preface" to the *Kokinshū* stood in strong contrast to the enthusiastic embracing of the ornate sophistication based on Chinese precedents during the eighth and ninth centuries. In turn, in *On the Ideal Orator* (*De oratore*) and the *Brutus,* which we already discussed in the previous chapter, Cicero uses narratives of decline to develop a highly original vision of a truly Roman *sapientia,* "wisdom," that aimed at restoring the lost balance between "philosophy" and "rhetoric," which Socrates had introduced; and he attacks those who propagated a new vogue of Greek, Attic classicism with claims that Roman oratory had its own glorious, independent past that called for emulation. But on the example of Horace's *Satires* we will explore what was a more frequent move in Latin literary culture: aggressive satirical attack on earlier, supposedly cruder Roman receptions of Greek culture that an author aimed to replace with a more polished form of Hellenism, which was preferable to older literature. From Horace's perspective, the good old and simple looks suddenly crude and embarrassing. Already Ennius claimed that his predecessor Naevius was old-fashioned and insufficiently Hellenized.

What does it mean to construct a "mutual virtual history?" Put simply, it means to create a virtual historical timeline with snippets of actual historical processes in different cultures. With a "*Kokinshū* moment" in Late Republican Rome and a "Horace moment" absent from early Japan we are creating a Sino-Japanese Greco-Roman timeline with the same virtual brush. With this tool we try to tease out the implications of the convergences and divergences of early Japanese and Latin literary cultures. Ideally, we will gain a deeper understanding of each of them, just as with a painter who can suddenly make a spacious landscape leap out by inserting as contrasting background a second picture, where we previously only saw a few scattered strokes on a single flat canvas. Let us now insert Cicero and Horace into our East Asian canvas.

3a. Undoing Socrates's Scalpel: Narratives of Decline and Cicero's New Roman Wisdom (*sapientia*)

Written in 55 BCE when Cicero had been back from exile for a couple of years but saw his hopes for Republican order wane under the power arrogated by the "triumvirate" of Caesar, Pompey, and Crassus, the long dialogue *On the Orator* has a special place in Cicero's lifelong writing about rhetoric.[35] Cicero wrote it during the final crisis of the Republic but set its events in 91 BCE, another period of civil war and crisis that peaked in Sulla's dictatorship. An ominous glitter of tragic destruction and exuberant vision hovers over the lengthy discussion about oratory led by foremost experts of the day, such as the two eminent orators Lucius

---

articles of the edited volume Ferguson 1997. It dwells on counterfactuals of wishful or apocalyptic thinking such as "what if the Cold War had been avoided?" or "what if Nazi Germany had defeated the Soviet Union?" This type of virtual history might have a cathartic function for dealing with historical traumas in the present. Little attention has been paid so far to the use of virtual history in the comparison of historically unrelated cultures or phenomena, which I am proposing here.
[35] For a concise introduction and bibliography about *De oratore* see Wisse 2002b. See also the excellent introductory matter in May and Wisse 2001. A stimulating reflection on the ingeniously ambivalent relation of Cicero to Greek cultural artifacts, such as oratory, is Zetzel 2003.

Licinius Crassus (140–91 BCE) and Marcus Antonius (143–87 BCE), and the legal expert Quintus Mucius Scaevola (168/160-ca. 87 BCE). In the dialogue Cicero gives voice to important mentors of his youth, who, as every reader would have known, would all be dead within a few years after the conversation recorded in the dialogue, either through illness or by Sulla's purge. Cicero combined a spirited homage and a preemptive requiem with the chance to articulate his own ideas through the mouths of his mentor figures. Indeed, in no other work does Cicero so forcefully sketch a vision of his oratorical ideal and boldly argue for going beyond the age-old struggle between "rhetoric" and "philosophy" that Plato had ignited so effectively.[36] *De oratore* is a complex work, and I will not even begin to discuss Cicero's clever take on the staples of Hellenistic rhetorical theory and practice of his day and his narrative powers to weave them into the complex dynamic unfolding between the various participants in the dialogue. We also need to keep in mind that Cicero's thinking about Plato and the relation between philosophy and rhetoric kept changing throughout his life. In *On the Republic*, for example, Cicero seems to worship Plato but also suggest that Plato distorted Socrates's ideas in crucial respects. But Cicero's opinions in his most pioneering work on rhetoric make for a more productive comparison with the *Kokinshū*. So for our purposes I will merely focus on the crucial narrative of decline in *On the Orator* that, put in the mouth of the charismatic elderly Crassus, is the dialectical basis on which Cicero's unique imagination of a new Roman *sapientia* is built:

> The people who discussed, practiced, and taught the subjects and activities we are now examining [namely "wisdom in action" and "wisdom in speech"] bore one and the same name (because knowledge of the most important things as well as practical involvement in them was, as a whole, called 'philosophy'), but he [Socrates] robbed them of this shared title. And in his discussions he split apart the knowledge of forming wise opinions and of speaking with distinction,[37] two things that are, in fact, tightly linked. [...] This was the source of the rupture, so to speak, between the tongue and the brain, which is quite absurd, harmful, and reprehensible, and which has resulted in our having different teachers for thinking and for speaking. [38]

> *Is eis qui haec quae nos nunc quaerimus tractarent, agerent, docerent, cum nomine appellarentur uno quod omnis rerum optimarum cognitio atque in eis exercitatio philosophia nominaretur, hoc commune nomen eripuit, sapienterque sentiendi et ornate*

---

[36] Current scholarship rarely makes the case for *On the Orator* as emphatically as James Zetzel: "*De Oratore* is not only the single greatest surviving work of classical Latin prose but also the most ambitious attempt of one of Rome's most original thinkers to provide a moral justification for Roman public life and to ground it in establishing a complex balance between Greek philosophy, past and present, and Roman ethics and history." See Zetzel 2005.

[37] May and Wisse translate ornatus (and its cognates) as "distinction," avoiding the more common Latinate English renderings as "ornament" or "embellishment." I do agree that Cicero thinks of "ornatus" as constitutive of content, not as an exterior application to it. However, translating Cicero's argument into a term that, like with the Chinese concept of wen, is highly ambivalent and avoiding any Latinate resonances obscures the issue at stake and Cicero's contribution to the debate. I would translate "ornate dicendi" as "speaking with sophistication" or "ornate speaking."

[38] *De oratore* III.60–61. Translation from May and Wisse 2001, 241.

dicendi scientiam re cohaerentes disputationibus suis separavit;...Hinc discidium
illud exstitit quasi linguae atque cordis, absurdum sane et inutile et reprehendendum,
ut alii nos sapere, alii dicere docerent.

As in the "Sino-Japanese Preface" to the *Kokinshū* we have a pristine age that is destroyed by the intrusion of a villain equipped with evil tools. In Cicero's dialogue, however, the pristine age was not distinctive because it was blessed by words of "substance," but because it could boast an original union between the "knowledge of forming wise opinions" (*sapienter sentiendi scientia*) and the "knowledge of ornate speech" (*ornate dicendi scientia*). This union resembles the balance between "substance" and "flourish" that Hamanari's manual praises as a mark of ancient waka poetry. It also locates the pristine age in Greece, unlike the *Kokinshū* Prefaces, which are little interested in matters Chinese, but evoke the grand past of Japan's Age of the Gods as "another country," to use L. P. Hartley's poetic words.

Second, Cicero's villain Socrates is Greek, not a fellow citizen, as Prince Ōtsu was for the Japanese writers. We can anticipate that Cicero has to accomplish a much greater feat with his new Roman sapientia than Yoshimochi and Tsurayuki with their domestic revival of waka poetry: Whereas Cicero proposes to atone for a crime committed on the territory of and by a representative of its ancient reference culture, Yoshimochi and Tsurayuki only settle matters on Japanese ground and with Japanese people. Third, the crime of intrusion is phrased in anatomical, not technological terms: While Socrates dissects tongue from heart/brain (*discidium...linguae atque cordis*) Prince Ōtsu introduces the destructive technology of writing in the form of Chinese letters. Socrates commits a crime against human anatomy, against the unity of the human body as much as against what Cicero sees as the integrity of human wisdom, *sapientia*. It is far more violent than Prince Ōtsu's "transport of Chinese characters" (*moji o utsushi* 字を移し) to the Japanese archipelago. This is an urgent and plastic rephrasing of the old struggle between rhetoric and philosophy into a criminal surgical procedure committed by, as Crassus of course points out, one of the greatest Greeks. It shows just how strongly Cicero feels about the fundamental importance of oratory to philosophy in Rome and how craftily he stages an anatomical spectacle before our eyes to prepare us for a triumphant vision of clinical recovery with himself in the role of the healer and Rome as the intellectual hospital.

After Crassus castigates Socrates's destruction of the natural unity between thought and speech, philosophy and rhetoric, he traces the "succession of philosophers," after Socrates in the fashion of Hellenistic scholarship, dwelling on Plato's Academy and Aristotle's Peripatos, the Cynics, Stoics, Cyrenaics, and Epicureans. All these schools were of Hellenistic derivation, not Roman origin, which might be one of the reasons why Crassus concludes his survey of the contemporary state of the field of philosophy with an ambivalent second allegory of division, this time not anatomical but geological:

> So, just as the rivers part at the watershed of the Apennines, the disciplines parted when flowing down from the common ridge of wisdom. The philosophers flowed into the Ionian Sea on the East, as it were, which is Greek and well provided with harbors, while the orators came down into our barbarian Tyrrhenian

Sea on the West, which is full of reefs and dangers, and where even Odysseus himself had lost his way.

Haec autem, ut ex Apennino fluminum, sic ex communi sapientium iugo sunt doctrinarum facta divortia, ut philosophi tamquam in superum mare defluerent Graecum quoddam et portuosum, oratores autem in inferum hoc Tuscum et barbarum, scopulosum atque infestum, laberentur, in quo etiam ipse Ulysses errasset.[39]

Crassus's proposed geography clearly gives the hegemony over philosophy and the Ionian Sea to the Greeks. Despite this concession, Crassus boldly declares the very backbone of the Italic peninsula, the Apennines, to be the "common ridge of wisdom," which in the previous passage was presumably Greek territory. And the Roman rivers of rhetoric go into the native Tyrrhenian sea, off the Western coast of Italy, which is stormier, more complex, and even leads the clever Greek Ulysses, one of those early Italic travelers, astray.

While conquering the "ridge of wisdom" with its rivers of philosophy and rhetoric for Rome, Crassus does not neglect to pay homage to undisputed Greek primacy in philosophical matters. The explosive ambivalence contained in Cicero's geological metaphor is reinforced in the continuation of the discussion, when Crassus recommends to aspiring orators who want to become a Pericles or Demosthenes to also master the power of Carneades, skeptic and leader of Plato's Academy in the second century BCE, or that of Aristotle. Socrates's destruction of the "miraculous communion between speaking and understanding" (*dicendi et intellegendi mirificam societatem; De oratore* III.73) is contrasted with the exemplary vision of Carneades (ca.214–129 BCE) and Aristotle, who like "those great men of the past, all the way down to Socrates, used to link the principles of oratory with the entire study and knowledge of everything that was relevant to human conduct, to human life, to virtue, and to the state."[40] Crassus balances his attack on Socrates with a praise of Aristotle. Cicero's vision of oratory owes indeed more to Aristotle's appreciation of rhetoric as a respectable form of popular philosophy and a tool to appeal to human emotions than to Plato's suspicion against rhetoric as that form of demagogy that brought down his teacher Socrates.[41]

In Crassus's final verdict about what kind of training is expected of the ideal orator, Crassus solemnly proposes a solution to the quarrel between rhetoric and philosophy:

But if we are looking for the one thing that surpasses all others, the palm must go to the learned orator. If they allow that he is also a philosopher, then the quarrel is over. If, however, they keep the two distinct, they will be inferior in that all their knowledge is present in the perfect orator, while the knowledge of the philosophers does not automatically imply eloquence. And although they

---

[39] Cicero *De oratore* III.69. May and Wisse 2001, 245–46.
[40] *De oratore* III.72. May and Wisse 2001, 246. *[V]eteres illi usque ad Socratem omnem omnium rerum quae ad mores hominum, quae ad vitam, quae ad virtutem, quae ad rempublicam pertinebant cognitionem et scientiam cum dicendi ratione iungebant.*
[41] On Cicero's relation to Aristotelian rhetoric in *De oratore* see Fantham 2004, 161–85.

scorn it, yet it is inevitably true that eloquence somehow sets a capstone upon their art.

Sin quaerimus quid unum excellat ex omnibus, docto oratori palma danda est. Quem si patiuntur eundem esse philosophum, sublata controversia est; sin eos diiungent, hoc erunt inferiores quod in oratore perfecto inest illorum omnis scientia, in philosophorum autem cognitione non continuo inest eloquentia; quae quamvis contemnatur ab eis, necesse est tamen aliquem cumulum illorum artibus afferre videatur.[42]

Crassus is in favor of a "learned orator," who combines the skills of rhetoric with the knowledge of philosophy, in short of an ideal Roman orator, an ideal Roman philosopher, or for that matter an ideal Roman citizen. In the words of Crassus Cicero does not solve the famous quarrel, but transcends it, literally, by Hegelian *Aufhebung*, sublation: Should the orator also be a philosopher, *sublata controversia est*. His Roman orator transcends both petty philosophy and petty rhetoric.

If until recently scholars felt that every argument of a Latin author must have a Greek precedent, some have claimed that Cicero's proposed synthesis of rhetoric and philosophy was adopted from Philo of Larissa, head of the Platonic Academy in the 90s BCE, whom the young Cicero heard lecture in Rome in 88 BCE. However, Jakob Wisse has forcefully argued for the originality of Cicero's synthesis.[43] It is not the idea of a synthesis of oratory and philosophy *per se* that is crucial in Cicero. His creation of a Greek narrative of decline from which to leverage off his proposition of a Roman solution to a Greek scandal makes his contribution to the quarrel so original and visionary. Moreover, Cicero's anatomical and geological metaphors for the interrelation between philosophy and rhetoric and Greece and Rome are powerful and distinctively Ciceronian tools of persuasion that Cicero puts to stunning use to sidestep and overcome an overdetermined quarrel on Roman grounds.

3b. Best Cato and Perhaps Demosthenes: Roman and Attic Simplicity in Cicero's *Brutus* (46 BCE)

Proposing an oblique Roman solution to a Greek problem is what links Cicero's *De oratore* to his *Brutus*. The introduction of a narrative of decline in the wake of Socrates's destruction of the natural unity of tongue and brain allowed Cicero to propose a highly original vision for a new Roman sapientia. In the *Brutus* ten years later, Cicero administers his ironic stabs at a new vogue of "Attic" styles of oratory, a classicist movement that rejected contemporary Hellenistic rhetoric and looked back to the great fifth and fourth centuries of classical Athens, in a dialogue that parades a vast ancestor gallery for Roman oratory. It is unclear to which degree the "Atticist" fashion of the mid-first century BC in Rome, of which Calvus seemed to have been a leading figure, was influenced or inspired by contemporaneous developments in

---

[42] Cicero *De oratore* III.143. May and Wisse 2001, 266.

[43] Jakob Wisse makes a case for the originality of Cicero's vision, while showing how Cicero might have been inspired in his vision by debates raging in the three main Greek philosophical schools of the Academy, the Peripatos, and the Stoa since the latter half of the second century BCE. Wisse 2002b, 396–97 and also Wisse 2002a, 361–64. For previous attempts to show Cicero's indebtedness to Greek sources see Wisse 2002b, 396, fn. 32.

Greece. Also, descriptions of what exactly constituted the "Attic" and the "Asiatic" style were often highly self-serving to the agenda of those who provided them. Furthermore, the very idea of what counted as "ornate" and what as "plain" was prone to slippage, one of the "paradoxes of ornateness" mentioned above. But it was clearly a debate about the virtues and vices of simplicity and ornateness, and for its Roman participants it was connected with the question of how much and what kind of Hellenization was permissible and desirable in Late Republican literary culture.[44]

In the last chapter I showed how Cicero in the *Brutus* fashioned Cato into a highpoint of a "natural history" of early Roman oratory in order to claim Roman independence from Greek oratory. In this chapter we sill see how Cicero's espousal of Cato was part of a larger scheme of self-defense against accusations that Cicero's style was too ornate and bombastic, in short too "Asiatic."

Cicero tackled this problem, which on the surface played out in the arena of Greek relative literary chronology and historical self-awareness, in a stunning fencing act. This unfolds in the course of the long dialogue between the fictional Cicero, Atticus and the young Brutus, who admired Cicero as much as they were enticed by the new Atticist vogue that looked to classical Greek models for emulation. Cicero performs six basic moves of triumphant self-defense: side with your opponents by demolishing what they hate; show the naïveté of your opponents' ideal; improve on it by proposing a new Greek one; praise your opponents' ideal over the top to make it insignificant; create a straw man who can be sacrificed in your stead, and first and foremost, replace their Greek ideal with a Roman one.

Here is how Cicero's fencing with "those Atticists," as he calls them, looks on the ground. First, Cicero indirectly supports the Atticist ideal when he calls the Asiatic style a traveling pest:

> For when once eloquence had sailed forth from Piraeus it traversed all the islands and visited every part of Asia, but in this process it contracted some stain from foreign ways and lost that wholesomeness, and what one might call the sound health, of Attic diction; indeed it almost unlearned the art of natural speech. From this source came the Asiatic orators, not to be despised whether for their readiness or their abundance, but redundant and lacking conciseness.

> *Nam ut semel e Piraeo eloquentia evecta est, omnis peragravit insulas atque ita peregri-*
> *nata tota Asia est, ut se externis oblineret moribus omnemque illam salubritatem Atticae*
> *dictionis et quasi sanitatem perderet ac loqui paene dedisceret. Hinc Asiatici oratores non*
> *contemnendi quidem nec celeritate nec copia, sed parum pressi et nimis redundantes.*[45]

Cicero's startling metaphor of the cankerous spread of an infected Attic oratory in the Eastern Mediterranean leaves no doubt that Attic *salubritas* and *sanitas* are

---

[44] For a brief overview of the main approaches to the thorny questions of where the Atticist movement started, where to look for its antecedents in Greece and Rome, and how it related to Late Republican intellectual culture see Wisse 2002a, 364–68, and Wisse 1995, 65–82. For a concise overview and bibliography regarding the *Brutus* see Narducci 2002. For an introduction to the issue of Atticism in relation to the *Brutus* see ibid., 408–12 and Narducci 1997, 124–33.
[45] Cicero *Brutus* 51. Translation from Hendrickson 1936, 53.

preferable to Asiatic contamination.[46] Yet he is careful to defend the quick wit and readiness (*celeritas*) and the preference for abundance (*copia*) in the Asiatic orators. Copious verbal display was certainly no good fit with the Atticist ideals of Brutus or Calvus, whom the *Brutus* mentions as a self-proclaimed Atticist. Cicero's praise of *copia* puts a sting into a narrative of decline that must have been agreeable to Brutus, even if perhaps couched in too lush figural language for his taste.

In a second move, Cicero attacks more directly and laughs at the naïveté of the followers of the new Atticist fashion, pointing out that there is no such one thing as "Attic":

> But because there are in the category of Attic other qualities better than these [i.e. meagerness, dryness and poverty that Cicero ascribes to the style of Calvus and his followers], one must beware not to overlook the gradations and dissimilarities, the force and variety of Attic orators. "My aim is," you say, "to imitate Attic models." Which, pray? For they are not all of one type. Who, for example, are more unlike than Demosthenes and Lysias? Than either of them and Hyperides, than all of these and Aeschines? Whom then are you going to imitate? If one only, do you mean that all the others did not speak pure Attic? If all, how can you imitate them when they are so unlike each other?

> *Sed quia sunt in Atticis alia meliora, videat ne ignoret et gradus et dissimilitudines et vim et varietatem Atticorum. "Atticos," inquit, "volo imitari." Quos? nec enim est unum genus. Nam quid est tam dissimile quam Demosthenes et Lysias? quam idem et Hyperides? quam horum omnium Aeschines? quem igitur imitaris? Si aliquem, ceteri ergo Attice non dicebant? si omnis, qui potes, cum sint ipsi dissimillimi inter se?*[47]

Cicero uses satirical diatribe to drive home his reasonable point that the styles of orators and writers of classical Athens were quite different and that they defy a single label of the "Attic." His fictional opponent looks like a pedantic simpleton: "My aim is to imitate Attic models (*Atticos volo imitari*)." Not only does he not understand the wide spectrum of Attic styles, but, more importantly, he foolishly thinks that old is automatically good.

Cicero goes on to compare this Atticist dunce to a person who desires both too young Falernian wine—the latest vogue of Atticist fashion—and too old Anicius wine—the imitation of the old historical prose of Thucydides in oratory:

> I hold that those friends of yours do well to shun this new oratory still in a state of ferment, like must from the basin of the wine-press, and conversely that they ought not to strive for the manner of Thucydides,—splendid doubtless, but, like the vintage of Anicius, too old. Thucydides himself if he had lived at a somewhat later time would have been mellower and less harsh.

> *Sic ego istis censuerim et novam istam quasi de musto ac lacu fervidam orationem fugiendam nec illam praeclaram Thucydidi nimis veterem tamquam Anicianam*

---

[46] Note, however, that he reserves for the "school of Rhodes" a close connection to Attic models, despite its geographical location. Given that Cicero studied under Molo of Rhodes, this is not an entirely disinterested move.

[47] Cicero *Brutus* 285. Hendrickson 1936, 247–49.

notam persequendam. Ipse enim Thucydides si posterius fuisset, multo maturior fuisset et mitior.[48]

Viniculture and literary composition compare in their "aging" and "fermentation," and in the sophisticated typology of appraisal that wine and word lovers develop to assess the "style" of their expert product. Ancient literature, like old wine, lacks the mellowness that makes moderately old literature more attractive for imitation and consumption.

Despite his debunking of the notion of a uniform "Attic style" Cicero, in a third move, unabashedly promotes Demosthenes as his Attic model against the Atticist pedants:

> "Should we then make Demosthenes our model?" There, by heavens, you have it! And what better I ask, do we seek, what better can we wish for? But we do not it is true succeed in our effort; these fellows however, our self-styled Atticists, quite obviously it would seem do succeed in what they have set themselves. They don't even see, not only that history records it, but it must have been so, that when Demosthenes was to speak all Greece flocked to hear him. But when these Atticists of ours speak they are deserted not only by the curious crowd, which is humiliating enough, but even by the friends and supporters of their client. So then if to speak in a pinched and meager way is Attic, why let them enjoy their title of Atticists.

> *"Demosthenem igitur imitemur." O di boni; quid, quaeso, nos aliud agimus aut quid aliud optamus? At non assequimur; isti enim videlicet Attici nostri quod volunt asse-quuntur. Ne illud quidem intellegunt, non modo ita memoriae proditum esse sed ita necesse fuisse, cum Demosthenes dicturus esset, ut concursus audiendi causa ex tota Graecia fierent. At cum isti Attici dicunt, non modo a corona, quod est ipsum mise-rabile, sed etiam ab advocatis relinquuntur. Qua re si anguste et exiliter dicere est Atticorum, sint sane Attici.*[49]

Without question, Cicero is also an "Atticist" in the sense that he does not want to let go of the label, even if he fills it with different content and shows how the new Roman Atticists fail in the face of a Demosthenes.

This prepares Cicero, in a fourth move, to so fully embrace the Attic as an ideal that it becomes devoid of content. He claims that any good oratory will be Attic anyway, when he imagines how his ideal orator wields his power over the emotions and reactions of the crowd, moving them to laughter and tears as he wishes:

> If this is what happens be assured that he is speaking like an Attic orator, that he is faring as we read of Pericles, of Hyperides, of Aeschines, of Demosthenes most of all. But if they prefer rather a style of speaking that is acute and judicious, while at the same time pure, sound, and matter-of-fact, which does not make use of any bolder oratorical embellishment, and if moreover they will have it that this

---

[48] Cicero *Brutus* 288. Hendrickson 1936, 251.
[49] Cicero *Brutus* 289. Hendrickson 1936, 251–53.

style is peculiarly and properly Attic, they are quite right in their approbation. For in an art so comprehensive and so varied there is a place even for such small refinements of workmanship. Our conclusion then will be, not that all who speak in an Attic style speak well, but that all who speak well deserve the title of Attic.

Haec cui contingant, eum scito Attice dicere, ut de Pericle audimus, ut de Hyperide, ut de Aeschine, de ipso quidem Demosthene maxime. Sin autem acutum prudens et idem sincerum et solidum et exsiccatum genus orationis probant nec illo graviore ornatu oratorio utuntur et hoc proprium esse Atticorum volunt, recte laudant. Est enim in arte tanta tamque varia etiam huic minutae subtilitati locus. Ita fiet ut non omnes, qui Attice, idem bene, sed ut omnes qui bene, idem etiam Attice dicant.[50]

Note that Cicero does not mention Brutus's and Calvus's most beloved model, the plain and prosaic Lysias; that his ideal orator looks a bit too emotional and "Asiatic"; that his support of the pure, sound, and "dried out" (*exsiccatum*) style his opponents would praise sounds ironic; and that his wholesale adoption of the "Attic" as the good diminishes rather than increases the value of the concept of the "Attic."

Fifth, once a self-declared "Atticist" himself, Cicero introduces a figure designed to replace him as the target of his opponents' attack on "Asiatic" excesses: Hortensius (114–50 BC), a consul and prominent orator whom Cicero had defeated in his famous case against Verres, the extortionary governor of Sicily. No fragments remain that would allow us to assess Cicero's claim that Hortensius was or saw himself as an "Asiaticus" in stylistic matters. (*Brutus* 95.325).[51] But that Cicero rids himself rhetorically of accusations of the "Asiatic," while imposing the term on Hortensius is of particular importance, because the figure of Hortensius frames the entire *Brutus*. It opens on the message of Hortensius's death and Cicero's grief and mourning of his loss; and he reemerges in Cicero's account of his own life toward the end of the dialogue, which shows how ambivalently their lives as rivals and peers were intertwined. The young Atticist reformers spoke out against the Hellenistic oratory of Cicero's generation and, though there is no evidence to judge, it is not implausible that in the *Brutus* Cicero wanted to pay homage to Hortensius's memory but also to construe him as the "Asiatic" in his generation in order to distract attention from himself.

The sixth and foremost move in Cicero's riposte to attacks by Atticists was his vision of what we would have to call a "Roman Atticism." I use the term here not in the usual sense that the participants in the debates about Atticism did at home in Rome. But Cicero proposes nothing less than an argument that true classicists should look to older *Roman*, not Greek, models.[52] He equates Cato with Lysias and laments that they are similar in oratorical achievement, although only Lysias is

---

[50] Cicero *Brutus* 290–91. Hendrickson 1936, 253–55.
[51] On our poor evidence for Roman orators independent from Cicero see Steel 2007, 237–49.
[52] The first Greek proponent of Atticism was Dionysius of Halicarnassus, who worked in Rome from 30 BCE onward, and this fact has fueled the debate about whether Atticism in Rome descended from a Greek version of the phenomenon, whether Greeks working in Rome pioneered it, or whether it was initiated by Romans and in turn inspired a Greek movement through figures like Dionysius. Wisse's hypothesis that Calvus himself was the originator of Atticism is controversial, but very attractive. Wisse 2002a, 366–67.

famous (*Brutus* 16.63). He despairs that Rome's Atticists are blind to what would be a true, desirable "Roman Atticism":

> But observe the ignorance of our Romans! The very men who find such pleasure in the early period of Greek letters, and in that simplicity which they call Attic, have no knowledge of the same quality in Cato. Their aim is to be like Hyperides and Lysias; laudable certainly, but why not like Cato?

> *Sed ea in nostris inscitia est, quod hi ipsi, qui in Graecis antiquitate delectantur eaque subtilitate, quam Atticam appellant, hanc in Catone ne noverunt quidem. Hyperidae volunt esse et Lysiae; laudo, sed cur nolunt Catones?*[53]

The fictional Cicero urges Brutus and Atticus to read ancient Roman orators and take them as their models rather than to blindly imitate Greek classical models. Although Atticus later laughs at him and considers his praise of Cato a joke (*Brutus* 85.293), Cicero holds on to his elevation of Cato to the highpoint of the "natural" history of Roman oratory and to the Roman Atticist equivalent of the Attic Lysias and adds that his speeches lacked only some "pigments" of rhetorical colors that "were not yet invented." (*Brutus* 87.298). But he holds on to his central claim to Cato as a cardinal figure of the dialogue.

To my knowledge nobody has so far taken seriously Cicero's rhetorical claim to a Roman homology for Atticism, let alone proposed the concept of a "Roman Atticism" to describe one of Cicero's central projects in the *Brutus*. However, the *Brutus* is first and foremost an exquisitely long lineup that features names and appraisals of several hundred Roman orators, weaving them into a history of Roman oratory that is presented not just for antiquarian purposes. Is Cicero desperately trying to expand the repertoire of materials and models for a potential future of a "Roman Atticism," as bold or ironic as this idea might sound?

Cicero's vision for a new Roman *sapientia* that would transcend the Platonic quarrel between rhetoric and philosophy, and his plea for a new Roman classicism that would counter Roman fashions of Greek Atticism, share with the Prefaces to the *Kokinshū* the imagination of a national literary culture that is aware and proud of its history—whether of the Republican or Divine age. Yet the self-confident audacity with which Cicero plays with notions of Greek and Roman identity and sensibility in *On the Orator* and the *Brutus* is foreign to the Sino-Japanese Preface to the *Kokinshū*, whose villain was Japanese and a domestic problem, unlike Cicero's Socrates. Also, Cicero's historical self-awareness with which he shifts between an absolute subordinating chronology of the Greco-Roman constellation, where a postclassical Greece coexists with a fledgling Rome, and a relative equalizing chronology of this constellation, where both Greece's and Rome's cultural histories unfold according to similar patterns in similar time spans, is not thematized in the Prefaces to the *Kokinshū*. There, Chinese-style poetry written by Japanese does not exist, let alone Chinese literature (except for the generic mention of its pernicious use by Prince Ōtsu).

Despite significant discrepancies, it is still meaningful to speak of Cicero as achieving a "*Kokinshū* moment" of sorts in *On the Orator* and the *Brutus*. However,

---

[53] Cicero *Brutus* 67. Hendrickson 1936, 65.

with Horace we move away from a comparability of early Japanese and Latin notions of simplicity and ornateness. Horace's *Satires* 1.4 and 1.10 lead us onto territory of self-reflection and self-aggression within a literary tradition that has hardly any equal in extant early Japanese texts.

3c. The "Horace Moment" That Never Was: Self-Reflexive Hellenism in the *Satires*

Despite thorough Hellenization since the earliest centuries of literary production it was common in Latin literary culture to phrase claims to innovation as "claims of an epiphany of Hellenic influence," to use Stephen Hinds's words and astute thinking on the topic.[54] Already Ennius (239–169 BC) in the proem to his epic history of Rome, the *Annals,* had Homer say that he, the Greek poet par excellence, had become reincarnated in Ennius. Subsequent Roman writers dramatized the epiphany of Hellenic influence by portraying themselves as the Roman "inventors" of certain Greek genres, applying a well-worn Hellenistic trope to the translation of genres from Greek into Roman literary culture. Ennius was the Roman Homer; Virgil was another Roman Homer with the *Aeneid,* but in his *Eclogues* also a Roman Theocritus. Propertius saw himself as the Roman Callimachus. And Horace claimed to be the Roman Archilochus in his iambic *Epodes* and a Roman Alcaeus or Sappho in his *Odes.*

The logic of what I would like to call the "inventor trope" had far-reaching implications. First, it drew a deceptively sharp line between an old Roman and a new Hellenized period, suggesting that before the iconic moment of "invention" there was a time when Rome—at least for a particular genre—was not yet Hellenized. Second, in stark contrast to the strangely amorphous linguistic and cultural continuity of an imagined Sino-Japanese space in early Japan, the inventor trope dramatized the act of translation from Greek precedent into Roman variant. It showed that translation of literary genres from Greek to Latin literary culture was an active act, not an automatic event. Third, it created a competition over entitlement to "invention" and enhanced the search for intellectual and generic lineages.

The dynamic of the inventor trope, which played no significant role for early Japanese writers' appropriation of Chinese precedents, underlies Horace's bizarre relation to his satirist colleague Lucilius in *Satires* 1.4 and 1.10. The relation of Horace to Lucilius has long puzzled scholars, because Horace's "satires" seem simply not funny enough to explain away a number of contradictions, such as the verbosity with which Horace himself tries to denigrate the copiousness of Lucilius's verbiage; Horace's overemphasis but also complete disavowal of Lucilius's particular form of Hellenism; Horace's veneration of Lucilius as the "inventor" of Roman satire, but also his downplaying of Lucilius's contribution as a satire writer by suggesting multiple lineages for the genre; and, of course, his dealing with Lucilius in a satirical text that was not just subject to the subversive rules of satire but also part of one of the most promiscuous and ill-defined genres of Latin literature.[55]

---

[54] Hinds 1998, 52.

[55] For a concise introduction to Horace's *Satires* with bibliography see Gowers 2005, 48–61. A classic study of the relation between Lucilius and Horace is Fiske 1920. His assumption of an "imitative" relationship between Lucilius and Horace was an important step away from dominant Romantic ideals of original genius in literary studies of his time. More recently, Kirk Freudenburg's exciting *The Walking Muse. Horace on the Theory of Satire* has contextualized Horace's Satires from as different

Lucilius (ca. 180/148–102 BC) was of aristocratic birth and had close links to the most avant-garde Hellenophile circles of his time. Not only had he studied in Athens and developed close ties to the leaders of the Platonic Academy. He was also part of the coterie around Scipio Aemilianus, which included the historian Polybius and the philosopher Panaetius. He must have had access to the first-rate Hellenistic library of the Macedonian kings that Scipio's father, L. Aemilius Paullus, had brought to Rome as booty from his victory at Pydna in 168 BCE. His Hellenic education could not have been more thorough or more up to date. Horace knew this all too well. If he wanted to criticize Lucilius's appropriation of things Greek in his works, his "Hellenism" so to speak, he could only do so by saying that Lucilius's was an outdated type of Hellenism. From what survives of his satires we can see that Lucilius was very receptive to the Hellenistic aesthetics of Callimachus.[56] But Horace turns the values of restraint, formal polish, and balance, key to the interpretation of Callimachus of his generation, against Lucilius:

> Herein lay his fault: often in an hour, as though a great exploit, he would dictate two hundred lines while standing, as they say, on one foot. In his muddy stream there was much that you would like to remove. He was wordy, and too lazy to put up with the trouble of writing—of writing correctly I mean; for as to quantity, I let that pass.[57]

These are Horace's complaints about Lucilius's writing: too wordy "like a muddy stream," too lazy to bear the "labor" of Horatian word polishing, and too unbalanced, because "just on one foot." In *Satire* 1.10, under the mask of a satirist, Horace further pontificates about how wrong and vain Lucilius's Hellenism was, intertwining the issue with the "inventor" discourse. Because not just Lucilius, but before him Ennius, had written satires, Horace could not possibly claim an "inventor" title for the genre of satire, the origins of which in Rome were anyway so varied and murky that Quintilian could claim it as the only genre in Latin literature of independent Roman origin.

However, the Horatian satirist could move in contradictory circles around Lucilius's satires often enough to make his merit as the most prominent early writer of the genre disappear in the ensuing mêlée. At the beginning of *Satire* I.4 Horace's satirist says that Lucilius depended completely on the free and funny spirit of Old Comedy writers like Aristophanes, "changing only meter and rhythm."[58] In the beginning of Satire I.10, the satirist corrects this after all complimentary

angles as popular drama, the Greek iambographic tradition, Late Republican stylistic theory, and Callimachean ethics. Niall Rudd reads Horace's interplay of homage and invective vis-à-vis Lucilius on a largely literal level and adduces evidence for Horace's criticisms of Lucilius. He reduces their differences to a "difference in theory" and "temperament" and does not consider the radically different stages of Hellenization that Roman literary culture experienced during the lifetime of both authors. Rudd 1966, 86–124.

[56] For an analysis of Horace's play with both anti-Callimachean and Callimachean moves in the context of Late Republican and Early Imperial poetry see Zetzel 2002, 38–52.

[57] *Satires* 1.4.9-13. Translation from Fairclough 1929, 49. *nam fuit hoc vitiosus: in hora saepe ducentos, / ut magnum, versus dictabat stans pede in uno; / cum flueret lutulentus, erat quod tollere velles; / garrulus atque piger scribendi ferre laborem, / scribendi recte: nam ut multum, nil moror.*

[58] On what Horace might known of Old Comedy and of Lucilius's own historical context see Goldberg 2005, 162–71.

association: Lucilius's satires make people grin with laughter, sure, which puts them on the level of plebeian popular mime, robbing Lucilius not just of more respectable literary status, but also of Greek precedent. Within a few dozen lines Horace spitefully proclaims Lucilius the "inventor" of satire. In the same breath he compliments himself on his success as the writer of satires:

> This satire, which Varro of the Atax and some others had vainly tried, was what I could write with more success, though falling short of the inventor [Lucilius]; nor would I dare to wrest from him the crown that clings to his brow with so much glory.[59]

Is Horace's satirist generously making fun of the inventor discourse and of people like Horace who proudly laid claim to the inventor label in his *Epodes and Odes?* Or is he spitefully disinheriting Lucilius despite theatrical investiture with the inventor crown? The satirist quickly adds that if scholars criticize Homer, and Lucilius criticized Accius (which we know he did) and laughed at Ennius, there is no reason not to criticize Lucilius. This could be a sign that much of the bile was indeed directed against Lucilius and not a subtle act of self-irony directed either at claimants of invention in general or Horace in particular. That Ennius is mentioned only in this context in Horace's *Satires* about Lucilius makes our satirist's failure to mention the older Ennius as a writer of satire preceding Lucilius and potential claimant to the inventor title all the more conspicuous.

The gap between the satirist's playful mask and Horace's serious face almost disappears toward the end of this satire, which concludes Horace's first book of satires, when Horace elicits the favor of a dozen figures of the literary scene, including Virgil and the three patrons Maecenas, Messala, and Pollio. For them he voices his classicist manifesto that only careful polishing and moderation makes sophisticated literature.

> Grant, say I, that Lucilius was genial and witty: grant that he was also more polished than you would expect one to be who was creating a new style quite untouched by the Greeks, and more polished than the crowd of older poets: yet, had he fallen by fate upon this our day, he would smooth away much of his work, would prune off all that trialed beyond the proper limit, and as he wrought his verse he would oft scratch his head and gnaw his nails to the quick.[60]

Horace is adamant in his aesthetic values of a very classicized, polished, and controlled new Hellenism that is characteristic of the Augustan Period: less is more and therefore one need to prune words, scratch one's hair and gnaw one's nails. And as much as this intolerance caused the satirist to decry the "crude," visceral

---

[59] Horace *Satires* 1.10.46-49. Fairclough 1929, 119. *Hoc erat, experto frustra Varrone Atacino / atque quibusdam aliis, melius quod scribere possem, / inventore minor; neque ego illi detrahere ausim / haerentem capiti cum multa laude coronam.*

[60] Horace *Satires* 1.10.64-71. Fairclough 1929, 121.... *Fuerit Lucilius, inquam / comis et urbanus, fuerit limatior idem / quam rudis et Graecis intacti carminis auctor, / quamque poetarum seniorum turba: sed ille, / si foret hoc nostrum fato delapsus in aevum, / detereret sibi multa, recideret omne quod ultra / perfectum traheretur, et in versu faciendo / saepe caput scaberet, vivos et roderet unguis.*

and copious Hellenism of Lucilius, there is much envy of Lucilius's freedom to spiteful attack, which had become rather restrained in early Imperial Rome.

That Lucilius was "quite untouched by the Greeks" is a hearty joke, especially because a few pages earlier the satirist is appalled at Lucilius's mixing of Greek and Latin words and his seeming attempts to "write in Greek." But it makes perfect sense if we take into account the logic that underlies the inventor discourse, which drew a deceptively sharp line between a supposedly old Roman and a new Hellenized period. Horace shaped a new Augustan decorum of Hellenism that strongly rejected earlier forms of Hellenism by declaring them as wrong or even void forms of Hellenism ("style untouched by Greeks"). The second characteristic of the inventor logic, the dramatization of the act of translation from Greek precedent into Roman variant becomes apparent in the *Satires*' constant wavering when it comes to the status of Lucilius and the satire genre in literary history. This is also a farcical rumination on the inventor logic and its coronation rites, which become all the more grotesque if, as a third characteristic of that logic, they rest on as divergent generic lineages as Greek Old Comedy or Roman popular mime.

But there is another, more important message in Horace's final pounding on pruning and polishing: Horace's satirist says that if Lucilius had lived in Horace's time he would have embodied Horace's aesthetic values. It is by this token of virtual history that Horace's *Satires* not just invent a figure of Lucilius: Horace, as reincarnated Lucilius, can claim the inventor label without tearing that crown from Lucilius's head.

In *Satires* 1.4 and 1.10, old Roman writers like Lucilius were depicted not as laudably simple, but had become simply crude. An ideology of restrained polish, which did not look ornate, but was highly formalized and sophisticated, made Horace intolerant, but also a bit envious toward the times, when Lucilius could liberally fool around with all those novel Greek words and concepts and draw sparks from them in his exuberant word games. In Horace's time the options for being a sophisticated Hellenized Roman were much more complex and restrictive; it is hard to imagine how an unbridled wordsmith and criticaster such as Lucilius would have fit in. That Horace briefly imagined Lucilius as a contemporary was yet another sign of the strange mix of admiring intimacy and derisory distance with which he treats his predecessor. From the vantage point of the obsessively self-historicizing and self-conscious literary culture of Late Republican and Augustan Rome such a complex set of gestures were highly attractive.

4. Outlook

This chapter has explored questions raised by the distinctive growth curve of the literature of "latecomers," younger literary cultures that develop in dialogue with highly sophisticated literary precedents of older reference cultures. In such cultures narratives of decline, and concepts of "ornateness" and "simplicity," helped writers to formulate their ambivalent stance toward the older reference cultures and, in the process, to shape a sense of their own historical and cultural identity. We have studied these issues through a small number of texts from Nara to mid-Heian Japan and Republican Rome, which offered particularly interesting or influential insights. We saw that some eighth century Japanese texts enthusiastically embraced "ornament" in the broadest sense and reveled in the expressive possibilities that highly ornate Chinese poetry of the Six Dynasties and early Tang Dynasty offered. Although the question was not discussed, we can hypothesize based on the surviving fragments of Lucilius's satires and the revulsion of the Horatian satirist against what he saw as Lucilius's verbose bombast and illicit mixing of Greek and Latin, that an old poet like Lucilius was apparently inspired in similar fashion by the expressive possibilities of Hellenistic literature.

Next, we saw how constructions of a presumed "simplicity" of beginnings in the Prefaces to the *Kokinshū* and Cicero's dialogues on oratory occurred only a few centuries *after* the onset of the younger literary cultures. By then they had gained enough historical depth that gave them the confidence to claim a more independent identity and the chance to envision a national tradition in the past and for the future: a new public stance of waka poetry at court, the successful union of Greek rhetoric and philosophy in a new Roman sapientia; or a truly Roman classicism that could brave the new fashion of Greek Atticism, at least as a thought experiment. True, in the first vernacular poetry anthology of the mid-eighth century, Yakamochi had already assumed a pose of simplicity that made him look both humbler and wiser (even wiser than his Chinese model Yang Xiong). But his mask of a literary simpleton was coached in too sophisticated terms to sound genuinely simple. Also, it did not entail a grand historical scheme of decline related to the balance of ornateness and simplicity, which both Hamanari's treatise and the Prefaces to the *Kokinshū* had articulated for their purposes.

We have also seen that narratives of decline were powerful platforms from which writers of the younger literary cultures could launch their call for a renewal or vision of their choosing: the promotion of vernacular poetry at court in the case of the *Kokinshū* that could stand on a par with the previously dominant formal genre of Sino-Japanese poetry; or the vision of a highly original Roman sapientia in Cicero's *On the Orator* that tailored Hellenistic rhetoric and philosophy into a Roman discipline of oratory designed to function as the central practice of Roman public life. In contrast, Cicero's narrative of the decline of Attic oratory through a contamination with "Asiatic stain" served as one move in the fencing game with those who criticized Cicero's style as too Asiatic. Though colorful and highly effective, this narrative of decline had a more local relevance then the narratives of decline discussed from the Prefaces to the *Kokinshū* and Cicero's *On the Orator*. In this it resembles the local importance of Yakamochi's pose of simplicity, which lacked connection to a historical scheme of decline with broader implications.

While discovering a surprising number of similarities in the ways issues of ornateness, simplicity, and narratives of decline preoccupied our Japanese and Latin authors, our close readings have also allowed us to discern fundamental differences between them. The lack of early Latin texts has forced us to match early Japanese texts up until the *Kokinshū* with Latin texts from Cicero, a sort of "*Kokinshū* moment," to Horace. I had called the chimera of a historical timeline with Japanese feet and Latin arms a suggestive example for a "mutual virtual history." Virtual history relies on counterfactuals to imagine radically different outcomes that did not actually happen, but that help us grasp the impact of inflection points in actual history. Such an approach mobilizes our imagination of historical events so that we can more clearly discern their true historical importance.

I would argue that the methodology of virtual history could be significantly enriched by including the practice of a "mutual virtual history." Asking "what would have happened if X (or not X)?" naturally yields answers that will be heavily informed, even if indirectly, by our knowledge of what actually happened: going by the simplest laws of logic it might be answered by imagining an increased, decreased, or antithetical result for a given phenomenon. In contrast, a mutual virtual history would flesh out and complicate the simplistic logical patterns of a virtual history of alternatives by inserting the complexity and richness of another culture's historical narrative.

This approach has allowed us to discern the difference of Cicero's arguments from those of the Prefaces to the *Kokinshū*. Cicero plays ingeniously with polar opposites: Greek versus Roman, Attic versus Asiatic, rhetoric versus philosophy. He transcends them rather than choosing between them, although he always sounds like someone with strong opinions. The challenging entanglement and closeness of these polar opposites is foreign to the Japanese texts discussed above. The *Kaifūsō* Preface does not even mention that vernacular poetry exists, although vernacular poetry was everywhere and was being anthologized into the voluminous *Man'yōshū* right around that time. And Yakamochi and Ikenushi, though writing in two idioms and four genres, do not thematize these differences or reflect on them as Chinese, Sino-Japanese, or vernacular Japanese practices. Equally, neither Hamanari's treatise nor Tsurayuki's preface acknowledges the existence of Sino-Japanese poetry alongside with waka. That Cicero's villain was Greek, while the villain in the Sino-Japanese Preface to the *Kokinshū* was Japanese, confirms that Greece appeared closer and more threatening, while China could be as close or as far as a Japanese author wished it to be. Japanese writers settled early into a pattern of *wa-kan* polarity, collecting waka and kanshi in separate anthologies and treating them in separate treatises. The consequence of the early compartmentalization of Japanese literature into vernacular and Sino-Japanese strands and the minimal physical contact between Chinese and Japanese people in early Japan was that the internal development of Japanese literature was more continuous and less disrupted by avant-garde fashion changes in China than the development of Latin literature, whose authors in the classical period were often trained in Greece or at least educated by Greeks and thus in close physical and intellectual contact with Greek intellectual trends.

This might be one of the reasons why a "Horace moment" did not happen in early Japan. Nara and Heian writers did not have the historical awareness that Latin writers had not just of their own old and contemporary literature, but, more importantly, of the radical differences between types of Archaic, Classical Athenian, and Hellenistic Greek literature. It would probably have been incomprehensible to an early Japanese author why Horace's satirist should go to such pains to play around with the Greco-Roman "inventor" discourse and make such a sophisticated fool of himself by both validating and devaluating Lucilius's status as inventor of the satire genre. Why bother debating to which degree an earlier compatriot had made proper use of Chinese precedents and their historical status? Emphasizing one's active, proud transposition and introduction of Greek precedents into Roman literary culture gained a Latin writer cultural capital. Roman writers enjoyed claiming to be the first to do something that someone before them had already claimed to have done for the very first time, and they developed ways to parse their firstness in ever more subtle and particular ways. Quite to the contrary, blurring the boundaries between the Japanese and the Chinese traditions constituted cultural capital for Japanese writers.

From our experiment with "mutual virtual history" we can say that Latin authors who wrote on ornament, simplicity, and decline were more conflicted in their relation to their reference culture Greece than their Japanese peers in relation to China. Paradoxically, they had to be both more aggressive and more diplomatic in their claims, because of the close political, physical, and intellectual symbiosis with Greece and Greeks.

This intimacy also meant that Late Republican and Early Imperial Latin writers probably felt more embarrassed about the humble beginnings of their literary art on Italic soil, which played some role in Horace's ambivalent railing against Lucilius. That even those Latin authors who pushed their praises of their old Roman predecessors to the limits of credibility contributed to the disparagement and oblivion of early Roman literature is one of the tragedies of this chapter. In the *Brutus*, a dialogue fraught with various tragedies and somber foreshadowing, Cicero admits to Brutus his hope for the future of Roman oratory:

> I have, I am sure, contributed some benefit to the rising generation in showing them a more elevated and more elaborated style, and perhaps too some harm, in that the older orations in comparison with mine have ceased to be read by the majority; not by me however, since I prefer them to my own.

> [C]erte enim et boni aliquid attulimus iuventuti, magnificentius quam fuerat genus dicendi et ornatius; et nocuimus fortasse, quod veteres orationes post nostras, non a me quidem—meis enim illas antepono—sed a plerisque legi sunt desitae.[61]

Cicero was to remain quite alone with his reading preferences. Much of early Latin literature was lost over the next few centuries, and another dozen centuries later we are forced to come up with methodological devices that allow us nevertheless to pursue a radically asymmetrical comparison between early Japanese and Latin writers and the ways in which ornateness, decline, and simplicity mattered to them.

---

[61] Cicero *Brutus* 123. Hendrickson 1936, 109–11.

CHAPTER 4 | City-Building or Writing?
How Aeneas and Prince Shōtoku Made
Rome and Japan

NATION STATES OFTEN HAVE a repertoire of founding figures who embody different aspects of collective memory and can be mobilized depending on occasion.
Japan's nationalist government celebrated the 2,600th anniversary of the foundation of the Japanese empire in 1940 and emphasized the mythical longevity of
the Japanese imperial institution by harking back to the legendary first emperor
Jinmu, who is shrouded in the mist of prehistory, which lasted for more than
another millennium after his debatable existence. Years later, in 2006, when no
male successor to the Japanese throne was in sight, those who agreed with Prime
Minister Koizumi about the introduction of a bill allowing women to succeed to
the throne could point to the comparably legendary Queen Himiko, mentioned in
Chinese chronicles of the third century, and the six female emperors of seventh-
and eighth-century Japan.

For Rome, Romulus had an undisputed authority as founder of the city that
embodied the power of the empire. Augustus harked back to the ambivalent figure of Romulus, and Mussolini, in turn, restored Augustus's Altar of Peace, the
Ara pacis, and included it into the pompous display of Augustan art arranged
for the bimillenial celebration of Augustus's birth in the late 1930s, leaving no
doubt that the Duce saw himself as a New Augustus. But those throughout history
who cherished Rome's Republican traditions would evoke Lucius Junius Brutus,
who in 509 BCE expelled the last king, Tarquinius Superbus, founded the Roman
Republic, and became one of its first consuls.

When looking over the candidates from the repertoire of Japanese and Roman
national heroes, Prince Shōtoku and Aeneas make a particularly compelling pair,
as they have a comparably exceptional profile as founding figures of the Japanese
and Roman state, respectively. First, they have complex connections with China
and Greece and are thus national figures with a "strategic foreign edge." Prince
Shōtoku was considered the reincarnation of the Chinese Buddhist patriarch
Huisi 慧思 (515–577), while the Trojan prince Aeneas escaped the burning Troy
when the Greeks took the city after a decade of warfare; he originated as a creature

of the world of the Homeric epic. Second, they both played a crucial role in the cultural transfer and introduction of religious practices: Prince Shōtoku is revered as the founder of Buddhism in Japan and he built the first temples to house Buddha images, while Aeneas carried not only his old father and infant son, but also the Penates, the Trojan households gods, out of the burning city and installed their statues in his newly founded city of Lavinium, about 30 km south of the later Rome. Third, despite great variations in the numerous legends that accrued around Shōtoku and Aeneas, both figures are not just much larger than life, but much larger than history. They are considered emblematic for Japanese and Roman civilization, respectively. Prince Shōtoku was an intuitive moral exemplar associated with various forms of literacy and writing, whereas Aeneas's prominent qualities included, most notably, his *pietas*, his "sense of duty," "righteousness" and "trustworthiness," or "devotion," but also his ability to build cities, give laws, and support agriculture.

This chapter compares the image of two respective national founding figures of Japan and Rome as presented in two particularly influential texts: the *Abridged Biography of Prince Shōtoku* (*Shōtoku taishi denryaku* 聖徳太子伝略) and Virgil's *Aeneid*. The two texts are radically different in scope, intended audience, and style.

The *Abridged Biography* is a sprawling work of hagiography, a treasure trove of legends about the prince's life and the lively religious cult that formed around him after his death. It was written some time during the tenth century—at least three hundred years after the prince's death—possibly by somebody from the Taira lineage who had close connections to the Shōtoku cult at Shitennōji temple, one of the temples founded by the prince near present-day Osaka. As such, it pays homage to Prince Shōtoku, the Buddhist saint, whose cult was by then well established and who looked quite different from Prince Kamitsumiya or Umayado, as Shōtoku was called during his lifetime. Just to point to one significant cosmetic correction of the image of the historical prince: in texts preceding the *Abridged Biography* we see a prince in often violent action, even killing his enemies. But the *Abridged Biography*, which celebrates the prince as the founder of Buddhism who introduced laws against taking the life of sentient beings into Japanese culture, sanitized this image considerably and presented a more saintly, pacific prince.[1] The biography uses the sober format of Chinese-style annalistic biographies, treating events in chronological order from the beginning of Emperor Bidatsu's reign (r. 572–585) to the beginning of Empress Kōtoku's reign (r. 645–654). Though there is no dearth of engaging anecdotal material, the text consists of simple, straightforward Buddhist prose, a far cry from the ornamental literary *kanbun* prose that contemporary courtier-poets of the mid-Heian Period such as Sugawara no Fumitoki or, later, Ōe no Masahira would have produced (and which would, from a stylistic perspective, be far more comparable to Virgil's *Aeneid*). The *Abridged Biography* is not a text of particular aesthetic purpose or value, but is a central text for the Shōtoku cult and the early history of Buddhism in Japan.

---

[1] On the formation of Shōtoku's image as a pious Buddhist avoiding bloodshed see Matsumoto 2007, 23–66. On the various legends about Shōtoku that precede the *Abridged Biography* see Iida 2000, 1–36.

In striking contrast, the *Aeneid* is a masterpiece of Augustan high literary culture and, as is sometimes argued, the most influential classic in Western literary history.[2] Into the twentieth century it has shaped the moral and aesthetic education, visions of valor and empire, notions of destiny and piety for generations; it has also been a thematic treasure trove for painters and composers; and it has inscribed itself into the English language through its rich translation history starting from the Renaissance translation by the Scottish bishop Gavin Douglas and Dryden's well-known 1697 translation, to Robert Fitzgerald's and, most recently Stanley Lombardo's, Robert Fagles's, and Sarah Ruden's rendering of the epic.

The *Aeneid* is one particular and obviously the most famous version of the many legends that accrued around Aeneas, who was destined to escape the destruction of Troy and find and defend a new home in Italy around the site of future Rome. After challenges by the Greek-loving and thus hostile goddess Juno, taxing travels, and amorous temptations by Carthage's Queen Dido, he manages to reach Latium, settles there and founds the Roman race. Around 30 BCE Virgil started working on the grand epic, which, as one of his early commentators claimed, served the purpose of "imitating Homer" and "praising Emperor Augustus, beginning with his ancestors." He continued working on it until his death in 19 BCE in the Apulian city of Brundisium (modern-day Brindisi) on his way back from Greece to Rome.[3]

Just how unfinished the *Aeneid* actually is has been subject to extensive debates, but the epic ends suggestively unfinished on several levels: in terms of plot it breaks off in the middle of battle, when readers hold their breath while Aeneas thrusts his sword into the breast of Turnus, the king of a local tribe in Latium who fights the arrival of the unwelcome strangers from Troy. In terms of Aeneas's destiny, the epic ends in the middle of the wars Aeneas has to endure in Latium to ensure his descendants' claim to rule; it does not reach the decisive moment of his foundation of the city of Lavinium and his marriage to Lavinia, daughter of the local king Latinus. Many legends struggle precisely with connecting the two unrelated threads of Aeneas the Homeric hero—who by Poseidon's prophecy in *Iliad* 20.307 ff. is destined to become king of Troy, the "second Troy" of Rome after the extinction of Priam's line—and the Italic Aeneas, the ancestor of a hybrid local lineage in his new home of Latium that eventually leads to Romulus and the actual founding of the city of Rome.

---

[2] In "What is a Classic?" T. S. Eliot claimed the *Aeneid* as "the classic of all Europe," pointing to its comprehensive sweep, its "maturity" and "universal" appeal in religious, political, and moral matters. Eliot 1957, 53–71. S. J. Harrison has extended this argument intriguingly to the ways Virgil integrated resonances of other genres into his epic: "The generic comprehensiveness...constitutes an equally powerful explanation of the endurance of the *Aeneid* over two millennia as an object of study and reading. The diversity of literary forms appropriated into Vergil's epic through generic enrichment ensures a complex and subtle poetic texture, which leads not only to the poem's own extraordinary afterlife but also to substantial evolution within its genre. After the intergeneric pyrotechnics of the *Aeneid*, Roman epic was both inspired and challenged by its example." Harrison 2007, 240. On the *Aeneid* as a classic in European cultural history over the past few centuries see Haynes 2010.
[3] For a concise and compelling introduction to Virgil and his works see Hardie 1998. This is closer to the "Augustan" interpretation of the *Aeneid* that has been so dominant and ensconced in public school education and against which Richard Thomas argues in Thomas 2001.

Aeneas was already popular in the Greek world by the sixth century BCE, when vase painters liked to depict Aeneas carrying his father Anchises to safety from the ruins of Troy.[4] He took on many different faces in the Greek and Latin legends that preceded Virgil's large-scale epic, but Virgil created his own version of the legend in the *Aeneid* in a very distinctive form: The reader of the *Aeneid* is faced with a double text, the Virgilian story of Aeneas and the subtext of Homer's *Iliad*, the epic story of the Trojan War projected onto the wars Aeneas has to fight in his new home, and Homer's *Odyssey*, the travels and tribulations of another survivor of the Trojan War, Odysseus. The highly sophisticated echoing, imitating, or overwriting of Homeric parallels and precedents is probably the most striking difference between Virgil's *Aeneid* and the anonymous biography of Prince Shōtoku. The authors of the *Abridged Biography* could pick and choose from different variants of the prince's legend, but they were not faced with a canonical subtext as Virgil who stepped up to the overawing stature of Homeric epic. Philip Hardie reminds us what an enormous audacity Virgil's comprehensive reimagination of the entire Homeric corpus was, because Homer was not only the earliest poet writing in the most authoritative genre of epic, but "he was a universal poet, the source of all later literature and wisdom, of almost god-like stature, and the one who saw into the deepest mysteries of the universe. It is a mark of the success of the *Aeneid*'s ambition that later centuries saw Virgil himself as a universal and almost divine poet."[5] Already Virgil's contemporaries understood the enormity of the poet's ambition, as is attested by Propertius's well-known exclamation that "something greater than the Iliad is being born (*nescio quid maius nascitur Iliade*)."[6]

Also, the *Aeneid* combines several subgenres in unique fashion, unlike the rather standard format of hagiographical biographies that the *Abridged Biography* follows: it is an epic of war, like the *Iliad*, as well as an epic of homecoming (Gr. *nostos*), like the *Odyssey*; but it is also an etiological poem in the Hellenistic tradition on the origins of a place and a people and thus imbued with antiquarian scholarship of sorts, even if Virgil chose from his sources what fit the vision of his *sujet*.

The *Aeneid* is a "double text" in yet another sense, in that it superimposes two planes of time: it is a national epic recounting the mythological origins of the Roman state, but also a personal imperial history pointing, however ambiguously at times, toward Augustus and his age. Julius Caesar and then his adopted son Octavian, the later Augustus, claimed that the Julian gens descended from Aeneas's son Iulus (Ascanius).[7] Virgil gave literary flesh to this claim of dynastic origins and used the Aeneas legend as a complex experimentation ground to thematize the fundamental problem of the relationship between the mythical and the historical, literature and ideology, Roman dependence and the surpassing of Greek history and its literary models.

---

[4] Anderson 1997, 63.
[5] Hardie 1998, 57.
[6] Propertius. *Elegies* 2.34.66.
[7] The identification of Ascanius with Iulus probably occurred late and was not universally accepted even during Virgil's time. On this and the different character profiles associated with the two names see Paschalis 1997, 61–63.

As should be clear by now, our heroes and texts are quite unalike. Aeneas is a founding figure *before* the actual founding of Rome who also referenced the genealogical claims of Augustus. The *Aeneid* made him into a complex synecdoche of Roman destiny and history and told his story through moments of proleptic narrative—as when he visits the site of future Rome in a vision of Virgil's contemporary Augustan city. Prince Shōtoku is a founding figure *after* the founding of the Japanese state, where the earliest chronicles trace back to the legendary Emperor Jinmu in the seventh century BCE, more than 1,200 years before Shōtoku's time. Also, rather than being in an explicit leadership position, the prince served his aunt, Empress Suiko (r. 593–628), as regent and never became the state's ultimate leader as emperor. The texts are yet more unalike: Virgil's is a highly self-conscious polished literary masterpiece in its inception (and of course reception), written in the most hallowed genre of epic (and infused with an inset-piece of the similarly authoritative genre of drama: the tragic love affair of Aeneas and Dido); the *Abridged Biography*, in contrast, is an aggregation of legends streamlined into a plain hagiographic biography.

Still, this does not render our comparison less valid. Even if Shōtoku postdated the mythical beginnings of the Japanese state, his role in the introduction of Buddhism to Japan made him into a comparable foundational figure and Shōtoku's veneration as a dharma king who protects the nation and helps it flourish gave him a central role on a metaphysical level.[8] Given that it is even hard to find another Latin text that matches Virgil's complex epic designs in the *Aeneid*, the discrepancy between the Virgilian epic and the Buddhist biography are hardly damaging to our comparison. What interests us here is a comparison of Aeneas's and Prince Shōtoku's portrayals as national founding figures in two texts that presented particularly influential versions of their stories. What are the character traits that make them attractive as founding figures in their respective cultures? How do the two texts under consideration present and illustrate these representative personality traits? And is the difference in their character traits a significant indicator of broader differences in the fundamental orientations of Latin and Japanese cultures?

1. *The Foreign Edge of National Founding Figures*

Prince Shōtoku and Aeneas share a common fate as national founding figures with a foreign edge that allowed them to show both independence of their own, younger culture, but also had them benefit from the authority that came with connections to the older reference culture. Prince Shōtoku (574–622) was considered to be the reincarnation of the Chinese patriarch Huisi 慧思 (J. Eshi) (515–677) of the Tiantai (J. Tendai) school of Buddhism. One of the earliest appearances of this belief occurs in a poem by the eight-century scholar and poet Ōmi no Mifune, who also wrote a biography of the Chinese monk Jianzhen 鑑真 (J. Ganjin), where he

---

[8] Michael Como also emphasizes that Shōtoku is the earliest figure onto whom national significance has been projected. To this day, Shōtoku has retained this position in Japanese public and academic culture and is sometimes instrumentalized by people with nationalist agendas. Como 2008, 6.

claims that Jianzhen was inspired to go to Japan and support fledgling Buddhism because he had heard that patriarch Huisi had reincarnated in that country. In his biography of Jianzhen, *Account of the Eastern Expedition of the Great Tang Priest* (*Tō daiwajō tōseiden* 唐大和上東征伝, 779), he has Japanese envoys seek out Jianzhen in China and address him as follows:

> "The Buddhist Law has spread east and arrived in Japan. However, although the Law exists now, there are no people to transmit it. In our country Prince Shōtoku once said, 'In two hundred years the sacred teaching will flourish in Japan.' Since this destiny has now been accumulated, we would like you to come east with us and bring the teaching to flourish." The Master (Jianzhen) replied, "I have heard long ago, that after the Master Huisi of Nanyue Peak passed on, he reincarnated as a prince in the land of Yamato, Japan, made the Buddhist Law greatly flourish and helped all sentient beings towards enlightenment."

> 「佛法東流、至日本國、雖有其法、而無傳法人。本國昔聖徳太子曰『二百年後、聖教興於日本。』今鍾此運。願和上東遊興化。」大和上答曰『昔聞。南岳惠思禪師遷化之後、託生倭國王子、興隆佛法、濟度衆生。[9]

Connecting Prince Shōtoku to the Chinese patriarch represented a formative moment in the making of his legend, as his profile now reached beyond Japan to China.[10] In earlier Chinese sources Huisi was known for his expertise in the *Lotus Sutra*, the central scripture of Tiantai (J. Tendai) Buddhism, for his retreat to Nanyue Peak in Southeastern China in quest for longevity, and for his superhuman abilities. Some sources claimed that Huisi had knowledge of his previous incarnations and also predicted that in his next life he wished to be reborn in a far-away land to help spread Buddhism.[11] The early ninth century saw further significant elaborations of the Shōtoku legend, when the founding figure of Japanese Tendai Buddhism, Saichō (767–822), called Shōtoku a "teacher of the nation" and positioned the Tendai School as a continuation of Shōtoku's work, arguing that it could therefore claim a privileged position among the various Buddhist schools. Saichō also further expanded Huisi's identity, suggesting that Huisi was the reincarnation of one of the innumerable people in the audience at Vulture Peak when the historical Buddha delivered the sermon that was recorded in the *Lotus Sutra*. Now Shōtoku's identity was traceable all the way back to India, the country of Buddhism's origin.[12] Shōtoku had now accumulated considerable historical and cultural karma, which gave him significant legitimacy beyond his historical existence as a Japanese prince living around the turn of the seventh century.

There is another sense in which Shōtoku's profile benefited from older Asian connections. As Michael Como, building on Tamura Enchō's work from the 1980s, has recently argued, Korean immigrant lineages in Japan played a major role in shaping and promoting the Shōtoku legends. This goes against frequent

---

[9] Takeuchi 1943–44, vol. 2, 896.
[10] On the development of the legend of Huisi's reincarnation as Shōtoku see Wang 1994.
[11] Como 2008, 144.
[12] Como 2008, 150–51.

assumptions that the Shōtoku cult was mainly product of imperial ideology. In seventh-century Japan kinship groups from the rival Korean kingdoms of Paekche and Silla were not just on the forefront of the propagation of Buddhism, but were also the dominant professional groups in control of literacy, which makes their involvement in the production of the Shōtoku legends all the more probable. Como argues that the fierce conflicts between the "Three Kingdoms" of Silla, Paekche, and Koguryo that ravaged Korea before the unification under Silla's rule in 668 were echoed in the conflicts between the Korean lineage groups living in Japan and that the early Shōtoku cult may have been bifurcated from its beginnings along ethnic lines: Paekche and Silla kinship groups would have used their temple building activities to highlight their distinctive identities and that the cult "was in part created and sustained by the inter-regional and inter-ethnic conflicts that con-vulsed Yamato in the middle years of the seventh century."[13] The narrative in the *Chronicles of Japan* of 720 emphasizes Prince Shōtoku's role and thus the impor-tance of the royal court in the establishment of Buddhism, but it bears clear traces of the influence of immigrant groups. The *Chronicles of Japan* date the introduction of Buddhism to 552, when Paekche sent a Buddhist statue to Japan. It came to be worshipped by the head of the Soga kinship group, themselves probably of Paekche descent. The Mononobe and Nakatomi, powerful conservative native kinship groups in competition with the Soga's influence at court, resisted the introduction of the foreign religion and claimed that it would make the gods of the Japanese Islands angry. When tensions between the Soga and Mononobe escalated into mili-tary conflict in 587, Shōtoku fought with the Soga on the pro-Buddhist side, vowing to build a temple in case of victory. Shōtoku's narrative in the *Chronicles of Japan* ends with the foundation of the "Temple of the Four Heavenly Kings" (*Shitennōji* 四天王寺) in Naniwa, present-day Osaka. Although the prince gets the main credit for the successful battle, the account of Shōtoku's foundation of the Temple of the Four Heavenly Kings is closely modeled on the foundation legend of the largest temple of Silla bearing the same name, another indication of the contribution of immigrant lineages to the making of Shōtoku's legends.[14]

The temples founded or promoted by Prince Shōtoku, which belong to the oldest Buddhist temples in Japan, had clear ethnic affiliations: The Silla immi-grant clans of the Kishi, Hata, and Abe seem to have played a large role in the early development of Shitennōji, while Paekche groups such as the Soga were influential at the temples of Horyūji and Asukadera. Thus, Shōtoku seems to have been a contested cultural hero to whom different groups tried to lay claim. These rivaling Korean immigrant groups brought Buddhism and the accompany-ing crafts of temple architecture and sacred sculpture to Japan; with their high proficiency in literacy and textual knowledge they contributed to Shōtoku's image in Japan.

Just as Chinese legends about Huisi facilitated the shaping of Shōtoku into a Japanese national hero and Korean immigrant lineages used the figure of

---

[13] Ibid., 23.
[14] For an account of the role of the immigrant lineages in the founding legend of Japanese Buddhism see Como 2008, 13–31.

Shōtoku to promote Buddhism and defend their distinctive identities, Greek legends of Aeneas were the point of departure for Roman elaborations of Aeneas's image.[15] In *Iliad* 20 Poseidon rescues Aeneas, presumably because the Trojan prince is destined to rule over Troy and needs to survive. This canonical prophecy preoccupied later writers, as they tried to connect Aeneas with the foundation of Rome. In the world of myth and Homeric epic Italy was associated with the travails of Heracles and Odysseus, who make their appearance in the *Aeneid*. For Aeneas Greek writers elaborated various scenarios: Dionysius of Halicarnassus, who wrote as a Greek in Augustan Rome, claimed Aeneas as a Greek, descended from Dardanus, whom he traced back to the ruling house of Arcadia. He revels about the Trojans: "One will not find a people more ancient or more Greek!"[16] But some people, like the geographer Strabo, Dionysius's rough contemporary, insisted on Homer's authority and were convinced that Aeneas had actually never left Troy.[17]

The Greeks of Magna Graecia, descendants of the Greeks who had colonized southern Italy since the eighth century BCE, were obviously particularly interested in insisting on a Hellenic connection of the foundation of Rome. In his work on the antiquities of Sicily and Italy a certain Alkimos from Sicily (ca. late 4th century BCE) connected the Greek legends around Aeneas to the foundation of Rome: "Alcimus says that Romulus was a son of Thyrrenia and Aeneas and that Alba, granddaughter of Aeneas, was born from him; her son Rhomus founded the city of Rome (*Alcimus ait Tyrrhenia Aeneae natum filium Romulum fuisse atque eo ortam Albam Aeneae neptem, cuius filius nomine Rhomus condiderit urbem Romam*)."[18] This is one of the earliest texts that connect Aeneas to Rome. Without overstretching what would have to be a complex comparison, the Greeks of Sicily and Southern Italy had a mediating role between Greek culture and the Roman state that was in some aspects comparable to the role of the immigrants from the Korean peninsula in Japan's appropriation of Chinese culture.

Roman historians and poets picked up on the connection their Greek colleagues had established between Aeneas and Rome and in the third century BCE it was still common to assume a close family relation between the Trojan prince and the founder of Rome proper: both Ennius and Naevius still made Romulus the grandson of Aeneas. But Fabius Pictor, the first Roman to write a history of his city (published around 210 BCE) filled the obvious gap between the fall of Troy, dated by Greek writers to the twelfth century BCE, and the foundation of Rome in the eighth century BCE with a long dynasty of Alban kings originating with Aeneas's son Ascanius and his foundation of Alba longa.[19] This was to become the customary version of Aeneas's relation to Romulus and Rome.

---

[15] For an introduction to the various Greek and Latin sources about Aeneas and the early history of Rome see Hillen 2003.

[16] Dionysius of Halicarnassus, *Roman Antiquities* I.89.2.

[17] In the following I rely on Gruen 1992b and Casali 2010. On the development of Aeneas's image particularly in Greek sources see Moreno 2007, 167–85.

[18] Jacoby 1923–58, 560 F 4.

[19] Feeney 2009, 143.

In his *Aeneid* Virgil added a few crucial twists to the wealth of variant Aeneas myths that featured in earlier historiography and epic.[20] He emphasized Aeneas's prospective lineage, claiming that Augustus's clan, the *gens Iulia,* derived from Aeneas's son Ascanius/ Iulus. Equally importantly, he retrospectively redirected the genealogical thrust of the Trojan prince's ancestor Dardanus, whom his contemporary Dionysius of Halicarnassus made Greek: Virgil's Dardanus is Italic. In Greek sources Dardanus was associated with Samothrace, Arcadia, and, in Homer, Troy, whose royal lineage he founded; but Virgil has him born in Corythus, an Etruscan city.[21] In Virgil's scheme Aeneas ventures not to foreign shores with his household gods but returns back home to his Italic roots, just as we expect in a typical nostos-narrative such as the *Odyssey*.[22]

While Virgil highlights Aeneas's Roman identity with a temporal vector—the Italic origins of his ancestor Dardanus—he puts the space of the future Rome into Greek limelight: Aeneas does not find virgin soil, but finds the humble Greek settlement of Pallanteum on the site of the future Palatine. Its ruler, the Arcadian Evander, welcomes Aeneas to his destined soil and introduces him to Rome's future history. Intriguingly, Evander is the protagonist in the epic who speaks the most after Aeneas, even more than Anchises, and he appears as the prototype of an erudite Greek historian who teaches the Trojan Romans-to-be about their future and past.[23] Evander must have been all the more appealing to Virgil's educated readers, as various Greek and Latin sources claimed that he civilized the Latins by introducing laws, music, and, most importantly, writing, to Italy.[24] Virgil maximized Aeneas's attraction as a Roman national founding figure by having his clan, literally, build on the cultural resources of the reference culture—the Greek Pallanteum, proto-Rome—while rechanneling genealogy in a way that designated Italy as the true home of the Trojan hero.

Whereas the foreign edge that Aeneas and Prince Shōtoku gained from their cultural, religious, and genealogical connection with Greece and China (and Sicily and Korea) legitimized them from the perspective of their older reference cultures in comparable fashion, two rather different devices propelled our heroes into their new national habitat of Rome and Japan: prophecy and reincarnation.

2. Prophecy

Prophecy and reincarnation are obviously fundamental, deep-seated cultural orientations rooted in religious beliefs and manifested in religious practices, whose

---

[20] On Virgil's possible use of mythographic manuals see Cameron 2004, 255–60.

[21] *Aeneid* 3.167–71.

[22] As J. D. Reed points out, an Etruscan Dardanus from Corythus might still in the end be Greek. Herodotus claims that the Etruscans were Lydian, and thus stemmed from Asia Minor like the Trojans, and Dionysius of Halicarnassus makes the Italian city of Cortona, with which Corythus has traditionally been identified, a Pelasgian, Greek city. Reed 2007, 11. This makes Virgil's choice of Dardanus's origin more complex and intriguing, but it does not put into question Virgil's clear intention to make the *Aeneid* into a nostos narrative: Aeneas and his gods "return home" to Italy and, by extension, Rome is both Aeneas's point of origin and his destination.

[23] Casali 2010, 39.

[24] Moreno 2007, 175. On the Latin side see *Livy* 1.18–19.

comparison would require multiple studies in their own right. For the purposes of this chapter we will focus very narrowly on how they work as narrative devices in the *Aeneid* and the *Abridged Biography*. What do these devices, as part not just of the cultural and religious matrix, but also as part of the narrative repertoire of Latin and Japanese literary cultures, allow and propel our protagonists to do, or discourage them from doing?

In the *Aeneid* prophecies come in many forms and through many mouths: gods exchange prophecies on Rome's future grandeur, or disclose future events to chosen humans; ominous dream visions or encounters with the dead point mortals toward what is to come; or "professional prophecies" are dispensed in wild oracular performances like that of the Sibyl at Cumae in Campania, a divinely inspired medium communicating the will of the gods similarly to the Greek Pythia at the temple of Apollo at Delphi.

Prophecies often function as narrative pivots: although they have the power to point toward the *telos*, the protagonist's ultimate destiny, they have equal power to distract him from it, most often because they are elliptic and underdetermined; the protagonist needs to grapple with their oblique meaning and can only gradually arrive at true understanding. In fact, as James O'Hara has argued, most of the predictions and prophecies in the *Aeneid* are deceptive, because they often suppress darker realities under a surface of optimism.[25] A good part of the pleasure of prophecies as narrative devices derives from the unequal access the protagonist, narrator, and reader has to their meaning. While Aeneas navigates through much suffering between clairvoyance and error in search of his prophesized destiny, the narrator initiates the reader of the *Aeneid* from the very first famous lines of the long epic into the protagonist's telos:

> Arms and a man I sing, the first from Troy,
> A fated exile to Lavinian shores
> In Italy. On land and sea, divine will—
> And Juno's unforgetting rage—harassed him.
> War racked him too, until he set his city
> And gods in Latium. There his Latin race rose,
> With Alban patriarchs, and Rome's high walls.[26]

Virgil nails down every part of his man's telos with predictive, not even prophetic, precision: that his fate is to reach Italian soil, found a city, introduce his gods to Latium and lay the foundations for the Latin race and the rise of Rome. That Virgil summarily gives it all away in a few lines shortcuts any expectation of linear narration or easy pleasures of suspense. Instead, the reader is asked to tally three different vectors of plot development against each other: there is the ultimate telos, of which she can be sure, unlike the protagonist; then there are the more mysterious prophecies, which captivate and guide her along like the protagonist; and, last,

---

[25] O'Hara 1990.
[26] *Aeneid* 1.1–7. Translation from Ruden 2008, 1. *Arma virumque cano, Troiae qui primus ab oris / Italiam fato profugus Lavinaque venit / litora—multum ille et terris iactatus et alto / vi superum, saevae memorem Iunonis ob iram / multa quoque et bello passus, dum conderet urbem / inferretque deos Latio; genus unde Latinum / Albanique patres, atque altae moenia Romae.*

there are the actual actions of the protagonist, which repeatedly make the reader wonder just how aware the hero is of his destiny.[27]

The shifting pattern of tension between these three vectors, which at times run parallel or counter to each other, or intersect, makes for a kind of three-fold linear plot development brimming with suspense despite the initial statement of the ultimate telos at the beginning of the epic. Yet more importantly, the reader not only knows what should and will happen to Aeneas in the future—understands the telos in a strictly historical, temporal sense—but she grasps that Aeneas's historical telos stands as *pars-pro-toto* for the eventual triumph of Augustan Rome—she has a synecdochal understanding of the plot. The reader's synecdochal understanding of the telos virtually always exceeds Aeneas's understanding of his destiny and heightens the reader's elation as she partakes in yet another, ultimate layer of the narrative privy to the protagonist's awareness. Most details of the prophecies in the Aeneas appear in previous historical or rhetorical works, but the focus on the synecdochal telos, the rise of Augustan Rome, is Virgil's invention.

Aeneas is easily taken off-course and the moments when we have the impression that he does know his destination can be treacherous. For example, already in Book 1, when he encourages his comrades after the huge storm whipped up against the Trojans by Juno's anger, he clairvoyantly promises Latium specifically as a second Troy and final destination:

> "Friends, we are all at home with suffering—
> Some worse than this—but god will end this too.
> . . .
>
> We fight through perils and catastrophes
> To Latium, where divine fate promises
> A peaceful homeland, a new Trojan kingdom.
> Endure and live until our fortunes change."
> Sick with colossal burdens, he shammed hope
> On his face, and buried grief deep in his heart.[28]

Aeneas shams (*simulat*) hope on his face, suppressing his anguish and lack of confidence in the gods' promise. This moment is particularly paradoxical, because Aeneas's mention of Latium specifically seems to confirm the reader's confidence in Aeneas's foresight but his pose of confidence puts this first impression into doubt. Aeneas's ambivalence and human limitations become all the more

---

[27] Repetition (or repetition with difference) rather than linearity is a major plot pattern in epic. As Philip Hardie has astutely remarked: "The epic strives for totality and completion, yet is at the same time driven obsessively to repetition and reworking." Hardie 1993, 1. David Quint divides the *Aeneid* into two cycles of repetition patterns: the "regressive repetition of the Odyssean wanderings" in the first half of the epic, where the Trojans try obsessively to recreate their lost city and the "successful repetition-as-reversal of the Iliadic war," when the Trojans lead wars in Latium and, this time, come out as victors. Quint 1993, 50–51. In contrast, here I am drawing attention to patterns of linearity in the epic that have less to do with plot (although, most obviously they relate to the *telos* of the narrative) than with a reader's expectation and reading experience.

[28] *Aeneid* 1.198–99 and 204–209. Ruden 2008, 7. "*O socii (neque enim ignari sumus ante malorum), / o passi graviora, dabit deus his quoque finem. / . . . per varios casus, per tot discrimina rerum / tendimus in Latium, sedes ubi fata quietas / ostendunt; illic fas regna resurgere Troiae. / durate, et vosmet rebus servate secundis.*" / *Talia voce refert, curisque ingentibus aeger / spem vultu simulat, premit altum corde dolorem.*

apparent, when shortly later the reader is initiated into the full-fledged divine plan with Jove's prophecy to Venus. Jove, accused by Aeneas's mother Venus of failing to support the quest of her son for his destiny in Italy, appeases the goddess (incidentally his daughter) and assures her that nothing has changed in the divine plans for her son. This time Jove not only predicts Aeneas' founding of the city of Lavinium and the Julian lineage leading up to Augustus, but he promises "empire without end (*imperium sine fine*)" for the Romans, "lords of the world, the race arrayed in Togas (*rerum dominos, gentemque togatam*)."[29]

Virgil keeps tantalizing his readers about the scope and nature of Aeneas's foresight in the yet more detailed prophecies of Rome's future in Book 6 and 8. After Aeneas visits Anchises in the Underworld, who discloses important milestones of Rome's history to his son, Virgil has Aeneas leave through a door of delusive dreams:

> There are two gates of sleep. The one, they say,
> Is horn: true shades go out there easily;
> The other—shining, white, well-crafted ivory—
> Lets spirits send false dreams up toward the sky.
> His speeches done, Anchises brought his son here,
> And the Sibyl too, and sent them through the ivory.[30]

Although Aeneas had followed attentively what the future has in store for Rome, Virgil potentially dims Aeneas's memory of the prophecy by sending him out the door of deceptive dreams.

In the *Aeneid*'s second grand procession of future Roman history, fleshed out in reliefs on Aeneas's battle shield in Book 8, Virgil uses a different strategy to blind the hero to divine knowledge and tickle his readers' speculations about Aeneas's awareness. Aeneas enjoys the scenes of Roman history depicted on the shield with which he will gain a first crucial victory in his new home country, launching not-yet-Rome on the path toward world domination. But he does not understand them:

> Aeneas loved these scenes on Vulcan's shield,
> His mother's gift—but didn't know the stories.
> He shouldered his descendants' glorious fate.[31]

Aeneas gazes at and shoulders the shield, the enormous weight of Rome's future, but his mind cannot grasp the significance of the scenes depicted on it. The joy he feels over the images matches his visceral premonition of destiny fulfilled. Aeneas has similar feelings when he visits the site of the future Rome with Evander: he is "entranced by the site, happily asking, learning, one by one, the legendary tales of

---

[29] *Aeneid* 1. 279 and 282.

[30] *Aeneid* 6.893–98. Ruden 2008, 143. *Sunt geminae Somni portae, quarum altera fertur / cornea, qua veris facilis datur exitus umbris, / altera candenti perfecta nitens elephanto, / sed falsa ad caelum mittunt insomnia Manes. / his ibi tum natum Anchises unaque Sibyllam / prosequitur dictis portaque emittit eburna.*

[31] *Aeneid* 8.729–31. Ruden 2008, 189. *Talia per clipeum Volcani, dona parentis, / miratur rerumque ignarus imagine gaudet / attollens umero famamque et fata nepotum.*

the men of old (*capiturque locis et singula laetus/ exquiritque auditque virum monumenta priorum*)."[32]

While the reader wonders throughout the *Aeneid* about Aeneas's grasp of his destiny, she sees him more often than not go astray. One of the biggest challenges for Aeneas in reaching his telos is a string of misunderstandings about its geographical location. The connection between geography, people, and place names is anything but obvious, because Aeneas travels on multiple maps—geographical, linguistic, mythical, genealogical—which do not always match. In the *Aeneid* a variety of resonant place names are associated with Aeneas's telos. On the map of Greek ethnography and myth he travels toward "Hesperia," an ancient Greek name for southern Italy; this name, "land in the west," already appears in the 6th century BCE in the poetry of Stesichoros, a Greek poet from southern Italy. Or he travels toward "Ausonia," a later Greek name for southern Italy associated with the Homeric world: Virgil's early 5th century commentator Servius relates it to Auson, son of Odysseus and Circe or Calypso.[33] The Greek toponyms are familiar to Aeneas the Trojan: his first wife Creusa, who dies in the flames of conquered Troy and thus never leaves the Greco-Trojan world promises Rome in her own, Greek terms: "the vast plains of the sea are yours to plow, until you will come to Hesperia, where Lydian Tiber flows smoothly through rich fields of warriors (... *et vastum maris aequor arandum; | et terram Hesperiam venies, ubi Lydius arva | inter opima virum leni fluit agmine Thybris*)."[34] When Creusa appears to him Aeneas has not yet left Troy and the Greek names of "Hesperia" and the "Lydian Thybris" (so-called because the Tiber passed along the borders of Etruria, which Herodotus considered a colony of the Lydians from Asia Minor) mean more to him than "Italia" and "Tiberis" would have at that point.

The place names on the Italic map lack resonance and are empty signifiers waiting for future fulfillment: The region of "Latium" is related to King Latinus, whom Aeneas only encounters at his final destination; as we saw above, Aeneas does use that name when he encourages his comrades in the big storm, but his confusion over his final destination in the following books suggest that Latium is still an unknown quantity to him. The city of "Lavinium," named after Aeneas's future wife Lavinia, the daughter of King Latinus, is a yet more unfulfilled geographic signifier, as the foundation of this city lies beyond the narrative of the *Aeneid*, which ends with Aeneas's victory over his rival in war and marriage, Turnus.

Most intriguing are the moments when Greek and Roman maps of Aeneas's telos overlap, as he gradually makes his way to his destined soil: in her prophecy the Sibyl of Cumae in southwest Italy promises the Trojans "Lavinium" but she also clothes her prophecy into an ambivalently Homeric cloak: a "new Achilles" is already born in Latium and again a "foreign bride" will be the cause of a vicious war. That the foreign bride points to Lavinia, a second Helen, is quite clear. But whether the "new Achilles" points to Aeneas or Turnus is left open.

---

[32] *Aeneid* 8.311-12. For several passages where Aeneas's marveling and joyfulness convey a premonition of fulfilled destiny see Binder 1971, 79–80.
[33] *Aeneid* 8.328 and 3.171.
[34] *Aeneid* 2.780-82.

Virgil's program of Homeric intertextuality insists that Turnus's allies become the Trojans and the Trojans Greek while Turnus becomes Hector and Aeneas Achilles. But throughout the later books Turnus persists in regarding his allies as Greek, himself as Achilles, and the Trojans as still Trojan. Obviously, he wanted to imagine himself on the winning side. Less confusingly, the Sibyl also promises that against all odds, Aeneas's man will receive help from a "Greek city"—Pallanteum, Evander's settlement on the site of the future Rome.[35]

The most fateful and resonant, but ultimately emptiest, geographical signifier of Aeneas's telos is undoubtedly "Troy." The rhetoric of Aeneas's destiny to found a "second Troy" originated with Poseidon's prophecy in the *Iliad* that Aeneas will once become king over Troy and is pregnant with Homeric plot expectations, but it is literally tautological or simply metaphorical and does little to help Aeneas to navigate his way to his destined land.[36]

Because the Greek maps of Aeneas's telos are imprecise and overpopulated (or populated with unwelcome associations) and the Roman maps are a tabula rasa pregnant with promise but of little navigational value, Aeneas is at times thrown back onto genealogical maps. The oracle of Apollo on the island of Delos tells him to "seek out the Ancient Mother (*antiquam exquirite matrem, Aeneid.* 3.96)," the land Dardanus, founder of the Trojan lineage. But genealogy can be treacherous. Where was Dardanus's homeland? Was it Arcadia, as Dionysius of Halicarnassus believed? Or Crete, as Anchises vaguely recalls in the *Aeneid*? Anchises's misunderstanding of the oracle prompts the party to go off on a tangent to Crete, where an ominous plague makes it clear that something went wrong. Finally, the Household Gods appear to Aeneas and set the party on the right track with a powerful cluster of place names in the short span of eight lines that point unmistakably to Italy: "Hesperia," "Ausonia," "Italia," and the land of the "Oenotrians."[37] (*Aeneid* 3.163–71).

When Aeneas finally does reach Latium after repeated false starts, Virgil makes sure to paint the fulfillment of the prophecy with great pathos: in a rare moment in the *Aeneid*, Ascanius makes a joke, comic relief from the sheer endless hardship they endured along the way; Aeneas hails his destined land, then introduces the Household Gods to their new home (*Aeneid* 7.120–22); bystanders realize with amazement that the day has come to found the promised city; and without even awaiting word from the local Latins who inhabit the land, Aeneas proceeds right away to the business of city-building: "... Where walls would rise, Aeneas dug a low ditch / On the shore and started their first settlement / With battlements and ramparts, like a camp. (... *ipse humili designat moenia fossa / moliturque locum, primasque in litore sedes / castrorum in morem pinnis atque aggere cingit.*" *Aeneid* 7.157–59. Ruden 2008, 149).

To make the fulfillment of the prophecies come full circle, also the local powers of Latium confirm that this time Aeneas has indeed reached his destination: King

[35] *Aeneid* 6.83-97.
[36] On Rome as "second Troy" see Henry 1989, 43–65 and Edwards 1996, Chapter 2.
[37] Oenotria was named after a Sabine or Arcadian king and for its good wine (Gr. *oinos*). O'Hara 1996, 127.

Latinus knows that Dardanus was born in Latium (*Aeneid* 7.205–7) and suddenly realizes the meaning of an earlier prophecy that had urged him to wed his daughter to a newcomer bound to arrive in Latium. Then, the River god Tiberinus gives him an unexpected welcome in a dream vision. He introduces himself as a local god and promises Ascanius's foundation of Alba, assuring Aeneas that his prophecy is correct (*Aeneid* 8.49)—he is well aware that they meet for the first time and Aeneas might harbor doubts about the predictions of an unknown god in a foreign land.

Had Aeneas had an Alexandrian etiologist in his company, versed in the rich geographical and ethnographical lore and the philological methods to interpret it, he would have been able to avoid a number of detours. But Aeneas must prove himself, slowly completing his path between human misunderstanding and divine prophecy, which keeps him moving even if he does not always comprehend it. But not just Aeneas faces challenges; even if we often know more than the protagonist, readers must navigate a complex set of plot planes, as Gian Biagio Conte has elegantly stated: "Virgil makes a heavy demand on his readers. They must appreciate the fated necessity of victory, and at the same time must not forget the reasoning of the defeated; they must view the world from a superior perspective (Jupiter, Fate, the omniscient narrator) and at the same time witness and participate in the sufferings of individuals; they must accept epic objectivity, which beholds from on high the great providential cycle of history, and at the same time accept tragic subjectivity, which reflects and matches against each other personal motives and relative truths."[38]

3. Reincarnation

In the East Asian context reincarnation became a basic cultural assumption with the advent of Buddhism. Although hinted at in pre-Buddhist early Chinese texts, such as the Masters Text *Zhuangzi* 莊子 (4th through 2nd century BCE), it first became a central concept with the arrival of Buddhism in China during the first centuries of the Common Era. Reincarnation eventually advanced to a favorite narrative device in story telling and fiction. By the early modern period the great classical Chinese novels, such as *Journey to the West* and *Story of the Stone* (also known as *Dream of the Red Chamber*), are unthinkable—both in macroscopic frame plot, and in miscroscopic shaping of the narrative—without the trope of reincarnation.

In terms of the relation between the author, his protagonists, and the reader, prophecy and reincarnation work remarkably similarly: the reader knows that Aeneas is destined to lay the foundation for Rome and her view resembles that of the omniscient gods, while Aeneas himself often loses sight of his destiny or fails to interpret prophecies correctly. Similarly, the reader of the *Dream of the Red Chamber* knows that the main protagonists Jia Baoyu, a scion of a wealthy family, is the reincarnation of a cosmic stone that many eons ago used to nourish a crimson pearl flower with the dew it accumulated on its surface. When the flower reincarnates as Baoyu's beautiful and frail cousin Lin Daiyu the protagonists are

---

[38] Conte 2007, 46.

mystified by her constant crying, but the reader, blessed with a broader vision granted by the narrator, knows that Daiyu is simply paying back the karmic debt of refreshing dew she received eons ago with voluminous tears in this life.

The central importance of prophecy in the narrative unfolding of the *Aeneid* is comparable to the role of reincarnation in Prince Shōtoku's biography. Like prophecy, reincarnation binds the protagonists to a higher purpose, a divine destiny; like prophecy, it allows them to straddle the cultural and physical gap between the world of the reference culture and the national task in the new context; and like prophecy, reincarnation is a splendid narrative ploy that spins out the respective stories in circles of repetitions with variations. How does reincarnation as a narrative strategy shape the image of our protagonist? What does it allow him to do, what image does it allow him to project?

First of all, reincarnation allows Shōtoku to be the most competent transmitter of Buddhism possible. Patriarch Huisi, himself a reincarnation of several people who had practiced Buddhism at Mt. Heng of the Nanyue mountain range, guarantees the most competent introduction of a completely foreign religion. Unlike Aeneas, who was raised in Troy and arrives in Latium with the statues of his gods and a mature knowledge of religious practice, Shōtoku is born in Japan before the advent of Buddhism. His recommendation to show reverence to a Buddha statue sent by the Korean state of Silla and his deep understanding of Buddhism appear plausible because we know he can access the memory of his former life when he was a Chinese patriarch.

This different constellation of Aeneas's and Shōtoku's roles as transmitters of religion is also reflected in the native resistance in Japan to the Buddhist statues: the native clans of the Mononobe and Nakatomi threaten that Japan's gods would become angry and jealous. There is no comparable resistance after Aeneas's arrival; quite to the contrary, Aeneas seamlessly participates in the Greek world of worship, mixed with local cults, when he meets Evander and the Arcadian people of Pallanteum. Also, unlike Aeneas, Shōtoku is not suspended between an omniscient narrator, the gods, the reader, and his own human limitations. He does not need to laboriously realize his destiny step by step (or step by misstep); he embodies manifest destiny from the moment of his birth. The linear unfolding of his destiny fits well with the straightforward annalistic format of his biography that takes the reader from his birth to after his death. Shōtoku is born under miraculous circumstances, a sage authenticated already by immaculate conception:

> The consort dreamt of a golden monk with utterly attractive features. He stood before her and said, "I wish to save the world. My wish will take temporary abode in Your abdomen." The consort asked, "Who are you?" to which the monk replied, "I am the world-saving Bodhisattva [Kannon]. My home is in the West." The consort responded, "My abdomen is filthy—how could it serve as abode to a precious person?" The monk said, "I don't mind the filth—I only hope to somehow get in close touch with the human world." The consort replied, "I dare not refuse. Your attendant follows your orders." The monk's face took on a joyful expression and leapt into her mouth. When the consort woke up with a start, it seemed as if her throat had swallowed something. The consort thought this extremely strange and

when she told the prince about it he remarked, "What you nurture inside must be a sage." Thereafter she realized she was with child.

妃夢有金色僧、容儀太艶。對妃[39]　而立、謂之曰「吾有救世之願、願暫宿后腹。」妃問「為誰？」僧曰「吾救世菩薩。家在西方。」妃答「妾腹垢穢、何宿貴人？」僧曰「吾不厭垢穢、唯望斟感人間。」妃答「不敢辭讓。左右隨命。」僧懷懽色、躍入口中。妃即驚悟、喉中猶似吞物。妃意太奇語皇子。皇子答云「你之所育、必得聖人。」自此以後、始知有娠。[40]

Prince Shōtoku's human father is Emperor Yōmei, but his spiritual lineage, the lump in the consort's throat, connects him to the Bodhisattva Kannon. Divine, immaculate conception is just one among many signs of Shōtoku's sagehood: his body emits light and even after a fresh bath he exudes a miraculous fragrance that for months perfumes the clothing of people who get close to him.[41] The strongest signs of the prince's sagehood are his sensational precocity and his supernatural self-awareness. At eight months of pregnancy words can be heard from his mother's womb; he speaks in his first year instead of blindly crying like all babies would, bows and pays obeisance to the Buddha in his second without being taught, and behaves like an adult with his fifth year. In his sixth year, when a certain Lord Ōwake, who had been sent to Paekche, returns with sutras and treatises along with a meditation master and a nun, the prince reveals the truth about his identity to the dumbfounded Emperor Bidatsu:

> "I desire to see the sutras and treatises that he brought." The Emperor asked him, "Why?" The Prince addressed the throne and said, "In the past I was in China and lived on the top of Mt. Heng. I went through several dozen lives, practicing Buddhism. As for the teaching of the Buddha, it is non-being and non-nothingness. Always strive to perform good deeds, and do not commit evil ones. That's why now I wish to see the Buddhist sutras and Bodhisattva treatises offered up by (the Korean kingdom of) Paekche." The Emperor thought this extremely strange and asked him, "You are not even six years old, and have exclusively been around me. When could you have been in China? Why do you tell such nonsense?" The Prince addressed the throne, saying, "My mind has awareness of my previous lives." The Sovereign applauded in great amazement. The various officials who heard this also voiced their admiration, applauded and thought this miraculous.

> 兒情欲見持來經論。天皇問之、何由。太子奏曰、兒昔在漢、住衡山峯。歷數十身、修行佛道。佛之垂教、非有非無、諸善奉行、諸惡莫作。故今欲見百濟所獻佛經菩薩諸論。天皇、太奇問之、汝年六歲、獨在朕前、何日在漢。何以詐言。太子奏曰、兒之前身、意之所慮。天皇、拍手大異。所聞群臣、亦大鳴舌拍手而奇。[42]

Later we learn that Prince Shōtoku has a very precise memory of a number of his previous lives, all somehow connected to Mt. Heng, the home of Huisi, the

---

[39] Using 妃 instead of the variant 己.
[40] *Shōtoku taishi denryaku*, 126. I generally follow the text in *Dai Nihon Bukkyō zensho*, vol. 71. I have also consulted Yoshida and Okuda 1995.
[41] *Shōtoku taishi denryaku*, 127.
[42] Ibid., 126.]

most important of his incarnations before becoming the Japanese prince: that he once was a person from a humble Chinese family, met a master of the Lotus sutra and decided to shave his hair and became a monk on Mt. Heng; that during the Jin Dynasty (265–420) he "lodged his soul" again into the womb of a woman from the Han clan and practiced Buddhism for more than fifty years on Mt. Heng; that during the times of Emperor Wen of the Song (420–479) he incarnated into a Liu clan, then moved on to a Gao clan, and again lived for many decades on Mt. Heng during the Qi Dynasty (479–502), the Liang (502–557), Chen (557–589), and the Zhou Dynasty of Empress Wu, which briefly interrupted the Tang (618–907).[43] After that particular life he wished "to be born in a country of the Eastern Ocean and disseminate the Buddhist Law (生 東海之國。流通佛法)."[44]

The little prince does not simply show off his supernatural identities and memory skills to impress. He takes advantage of the incredulous gasps of his bystanders and the authority his precocious performances endow him with to effect change and introduce Buddhism to the marginal, fledgling state of Japan. Thus, in his seventh year, he convinces the emperor to introduce the crucial Six Precept-Observing Days, during which the taking of life is forbidden:

> Several hundred volumes of sutras and treatises were brought from Kudara and submitted to the throne. In the second month of spring the Prince burned incense and began to read them. At one or two volumes a day, he had finished to read them all by the winter. Again he addressed the throne, saying, "The 8th, 14th, 15th, 23rd, 29th, and 30th day of each month are the Six Precept-Observing Days. On these days, Brahma and Indra descend to inspect the country's administration, so you should therefore forbid the taking of life. This is the basis of benevolence. Benevolence and sageliness are close in essence." The sovereign was greatly delighted, and handed down a proclamation to the realm, ordering to forbid the taking of life on these days.

> 百濟經論數百卷、持來上奏。春二月、太子燒香披見。日別一二卷、至冬一 遍了。又奏曰、月八日・十四日・十五日・廿三日・廿九日・三十日、是為 六齋。此日梵天・帝釋降見國政、故禁殺生。是仁之基也。仁與聖其心近 矣。天皇、大悅。下勅天下、此日令禁殺生事。[45]

The prince's deep familiarity with current Buddhist practice, gained during his many lives on Mt. Heng in China and apparently nourished by his own continued study of sutras in Japan, gives him a different view of reality: he is more omniscient than the narrator or anybody else.

He uses his supernatural knowledge to decry human acts of ignorance: for example, he claims that the Mononobe and Nakatomi clans, who strongly opposed the introduction of Buddhism and whom the prince fought in a war together with the Paekche-descendant Soga clan, do not understand the cosmic law of retribution.

---

[43] Ibid., 136.
[44] Ibid., 136.
[45] Ibid., 126.

He repeatedly treats strangers with unusual intimacy, just to declare that they are former friends from one or the other life on Mt. Heng who, like him, have moved on to other existences. And he has full command over his previous and current life: he carefully stages his death, the path toward his next transmigration, with his consort:

> The prince was in Ikaruga Palace. He ordered his consort to take a bath, and he himself took a bath. He put on a clean set of robes and said to his consort: "Tonight I will transmigrate. You can come along." The consort also put on a clean set of dress and went to sleep on the bed next to the prince. Next morning the prince and his consort did not get up for a long time. When the attendants opened the doors of the chamber they understood that he had transmigrated.

> 太子在斑鳩宮。命妃沐浴。太子亦沐浴。服新潔衣袴、語妃曰:「吾今夕遷化矣。子可共去。」妃亦服新潔衣裳、臥太子副床。明且太子并妃久而不起。左右開殿戶、乃知遷化。[46]

That he carefully times and celebrates his own and his consort's death with a ceremonious purification is just another sign of Shōtoku's supernatural sagehood. He leaves the world as miraculously as he had entered it: his body is surrounded by an overpowering fragrance, and his corpse is virtually weightless and looks alive.

The prophecies that guide Aeneas's action and the law of reincarnation that underlies Prince Shōtoku's existence are comparable narrative devices in that they articulate our protagonists' fate and guide their divine destiny. But their inverse time vectors, among other things, make the *Aeneid* and the *Abridged Biography* into very different narratives. Prophecies point Aeneas toward the future, the promised telos that motivates him to find his path toward their fulfillment. Reincarnation, in contrast, points Shōtoku toward a past existence that informs his current life as a root cause and predetermines its pattern. The most prominent difference between the providence of the Greco-Roman gods (and Roman history) and the Buddhist Law is that reincarnation is based on an impersonal cosmic law, not on the personal caprices and prejudices of an all-too-human and emotionally often immature pantheon. Although the Greco-Roman gods are cosmic forces, they also represent historical law: their sympathy for or antipathy against Aeneas depend on their previous experiences with each other and with their human heroes in the Trojan War; and, from a Virgilian standpoint, the gods give Aeneas a destiny that stands in for the historical realization of the Roman empire under Augustus. The Buddhist Law, however, is timeless, universal, and impersonal. In short: cosmic. True, Shōtoku's incarnations as a Buddhist practitioner and even patriarch in China are historically bound and so is the "cultural karma" that he gains from his previous life when he reincarnates as a Japanese prince. But his cosmic omniscience and flawless sagehood puts him not just above Aeneas's human limitations, but even beyond the omniscient, biased, and capricious Greco-Roman gods.

The *Abridged Biography* is infallible manifestation of the predictable circles of reincarnation, whereas the *Aeneid* gives us the excitingly fallible, often misleading and only gradual realization of prophecy. This makes the narrative of the *Abridged*

---

[46] Ibid., 137.

Biography look simplistic when read side by side with the complex discursive maneuvers of the *Aeneid*. But narrative complexity and literary artifice was hardly important to the authors of Shōtoku's biography. Rather, they looked for strategies that would explain the reception of Buddhism from the continent to Japan and that would at the same time create a cultural and religious founding figure who could strategically reverse the very cultural hierarchies that made the reception of Buddhism in Japan possible.

To better understand the significance and potential of the narrative device of reincarnation in Japanese literary culture it might help to look beyond solemn hagiographies to entertainment literature: vernacular tales and fiction. In the eleventh-century *Tale of Middle Councilor Hamamatsu* (*Hamamatsu Chūnagon monogatari* 浜松中納言物語) a Japanese official pays his late father a filial visit in his newly reincarnated form as a young Chinese prince. Age and cultural hierarchies are reversed as Japan is shown as civilized, elaborate, complex and China as unsophisticated, rough, and simple; and distinctions between China and Japan are leveled out as Chinese women recite not just Sino-Japanese kanshi, but even Japanese waka—a wonderful wishful reversal of the mainstream cultural flow from China to Japan.[47]

Different as they might be, prophecy and reincarnation launch our protagonists on the paths to their national destiny in equal fashion. Now, what are the core qualities that Aeneas and Shōtoku bring to their respective tasks?

4. City-Building

One of Aeneas's most prominent character traits is his *pietas*, his sense of duty and devotion. Although already ancient authors pointed out impious aspects of Aeneas's behavior, his sense of duty has become proverbial and has received abundant critical attention.[48] Another prominent aspect of Aeneas's profile is his skill—and obsessive desire—to found and build cities. As we saw above, his achievement as a city-builder is mentioned in the opening lines of the epic, although the *Aeneid* ends before he gets the chance to found Lavinium. Scholars have connected the motif of city-founding to legends surrounding the Great Greek colonization of the Mediterranean from the eighth century BCE onward, which, via the Homeric epic, made it into the world of the *Aeneid*.

The affinity between the genre of epic and cities is well known—already the Mesopotamian *Epic of Gilgamesh*, which arguably belongs to a broader Mediterranean epic tradition, focuses on one hero—King Gilgamesh of Uruk—and his city. And a number of heroes of the Trojan War are associated with the foundation of cities in Italy: Diomedes from Argos later founded Arpi, Sipontum, Canusium, Benevent, Venusia, Venagrum, and Aequum Tuticum; Philoctetes, who had been abandoned on the island of Lemnos when his snake bite became

---

[47] For a more detailed discussion of this tale see Chapter 1 of Atsuko Sakaki's groundbreaking book Sakaki 2006.

[48] For classical sources critical of Aeneas's piety see Chiappinelli 2007. On the significance and reception of Aeneas's *pietas* see Garrison 1992.

pungent, but is rescued in the tenth year of the Trojan War and ultimately kills Paris, supposedly founded Petelia, Krimisa, and Chone in southern Italy; Idomeneus, leader of the Cretan contingent against Troy, settled Uria and Castrum Minervae on the east coast of southern Italy, and Epeios, the architect of the wooden horse, is associated with the foundation of Pisae in northern Etruria.[49]

The motif of the building and destruction of cities is prominent already in the Homeric world, but it is particularly poignant in the *Aeneid* because it resonates so obviously with Augustus's feverish building program that resulted in the emperor's reported bragging that he found a city of bricks and left a city of marble. James Morwood has listed parallels between descriptions of buildings in the *Aeneid* and Augustus's building and restoration activities not just in Rome, but also in Cumae and Actium.[50] Reflecting on the significance of this motif, he argues that Virgil intended to draw attention to three founders of Rome's grandeur: Aeneas, founder of the Roman race; Romulus, founder of Rome proper; and Augustus, founder of imperial Rome. This is certainly indisputable, but we might want to press our quest for understanding the significance of the city-building motif in the *Aeneid* even further and ask: What does it mean that the Augustan hero Aeneas in Virgil's epic is obsessed with city-building? That he marks out city walls, gives laws, and founds institutions at any possible occasion and is *not* a poet or philosopher—Greek models of entitlement to social or political leadership? That he does not feature as a hero of writing, though perhaps not illiterate? That for the sophisticated and highly literate Virgil and his audience the relative absence of references to Aeneas as a reader or writer was unproblematic and acceptable?

Let us examine a few high points of Aeneas's obsession with city-building and see how the motif unfolds in the *Aeneid* before returning to these suggestive questions. Hardly has Aeneas left Troy and headed along the Asian coast straight up north to Thrace with his household gods, father, son, and companions that he attempts to found his first city. This area, formerly ruled by a certain Lycurgus, was one of Troy's allies, with "allied household gods" (*socii Penates*): "...I landed, set my first walls / On the curving shore, and shaped a name from mine, / 'Aeneas' Town'—but fate was hostile here."[51] Here Aeneas is not shy to tell Queen Dido, to whom he recounts his trials between the flight from Troy to the arrival in Carthage, of his first failed attempt at city-building, although he knows at this point that fate had other things in store. Building the walls, naming the city—almost pretentiously—after himself all seems deceptively easy, but a terrifying omen soon presses Aeneas on to new shores: when he tries to collect boughs to decorate the sacrificial altar, dark blood oozes from the roots of the brush and the ghost of a fellow Trojan, Polydorus, who was raised in Thrace but murdered by the Thracians when the victorious Greek fleet passed by after the fall of Troy, appears from his grave mound and tells of his gruesome

[49] Hillen 2003, 46–49. In *Fasti* 4.64–80 Ovid lists famous examples of various Greek foundations of cities on Italian soil, to show that Italy was nothing but Greater Greece.
[50] Morwood 1991, 218–21.
[51] *Aeneid* 3.16–18. Ruden 2008, 48–49. *...feror huc et litore curuo / moenia prima loco fatis ingressus iniquis / Aeneadasque meo nomen de nomine fingo.*

fate. Terrified, Aeneas convenes the first symbolic meeting of a senate-like council of elders to take a collective decision in Roman Republican fashion:

> ... When I'd stopped quaking,
> I told our leaders—first of all my father—
> About the omen here and sought advice.
> They said that we must sail with the south wind
> And leave this evil land where guests were outraged.[52]

The first attempt at founding a city is ill-fated, because the Thracian soil is cursed with the bloody aftermath of the Trojan War, not ready to become the site of a new foundation. The party continues its flight, finds temporary shelter in Delos, and receives the ambiguous prophecy to "seek out their ancient mother," which, as we saw, sends the company erroneously off to Crete, which Anchises wrongly identifies as the homeland of the Trojan ancestor. They arrive swiftly in Crete and Aeneas goes to work with great enthusiasm:

> Greedy for work on yearned-for Pergama—
> A welcome name—I urged my race to love
> The homes and fill the citadel with rooftops.
> The ships were on the shore and almost dry,
> Marriage and farming occupied the young,
> Laws and allotments me; when suddenly
> That sky rained wretched, rotting sickness on us.
> The trees and fields grew only death that year.[53]

The second city founding is equally unsuccessful and partly complementary to the first. Aeneas has learnt that hastily drawing up city walls and naming a city after himself ("*nomen de nomine*") is too simple; he now chooses the *cognomen* of his home city Troy: Pergamum, the name of the Trojan citadel. Also, Virgil makes this not a city of the elite—the proto-senate featuring in his first city-building adventure—but of the people. Aeneas encourages agriculture and the building of homes and hearths, and he promotes weddings, perhaps a hint at Augustus's reforms of agriculture and marital laws. This time Aeneas's attempt to build a city is not haunted by history—the dark blood and ghost of Polydorus—but by providence—the curse of a plague striking down from the sky. Aeneas understands this sign from the gods and the party hastily moves on.

As Aeneas's ships get closer to Italy and he gradually understands the will of the gods from further prophecies, his attempts at founding cities stop. Instead, we see him observe and evaluate recently founded cities he encounters along the way in preparation for his own future community.

---

[52] *Aeneid* 3.132–39. Ruden 2008, 52. ... *postquam pavor ossa reliquit, / delectos populi ad proceres primumque parentem / monstra deum refero et, quae sit sententia, posco. / omnibus idem animus, scelerata excedere terra, / linqui pollutum hospitium et dare classibus Austros.*

[53] *Aeneid* 3.132–39. Ruden 2008, 52. *ergo avidus muros optatae molior urbis / Pergameamque voco, et laetam cognomine gentem / hortor amare focos arcemque attollere tectis. / iamque fere sicco subductae litore puppes; / conubiis arvisque novis operata iuventus, / iura domosque dabam: subito cum tabida membris, / corrupto caeli tractu, miserandaque venit / arboribusque satisque lues et letifer annus.*

Buthrotum of Epirus, on the northwestern coast of Greece, leaves Aeneas to wonder whether an imitation of Troy—be it in name or reality—is ultimately desirable. He meets face to face with the tragic Trojan past, since the city is ruled by nobody other than Andromache, wife of Hector, and Helenus, another of Priam's sons and thus her brother-in-law. Andromache is lucky to be married to a Trojan again, after being forced into marriage with the Greek Neoptolemus (or Pyrrhus), the son of the very Achilles who killed her husband. The visit at Buthrotum is filled with sweet nostalgia, but also the bitter realization that this is in many ways a wrong Troy.

> Now I approached a little Troy, a tower
> Shaped like the great one, and a dry stream, 'Xanthus.'
> I kissed the threshold of a 'Scaean Gate.'
> My Trojans too enjoyed their kindred city.[54]

The sight of scenic elements of Troy and the welcome by fellow survivors of the Trojan War is deeply moving, but its queen has been raped by war and forcibly married to the son of the very Greek hero who killed her husband. The city is small, a "simulated," fake miniature (*simulata*), a desperate attempt to mimic what has been irretrievably lost: the mighty towers, the impressive Xanthus, reduced here to an arid brook, the Scaean Gate. The "second Troy" that Aeneas is seeking and Augustus will realize to its fullest will be the opposite: monumental and unprecedented, not a nostalgic copy of a lost homeland built by war victims, but a uniquely imposing new creation of victors.[55]

Although Buthrotum is a violated, reduced remnant of Troy's former splendor, it is here that Aeneas receives one of the longest and most explicitly reassuring prophecies of his path ahead. Helenus's prophecy charts the crucial transition from Greece and Epirus to Italy and Latium. Unlike previous prophecies that had mystified Aeneas's party with enigmatic innuendos, it is an explicit travel description, spelling out the dangers along the way, such as hostile Greeks or the monsters Scylla and Charybdis, and sending the hero off to the next checkpoint, Cumae's Sibyl, for more detailed prophecies on the wars Aeneas will have to face in Latium.

The departure from Epirus is a last, dramatic moment of sharing in his Trojan past, before Aeneas moves on to become a more distinctly Italic hero. Andromache and Aeneas part with direct comparisons of their fates and cities. Andromache sees her dead son in Ascanius: "You are the only image of Astyanax / Left to me—with his hands and his expressions / And eyes; he'd be at boyhood's end, like you."[56] Just as the city is a "simulated Troy," Ascanius is a living trace, an *imago*, of Hector's son. In response, Aeneas points to their common fate and

---

[54] *Aeneid* 3.349–52. Ruden 2008, 58. *procedo et parvam Troiam simulataque magnis / Pergama et arentem Xanthi cognomine rivum / adgnosco, Scaeaeque amplector limina portae. /nec non et Teucri socia simul urbe fruuntur.*

[55] With the *Aeneid* Virgil linked the image of Buthrotum firmly to Troy, to the foundation history of Rome, but also to Augustan Rome, as it featured as a counterpart to Augustus's city of Nicopolis near Actium, the site of Octavian's final decisive victory. See Hansen 2011.

[56] *Aeneid* 3.489–91. Ruden 2008, 62. *o mihi sola mei super Astyanactis imago. / sic oculos, sic ille manus, sic ora ferebat; / et nunc aequali tecum pubesceret aevo.*

promises to unite his purpose of a second Troy and their purpose of a little Troy into one:

> Be happy, since your destiny is finished.
> We are called on to one and then another.
> You have your peace: no ocean field to plow,
> No land to seek that falls away from you
> Forever. You've made images of Xanthus
> And Troy with your own hands—with better omens,
> I hope, than Troy, and out of reach of Greeks.
> And if I ever come to Tiber's country
> And see the ramparts granted to my people,
> We'll make Epirus and its neighbor Italy,
> Which share a history and a founder too—
> Dardanus—brothers in their souls: we'll make
> A single Troy. Our heirs must see to this.[57]

If Little Troy looked reduced upon arrival, it fills Aeneas with some envy upon his departure. *Fortuna peracta!* Their destiny is already finished, they have their images and replica (*effigies*) of Troy in a more sheltered place than the original Troy, while Aeneas has yet to realize his. The promised pact between little and future second Troy will yield "a single Troy" joined by the same ancestor, by common fate, and pragmatic political alliance. Aeneas proves himself here as a builder of city alliances; and the pact he seals with Andromache and his Trojan past allows him to move on more swiftly to his Italic future.

This becomes clear with the next city-building project he encounters along the way to Italy (and almost joins for good): Dido's Carthage. Dido had fled the Phoenician city of Tyrus and founded the city of Carthage after her oppressive brother, king Pygmalion, killed her husband Sychaeus. When Aeneas and Achates climb a steep hill to take a first look at the city, Venus shrouds them in mist so that nobody will become aware of the strangers' presence. They see an enterprising people devoted to building their city and its institutions:

> Aeneas was amazed at those great structures
> Where huts had been: the gates, paved roads—the hubbub!
> Some Tyrians feverishly laid out long walls
> Or rolled rocks in to raise the citadel;
> Others chose sites and bordered them with trenches.
> Laws, offices, a sacred senate formed.
> A port was being dug, the high foundations

---

[57] *Aeneid* 3.493–505. Ruden 2008, 62–63. '*vivite felices, quibus est fortuna peracta / iam sua; nos alia ex aliis in fata vocamur. / vobis parta quies; nullum maris aequor arandum, / arva neque Ausoniae semper cedentia retro / quaerenda. effigiem Xanthi Troiamque videtis, / quam vestrae fecere manus, melioribus, opto, / auspiciis, et quae fuerit minus obvia Grais. / si quando Thybrim vicinaque Thybridis arva / intraro gentique meae data moenia cernam, / cognatas urbes olim populosque propinquos, / Epiro Hesperiam, quibus idem Dardanus auctor / atque idem casus, unam faciemus utramque / Troiam animis; maneat nostros ea cura nepotes.*'

Of a theater laid, great columns carved from cliffs
To ornament the stage that would be built there.. .
　"What luck they have—their walls grow high already!"
Aeneas cried, his eyes on those great roofs.[58]

Again, Aeneas envies those who are further ahead in their destiny as city build-
ers. Although this is a Phoenician city, its description sounds distinctively
Roman: Rome's political institutions are in place and the great stone columns
for the theater remind us that the first stone theaters in Rome were built during Virgil's lifetime.[59] Dido's Carthage looks civilized and imperial compared to
Evander's rustic Pallanteum that Aeneas will encounter on the site of the future
Rome. Rather than only being counter-images of each other as is often pointed
out,[60] Evander's huts on the Palatine and Dido's city of stone and refinement incidentally also represent two faces of Rome: the pristine simplicity and frugality
of old Rome with its values of restraint and the spectacular splendor that Rome
gained during the early empire.

Carthage's imperial touch moves Aeneas clearly toward his Roman future.
True, the reliefs in the Juno temple located in the grove above the city, where
he meets Dido for the first time, take Aeneas back to the Trojan War, but note
that unlike with Buthrotum, where Aeneas met some of the actual players of
the Trojan War, by the time he arrives in Carthage the Trojan War has become
a monument in stone and Andromache's husband Hector an epic hero in a
frieze. In this way the friezes depicting the Trojan War can also be read as a
step away from Aeneas's past and a further, liberating step toward his Roman
destiny.

While in Carthage Aeneas is not just confused, as is so well-known, by his love
for the queen, but also by their contiguous fate as city-builders. (see Figure 4.1)

This common enterprise almost has him stay in Carthage for good. When
Aeneas sees Dido for the first time she is seated in front of the temple and
is busy with typical activities associated with city-building, "giving decrees
and laws to her people (*iura dabat legesque viris*)" (*Aeneid* 1.507); and the first
words the Trojans address to the queen describe her city-founding mission
in suggestively close terms to the prophecies guiding Aeneas's destiny: "Your
highness, we poor Trojans plead with you: / Jove let you found a city and bring
justice / To lawless tribes…"[61] Encouraged by this congeniality in fate, the
queen makes an intriguing offer. She will either help the Trojans reach their

---

[58] *Aeneid* 1.421–29 and 437–38. Ruden 2008, 13–14. *Miratur molem Aeneas, magalia quondam, / miratur
portas strepitumque et strata viarum. / Instant ardentes Tyrii, pars ducere muros, / molirique arcem
et manibus subvolvere saxa, / pars optare locum tecto et concludere sulco; / iura magistratusque legunt
sanctumque senatum; / hic portus alii effodiunt, hic alta theatri / fundamenta locant alii, immanisque
columnas / rupibus excidunt, scaenis decora apta futuris/…/ "o fortunati, quorum iam moenia surgunt!"
Aeneas ait et fastigia suspicit urbis.*
[59] Morwood points out that Hannibal's Carthage was also governed by a senate and had artificial
harbors, but he also emphasizes that Dido's Carthage "belongs very much to the Roman world of
Virgil's day." Morwood 1991, 213.
[60] See for example Gransden 1976, 123.
[61] *Aeneid* 1.522–24. Ruden 2008, 16. *o regina, novam cui condere Iuppiter urbem / iustitiaque dedit gentes
frenare superbas, / Troes te miseri…/ oramus.*

FIGURE 4.1 *Aeneas and the Building of Carthage*
Vergilius Vaticanus, early 5th century. Vat.lat.3225.F 13recto © Biblioteca Apostolica
Vaticana, Rome.

promised Hesperia and found their own city or she wants them to share in the
building of Carthage:

> To Saturn's fields, the great lands of the West,
> Or the kingdom of Acestes next to Eryx[62],
> I'll send you off secure and well-supplied.
> Or would you settle here and share my kingdom?
> This town I found is yours too. Land your ships.
> To me, you will be equal to my own.[63]

For quite some time Aeneas seems to settle for joint city-building rather than
for his own destiny and the reader begins to worry how he will reach his telos after

---

[62] The Sicilian Eryx, where the fellow Trojan Acestes rules, is the next port of call after Aeneas leaves
Carthage. This is where Aeneas founds a city to accommodate the frail and elderly Trojans and
celebrates the funeral games for Anchises.
[63] *Aeneid* 1.569–74. Ruden 2008, 17. *Seu vos Hesperiam magnam Saturniaque arva, / sive Erycis
finis regemque optatis Acesten, / auxilio tutos dimittam opibusque iuvabo. / voltis et his mecum
pariter considere regnis? / urbem quam statuo vestra est; subducite navis; / Tros Tyriusque mihi
nullo discrimine agetur.*

all. Finally Mercury, sent by worrying Jove, finds Aeneas engaged in building towers and new houses. The divine messenger lashes out at him:

> ... You, so now you lay
> foundation stones for the soaring walls of Carthage!
> Building her gorgeous city, doting on your wife.
> Blind to your own realm, oblivious to your fate!
> The King of the Gods, whose power sways earth and sky—
> he is the one who sends me down from brilliant Olympus,
> bearing commands for you through the racing winds.
> What are you plotting now?
> Wasting time in Libya—what hope misleads you so?[64]

The most damning verbs Mercury hurls at Aeneas's feet are cognates of *struere*, "to build, to plot." Why does he "build up" (*exstruis*) a beautiful city for his wife, and what is he "plotting" (*struis*) now, wasting his time? The very quality of Aeneas, city- and community-building, becomes a weakness if applied to the wrong place and people.

The only city Aeneas is allowed to found with the blessings of the gods before reaching Latium is Acesta (Segesta) in Sicily. There are practical reasons: While the men celebrate the funeral games for Anchises Juno instigates the Trojan women to burn the ships so that they can finally settle down and found a Trojan city. Encouraged by the aged Nautes and an apparition of Anchises, Aeneas decides to found a "city of mercy" where the elderly Trojans can find peace, while he moves on with the young and strong in his party to face the challenging wars that await the Trojans in Latium. There are also religious reasons: since Anchises dies before they reach Latium, Aeneas must leave his father's tomb behind. In addition to founding Acesta and entrusting it to Acestes, a fellow Trojan who had previously settled in the area and hosts Aeneas's party when they pass by, Aeneas establishes a temple for his mother Venus and a sacred precinct next to his father's tomb. He assigns a priest to the tomb, so that Anchises's gravesite is not left by the wayside but tended for by a community consisting of compatriots.

City-building is the most prominent activity Aeneas engages in wherever he goes. At first, he is eager to found his city on every occasion. Even as Aeneas's city-building instinct diminishes, as he understands better where exactly Jove wants him to found his city, city-building stays the guiding thread that leads him from one place to another, from his old home to his new home: whether he is touched by Little Troy, contributes to Dido's city building, or authorizes a city for the elderly Trojans near the gravesite of his father, city-building stays a consistent motif that allows the reader to see Aeneas change from a defeated Trojan prince caught in a Greek world of traumatic memory into a victorious Roman hero who comes to gradually understand, reach, and inhabit his new home.

---

[64] *Aeneid* 4.265–71. ... 'tu nunc Karthaginis altae / fundamenta locas pulchramque uxorius urbem / exstruis? heu, regni rerumque oblite tuarum! / ipse deum tibi me claro demittit Olympo / regnator, caelum et terras qui numine torquet; / ipse haec ferre iubet celeris mandata per auras. / quid struis? aut qua spe Libycis teris otia terris? To better highlight my argument here I use Robert Fagles's translation. Fagles 2006, 136–37.

5. Literacy

Aeneas's tireless attempts at city-building constitute a central *leitmotif* of the *Aeneid*, just as the theme of literacy dominates Prince Shōtoku's image.[65] The prince is a supreme reader and creator of signs, a master of "literacy" in the broadest sense. Central to the understanding of signs in premodern East Asia was the concept of "pattern" (Ch. *wen*, J. *bun* 文), whose development in early Japan we explored through key texts in Chapters 2 and 3. Shōtoku is expert in interpreting the patterns of heaven, earth, and mankind (Ch. *tian di ren* 天地人), an all-encompassing cosmic triad that ultimately went back to the *Classic of Changes* and cosmological debates in Masters Texts of China's Warring States Period (403–221 BCE). As a young boy he explains astronomical phenomena to the dumfounded emperor, revealing his expertise in "heavenly patterns" (*Shōtoku taishi denryaku*, 127). Later he analyzes the occurrence of an earthquake based on Yin-Yang cosmology, evidence of his understanding of "earthly patterns" (131). He also shows himself an expert physiognomist, reading the emperor's body patterns. (129).

Shōtoku's most brilliant expertise, which is particularly highlighted in the *Abridged Biography* but also characterizes him in almost all other sources, is in the area of "human pattern." This includes his precocious command of proper ritual behavior: he amazes the court when he performs ritual postures with the maturity of an adult at age four (126). It also encompasses his building of political institutions: he reputedly was the first to set up the system of twelve court ranks, which became the backbone of the imperial court administration. But the heart piece of his expertise lies in a narrower, most distinguished type of "human pattern": textual expertise. Episodes showcasing various forms of his literacy dot the biography. His career as a master of calligraphy starts at age four:

> In Autumn in the ninth month the prince said to his nurses, "I should practice writing. Why don't you bring me brush and ink?" The nurses consulted the crown prince [Shōtoku's father, the later Emperor Yōmei], who gave him an ornate brush and a calligraphy manual. Every day he would practice a thousand characters. Three years later he studied the calligraphy of Wang Xizhi (ca. 303–361) and had already attained its "boniness" and "full body." He made his brush flow like lightning, and people at the time found it truly extraordinary.

秋八月、太子語嬭母曰「小子須習文書。何不持來筆墨耶」嬭母諮皇子、即賜文筆書法。日別習書數千字。三年以後、學王右軍書、既得骨體、流筆如電。時人大異。[66]

This time the prince's age is fairly close to when Heian boys would have started with basic calligraphy training and is not set at a supernaturally precocious age. What is, however, supernatural is that the little prince requests calligraphy training, that there is no teacher beside him, and that within three years he masters the style of Wang Xizhi, one of the most revered Chinese models for calligraphy

---

[65] For further treatment of this theme see Lurie [Unpublished paper].
[66] *Shōtoku taishi denryaku*, 126.

FIGURE 4.2 *Prince Shōtoku Lecturing on the* Lion's Roar Sutra
Kamakura Period, thirteenth century. Hankyūji, Hyōgo Prefecture, Japan © Nara
National Museum.

in East Asia. The little prince knows what he needs to learn and merely requests
the resources necessary for his self-education—ink, brush, and a calligraphy text-
book with models for imitation. Here, as throughout the biography, there is a
conscious erasure of authority figures from whom Shōtoku would have learnt,
further emphasizing his self-contained sagehood and the layers of Chinese karma
and superior learning the young prince has under his Japanese skin.

Traditional wisdom regards Shōtoku as the first "author" in Japanese history.
He allegedly wrote a foundational text of statecraft, the so-called "Seventeen Article
Code of Conduct (*Jūshichijō kenpō* 十七条憲法), while serving as regent to his aunt,
Empress Suiko (r. 592–628). It outlines rules for virtuous government officials,
freely mixing concepts and phrases mainly from Confucian, Legalist, and Buddhist
texts. He is an expert interpreter of Buddhist sutras—we saw him above requesting
to examine the sutras a Japanese envoy brought from Paekche and deploying the
knowledge he derives from their systematic study to introduce new policies, such as
rules against killing. Even more importantly, he became famous as a sutra commentator and author of "The Three Sutra Commentaries" (*Sangyōgisho* 三経義疏): one
on the *Lotus sutra*, most famous since it is a central text of Tendai Buddhism, one on

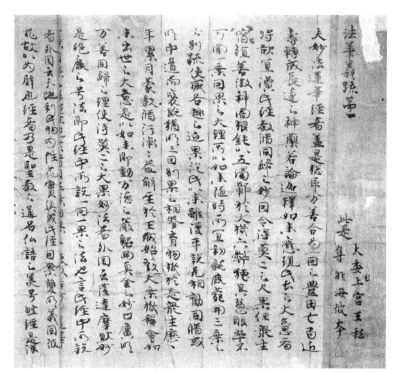

FIGURE 4.3 *Commentary on the* Lotus Sutra *attributed to Prince Shōtoku*
Asuka Period, early seventh century. © Imperial Household Agency, Tokyo.

the *Lion's Roar Sutra* and one on the *Vimalakirti Sutra*.[67] In the *Abridged Biography* Shōtoku features repeatedly as careful reader of sutras, as lecturer about them at court, and as author of these sutra commentaries.

The episode about the *Lotus Sutra commentary* in the *Abridged Biography* enables the authors to show Shōtoku as a facilitator of East Asian diplomacy, and to tell a bold tale of cultural reversal of the customary flow from China to the cultural periphery, Japan. To briefly sum up the chain of events: When collating a copy of the *Lotus Sutra* the prince proclaims he needs the sutra copy he used in China when he was Huisi, because all copies outside China are missing one particular character of the text. Shōtoku therefore sends a certain Ono no Imoko, whom we know as historical figure and ambassador to China from other sources—and instructs him to collect the copy from his former life. Shōtoku helps draft the diplomatic letter for the Sui Emperor—yet another specialized type of literacy—and Imoko leaves. The following year, 608, Shōtoku goes into a week-long trance in the "Dream Hall" (*yumedono* 夢殿) of his residence. He reemerges with a sutra copy that contains the missing

---

[67] For an introduction to the issues surrounding the sutra commentaries see Nakamura 1992, 157–92.

character. Although Imoko had collected a sutra and other objects the prince owned when he was Huisi from monks who still knew him on Mt. Heng, Shōtoku knows that the sutra he brought was the wrong one. After a second trip to China Imoko reports that the monks at Mt. Heng saw the prince flying down from the sky in a blue dragon chariot, flanked by five hundred servants, retrieving Huisi's sutra copy and leaving his own *Lotus Sutra* commentary in its stead. Shōtoku revises his commentary based on Huisi's copy and sends it off to Korea with a priest from Koguryo. The prince's text has now reached both China and Korea.

This fantastic tale of the flow of people and texts between Japan and the continent does not appear in previous accounts of Shōtoku's life and can be read as an attempt to assert the independence of Japan's religious authority from China. By the time the *Abridged Biography* was written in the tenth century a Japanese monk, Ensai 圓載 (d. 877), had indeed brought a manuscript of the *Lotus Sutra Commentary* to a monastery on Mt. Tiantai.[68] Whether Ensai's act inspired the episode in the *Abridged Biography* or not is unclear, but Shōtoku's biography shares with Ensai the desire to proudly offer the Chinese something that could testify to Japan's indigenous religious sophistication.

Considering that Shōtoku was famous first and foremost as the founder of Buddhism in Japan it is no surprise that the central episode of literacy in the *Abridged Biography* throws limelight on his activities as an exegete and commentator of Buddhist sutras. But there is yet another form of Shōtoku's expertise in "human pattern," and writing in particular, that the *Abridged Biography* highlights in unusual ways: Shōtoku as sponsor of court poetry banquets.

On the first day of the snake, third month, the Prince addressed the throne, saying, "Today is the day when the Tang emperor sponsors a drinking event." He then summoned the court from the great ministers on down, and sponsored a winding stream banquet. Inviting virtuous monks from vassal states and literati from China and Paekche, he had them compose Chinese-style poems. He asked the throne to bestow rewards based on distinction. In the fall, the ninth month, he again set out a great banquet at the Prince's palace. The emperor graced the event with his presence. All the ministers presented poems of this land.

三月上巳、太子奏曰、今日唐家天子賜飲之日也。即召大臣已下、賜曲水之宴。請諸蕃大徳并漢百濟好文之士、令裁詩。奏賜祿有差。秋九月、太子之宮、復設大宴。天皇臨而御之。群臣各上當土之歌。[69]

Shōtoku appears here as the founder of two cardinal annual festivals in spring and autumn that included poetry banquets: the third day of the third month, the so-called "Winding Stream Banquet" when courtiers floated cups with wine down little artificial stream sceneries, and the ninth day of the ninth month, the "Double Ninth Festival." Eighth-century portrayals of the prince did not mention the prince's interest in poetry and belles lettres: The *Chronicles of Japan* of 720 lacks any reference to it and the Preface to the *Florilegium of Cherished Airs* (*Kaifūsō*

---

[68] Groner 2007, 23.
[69] *Shōtoku taishi denryaku*, 137.

懐風藻) of 751 even denied Shōtoku the role of a supporter of belles lettres, claiming that he was busy promoting Buddhism and had no time for such trivial pursuits. But by the early tenth century, poetry events under imperial auspices had become so central to the vision of the court and the emperor's role in it that it was certainly desirable to give the prince just one more, probably the most "contemporary," edge of literacy that was added in the Heian Period.

5. Conclusion

In the end we are left with the fundamental question: Why was literacy and textual expertise so important for a Japanese national hero, but not as crucial for a Roman one? Apparently there was little advantage in emphasizing Aeneas's literacy and textual expertise, even for an Augustan author who inhabited and came to define the standards of highest literary culture, whereas it was highly profitable to make a Japanese figure of state foundation into a brilliant writing specialist. From a Chinese perspective the technology of writing was not just a human skill that enabled the beginning of history and civilization, but a cosmic manifestation of nature as expressed through "human pattern." Since the Han Dynasty (206 BCE-220 CE), legends became popular that credited the legendary sage Fu Xi or Cang Jie—in some accounts the scribe of the Yellow Emperor who stands at the beginning of Chinese history in Sima Qian's *Historical Records*—with the invention of writing. They emphasized that writing was actually not invented, but simply "discovered" in natural patterns such as the tracks of birds, and their imitation adapted to human usage. As we saw in Chapter 2, the earliest Japanese accounts of the development of literature downplayed the importation of the technology of writing from China by relying on Chinese arguments that "naturalized" writing and claimed for Japan a literacy *avant la lettre,* or, as I called it, a "hexagrammatic literacy." In this view writing was cosmic and universal, not historically and culturally conditioned. It was thus a highly attractive attribute for anyone in East Asia who wanted to claim universal political rule.

Beyond its appeal for state ideology, writing had a crucial practical function in the "Sinographic sphere" that defined East Asian interstate politics. The use of Chinese characters and protocol of Chinese administrative, religious, and literary genres allowed the Japanese access to the continuous world of East Asian literacy and culture. Oral communication between the elites of China, Japan, the various Korean states, and Vietnam was typically impossible except for rather rare individuals who were multilingual and knew several vernaculars. Usually, people communicated through "brush talk," writing their messages up in literary Chinese and passing sheets of paper back and forth in the fashion of an oral conversation.

Lastly, literacy had intimate connections to the most important venues of social and political success in early Japan. Literacy here does *not* mean the basic mastery of a certain number of Chinese characters, which modern alphabetization campaigns have aimed for. In premodern East Asian elite culture it referred to the mastery of a great variety of literacies, each defined by genre and social context. Shōtoku embodies the most central forms of literacy: the mastery of diplomatic and administrative genres, philological expertise and Buddhist exegesis, composition of poetry at court events, and, not to forget, expert calligraphy.

In contrast, the writing system and its skillful manipulation was probably not as defining a cultural concept for Greco-Roman elite culture. Unlike with China, one of the few civilizations that invented script, Greek writing was borrowed from the Phoenician script and was derivative. Partly for that reason, the Greeks were self-conscious vis-à-vis their writing system, because they were acutely aware of the radically different logographic writing systems of the older Egyptian and Mesopotamian civilizations. This led to two contradictory perceptions of writing: on the one hand authors such as Plato and Herodotus acknowledged that the most powerful type of writing was not to be found in alphabetic writing but in "signs" that were mysteriously potent and "sacred," in short: "hieroglyphs." Deborah Steiner has even argued that this ambivalent form of admiration helped the Greeks associate potent writing and textuality with Oriental despotic regimes—thus ultimately devaluing logographic writing—and asserting their own, phonographic literacy and an emphasis on the oral.[70] Parallel to this ambivalent admiration there developed a critique of writing, most famously articulated in Plato's *Phaedrus,* which saw writing as the poor trace of the fullness of the human voice and mind and celebrated the living word over textuality, phonocentrism over graphocentrism. Denis Feeney wittily detects this lingering Platonic prejudice in modern scholarship:

> Much modern theory is saturated with nostalgia for some lost plenitude, a time of grace and wholeness before the invasion of all kinds of serpents (language, gender, class, culture, self-consciousness). Among Hellenists who are inclined this way, the favoured candidate for serpent is writing, held to mark the fall from fullness of presence, shared community and immediacy of communication, as an oral-performance culture inexorably gives way to the dusty culture of the book.[71]

Without touching upon the vast theoretical debates around orality and phonocentrism that Plato's legacy has triggered all the way up to postmodern theory-making, it is safe to say for our purposes here that a scribe and master of literacy would have made for a less effective national hero in the Greco-Roman context. More specifically for the *Aeneid*, writing was no central attribute of our hero, because it had little importance in its model text, the Homeric epic. Barry Powell reminds us how strange, in fact, the absence of writing from Homer's really is, although we tend to take it for granted in both Homer and Virgil. As he points out, writing and written documents play a key role in the literatures of Egypt and the Near East and scribes and writers are often central protagonists. Unlike Feeney's Hellenists who revel in the prelapsarian world of oral community before writing, Powell sees the virtual absence of writing in the Homeric epic as a testimony to Hellenic provincialism—the Greek epic poets almost as primitive in comparison to their Near Eastern and Egyptian sophisticated, literate colleagues.[72] Powell's views on Homer and literacy do certainly not represent mainstream opinion, but they are worth considering, especially because they come from someone belonging to the

---

[70] Steiner 1994.

[71] Feeney 2000, 9.

[72] Powell 2002, 8–10. It is interesting to note that, while Virgil respects this Homeric convention, Naevius (ca. 270-201 BCE) in his *Punic War (Bellum Punicum)* violates it by having Venus give books of prophecy to Anchises. *Fragmenta Poetarum Latinorum,* fr. 4.

small minority of classicists who read contemporary nonalphabetic languages and literatures such as Egyptian and are able to place the Greek tradition in a broader Mediterranean and Middle Eastern context.

Virgil inherited the oral framework of Greek epic and the "aesthetics of presence," as Michèle Lowrie has called it, which came with it. It starts already with the first verb in the Aeneid, "Wars and a man I sing (*cano*)." As Lowrie notes, this might be the most famous speech act in Roman literature and yet, we know that it is literally wrong and that Virgil wrote or dictated, but certainly did not sing.[73] But Homer and early Greek epic poets did; and the archaic topic of Virgil's epic made song obviously into the preferred medium. Lowrie tries to rescue the very few clues to writing in the *Aeneid*: prophecies uttered by the Parcae and Jove about Aeneas's and Rome's fate are read from book rolls.[74] Also, at Actium Aeneas has a shield taken from the Greek warrior Abas nailed to the gates with an inscription on it (*Aeneid* 3.286–88). Thus, we know that he and his fellow men to whom the inscription was addressed were probably not illiterate. Also, interestingly, Virgil "oralizes" the one explicitly literate human figure that appears in the *Aeneid*: the Sibyl of Cumae. When Helenus sends Aeneas off from Buthrotum to the Sibyl he advises Aeneas to ask the Sibyl to sing (the epic *canere*) herself and not write her oracle on leaves, as she usually does, because the wind might disturb the order of the leaves and make the oracle illegible. Although this is for a practical reason and the Sibyl usually gives her oracles in writing, which hints at a fairly literate clientele, Virgil still has Helenus vote for the oral over the written word in this particular situation. Note that, possibly in resonance with the Greeks' ambivalent admiration of oriental, sacred graphs, the Sibyl usually does not "write," but "commits her vision to words, to signs on leaves" (*foliisque notas et nomina mandat. Aeneid* 3.444). When Aeneas reaches Cumae he does as advised. Aeneas asks her not to commit her "songs" to leaves but to chant them herself (*foliis tantum ne carmina manda...ipsa canas oro Aeneid* 6.74–76). Though Aeneas is not illiterate, there lingers here nostalgia for some bygone preliterate world that gives power to song, not text. These are the few fleeting incidents in the *Aeneid* that relate to literacy. When we compare them to the biography of the full-fledged hero of literacy, Prince Shōtoku, they are of minor relevance. It is no exaggeration to say that Virgil's epic has fundamentally an a-literate—though not illiterate—framework.

Regardless of the salient differences that helped Aeneas and Prince Shōtoku "make" Rome and early Japan, they are in the end both superhumans with their own share of "humanity": Dutiful Aeneas is humane in caring for his companions and for the fate that awaits him in Latium. He is human in forsaking his home, wife, lover, and his old identity for the sake of his new home, a new imperial, Augustan Rome for which he vouches. His "city-builder" identity was a perfect allegory for Augustus's ideological and physical rebuilding of Rome after the destructive period of the civil wars and allows him to gradually transform himself from a Trojan into a Roman hero. Brush-wielding Prince Shotoku, in turn, is humanist: his acquisition and display of ever new forms of textual mastery endowed him with the most coveted ornaments of civilizing power in ancient East Asia.

---

[73] Lowrie 2009, 1–8.
[74] Ibid., 4–5.

| Rome and Kyoto
Capitals, Genres, Gender

Rome, smile on me! For you rises my opus! Citizens, grant me a fair omen, and let a bird on the right augur success for my undertaking.

Roma, fave, tibi surgit opus; date candida, cives, omina; et inceptis dextera cantet avis!

PROPERTIUS _ELEGIES_ IV.1A. 67–68

Topics for poetry: The Capital. _Kudzu_ Vines. Water burr. Horses. Hail.

歌の題は：都。葛。三秋草。駒。霰。

SEI SHŌNAGON. _THE PILLOW BOOK_ 67

AFTER LOOKING AT DEPICTIONS of Prince Shōtoku and Aeneas as icons of national identification, for whom close ties to the Chinese and Greek world were claimed, respectively, we turn now to the capital cities, Kyoto and Rome, where Shōtoku's and Aeneas's legacy were preserved and shaped. During Prince Shōtoku's time, the Asuka Period (592–710), the center of power on the Japanese archipelago was in the vicinity of Asuka, about forty miles South of Kyoto, and Kyoto had to wait another two centuries for its foundation; similarly, Aeneas only founded Lavinium, a small city in Latium named after his second wife Lavinia, and the foundation of Rome was left to his descendants. But without Kyoto and Rome, Prince Shōtoku and Aeneas would hardly have gained their characteristic historical significance.

Kyoto and Rome can undoubtedly lay claim to belonging to the most successful capital cities in Japanese and European history. Kyoto, founded as Heian-kyō, the "Capital of Peace" by Emperor Kanmu in 794, was the seat of the imperial court from 794 to 1868, when the Meiji Emperor moved the capital to Tokyo. Japanese history after the Heian Period (794–1185) consisted of complex power arrangements between warrior families, who lay claim to political power, and the imperial court, which was respected as the nation's ceremonial center. Political power shifted back and forth between the eastern region of Kantō and Kyoto in the West. The Kamakura shoguns (1185–1333) ruled from Kamakura, south of today's Tokyo, the shoguns of the Muromachi Period (1333–1568) established themselves in Kyoto and graced the city with lavish buildings and temples that continue to give the city its historic face, and from 1600 to 1868 the Tokugawa shoguns chose Edo, the later Tokyo, as their power base. Yet Kyoto remained the ceremonial center throughout and, with the Meiji Emperor making a point of moving into the castle of the former Tokugawa shoguns in Tokyo, thus marking the unification of political and ceremonial power in the figure of the emperor after centuries of dual rule, Kyoto is still a symbolic capital of sorts. Political power has once again shifted to Tokyo, where even the emperor resides now, but the Imperial Household Agency administers Kyoto's Imperial Palace, Villas, and Mausoleums, which are regularly visited by the imperial family; and coronation ceremonies are to be held in Kyoto, rather than Tokyo.[1]

Rome, by some accounts believed to have been founded in 753 BCE, is still the capital of two empires, a significantly shrunken and a still expanding one: the successor state to the Roman Empire is now a state within the European Union, most of whose territory it conquered at some point in antiquity; the Vatican City State presides over the Roman Catholic souls of the world, whose numbers, though decreasing back in Europe, are increasing in other parts of the world, such as today's China. In antiquity Rome was the undisputed capital until the foundation of Constantinople in 330 CE and the division of the empire into Eastern and Western parts following the death of Theodosius in 395 CE. From a rustic village under Romulus in the eighth century, if we believe the record, it became the ruler of the region of Latium and Central Italy by the fourth century BCE, of all of Italy by the third century BCE, and gradually the overlord of the entire Mediterranean after the second century BCE. Despite the end of the Western Roman Empire in 476, when the last Roman Emperor with the ominous name Romulus Augustulus was deposed by the northern tribesman Odoacer, Rome retained a great symbolic significance as the papal residence for the medieval emperors of the "Holy Roman Empire of the German Nation," until it reemerged after centuries of limited political importance as the national capital of a new reunited Italy in 1870. Unlike with Kyoto, which has been reduced to a ceremonial and cultural capital of sorts, Rome is again the capital and as the seat of the government of the state of Italy, confidently puts on display the complex layers of her various splendid pasts.[2]

If we escape the vigilant eyes of the guardians of national cultural heritage, we can touch the fragrant Japanese cypress pillars of the Phoenix Hall of the Byōdōin 平等院, a Buddhist temple south of Kyoto and one of the very few buildings in the former capital area that actually dates to the Heian Period (794–1185) and has not gone through cycles of destruction and complete rebuilding. We can run our fingers over what is left of the Temple of Vesta on the Forum Romanum with even

---

[1] The most multifaceted and lavish treatment of Kyoto in any Western language to date is Fiévé 2008. For a survey of Kyoto's political and cultural history see Yoshikawa 2002 and Hall 1974, 3–38. For an urban anthropology of Heian Kyoto see Nishiyama 2004. For concepts of the capital in early modern and modern Japan see Smith 1978, 45–80.
[2] A particularly vivid and perspicacious introduction to the history of Rome is Hibbert 1985. On the development of ancient Rome see Stambaugh 1988.

FIGURE 5.1 *The Cherry Tree in the Inner Imperial Palace*
Woodblock print by Utagawa Yoshiiku (1833–1904) depicting the shogun's visit at the imperial palace in 1863. © Private owner.

more impunity. Italian guards are by nature more insouciant in their protection of the past. They can afford to do so, because the times have treated more kindly Greco-Roman stone architecture than the wooden structures in China and Japan, which burnt down at regular intervals due to fire, warfare, or even arson, as it happened with one of the touristic highlights of Kyoto, the Golden Pavilion. Despite this furtive attempt to be in touch with the past, old Kyoto and Ancient Rome will always elude us. Not only because they have obviously lost any resemblance with their faces in antiquity, but because they have so selectively preserved certain aspects of the past, often through centuries of reimagination and reconstruction. Cities, especially capital cities, the miniatures of the realms they preside over, are sites of great value amplitude. Among worthless urban rubble of huts and stores, shady streets and entertainment establishments that came and went with the times, there were buildings and sites endowed with symbolic value that demanded preservation and reconstruction at all costs, at least as long as the regimes and ideologies that propagated their value lasted. These included obviously palaces of rulers and buildings of political administration as well as temples and religious sites, but also more curious elements of the cityscape.

Quite possibly, no trees on the Japanese archipelago during the Heian Period received as much veneration and care as the famous Tachibana Orange Tree (*ukon no tachibana* 右近の橘) and Cherry Tree (*sakon no sakura* 左近の桜) right and left to the entrance of the *Shishinden* 紫宸殿, the main ceremonial building of the Inner Imperial Palace, where the emperor conducted government affairs. (see Figure 5.1)

In the early chronicles and in the *Man'yōshū*, the Tachibana orange appears as a miraculous golden fruit brought from the fabled "Land of Everworld" (*tokoyo no kuni* 常世の国), realm of the immortals, at the behest of an early emperor and it was possibly associated with Korea.[3] Emperor Kanmu, the founder of Heian-kyō, had first planted a Chinese plum tree, which half a century later was replaced with a cherry tree, indicating an aesthetic shift away from Chinese precedent to a tree that during the Heian Period became the most popular and poetically most productive tree of Japan until this day.[4] The trees were reverentially cared for by the Bodyguards of the Right and the Bodyguards of the Left, respectively. They were subject to official imperial inspections, which would be followed by a banquet that included the composition of poetry at imperial command.[5] And they would be faithfully replanted each time the palace buildings burnt down, like during the reigns of Emperors Murakami (r. 946–967) and Horikawa (r. 1086–1107).

In Rome, no hut was more precious than the "Hut of Romulus" (casa Romuli), a structure on the Palatine, which according to Varro was revered by Romans at least by the third century BCE, and was located in the proximity of the Lupercal at the foot of the Palatine, where the twins Romulus and Remus were presumed to have been found. (see Figure 5.2)

It was close to the equally venerated *ficus ruminalis*, the fig tree where the basket carrying the baby boys Romulus and Remus came to rest, and where the wolf suckled the twins and prepared Romulus for his fate of founding Rome. It gained particular significance when Augustus built his palace on the Palatine and reinforced the connection between Romulus and the emperor, the mythic past and the political present. The hut was cared for by the *pontifices*, the eminent high priests in Rome, whose ancestor was nobody other than King Numa Pompilius, the successor of Romulus on the throne. Because its building material was closer to that of Japanese palaces and not to the brick and marble of Augustan Rome, the hut was repeatedly destroyed by fires, as in 12 BCE when it went up in flames because crows had dropped burning meat from some altar fire on its vulnerable straw roofing.[6] Yet as a physical symbol of the *mos maiorum*, the uncorrupted ancient Roman customs and values, it was faithfully rebuilt and was still carefully tended to until at least the fourth century CE.[7] Dionysius of Halicarnassus, a Greek writing

---

[3] For a panegyric poem on the Tachibana tree see Ōtomo no Yakamochi's "Long Poem on the Tachibana Tree"; *Man'yōshū* 18.4111–12. Cranston 1993, 464–66.
[4] For a now rather old treatment of the history of the cherry tree in Japan see Yamada 1942. Pages 27–37 deal with the palace cherry tree in the Heian Period.
[5] For a glimpse of such an event see chapter 8 "Under the Cherry Blossoms" (*Hana no en* 花の宴) of the *Tale of Genji*.
[6] Cassius Dio *Roman History* 54.29.8.
[7] For discussion of Romulus's hut in literary sources see Edwards 1996, 32–42.

FIGURE 5.2 *Remains of the casa Romuli?*
Excavations revealing eighth-century BCE foundations of hut-like structures. Palatine, Rome. © Giovanni Lattanzi/ArchArt.

in Augustan Rome, informs us that the preservation of a consciously archaic simplicity and the faithfulness to its previous form was the goal of these repeated restoration efforts:

> it is preserved holy by those who have charge of these matters; they add nothing to it to render it more stately, but if any part of it is injured, either by storms or by the lapse of time, they repair the damage and restore the hut as nearly as possible to its former condition.[8]

> ἣν φυλάττουσιν ἱερὰν οἷς τούτων ἐπιμελὲς οὐδὲν ἐπὶ τὸ σεμνότερον ἐξάγοντες, εἰ δέ τι πονήσειεν ὑπὸ χειμῶνος ἢ χρόνου τὸ λεῖπον ἐξακούμενοι καὶ τῷ πρόσθεν ἐξομοιοῦντες εἰς δύναμιν.

As an artificial icon of programmatic immutability in the urban sea of change, the hut obviously served the thirst for origins and necessary connections between the coincidence of a city and the absoluteness of a state and the ideologies that support it. Would Romulus's hut ever have been preserved if some menial Rufus had lived there? Certainly not. But it probably looked just like the humble shack of such a Rufus, even if its symbolic value was higher than almost all of the marble and gold the city amassed during centuries of military expansion and colonization.

Had the Roman Empire and the imperial cult continued until this day, the hut might indeed have survived intact and there would have been no need for

---

[8] Dionysius of Halicarnassus. *Roman Antiquities* 1.79.11. Cary 1937-50, vol. 1, 270–71.

rediscovering it. Modern excavations on the Palatine have produced a series of hut-like structures datable to the eighth century and recently archeologists even claimed to have located the Lupercal Cave, but scholarly opinion is divided on how to relate the archeological artifacts to literary sources about the early mythical history of Rome and its foundation.[9] Since the Japanese imperial institution did survive, both the Imperial Palace in Tokyo, the official residence of Emperor Akihito, and the Imperial Palace in Kyoto still have their Tachibana and Cherry Tree, although neither of them stands at the original site of the Heian Imperial Palace.

The palace trees and Romulus's hut are just two pointed examples of the exceptional value scale intrinsic to capitals, where huts and trees can simply be huts and trees and disappear in a generation, or be the Hut and the Tree, which need to be tended, restored, rebuilt, or replanted at all costs for centuries. Kyoto and Rome are thus not just elusive for what has disappeared, but for what has been preserved and how and why it has come down to us. Archeologists of the past can help us imagine urban structures that have disappeared, but as observers of the present we need to constantly remind ourselves that what we cherish as old is just another face of the present, yet more complicated than an outright modern structure, because it has accrued over time through the needs of many "presents" in constant change that we might have no or little detailed record about.

***

If we move from the physical cityscapes of capitals to their representation in literary texts, a whole new type of elusiveness comes into play. Cities are never really represented in literary texts, but strangely refracted through the literary patterns of the textual genres in which they appear. They have different faces depending on whether they feature in historical annals or epic poetry, praise paeans or biting satires, whether they are evil incarnate to the bucolic poet or the cosmopolitan playground for the poet of love elegies.[10]

The goal of this chapter is to, first, remind us how very unlike Kyoto and Ancient Rome were as capital cities of the Heian Court and Augustan Empire, respectively, and then to explore how these differences informed the writing of a few authors during two high-points of their respective literary history: eleventh-century Japan and Augustan Rome. Kyoto and Rome were both capitals of an empire, but of radically different sorts. They were both at the center of their empires, surrounded by territories and a countryside, whose image their writers shaped as a contrast to their capital experience, but the link between capital and periphery was of different nature. They were both at the center of the ideology and teleology that their political elites endowed their states with, in the grander scheme of the legitimization of rule, but this

<hr />

[9] For an overview of archaeological traces of the origins of Rome see Cornell 1995, 48–80.
[10] On images of Rome in literature see Edwards 1996 and Lowenstein 1965, 110–23. On Rome as a literary space see Woolf 2003, 203–21. Nishimura Satomi discusses various aspects of Kyoto as a literary space in Nishimura 2005.

teleology was at times, as I would like to show, inverse. And they were both the center of an empire of letters, a magnet and subject for writers who were born there or otherwise flocked to live there, but the genres through which they refracted the capital, and even the gender of the authors who wrote most extensively about it, differed.

This chapter aims to showcase those differences along two vectors: the vector of time and the vector of romance. How did Heian authors and how did Augustan authors locate the capitals they inhabited in time? With what kind of teleologies, vectors of destiny, did they endow their cities and how did the genres they chose inflect their capital visions? Out of the many possible perspectives on this question I choose two cases of particularly strong contrast: We will juxtapose visions of Rome in Virgil's *Aeneid* with visions of the capital in the *Wakan rōeishū* 和漢朗詠集 (Collection of Japanese and Chinese-style Poems for Recitation), an eleventh-century anthology of Chinese, Sino-Japanese, and Japanese poetry arranged by encyclopedic topics. In contrast to the powerful prospective teleology of Virgil's *Aeneid*, which anticipates the splendor of Augustan Rome during Virgil's lifetime, the *Wakan rōeishū* is suspended in a retrospective aesthetic of abandoned earlier capitals and a floatingly timeless vision of the Heian court painted with contrastive Chinese or Japanese brushstrokes where deemed fitting.

While the capital could be depicted with inverse time vectors, one prospective and the other retrospective or atemporal, both mid-Heian Kyoto and first-century BCE Rome were the sites of literary revolutions that were intricately connected with the urban fabric and capital culture: a new culture of romance. In tenth- and eleventh-century Kyoto the rise of vernacular prose literature culminated in masterworks of amorous psychography such as Murasaki Shikibu's *Tale of Genji*. These new tales (*monogatari* 物語) and vernacular diaries (*kana nikki* 仮名日記) were often written by women and expanded the vocabularies and registers of romance far beyond what had ever been written in Sino-Japanese genres, the so-far dominant modes of prose writing. Comparably, the rise of Latin love elegy in first-century BCE Rome made passion and romance into a proud way of life, which flew in the face of traditional Roman values of civic duty and, though having roots in Greek elegiac poetry, resulted in a distinctively Roman discourse of love. What were the rules and assumptions of this new, "vernacular" we might say in both cases, game of love? Who were the players and how do the capital sides collude in the love affairs of our writers? Again, to show range rather than equitability, we will explore romance in the respective capitals through two unlikely bedfellows: the stormy Propertius (ca. 49–16 BCE), ever hopelessly in love and tormented by his Cynthia while later in his life also singing the praises of the splendors of Rome, and Sei Shōnagon (ca. 966–1017), the subdued yet saucy lady-in-waiting of an imperial consort and author of the *Pillow Book* (*Makura no sōshi* 枕草子). No topic in this book is more accessible to our senses today than Kyoto and Rome. Let us hope that our authors can alleviate the sense of elusiveness of old Kyoto and Ancient Rome and bring us closer to their ancient incarnations.

1. Unequal Capitals

Both Japan and Augustan Rome were divinely legitimated empires that traced their lineages to the sun goddess Amaterasu and Venus, respectively. But apart from the divine sanctification of the imperial figure, which in Rome was preceded by the early kings and the Roman Republic (509–27 BCE), little was similar in these two "empires" of sorts. The portrayals of the early Roman kings in Livy's (59–17 BCE) history with their pioneering exploits of mythical proportions are not unlike the larger-than-life images of the earliest Japanese emperors in the first Japanese court chronicles, the *Record of Ancient Matters* (*Kojiki* 古事記, 712) and the *Chronicles of Japan* (*Nihon shoki* 日本書紀, 720). But the Republic, which in Livy's history was the *telos* of Rome's early development, the triumphant moment when tyrannical kings were replaced with Republican institutions, had of course no equivalent in Japan, where the eighth-century annalists, quite to the contrary, were keen on constructing a continuous imperial line reaching back to the fabled emperor *Jinmu* 神武 (traditionally dated to 660–585 BCE), the first human ruler, in order to sanction the current emperors. Livy clearly idealized the early and middle Republic, which despite its Republican institutions—the magistrates such as the consuls, praetors, aediles, and quaestors, the popular assemblies, and the most powerful assembly, the Senate—had a strongly aristocratic character.

Yet the notion of a meritocratic bureaucracy, in which officials qualify for office both through a prescribed *cursus honorum*, or rigid system of ranks, as well as through their financial and aristocratic ties, made the earlier Roman Republic not completely unlike Nara and Heian Japan. The Japanese emperor was not an absolutist ruler, but during the seventh century became the apex of the so-called *ritsuryō* 律令 system, or "statutory law system." This was an intricate government form based on Chinese legal precedents, which was built on a hierarchical rank system and an extensive imperial bureaucracy designed to apply and regulate the extensive civil and criminal law codes and the complex land allotment and taxation system. Although originally introduced as a forceful measure for political centralization during the seventh century, it also significantly limited the arbitrary power of the emperors. The architecture of the Imperial Palace complex was a living testimony to this: actually only a small part of the complex, the Inner Palace (*dairi* 内裏), was reserved for the emperor. The greater part housed the *ritsuryō* bureaucracy: the Council of State (*daijōkan* 太政官), the supreme organ of government comparable to the Senate, with its executive organs, the Controller's Office of the Right, the Lesser Counselors' Office, and the Controller's Office of the Left, and other subordinate organs of government such as the Eight Ministries, which included the Central Affairs Ministry, the Ministry of Ceremonial, the Civil Affairs Ministry, the Popular Affairs Ministry, the War Ministry, the Punishments Ministry, the Treasury Ministry, and the Imperial Household Ministry.

Right outside the main gate of the Imperial Palace was the State Academy (*daigakuryō* 大学寮), the university that was established as part of the *ritsuryō* system and where the male elites were trained in the Confucian canonical texts on which the system was predicated. The power of the emperor declined considerably since the tenth century, when one aristocratic family, the Fujiwara, managed to overrule the *ritsuryō* system and forced the emperors to accept them as "regents." This position did not exist in the legal codes and it gave those Fujiwara who held it de facto more power than the emperor; they enhanced their authority even more by seeing that their daughters married into the imperial family and produced the next generation of emperors.[11]

The Japanese government system of the Nara and Heian Periods was neither that of the Roman Republic, nor that of the Roman Empire, but had something of both.[12] Yet the most significant difference between the two states, which gave an incommensurate face to early Japan and Rome, was not their political system, but Rome's military expansion and the changes it brought to the economic networks and social fabric. Through centuries of its conquest of, first, Latium, then the Italic Peninsula, the Mediterranean, and good parts of Northern and Eastern Europe, the Roman state became highly militarized and designed to conquer and govern new territories. The military expansion had far-reaching effects on the everyday life of the inhabitants of Rome and its surroundings.[13] Peasants who were drafted into the army for long wars returned home to find their farms in dereliction; many migrated to the city and became part of the rapidly growing proletariat. In turn, urban elites grew rich from the conquests, appropriated the public land (*ager publicus*), and founded large-scale estates for whose operation they imported a large amount of slaves. The conquests changed the cityscape: gorgeous statues looted from the conquest of Hellenistic territories were inserted into Rome's proud façades,[14] lavish building programs altered the face of the city and supplied it with large-scale theaters for gladiatorial games and popular performances, and luxury goods came across continents to Rome and were sold to its wealthy citizens. The huge social disparities that resulted from the conquests led to bloody clashes: first in social wars, then slave revolts, and, by the first century BCE, civil wars.

Against the backdrop of the vertiginous scale of territorial, economic, and social changes that Rome underwent during its centuries of rapid military expansion, early Japan appears remarkably stable. It experienced a process of consolidation rather than expansion: until the twentieth century Japan did not reach beyond its archipelago and already by the fifth century CE chieftains in the Yamato region, in today's Nara Prefecture, had expanded their rule to northern Kyushu in the southwest and the Kanto plain in the northeast. By the early eighth century the

[11] For a portrayal of the geographical, social, and economic structure of Heian-Period Kyoto see McCullough 1999 and Hérail 1995. For a concise sketch of the rank system and the bureaucracy of Heian Japan see McCullough and McCullough 1980, 789–831. Morris 1969 is a vivid portrayal of the Heian world and its capital.

[12] As a multiethnic empire China makes obviously for a better comparison with Rome. See the pioneering comparative volume Scheidel 2009.

[13] For a systematic overview of Roman economic history see Scheidel, Morris and Saller 2008. For a compilation of primary sources relating to nature, motivations, and consequences of Roman imperialism see Champion 2004. For a new view of urbanization and Roman expansion that emphasizes the importance of urban, not rural, slavery see Jongman 2003.

[14] Edwards 2003b.

archipelago was under the imperial rule through a divine ruler who acted within the statutory government system and stable capital cities based on Chinese precedent were founded, replacing the previous custom to move the court upon the death of an emperor. There were a number of rebellions, internal challenges to power, and still, during the Heian Period, the Northern Frontier against the Emishi tribes 蝦夷 (also called Ezo or Ebisu 夷) was occasionally unruly and the target of expensive military campaigns.[15] But in comparison to Rome, it is fair to say that the Heian capital was literally a "Capital of Peace": all of the War Ministry's subordinate bureaus, which in Tang China had significant importance, were gradually abolished through the course of the Heian Period and were left to perform decorative tasks such as choosing the contestants for archery competitions at court.[16] If belligerence continued in Heian Japan, it was embodied in the fierce struggle over the imperial lineage, enhanced by polygyny, which had the empress, various consorts, and intimates of the emperor compete in the promotion of their sons to the role of Crown Prince. But there were few social upheavals, and city growth due to migration processes were nothing to speak of in comparison to Rome. In fact, between the ninth and the eleventh centuries Japan's population was actually shrinking due to famine and epidemics.[17] Economically, although the city planners of Kyoto had reserved large spaces in the southern part of the city east and west of the central city axis, Suzaku Avenue, for the "Eastern" and "Western Market," Kyoto's markets were modest and never played a significant role in the state's economy, in contrast to the thriving markets of the same name in the Tang capital of Chang'an where exotic goods poured in from the Eurasian continent via the Silk Road. Japan was part of an overseas commercial network and traded for spices, medicines, cosmetics, gold, iron, fur, and other goods with the Korean state of Silla and with the state of Parhae in modern Manchuria, in addition to the strictly regimented tribute trade with the Chinese Empire. But overseas trade must be called insignificant compared to the overseas economy of the Roman Empire.

In addition to the political, economic, and social differences between the stable insular state of Japan and the conquest empire of Rome, the origin, topography, and ideological significance of their respective capitals differed considerably. First, while Kyoto was at its foundation just one of many previous capitals, Rome was the sole capital until the division of the empire in late Antiquity. Livy reports that Servius Tullius (578–534 BCE), the sixth king of Rome, persuaded the leaders of surrounding Latin city-states to jointly build a temple to Diana of Ephesus in Rome, and he interprets this joint devotional act of polities with which Rome had for long been at war as a sign that they finally recognized Rome as a capital of sorts (*ea erat confessio caput rerum Romam esse,* *Livy* I.45.3). But this time was buried in Rome's mythic past, preceding Fabius Pictor, the earliest historian of Rome and its right to rule, by more than three centuries. Thus, for as long as Romans could think, or at least write about

---

[15] For a timeline of military events on the northern frontier see Takahashi 1963, 300–314.
[16] McCullough and McCullough 1980, 810.
[17] For the social and economic history of Heian Japan see Farris 2009; on overseas trade see Batten 2006 and von Verschuer 2006.

themselves, Rome was simply the one and only capital. Even if its role as capital was at times disputed—such as when the Gauls sacked Rome in 390 and triggered a debate over abandoning the city and relocating to Veii or when Augustus contemplated moving the capital to the east—Rome remained capital and it had a halo of destiny on its side.

At its founding Kyoto had no trappings of sacred fate, first of all, because there had been many capitals preceding it. Richard A. Ponsonby-Fane (1878–1937), private secretary to the British Crown in various colonies of the Empire and the first Western scholar to write with extensive devotion on the city of Kyoto and previous Japanese capitals, counts forty-three changes of capitals before the foundation of Nara in 710 recorded in the early chronicles.[18] Most of them were in the Yamato region, the power base of the Kinai rulers, and were probably not much more than a modest residence of the ruling sovereign. Early Japanese capitals shifted with each new court after the death of the sovereign, probably as an act of avoiding pollution, until the foundation of the first stable capital at Heijō, Nara, in 710. Practices rooted in similar ideas still survive in the regular rebuilding and ritual moving of major Shinto sanctuaries, such as the Ise Shrines, devoted to the sun goddess Amaterasu and the imperial line, whose twenty-year turn to move has come again in 2013.

The second reason for Kyoto's lack of charismatic destiny at its foundation was that it was not just one of many preceding capital cities, but was the sixth capital built on Chinese precedent. Just during the century leading up to Kyoto's foundation, six new capitals were built: Fujiwara (694–710), Nara (710–740 and 745–784), Kuni (740–44), Naniwa (744–45), Nagaoka (784–94), and, finally Kyoto (794–1868).[19] It was just one more of those Japanese capitals that imitated the basic pattern of Chinese capitals: a large rectangle with the imperial palace complex looming over the city from the north, a central avenue leading up to it, flanked by four large avenues that cut across the city from north to south, which produced a generic grid by intersecting with nine large streets running from east to west, complete with the "Eastern" and "Western Market" areas in the South of the city.[20] (see Figure 5.3) Fujiwara was probably based on the Luoyang of the Wei Dynasty (220–265), where the palace complex was located right at the heart of the city, but the generic checkerboard structure of the cityscape was the same.[21]

In contrast, Rome was topographically one of its kind. It was not modeled on Hellenic precedents of urban planning—if we accept Rome's traditional date of foundation during the eighth century, Greece itself was on the threshold of history and had hardly any urban centers that could have served as such a model, let alone urban centers with seven hills. Although later many features

---

[18] Ponsonby-Fane 1979, 9. Although dated due to the wealth of archeological discoveries over the last decades Wheatley and See 1978 is still valuable as an account of the early court-capitals.

[19] For the political context of the moves to Fujiwara and to the short-lived Kuni and Nagaoka see Piggott 1997, chapters 5 and 7, respectively.

[20] For a basic plan of a Chinese-style capital city see van Goethem 2008, 140. For early Chinese cities see Lewis 2006, Chapter 3 "Cities and Capitals." For the Chinese imperial tradition of city building see Steinhardt 1990.

[21] For maps of the Chinese-style capitals and their relation to Chinese precedent see Fiévé 2008, 40–51. See also Satō 1974 and, for Nara, the images and maps in Tsuboi and Tanaka 1991.

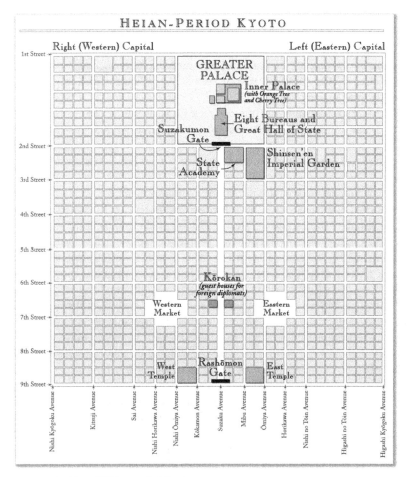

FIGURE 5.3 *Map of Heian-period Kyoto*

of Hellenistic cities, such as public colonnades and temples, theaters, libraries, gymnasia, and baths became part of the Roman cityscape, serving the needs of an increasingly Hellenized Roman population, they were fitted into the Roman landscape of the Seven Hills, rather than reproducing any part of a model Hellenistic city. Rome's Seven Hills on the Tiber made it unique and already in its earliest period of existence embodied her ethnic and social diversity: Livy reports that in the latter half of the seventh century BCE the Palatine was the quarter of the original Romans, the Capitol and Citadel were inhabited by the Sabines, while the Albans occupied the Caelian Hill. Since the Aventine was apparently still available, Ancus Marcius, the fourth king of Rome, settled there the remainders of the population of the Latin cities of Politorium, Tellenae, and Ficana, after inflicting a crushing defeat, thereby "following the custom of the early kings, who enlarged the Roman state by making her enemies to citizens (*secutusque morem regum priorum, qui rem Romanam auxerant hostibus in civitatem accipiendis, Livy* I.33.1)."

At that point in history there was apparently still ample free space and, even though conquered, one could be graced with some private ethnic space of one's own in the unique cityscape of emerging Rome.[22] As the proverb goes, Rome was not built in one day, nor by the fiat of one particular sovereign as was Kyoto, but her gradual growth and construction was a layered mirror of Roman imperial building. (see Figure 5.4)

From Livy's description of the early settlings of Rome's Seven Hills, it was ideologically not far to Ovid's famous *dictum*, which he wrote in his *Fasti*, a ritual calendar of the city and declaration of love to the home he was about to lose when sent into exile shortly after: "The extent of the City of Rome and the world is one (*Romanae spatium est urbis et orbis idem*)." (*Fasti*, II.684)

This would have been the most striking difference had somebody from Heian Kyoto visited Augustan Rome: the overwhelming presence of foreigners, the prominence of public spaces, and the wealth of mass public events. Rome was a miniature of its empire; each of its conquered people was represented in the capital. And for them, as for Romans, spectacles that put in scene the mightiness of Rome's empire shaped daily life. There was the Forum, place of grand speeches, court litigations, state sacrifices, and site where generals, dictators, and emperors celebrated their victories over distant territories in magnificent triumphs, and paraded their war spoils, along with foreign chieftains, strange animals, and other booty. Then there were the theaters and the game arenas, the public baths, and public lectures. Women were moving freely and parading their new fashions—including Asian silk—on the street instead of hiding in carriages or behind screens and sliding doors as in Kyoto. Life in Heian Japan was lived with much less public visibility. The highly official annual festivals and regular court events were mostly limited to courtiers. And there was nothing comparable to the great number of publicly sponsored theater performances and sumptuous games for people of all classes. We do have a vivid description of a popular festival in Fujiwara no Akihira's 藤原明衡 (989–1066) *New Monkey Music* (*Shin sarugaku ki* 新猿楽記), which parades pantomimes, exorcists, magicians, dancing midgets, and acrobats in front of the reader's eye. But the text is unique and idiosyncratic, and ironically the real sight of the popular festival are not even the performers, but the spectators, namely the outrageous family of an Outer Palace Guard with his three wives and numerous descendants, who are described in sometimes bawdy detail. Noh Theater only developed much later in the fourteenth century. Thus Kyoto remained something of an aristocratic palace city in contrast to the cosmopolitan public stage that was Rome.

Third, and most importantly, Kyoto could not have had a halo of destiny because it was founded in the broad daylight of history at the end of the century that saw the first explosion of literacy and the compilation of two large chronicles, poetry anthologies, local gazetteers, and other sophisticated literary works. It was not just founded in a literate era, but its very foundation was effected through writing, namely *par ordre de* Kanmu. After finding a fitting construction site, he

---

[22] For surveys of the development of the city of Rome see Cornell 1995, and John E. Stambaugh 1988, 1–85.
[23] *Nihon kiryaku*: Enryaku 13/10/28. Kuroita 1965b, 268.

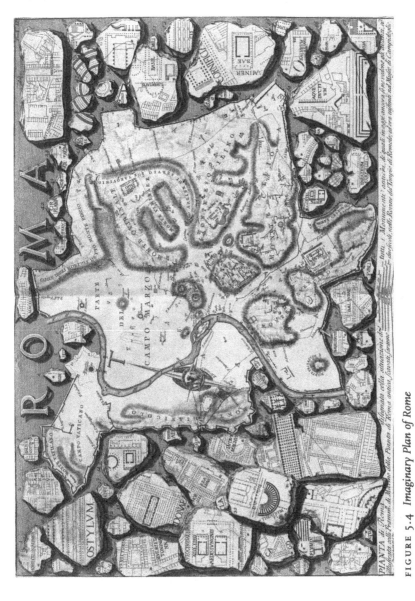

FIGURE 5.4 *Imaginary Plan of Rome*

Giovanni Battista Piranesi (1720–1778). From *Le antichità romane.* © Master and Fellows of Trinity College Cambridge.

announced the moving of the capital from Nagaoka to Kyoto on the twenty-eighth day of the tenth month of 794:

> The location of the Grand Palace of Kadono has beautiful mountains and rivers and is convenient in terms of traffic for people from all four directions of Our realm.

> 葛野大宮地者。山川麗。四方國百姓參出來事便。 [23]

We have detailed descriptions of two years of moving preparations following the selection of the new construction site in the Kadono district of Yamashiro Province. A great amount of laborers and lumber had to be secured, ancestors and deities had to be informed of the move, and peasants were compensated for giving up their land for the construction of the new capital. It was an enormous financial feat, especially because a mere decade before the foundation of Heian-kyō Kanmu had moved from Nara to the new capital of Nagaoka. One can fathom the struggles from the fact that Kanmu repeatedly issued edicts to ensure tax payments, which were crucial to the financing of the expensive new capital project. He forbade, for example, people changing their names as an attempt to evade taxes.[24]

Despite the wealth of detail about the construction of the new capital and Emperor Kanmu's keen interest in the process, the sources are close to silent about the reasons for the move.[25] The Kyoto basin certainly provided an excellent plane on which to project a Chinese-style capital layout and was favorable from the perspective of geomancy. Other motives might have included that the Hata family, a powerful immigrant clan from the Korean Peninsula with its home base in the northwest of modern Kyoto, cut funds for the Nagaoka capital construction and tried, successfully, to draw Kanmu to their own power base, the future Heian-kyō. There was also the assassination of Fujiwara no Tanetsugu, the mastermind of the move to Nagaoka, and a series of natural disasters, which were associated with the vengeful ghost of Kanmu's brother Prince Sawara, who had died in exile, making Nagaoka into an inauspicious capital site.

Moreover, Nagaoka was by nature an inconvenient site, because it was prone to flooding. The main question remains why Kanmu left Nara in the first place, and among the various geographical, economical, political, and religious reasons that have been advanced over the years a particularly convincing reason was Kanmu's family background and his vision of his imperial mission. Kanmu came from the imperial line of Emperor Tenji, which was pushed aside by his brother Tenmu in 672. Tenmu's lineage remained in power for a century until the inthronization of Kanmu's father, and Kanmu carefully positioned his reign as a new beginning. Appealing to Chinese calendrical numerology, he chose the year 784 as the moment to leave the Nara area, power base of the Tenmu lineage, for sites that were close to his forefather Tenji's short-lived capital of Ōmi (670–72) on the Biwa Lake: Nagaoka and then Heiankyō.

---

[24] van Goethem 2008, 253.
[25] On the building process and theories about reasons behind the capital move see van Goethem 2008, 213–58 and Toby 1985.
[26] *Nihon kiryaku*: Enryaku 13/11/8, Kuroita 1965b, 268.

Kyoto was founded in the daylight of history and therefore brought into being by physical as well as textual manipulations. On the eighth day of the eleventh month of 794 Kanmu baptized his new city in an edict:

> This province, enclosed by mountains and streams like with collar and sash, makes a natural citadel. Because of this fortunate configuration, we should devise a new name for it: let *Yamashiro Province* 山背國 ("Province Behind the Mountains") become *Yamashiro Province* 山城國 ("Province of the Mountain Citadel"). Moreover, flocks of people and singers of praise songs raise their different voices in identical words, naming this the 'Capital of Peace (*Heiankyō*).'
>
> 此國山河襟帶。自然作城。因斯形勝。可制新號。宜改山背國為山城國。
> 又子來之民。謳歌之輩。異口同辭。號曰。平安京。 [26]

As in other edicts, Kanmu praises the new capital for its natural blessings and calls on his subjects to spread word of the auspicious new name. More subtly, he changes the spelling of the province into which he inserted his new capital: the name "Yamashiro" is unchanged, but the modestly descriptive character "behind (*shiro* 背) the mountains" is exchanged with the politically pregnant character "citadel (*shiro* 城) in the mountains." With the words of Kanmu's edict, the provincial countryside was now ready to take control and make history.

Although Kyoto did not start out with a halo of destiny, it quickly acquired one as the indispensable stage on which the refined Heian court culture unfolded. When at the end of the Heian Period in 1180 Kiyomori of the powerful warrior clan of the Taira forced the emperor to leave Kyoto and set up a new capital at his own power base in Fukuhara, the eminent courtier Fujiwara no Kanezane warned that Emperor Kanmu had founded this capital after careful consideration of its strategic location and with the divine protection from deities on its East and West borders. He emphasized that this went beyond the fathoming of men and that a move of the capital would endanger the survival of the state because Kyoto was an "area that heaven had made such (天之令然之地)." [27] Due to unrest and protests from various fronts, Kiyomori had to give up Fukuhara and return the court to Kyoto after six months. Kyoto's cityscape had become symbolic for the aristocracy and could not easily have been done without. One of the reasons given for the move back to Kyoto was that there was apparently no building at Fukuhara that could possibly have accommodated the intricate imperial New Year's ceremony. [28] A few years later, Minamoto no Yoritomo and his warriors vanquished the Taira clan and set up Japan's first shogunal government in Kamakura, but the imperial court and capital remained in Kyoto.

2. *Unequal Time Vectors*

Given the different nature of the Roman and Japanese Empires and their respective capitals, how did writers of the two traditions relate to their capitals and to their capitals' place in the empire? Historians and poets of the Augustan Period

---

[27] Nishimura 2005, 23.
[28] Hall 1974, 23.
[29] Polybius. *Histories* I.5-6. Translation from Paton 1922–1927, 3-5.

had the fantastic challenge to narrate and explain the meteoric rise of Rome from Romulus's hut to Augustus's marble city, gleaming of gold and imperial pride. The city's extraordinary success in conquering a world is the starting point for the great histories of Rome. Already Polybius (ca. 199–120 BCE), himself a Greek who, captured in the process of Roman conquests, passed much of his life in Rome, took the Roman miracle as the point of departure for his *Histories*. He thought that understanding its origins and causes was one of the most exciting goals of his enterprise:

> For who is so worthless or indolent as not to wish to know by what means and under what system of polity the Romans in less than fifty-three years have succeeded in subjecting nearly the whole inhabited world to their sole government— a thing unique in history? Or who again is there so passionately devoted to other spectacles or studies as to regard anything as of greater moment than the acquisition of this knowledge?

> τίς γὰρ οὕτως ὑπάρχει φαῦλος ἢ ῥᾴθυμος ἀνθρώπων ὃς οὐκ ἂν βούλοιτο γνῶναι πῶς καὶ τίνι γένει πολιτείας ἐπικρατηθέντα σχεδὸν ἅπαντα τὰ κατὰ τὴν οἰκουμένην οὐχ ὅλοις πεντήκοντα καὶ τρισὶν ἔτεσιν ὑπὸ μίαν ἀρχὴν ἔπεσε τὴν Ῥωμαίων, ὃ πρότερον οὐχ εὑρίσκεται γεγονός, τίς δὲ πάλιν οὕτως ἐκπαθὴς πρός τι τῶν ἄλλων θεαμάτων ἢ μαθημάτων ὃς προυργιαίτερον ἄν τι ποιήσαιτο τῆσδε τῆς ἐμπειρίας.[29]

About a century later Livy, the major Latin historian of Rome, writes his monumental history of the city from its foundation to Livy's own time in 142 books, because he feels the need to record the Roman miracle in detail. He shudders at the greatness of this task in the preface to his monumental work, on which he worked for over forty years, on this awe-inspiring note:

> I am not quite sure whether I will create anything worthy of the labor, when I write up the affairs of the Roman people since the beginnings of the city ... Yet, it will bring satisfaction to commemorate the deeds of the world's foremost people with all my might; and if among such a crowd of writers my fame should remain obscure, I will console myself with the excellence and greatness of those whose renown will overshadow mine.

> *Facturusne operae pretium sim, si a primordio urbis res populi Romani perscriperim, nec satis scio [...] iuvabit tamen rerum gestarum memoriae principis terrarum populi pro virili parte et ipsum consuluisse; et si in tanta scriptorum turba mea fama in obscuro sit, nobilitate ac magnitudine eorum me qui nomini officient meo consoler.*[30]

Rome's splendor is such that it threatens to obscure those who flock to write about it and compete in fame when expounding the city's prominence. Historians' explanations of the Roman miracle varied, but two concepts seemed particularly attractive to make sense of it: did Rome succeed because of some divine destiny or because of its military and political worth? Plutarch (ca. 45–125), who as a Greek

---

[30] *Livy, praef.* 1–3. The translation is mine.
[31] On this point see Swain 1989.

under Roman imperial rule was particularly sensitized to the question of Rome's imperial success, discusses the two poles of divine fortune (*tychê*) or virtue (*aretê*) in his *On the Fortune of the Romans* (*Peri tês Rhômaiôn tychês*) as explanatory options. Although the essay clearly bears traces of a well-formed exercise in epideictic rhetoric, it is not a half-hearted product of rhetorical pedagogy designed to teach the art of praise speeches, but discusses issues that deeply preoccupied Plutarch throughout his life.[31] Plutarch gives credit both to divine destiny as well as to Roman genius, but seems at times more strongly attracted to destiny. Regardless of where, exactly, we would pin him down if we could, his essay exemplifies that the Roman miracle demanded an explanation and that writing Rome's history was always caught up in the question of how to explain Rome's meteoric rise to greatness.

Rome's greatness allowed its writers a degree of bold imagination and sweeping adventurousness that no Heian Japanese, speaking from the Heian capital out to the world, would ever have had cause to dream of. The expanses of the Roman realm guaranteed its writers a globe-spanning audience of most various *couleurs*:

> The Colchian will know me, and the Dacian who pretends not to fear a cohort of Marians, the Geloni at the ends of the earth, the learned Iberian, the Rhône-swigger.

> *me Colchus et qui dissimulate metum / Marsae cohortis Dacus et ultimi / noscent Geloni, me peritus / discet Hiber Rhodanique potor.*[32]

Horace cannot complain about a lack of audience and uses this publicity map of future readership to explain why he does not want a tomb or elaborate funeral dirges. The circulation of his books will grant him the immortality that funeral rites cannot bestow. The imperial gesture with which Horace sings the praise of his own poetry is made tolerable, even delightfully comic, thanks to the image he uses to describe the spread of his fame: he himself, as a "tuneful bird" (*canorus ales*), carries his song into the world. He foresees his imminent transformation into the bird because of the wrinkly skin at his feet, his swan-white snowy hair, and the "soft plumage" that slowly takes the better of his arms and shoulders. His physical demise allows his fame to fly out into the world and his name to become immortal.

The greatness of the Roman Empire allowed Roman authors not just to imagine the spread of their works through the world. It gave them the opportunity to radically change their lifestyle and develop imperial tastes themselves. Horace chides a certain Iccius for marching out into the empire for new exploits, which are, deplorably enough, financed by the pawning of his precious copies of philosophical literature:

> Iccius, are you now envying the rich treasures of Arabia, preparing a ruthless campaign against kings of Sheba never before subdued, and weaving chains for the fearsome Mede? What barbarian virgin will be your slave, mourning her bridegroom killed in battle? What boy of the court brought up to stretch Chinese arrows on the bow of his fathers will take his place by your cup with rich oils on

---

[32] Horace, *Odes* II.20.17–20. Translation from West 1997, 74.
[33] Horace, *Ode* I.29. West 1997, 49.

his hair? Who would deny that down-rushing rivers can flow up steep mountains and Tiber reverse his course when you are in such haste to exchange for Spanish breastplates the Socratic school and the works of great Panaetius collected from all over the world—you promised better things.

Icci, beatis nunc Arabum invides / gazis, et acrem militiam paras / non ante devictis Sabaeae / regibus, horribilique Medo / nectis catenas? quae tibi virginum / sponso necato barbara serviet? / puer quis ex aula capillis / ad cyathum statuetur unctis, / doctus sagittas tendere Sericas / arcu paterno? quis neget arduis / pronos relabi posse rivos / montibus et Tiberim reverti, / cum tu coemptos undique nobilis / libros Panaeti Socraticam et domum / mutare loricis Hiberis, / pollicitus meliora, tendis?[33]

Horace does seem scandalized by Iccius's decision to change his life from that of a scholar to that of an Oriental conqueror. He had "promise of better things." It is particularly outrageous that he bought Spanish corselets at the price of his hard-earned collection of the works of Panaetius (185–109 BCE), head of the Stoa in Athens and, more importantly, crucial transmitter of Greek philosophy to Rome through his connection with the Scipionic circle and his life spent in Rome. Yet Horace does not refrain from imagining the pleasures awaiting Iccius in his new life: Arabian treasures, conquered Sabaean kings, young cup-bearers of Oriental royal blood, or barbarian maidens. Horace, who throughout his *Odes* is a master in handling hyperbolic imperial praise with an elegant iridescence of grandeur and irony, both scolds and relishes Iccius's thirst for private imperial exploits; and in this ode both Rome and Iccius have supernatural powers: "who'll deny" that in the city on the Tiber simply anything is possible, including the reversal of the Tiber's flow? That Horace clamorously shatters the commonsensical *adynaton*, rhetorical trope of the "impossible," expresses not just Horace's exasperation at Iccius's change of lifestyle. Rather, it makes Iccius into a grand and scandalous example of the power of Rome's imperialism and the imperial fantasies that it allowed its subjects, to the point of bending the laws of nature.

It is this grandeur, Rome's splendid pretentiousness, which underlies in particular Augustan literature in all its elevating, satirical, or scandalizing modes. This grandeur became destiny, an inescapable telos. Virgil's *Aeneid* shows that the effects of this telos could become all the more miraculous the further back in time one applied it. The thrust of the telos allowed for inversions of most fundamental categories of common sense, such as temporal succession. In the Homeric epic Achilles received his famous shield with scenes of the cosmos and societies in peace and war, and Ulysses visited the underworld, receiving a prophecy about his personal further destiny and meeting the mythical heroes of the past, including his dead companions from the Trojan war; but when Aeneas receives his shield and visits the realm of the dead in the *Aeneid*, the Homeric tropes become filled with majestic sketches of Rome's rise and the contemporary Augustan empire. As we discussed in the previous chapter from a different angle, the *Aeneid* lives off the moments of prophecy and proleptic imagination. When Aeneas goes to the

---

[34] Virgil. *Aeneid* VI.756–759. Ruden 2008, 139.

underworld, he witnesses the historical procession of Rome's future, announced by the shadow of his late father Anchises:

> Come, hear your destiny, and the future glory
> Of the stock of Dardanus, all the descendants
> That we will have from the Italian race—
> Great souls who will be born into our family.

> *Nunc age, Dardaniam prolem quae deinde sequatur / gloria, qui maneant Itala de gente nepotes, / inlustris animas nostrumque in nomen ituras, / expediam dictis, et te tua fata docebo.*[34]

As if learning a teachable skill or craft, Anchises "teaches" his son the art of "destiny" (*tua fata docebo*) or, to translate it more soberly, "informs" him of his "destiny." Starting with Aeneas's Italic son Silvius, by his new wife Lavinia, Aeneas's male descendants down to Romulus pass before his eyes. With Romulus, capital and the world, *urbs* and *orbis*, join fates, as they do with Augustus, to whom Anchises jumps directly before even telling of the kings succeeding Romulus, who will appear later in the procession. At last Anchises entrusts his son with the ultimate lesson about the duties resulting from Rome's fate:

> Others, I know, will beat out softer-breathing
> Bronze shapes, or draw from marble living faces,
> Excel in pleading cases, chart the sky's paths,
> Predict the rising of the constellations.
> But Romans, don't forget that world dominion
> Is your great craft: peace, and then peaceful customs;
> Sparing the conquered, striking down the haughty.

> *Excudent alii spirantia mollius aera / (credo equidem), vivos ducent de marmore voltus, / orabunt causas melius, caelique meatus / describent radio et surgentia sidera dicent: / tu regere imperio populos, Romane, memento / (hae tibi erunt artes), pacique imponere morem, / parcere subiectis et debellare superbos.*[35]

Not the Greek art of sculpture or of rhetoric, and not the Chaldean art of astronomy is Roman destiny, but Rome's is the art of destiny, of the destiny to rule and to dispense peace and war justly. For plot purposes, Aeneas exits the underworld through a gate of sleep that ensures that he forgets the great destiny laid out for Rome summoned up by his late father. Thus he has not to either worry over the challenges that await him on the shores of Latium or grow lazy, because he knows that destiny to spectacular fame is self-fulfilling anyway. As discussed in the preceding chapter, when he examines the depictions of Roman history on the shield that his mother Venus has made for him he has a sense of prescient pleasure, but no foreknowledge. Just as he had carried his hearth gods, the Penates, and his father Anchises on his arms out of the burning Troy, he now carries, unknowingly,

---

[35] Virgil. *Aeneid* VI. 847–853. Ruden 2008, 141.
[36] Morris 1994, 21.

the load of Rome's future on the shield. It is these clever gestures of prescience and proleptic history that run through Augustan literature, even though in different modes and moods, and if we have grown up with the *Aeneid*, the temporal *adynata*, impossibilities, which are the springs for Aeneas's launching of Roman destiny, do not even appear distorted or hyperbolic.

In remarkable contrast, Kyoto had no such spectacular historical legacy calling for philosophical reflection or historical explanation. Not that the Heian elite lacked pride in Kyoto. The city became the incarnation of all things refined and was at the center of virtually all literary activity. By the tenth century it became the splendid stage for the new vernacular tale literature (*monogatari* 物語) such as the *Tale of Genji*, written by the court lady Murasaki no Shikibu in the early eleventh century. As Ivan Morris has aptly observed:

> In the *Tale of Genji*, then, the nature of Heian Kyo and its environs is no mere static background which the author introduces for decorative effect. It is a vital force, exerting a constant influence on the characters; and it is in terms of this nature that Prince Genji and the others perceive and express their emotions.[36]

The city and its locales do weave themselves subtly into the fabric of all Heian literature, but in less ostentatious and triumphant ways.[37] There are no histories like Polybius's or Livy's, which proclaim and try to understand the Roman miracle, nor is there a Virgilian epic, which gives us Aeneas's story as the Augustan synecdoche for that miracle.

More significantly, there are also no signs of grandiose rhapsodies (*fu* 賦) that would have lavished their hyperbolic praises on the Japanese capital as we know from the Chinese tradition. Not coincidentally, the genre of rhapsodies originally thrived during China's first grand empire during the Han Dynasty, when parts of Korea, Vietnam, and Central Asia were conquered by Chinese armies. The imperial expansion triggered disputes over the ethics of empire: should one indulge the pleasures of exotic luxury goods and grandiose displays of imperial violence in war or hunt, or should one, to the contrary, practice the virtues of restraint, civil decorum, and intellectual sublimation? These questions cut right through the narrative nerves of the subgenre of rhapsodies on capital cities. Because the capital rhapsodies made up the opening books of the *Wenxuan* 文選 (*Selections of Refined Literature*), a sixth-century Chinese anthology that was a central text in Heian elite education, Heian writers were thoroughly familiar with this subgenre. They could have had every reason to write capital rhapsodies on their capital, precisely because they knew well that rhapsodies stood at the top of the genre hierarchy in Chinese canonical anthologies such as the *Wenxuan*. Yet no capital rhapsodies survive from Japan and the rhapsody genre, in particular in its long and exuberant Han Dynasty style, never quite took off in Japan.

There are, however, powerful praise poems of emperors, their palaces, and short-lived capitals in the vernacular anthology *Man'yōshū*, compiled about 150 years before the foundation of Kyoto and thus containing poems from a period with

---

[37] On Kyoto as backdrop in Heian literature see Shinma 2009, 317–34.
[38] On the praise poems on Yoshino Palace see Denecke 2005, 165–89.

frequent capital changes between the mid-seventh to the mid-eighth centuries. There are famous praise poems by Kakinomoto no Hitomaro 柿本人麻呂 (ca.-708), composed when he followed in the retinue Empress Jitō on her excursions to the Detached Palace at Yoshino outside the capital. Although Hitomaro and other court poets who praise Yoshino after him evoke the imposing mountains and clear waters of Yoshino and its palace, these praises serve to set off the towering imperial figure and are thus praises of imperial power rather than of the palace, which was anyway only a place to accommodate the emperors during occasional visits.[38] The series of poems composed on Kuni, capital between 740 and 744,[39] and Naniwa, capital between 744–45,[40] are tragic traces of capitals that had but the shortest fate in Japanese history. Because of the frequent change of capitals and the abandonment of previous capital sites, capital laments—a genre that had precedents in China, but, more importantly, was highly relevant to the early Japanese history of shifting capitals—became almost more frequent than capital praises. In *Man'yōshū* VI.1059–61 Kuni is lamented again as soon as its founding had been praised, and *Man'yōshū* VI.1044–50 laments the abandonment of Nara.

But the most poignant capital lament poem is arguably Hitomaro's dirge on the capital of Ōmi, the site on the shores of the Biwa Lake far away from the previous capital in Asuka that Emperor Tenji, the forefather of Kanmu, the founder of Kyoto, had chosen as his capital from 667 to 671. When Hitomaro passed the ruins of Ōmi perhaps sometime in the early eighth century, Ōmi was a political problem, because it symbolized the war of 672 during which the brother of Emperor Tenji seized the throne for his lineage and his wife, Empress Jitō, during whose reign Hitomaro was writing. Ōmi was therefore a doubly sad place.

近江の荒れたる都に過る時に、柿本朝臣人麻呂が作る歌

A poem composed by Kakinomoto no Hitomaro on passing the ruined capital of Ōmi

玉だすき	From that hallowed age
畝傍の山の	When the monarch Suzerain of the Sun
橿原の	Reigned at Kashihara
聖の御代ゆ	By Unebi, called the Jewel-sash Mount
生れましし	Each and every god
神のことごと	Made manifest in the world of men,
つがの木の	One by one in evergreen
いや継ぎ継ぎに	Succession like a line of hemlock trees,
天の下	Ruled under heaven
知らしめししを	All this realm with uncontested sway:
天にみつ	Yet from sky-seen
大和を置きて	Yamato did one depart—
あをによし	Whatever may have been
奈良山を越え	The secret of his sage intent—

---

[39] *Man'yōshū* VI.1050–58.
[40] *Man'yōshū* VI.1062-64. The date of the poems is unclear.
[41] *Man'yōshu* I: 29–31. Translation from Cranston 1993, 190–92.

いかさまに	And passed across
思ほしめせか	The slopes of blue-earth Nara Mountain
天離る	To a land, remote
鄙にはあれど	Beyond the distant heaven,
石走る	The land of Ōmi
近江の国の	Where water dashes on the rocks,
楽浪の	To the palace of Ōtsu
大津の宮に	In Sasanami of the gently lapping waves;
天の下	And there, as it is said,
知らしめしけむ	He ruled this realm beneath the sky:
天皇の	That sovereign god,
神の尊の	August ancestral deity—
大宮は	His great palace stood
ここと聞けども	Upon this spot, as I have heard;
大殿は	Its mighty halls
ここと言へども	Rose here, so all men say;
春草の	Where now spring grasses
繁く生ひたる	Choke the earth in their rife growth,
霞立ち	And mists rise up
春日の霧れる	To hide the dazzling springtime sun;
ももしきの	Now I view this site
大宮所	Where once the mighty palace stood,
見れば悲しも	And it is sad to see.

Envoy poems:

楽浪の	Still Cape Kara stands
志賀の唐崎	In Shiga of the gently lapping waves,
幸くあれど	Changeless from of old;
大宮人の	But it will wait in vain to see
舟待ちかねつ	The courtiers' boats row back.

***

楽浪の	Broad the waters stand
志賀の大わだ	By Shiga of the gently lapping waves:
淀むとも	The lake is still;
昔の人に	But how can it ever meet again
またも逢はめやも	The men of long ago.[41]

The drama in this poem unfolds along the axes of continuity and change: there is the continuity of the imperial lineage spanning from the first human emperor Jinmu and his palace in Kashiwara, to Emperor Tenji. Beautiful "pillow words," poetic epithets, spell out that continuity: there is sacred Mount Unebi, the "Jewel-sash" Mount and the many generations that have ruled the empire (the "realm beneath the sky") from the area of "sky-seen" Yamato. Yet Tenji breaks this heavenly

---

[42] On this term and the distinctive features "couplet culture" took in Japan see Denecke 2007.

harmony on earth and decides to leave for a barbarous place: Ōmi. It is inaccessible—beyond the green hills of Nara—and unruly; it sports racing rocks and lapping waves and is, most unfortunately, "beyond the distant heaven." Hitomaro seeks continuity: he gazes sadly at the palace ruins and is puzzled over Tenji's motives for breaking heavenly harmony. In fresh contrast to the dereliction of the place, which after all had only served as capital for a few years, it is spring grass and spring haze that makes it delicately rustic, infuses it with a touch of temporary reawakening. The two envoys play a yet more paradoxical game with continuity and change: Hitomaro clings to constant elements in the landscape: Shiga and the firm Kara Cape. The still waters of the lake serve as pivot for our perception of time. On the one hand their stillness suggests serene constancy; on the other hand the lack of movement in the water proves that those courtiers' boats of the Ōmi court are long gone and that the flow of time has stopped. After Hitomaro's empathy with Emperor Tenji's decision to move away from heaven-close Yamato, in the last envoy stanza he bemoans that he cannot meet people of the past.

By the early eleventh century Kyoto and the concept of a stable capital were more than two centuries old. Kyoto flourished under the regency of Fujiwara no Michinaga, whose glorious era was immortalized in the *Tale of Flowering Fortunes* (*Eiga monogatari* 栄華物語), a memoir written by a woman who had been in the service of his principal wife. The cultural confidence in the artistic, aesthetic, and literary refinement that Heian court society had produced radiates from works of that period. If in Rome the new cultural confidence of the Augustan Period inspired writers to take on the language of legends and engage historical subjects of mythic proportions, Japanese writers of the eleventh century convey their pride in more subdued colors. They resort to complex schemes of balancing Chinese-style and indigenous artistic repertoires, public and private registers, and female and male domains.

One of the most dazzling and influential literary balancing acts of the eleventh century is the *Collection of Japanese and Chinese Texts for Recitation* (*Wakan rōeishū* 和漢朗詠集, hereafter *Collection*), an anthology of literary excerpts culled from texts by Chinese and Japanese authors compiled by Fujiwara no Kintō (966–1041) around 1013. The very form of this text makes it incomparable to any Greek or Latin text that has come down to us. It consists of some 800 short excerpts from poems and various prose genres organized by 125 topics in two books. The topics in the first book go through the various phases of the four seasons and the relevant seasonal changes such as festivals, customs, plants, or animals related to them. The second book treats topics selected from nature and human society, ranging from meteorology, botany, and zoology, to phenomena of human society such as letters and wine, houses and temples, emperors and ministers, friends and courtesans, to more abstract themes such as the impermanence of all things or the ultimate closure to the collection, the topic of "whiteness." Although many topical categories are borrowed from Chinese encyclopedias, Kintō added some of his own and arranged them in unique fashion.

Producing anthologies of beautiful couplets culled from poems was a practice that Heian Japanese took over from China and enthusiastically applied to their own literary culture. It was part of what I have elsewhere called "couplet culture," an aesthetic vision that prized the appreciation of poetic fragments.[42] But it was completely unprecedented to cull passages from texts written between the Western Han Dynasty (206 BCE to 20 CE) and Kintō's own time, systematically juxtaposing snippets from Chinese, Chinese-style, and Japanese texts, and unleashing resonances, which were not intended by their original authors.[43]

The effect was stunning: Within a century of its publication commentaries started to be written on the *Collection* and it quickly became a schoolbook that could teach the array of skills necessary for courtiers all at once: it became a primer for poetry chanting and calligraphy practice, and was committed to memory as a sort of dictionary for literary references, anecdotes and elegant diction. In this way it became an internalized poetic mind-map of common topics and examples of their most successful treatment and also served as a schoolbook to learn writing "Topic Poetry" (*kudaishi* 句題詩), the mainstream genre male courtiers used in Heian Japan when composing poetry at official occasions.[44]

Although abandoned capitals were a thing of the past for Kintō and his contemporaries living during the highpoint of Kyoto's court culture, Kintō includes the topic "Old Capitals" rather than introducing a topic category for the current capital. The retrospective teleology of appreciating things ruinous and abandoned instead of boasting the splendors of the present is elevated in Kintō's anthology from historical necessity of Hitomaro's time in the seventh century (and certainly a literary *topos* well know from China) to aesthetic principle three centuries later. The topic "Old Capitals" is embedded in a sequence of related topics. It is prefaced by eleven passages selected for the topic "Water; with Fishermen appended," and seven passages on "Forbidden City/Imperial Palace," and is followed by ten passages on "Old Palaces; with Derelict Residences appended" as well as fourteen excerpts on the topic "Immortals, with Daoists and Hermits appended."

What at first look seems like an absurdist list straight out of Borges's Chinese encyclopedia has nevertheless a clear architecture of contrasts and superpositions: the "Palace," the seat of the court in the "Forbidden City" is at the center of the realm, and overlaps with other realms such as the world of humble fishermen and clear streams, the quietist double of the court, where already Chinese sage rulers of high antiquity found wisdom and discovered brilliant advisors of uncorrupted simplicity. Another metaphoric double of the court was the world of Immortals, which furnished fancy metaphors for the hyperbolic description of the court in this world. That both the realm of the Fishermen near the water and the world of the Immortals in the mountains were farthest away from—a far cry indeed—and identical with the court made them attractive as powerful metaphorical spaces, where their tensions could have full play. In between the court and the immortals two topics are set in the past: "Old Capitals," and "Old Palaces." They give the current palaces and its two alternative incarnations temporal depth.

---

[43] On Kintō's creation of new meanings through juxtaposition of excerpts from different literary traditions see Tanaka 2006, 1–26.

[44] Satō 2006, 35–48.

The *Collection* is unique and idiosyncratic, but it is worthwhile looking carefully at the sequence related to "Old Capitals" for various reasons. First, because it is certainly the most complex poetic geography of the capital in any Heian text; second, because the mind-map it provided of the capital as a poetic topic was highly influential and inscribed itself into the memory and imagination of generations of readers from the Late Heian Period through the Meiji Period; and third, because it is a literary experiment with such a unique structure that it is interesting to think about it as an experiment in cognitive poetics. Certainly, choosing a poetry anthology that, like a kaleidoscope of glass pieces, shakes up excerpts from three different literary canons and arranges them in ultimately subtle and overdetermined topical order, is likely to produce an image of the Japanese capital that will be blinded by its own iridescence and indeterminacy of meaning. Yet an exploration of the image of the capital in the *Collection* allows us to analyze the workings of an aesthetic device that was not used in the Greco-Roman literary tradition.[45]

To my knowledge there are no poetic anthologies that juxtapose Greek and Latin poetry and rearrange them in a topical framework into a larger narrative: in the *Collection* the base text are the raw poetic excerpts, whose juxtaposition creates a supernarrative, which, in turn, is topped by the hypernarrative of the topic headings. Literary anthologies with sophisticated topical arrangements, one of the master formats of Chinese and especially Japanese literary traditions, were not a prominent medium of Hellenistic and Roman literary cultures and there are no indications that there was a multiliterate anthology including various genres of Greek and Latin poetry.[46] The closest literary phenomenon to the *Collection* is perhaps the Cento, "patchwork poems" made of literal allusions mostly to Homer and later Virgil that became popular in Hellenistic and Latin literature since the second century CE. But, unlike the *Collection*, they are most often parodical, only focus on the most canonical texts, are not inserted into yet another framing layer of topical headings, and are monolingual, that is, either in Greek or in Latin.

Let us now start to sketch the outlines of the capital location in the *Collection* by diving into the "Water; with Fishermen Appended" chapter, a companion chapter both to the preceding "Mountain and Water" and the actual "Forbidden City" that follows it. Within the short span of a dozen poetic excerpts it moves the reader

---

[45] Despite its great importance, there is little scholarship in Western languages on the *Collection*. The front matter of Chaves's and Rimer's translation (see below) gives insight into the Chinese poets included in the anthology, about the chanting practices and the *Collection*'s connection to the art of calligraphy. See also Smits 2000a and Smits 2000b and reflections on the *Collection* in part 2 of LaMarre 2000.

[46] There is of course *the* Anthology, the *Anthologia Palatina*, a codex containing ca. 3,700 epigrams, compiled around 930. But it is, as the definite article indicates, an exceptional collection; and it only contains Greek poems, is limited to the brief genre of epigrams (comparable in that aspect to the brief genres of Chinese and Japanese poetry), and is arranged by functional subgenres, such as dedicatory, funerary, protreptic, sympotic, and pederastic epigrams, an arrangement designed to satisfy practical purposes rather than to produce a complex hypernarrative that is equally "text" as the literal text itself. We know of a number of Hellenistic anthologies of epigrams and epigrammatists, but the closest analogy to the carefully constructed Japanese poetry anthologies is Meleager's Garland (Stephanos), compiled around the first century BCE, which arranged epigrams from the entire Greek tradition under topical headings and juxtaposed originals and imitations. Anthologization has received accordingly little scholarly attention in Classics. For a book-length study of Hellenistic epigram anthologies, including Meleager's, see Gutzwiller 1998.

from the limits of the known world to the imperial palace in Kyoto. This telescopic sweep opens in the farthest spot of the imagination with a couplet from a "Rhapsody on daybreak" by the Chinese poet Xie Guan 謝觀, which evokes a river near a fortified town somewhere on China's unruly northern frontier. From this generic vignette of Chinese frontier lore the reader's eye is led through the highlights of Chinese lake landscapes in the next three couplets, all from different poems by the Chinese poet Bo Juyi (772–846): dozing mandarin ducks at the Kunming lake in Yunnan (no. 511), the rainy season at the Qingcao Lake at the southern tip of the much-sung Dongting Lake in Hunan (no. 512), and travel spots near a lake associated with the legendary ancient southern state of Yue in the vicinity of Suzhou (no. 513). So far the reader has traveled from China's bleak and belligerent Northern frontier to its Southeastern cultural centers pregnant with poetic imagination. The next couplet, a sort of watershed between the first four Chinese and the following four Sino-Japanese excerpts of the chapter, enables the transition from China to Japan and from the Chinese periphery to the Japanese capital. The pivotal couplet is extracted from a poem by the Chinese poet Du Xunhe 杜荀鶴 (846–907), and effects the transition thanks to the intervention of the generic fisherman, a venerable topic of the Chinese tradition and an attractive figure of a life led with simple wisdom in undisturbed serenity:

菰蘆杓酌春濃酒。 　With your gourd ladle, you pour yourself some
　　　　　　　　　　spring-ripened wine
舴艋舟流夜漲灘。 　And with your tiny skiff you float along with the
　　　　　　　　　　night-swelling tides.

WAKAN RŌEISHŪ NO.514[47]

Du Xunhe's vision of the insouciant fisherman's life in this couplet seems to go along with the typical fisherman cliché: a life with good wine in free float. However, for those who know the entire poem, it is actually a double reversal of the fisherman cliché and is for good reason entitled "Sent to a fisherman in jest (*zeng xi yujia* 贈戲漁家)." In the closing couplet he laughs at the fisherman, who has apparently complained about his hard life, and claims that his own life as an official in the capital of Chang'an in the midst of political strive is much harder. Du Xunhe has apparently met a real-life fisherman, who looks strikingly different from the serene fisherman ideal in the imagination of urban poets. Thus Du Xunhe reverses expectations on both sides: his poem tells the urbanized poets that the fisherman believes his life is much tougher than they ever imagined, and he lectures the fisherman and his family that they have no idea how hard capital city life really is. Du Xunhe's ironic couplet joins the fate of the periphery to the world of the capital, so that the reader glides plausibly into the next excerpt, a glimpse of autumn at the residence of the retired Emperor Uda (r. 887–897) in Kyoto:

---

[47] My translations rely on Sugano Hiroyuki 1999, *Wakan rōeishū* SNKBZ 19. I have also consulted Ōsone Shōsuke's *Shinchō Nihon koten shūsei* edition and Kawaguchi Hisao's NKBT edition. For a basic complete English translation see J. Thomas Rimer, and Jonathan Chaves, *Japanese and Chinese Poems to Sing: the Wakan rōeishū* (New York: Columbia University Press, 1997).

閑居属於誰人。紫宸殿之本主也。 This abode for retirement—to whom
does it belong? To the former Lord of the
Purple Imperial Hall.
秋水見於何処。朱雀院之新家也。 The autumn waters—where can we
see them? In his new residence, the
Vermilion Bird Courtyard.

WAKAN RŌEISHŪ NO.515

The eminent scholar-official and poet Sugawara no Michizane, to whose exile poetry the next chapter of this book is devoted, wrote these lines for the annual autumn festival on the ninth day of the ninth month in 897 in praise of the retired emperor's new residence to which his majesty had recently moved. The following three Sino-Japanese excerpts do not explicitly refer to locations in the Japanese capital, and no. 517, by the Japanese poet Ōe no Asatsuna (886–957), describes a beach scene with gulls and geese from a poem written about the Chinese Dongting Lake. This couplet returns us to the southern Chinese lake highlights of the opening passages, though we look through the eyes of a Japanese poet who never visited China, but gazed poetically at Dongting Lake across the far ocean. Nevertheless, Michizane's four lines had brought the topic "Water; with Fishermen appended" firmly into the heart of the Japanese capital. Kintō's emphatic placement of Michizane's excerpt on the imperial residence in the middle of the chapter is echoed in the closing poem, a waka by Sone no Yoshitada 曽禰好忠 (fl.980s) that evokes another emperor's residence:

水上の The headwaters
さだめてければ are clearly determined:
君が代に in your august era
ふたたびすめる it is the second time
ほりかはの水 that you reside near the clear waters of the Horikawa River.

WAKAN RŌEISHŪ NO.520

The Imperial Palace burnt down twice during the reign of Emperor En'yū (959–991; r. 969–984), and as a make-shift solution the emperor moved twice into the "Horikawa Residence" of the powerful regent Fujiwara no Kanemichi 藤原兼通 (925–977) near the Horikawa River in the middle of the city. This plain waka celebrates the second move of the emperor. With this closing poem, the chapter, which had started on the Chinese Northern Frontier, is brought to conclusion back home on the imperial stage of the Japanese capital. And it adds another polar element, by ending the chapter on "Water" with two palace "fires," balancing it with the Chinese-style cosmology of the "Five Elements."

Yoshitada's waka leads us from a makeshift palace right into the next chapter on the actual "Forbidden City/Imperial Palace." As if wanting to add splendor to the Japanese Imperial Palace, which was significantly more modest than its Chinese models, Kintō borrows the imposing scenery of the Tang capital from Chinese poems in the opening excerpts of the chapter: In a couplet by Bo Juyi there is "Phoenix Pond" close to his office building in the Central Secretariat, in charge among other things of drafting the emperor's edicts, and the "Dragon Tower-Terrace" flanking the gate of the majestic Weiyang Palace from the Han

Dynasty (no. 521), and excerpt no. 523 evokes Han-yuan Hall, the state ceremonial hall in the most important of the various Tang Palaces, the Daming Palace. With a perimeter of 7, 7 kilometers the Daming Palace alone occupied a space that was about a third of the entire city of Kyoto. Kintō's opening selections evoke imperial grandeur through the image of China's majestic palaces.

Yet the remainder of the chapter does not follow up on this invitation to imperial praise clad in Chinese-style grandeur. The Japanese emperor does not once figure in the chapter until the very last poem, and there he appears only indirectly. Instead, the "Forbidden City" chapter shows the Imperial Palace as the everyday workplace of the official bureaucracy. The excerpt sequence of nos. 523, 524, and 525 is associated with the painful *rite de passage* of the later Chinese bureaucracy, the civil service examination. Although Japan's State Academy (*daigakuryō* 大学寮) was founded in the late seventh century on the model of medieval Chinese educational institutions, the exam system never developed into an important tool of career advancement as it did since the Tang or particularly the Song Dynasty (960–1279) in China. Birth into the powerful family lineages was the major factor in one's social standing in Heian Japan, yet the exams remained important for the hereditary scholarly families such as the Sugawara, the Ōe, and a branch of the Fujiwara clans; and scholarly success did ensure a good reputation and opportunities to be invited to high-profile court events to compose poetry on the occasion.

The exam-related sequence combines a hodge-podge of genres, juxtaposing a couplet from a Chinese poem with four lines from an actual examination essay written by a Japanese scholar and a slightly satirical, anonymous Japanese "linked poem" (*renku* 連句). The Chinese couplet (no. 523) shows successful exam candidates in the palace and with no. 524 we see from a Japanese candidate what kind of procedure the Chinese candidates might just have gone through: the examination essay by Miyako no Yoshika 都良香, a prominent scholar-official and older contemporary of Michizane's, is devoted to the topic of time measurement and water clocks:

鶏人暁唱。声驚明王之眠。 The "rooster man" cries out at dawn: its sound startles the enlightened ruler from his sleep.

鳧鐘夜鳴。響徹暗天之聴。 Master Fu's bell rings in the evening: its echo penetrates all hearing beneath the dark sky.

WAKAN RŌEISHŪ NO.524

Miyako no Yoshika eagerly shows off his bookish knowledge: both the "rooster man" and "Master Fu's bell" appear in the *Rituals of the Zhou (Zhou li* 周禮), one of the Chinese Confucian Classics. The "rooster man" was a time-keeping official in the Heian Palace, who ensured in particular on days of important ceremonial functions that the court would be on its feet in time. Master Fu's bell, however, was the stuff for antiquarians: the *Rituals* mention that a certain person named Fu invented this particular type of time-keeping bell, but it does not seem to have been part of the Heian Palace accessories. Kintō interrupts Miyako's erudite lecture on the chronometric soundscape of the Heian Palace with a light "linked verse," a popular poetic game where people would take turns writing lines or couplets:

朝候日高冠額抜。	. The officials, off to morning court when the sun is already high up in the sky, have their caps pulling from their foreheads!
夜行沙厚履声忙	The night patrol, on the heavy sand, busily scuff their clogs.

WAKAN RŌEISHŪ NO.525

This vignette satirizes the busybody officials scurrying about on the palace grounds and adds comic touches to the palace scenery: apparently the "rooster man" has not done his job, since the gentlemen are late on their feet for morning court. The awkwardness of their caps pulling from the heads in haste in the morning matches their clumsy clogs at night, certainly not an image that would inspire confidence in these officials at any other time during the day, either. At this moment of comic relief Kintō abruptly turns away from the serious business of the civil servants and inserts a seething vernacular love poem, with little more than a metaphorical excuse:

御垣守る	Although it is not
衛士のたく火に	like the fire of the guards
あらねども	protecting the imperial precincts
われも心の	in my innermost heart
うちにこそたけ[48]	burns my longing.

WAKAN RŌEISHŪ NO.526

The metaphor that justifies and dramatizes the sudden thematic break is the torches of the imperial guards, held up as a kenning of the burning love that this poem declares. Does Kintō proceed from social satire of the Chinese-style bureaucracy to an emotional satire of that satire, gliding into the vernacular voice of love coached in a waka poem on the flimsy bridge of the guards' metaphorical fire? Does the vernacular waka look more ridiculous than the satirized bureaucrats? Or do the satirized bureaucrats look yet more out of place because of the waka poem? Ironically, this ambiguous coupling of excerpts provides leeway into the most venerable subject of the Forbidden City, which the Chinese and Sino-Japanese poems had left unmentioned: the Emperor.

The second and concluding waka of the chapter continues the theme of longing, but transfers it from a couple of lovers to a courtier yearning for his nearby emperor.

ここにだに	Even right here
光さやけき	its light shines bright:
秋の月	the autumn moon,
くもの上こそ	I keep thinking,
思ひやらるれ	must be yet brighter "above the clouds."

WAKAN RŌEISHŪ NO.527

The waka is by Fujiwara no Nobuomu 藤原経臣 (fl. ca. 900?), who watched the moon at the chamberlain's office on the night of the fifteenth day of the eighth month, when the moon was at its brightest and the customary "Moon Festival"

---

[48] Following Ōsone Shōsuke's *Shinchō Nihon koten shūsei* edition.

was held. As a chamberlain he worked in an agency that functioned as a private secretariat to the emperor and allowed unusually close interaction with the sovereign, but his low, fifth, rank meant that he was mostly carrying around imperial messages and was not allowed into the *Seiryōden* 清涼殿 ("Hall of Clarity and Coolness"), the emperor's private residence, where Emperor Daigo (885–930; r. 897–930) was celebrating the moon festival at the moment when Nobuomu composed his waka. Although the chamberlain's office was immediately south of the *Seiryōden* and the physical distance between the emperor and the poet was minimal, the social and poetic distance between the emperor's presence "above the clouds" and the poet's "right here" is insurmountable.

Although the moon in the poem was first and foremost the autumn moon celebrated on the night of the festival, the moon could also function as an image for the emperor, making the poem both into a praise of the moon and of the emperor, who bestows his radiant grace on his subjects. At the same time, watching the moon had erotic associations: it was something one did with a lover, or one lamented not doing if one was separated from one's lover on a beautiful moon night. The iridescence of the poem's moonlight gives this simple poem more depth than expected: the rays on the night of the festival blend with the splendor of imperial grace in an ambiance of amorous yearning, which is not an unusual image in the political erotics between ruler and subject.

It is masterful how in this chapter Kintō creates a vignette of the Imperial Palace that plays through such varied majestic, solemn, comic, and eulogistic modes to capture the Heian Palace as a physical and social space. But Kintō defers the appearance of the emperor, the sovereign of the palace and the symbolic center of Heian political culture, until the closing poem, where he appears only as a distant presence in absence.

The chapter on the Imperial Palace makes a diptych with the following chapter on "Ancient Capitals." This chapter, only two excerpts short, is one of the few chapters in the *Collection* that start with a Japanese rather than Chinese author. If in the "Imperial Palace" chapter Kintō brought the narrative from the borderlands of China to the imperial palace in Kyoto thanks to a passage by the eminent scholar-official Sugawara no Michizane, it is his talented grandson Sugawara no Fumitoki (899–981) whose couplet opens "Old Capitals":

緑草如今麋鹿苑。　Green grasses—now like a garden for large deer.
紅花定昔管絃家。　Red blossoms—in the old days certainly houses filled
　　　　　　　　　with the music of pipes and strings.

WAKAN RŌEISHŪ NO.528

Fumitoki apparently wrote these lines when passing the former capital Nara and it is a typical treatment of the abandoned capital topos. Weeds have grown over the former palaces and deer, still today part of Nara's cityscape, have settled in. The red blossoms, an afterglow of former aristocratic residences and their extravagant feasts, connect Fumitoki's couplet to the second poem in the chapter, an anonymous waka:

いそのかみ　　　When I come to gaze at

古き都を	the capital, of times immemorial
きてみれば	like Isonokami
むかしかざしし	I find those flowers, with which they decorated [their hair]
花さきにけり	blooming afresh.

WAKAN RŌEISHŪ NO.529

Both Fumitoki's couplet and the waka gaze with nostalgia over the former capital site and zoom in on the blooming flowers, symptoms of painful change and vigorous continuity at once. The waka gets some inches closer to the former capital, seeing the flowers before the eyes of the poet in the hair of the former capital inhabitants during their festive celebrations. But the most significant distinction between the kanshi couplet and the waka poem is the contrast between the particular and the generic that is rooted in the different rhetorical repertoire of kanshi and waka, respectively. Fumitoki wrote his capital lament specifically on Nara, though tapping into the generic resources of Chinese and Chinese-style capital laments. The waka poet, in contrast, creates a vignette of the literary topos of the abandoned capital thanks to a rhetorical device specific to waka, the so-called "pillow word," *makura kotoba* 枕詞. Pillow words served as amplifying epithets to expressions that deserved particular decoration, such as venerable landmarks or objects related to the gods or emperors. Most often consisting of five syllables, and thus a short line in the 5-7-5-7-7-syllabic scheme of waka, these pillow words were set phrases that gave the poems solemnity, but also inspired playfulness and literary sophistication. "Isonokami," the "pillow word" in the waka at hand and a place nowadays in the area of *Furu* 布留 in Tenri City of Nara Prefecture, had indeed been the location of the palace capitals of Emperors Ankō and Ninken, two fifth-century emperors of hoary antiquity by Kintō's standards. Mentioning this place name allowed the poet to insert a clever pun: when he writes about the *furuki miyako*, the "old capital," his mind wanders along with his tongue and he ends up writing about that *Furu miyako*, Isonokami in the area of *Furu*. Thus, Isonokami is not so much a place name, but a "pillow word" that serves as a generic cushion for just about any old capital. Through the power of this rhetorical device the waka distills the literary *topos* of the abandoned capital into an aesthetic phenomenon, shedding its historical specificity. This retrospective aesthetic of the destroyed past continues in the next chapter, which follows the mood of the "Old Capitals" chapter and is devoted to old palaces and dilapidated residences.

Without doubt, there is no limit to the meaning one can insert into the spaces between the juxtaposed poetic excerpts of Kintō's *Collection*. Not doing so reduces Kintō's ingenious work to a heap of fragments (which it technically is). If we can talk about a "literary epistemology" behind the unique format of the text, it probes the limits of what literary fragments quoted-out-of-context can be brought to say when placed under the terse control of a lineup of topic headings. Despite the fact that Kintō's collection is such a play with unleashed and controlled indeterminacy, the contrast between Kintō's mind-map of the Heian court and capital in the *Collection* and Virgil's road-map toward Augustan Rome in the *Aeneid* is clear. In curious parallel to the structure of Kintō's *Collection*, my discussion of the image of Kyoto in the *Collection* and the image of Rome in the proleptic moments of the *Aeneid* seem to make a suggestive juxtaposition rather than a good comparison.

Yet the opposite direction of the time vectors, which these extremely influential images of the respective capitals engraved into the minds of generations of their readers who knew them by heart, is significant and should be taken seriously.

The breathtaking proleptic foresights of Augustan Rome in the *Aeneid* were only meaningful as dramatizations of the Roman miracle, the spectacular success at world domination. In contrast, the Heian capital is subtly suspended in a retrospective aesthetic of dereliction and a web of metaphorical parallel realms such as the uncorrupted realm of fishermen and immortals, exam candidates or funny officials. This mind-map of the capital, refracted as it is through excerpts in different literary languages, responded to a different preoccupation, not with the vertical timeline of political success, but with the horizontal coexistence of multiple aesthetic and literary traditions and linguistic and rhetorical choices in Japan.

3. Unequal Romance

What else was comparably unequal in Kyoto and Rome? In tenth-century Kyoto and in first-century BCE Rome literary revolutions took place. One of them, in both places, concerned the relation between literature, the capital, and romance. In Japan, the newly developed *kana* syllabary, based on simplifications of Chinese characters, enabled the rise of new genres, in particular tales (*monogatari*) and vernacular diaries (*nikki*), written predominantly by women. These genres were closely related to the social rise of waka poetry in the late ninth century. At the beginning of the tenth century the first imperially commissioned waka anthology, the *Collection of Ancient and Modern Poetry* (*Kokinshū*), had elevated "love" to a major topic of the poetic production at court. And in the new tales and diaries we can see waka in social action, functioning as an elegant go-between of lovers who spent most of their time apart from each other due to the prevalent segregation of sexes. Waka poetry became a fundamental social practice in Heian society, both as opportunity to excel at courtly banquets, where waka and kanshi were composed, and as means of communication in amorous affairs. Written mostly by ladies-in-waiting at the imperial court, the new forms of prose fiction and confessional accounts allowed women to record, lament, or creatively reimagine the romantic on-goings and the fierce marriage politics between members of the Heian elite. These women served in the lavishly equipped entourage of the daughters of the leading Fujiwara families, who competed for the emperor's attention. Because they were often the daughters of mid-level aristocrats, who had not succeeded in making a career at court and thus served as governors in the provinces, they had both a duty to praise their powerful patrons and a desire to criticize the power games of court culture and the vulnerable position of women in it. This dilemma makes for some of the most memorable moments in Murasaki Shikibu's *Tale of Genji* and Sei Shōnagon's *Pillow Book*.

In turn, late first-century-BCE Rome saw the fulminant flourishing of Roman love elegy, a programmatically subjective genre of love exaltation written mostly by men who had lived through the bloody civil wars and vowed to replace the now questionable life of civil service with a new type of service, the *servitium amoris* to their *puella* or *domina*. Elegy, one of the most disputed and complex genres in Greek and

Latin literature, was written in elegiac couplets, alternating a dactylic hexameter with a pentameter. It was metrically close to epic poetry and its Greek origins went back to the seventh century BCE. Greek elegists treated a large variety of themes and wrote elegies for festive or funerary occasions and on erotic, political, mythical, and etiological themes. The surviving Roman elegists of the first century BCE, Tibullus, Propertius, and later, Ovid, shared much with Catullus and neoteric poetry of the late Republic. In particular, Propertius and Ovid elevated their gusto for moral rebellion, their retreat from political engagement and the mythological elevation of love, with its ecstasies, disenchantments, and volatile capriciousness, into a way of life.[49] Roman love elegy was a short-lived phenomenon and produced incomparably less literature than the new vernacular genres in Japan: although vernacular tales and diaries were considered a popular literature of sorts in their own time, in contrast to the high status of Sino-Japanese writings, these genres produced a vast body of literature, and starting in the thirteenth century the two principal tales, the *Tale of Genji* and the *Tales of Ise*, were canonized and moved up in the genre hierarchy.[50]

Japanese vernacular tales and diaries and Roman love elegy share significant common features that are worth juxtaposing. First, they were new or unfolded in ways independent of their reference culture. Japanese tale and diary literature was written in the vernacular and had no direct genre correlate on the Chinese side. Although Chinese poems and stories of passionate love had a deep impact in terms of plot elements and the logic of tragic love affairs on Japanese tales such as the *Tale of Genji*, there was no long prose genre in Chinese literature at the time. It took a few more centuries in China before novels of the length and complexity comparable to Murasaki Shikibu's *Tale of Genji* came to be written.[51] The independence of Roman love elegy from Greek elegy is a more complex question that has been much debated, but the hypothesis that it might derive either from Hellenistic subjective-erotic elegy or from the Hellenistic epigram tradition is generally rejected today, although they share many traits.[52] Already by the end of the first century CE the magisterial teacher of oratory Quintilian had declared proudly that "Also in elegy can we challenge the Greeks (*elegia quoque Graecos provocamus*)."[53] What seems to make Roman love elegy distinctively Roman is the unique combination of a rather carnal autobiographical pose, with the projection of one's love into the elevated realm of myth, and the proud literary celebration of a life lived in absolute devotion to the cause of love, which most often humiliates the poet in the eyes of civic morality.

Second, Japanese tales and diaries and Roman love elegy allowed the experimentation with emotional intensity and transcendental passion that previously had hardly any extensive, let alone distinctive venues of expression.[54] Also, in both cases the pose

---

[49] For a quick introduction to the genre of Roman love elegy see Gibson 2005 and Conte 1994b, 321–39.
[50] On the modern canon formation of classical Japanese literature see Shirane and Suzuki 2000a.
[51] On the *Tale of Genji* in the context of previous tale literature see Shirane 1987. On the relation of the *Tale of Genji* to Chinese literature see the studies of Shinma 2003 and Shinma 2009.
[52] On recent debates regarding the origin of Latin love elegy in relation to Propertius's work see Cairns 2006 and Hollis 2006.
[53] *Institutio oratoria* 10.1.93.

of the autobiographical—whether true or retouched, authenticated or consciously overdramatized—was crucial to the authors' voice and to the genres' attraction and credibility.

This relates to a third resonance: because the Japanese vernacular tales and diaries did not dwell on grand themes of Confucian governance and public morals that were de rigueur in Sino-Japanese genres of the time, and because Roman love elegy and its authors renounced a life and literature elevated by epic grandeur and displays of virtuous Romanness, these genres developed their own versions of *recusatio*, or tropes of literary "refusal." Their authors eloquently conceded the inferiority of their amorous subject matter to the grand literary themes treated in the genres at the top of the respective genre hierarchy, namely Chinese-style literature in the Japanese, and epic poetry in the Roman case. Yet the trope of refusal allowed at the same time to celebrate the immediacy of passion, which required a lighter muse, and to practice the sophisticated art of ostentatious understatement.

Fourth, Heian vernacular literature and Roman love elegy had an intimate urban connection. Although in both cases literary production centered on the capitals, where authors were either born or came to receive their education, make a living, and spend their lives, Japanese tales and diaries and Roman elegy spoke about and through the capital. Most often, this was where lovers lived, met, made love, or pined away in neglect, and this was where readers and literary fame intersected with the opportunities for sophisticated romance. In short, the new literature of romance was unthinkable without the urban fabric of the capital. True, stories about love adventures in the countryside abound in the *Tales of Ise* (ca. 947), but if anything, they often serve to underscore the elegance of urban life in the capital and to show that living in the provinces was to be considered an exile of sorts. Similarly, Tibullus (ca. 50–19 BCE), the elegist who likes to express his yearning for serene rural life, does so because of his experience of city life, and his sweetheart Delia appears as a lady of worldly tastes, fond of luxury and full of capricious surprises, to be expected from a city dweller, not a country girl. Clearly, both Heian tales and diaries, and Roman love elegy, sported a *goût* for urban refinement and aesthetic sophistication.

Needless to say, there are significant differences between the Japanese genres and Roman love elegy and the conditions of their respective rise in Kyoto and Rome. Most importantly, the authors' gender and their social contexts differed radically: in the case of Japan the main proponents of this new world of romance were women writers. True, the earliest tales were probably written by men, and

---

[54] Love discourse had only very limited space in Sino-Japanese literature. In Japanese tales and diaries the absoluteness of love is often expressed more obliquely than in Roman love elegy, but there are also moments of spirited assertiveness, like in Sei Shonagon's *Pillow Book*: "There was a large and distinguished gathering at Her Majesty's, of various family members, nobles and senior courtiers. I was sitting leaning against an aisle pillar talking to some of the ladies, when Her Majesty tossed me a note. Opening it, I read, 'Should I love you, or should I not? How would it be if you were not loved above others?' This was a reference to something I had said in passing in Her Majesty's hearing. 'I absolutely must be first in someone's heart,' I'd declared. 'If not, I'd prefer to be loathed and treated like dirt. I'd rather die than be second or third in a person's affections. It's first or nothing, for me.' Hearing me, some of the ladies had joked, 'She's Lady *Lotus Sutra*—there can be no other Law.' (section 96; McKinney 2006, 104.)

the first diary, the *Tosa Diary* (*Tosa nikki* 土佐日記, ca. 935) was written by a man, though in the voice of a woman, which reveals the general assumption at the time that such texts would be written by women. There is also evidence that a lineage of poem collections, tales and diaries that influenced the *Gossamer Diary* (*Kagerō nikki* 蜻蛉日記, 974), which is seen as the fountainhead of women's confessional diaries, were written or commissioned by men of the powerful Regent branch of the Fujiwara family to glorify the poet and amorous exploits of their clan.[55] This shows the strong grip that men did have on women's writing. Yet, even if the author, whom we only know by the name of "Mother of Michitsuna," had perhaps been asked to compile a flattering poetry collection of her husband Fujiwara no Kaneie (929–990), the diary she produced instead detailed her unhappiness and reproached him for his neglect of her. And most of mid-Heian vernacular literature was written by women. They worked as ladies-in-waiting for the courts of the Fujiwara imperial consorts and were usually handpicked for their beauty and skills in poetry, music, and witty conversation; their writing was an integral result of their participation in court life.

Meanwhile in Rome, the love elegists were almost exclusively men (the elegist Sulpicia being the exception that confirms the rule). They acquired fame for themselves and for their Delias, Cynthias, or Lycorises. But the women behind these figures did not write or leave anything that would give us the female perspective on their romantic affairs. Also, the Roman love elegists rejected a public career and portrayed themselves as rebellious bohemians and their lovers as either free women or courtesans. In contrast, the Japanese tale and diary writers served at the heart of the Heian political establishment, were part of court society, and were left to criticize it indirectly and from within.[56]

A second difference is that the boundary between the new genre of romance and the genres of higher canonical standing in the Japanese and Roman genre hierarchy had a different edge. There is a much more pronounced permeability between epic and love elegy, in meter, diction and its recourse to the plot resources of myth. On the Japanese side, it was after all women who were writing a *new* type of literature, not men who wrote a *different* type of literature and the social and linguistic gulf between the new vernacular genres and the canonical status of Chinese-style literature was much wider. We do of course find many references to Chinese and Chinese-style literature and hilarious parodies of the scholarly world of Chinese-style writing, as we shall see in Chapter 7 of this book, but they do not become a carrying force of articulation in the vernacular tales and diaries, as the play with epic conventions becomes in Roman love elegy.

As a third divergence, Roman love elegy *depicts* their protagonists and their amorous adventures in text. Japanese tales and diaries go beyond that by including

---

[55] For a translation of the *Tosa Diary* see McCullough 1990, 73–102. For the *Gossamer Diary* see Arntzen 1997. For translations of early diaries written between the *Tosa Diary* and the *Gossamer Diary* and a discussion of the gender dynamics and political purposes behind their production see Mostow 2004.

[56] On marriage customs and the social status of elite women in Heian Japan see McCullough 1999, 134–42.

the actual *corpora delicti* of the affairs in the text. In the case of autobiographical diaries, men were not just described by female authors, but the actual poetry with which they courted their ladies was usually included, thus preserving the male voice in a text, which is otherwise told from the female perspective. Propertius's Cynthia might love her man—so the voice of Propertius tells us—because he writes about her and is immortalized as his muse. In contrast, those males who might have been Sei Shōnagon's lovers are not just described through the pen of a woman in her *Pillow Book* but speak through their poems. As the social practice of poetry was the linchpin of romantic affairs, the inclusion of the lover's poems was an essential element of the romantic plot: a romance of, not just in writing.

Propertius's *Elegies* and Sei Shōnagon's *Pillow Book* are worth juxtaposing to get a more palpable sense of the difference between the romance of writing and the romance in writing and, more broadly, of the intersections and gaps between romance in Heian vernacular diaries and Roman love elegy. Propertius and Sei Shōnagon seem to make an apt pair, because they both enjoy parading their literary wit and surprising their readers with unexpected turns of events or phrases. Propertius's four books of elegies, published separately between 28 and 16 BCE, start out with the name of his muse, Cynthia, who dominates the first book. She is still at the center of the second and third books, often in her unpleasant and capricious moods, and fades out in the fourth book, which is mostly devoted to elegies on the myths and religious ceremonies of the Roman and Italic tradition. This overall narrative arch has been seen both as a reflection of the rise and fall of Propertius's affair with Cynthia and as an increasing integration of Propertius into the Augustan establishment that went along with his participation in the famous circle of Maecenas, where he met Virgil, and Horace.

While Propertius's books were immediately recognized as centerpieces of the genre of Roman love elegy and already mentioned by his immediate successor Ovid, Sei Shōnagon's *Pillow Book* is unusual among the diaries of Heian court women.[57] It was probably finished around 1005, after the death of her patron Empress Teishi and the demise of the literary salon of the Empress in the face of the rival Empress Sōshi, who outshone Empress Teishi at court and had writers such as Murasaki Shikibu, Izumi Shikibu, and Akazome Emon in her service. It consists of three types of entries, namely catalogues of objects and moods, essayistic reflections, and diary entries. In the Nōin and Sankan variants of the text, which have become canonical, these different materials are mixed and not presented in chronological order. This unusual format makes it impossible to categorize it as belonging to one single genre, but it shares much with tale literature, the diary tradition, and later medieval essay writing (*zuihitsu* 随筆). In contrast to Propertius, whose first book of elegies, the *monobiblos*, caught Maecenas's attention and led to his introduction into the most powerful literary salon of the time, Sei Shōnagon wrote the *Pillow Book* in memory of her late patron Empress Teishi and focused on those happy years when Teishi's standing at court was at its height, in ominously silent awareness of the tragic demise that was to follow.

---

[57] For an overview of research trends in the scholarship on the *Pillow Book* and a reading of the *Pillow Book*'s headstrong portrayal of Empress Teishi's court in the "diary" type entries against the backdrop of historical sources see Naomi Fukumori 1997, 1–44.

Let us try to capture a bit of the romantic games that Propertius and Sei Shōnagon play in their writing.[58] Propertius's passions are profoundly connected to Rome. In elegy II.6 he exclaims, after explaining that the vices of love and jealousy led to wars such as the one at Troy:

> Why seek I precedents from Greece? You, Romulus, nursed on the harsh milk of a she-wolf, were the instigator of the crime: you taught us to rape the Sabine virgins with impunity: through your fault Cupid dares any outrage at Rome.
>
> *Cur exampla petam Graiūm? tu criminis auctor, / nutritus duro, Romule, lacte lupae: / tu rapere intactas docuisti impune Sabinas: per te nunc Romae quidlibet audit Amor?*[59]

Thanks be to divine Romulus that not just Cupid but also Propertius can afford to engage in extravagant love affairs in his Rome. It isn't just Propertius who benefits from Rome's history, which gives him much sexual license thanks to the precedent of Romulus and the rape of the Sabines. Note that in elegy I.8 it is actually Rome, too, who profits in *her* reputation from *his* love affairs:

> She (i.e. Cynthia) loves me and because of me loves Rome of cities best, and says that without me even a kingdom would not please her. She has preferred to lie with me, though narrow is my bed, and to be mine, whatever our style of life, than to possess the ancient kingdom that was Hippodamia's dowry and all the wealth horse-pasturing Elis had amassed.
>
> *illi carus ego et per me carissima Roma / dicitur, et sine me dulcia regna negat. / illa vel angusto mecum requiescere lecto / et quocumque modo maluit esse mea, quam sibi dotatae regnum vetus Hippodamiae, / et quas Elis opes apta pararat equis.*[60]

Cynthia loves Rome because she loves Propertius. Without him, Propertius claims, Rome would be nothing to her. Not just Rome, but even more fabled kingdoms such as the ones of the Homeric heroes of the House of Atreus, Agamemnon and Menelaos, the descendants of Hippodamia, would be nothing to her. Thus, according to Propertius's Cynthia, Propertius's worth exceeds all fabulous kingdoms, past and present, Greek and Roman. If in this elegy Propertius has his Cynthia set the price of his love far beyond that of the Roman Empire, Propertius repays the hyperbolic compliment in Elegy II.1, where she is a goddess, his muse, his *puella* and wrestling partner in bed:

---

[58] On Propertius elegies Hubbard 1974 is still important. For recent scholarship, Johnson 2009 is a vivid and thoughtful discussion of Propertius's work in the ideological and literary context of the late Republic and the Early Empire. James 2003 explores Roman love elegy from the perspective of female readership and opens compelling ways to look beyond what she calls "the sincerity requirement" of elegy, thus moving from the autobiographical fallacy to the rhetorical and literary workings of the genre. A similar fallacy can sometimes also be detected in too literal readings of Heian women diaries and the *Pillow Book*.

[59] *Propertius* II. 6. 19–22. All translations from Propertius are from Goold 1990, 137.

[60] *Propertius* I.8B. 31–36. Goold 1990, 69.

You ask how it is that I compose love poems so often, how it is that my book sounds so soft upon the lips. It is not Calliope, not Apollo that puts these songs in my mind: my sweetheart herself creates the inspiration. If I have seen her step forth dazzling in Coan silks, a whole book will emerge from the Coan garment; if I have seen the locks straying scattered on her brow, I praise her locks and for joy she walks with head held high; if with ivory fingers she strikes the melody of the lyre, I marvel how skillfully she applies her easy touch; or if she lowers eyelids that fight against sleep, the poet in me finds a thousand new conceits; or if, her dress torn off, she struggles naked with me, then, be sure of it, I compose long Iliads: whatever she has done[61], whatever she has said, from absolutely nothing is born a grand legend.

Quaeritis, unde mihi totiens scribantur amores / unde meus veniat mollis in ora liber.
/ non haec Calliope, non haec mihi cantat Apollo: / ingenium nobis ipsa puella facit. /
sive illam Cois fulgentem incedere vidi / totum de Coa veste volumen erit; / seu vidi ad
frontem sparsos errare capillos / gaudet laudatis ire superba comis; / sive lyrae carmen
digitis percussit eburnis / miramur, facilis ut premat arte manus; / seu compescentis
somnum declinat ocellos, invenio causas mille poeta novas; / seu nuda erepto mecum
luctatur amictu / tum vero longas condimus Iliadas: / seu quidquid fecit sivest quod-
cumque locuta / maxima de nihilo nascitur historia.[62]

Propertius paints his sweetheart with the colors of an alternative Calliope, muse of epic poetry and warfare. Each part of her portrait creates writing: the famous silk from the island of Cos—a book; her locks—a panegyric on her pride; her fingers on the lyre—an ode to her skillfulness; her eyelids—a thousand new conceits; best of all, once all covers (except for natural ones like her drowsy eyelids) fall and she is naked, Iliads emerge, in the rare plural. Whatever she does, the poet will extract a *historia*. Propertius and the other elegists clearly fashioned their literary loves to serve their own purposes.[63] This flattering portrayal would certainly appeal to female vanity, too, but it also serves the poet's own literary vanity, because it allows him to launch on a grand gesture of *recusatio*, the ostentatious refusal to compose in grandiose epic fashion on grand legendary themes.

There is a complex zigzag pattern of recusatio and re-recusatio in this elegy. Let us follow the moves of this play with romance and recusatio. First, as we saw, Propertius dresses Cynthia up as the new Calliope, inspiring the poet to write much and in many modes. Second, enter a new character, Maecenas, Propertius's patron and Augustus's intimate friend. Propertius promises Maecenas that he would use his new muse to tell of Augustus's and Maecenas's policies and exploits (*Propertius* II.1.17–26). He promises to produce an epic on the patron and the patron's patron. In a list of quick references to Octavian's victories from the 40s to the 20s BCE, Propertius highlights Maecenas's role in the military exploits and his loyalty, *fides*, to Augustus. This pivot word, which connects war and love discourse,

---

[61] The Loeb edition has erroneously "said."
[62] *Propertius* II.1.1-16. Goold 1990, 117.
[63] Maria Wyke has debunked the common assumption of autobiographical realism and has convincingly traced hints at the fictional nature of Propertius's lover throughout his corpus. Wyke 1987.

is, third, the right moment for Propertius to jump from promises to epic to his light Muse and return to outrageous recusatio: "I for my part wage wars within the narrow confines of a bed: let everyone spend his life in the trade he practices best (*nos contra angusto versamus proelia lecto: / qua pote quisque, in ea conterat arte diem, Propertius* II.1.45–46)." His *fides* goes to his *puella*, but also to his trade as an elegiac poet. And ultimately his loyalty goes to death: "To die in love is glory: and glory yet again to enjoy a single love… (*laus in amore mori: laus altera, si datur uno / posse frui…; Propertius* II.1.47–48)."

What looks like an audacious recusatio is actually none at all, because Propertius claims the realm of war for love, and the realm of epic for love elegy. In a fourth move, to give death epic dignity, Propertius projects the prophecy of his death into the choicest examples from myth: he wouldn't mind to die by the poisonous potions of the likes of Phaedra, Circe, and Medea, who killed because of love and jealousy. Medicine, able to cure all human pains, would not cure Propertius. He can only be healed by that physician who could heal poor Tantalus, whom the gods in all eternity tortured with thirst and hunger, who could wash away the sins of the Danaids, from whom the gods in all eternity withheld water vessels, and who could protect Prometheus from the vulture, whom the gods had sent for all eternity to peck out his liver. Only the impossible reversal of divine fate by myth's sanction could save Propertius, in short, nothing.

> When, therefore, fate claims back from me my life, and I become a brief name on a tiny marble slab, then, Maecenas, hope and envy of Roman youth, my rightful pride in life and in death, should your travels chance to bring you close to my tomb, halt your British chariot with its figured harness, and, shedding a tear, pay this tribute to my silent embers: "An unrelenting girl was the death of this poor man!"

> *Quandocumque igitur vitam me fata reposcent, / et breve in exiguo marmore nomen ero, / Maecenas, nostrae spes invidiosa iuventae, / et vitae et morti gloria iusta meae, / si te forte meo ducet via proxima busto, / esseda caelatis siste Britanna iugis, / taliaque illacrimans mutae iace verba favillae: / "huic misero fatum dura puella fuit."*[64]

Propertius seems to have waited all along to paint this final scene and indulge a vision of his posthumous self: like a soldier, he has met his fate and died in battle. Death is not so bad after all, since his name is immortalized on a marble slab and a tomb close enough to a grand avenue where Maecenas could ride by on a triumph to pay his warrior tribute in a "British chariot." Maecenas is the executor of Propertius's last will, his desire for a public lament. Maecenas should shed tears in his chariot, Propertius will be nothing but silent ashes, and the incriminating finger will point at Cynthia. The poet's unepic death is dignified by an epic hero coming home from battle. And even if Propertius's playfulness should keep us from taking his pompous self-lament all too seriously, he looks nobler for it. Because he had dressed up his *puella* as the epic muse in the opening lines of the elegy, his death is both due to a hard-hearted lover and the hard-hearted muse.

---

[64] Propertius II.1. 71–78. Goold 1990, 123.

Let us quickly sum up some decisive elements of the dynamics of romance in this elegy, before plunging into the love world of eleventh-century Japan. First, romance unfolds here in a triangle: rather than addressing his lover directly, the poem is addressed to Propertius's patron Maecenas. Yet Propertius certainly wanted Cynthia to hear his accusations against her harshness through Maecenas's mouth and his public lament. That the verdict is delivered from a war chariot relates to the second point: romance in this elegy lives off the language of war and the epic literature that depicts it. War and epic are the things that Propertius claims not to be able to do, but at the same time precisely claims to be much abler to do than the real warriors and epic poets. There is a more clamorous and exhibitionist deployment of recusatio in Propertius's elegies than in the poetry of Horace, who, like Propertius, spent his life writing anything but epic. Cynthia is a much complimented and necessary element of the romantic game, but Propertius seems more occupied with his own immortality, luckily enabled by the cruel death in love, and his playful relationship to the grand tones and themes of epic. This means, moreover, that his recusatio is not simply a way to justify his indulgence in love elegy; rather, he designs himself a life where his passion has a degree of primacy and absoluteness that only uncompromising genres like the epic and the language of myth are able to express. He builds up a strong ground for epic love in his elegies that enables him, with more or less irony at times, to live an absolute life, a life of love of epic proportions.

Entering the world of Sei Shōnagon's *Pillow Book* from Propertius's *Elegies* is not just a long stretch; it is a jump, which is worth exploring because the rise of new discourses of love connected to the urban cultures of the capitals of tenth-century Japan and first-century BCE Rome provides enough of a frame to appreciate the juxtaposition.

The instructive dissimilitude starts with the simple fact that in the scene from the *Pillow Book* to which we turn now there is no Cynthia, no figure beguilingly praised, undressed, cursed, and divinely adored. Sei Shōnagon's love life remains a mystery. The center of romantic attention in this scene is Fujiwara no Tadanobu (967–1035), a senior courtier well known for his literary wit and poetic skill. From the way he appears in the *Pillow Book* it seems likely that he and Sei Shōnagon were lovers at some point: they like to tantalize each other with private jokes and she tells of being hopelessly enraptured with a particular incense he was wearing that day.[65] But the man she might have been married to for a short while and who probably was the father of her child was an undistinguished man named Tachibana no Norimitsu, whom Sei Shōnagon repeatedly mocks for his lack of poetic sensibility.[66] From the way Sei Shōnagon conveys wisdom about affairs of the heart, we should infer that she had quite a few lovers. But compared to the adventures described by Catullus or Propertius, romantic affairs in Japanese diaries and tales, whether autobiographical or fictional, are painted in pastel colors. They often withhold identities, and hardly ever expose any flesh. Even in the case of the stormy lover Prince Genji, the reader

---

[65] See sections 128, 154, and 189, respectively. Kamens 2007 very compellingly uses Tadanobu's multifaceted writings as a way to explore the complexities of Japan's biliterate literary culture on the example of the eleventh century.
[66] See sections 79 and 126.

has to be able to read the subtle code of passions to understand whether Genji only exchanged flirtatious remarks, shared a bed, or even coincidentally impregnated his lover, so subdued and indirect is the language of love at times.

The following scene, probably from the autumn of 994, shows the subtlety of the culture of romance in the Heian capital.[67] Sei Shōnagon had for a while been agonizing over rumors about her character that had presumably led Tadanobu to make disdainful remarks about her in public. Then, on a dreary autumn night in the midst of rain and boredom, a soaking-wet messenger with a letter from Tadanobu bursts into the chatty round of ladies-in-waiting cuddled around the brazier after her Majesty, Empress Teishi, had retired to bed. Although the messenger urges Shōnagon to quickly reply to Tadanobu's letter, she tucks it away, afraid that it will contain nothing friendly. Only when the messenger appears a second time and announces that Tadanobu expects either to get an answer or to receive his letter back does she open the letter:

> This is just like something out of one of the old tales, I thought wryly. I looked at the letter, and found it to be written very beautifully, on thin blue paper. There was nothing in it to justify my nervousness. He had written the line from Bo Juyi,
>
> "You are there in the flowering capital, beneath the Council Chamber's brocade curtains," and added, "How should it end, tell me?"
>
> "What on earth shall I do?" I wondered. "If Her Majesty were here I'd most certainly show this to her. It would look bad to parade the fact that I know the next line by writing it in my poor Chinese characters." I barely had time to turn the problem over in my mind before the messenger was distracting me again with his urgings to be quick, so I seized a piece of dead charcoal from the brazier and simply wrote at the end of his letter, in Japanese script, "Who will come visiting this grass-thatched hut?"
>
> The messenger duly carried it off, but there was no response.

> 「いをの物語」なりやとて、見れば、青き薄様に、いと清げに書きたまへ
> り。心 ときめきしつるさまにもあらざりけり。「蘭省花時錦帳下」と書き
> て、「末はい かに、末はいかに」とあるを、「いかにかはすべからむ。御
> 前おはしまさば、御 覧ぜさすべきを、これが未を知り顔に、たどたどしき
> 真名書きたらむもいと見苦 し」と思ひまはすほどもなく、責めまどはせば
> 、ただその奥に、炭櫃に、消え炭 のあるして、「草の庵を誰かたづねむ」
> と書きつけて取らせつれど、また返事も 言はず。[68]

Shōnagon reads Tadanobu's letter with the mind of a protagonist in a romantic tale, a *monogatari*. Before reading the content of the letter, she examines Tadanobu's taste and finds the quality and color of the paper and the style of his written characters to her satisfaction. Only then does she notice with relief that its content is flirtatious rather than reproachful. As a senior official, Tadanobu

---

[67] For Japanese discussions of this famous passage see Inaga 2008, 245–48; and the bibliography included in Amagai 2001, 319–22.
[68] *Makura no sōshi*, p.136. Translation from McKinney 2006, section 77.

is secluded in the emperor's private residence in order to avoid evil influences predicted by Yin and Yang divination, and sends a message to Shōnagon, who is on service at the residence of Empress Teishi. Tadanobu pitches his romantic inquiry through the words of the Chinese poet Bo Juyi (772–846), at the time the most popular Chinese poet in Japan. The line is taken from a poem Bo Juyi sent to a friend in the capital from far-away Jiangzhou (modern-day Jiangxi Province), where he had been exiled. Shōnagon immediately recalls the next line to the famous poem: After Tadanobu's "You are there in the flowering capital, beneath the Council Chamber's brocade curtains" the poem continues "I sit on a rainy night in my grass-thatched hut beneath Lu Shan Mountain." It plots Tadanobu, who is with the emperor in the heart of the palace complex, inversely in the role of the exiled Bo Juyi in his famous hut on Lu Mountain and Shōnagon in the role of Bo Juyi's male friend who serves as an official in the capital at the Department of State Affairs. Tadanobu projects Bo Juyi's double longing—for the capital and for his friend—onto Shōnagon, and his question of where it all should end concerns both the Chinese poem and his romantic affair.

Shōnagon has several challenges to tackle at once: Most immediately, how does she want Tadanobu to feel about their affair? It is easy for Tadanobu to ask where things should go, but the burden is now on her to suggest a new direction after the longer period of smoldering dismay and mutual suspicion. More trickily, since Tadanobu has pitched his question through a line in Chinese that implies the friendship between two male officials, how should she adapt Bo Juyi's poem to her role as female, confined to the "women's hand" of the vernacular language? Although Heian elite women like Sei Shōnagon and Murasaki Shikibu were often highly educated in Chinese literature, they did not produce Chinese-style literature, but wrote in vernacular Japanese genres such as waka, diaries and tales. Elite men, in contrast, were normally educated and productive in both. Sei Shōnagon knows that it befits her to keep to the vernacular *kana* letters and avoid writing in her "poor Chinese characters." But quite apart from that, simply supplying the second line of the poem would be a dull solution.

Lacking the opportunity to confer with her patron about the matter and under pressure from Tadanobu's impatient messenger, she comes up with a brilliant conceit. That she uses a piece of dead charcoal from the brazier is in tone with the message of her reply: she reproaches Tadanobu for not having visited her recently and having let the flames of the affair die. The piece of charcoal is also an elegant solution to another challenge she is facing: it gives her *kana* letters the rustic sheen that justifies her switch of roles: now *she* is suddenly Bo Juyi, exiled and abandoned in his grass hut on Lu Mountain. She tackles the challenge on various levels. First, she writes in *kana* letters, as expected, while showing with her mention of the "grass-thatched hut" that she knows Bo Juyi's poem all too well. Second, she reproaches Tadanobu for his distance by changing her role to that of Bo Juyi—those away from the capital are always more pitiable and can more easily lay claim to feeling abandoned. Third, she challenges Tadanobu to a contest of poetic knowledge and wit. Her answer of twice seven syllables is the second half of a waka poem. Having answered his Chinese line with one half of a vernacular poem, she now expects Tadanobu to respond with the next lines of Bo Juyi's poem.

As Sei Shōnagon learns the next morning, the challenge proved too great for Tadanobu and his colleagues, which explains why she failed to receive an immediate answer.

> We all went to bed, and the first thing next morning I went back to my room. Not long after I arrived, the Minamoto Captain was heard crying in grandiose tones, "Is 'Grass-thatched Hut' present?" "How extraordinary," I said. "Why should you think anyone with such a depressing name might be here? Now if you'd asked for 'Jewelled Palace,' you might have got an answer."

> みな寝て、つとめていととく局に下りたれば、源中将の声にて、「ここに草の庵やある」と、おどろおどろしく言へば、「あやし。などてか、人げなきものはあらむ。『玉の台』ともとめたまはましかば いらへてまし」と言ふ。[69]

That Sei Shōnagon's extempore answer to Tadanobu has been spectacularly successful is clear from the fact that Minamoto no Nobukata (d. 998), another senior courtier who might have had some interest in Shōnagon, has transformed her answer into a decorative epithet for the winner of the poetic game.[70] Now in stronger spirits, Shōnagon sheds her rustic pose from the night before and, with urban confidence, styles herself "Jewelled Palace." This is again a witty solution, because the name breathes Chinese-style poetic elegance, but also picks up on waka poems that play on both epithets under discussion such as this poem:

> Today when I look / I find no jeweled palace / but see here only / this lowly hut / thatched with iris leaves.

> 今日見れば 玉の台も なかりけり 菖蒲の草の 庵のみして[71]

By now it has become totally clear that the game is about names, and that Sei Shōnagon has gained for herself an admiring epithet. Shōnagon receives two excited visitors in a row—the Minamoto Captain and the Assistant to Palace Repairs Tachibana no Norimitsu, supposedly Shōnagon's husband—who tell her about the smashing success her letter has achieved. She learns that Tadanobu had wanted to put her to a test once more before deciding whether to give up on her. The Minamoto Captain emphasizes that Tadanobu's colleagues made it clear to him that she is worth pursuing:

> Everyone gathered round to look, and made a great fuss. "What a clever rogue she is!' we said. 'No, you really can't give her up.".. .

> 「みな寄りて見るに、『いみじき盗人を。なほえこそ思ひ捨つまじけれ』とて見さわぎて...[72]

[69] *Makura no sōshi*, p.136. McKinney 2006, section 77.
[70] In section 154, at least, he is jealous of Tadanobu's and Shōnagon's exchange of jokes.
[71] Poem no. 110 from the third imperial waka anthology, the *Collection of Gleanings* (*Shūiwakashū* 拾遺和歌集), compiled between 1005–1007.

But then it turns out that nobody of those present passes Sei Shōnagon's test: nobody remembers the remaining lines of Bo Juyi's poem. They turn their shame into veneration of her wit, and although she feels very flattered, fear of potential failure grips her belatedly:

> When I contemplated how innocent I'd been of this full-scale involvement in the plot, it made me nervous all over again to think how easily I could have disgraced myself. And I hadn't realized that this "sister-brother" relationship[73] was known to even the Emperor, and that the senior courtiers would call him this rather than refer to him by his post! While we were talking, a message came from Her Majesty summoning me immediately, so I went and presented myself. She too wanted to talk about the incident. It seems His Majesty had laughed about it and told her the story. "All the gentlemen have written your reply on their fans," she informed me. I was amazed, and could only wonder what had possessed me to make me produce such a brilliant response. Anyway, after that Tadanobu no longer raised that shielding sleeve when we met, and seems to have quite changed his mind about me.

> げにあまたしてさる事あらむとも知らで、ねたうもあるべかりけるかなと、これらなむ胸つぶれておぼゆる。 この 「いもうとせうと」 といふ事は、上までみな知ろしめし、殿上にも、司の名をば言はで、せうととぞつけられたる。 物語 などしてゐたるほどに、 「まづ」 と召したれば、まゐりたるに、この事仰せられむとなりけり。 上笑はせたまひて、語りきこえさせたまひて、 「男どもみな扇に書きつけてなむ持たる」 など仰せらるるにこそ，あさましう、何の言はせけるにかとおぼえしか。 さて後ぞ、袖の几帳なども取り捨てて、思ひなほりたまふめりし。[74]

The romantic irritation between Tadanobu and Shōnagon has vanished and Shōnagon is proud of her success: the courtiers display her reply on their fans, her patron is well pleased, and the affair has even reached the Emperor.

How can we relate these so dissimilar scenes of romance, a poem by a male elegist of first-century BCE Rome, and a diary entry by a female court lady in eleventh-century Kyoto? A first point of comparison is the collusion of romantic and literary ambition and the role of the writers' respective societies in it. It is fair to say that both Sei Shōnagon and Propertius are as much in love with their clever writing as they are with the objects of their romantic interests. Yet that pride takes different shapes. Propertius dreams of a marble slab inscribed with his name, announcing his physical mortality and literary immortality. In turn, the fans of the Heian courtiers, inscribed with Shōnagon's challenge both to Tadanobu and Bo Juyi, signal her brilliant escape from embarrassment and an imperial celebration of her poetic acumen, although in an entirely social, and not monumental, mode of fame (the inscribed fans will presumably be thrown away soon, overwritten with next month's most witty poem).

---

[72] *Makura no sōshi*, p.137 and McKinney 2006, Section 77.
[73] Emperor Ichijō had apparently heard that Norimitsu and Shōnagon were calling each other endearingly "brother" and "sister."
[74] *Makura no sōshi*, 139–40 and McKinney 2006, Section 77.

Thus, both Propertius and Shōnagon are very concerned with their name and literary fame—the scene from the *Pillow Book* turns in fact around the play with epithets. But the degree to which the surrounding societies of the Roman and Japanese author participate in their love games differs vastly. Maecenas is the only other person partaking in the romantic game with Cynthia, while all the other protagonists are muses, gods, and heroes living beyond Rome proper. In contrast, Shōnagon lives in the palace with a group of gentlewomen and is trapped in spaces only structured loosely by movable paper sliding doors, thus inhabiting a world where romantic affairs can hardly be kept secret, but are intercepted by a host of collateral protagonists who facilitate and obstruct, inflame or deflate, approve or disprove of the passions that unfold around them. And there are not just the other ladies-in-waiting, but servants, messengers, visitors, and of course the emperor and his empresses and consorts. It is a world of rumors and whispers that determines one's status in court society.

A second point of comparison is the different presence of the physical world in the texts describing the romantic game. The central role of poetry exchanges in the dynamic of love affairs makes them a romance of and not just in writing. In Japan both sexes are writing and material objects other than poetry participate in the love game. Propertius might drape Cynthia in Coan silk, but the Coan silk is the decoration, not the plot device of the game. By contrast, romantic liaisons in Heian Japan could be made or broken by the proper flower attached to the right paper with the proper calligraphy. Had Sei Shōnagon not chosen charcoal to write out her "Grass-thatched hut" response, it would not have been half as brilliant; had she not feared that her characters would come out ugly on the physical page, she would perhaps have come up with an erudite Chinese response to tease the men, and again, she would not have convinced Tadanobu of her worth. This intrusion of the material world into textual space was crucial to vernacular literature, and this was both a reflection of social patterns of courtship, and also the manifestation of a material aesthetics that makes the Japanese poetic tradition particularly interesting.[75]

A third point of comparison is Shōnagon's and Propertius's recourse to recusatio in their romantic dealings. Both are caught in a situation where they have to ostentatiously reject certain literary genres and registers. With much saber-rattling imagery, Propertius rejects (and relies on) a discourse that demanded a way of life—one of epic valor and civic devotion—that was not attractive to him. Shōnagon, in turn, cleverly engages a discourse and a—male—way of life that might have been attractive, but that wasn't accessible to her. She engages in a *recusatio* of sorts, when she responds with half a waka to Tadanobu's Chinese line and elegantly plays rustic innocence to reproach Tadanobu for having neglected her. In both cases the recusatio produces spectacular results. Shōnagon's apparent rejection of Chinese-style registers is followed by the embarrassing defeat of the men

<hr />

[75] Edward Kamens discusses the role of the material in waka poetics in his excellent study Kamens 1997. Both Catullus and Martial (in two cycles of epigrams written to accompany gifts, book 13 and book 14) deal with the materiality of everyday objects and literary texts, but these examples are rather specific to the author or the occasion and do not represent an entire genre aesthetic, as is the case with Japanese waka. See Roman 2001.

on their own ground: they don't know their Bo Juyi, as they should, but Shōnagon does, although she needn't. Yet Shōnagon's recusatio is much more confined and anxious. Luckily, she did come up with a great response, but once she hears the plot behind the poetic game with Tadanobu she worries about the consequences a failure would have brought her. Although she luckily passes the "test" Tadanobu and his colleagues had put her to, she is still worried that her proud recusatio, her improvised half-waka, where she posed as a rusticized Bo Juyi and abandoned lady, might bite back; she shudders at the thought of going down in history with the "awful name" of "Grass-thatched hut."

Also, her dependence on the numerous intermediaries witnessing, helping or obstructing, and gossiping about the romantic couple, make her success more public and satisfying, but would precisely have produced infinitely more embarrassment had she not stood the test. Thus, although both Propertius and Shōnagon engage in a complex battle of the sexes with their pen and brush, respectively, Shōnagon has to fight much more subtly, from the circumscribed social space she was confined to as a Heian elite woman, in a complex balancing act to make her talents shine or to keep them back, as circumstances demanded.

4. Outlook

We have now covered quite some ground, starting from the juxtaposition of two particular capital cities in Ancient East Asia and the Mediterranean, and closing on the significance of decorated fans and inscribed marble slabs. What value has this swift parcours added to our understanding of Sei Shōnagon and Propertius, and Kyoto and Rome?

My confrontation of Sei Shōnagon's *Pillow Book* and Propertius's *Elegies* has had several aims at once. First there was of course the thrill of bringing two so improbable bedfellows into the same chamber—some of the more carnal and perverted twists of Propertius's love discourse would undoubtedly have scandalized Shōnagon. Yet the real interest of the comparison doesn't lie in the blatant differences between the works of a well-adjusted Heian court lady and diarist, and a tempestuous Roman love poet. Instead, I wanted to tease out the striking similarities that become visible only when we allow the comparison to penetrate into the deeper tissue of their respective literary and romantic projects. Only then do we see that both authors wrote in modes different from the literary repertoire of their respective reference cultures, China and Greece; we saw that they experimented with a new form of love discourse that developed during those periods of Japanese and Latin literature, namely mid-Heian Japan and Augustan Rome, which quickly came to be considered the golden classical mean of their respective literary traditions. And we saw that they both resorted to complex strategies of recusatio to defend (and aggrandize) their projects, and that they both wrote as proud inhabitants of their respective empire's capitals, Kyoto and Rome.

These points of similarity establish our literary lovers' comparability, while not playing down difference. Especially the gestures of recusatio have a different edge in Shōnagon's *Pillow Book* and Propertius's *Elegies*: On the Roman side, there is a much more pronounced permeability and interplay between the high registers of epic and the light Muse of love elegy in meter, diction, and their recourse to the plot resources of myth. In contrast, Japanese women were writing a *new* type of literature, not, like Roman men, just a *different* type of literature. There was a much wider social and linguistic gulf between the new vernacular genres promoted by women and the canonical status of Chinese-style literature. We do of course find many references to Chinese and Chinese-style literature in Japanese vernacular prose (and even hilarious parodies of the world of puffed-up Japanese scholars of Chinese) but they rarely become a carrying force of articulation in the vernacular tales and diaries, in the way we can see in the Roman love elegy's play with epic conventions.

The growing distance in Propertius between the modes of love elegy and patriotic praise elegy has often been seen as an intellectual and literary contradiction, to be explained away biographically: presumably, Propertius's affair with his Cynthia went downhill and, so goes the argument, his interests shifted to the wellbeing of the Roman state, as he became increasingly involved with the literary circle of Maecenas and with Augustan ideology after the publication of his first book.[76] However, when viewed through Sei Shōnagon's world, Propertius's witty shifts between gestures of epic and gestures of love elegy seem much more in tune with each other than much scholarship wants us to believe. They are shifts on the modest scale of a "back-and-forth," between which the male elegiac poet can smoothly criss-cross. Shōnagon, in contrast, is bound up in the dynamic of an "inside-outside," where she is valued for her knowledge of the outside—the male world of Chinese scholarship and literature—but is expected to stay inside of her female world and voice when writing. The membrane between the inside and the outside is not equally permeable to both sexes.[77]

I would argue that this complex literary physiology makes the Japanese literary tradition interesting from the perspective of the world's literary traditions, in ways that scholars have yet to fully realize and explore. The overwhelming majority of Japanese literature scholars study the vernacular literature of the Heian Period, which for the most part was canonized much later, and only a waning minority specializes in the most esteemed literature of the Heian Period as it was

---

[76] For examples of how Elegy 2.1 in particular is often read as a significant break with Propertius's first book and how his love poetry and courtly praise elegies are construed as opposite poles see Johnson 2009, 102 ff. Welch 2005 makes the interesting argument that Propertius's poems on Roman monuments and institutions that dominate and set apart the last book of his elegies was not an alignment with Rome's ruling power, but an attempt to establish himself as a rival to Augustus in the creation of the image and identity of Roman urbanism. This opens new ways to see a unity in Propertius's work, which has so often been denied. See in particular pp. 10–12. "Propertius' achievement of Book 4—its multivalence, its artistry, and its relevance to the self and to society—had never been seen before in Latin elegiac poetry and, arguably, would never be seen again. [...] The elegies in Book 4 make audible the process of self-expression, individuation, and even defection all but drowned out by the overwhelming—and persuasively symphonic—legacy of Augustus' city of marble. In this way, Propertius' final book is more than Propertius' own triumph: it is the acme of personal elegiac poetry." 12.

[77] Too little attention has been paid to the fact that Shōnagon's play with Chinese texts and allusions is particularly prominent in the most intimate romantic moments. This is the case in her interactions with Tadanobu, and also in her flirtations with Yukinari, another romantic interest of hers (see e.g., Section 46).

understood in the Heian Period itself—mostly Chinese-style literature written by Japanese authors. This situation is beginning to change, but there is still too little real engagement and conceptual dialogue between the two camps, so that the physiology of this Sino-Japanese membrane gets far too little scholarly attention.[78] I hope that Propertius has thrown this literary physiology into much crisper view than it appears when merely seen in the context of Heian Period Japanese literature alone. We will leave Propertius and Shōnagon here, with the wish that our comparison can allow us to see less contradiction in Propertius's corpus of *Elegies* and create more contradiction in Shōnagon's *Pillow Book*.

I hope to have shown the fruitfulness of moving from a comparative approach that relies on detecting *ellipsis*—the absence of something that makes one of the cultures look deficient—to an approach that profits from *catachresis*—the temporary application of an existing name to something that does not have one. It is surprising how ingrained the rhetoric of ellipsis still is in thinking about East Asia, and in particular China (in the style of "China didn't have x,y,z," with x,y,z being epic, science, transcendence, potatoes?). Ellipsis is a trope of the surface, and it often doesn't get us very far: had the logic of ellipsis guided my exploration of romance in Kyoto and Rome, Sei Shōnagon and Propertius would not have qualified as a promising couple for comparison. Where's the bed-wrestling, the carnal hymns and curses, and the whole language of the flesh that we enjoy in Propertius? Instead of the surface comparisons of ellipsis, catachresis offers us a trope of mutually expanding depth. If we apply Propertius and Shōnagon to each other catachrestically, and feel our way into gauging their respective textures against each other, they gain depth in the process. They can suddenly appear with more clarity, thrown into more dramatic relief than if we view them only through their own literary traditions and the scholarship that has accrued around the master narratives of Japanese or Latin literatures alone. In unfolding a literary dynamics of a "back-and-forth" versus an "inside-outside" recusatio in Propertius and Sei Shōnagon, I have tried to venture into a "deep comparison" of these writers and their literary cultures.

---

[78] As mentioned above, Edward Kamens's "Terrains of Text in Mid-Heian Court Culture" can serve as a fine example for future explorations. The three Anglophone studies that have broken major ground for the analysis of what has been called the *wa-kan* (Japanese-Chinese-style) dynamic in Japanese literature are Pollack 1986, LaMarre 2000 and Sakaki 2007. Smits 2007 proposes a view of developments on the Chinese-style side of the membrane during the mid-Heian Period. In most scholarship the *wa-kan* dynamic is not seen as a defining characteristic of the pillow book, and Chinese literature mostly comes to the fore in discussions of her educational background, not in its literary dimensions in her work. When the "essence" (*honshitsu* 本質) of the *Pillow Book* is discussed in articles such as the contributions by Akiyama Ken and Tsukahara Tetsuo in Mitamura 1994, that issue never comes up. How little the subject of her *kanbun* education is part of a more general approach to the *Pillow Book* can be showcased by Kuboki Tetsuo's interesting article in the same volume on Shōnagon's strategies of self-praise: it does not even raise the issue of her pride in *kanbun* learning, although it does play an important role in her self-image.

| Poetry in Exile
Sugawara no Michizane and Ovid

1. From Capital to Exile

Ovid was only relegated, not officially exiled, and thus did not lose his property. But he tells us that when he had to leave Rome for Tomis on the Black Sea at the order of Emperor Augustus, on an early winter night of 8 CE if we are to believe him, he lost everything, which had meant his life and livelihood. He later compared this last night to a "noisy funeral" and gave a dramatic portrayal of himself hastily leaving his house and wife: "So I made my exit, dirty, unshaven, hair anyhow—like a corpse minus the funeral (*egredior, sive illud erat sine funere ferri / squalidus inmissis hirta per ora comis*)."[1] For Ovid, leaving Rome meant virtual death and was a catastrophe of epic proportions. Thus, it was no surprise that he claimed the uproar in his house on the last night was equal to the fall of Troy. He does apologize for drawing such an immodest parallel between his personal fate and the archetypal site of Rome's legend of origins. But the epic truth, which he was to repeat again and again in the poems he wrote in exile, was that life as he had known it and loved to live it, had ended on the night of his forced departure from Rome. In the next ten years before his death in exile, illness, depression, and repeated death wishes haunted a man who had already left the world, although in his poetry he appears a man who kept alive by almost obsessively writing about himself and his shifting hopes for returning to Rome.

When Sugawara no Michizane was sent into exile by imperial edict on the twenty-fifth day of the first month of 901, his demotion meant first and foremost political death. Overnight, he was declared enemy of the state and the former Minister of the Right, the second highest office at the imperial court in Kyoto, was forced to accept a punitively low position as "supernumerary governor general of Dazaifu," an outpost on Japan's southernmost island of Kyushu. His pride as a civil servant was shattered and he, too, compared his exile to painful death:

---

[1] *Tristia* I.3.89-90. All translations from Ovid are from Green 2005. The Latin text is based on Goold and Wheeler 1988.

法酷金科結	The application of the law was more cruel than usual measure
功休石柱鐫	And my accomplishments will cease to be carved on stone monuments.
悔忠成甲冑	I regret that I made loyalty my armor and helmet
悲罰痛戈鋌²	And bemoan that my punishment was more painful than a stabbing dagger.

Michizane's "armor of loyalty"—a metaphor for the ideal Confucian civil servant from the Chinese ritual classic *Record of Rites* (*Liji* 禮記)—was useless against the fatal blow of the imperial edict and he bitterly bemoaned that his enemies at court had succeeded in slandering him to remove him from power.

Although exile cut through the lives of these two extraordinary poets with similarly deadening harshness, Ovid and Michizane's paths to exile had been quite different. Ovid was born in 43 BCE in Sulmo, an idyllic town a hundred miles from Rome, and was proud to come from an old equestrian family.³ His parents saw to his education by leading rhetoricians in Rome, and after educational travels in Greece, which was a customary part of Roman elite upbringing, he took up several minor posts in civil law administration. But he soon abandoned a career in law and politics for poetry and joined the literary circle of Messalla Corvinus, quickly becoming one of the most celebrated contemporary poets. Ovid's precocious pen could dispense phrases of scintillating virtuosity and throughout his life he wrote in a great number of genres, spanning the spectrum from the rather personalized and confined world of the love elegy and didactic works on love, to the *Metamorphoses*, his own version of epic, and the *Fasti*, a didactic poetic calendar of Roman beliefs, customs, and monuments, which remained unfinished due to his exile. From the pinnacle of poetic success and conjugal happiness (with his third wife), he was suddenly banished to Tomis, nowadays a Romanian beach town on the shores of the Black Sea.

The emperor's reason for banishing the adulated poet are unclear, although Ovid often rehearses the verdict and regrets a "poem and an error" (*carmen et error*, *Tristia* 2.207). Rather than the alleged immorality of his *Art of Love* (*Ars amatoria*, ca. 1 BC to 1 CE), which could have served as a good excuse to get rid of him, he might have known too much about a sexual scandal involving Augustus's granddaughter; or he might have been involved in the political plot against the Claudian succession to Augustus, propagated by Augustus's third wife Livia, who worked, ultimately successfully, to have Tiberius, her son from a previous marriage and thus Augustus's stepson, enthroned.⁴ Although we will never know the cause for sure, the effect was dire: in Ovid's exile poetry, embellished by ethnographies about the grim Scythians as they appear in Herodotus and Virgil, Tomis came across largely as a hopelessly outlandish place cursed with eternal cold and winter,

---

² *Kanke bunsō, Kanke kōshū* no. 484. All translations from Michizane's poetry in this chapter are mine.
³ For an introduction to Ovid's biography and works see Conte 1994b, 340–66 and von Albrecht 2003; for an introduction to Ovid's exile work see Peter Green's introduction to his translation and Williams 2002, 337–81.
⁴ For some of the voluminous scholarship debating the cause for Ovid's exile see Williams 2002, 337.

threatened by attacks from various raiding local tribes, and inhabited by a mixture of indigenous Getes and remote descendants of Greek colonists from Miletus on the Ionian Coast who had settled at this end of the world as early as 600 BCE.

In legal terms Ovid was merely relegated, not officially exiled, which meant that he was entitled to keeping his citizenship and his possessions. His wife, connected to the patrician clan of the Fabii, stayed behind to look after their house and work for her husband's amnesty and recall. Even the hope to relocate to a less harsh place of exile, which Ovid expresses repeatedly in his exile poetry, was not fulfilled, and he died around 17 or 18 CE in Tomis after a decade of desperation, and a painful process of slow and inconsistent realization that he was never going to see his beloved Rome again. His *Tristia* (five books with fifty elegies; 8–12 CE) and his *Black Sea Letters* (*Epistulae ex Ponto*; four books with 46 elegies; between 12 CE and his death) are an extensive canvas on which to trace Ovid's tempestuous psychological trajectory in exile, from leaving his house in Rome as a "corpse" to his actual death on the shores of the Black Sea a decade later.

Sugawara no Michizane (845–903) came from a family of remarkable scholars, who had served as professors at the State Academy in Kyoto, which focused on the study of the Chinese Classics.[5] After passing the academy examinations, he served in minor court positions, helping draft administrative documents, before being appointed professor at the State Academy in his early thirties in 880. Although the Sugawara clan was renowned for scholarship and the composition of Chinese-style poetry, they had only been of middle rank and never held the highest offices at court. These posts were coveted by members of the powerful northern branch of the Fujiwara family, who had set themselves up as regents with de facto power, which often exceeded even that of the emperors, and married their daughters into the imperial family. The Fujiwara managed to purge some thirty non-Fujiwara office holders to create vacancies for their own clan in 886. This led to the first banishment of Michizane, who was sent off to serve as the governor of Sanuki Province on Shikoku, one of the four main islands of Japan. This degradation in office was by no means a harsh punishment: Michizane had a well-provided official post, which was not even so distant from the capital. But his poetry from the period as governor of Sanuki is filled with plaint and resistance to this forced absence from the capital and its vibrant court culture. When Michizane returned after his four years of service in Sanuki, he became a close confidant of the newly enthroned Emperor Uda (r. 887–97) and quickly received increasingly high-ranking posts. This led to the beginning of the end in 899, when Michizane was appointed Minister of the Right, now inferior only to the equally newly appointed Minister of the Left Fujiwara no Tokihira, the son of the Fujiwara Regent who had caused Michizane's demotion to Governor of Sanuki in 886.

Michizane was aware of the danger of his rise at court and the jealousies it inspired. He tried to decline the post, but in 901, some two weeks after receiving

---

[5] For a commanding portrayal of Michizane's life and work see Borgen 1986. To date there is no complete translation of Michizane's personal poetry collection (of about 680 pieces of poetry and prose) into any Western language, but Borgen translates a generous amount of Michizane's poetry and Rabinovitch and Bradstock 2005, 121–40 also contains selections.

yet another promotion in rank along with Tokihira, Michizane was stripped of all of his titles and ordered to go into exile in Dazaifu in Kyushu. Even the Retired Emperor Uda, Michizane's staunch supporter, who had abdicated to his young son Daigo in 897 but remained a strong presence at court, could do nothing: he was barred from entering the palace when he tried to protest the imperial edict, and was left waiting on a lawn before the palace for an entire day (and an entire night a few days later). The proclamation drawn up by Michizane's enemies at court accused him of plotting against the emperor and of dangerous political ambition. He was only considered exempt from capital punishment because of his previous services to the court.

This time he was not just demoted and sent away from the capital, but he and his entourage were considered criminals: four sons and nine of his associates were exiled to different places, Michizane was taken from the capital by a military escort, post stations along the way to his exile in Kyushu were forbidden from providing food or horses, and he was put under house arrest during his two years in Dazaifu, where he seemed to have suffered from material want and malnutrition.[6]

The shock of exile that Ovid and Michizane suffered was comparable: the sudden fall from grace; the expulsion from the sophisticated cultural milieu of the capital; the hardships of travel to a distant, unwelcome destination; the predictable disdain for the more primitive living conditions; anxiety, depression, impulses of self-reflection and self-defense; and, lastly, writing as a familiar practice, which suddenly took on a new tone and importance as a channel for, variously, expressing outrage, finding consolation and reconfiguring the glorious poet's former persona. Yet as much as the severe punishment of exile triggered universally visceral reactions in Augustan Rome and Heian Japan, poets were equipped with different coping strategies by their respective literary cultures and personal temperament.

In this chapter I argue that both Michizane and Ovid experienced a similarly new challenge when writing in exile. On the one hand, exile was an irreversible inflection point, after which no sentence, no poem, no word could ever quite mean the same. The new reality—the sense of humiliation and blotted reputation, the different climate, food, life rhythm, commodities (or absence thereof), and the effects of disease and depression—clouded their formerly radiant life paths and shook their confidence.[7] On the other hand, they had to cope with their new situation with the tools they had acquired throughout their lives in the capital: a sense of their social and poetic selves and the entitlements that came with it, genres and rhetorical tropes of their literary traditions and from their previous oeuvre that allowed them, now, to capture the exilic condition and try to mend it, and models from poetic lore or mythology that invited comparison to their own fate and afforded—or withheld—consolation.

Though the two poets faced a similar creative challenge in exile, their reactions in poetry differed greatly, not the least because their literary cultures had endowed them with a different social persona and distinctive rhetorical and genre

---

[6] Borgen 1986, 278–79. On Michizane's fall from power and exile see Fujiwara 2002, 237–81.
[7] Occasional arguments that Ovid actually never went into exile but only lived it out in literary fantasy have not been convincing. For related literature see Williams 2002, 341.

resources, as well as shaping their temperaments into very different poetic personalities. In this chapter I explore how Michizane and Ovid coped with a similar challenge in different ways. How did Ovid, the poet-provocateur, deal with exile differently from Michizane, the court-employed poet-official? How is our reading of their exile oeuvre tinged by the ways scholars situate their exile oeuvre within their entire work and within the values of Latin and Japanese literary cultures? With whom, by which rhetorical means, and to which end do Ovid and Michizane enter into a dialogue as compensation for their separation and isolation? And how do they use poetic and mythological lore in the process?

2. *The Poet-Provocateur and the Poet-Official*

When reading Ovid's and Michizane's exile poetry face to face their authors seem grossly incongruous: we have the extravagant Latin poet, darling of refined and at times risqué audiences and author of piquant works of amatory didactics, confront the rather straight-laced Japanese statesman and scholar, a court poet who arranged his grandfather's, father's, and his own poetry into an authoritative family collection, which he presented to the emperor in 900 in his function as a high-ranking courtier and subject of the emperor. One was banished for corrupting Rome with his sexually audacious writings (at least on the surface; and was it not a much more romantic reason to be banished for a leading poet of love elegy and didactics?), the other fell prey to political rivalries with the powerful Fujiwara regent clan increasingly dominating the imperial court.

True, we have here poets of different individual temperament, but that explains only part of the discrepancy. More importantly, poets had different positions in the Heian and Augustan sociopolitical landscape. Whereas Heian court life centered on festivals and events that included official poetry composition by officials who also served in the courtly bureaucracy, Augustus did not call on poets for literary banquets. Certainly, some of his successors, such as Nero, did institute festivals for poets to display their talent, but this is not comparable to the predominantly institutionalized, largely collective poetic production of early Japan. In contrast, patrons played a central role in Augustan Rome (and much of the history of Roman literature). They enjoyed the poets' company during their leisure hours (*otium*). Often the relationship had no economic necessity: many poets could live off inherited property or invested capital, in particular those poets whose assets qualified them as knights (*equites*), as was the case with Horace, Tibullus, and Ovid during the Augustan age. Roman poets might have received occasional monetary gifts from their patrons, but they usually received no regular "stipend" or were engaged in other professional occupations, unlike the Heian poet-officials.[8]

As a consequence, while there was a long tradition of exiled poet-officials in China and Japan, Rome exiled political figures rather than poets per se. Michizane could look back to towering models for his exile, beginning with Qu Yuan (ca. 340–278 BCE), a virtuous minister who lost favor with his king,

---

[8] On patronage see White 1993 and Fantham 1996, 67–84.

committed suicide after presumably composing his expansive poetic plaint "Encountering Sorrow" (*Lisao* 離騷) for which he came to be considered the first lyrical poet of China. More recently, many Tang poets lived and wrote through phases of exile, for example Bo Juyi, a crucial model for Michizane's life and work. Exile was certainly a pervasive means of punishment in Greece and Rome, too. But in the line of prominent political exiles such as the early Republican patrician statesman Camillus, the legendary general Coriolanus, Scipio, Cicero, Pompey the Great, Cato the Younger or later Seneca, Ovid was the exceptional poet.

The difference of the social profile of poets in Heian Japan and Augustan Rome affected their exile poetry: Although Ovid's and Michizane's outrage over the injustice that had befallen them was probably comparably strong, Michizane often attributes his misfortune to dark and abstract powers of fate, as if exile was sent down from heaven and would strike anybody sooner or later. Sadly, it was a predictable part of the political system and Michizane could console himself by evoking the remarkable exile poets of the Chinese past. Ovid, in contrast, took his exile very personally, was not shy to fault Augustus personally for his misery, and had mythological models to identify with, rather than previous Roman exile poets in whose company he could feel honored and a bit consoled.

The first poem in Michizane's exile collection shows poignantly how intensely Michizane felt wronged but how he turned away from personal accusation to an overpowering sense of cosmic law:

自詠	Composed to Myself
離家三四月	Away from home for three, four months now
落涙百千行	My tears fall in hundreds, thousands of streams.
万事皆如夢	The ten thousand things that happened are all like a dream
時時仰彼蒼[9]	Time and again I gaze up to Dark Heaven.

The algebraic crescendo that builds up from the time span in exile, to the number of streams of tears and the bewildering number of small events adding up to the sudden reality of life in exile culminates in one thing: Dark Heaven, a somber power that evokes the poem "Yellow Bird" (*Huang niao* 黃鳥) from the Chinese *Classic of Poetry* (compiled ca. 600 BCE). In the poem, each time the bird cries, a valiant warrior of the harsh state of Qin (which later founded the first Chinese empire in 221 BCE) is sacrificed to follow his lord into death. The speaker cries out in vain:

彼蒼者天	You Dark Heaven,
殲我良人	You destroy our best men.
如可贖兮	If this one could be ransomed:
人百其身	A hundred men just for his life.[10]

Each time Michizane looks up to the ominous heavens over Dazaifu, he becomes a political victim chosen by cosmic law, and knows that no human power would be able to pay the ransom—"a hundred for one." Amplified by the grisly plot of

---

[9] *Kanke bunsō, Kanke kōshū* no. 476.
[10] The translation is mine.

"Yellow Bird," Michizane's parsimonious pentasyllabic quatrain hides a brute force behind a simple façade of counting and sky-gazing. Yet, the desperate call for ransom that the poet voices through his allusion to the *Classic of Poetry* is not hurled at Emperor Daigo, Michizane's rival Tokihira, or anybody else. The title "Composed to Myself" keeps this force internal to Michizane. But where Michizane's model Bo Juyi used this exact title to write casual poems of entertaining self-reflection, Michizane composed a dire poem of heavenly doom to exile, a death of sorts.[11]

Ovid looks much closer for culprits responsible for his misfortune: His talent and Augustus.

> Books, my unlucky obsession, why do I stay with you
> when it was my own talent brought me down?
> Why go back to those fresh-condemned Muses, my nemesis? Isn't
> one well-earned punishment enough?
> Poetry made men and women eager to know me—
> that was my bad luck;
> poetry made Caesar condemn me and my life-style
> because of my *Art [of Love]*, put out
> years before: take away my pursuit, you remove my offences—
> I credit my guilt to my verses. Here's the reward
> I've had for my care and all my sleepless labour:
> A penalty set on talent.[12]

Book 2 of the *Tristia*—a single long letter to Augustus, unlike the other books, which contain several epistolary elegies—opens with a quantum of self-pity seasoned with self-praise. The letter is a remarkable tour de force that blends flattery of the emperor with Ovid's self-compliments, self-defense with outright accusation, and touches of humility and gratitude with moments of mordant mockery.[13] His pose of supplication is directed at the godly emperor by reminding the gods, the Muses, that they owe him: "and the Muse, having stirred that wrath, may now assuage it: poetry often moves the gods on high. (*Musaque, quam movit, motam quoque leniet iram: / exorant magnos carmina saepe deos*)." (*Tristia* II.21–22).

He does admit that he committed an error and deserves Augustus's wrath, but his seeming concessions come rarely without barbs: As he points out, Ovid's error gives Augustus the splendid chance to live up to his proverbial mercy; Augustus's military campaigns and glorious political maneuvers leave him no time to read Ovid's "frivolous works" (what was he thinking, banishing

---

[11] See Hatooka 2005, 384–86.

[12] *Tristia* II.1-12. Green, 25. "*Quid mihi vobiscum est, infelix cura, libelli / ingenio perii qui miser ipse meo? / cur modo damnatas repeto, mea crimina, Musas? / an semel est poenam commeruisse parum? / carmina fecerunt, ut me cognoscere vellet / omine non fausto femina virque meo: / carmina fecerunt, ut me moresque notaret / iam demi iussa Caesar ab Arte mea. / deme mihi studium, vitae quoque crimina demes; / acceptum refero versibus esse nocens. / hoc pretium curae vigilatorumque laborum / cepimus: ingenio est poena reperta meo.*"

[13] For a close reading of this letter and the question of the ambiguity of Ovid's treatment of Augustus here and in other works see Williams 1994, 154–209.

Ovid for a book he hasn't read?); and Augustus is a generous sponsor of public games and farces, without apparently realizing they are full of adultery and the kind of stuff for which Ovid was exiled. Ovid's main line of defense is to draw up a list of venerable authors, both Greek and Roman, who treat adultery and lust without receiving punishment like Ovid. Even Homer does not go unsullied: "What's the *Iliad* but an adulteress, battled over by husband and lover?…What's the *Odyssey* but the wooing of one woman, in her husband's absence, by a crowd of men and all for love? (*Ilias ipsa quid est aliud, nisi adultera, de qua / inter amatorem pugna virumque fuit?… aut quid Odyssea est, nisi femina propter amorem, / dum vir abest, multis una petita procis?*)." (*Tristia* II.371–77) What in other contexts could be an innocent list of erudite exempla can here be read as a nail-by-nail accusation of the Princeps of either not knowing or not wanting to know that, if the emperor is right, Tomis should be a populous colony of culprits akin to Ovid. But Ovid is the only one hit by the imperial thunderbolt.

There could hardly be a more dissimilar way of coping with exile in these two poems: Ovid's sprawling, mercurial eloquence, spurting forth from a wounded soul with a most intact double-edged tongue directed at the emperor; and Michizane's introverted evocation of a heavenly law and fault per force of an ominous brutal allusion to a Chinese Classic.

Not only is Michizane *not* launching into a querulous persuasion attempt of Emperor Daigo, whose edict banished him. But one of his most famous exile poems has traditionally been read as proof of Michizane's unshaken loyalty to the emperor. On the ninth day of the ninth month of 900, the annual "Double-Ninth Festival," poets gathered in the palace for this major autumn festival, enjoying chrysanthemum flowers and composing poetry on a set topic in tune with the season. The next day the courtiers met again and composed on "Autumn Thoughts" and Michizane's poem moved the sixteen-year-old Emperor Daigo so much that he bestowed on his senior minister Michizane, at the time aged fifty-six, a robe as a token of special favor. Michizane remembers the incident a year later, now from the beyond of exile:

九月十日	Ninth month, tenth day
去年今夜侍清涼	This night last year I was in attendance at the Hall of Clear Coolness
御在所殿名。	This is the name of a hall in the Imperial Palace.
秋思詩篇獨斷腸	and in my poem on "Autumn Thoughts" I felt alone heartrending grief.
勅賜秋思賦之。臣詩多述所憤。	We were asked by the emperor to present a poem on "Autumn Thoughts." My humble poem set forth much resentment.
恩賜御衣今在此	The robe bestowed on me by imperial grace is here with me now—
捧持每日拜餘香	Each day I raise it in reverence and pay homage to its lingering fragrance.

宴終晚頭賜御衣。今隨身在箇中，故云。[14]

When the festival was over and it was late [the Emperor] bestowed this robe. Even now I have it at hand in a chest. That's why I say this.

In the poem composed at the poetry event hosted by Emperor Daigo the previous year, Michizane had lamented the sadness of the season and his progressive aging, and tried to console himself with the grace of the Emperor—a lexical item de rigueur in this kind of poetry—and Bo Juyi's "three friends" of wine, lute playing, and poetry.[15] The poem stays within the boundaries of the conventions of courtly autumn laments and does not mention anything in specific, but Michizane—though still in favor with the retired emperor Uda, his lifelong generous patron, and the young reigning Emperor Daigo—suffered from increasing political isolation due to the fierce lobbying of the Fujiwaras and had probably forebodings that his high rank and accumulation of titles would arouse envy.

The assigned topic of "Autumn Sadness" gained an entirely new significance when Michizane remembered the splendid Double Ninth Festival at court a year later in Dazaifu. It would be hard to read into this poem double entendres of lurking resentment or querulous criticism of the emperor à la Ovid. But must we really understand it as a celebration of Michizane's loyalty to the emperor who banished him, as has traditionally been done?[16] Might Michizane not, again, be "composing to himself"? Unlike Ovid's *Tristia* II, Michizane does not turn to the emperor at all: he seems to be addressing himself, an impression that is further reinforced by the fact that the poet added a self-commentary. Writing interlinear comments to one's own poetry was not common practice before Michizane's time. Michizane adopted it from the mid-Tang poets Yuan Zhen, Liu Yuxi, and, in particular, from Bo Juyi, who introduced this practice into Chinese literary culture.[17]

What was the point of the self-commentary? Note that the explanatory glosses to lines one and four explain items that need no explanation: Any of Michizane's readers would have known that the "Hall of Clear Coolness" was used for many official events—why mention that it was the name of a hall in the palace? The pedestrian explanation of the hall's name does not convey necessary information. Instead, it allows Michizane to imagine, visualize the hall as a *pars pro toto* for the palace, the capital, and all he had lost within the short span of a year. And from the poem's closure the reader must assume that Michizane still has the robe in his possession—why say that he keeps it in a chest close at hand? The gloss to the second line does provide the helpful information that the previous year courtiers had composed on "Autumn Thoughts," something that only readers who read or heard Michizane's composition from the previous year could have known. More importantly, this gloss points to the disjunction between poetic plaint and real-life

---

[14] *Kanke bunsō, Kanke kōshū* no. 482.
[15] *Kanke bunsō, Kanke kōshū* no. 473.
[16] Hatooka Akira also steps away from the traditional interpretation and draws attention to its value for Michizane's memory of the capital and his identity as a courtier. For his reading of the poem and the occasion see Hatooka 2005, 91–110.
[17] See Gotō 1993b, 75–94.

plaint. Back then, at the height of his power, Michizane "expressed much resentment." We can imagine Michizane casting a sarcastic glance back at himself as if to say: what did I know of suffering back then? The successful poet of sorrowfulness could not have imagined the exiled man of sorrow. What is the traditional poetics of mournful autumn in the face of exile during autumn, framed in poetry?

Based on this reading of the self-commentary Michizane is clinging less to the emperor than to the robe: its incantatory fragrance of better times and better places and its ability to transport Michizane into the realm of a happy past just for a brief moment each day when he takes it out. Worshipping the robe had become a daily routine to make the past present and imagine for a short moment that exile had not happened. Michizane is in dialogue with his own poetry and with the imperial token that gives his life in exile a fleeting glimpse of his former self, Michizane the minister and courtier. In *Tristia* II Ovid lets no opportunity pass to immediately spend the persuasive capital he has gained on reminding the emperor of his innocence and asking if not for amnesty, at least for a better exile. In his juxtaposition of two Double Ninth Festivals—captured in two poems at radically opposite poles of his life—Michizane does not spend his persuasive capital on anything. There is even a certain satisfaction, a tragic pleasure in a daily ritual that gives past meaning to present catastrophe, without working for change. And a ritual continues to this day: in commemoration of Michizane and his exile, priests at the Kitano Tenmangu Shrine in Kyoto—a major temple of the worship of Tenjin, the deified Michizane, god of scholarship—celebrate every year the "Lingering Fragrance Festival" (*yokōsai* 余香祭), where guests from all over Japan come and recite waka poems (nowadays not kanshi any more) on the day Michizane had written his poem on the fragrant robe from exile.

It is striking that the only poem in Michizane's exile work to use a term of legal accusation (*uttaeru* 訴へる) is addressed to Heaven (later legends claim that Michizane wrote a *saimon* 祭文, a prayer text, claiming his innocence, climbed up high and brought his case before Heaven[18]). Note the growing circles of darkness in this poem:

燈滅 二絕 其二	Lamplight Gone (second of two quatrains)
秋天未雪地無螢	In the autumn sky no snow yet and no fireflies on the ground[19]
燈滅**抛**書淚暗零	With lamplight gone I toss away my book, tears fall in silent obscurity
遷客悲愁陰夜倍	For me exiled man sorrows double in the black night
冥冥理欲訴冥冥[20]	Those deep dark principles—I want to bring suit before deep dark Heaven.

This poem drills itself deeper and deeper into darkness: the extinguished lamp light, the absence of indirect light from snow or fireflies is still an elegant negation

---

[18] Kawaguchi 1966, 739.
[19] Proverbially, the students Sun Kang and Che Yin were too poor to buy lamp oil and used these natural sources of light to study for the exams.
[20] *Kanke bunsō, Kanke kōshū* no. 509.

of beautiful light imagery. But the tears in darkness, the doubling of sorrows during night bring a somber tone to the scene until finally darkness takes over in the last line, which repeats four times the same word *mei*, "dark," in the short span of a seven-syllable line. The "deep dark" (*meimei* 冥冥) principles of fate, which are privy to humans, and the "deep dark" (*meimei* 冥冥) heavens are different entities, but they feature the same characters.[21] The four-time repetition of the same character in one line hammers home both Michizane's conviction of his innocence and the impenetrable inscrutability of heaven and its principles. In the end Michizane's gesture of legal accusation is dramatized but also cut short by the quadruple tautology in the last line, channeling his despair into complaints against a system—fate and cosmic forces.

3. Realism of Exile—Fallacy or Felicity?

So far we have explained the difference between Ovid's and Michizane's exile poetry on the grounds of the different sociological position of the poet in Augustan Rome and Heian Japan and Ovid's particular profile as a skillful provocateur, a role he continued to live up to even in exile. Still, both poets were in their own way jolted into a new, painful reality. By the time of exile both were in their fifties and at the highpoint of their careers and confidence and had to struggle with how to use their poetic craft under new circumstances and for new purposes. Modern scholars have sometimes captured this sudden shift by detecting a greater "realism" in Ovid's and Michizane's poetry, presumably a response to the sobering humiliations of exile. Nobody would deny that there are traces of the autobiographical in Michizane's and Ovid's exile poetry, but their poetry, *qua* exile poetry, has been more easily read with embarrassing literalism, to intriguingly opposite effect.

For classicists this alleged "realism" signaled a loss of Ovid's creative energies and poetic virtuosity and has partly led to a low regard for Ovid's exile oeuvre. Peter Green astutely captures this disappointment with Ovid, the exile author:

> The fashionable *flâneur* whose nearest approach to reality had been a fantasy-manual of seduction, whose most sustained creation was centred on *outré* metamorphoses and the ironic mockery of traditional myth, now found that Life, in its crudest form, had invaded his library and at one stroke deconstructed his lovingly fashioned literary persona. He became querulous, repetitive, self-pitying and self-obsessed, humourless. The egotism that had been a lightweight joy in Rome's *enfant terrible* of the boudoir became an embarrassing aberration when exercised, without elegance or proportion, at the expense of his wife. Tomis no longer let him be funny. The *praeceptor amoris* with his mask of myth, wit and literary allusion was now an all-too-human husband in a real-life situation.[22]

Ovid's exile poetry is simply too "real," embarrassingly real for a poet whose forte lay in literary seduction and creative pretension. Most studies of Ovid's exile poetry published over the last few decades have lamented this prejudice against Ovid's

---

[21] On resonances with Buddhist and Daoist associations of "darkness" in this poem see Hatooka 2005, 217–18 and 414–17.
[22] Green 2005, xxxvi.

last two works and have aimed to unmask the assumption of realism as a fallacy.[23] They have shown that Ovid's literary artistry is on a par with his masterful works before exile and, in turn, blame scholars for their too literalist acceptance of Ovid's disingenuous laments that his creative powers are waning and his command of Latin declining under the influence of the barbarian environment.

What Ovid scholars consider a literalist, realist fallacy in need of redress is welcomed by many Michizane scholars as a felicity. The poetry Michizane composed during his exile in Sanuki Province from 886 to 887 and in Dazaifu from 901 to his death in 903 is regarded as distinctive and given exceptional importance in Michizane's poetic oeuvre. Away from court and its numerous occasions for the composition of formal poetry, Michizane was forced to discover new poetic *sujets*: common people, local customs, a new landscape, the sorrows of travel and separation from home, and worries over advancing age and lack of career success.[24] This becomes exacerbated in the forty-six poems Michizane wrote in Dazaifu, which the poet compiled into a separate collection entitled *Later Collection of the Sugawara Family* (Kanke kōshū 菅家後集) and sent off to his friend Ki no Haseo in the capital shortly before his death. Hatooka Akira has argued that, while the Sanuki Period broadened the scope of Michizane's poetry and brought him into closer poetic dialogue with Bo Juyi— himself poetically productive when exiled to Jiangzhou in Southern China in 815— the Dazaifu experience pushed Michizane to his limits and beyond Bo Juyi, where poetry became a tool for distinctive expressions of sorrow and despair.[25]

In traditional Chinese poetics suffering gave a cachet to good writing. One of the earliest formulations of this influential view comes from China's grand historian Sima Qian (ca. 145–85 BCE), who wrote a letter of self-defense when he himself was harshly punished by castration for a political misstep and chose the humiliation of castration over execution in order to finish writing his monumental history of China, the *Historical Records* (*Shiji* 史記). Hoping to ultimately gain immortality through writing, Sima Qian draws up an impressive list of venerable sages who, like him, produced superlative works in dire straits:

King Wen of Zhou (11th century BCE), when Earl of the West, was in captivity and elaborated the *Classic of Changes*; Confucius (5th century BCE) was in a desperate situation and wrote *The Spring and Autumn Annals*; Qu Yuan (3rd century BCE) was banished, and only then composed "Encountering Sorrow"... The three-hundred poems of the *Classic of Poetry* were for the most part written as the expression of outrage by good men and sages. All of these men had something eating away at their hearts; they could not carry through their ideas of the Way, so they gave an account of what had happened before while thinking of posterity.

蓋西伯拘而演周易；仲尼戹而作春秋；屈原放逐，乃賦離騷...詩三百篇，大氐賢聖發憤之所為作也. 此人皆意有所鬱結，不得通其道，故述往事，思來者.[26]

---

[23] See for example Froesch 1976, Nagle 1980 and Williams 1994.

[24] On Michizane's poetry in Sanuki see Hatooka 2005, 292–313 and Fujiwara 2002, 111–74.

[25] Hatooka 2005, 351–54.

[26] *Hanshu* 3460.2735. "Letter in Response to Ren An," translated by Stephen Owen (with modifications). Owen 1996a, 141.

This poetics of suffering, which linked great writing to hardship and, ultimately, immortal fame, became a powerful traditional assumption throughout East Asia and it certainly contributed to singling Michizane's exile poetry and its implied "emotional realism" out for distinction. (Incidentally, it also resonates with modern myths of literature in exile, partly inherited from nineteenth-century European romanticism, which might incline modern literary critics yet more to value Michizane's exile poetry).

In short, Ovid's image is dominated by the artistic brilliance of the *Metamorphoses* and his elegiac and didactic treatments of love, while his exile poetry, with its grim real-life edge, has proved of least interest to Ovid enthusiasts through the ages, in turn inspiring modern scholars to try to save its reputation. In contrast, Michizane's exile poetry is precisely treasured because of the traditional poetics of suffering and an assumed emotional realism and because modern critics long to hear the courtier trained in the panegyrical court style with its protocol of assigned topics, seasonal events, and prescribed rhyme words speak from closer to his palpitating heart.

A favorite example to show Ovid's fictionalizing craft in the exile poetry has been analyses of his portrayal of Tomis. If we take Ovid's accounts at face value, we might well shudder at the barbarity of the place: it appears to be a region of eternal winter and climatic extremes, at the opposite end of Roman civilization, torn by warfare between wild tribes, and utterly lacking in any natural harmony or balance. But recent archeology has shown that Tomis had a fair amount of Hellenistic culture: a gymnasium, elegant civic buildings, and inscriptions in Greek and Latin that show that its inhabitants were familiar with Euripides, Theocritus, and other Greek authors.[27] Ovid's description of Moesia, the area around Tomis, which was first brought under Roman control shortly before Ovid's arrival in the late first century BCE, seems far from Tomitan reality and relies instead on ethnographic and literary lore, such as the vibrantly exotic and barbaric Scythia as imagined in Virgil's *Georgics* 3 (349–83).[28] (See Figure 6.1.)

Although Dazaifu had its place in early literary history as a site where a few prominent poet-officials served, it was a sober place lacking any sensationalist ethnographic lore. One decisive reason for this was that Dazaifu had been a solid part of Japan for many centuries. Here Japanese was spoken and the overall culture, though provincial, was familiar. It even had an advantage for a Sinophile scholar like Michizane: Despite its peripheral location on the Southernmost island of the Japanese archipelago, the flourishing government quarters at Dazaifu had at least since the sixth century been the gateway for embassies going back and forth among Japan, states on the Korean Peninsula, and China. Dazaifu was therefore considered a "distant capital" of sorts. *Man'yōshū* poets such as Ōtomo no Tabito and Yamanoue no Okura, who served as officials in Dazaifu in the eighth century, benefitted greatly from their close exposure to newest developments on the continent and experimented with Chinese-style themes and forms. In this sense

---

[27] For relevant literature see Williams 2002, 340.
[28] On Ovid's literary crafting of the image of his exile see in particular Williams 1994, Chapter 1 "The 'unreality' of Ovid's exile poetry."

FIGURE 6.1 Delacroix had obviously read his Herodotus, who describes how the Scythians, barbarian pastoralists as he highlights, prepare mare's milk cheese. Little did the painter know that twentieth-century archeology would uncover a fair amount of Hellenistic urban infrastructure at the site of ancient Tomis.

Eugène Delacroix (1798–1863). Ovid Among the Scythians, 1859. © National Gallery, London/Art Resource, NY.

Dazaifu, though far from the capital, was as close as Japanese could get to the continent and China, without leaving home, unlike Tomis, which contrary to its past Greek colonization certainly did not represent the refinement of Hellenistic civilization despite the lingering Hellenistic influence.

Michizane does express his shock over the vulgarity of his exile location: in an expansive poem of one hundred couplets describing his banishment up to his first fall in exile and modeled on a poem composed by Bo Juyi in exile, Michizane complains about the greedy officials, his alienation from the locals, bad food, and his attempts to find solace in reading, Buddhism, and Daoism. There are also more subtle offenses to the courtier such as abalone stench and an elegant *koto*-lute out of tune.[29] These are failures of civil morals and tastes by capital standards: while in Sanuki Michizane wrote a poem lamenting the botched performance of the annual ceremony for Confucius, the *sekiten* 釈典. Ritual and music were considered complementary civilizing arts in the Confucian world. However, Dazaifu also afforded unexpected surprises and treasures thanks to its closeness to the continent:

題竹床子	On a bamboo armchair
通事李彥瓙所送。	Sent by the interpreter Li Yanhuan[30]

---

[29] *Kanke bunsō, Kanke kōshū* no. 484. For a translation of the poem see Borgen 1986, 296–301.
[30] His identity is unclear. He might have been a Chinese merchant and interpreter.

彥環贈與竹繩床	The bamboo chair Yanhuan sent me
甚好施來在草堂	Is just right to furnish my humble abode.
應是商人留別去	Those merchants must have left it behind when they took off
自今遷客著相將	So from today on this exiled stranger will have it.
空心舊為遙踰海	Its "empty heart" is old, because it crossed the seas from far
落淚新如昔植湘	But my staining tears are new, like those on the bamboo planted next to the Xiang River long ago.
不費一錢得唐物	Without paying a single coin I got myself something Made-in-China
寄身偏愛惜風霜[31]	I will entrust my body to it, cling to it in love, and lament the wind and frost (it has endured).

In a rare moment of (still tearful) pleasure in exile, Michizane celebrates a bamboo armchair he received from a Chinese acquaintance. Such poems on everyday objects were rarely written before Michizane, who picked up this habit in response to Bo Juyi's infatuation with everyday events and material culture. But here the bamboo wicker chair is everything from quotidian object to mythical projection ground and metaphysical force.

The physical object might be banal, especially in the first two couplets: Michizane explains where he got the chair, and that it's simply perfect for his home—the banality is mirrored in the fresh colloquial twang of the second line. Then there is a glimmer of bargain instinct: Michizane snatches up an object left behind by Chinese traders on the move who left him a *karamono*—a fabulous "object from Cathay," a "thing made-in-China." Obviously, "made-in-China" sounds reverse to our ears. Whereas today, or at least until recently, this referred to cheaply mass-produced low-quality products from a Communist country with artificially low wages, to Michizane it was a precious object from the venerable civilization of China. Like Bo Juyi, who was one of the first Chinese poets with an interest in talking about money, possessions, and laments in his poetry—for instance, the steep prices of peonies at the flower market—Michizane also presents the chair as an economic token and chuckles with delight that he got it for free.[32]

But the chair starts taking on mythical, metaphysical, and poetic dimensions in the last two couplets. Michizane imagines how his tears in exile will inscribe his pain into the chair, producing "dappled bamboo" that grows in the Xiang River area in Southeast China and that became tear-stained when the two wives of the legendary Emperor Shun of high antiquity bemoaned his death. The temple associated with the two lady-goddesses is also suggestively close to the area where Qu Yuan, the most poignant identification figure for officials out of favor in premodern East Asia, committed suicide. Michizane's fresh tears rework the ancient bamboo from China, which has an "empty heart" unencumbered by emotional or

[31] *Kanke bunsō, Kanke kōshū* no. 501.
[32] On the new importance of ownership and economic value in mid-Tang poetry see Owen 1996b, 24–33.

material attachments and is thus—as far as chairs can be—in a state of Buddhist enlightenment. The last line produces a climax that merges China and Japan, the old and the new, the metaphysical and the economic, poet and object: because bamboo stays green and unperturbed in the face of wind and frost, it embodies sturdy resistance in poetic lore and allows Michizane to transform the chair into a cipher for himself. The bamboo chair and the poet who uses and cherishes it are equals, because they have both endured hardship.

In this innocent poem on an everyday object, Michizane spins out a fantasy of economic, mythical, spiritual, and poetic connection to China that ennobles, consoles, and entertains him. Obviously, Ovid's and Michizane's location of exile in relation to the imperial center and its respective reference culture led one to feel utterly isolated and allowed the other to console himself at least now and then. One suffered and died at what he considered the end of the civilized world, whereas the other, though suffering and dying far from Japan's capital down South, ended his life at least in vicinity to China.

4. The Address from Exile

One trait that distinguishes the exile poetry of Ovid and Michizane from their previous work and that stands particularly out in comparison between the two poets is their different addressivity, to use Mikhail Bakhtin's helpful term: their ways of inscribing the audience into their lines.[33] There are moments in Michizane's exile poetry where he does address others: a response to a letter from his family in the capital, laments for colleagues or friends whose news of death reached him in Dazaifu. But the first few poems in the *Kanke koshū*, such as the "Poem composed to myself" discussed above, set the tone for the inward gaze of Michizane's exile work. Michizane rarely addresses his poems to people and does not ask for their help in improving his exile condition. He sometimes even makes fun of his poor skills of companionship: when composing a creative response to Bo Juyi's poem on the "three friends" of a gentleman, namely lute playing, wine, and poetry, he confesses that he has had little company of lute playing or wine and that only poetry remains as his friend.[34] And Michizane takes this friendship to its ultimate destination with a sober, somber pun: His friend Poetry (*shiyū* 詩友) is his death friend (*shiyū* 死友), perhaps the only one who will stand by him until the end.

In contrast, Ovid's entire exile poetry is cast into the genre of epistolary elegy, a dialogic genre oriented toward the implied addressee, although we only get to hear Ovid's monologues and lack any possible responses.[35] Even the first book of the *Tristia*, which takes the reader from Rome on the long exodus to Tomis during a forbiddingly cold winter, exposed to the whims of the Adriatic and Aegean, is not an introverted travel diary, but an epic exile drama staged for his readers back

---

[33] Bakhtin 1986, 95.
[34] *Kanke bunsō, Kanke koshū* no. 477.
[35] Claassen therefore uses the term "secondary epistle" for Ovid's verse letters, because they are practically monologues where the addressee has little voice but is more of a literary device. Claassen 1999, 23.

home. And with the second book, the letter addressed to Augustus to relieve Ovid of unfair charges and exile, Ovid moves explicitly into the epistolary mode. Except for Augustus, and a certain Perilla, possibly his stepdaughter and the addressee of poem 3.7, none of the addressees of the elegies in the *Tristia* are named, because Ovid apparently feared that associations with the disgraced poet would harm his friends in the capital. Several poems are addressed to Ovid's wife but, ironically, we do not know her name. The four books of *Black Sea Letters*, instead, embrace the letter form explicitly: composed after three or four years in exile, Ovid mentions the addressees of his letters now by name.

Ovid's choice of the letter genre in exile has interesting precedents in the literary tradition and in Ovid's own work. Jo-Marie Claassen traces connections between the letters Cicero wrote when exiled in 58–57 BCE for his harsh handling of some members of the Catiline conspiracy, and Ovid's epistolary elegies. She shows how Ovid expands what she calls the "myth of exile" established by Cicero.[36] Ovid shares with the exiled Cicero the literary expression of death wishes, the panic over the greatness of the fall, remorse, grief, reaching out to his wife and, last but not least, the image of the exiled man as a "living corpse."[37]

The major form of exile literature before Ovid had been consolatory letters using philosophical arguments to deal with bereavement and exile, a tradition that eventually came to include, most famously, Cicero's *Tusculan Disputations*— written to console himself after the death of his beloved daughter Tullia— and later Seneca's *Consolations* and Boethius's *Consolations of Philosophy*. But *Tristia* and the *Black Sea Letters* had little in common with these philosophical consolations and were something new. Intriguingly, they resonate closely with Ovid's youthful love elegies, the *Amores,* and the *Heroides,* a collection of fictional verse letters put in the mouth of famous women and lovers from Greek myth. Ovid invented the genre of elegiac epistles for the *Heroides* and, as Nagle puts it, "The behavior patterns of the *Heroides,* the *Amores,* and the exilic poems are similar— unfulfilled erotic desires and the exilic homesickness."[38] But what in the *Heroides* was still an exciting literary experiment turned to a literary obsession in the exilic elegies, where Ovid became the excluded and isolated lover asking for the pity of his beloved. In the *Heroides* he could play with fine literary portrayals of the distinctive sufferings of a Penelope, a Medea, or a Dido, but in *Tristia* and *Black Sea Letters* he changed into the only and his only case of abandoned love. Ovid leaves out no opportunity to remind his wife, friends, and colleagues in the capital that they have to work hard on lobbying for his recall to Rome, or at least on a revision of the verdict and transfer to a better location. In the—possibly spurious—poem *Ibis* he scathingly attacks an unknown enemy for forsaking him and, again and again, devotes poems to unnamed foes and throws thunderbolts at them for their betrayal or attack.

---

[36] Claassen 1999, 183–90.
[37] See Nagle 1980, 33–35.
[38] Nagle 1980, 21–22.

The different quality of addressivity in Michizane's and Ovid's exile poetry is particularly obvious in the ways the two poets deal with their wives. In response to a letter from his wife, Michizane writes the following poem:

讀家書	Reading a letter from home
消息寂寥三月餘	Sad, without news for more than three months,
便風吹著一封書	A favorable wind now blew along this letter.
西門樹被人移去	"The tree at the west gate was taken away by people (to sell),
北地園教客寄居	And I had a stranger come live in the northern plot of our garden."
紙裹生薑稱藥種	You call the paper-wrapped ginger a medicine of sorts
竹籠昆布記齋儲	And mention that the *konbu* kelp should serve as my ascetic fare.
不言妻子飢寒苦	The letter doesn't speak of your, my dear wife's, suffering of hunger
為是還愁懊惱余[39]	That's why I fret even more—it makes me miserable with worry.

Michizane's initial relief at receiving a letter from home after many months of silence gives quickly way to more worries. Apparently his wife had to sell a tree and rent out parts of their beautiful residence, the Senpūbō 宣風坊 at the intersection of Kyoto's Fifth Avenue and Nishi no Tōin street, to support herself. That she cared to send him *konbu* kelp and ginger—which he seemed to have liked—comes as a welcome gift for a man in his fifties who probably suffered from various ailments during exile. But the sight of the gifts, in conjunction with the alarming news about his wife's lack of funds, raises a worse suspicion in Michizane: while scrapping together food and medicine for him, she must be suffering hunger and hardship herself. Michizane appears here as a responsible husband and head of a once thriving household, though probably not as interesting a poet. He might have preferred composing a poem over responding with a prose letter, because the poem was a traditionally more urgent form to express personal distress and sorrow.

While this is the only extant poem Michizane addressed to his wife from exile, Ovid wrote many verse letters from Tomis to his wife. The third elegy of the fourth book of the *Tristia* gives a good taste of how Ovid uses his marital relation as an opportunity for poetic spectacle:

> . . . Do your feverish night-hours
> stretch out to eternity? Do you toss and turn
> till your weary bones are aching? That you suffer such symptoms
> I have no doubt, that your love betrays sorrow's pain,
> that your crucifixion surely matches Andromache watching
> Hector dragged in his blood at Achilles' chariot-tail.
> Yet what prayer to utter I know not, I cannot determine
> just what attitude I'd wish you to take.
> Are you sad? I'm angry at being the cause of your heartache.

---

[39] *Kanke bunsō, Kanke kōshū* no. 488.

Not sad? Yet your husband's loss
should affect you. Ah yes, lament your bereavement, sweetest
of wives, live through a season's grief
for my troubles, bewail my lot—there's some pleasure in weeping,
sorrow's worked out and relieved by tears.[40]

In contrast to Michizane's sober, marital concern over his wife's well-being, Ovid gives his wife a premier role in the spectacle of his exile. There is a hint of voyeuristic sadism in imagining her bones worn out from bad sleep, and a touch of pathetic masochism in elevating their plight to epic heights, envisioning himself a dead Hector dragged behind Achilles' chariot circling around Troy, watched by his helpless wife Andromache. Ovid does express regret to have to cause her heartache, but immediately prescribes unrestrained weeping over *his* sad fate. Similarly, when Ovid feels ashamed for his exile and the loss of reputation his wife incurs due to it, he takes that feeling as a welcome opportunity to parade his talent and male pride:

It cuts me to the quick if being spoken of as an exile's
wife makes you blush and turn your face aside;
it cuts me to the quick if you feel that to have our marriage
known, now, brings you disgrace, if you're ashamed,
now, of being mine! Gone, gone are the days when you boasted
about your husband, never hiding his name;
gone are the days when you (do you mind being reminded?)
were glad (I recall) to be, to be known as, mine.
As befits a true wife, you loved my every talent, your partial
love added many to the true ones. I
ranked so high in your eyes that there was no man living
you set above me, more coveted for your own.[41]

...

No: rather rise up in defence of me, make it your business
to be, for me, the model of a dutiful wife,
imbue these unhappy circumstances with your virtues:
high-striving glory climbs the steepest paths.

...

My misfortune gives you a chance for fame, it offers

---

[40] *Tristia* 4.3.25-38. Green 2005, 69–70. *et veniunt aestus, et nox inmensa videtur, / fessaque iactati corporis ossa dolent?/ non equidem dubito, quin haec et cetera fiant, / detque tuus maesti signa doloris amor, / nec cruciere minus, quam cum Thebana cruentum / Hectora Thessalico vidit ab axe rapi. / quid tamen ipse precer dubito, nec dicere possum, / affectum quem te mentis habere velim. / tristis es? indignor quod sim tibi causa doloris: / non es? at amisso coniuge digna fores / tu vero tua damna dole, mitissima coniunx, / tempus et a nostris exige triste malis, / fleque meos casus: est quaedam flere voluptas; / expletur lacrimis egeriturque dolor.*
[41] *Tristia* 4.3.49-60. Green 2005, 70. *me miserum, si tu, cum diceris exulis uxor / avertis vultus et subit ora rubor! / me miserum, si turpe putas mihi nupta videri! / me miserum, si te iam pudet esse meam! / tempus ubi est illud, quo te iactare solebas / coniuge, nec nomen dissimulare viri? / tempus ubi est, quo te—nisi non vis illa referri— / et dici, memini, iuvit et esse meam? / utque proba dignum est, omni tibi dote placebam: / addebat veris multa faventis amor. / nec, quem praeferres—ita res tibi magna videbar— / quemque tuum malles esse, vir alter erat.*

your loyalty room to raise its head, to make
itself conspicuous. Use this crisis—your gift, your godsend:
How wide a field lies open for your praise![42]

The wife in this poem exists for the sake of her husband and the sake of the poetic drama of exile. Thanks to him she gets *her* chance at fame and an opportunity to live up to the role of a paragon of marital virtue. It is ironic, as has been remarked, that of all Augustan poets Ovid, the love-inclined *enfant terrible* of Rome's literary scene, was the only one who tried marriage (even three times); and in this plea Ovid paints her according to the moralistic Augustan ideals of marriage that the Princeps had introduced with several marital laws promulgated in 18 and 17 BCE, which encouraged marriage and childbearing, and punished adultery.[43] This is again evidence that the much-debated question of Ovid's stance for or against Augustan ideology is often a matter of pragmatic poetic expediency rather than of political or moral principle. Who would not want to depict his wife loyally devoted to the cause of her husband at home when he pines away in exile? The gagging praise of his wife in this epistolary elegy is the most extreme case of the aggressive addressivity of Ovid's exile poetry: the letter's addressee is virtually strangled by the poet's desperate poetic drama of calling on her for help.

5. Ovid's Pleas: The Poet and Roman Oratory

The urgency of Ovid's addressivity is enhanced by a part of Roman literary culture and public life, which in this form did not exist in Japan: oratory and the practice of litigation. To work for his recall Ovid pleads with everybody and everything: the emperor Augustus, great beyond human power and inhuman in his verdict; the Muses, whose blessing with talent led to his exile due to poetry in the first place, but who at times help him through exile, giving him poetry as the only way to survive the ordeal; Amor—inspiration for the *Art of Love*—whom he accuses of causing his exile, when the divine boy visits Ovid in a dream vision; or, nearer to the ground, people who had close ties to the court, such as Messalinus, the son of his former patron Messala, Paullus Fabius Maximus, married to a first cousin of Augustus, or the influential consul Sextus Pompeius; Ovid's editor in Rome and literary executor of sorts, Brutus; a varied assortment of friends and fellow poets such as Cotta Maximus, Macer, or Cornelius Severus; from his family his wife and his stepdaughter Perilla (whom Ovid encourages to pursue her poetic talent despite his bad example of where it can lead); and, last but not least, anonymous enemies, unidentified friends who are too lazy to write to him, and future readers, posterity *tout court.*

---

[42] Tristia 4.3.71-74 and 81–84. Green 2005, 71. *sed magis in curam nostri consurge tuendi / exemplumque mihi coniugis esto bonae / materiamque tuis tristem virtutibus imple: / ardua per praeceps gloria vadit iter....dat tibi nostra locum tituli fortuna, caputque / conspicuum pietas qua tua tollat, habet. / utere temporibus, quorum nunc munere facta est / et patet in laudes area lata tuas.*

[43] For the content and implications of Augustus's marriage laws see Thomas McGinn, *Prostitution, Sexuality, and the Law in Ancient Rome* (Oxford and New York: Oxford University Press, 1998), chapters 3–6.

Training in judicial rhetoric and public declamation had a formidable role in the education of the Roman elite and, accordingly, patterned the poets' articulation and style and the perception of the reading public. Ovid came from an old equestrian family and had started on a public career, serving in minor legal jobs that would have involved him in the repression of crimes such as murder, theft, and arson. Although he did not plead cases from about age twenty-five to the time of his exile, he participated in jury panels settling private suits such as property disputes and inheritances, and possibly criminal cases. He obviously chose to continue playing an active civic role in the Augustan state even after he abandoned a senatorial career to devote himself exclusively to writing.[44]

Let us explore two examples of how Ovid uses the world of oratory in his addresses from exile. One verse letter is written for Cassius Salanus, the oratory tutor of the gifted and hapless Germanicus, on whom Ovid pinned his hopes as a successor to Augustus (which did not help his recall during Augustus's reign and after his death in 14 CE, because Augustus's wife Livia successfully forced her son Tiberius from her first marriage on the throne). During his exile Ovid continued to work on his *Fasti*, a didactic calendar of Roman religious festivals in chronological succession, and adopted parts of its calendrical underpinnings and didactic model from the astronomical calendar *Phaenomena* (c. 276 BCE) by the Hellenistic poet Aratus. Ovid produced a verse translation of the *Phaenomena* into Latin and rededicated his *Fasti* at some point to the young Germanicus who himself had produced a Latin translation of Aratus.[45] So there must have been both an intellectual and political resonance between the two, and Ovid praises Cassius Salanus's brilliant disciple, who would certainly have been flattered by Ovid's compliments and appeals to the commonalities between orators and poets to convince the orator to continue putting in a good word for him:

> … You too, my studious friend, must
> study the Muses: being talented yourself
> you favour my talent. Our work, though different, still issues
> from a common source: we both pursue liberal arts.
> My business is with the thyrsus, yours with the laurel,
> yet both of us need that spark,
> and just as your eloquence lends my verses muscle,
> so I impart a lustre to your words,
> and you're right to think that poetry borders on your studies,
> that as brothers-in-arms we should worship the same gods.[46]

Talent, creative spark, eloquence, connection to the divine: Ovid proposes here a theory on the synergy between private poetry and public eloquence. If one believed

---

[44] White 2002, 2–4. White also emphasizes that "[i]n range and frequency, Ovid's exploitation of legal imagery far exceeds that of other Augustan poets." Ibid., 4.

[45] Gee 2000, 3–4.

[46] *Ex Ponto* II.5.63-72. Green 2005, 142. *Tu quoque Pieridum studio, studiose, teneris / ingenioque faves, ingeniose, meo. / distat opus nostrum, sed fontibus exit ab isdem: / artis et ingenuae cultor uterque sumus. / thyrsus abest a te, gustata est laurea nobis, / sed tamen ambobus debet inesse calor: / utque meis numeris tua dat facundia nervos / sic venit a nobis in tua verba nitor. / iure igitur studio confinia carmina vestro / et commilitii sacra tuenda putas.*

that his young disciple would succeed Augustus, approaching Germanicus's tutor was certainly a strategic move. Ovid had apparently little prior acquaintance with him, but he addressed him as a professional colleague, a specialist of oratory who could display his eloquence's "muscle" (*nervos*) to work for Ovid's recall. Ovid, specialist of literary rhetoric, has "lustre" (*nitor*) to offer, but what he really needed was the physical force of a specialist in legal and juridical rhetoric, hence the appeal to their fraternal bond as "brothers-in-arms" (*commilitii*) who share the one goal of victory while contributing complementary fields of expertise. Thus, the world of Roman oratory allowed Ovid here to declare professional comradery with litigation specialists with attractive ties to the imperial establishment.

But the world of oratory could take on a much larger role than one of political expediency, providing the frame for a triumphant self-defense, an acquittal from all charges that was not forthcoming from the emperor but that the poet could freely administer to himself. This is how Ovid opens the large-scale *apologia* of his life and art, merging the roles of defendant and defense lawyer:[47]

> Who was this I you read, this trifler in tender passions?
> You want to know, posterity? Then attend:—
> Sulmo is my homeland, where ice-cold mountain torrents
> make lush our pastures, and Rome is ninety miles off.
> Here I was born, in the year both consuls perished
> at Antony's hands; heir (for what that's worth)
> to an ancient family, no brand-new knight promoted
> just yesterday for his wealth.[48]

Ovid opens with a direct address—an *apostrophe*—to the audience in his court room: his readers and posterity. Although this elegy is usually called an "autobiography" and justly famous as our most important source for details of Ovid's life, it would be more appropriate to call it an "auto-apology" and indeed, as we will see, "auto-apotheosis" for Ovid the poet.[49] Like in a standard *prosopopeia* in court speeches, where the orator speaks in the voice of somebody else for greater rhetorical effect, the exile poet speaks in the voice of an imaginary defendant Ovid of the past trial and future glorious triumph to an imaginary courtroom in Rome. The defendant proudly dates his birth in relation to the death of two consuls and highlights his family's ancient patrician roots.

After recounting his path away from a senatorial career to poetry and the Muses and telling his family's fortunes, Ovid's wishful fantasy of a trial that would absolve

---

[47] Fairweather has suggestively argued that this elegy is structured as an *apologia* that trims the account of Ovid's life to coincide with Augustus's own career as depicted in the fragments preserved of Augustus's lost autobiography *De Vita Sua*. Fairweather 1987, 181–96. Modeling one's defense on one's prosecutor's defense of his own life in another context is in principle a safe strategy, unless the prosecutor is the emperor. In that case the pretentiousness alone is probably offense enough.

[48] *Tristia*. IV.10.1-8. Green 2005, 79. *Ille ego qui fuerim, tenerorum lusor amorum, / quem legis, ut noris, accipe posteritas. / Sulmo mihi patria est, gelidis uberrimus undis, / milia qui novies distat ab urbe decem. / editus hic ego sum, nec non, ut tempora noris, / cum cecidit fato consul uterque pari / si quid id est, usque a proavis vetus ordinis heres / non modo fortunae munere factus eques.*

[49] For recent scholarship that corrects reading this elegy as an autobiography at face value see Green 2005, 269.

him from the accusations that caused his exile turns serious: Ovid imagines his judgment at the Stygian court in the Underworld and there assures his dead parents that he has committed no crime, just an error:

> ... Yet if there survives from a life's extinction
> something more than a name, if an insubstantial wraith
> *does* escape the pyre, if some word, my parental spirits,
> has reached you about me, if charges stand to my name
> in the Stygian court, then understand, I implore you
> —and you I may not deceive—that my exile's cause
> was not a crime, but an error. So much for the dead. I return now
> to you, my devoted readers, who would know
> the events of my life.[50]

As in a *suasoria*, a speech aimed at persuading the audience of the defendant's innocence, Ovid tries to convince his dead parents and the audience in the imaginary courtroom that he committed no crime. He ends his grand auto-apology with nothing less than a poetic auto-apotheosis:

> So the fact that I live still, to grapple with such grim hardships,
> unwearied, yet, of the light and all it brings,
> I owe, my Muse, to you: it's you who afford me solace,
> who come as rest, as medicine to my cares;
> you my guide and comrade, who spirit me from the Danube
> to an honoured seat on Helicon; who have
> offered me that rare benefit, fame while still living,
> a title rarely granted till after death.
>
> . . .
>
> There are many I'd rank above me: yet I am no less quoted
> than they are, and most read throughout the world.
> So if there's any truth in poetic predictions, even
> should I die tomorrow, I'll not be wholly earth's.
> Which I was it [that] triumphed? True poet or fashion's pander?
> Either way, generous reader, it is you I must thank.[51]

Although the underworld court would have ruled over the verdict associated with the missteps that caused Ovid's exile, by the end of the elegy the object of the trial has changed to a verdict over Ovid's immortality as a poet. Acquittal and triumph are in sight, and so is a transfer to a far better place than exile: Ovid sees himself

---

[50] *Tristia* IV.10.85-93. Green, 82. *si tamen extinctis aliquid nisi nomina restat, / et gracilis structos effugit umbra rogos, / fama, parentales, si vos mea contigit, umbrae, / et sunt in Stygio crimina nostra foro, / scite, precor, causam (nec vos mihi fallere fas est) / errorem iussae, non scelus, esse fugae. / Manibus hoc satis est: ad vos, studiosa, revertor / pectora, qui vitae quaeritis acta meae.*

[51] *Tristia* IV.10.115-122 and 127–32. Green 2005, 82–83. *ergo quod vivo durisque laboribus obsto, / nec me sollicitae taedia lucis habent, / gratia, Musa, tibi: nam tu solacia praebes, / tu curae requies, tu medicina venis. / tu dux et comes es, tu nos abducis ab Histro, / in medioque mihi das Helicone locum; / tu mihi, quod rarum est, vivo sublime dedisti / nomen, ab exequiis quod dare fama solet.... cumque ego praeponam multos mihi, non minor illis / dicor et in toto plurimus orbe legor. / si quid habent igitur vatum praesagia veri, / protinus ut moriar, non ero, terra, tuus. / sive favore tuli, sive hanc ego carmine famam, / iure tibi grates, candide lector, ago.*

whisked away from miserable Tomis to an "honoured seat on Helicon," the mountain of the Muses, and is proud to be read throughout the world and to have gained a name that will stand the test of times.

Although Ovid uses the frame of a legal case and during the evocation of the Stygian court in the Underworld one is tempted to focus on Ovid's attempt to enact poetic justice on the accusations that sent him into exile, the ultimate verdict is a prophecy of immortality, not an absolution from error. His audience is posterity and the fictional court defense turns into a poetic self-deification. Ovid does end on a weighty rhetorical question ("Which I was it [that] triumphed? True poet or fashion's pander?"), a question that ironically has indeed had resonance occasionally in Ovid's scholarly reception. But like in a *suasoria* that passionately argues the defendant's side but woos for the audience's sympathy by at least rhetorically giving them a choice, Ovid is sure of his victory, of the triumphant verdict that he is a true poet. And he thanks two groups of supporters in his imaginary courtroom: the Muses and his fans, the generous readers.

6. Michizane's Pleas: Poets and Plants

Against the background of the importance of oratory in Roman education and Ovid's early career, his mobilization of rhetoric in his exile poetry is little surprising, although perhaps distinctively Ovidian. Yet the contrast to Michizane should make us appreciate more that public oratory is a distinctively Greco-Roman cultural art and that the intersections between public and poetic space could take radically different shapes in other literary cultures. Although Michizane, as a scholar and poet-official, was carefully trained in drafting administrative documents, such as the deliberations (*gi* 議), imperial edicts (*shōchoku* 詔勅), or petitions to the throne (*sōjō* 奏状) that are included in the personal collection of his works he compiled, they belong to the world of the imperial bureaucracy, a predominantly textual culture unlike oral declamation and popular litigation in the Roman public sphere. That Heian poets include samples of these bureaucratic genres into their collected works alongside their poetry shows that these genres, written in ornate prose, testified to their authors' practical political as well as literary skills.

But Michizane does not mobilize the language of the imperial bureaucracy in his exile poetry for political, dramatic, or fictionalizing effect, as we have seen in Ovid. These are separate worlds of reflection and argument. Michizane does not even seize the opportunity to defend himself with tropes of official discourse under the most tantalizing circumstances, such as when Emperor Daigo announces a new imperial era, the Engi Era (901–923), and proclaims a general amnesty for all enemies of the state except for Michizane. Michizane does not defend himself, does not address himself to the emperor or anybody who could speak for him; he does not make this moment into political capital for his recall. Instead, in the poem "On Reading the Imperial Edict Announcing the Beginning of the New Era", he merely complains about metaphors, in particular about the fact that the edict refers to him as a "giant whale," an unsavory image for evil and corrupt ministers. In the last two couplets of the poem Michizane straightens the metaphoric record:

吞舟非我口	Swallowing boats? My mouth can't do it.
吐浪非我聲	Spitting out waves? I don't have that voice.
哀哉放逐者	Ah, how deplorable, me in exile!
蹉跎喪精靈[52]	My steps are faltering and I am losing my life spirit.

Michizane sarcastically ridicules the edict by literalizing the metaphor and gives rein to his despair, but he does not use the momentum of his indignation to argue or plead.

Let us contrast Ovid's frontal pursuit of his family, friends, supporters, and the emperor that we sampled above with a surprising form of addressivity that comes to the fore in Michizane's exile poetry. It will show how Michizane blended the literary resources of the Chinese and Japanese literary traditions, his reception of Bo Juyi and his own creative temperament into an intriguing, fresh novel poetics of exile. In comparison with Ovid's clamorous addressivity we saw that Michizane's poetry from exile appears introverted, as he often addresses himself, or dark forces of fate and heaven. Yet he creates for himself a curious lineup of dialogue partners: he starts talking to passing geese, going South in autumn, and is envious that they know their date of return, unlike the banished poet (no. 480). He thinks of the bamboo back in his residence in Kyoto and addresses it like a person left behind due to his exile (no. 490). In another autumn poem he does not speak to the flowers directly, but plants himself in his garden back home in Kyoto in the middle of yellow chrysanthemums and wilting flowers—imagining how his white tuft would fit into the plot (no. 512). Some of his more distant dialogue partners in nature even answer him. Here is a dialogue in quatrains where he converses with the moon:

間秋月	Asking the Autumn Moon
度春度夏只今秋	You passed spring, you passed summer, here you are in autumn:
如鏡如環本是鉤	Like a mirror, like a jade ring, but a crescent before.
為問未曾告終始	May I ask you, who has never announced an end or beginning,
被浮雲掩向西流	Why do you, covered in floating clouds, disappear in the West?

代月答	Answering for the Moon
黃發桂香半且圓	The "fortnight plant" is opening, my laurel is fragrant, I'm half, then full again[53]
三千世界一周天	The three-thousand Buddhist worlds I pass in my circles around heaven.
天廻玄鑑雲將霽	Where heaven turns its penetrating gaze clouds will dissipate,
唯是西行不左遷[54]	But I only go West, I'm not banished.

---

[52] *Kanke bunsō, Kanke kōshū* no. 479.
[53] Poetic lore related to the moon: a laurel tree is said to grow on the moon and the "fortnight plant" (*mei* 莢) opens for a fortnight and wanes again for the second half of the month. The legendary Chinese Emperor Yao supposedly fixed the calendar based on its blossoming rhythm.
[54] *Kanke bunsō, Kanke kōshū* no. 510-11.

The moon is a good person to ask about exile: like Michizane, it can be covered in—slanderous—clouds and it disappears in the West—Michizane's trek down from the capital to Dazaifu in the Southwest. But the moon regards the poet with both empathy and cosmic indifference. That Heaven will ultimately dissipate the clouds might console the poet: right and wrong, truth and slander will not stay concealed and the poet's innocence will become manifest at least in the broader, cosmic picture, even if the current "Heavenly Sovereign" Emperor Daigo has kept him exiled. But the moon's mobility reaches into all three thousand Buddhist worlds, in sharp contrast to Michizane's confinement in Dazaifu, and the moon is quick to point out that its westbound trajectory is a physical law, not a political punishment.

Michizane's fictitious dialogue with the moon is only one example of his larger engagement with plants and objects in the natural world, which holds a curiously prominent place in Michizane's exile poetry. They can be poetic objects signaling empathy and carriers of a possibility for pardon, like the moon or the geese above. They can be painful, but still consoling reminders of the time before and, hopefully, after exile: thinking of the bamboo or plum tree back home in his residence in Kyoto has the sweetness of nostalgic reminiscing, but it is painful as a deceptive counterfactual: in one poem Michizane remarks that while the blossoms can still at least smile, he is all sad (no. 495).

Some of the poetic lore around plants that Michizane uses had a long-standing connection to exile in the Chinese tradition and had early on become part of the poetic repertoire in Japan. Chrysanthemums—already flowers of autumn, decline, and sorrow—were particularly poignant reminders of exile. Qu Yuan, the paragon of Chinese exile poets mentioned above, said in "Encountering Sorrow," which he composed supposedly before his suicide, "in the morning I drank dripping dew from the orchids and in the evening dined on fallen petals of autumn chrysanthemums 朝飲木蘭之墜露兮, 夕餐秋菊之落英."[55]

The exotic flora of the Chinese South plays a central role in Qu Yuan's final plaint: they are part of the scenery through which Qu Yuan travels in a desperate search of a ruler who appreciates him and he might eat or drink from them, adorn himself with flower garlands, or use them as tissue paper to dry his tears, as occasion demands; also, Qu Yuan is a gardener and plants fragrant flowers, hoping they will not be overtaken by evil weeds. This mode of a very embodied, material use of plant metaphors—where Qu Yuan's cultivation of plants proves his moral "fragrance" and innocence and evil and stinking plants are kennings for slanderous ministers at court who brought about his downfall—had become a standard trope in Chinese literary culture and was early on adopted into Japanese literature.

But Michizane also picked up on new forms of dealing with objects in nature, for example conversing with them. Bo Juyi liked to engage "spring," "crane," or "autumn light" in poetic dialogue, occasionally speaking "for" them. There can be no doubt that Michizane wanted his readers to be thinking of Bo Juyi

---

[55] Ma 1993, 23.

when hearing his poetic diaologue with the moon.[56] Gotō Akio has shown that Michizane was the first Japanese poet to write numerous poems on the topic of bamboo. He echoed Bo Juyi, who enjoyed writing about the bamboo plants that surrounded him in many of the places he lived and who himself helped establish bamboo as a prominent poetic topic in Chinese poetry. Although Michizane's tutor Shimada no Tadaomi did write about bamboos, he relied on traditional poetic lore, referring for example to the third-century CE extravagant "Seven Sages of the Bamboo Grove." The novelty of Bo Juyi's and also Michizane's bamboo poetry was that they cut their plants fresh: they established them as topics in their own right and cut them loose of the clichéd poetic lore and addressed them as everyday objects existing in material space. Bo Juyi famously wrote about his love for eating cheaply purchased bamboo sprouts; and Michizane planted bamboo in front of his study in Kyoto, an homage to Bo Juyi's life spent among bamboo.[57]

But, as Gotō and several other scholars have pointed out, Michizane, with his plant poetry from exile, was not just a disciple of Bo Juyi. Michizane's poem "Longing for my bamboo at home on a snowy night" (no. 490) is not a traditional "poem on things" (eibutsushi 詠物詩) loaded with erudite poetic lore. Neither is it a chatty snapshot of everyday life à la Bo Juyi. It uses the moral qualities associated with bamboo—steadfastness, persistence—and entrusts Michizane's plaintive voice to the bamboo and is in this way a novel form of the "Expressing one's inner feelings" subgenre of poetry (jukkaishi 述懷詩), a true breakthrough in Michizane's Dazaifu poetry.[58] Ōsone Shōsuke locates Michizane's highpoint as a poet in the way Michizane can convey everyday life scenes that use plant imagery to limitless depth and sadness in his exile poetry.[59] Fujiwara Katsumi discusses the "mysterious, sad brightness" in Michizane's exile poetry and associates this with a very distinctive metaphorical mode.[60] So there is a clear sense among Michizane scholars that the poet developed a new repertoire of rhetorical tools in exile.

Let us look at "Planting Chrysanthemums," to see some of this distinctive mode at play. Here is Michizane, gardening in front of his home in Dazaifu:

種菊	Planting chrysanthemums
青膚小葉白牙根	Dark-skinned their small leaves, white-toothed their roots:
茅屋前頭近逼軒	(I plant them) in front of my cottage, pressing close to the railing.
將布貿來孀婦宅	I traded cloth for them: from the dwelling of an old widow
與書要得老僧園	Got them for books: from an old monk's garden.
未曾種處思元亮	Planting them here I did not even think of Tao Yuanming.
為是花時供世尊	When they blossom I will offer them to the Buddha.

---

[56] See the commentary on this poem in Kojima and Yamamoto 1998, 171 f.
[57] Gotō 1993a, 102–34.
[58] Gotō 1993a, 131.
[59] Ōsone 1998a.
[60] Fujiwara 2001, 288–293.

不計悲愁何日死　　In the midst of sorrows I can't fathom the day I die,
堆沙作壙荻編垣[61]　So I just gather sand to make a moat and bind reeds into
　　　　　　　　　a fence.

As with the Chinese bamboo chair, Michizane places the chrysanthemums into a context of trade exchange: he received them in return for cloth and books from acquaintances who each carry their own lot of hardship: a widowed neighbor and an old monk. And he plants them in a cramped space in front of his simple residence. In the last two couplets these "tradable" (*kaekitaru* 貿へ来る) objects of economic value suddenly function as poetic and religious capital: Qu Yuan and Tao Yuanming (365–427) are the foremost poets who come to mind when speaking of chrysanthemums.[62] Tao Yuanming retreated from public office and returned to live his life on his family farm in the countryside, enjoying the farm work and the charms of the rustic environment that allowed him to garden, read, drink, and write poetry. For the pleasures of a balanced life of gardening, Tao Qian was a perfect model of identification, although he was not exiled, but writes much of his poetry about how he made this life-changing choice. But in this poem Michizane consciously renounces the poetic lore of chrysanthemums: he omits Qu Yuan completely and mentions Tao Yuanming, only to say that he was *not* thinking of Tao Qian when planting his chrysanthemums, but prefers offering the flowers to the Buddha once they bloom. This moves Michizane from the consolation through the poetic tradition to the desire for religious salvation, which becomes a prominent concern for the aging poet in exile. In the last couplet the poem takes a lugubrious turn: although a pile of sand, a mound, and a fence could all be innocent elements of landscape gardening, we are not sure how they relate to his forebodings of death. Is he already grave digging while gardening?

This is just one example of Michizane's intricate mobilization of plants as creatures of botanical, economic, poetic, and religious significance with various degrees of physical and metaphorical value. Plants enabled a form of addressivity in Michizane's exile poetry that is quite unthinkable in Latin literary culture, just as oratory and court rhetoric was a form of social and literary practice that in its distinctive Greco-Roman form did not develop in Japan.

7. Conclusion

After their death in exile Ovid and Michizane came to live on as exile poets par excellence. Already a century after Michizane's death, Murasaki Shikibu's *Tale of Genji* evokes Michizane (and Bo Juyi) to capture the mood of the protagonist's exile in Suma, when Genji has to leave the capital for sexual liberties he took with the sister of his archenemy. And Ovid's nostalgia for Rome in his exile poetry became particularly attractive after the fall of the Roman empire during periods when Ancient Rome was consciously evoked as a political model for the present—for

---

[61] *Kanke bunsō, Kanke kōshū* no. 497.
[62] In a chrysanthemum poem composed during Michizane's exile in Sanuki, which describes his despair when thinking of the chrysanthemums in his garden back home in Kyoto, he mentions Tao Qian and Qu Yuan together. *Kanke bunsō, Kanke kōshū* no. 269.

example, during the Carolingian Renaissance of the ninth century and during the Middle Ages.[63] Although the overall popularity of Ovid's exile poetry dropped with the Renaissance and remained low into the twentieth century until its rehabilitation by scholars over the last few decades, it always remained an intensely personal point of reference for writers who suddenly found themselves out of favor in some form of exile.

From the perspective of the poetics that both poets developed in exile their afterlife appears ironically inverse. Ovid's intense addressivity was not rewarded: he was never pardoned in life or death although posterity and later readers stood by him, as he had anticipated. Michizane, however, who had kept more to himself or contented himself with metaphorical addresses to objects in nature, died a criminal, but was rehabilitated and became a god within a few decades of his death, after a stream of ominous disasters was attributed to his vengeful spirit: Tokihira's death in his prime, the death of the young crown prince, the son of Emperor Daigo and Tokihira's sister, Daigo's own death, and thunder and lightning that struck the palace and killed several courtiers, among others.[64] In 947 the Kitano Shrine in Kyoto was dedicated to Michizane, where Michizane merged with Tenjin, a general deity of thunder. The court rehabilitated the scholar-official by conferring two final posthumous promotions in 993: to minister of the left and to grand minister of senior first rank, the highest possible court rank and office in Heian Japan. Today, Michizane is one of the most popular Shinto deities, worshipped in thousands of shrines throughout Japan and in particular demand during the season of school and university entrance examinations when throngs of students come and pray to the god of scholarship to be accepted into prestigious schools of their preference. What Ovid had dared to imagine in poetry—his apotheosis—happened to Michizane in real afterlife, though of course thanks to a radically different horizon of cultural possibilities. Michizane did not become an immortalized poet on the East Asian equivalent of Mount Helicon and its Muses (there is none), but was gradually transformed from an angry spirit into a form of previously extant thunder deities, retaining the scholarly trait that the historical Michizane embodied.

Not just the exile poet was rehabilitated and survived in divine form. The form of adressivity directed at plants and nature that he had developed in his exile poetry took on its own afterlife. The spatial disjunction between flowers and the poet, and the flowers' ability of emotional empathy became a major trope in later Michizane lore and several of his most famous, possibly spurious waka, play on this. (see Figure 6.2)

When Michizane was about to leave his home for exile he presumably addressed the following waka to the plum tree in his garden:

東風吹かば	When the east wind blows,
にほひおこせよ	Send along your fragrance,
梅花	Plum blossoms!
主なしとて	Though without master,
春を忘るな	Don't forget the spring.[65]

[63] On Ovid's late antique and medieval reception see Dewar 2002 and Hexter 2002.
[64] For a brief introduction to the highly complex process of Michizane's deification into Tenjin see Borgen 1986, 307–36.
[65] *Shūiwakashū*, no. 1006.

FIGURE 6.2 *Michizane Bidding Farewell to his Red Plum Tree in Kyoto When Departing for Exile*
Picture Scroll of the Origins of Matsuzaki Tenjin Shrine (*Matsuzaki Tenjin engi emaki*). Kamakura Period, 1311. © Hōfu Tenmangū, Yamaguchi Prefecture, Japan.

The earliest surviving version of this poem stems from an eleventh-century imperial anthology, so that the poem belongs most probably to Michizane lore rather than to his poetic oeuvre. A later flourish of the legend claimed that the plum tree was so touched by his master's poem that it flew down to Kyushu to be with his master. That very tree, visitors nowadays are told to believe, is still revered in the Tenjin shrine in Dazaifu. Tenjin shrines are usually covered with emblems of the plum, Michizane's symbol, and in today's sleepy provincial town of Dazaifu "Plum Branch Cakes" can be sampled at any street corner. The plum continues to hold particular significance for Michizane lore, but there were similar legends and poems cropping up around Michizane's cherry tree and pine tree.[66]

Although these are later stories associated with Tenjin, the god of scholarship and of thunder, that are often kept apart from Michizane the living poet, we can see a suggestive line from Michizane's addresses to plants to the growth of legends that put flesh around the late poet's rhetorical gestures in his exile poetry, even to the point of conceiving of flying trees that consoled the homesick Michizane in exile.

This chapter has been a controlled experiment devoted to the hypothetical question, what happens if you force poets socialized in very different literary cultures, equipped with very different generic, rhetorical, poetic tools and different personal temperaments and identities into a comparably shocking situation like exile? As we saw, though the catastrophe of exile was comparable, Michizane's and Ovid's poetic reactions were rather different. And we discovered that this holds not only for our poets: modern scholars will have accordingly different, possibly even inverse expectations in reading exile poetry from Rome or Japan, as I showed when discussing the question of the "fallacy" or "felicity" of emotional realism projected onto the exile poetry.

---

[66] Borgen 1986, 290–95.

The reasons for the contrast between Michizane's and Ovid's different addressivity are complex and hard to determine. They would include sociopolitical aspects such as differences in the legal system, structure of the public sphere, the social profile of poets, and forms of civic participation (such as oratory). Equally important are differences in the structure of Japanese and Roman literary cultures: a lengthy elegy says different things and allows the poet to voice them differently from a terse Sino-Japanese quatrain. And lastly, their respective literary cultures shaped their personal creative temperament differently: Ovid's invention of the epistolary elegy for the *Heroides* before his exile and his startling application of the emotive potential of this form in his exile work contrasts with Michizane's distinctive reception of Bo Juyï's poetry in his exile verse. Exploring these various reasons for the difference between the addressivity of Ovid's and Michizane's exile poetry would have required a book-length study in itself. Or it might have provided one of many alternative structures for writing this book. Nothing is better than exile for being forced to see alternatives.

| Satire in Foreign Attire

The Ambivalences of Learning in Late
Antiquity and Medieval Japan

1. *"Our Satire, Their Philosophy"*

In the last two chapters of this book we move from perspectives on the symbolic centers of the Roman and Japanese Empires that we explored in the last three chapters—founding figures of state formation, the respective capitals as sites of literary production, and poets and poetry in exile—to two particular modes through which younger cultures defined themselves in relation to their reference culture: satirical invectives against the older reference culture, in this chapter, and texts that juxtapose both cultures for comparative and contrastive effect, in the final chapter.

Philosophers and Confucian scholars were iridescent figures in Ancient Rome and Japan. On the one hand, they were impersonations of a highly respected foreign regime of knowledge. On the other hand, they were derided as impractical, stilted, ludicrously cerebral, and aloof from the society they inhabited. Romans were aware that *philosophia* was a Greek invention with a Roman intervention and aftermath. Recently, scholars have increasingly emphasized the existence of a "Roman philosophy" in its own right that goes far beyond the translation and adaptation of Greek philosophy into the Latin language.[1] Yet all originality granted, philosophy in Rome *did* develop within the framework of the long-established Hellenistic schools of the Academics, Peripatetics, Epicureans, and Stoics. Similarly, the Confucian Classics and philosophical masters were of Chinese origin and, while the traditional Japanese elites made them their own by using their ideas and phraseology in virtually all texts and contexts, early Japan did not produce a Confucius or any other "school of thought" similar to the Chinese Mohists, Daoists, Logicians, Legalists, or the Yin-Yang-school.

If philosophers in Rome and Confucian scholars at the Academy in Kyoto represented a not really home-grown regime of knowledge, Romans and Japanese

---

[1] Important markers of this paradigm shift are Griffin and Barnes 1989 and 1997, Morford 2002, and Sedley 2003.

could boast something that seemed less developed in their reference cultures Greece and China: satire. Certainly, satirical invective pervades Greek old comedy, iambic verse, and the so-called "Menippean satire," associated with the Syrian cynic philosopher Menippus of Gadara (3rd cent. BCE), but the Roman rhetorician Quintilian (35–95) claimed famously, in a gesture of Roman self-assertion, that "at least satire is all ours."[2] And indeed, Latin verse satire as represented by Horace, Persius, and Juvenal stands out as a quite clearly defined uniquely Roman genre, although its relationship to Greek precedents (and to satirical registers of other Latin genres such as comedy or the epigram) is extremely complex.

In Ancient Japan nobody claimed satire as a uniquely Japanese phenomenon and there is no genre equivalent to Roman verse satire. Neither was it a genre in China. Certainly, "political satire" as an instrument to criticize (*feng* 諷) wanton rulers was one of the crucial functions of poetry according to the "Great Preface" to the *Classic of Poetry*. But little before the Early Modern Period, which saw the rise of a whole subgenre of satirical novels such as Wu Jingzi's hilarious *The Scholars* (*Rulin waishi* 儒林外史), makes us laugh like some lines from Persius or Juvenal. The relative poverty of Chinese satirical genres becomes clear in contrast to Japan. Since the medieval period, "comical plays" (*kyōgen* 狂言) served as intermezzi in Noh theater and the *haikai* 俳諧 culture of the Early Modern Period celebrated parodic transgression against the established canon of classical court culture in painting, poetry, and lifestyle. Haikai poetry (later called haiku) was a parodic genre, parasitic upon classical poetry that had thrived under imperial support since the Heian Period (794–1185) and had established a fixed decorum of diction, topics, and occasions. Haikai poetry relished the transgression of this fixed poetic cosmos by throwing in seemingly highbrow Sino-Japanese words, bantering vernacularisms, and other previously inappropriate language.

The Heian Period, during which the aesthetic of court poetry developed, later becoming the very target of Edo Period (1600–1868) parodic genres like haikai, had produced subtler forms of parodic satire.

Again, satire was certainly not absent from Chinese literature that influenced Heian Period literary production. From satirical texts that turned up in the vast provincial library of Dunhuang, the Chinese outpost of the Silk Road in north-western China, we understand that satirical pieces had low social prestige and were therefore probably not transmitted in great numbers. Thus, we cannot be sure whether a vast amount of Chinese satires that influenced Heian literary production are just lost or whether there were not so many in the first place. What we can say is that, in contrast to China, in Heian Japan satires and parodies were included in canonical anthologies and were thus elevated to a respectable literary register that coexisted strangely with the choice of exemplary literary works surrounding them. The contrast is obvious in the case of the Chinese *Literary Selections* (*Wenxuan* 文選, 5th century). It became a model of diction, style, and generic decorum in China, and then in Japan. When the Japanese courtier

---

[2] *Satura quidem tota nostra est* (*Institutio oratoria* 10.1.93). On the disputes over the uniqueness of Roman satire see Freudenburg 2005, 1–30.

Fujiwara no Akihira (989–1066) modeled his Sino-Japanese anthology *Literary Essence of Our Court* (*Honchō monzui* 本朝文粋) on the *Literary Selections* with the intention of creating an authoritative panoramic view of Japanese literary production, he slipped in a small number of obviously tongue-in-cheek pieces. Some were erotic satires such as a rhapsody on the pleasures of conjugal sex, or an official biography authored by a fellow named "Organ Extraordinary" (*Ratai* 羅泰), the "Former Governor of 'Goose Head' [Glans Penis]" that lavishes praise on the male organ under the suggestive title "Biography of the Iron Hammer."[3] He also included pieces—such an examination essay on "Monkey Music" (*sarugaku* 猿楽, *sangaku* 散楽)—that would not be funny for modern readers but must have been delightful to their Heian audience in the ways they play with genre confusion and transgress established cultural boundaries. "Monkey Music," a popular folk revelry that included dance and music, was certainly a most unlikely topic for the official examinations at the capital's Academy, which tested its candidates' knowledge of the Chinese classics, such as the canonical *Literary Selections* and the *Three Histories* (*Sanshi* 三史) Even if the examination system in Japan never became the recruitment strategy for government service as it did in China, it obviously gained those who mastered it social distinction as a well-educated elite. So the choice of a solemn scholarly genre for a low-class carnivalesque topic is the trick of the piece, which demands considerable knowledge of the cultural context for its modern reader to reach a hard-earned moment of erudite laughter.[4]

Yet why did Heian elites laugh at themselves and canonize this laughter in their model anthologies? How could the comic and the canonical collaborate so smoothly in Japan? What was funny about this less bawdy but rather cerebral and belabored attempt to elicit laughter from the very highbrow audience the pieces are parodying? This paradox is captured by Linda Hutcheon in a fitting mythological chiffre: "I recall a friend once saying that the god of parody, if there were one, would have to be Janus, with his two heads facing in two directions at once. Increasingly though, I find myself invoking Hermes, the mediating messenger god, with his winged sandals and paradoxically plural functions, for Hermes is the god of both thieves and merchants, cheating and commerce. What better deity to preside over the thinking about parody's transgressing and authorizing impulses, its challenges to as well as its reinscriptions of authority?"[5]

As we will see, nobody less than Hermes/Mercury will guide us to explore how and to what effect the canonical and pedagogical can collaborate with the comic and subversive within one and the same text. In this chapter I will approach these

---

[3] On this biography and its relation to Japanese and Chinese erotic literature see Borgen 2004.

[4] See also the parodic examination essay on waka poetry in *Zoku Honchō monzui*, 46–47. Since the early tenth century waka poetry enjoyed imperial support. It was thus an elite genre, unlike the "Monkey Music," but texts in classical Japanese were not included in the Academy's official examinations, for which candidates wrote Sino-Japanese essays on Chinese canonical literature. The piece's comic effect results from its inappropriate language choice (Sino-Japanese, not Japanese vernacular, the language of waka poetry) for a discourse on a text in a wrong language (in Japanese, not Chinese-style) cast into a mismatched genre (a purely Sino-Japanese genre that did not have a Japanese equivalent)—quite an academic exercise that is unlikely to arouse visceral responses of exhilaration in a modern reader.

[5] Hutcheon, 2000, xvii.

questions through two texts, which wed the pedagogical with the satirical in puzzling ways and which, for that very reason, have both been marginalized in their own ways.

2. An Odd Couple: *The Sino-Japanese Poems on the Tale of Shining Genji* and Martianus Capella's *The Marriage of Philology and Mercury*

The *Sino-Japanese Poems Composed on the Tale of Shining Genji* (*Fu Hikaru Genji monogatari shi* 賦光源氏物語詩, hereafter *Genji Poems*) are a medieval retelling in poetic form of the *Tale of Genji*. Written by the court lady Murasaki Shikibu (ca. 978–1014) in Japanese vernacular, the *Tale of Genji* recounts the numerous love affairs (and their implications in following generations) of the main protagonist Genji, son of an emperor and a low-ranking concubine. The *Genji Poems* were written in 1291 during the Kamakura Period (1185–1333), when de facto power was in the hands of the shoguns at Kamakura, outside of modern-day Tokyo, and symbolic ceremonial power resided with the emperor in Kyoto.

During the Heian Period (794–1185) the imperial court—though increasingly dominated by powerful Fujiwara regents at the expense of imperial power—was the center of cultural life with its exuberant literary and musical performances and ritual celebrations. The splendor of the Heian court had given place to an austere warrior regime, and post-Heian Period also meant a quantum leap in the development of Sino-Japanese poetry. While Heian Sino-Japanese poetry had developed in response to Chinese court-centered poetry of the third through eighth centuries and was mostly composed by courtiers educated at the Academy in the Heian capital, Sino-Japanese poetic production during the ensuing medieval period shifted to temples outside the capital and their monks. Catching up on new poetic styles in China, religious meditation, personal musings, and a new aesthetics of nature replaced the Heian Period's ornate decorum of ceremonial propriety, courtly landscape, and self-assertion.

The shift from ornate court culture of Confucian courtiers to warrior government surrounded by poet-monks is the broader canvas against which to appreciate the *Poems* on the *Tale of Genji*. The text picks up on the ornate registers of Heian court poetry and applies the Heian genre of Sino-Japanese poems composed on canonical Chinese texts to a noncanonical Japanese text, claiming in passing that the *Genji* is nothing less than a piece of official historiography. The effect of this maneuver is quite odd. Does the author seriously mean to place the *Tale of Genji* on the same authoritative footing as the Chinese Classics? That must have been quite a leap of faith in a period when the *Tale of Genji* had gradually been gaining authority as a manual for the composition of vernacular waka poetry, but existed realms below the canonical status of the Chinese Classics. Or is the author mostly enjoying his own provocative play with inverting the conventional genre hierarchy? Authorial intention of an anonymous author is even harder to fathom than of a known one, and it is itself symptomatic that the piece is anonymous—a rather unusual fact in Sino-Japanese poetry where texts usually *need* to have authors (and attract believable attributions if they don't).

Apparently nobody wanted to take responsibility for such an eccentric text. Equally wisely, scholars have avoided taking responsibility for its interpretation. This is highly surprising, given that the piece offers itself as a fabulous niche in *Genji* scholarship, which certainly equals the amount and complexity of Shakespeare studies. That there is virtually no scholarship on this text—although I argue that it is a suggestive contribution to early *Genji* criticism—and that it does not even appear in major modern dictionaries to the *Genji* proves that something is seriously wrong with it. What is the problem with the *Genji Poems*? How do they upset the genre hierarchy to the degree of discrediting themselves? Is this text another of the cerebral and erudite satires or a genuine case for the *Genji*'s canonicity, or both? As you will see I argue it is ingenuously both, even if it might lose some of its readers along the way.

The *Marriage of Philology and Mercury (De Nuptiis Philologiae et Mercurii)* is a similarly odd text, although, in stark contrast to the stunning obscurity of the *Genji Poems*, it became a bestseller for medieval curricula of the Seven Liberal Arts and also had considerable impact on the medieval *chantefable* tradition and on the development of allegorical fiction. It was written sometime between Alaric's sack of Rome in 410 and the Vandal occupation of Carthage in 439 by the African author Martianus Capella from Carthage, whom scholars have made everything from eloquent peasant to dignified proconsul.[6] The book is a systematic treatment of the Trivium, the arts of Grammar, Dialectic, and Rhetoric and the Quadrivium, the sciences of Geometry, Arithmetic, Astronomy, and Music. The treatment of the disciplines is framed by an allegorical tale of Mercury's betrothal—confirmed by a council of the gods—to the brilliantly erudite maiden Philology, who receives as part of her dowry seven handmaidens, the Seven Liberal Arts.

Although the tremendous influence of Martianus's encyclopedic schoolbook is beyond question, its framing as an allegorical tale of marital union has irritated scholars. William Stahl, who has produced a meticulous translation and thorough study of the text, states:

> One cannot read Martianus' book cursorily—one must tackle it—and the reader is immediately at a loss to explain how a book so dull and difficult could have been one of the most popular books of Western Europe for nearly a thousand years. We moderns may be repelled by the style and content of the *De nuptiis*, but vernacular readers and medieval students seeking an introduction to the learned arts and finding in Martianus' work a fairly compact treatise dressed in fantasy and allegory were both charmed and edified by it. Martianus understood the tastes of his readers much better than the modern critics who have been puzzled by this apparent enigma. (Stahl, 21)

H. J. Rose in his *Handbook of Latin Literature* of 1936 is even more to the point: "It is the dullest and poorest stuff imaginable." (458).[7] Only the recent scholarly

---

[6] For a condensed overview of the work's reception history see Stahl 1971, 55–71. For disputes over dating of the text and biographical details of Martianus see ibid., 9–20.

[7] I also like the damning statement that it is a "sad classic in the history of didactic literature." (Richard Johnson in Stahl 1971, 84). Banality, puerility, bad taste—Johnson does not spare Martianus's oeuvre any *epitheton deformans*.

appreciation for the period of Late Antiquity, which no longer embodies either the last sad stage of classical decadence or the embryonic and sketchy seed of the "dark" Middle Ages, has yielded more sophisticated judgments of Martianus's accomplishment. Martianus's *Marriage* has been recognized as a text of formidable broad sweep, that works through Neo-Platonist metaphysics, plots out numerological schemes, delights in correlative systems that harmonize the pantheon of Greco-Roman, Egyptian, and many other Mediterranean religious traditions, and clothes this bursting universe of Late Classical encyclopedic knowledge into an allegory of harmony and union of cultures, religions, disciplines, and genres.[8] It is the unique mixture of genres crossing path in the *Marriage* that makes it hardest to disentangle the agenda of the work: humble schoolbook, erudite encyclopedia, allegorical fable and Menippean satire—where is the reader's intended place in that labyrinth of contradictory gestures? It is the intersection of the pedagogical with the satirical that will interest us here.

A complex map of differences and similarities between the *Genji Poems* and Martianus's *Marriage* emerges. Facing East, toward Egypt and Chaldea, we have a long Latin text from Late Antiquity by an author from the cultural fringe concocting a new genre of allegorical pedagogics that was to become highly influential during the Middle Ages and beyond. Facing West, toward China, we have a short Sino-Japanese piece from medieval Japan, which employs the authoritative genre of Chinese-style prefaces and poetry on a canonical Chinese work in order to legitimize a vernacular tale by a Heian court lady, and which received close to no attention, although it did at least survive.

But the odd couple shares a curious intersection of the pedantically pedagogical with the subversively satirical. It also shares the status of being a misplaced text in modern scholarship. The *Marriage* has been adopted away from its late classical context by the concerns of medieval scholars and the *Genji Poems* are yet awaiting adoption by Genji scholars in search for new soil far from overworked terrain.

3. Translating In and Out of Genji's World

The *Tale of Genji* provides a highly peculiar view of the Heian aristocratic world. Unlike Heian courtier diaries written in Sino-Japanese by members of the male elite, which record court protocol in annalistic and so prosaic fashion that they could be used as ritual handbooks, and also unlike diaries in vernacular Japanese by female authors, which cultivated the confessional, plaintive, private, and anecdotal, Murasaki Shikibu's *Genji* creates a narrative space in between both worlds. The Heian universe was divided into "public" (*hare* 晴) (originally meaning "bright") and "private" (*ke* 褻) (originally meaning "subdued") phenomena that

---

[8] Among the recent appreciations is Shanza 1986, which reads the work as a "crypto-pagan mystagogic compendium," whose self-parody serves as a cover-up for pagan knowledge under Christian Vandal rule. Joel Relihan 1993, 137–51 carefully lays out the satirical elements of Martianus's allegorical frame narrative. That Grebe 1999, a nine-hundred-page long study of Martianus's work, devotes a mere ten pages to the elements of Menippean satire in the text, is symptomatic for much of the scholarship on Martianus, which either focuses on the satirical framing or on the treatment of the liberal arts.

mapped onto linguistic, aesthetic, and social aspects of life. While the "official" world was broadly associated with the Sino-Japanese language, Chinese-style artistry, official events and performance at court, the "private" world was reserved for the female and intimate sphere, indigenous artwork and cultivation of Japanese vernacular poetry. These lines were asymmetrical and blurred, as in the case of waka poetry that could be public or private, and associated with male or female performance at court. Yet it is important to keep in mind that the discourse around the "public" and "private" was highly pliable and did not necessarily map onto social reality. Thus, Murasaki's work is not only fictional because it contains fictional events, but because it creates a fictional space governed by the two discursive poles of "public" and "private."

Transgressing her own social boundaries in a highly gender-sequestered world, Murasaki creates (and sometimes ostentatiously denies herself) access to female and male emotions, private and official events, and, to a lesser degree, Sino-Japanese and Japanese idioms. The *Genji* both enacts and contradicts the division between these two worlds in fascinating ways. In his amorous adventures, Murasaki shows us the "private" half of her male hero's "official" male court existence, and throughout the long narrative in fifty-four chapters annual court observances and ritual events relating to births, deaths, illnesses, and anniversaries provide ample opportunity to weave in and out of the "public" and "private" spheres and produce ever new constellations of this dynamic.

Because "Chinese-style" and "Japanese" aspects of Heian life did not exist in rigid isolation, exploiting their creative tension and and creating ever new controlled interplay was one of the favorite pastimes of Heian court society. Also, they intersected in different proportions on the linguistic, social, and gender level and were never mapped symmetrically. Vernacular waka poetry, for example, developed linguistically in active contrast to Sino-Japanese poetry. Sino-Japanese diction and, occasionally, certain topics (e.g., wine and, to some degree, love), were kept strictly apart from a purified space of Japanese poetry and poetics. This set the stage for the haikai/haiku revolution in the early modern period, which precisely made the transgression of these linguistic and thematic boundaries into its hallmark. Yet, socially, waka poetry had since the late ninth century gained a public platform at court in the form of "poetry competition" events and imperial anthology compilations. Quite apart from asymmetrical mappings of the "public" and the "private" onto language choice, gender distribution, style, and social occasion, there were genres that purposefully or playfully erased the line between these two poles. On the linguistic level, some genres included both Sino-Japanese and Japanese parts and were based on creative juxtaposition of the two idioms in the spirit of an authorized transgression.

One rather rare form of authorized transgression was poetic translation. The late ninth-century *Chisato Collection* (*Chisatoshū* 千里集) by Ōe no Chisato juxtaposes individual couplets from famous Chinese poems with a paraphrase into an integral waka poem. This process is a poetic translation, because snippets from longer Chinese poems are transformed into integral Japanese poems. The strong length difference between Japanese and Chinese poetic forms made what might seem like a literal translation into a true poetic experiment. A more common sanctioned intersection of the dividing line between Chinese-style and Japanese modes was aesthetic juxtaposition of Chinese and Sino-Japanese poems with vernacular waka poems based on similarity in mood or topic. We see this most famously in the eleventh-century *Wakan rōeishū* 和漢朗詠集 (*Collection of Japanese and Sino-Japanese Poems For Recitation*), discussed in Chapter 5, and its twelfth-century sequel. A third form of authorized transgression were composite genres, such as prefaces written in Sino-Japanese followed by a collection of vernacular poems.[9] The fourth and most derivative mode of sanctioned transgression can be called "poetic elaboration." Phrases from famous Chinese or Sino-Japanese texts would serve as "topics" for the composition of *vernacular* poems. This hybrid genre originated from the practice of composing *Sino-Japanese* poems on Chinese topics at official poetic banquets, a practice that connected vital parts of Heian court reality, namely seasonal ritual observances, diplomacy, and the Academy, the prime institution of Chinese education in the capital. Poetic banquets at certain seasonal junctures, in honor of Korean envoys, or at the Academy in reverence for the Confucian *Analects* and other Chinese canonical texts, provided the courtiers with a stage on which to gain imperial favor, parade one's poetic talent, and display one's Chinese erudition.

Transgressions between the "public" and "private" worlds were ripe with satirical potential, because mismatches among language choice, topic, and occasion produced a hilarious, often defamiliarizing double vision. Similar to exotic snapshots in imaginary travelogues chronicling excursions to strange tribes or lunar realms, Japanese scholars of the Chinese Classics dressed in Japanese language could look like creatures from another planet. In the *Tale of Genji* Confucian scholars seem to be envoys of a powerful but outlandish foreign regime: strangely dressed, socially awkward, and too erudite to speak normal Japanese. The main character, which Murasaki Shikibu employs as a window unto the world of Confucian scholarship, is Genji's son Yūgiri.[10] Yūgiri is the son by Genji's first wife Aoi, one of the few women in the tale without any particular charms and with no poetry attributed, a clear statement of distance in a narrative where the most crucial communication happens through poetic exchanges. Yūgiri is further distanced from his father because of his multiple associations with the powerful northern branch of the Fujiwara family, who since the mid-Heian Period became de facto rulers in their service as regents to the emperor.

Yūgiri's mother is a Fujiwara, Yūgiri is particularly treasured by his Fujiwara grandmother, and he marries the daughter of his Fujiwara uncle Tō no Chūjo, a close teenage friend of Genji, from whom Genji gets increasingly estranged in adulthood. Thus, Yūgiri is an anti-Genji of sorts on the political level, standing closer to the Fujiwara than to Genji and the imperial lineage.[11] Also, in contrast to his father's tantalizing alternation between amorous adventurism and responsible

---

[9] For example waka poems on the *Chronicles of Japan* (*Nihon shoki* 日本書紀) and on the Chinese primer *Mengqiu* 蒙求.

[10] For a rich view on the various aspects of Yūgiri in the *Genji* see Shirane 1987, 32–40, 100–103, 116–19.

[11] On this see Okada 1991, 363.

care for the women he courts, Yūgiri only possesses his father's responsible side. When jealousies break out between his first and second wives, Yūgiri proves incapable of easing the tensions by using the fickle and inventive charms, which his father always brings into play so effectively.

The last and for our purposes most relevant contrast between father and son is Yūgiri's academic education, for which Genji himself is actually responsible. Whereas Genji is early on decorated with high court rank due to the special favor of his father, the Kiritsubo Emperor, Genji forces Yūgiri to take the more onerous path of passing the examinations at the Academy instead of awarding him a higher rank right away based on birth. The effect is twofold: Yūgiri indeed turns out to be a brilliant student of extraordinary talent, but despite his success he also feels humiliated before his peers who inhabit a world where academic studies were inconsequential for the access to powerful positions in the imperial bureaucracy. The Academy in the capital, where the four tracks of "Classics" (myōgyōdō 明経道), "History and Literature" (kidendō 紀伝道), "Law" (myōbōdō 明法道), and "Calculus" (sandō 算道) were taught, was established in the seventh century and lived through its heydays in the ninth century.[12] By Murasaki's time the Academy was no longer a springboard to high office, but served mostly the male members of the Sugawara, and Ōe families to gain academic degrees, which secured the candidates middle-rank office or a scholarly career at the Academy. Although the examination system in Japan, especially after the ninth century, never provided regulated access to political power like in China, the Japanese "Confucian scholars" (jusha 儒者) and Academy students possessed much symbolic power as experts of highly revered Chinese learning. Many of them would be called upon to participate in poetic banquets at court.[13]

While appearing to be paragons of the most authoritative kind of learning within the Sino-Japanese "public" Heian world, once brought into Murasaki's vernacular "private" space they become pitiable creatures, which lack confidence, talent, intuitive judgment, and taste. When Genji and his friend Tō no Chūjo compose Sino-Japanese poetry together with literati from the Academy in honor of the cherry tree in front of the Imperial Palace (which we discussed in Chapter 5), the doctors make their first ludicrous appearance in the tale:

> It was a lovely day, with a bright sky and birdsong to gladden the heart, when those who prided themselves on their skill—Princes, senior nobles, and all—drew their rhymes and began composing [Sino-Japanese][14] verses. As usual, Genji's

---

[12] On the Academy in the tenth century see Steininger 2010.

[13] In that function they were called "literati" (bunjin 文人). In contrast to China, where the same term referred more generally to individuals with extraordinary literary and artistic talent, the Japanese term in the Heian Period referred to individuals whom the emperor invited to compose Sino-Japanese poetry at official banquets. On the specific meaning of the term "literati" during the Heian Period see Kudo 1993, 75–110.

[14] Throughout I have replaced Tyler's translation of "Chinese" with "Sino-Japanese" whenever he refers to poems composed by Japanese authors. Due to the existence of a Japanese vernacular, Sino-Japanese was a hybrid idiom that originated from Literary Chinese, but developed a dynamics of its own. It should therefore not be called "Chinese," because that term fails to describe the Japanese identity of the authors and the often hybrid nature of the language they use.

very voice announcing, "I have received the character 'spring,'"[15] resembled no other. The Secretary Captain came next. He was nervous about how he might look, after Genji, but he maintained a pleasing composure, and his voice rang out with impressive dignity. Most of the rest appeared tense and self-conscious. Naturally, those belonging to the lesser ranks were even more in awe of the genius (*zae* 才) of His Majesty and the Heir Apparent, which stood out even then, when so many others excelled at that sort of thing. They advanced in dread across the immaculate expanse of the broad court, only to make a painful labor of their simple task. His Majesty was touched by seasoned performances from the shabby old Doctors, and he derived great pleasure from them, too.[16]

Genji's incomparable voice dominates the scene and the doctors—usually of middle rank, who are presumably experts of Sino-Japanese composition—are terrified by the presence of the court nobles of the third and higher ranks. Their uninspired efforts are tragicomic, but the pleasure the Emperor, Genji's father, derives from their sad performances is equally ambivalent. The reader cannot be quite sure whether the joke is at the expense of the doctors or also of the Emperor, who is magnanimous enough to enjoy their labors.

One gets an even more ambivalent glance at the "shabby old doctors" when Yūgiri receives his academic sobriquet, a Chinese-style name, which was conferred upon entering the Academy:

With desperately affected composure they shamelessly wore odd, ill-fitting clothes that they had had to borrow elsewhere, and everything about them presented a novel spectacle, including their manner of taking their seats with grave voices and pompous looks. The younger nobles could not stifle their grins. Genji had chosen only quiet, collected men to pour their wine, men unlikely ever to give in to mirth, but even so the Commander of the Right, the Lord of Civil Affairs, and the others who so earnestly kept their cups filled got a fine tongue-lashing. "Fie upon your manners, sirs! You presume to serve His Majesty, yet you fail to know a man of my renown? You are fools, sirs!" The company broke into laughter. "Silence! I will have silence! Your conduct is disgraceful! Sirs, I must require you to leave!"[17] Such magisterial censure was great fun. Those who had never heard anything like it before thought it a rare treat, and the senior nobles who had come through the Academy beamed with

---

[15] The participants of the banquet advanced in order of rank and drew a "rhyme character" in a lottery. They then used the rhyme character as basis for the rhyme structure of their poems and often also—as can be imagined with the rhyme character "spring" during a banquet at the beginning of the year—as topic.

[16] Tyler 2001, 155. *Genji monogatari*, "Hana no en," 353–54. 日いとよく晴れて、空のけしき、鳥の声も心地よげなるに、親王たち、上達部よりはじめて、その道のはみな探韻賜りて文作りたまふ。宰相中将、「春といふ文字賜れり」とのたまふ声さへ、例の、人にことなり。次に頭中将、人の目移しもただならずおぼゆべかめれど、いとめやすくもてしづめて、声づかひなどものものしくすぐれたり。さての人々は、みな臆しがちにはなじろめる多かり。地下の人は、まして、帝、春宮の御才かしこくすぐれておはします、かかる方にやむごとなき人多くものしたまふころなるに、恥づかしく、はるばるとくもりなき庭に立ち出づるほどはしたなくて、やすきことなれど苦しげなり。年老いたる博士どもの、なりあやしくやつれて、例馴れたるもあはれに、さまざま御覧ずるなむ、をかしかりける。

[17] The passage is replete with academic diction strikingly different from the language of the other courtiers.

satisfaction. Everyone felt it was a wonderful thing that His Excellency [Genji] should have chosen this course for his son. Was there a buzz of talk? They put a stop to it. A cheeky remark? They issued their rebuke. But as the night wore on and their stridently disapproving expressions stood forth a little in the lamplight, they took on instead a pathetically comical sadness, and this among other things made the occasion a strange and curious one indeed.[18]

The reader cannot help chuckling at the ridiculous manners of these lamentable creatures, but is also drawn into the mixed feelings of the attending nobles. Those who are unfamiliar with the isolated world of the Academy are amused by the curious scene. But those who attended the Academy are momentarily proud of their academic education and sympathize with the hardships of study awaiting Yūgiri, but not without clandestine gloating. Yet as the evening drags on, even they have had their dose of professorial fun and get depressed.

The deep rift between courtiers and academicians and the disjunction between political power and cultural capital is epitomized in the figure of Yūgiri's tutor on the day Genji tests his son in preparation for the first exam:

> The tutor was glad and proud at the sight. His face in his drunken daze—for the Commander kept his cup filled—was awfully thin. He was too great an eccentric to have found employment commensurate with his learning, and he lived in poverty and neglect, but Genji had singled him out that way because he saw something in him. The man seemed destined for even greater things in the future, considering that he now enjoyed Genji's favor far beyond his station and that he therefore owed to his young charge this sudden renewal of his life.[19]

In a society that at least expected that power would coincide with taste, manners, and talent, the academicians are a painful violation of that rule, because their outstanding erudition does not match their low station, which alienates them from the center of court life. Even more distressing, their erudition does not yield the fruits of superior taste and aesthetic refinement. Although their poverty might excuse them from wearing elaborate attire, their shameless appearance in ill-fitted rental clothes

---

[18] Tyler 2001, 381–82. *Genji monogatari*, "Otome," 24–25. 家より外にもとめたる装束どもの、うちあはずかたくなしき姿などをも恥なく、面もち、声づかひ、むべむべしくもてなしつつ、座につき並びたる作法よりはじめ、見も知らぬさまどもなり。若き君達は、えたへずほほ笑まれぬ。さるはもの笑ひなどすまじく、過ぐしつつ、しづまれるかぎりをと選り出だして、瓶子なども取らせたまへるに、筋異なりけるまじらひにて、右大将、民部卿などの、おほなおほな土器とりたまへるを、あさましく咎め出でつつおろす。「おほし、垣下あるじ、はなはだ非常にこ。はなはだをこなり」など言ふに、人々みなほころびて笑ひぬれば、また、「鳴り高し。鳴りやむむ。はなはだ非常なり。座を退きて立ちたうびなん」など、おどし言ふもいとをかし。見ならひたまはぬ人々は、めづらしく興ありと思ひ、この道より出で立ちたまへる上達部などは、したり顔にうちほほ笑みなどしつつ、かかる方ざまを思し好みて、心ざしたまふがめでたきことと、いとど限りなく思ひきこえたまへり。 いささかもの言ふをも制す、なめげなりとても咎む、かしがましうののしりをる顔どもも、夜に入りては、なかなか、いますこし揭焉なる灯影に、猿楽がましくわびしげに人わろげなるなど、さまざまに、げにいとなべてならず、さま異なるわざなりけり。

[19] Tyler 2001, 383–84. *Genji monogatari*, "Otome," 29. おし拭ひたまふを見る御師の心地、うれしく面目ありと思へり。大将盃さしたまへば、いたう酔ひ痴れてをる顔つき、いと痩せ痩せなり。世のひがものにて、才のほどよりは用ゐられず、すげなくて身貧しくなむありけるを、御覧じうるところありて、かくとりわき召し寄せたるなりけり。身にあまるまで御かへりみを賜りて、この君の御徳にたちまちに身をかへたると思へば、まして行く先は並ぶ人なきおぼえにぞあらんかし。

betrays their aesthetic numbness. The paragons of Sino-Japanese high culture offend Japanese taste.

Did Genji, who never fails to be the irresistible embodiment of Japanese tastefulness, really want his son to be in that filthy company? Murasaki has it both ways: She adds one more sparkling feather to Genji's image by making it into his genuine intention. Genji seems to really believe in the value of a solid Chinese education that he laments not having received himself: "After all, [Chinese] learning is what provides a firm foundation for the exercise of Japanese wit." (Tyler, 381) This precisely entitles her, in an ultimately more forceful countermaneuver, to show the uselessness of academic education. After the sobriquet ceremony, the party company composes Sino-Japanese poems and Genji's, not the doctors', poem is singled out for special praise by the audience.

After this quick exchange of contradictory blows, Murasaki cleverly retreats from the narrative scene into her confined female social role: While the reader is burning to read Genji's lavishly praised poem, Murasaki smilingly disappoints us by stating "[A] woman has no business repeating what she cannot know, and since I do not wish to give offense, I have omitted it." (Tyler, 383). Our author excuses herself elegantly for her temporary intrusion into—no, conquest of—the "public" male space of Academy ceremonies, which certainly excluded female presence.

Murasaki's risky play with both brightening the "subdued" and subduing the "bright" world gets more complex when the flavor of the academic is embodied in a woman. In the famous "rainy night discussion," during which Genji and his friends exchange stories about amorous experiences in the past and erotic prospects for the future, a Chief Equerry, a senior officer in charge of the Imperial Stables, offers to his unbelieving companions his adventures with a scholarly lady, who in the end scared him away with all her erudition. This daughter of his private tutor during his time as a student at the Academy turns out to be the Chief Equerry's most efficient instructor in preparation for his exams:

> She was very good to me. Even while we lay awake at night, she would pursue my edification or instruct me in matters beneficial to a man in government service, and no note from her was ever marred by a single one of those *kana* letters, being couched in language of exemplary formality. What with all this I could not have left her, because it was she who taught me how to piece together broken-backed [Sino-Japanese] poems and such, and for that I remain eternally grateful. As to making her my dear wife, however, a dunce like me could only have been embarrassed to have her witness his bumbling efforts.[20]

The object of his romantic affection turns out to be a real turnoff, who does nothing a reputable Heian woman would do. She doesn't write in Japanese *kana* letters, but uses Chinese characters, and her formal "public" tone puts the literary

---

[20] Tyler 2001, 33. *Genji monogatari*, "Hahakigi," 86. いとあはれに思ひ後見、寝覚めの語らひに
も、身の才つき、朝廷に仕うまつるべき道々しきことを教へて、いときよげに消息文にも仮名
といふもの書きまぜず、むべむべしく言ひまはしはべるに、おのづからえまかり絶えで、その
者を師としてなむわづかなる腰折文作ることなど習ひはべりしかば、今にその恩は忘れはべら
ねど、なつかしき妻子とうち頼まむに、無才の人、なまわろならむふるまひなど見えむに、恥
づかしくなむ見えはべりし。

efforts of the struggling Chief Equerry to shame, who should be the one taking the exams. He continues his courtship without the slightest sense of romantic adventure, but it all comes to a sudden end through a combination of the scholarly lady's erudition and foul smell:

> Well, I had not been to see her for a long time when for some reason I went again. She was not in her usual room; instead she spoke to me through an absurd screen. Is she jealous, then? I wondered, at once amused by this nonsense and perfectly conscious that this might be just the chance I was looking for. But no, my paragon of learning was not one to indulge in frivolous complaints. She knew the world and its ways too well to be upset with me. Instead she briskly announced, 'Having lately been prostrate with a most vexing indisposition, I have for medicinal purposes been ingesting *Allium sativum* (Garlic), and my breath, I fear, is too noxious to allow me to entertain you in my normal fashion. However, while I cannot address you face-to-face, I hope that you will communicate to me any services you may wish me to perform on your behalf.' It was an imposing oration. What could I possibly answer? I just said, 'Very well,' got up, and started out. I suppose she had been hoping for something better, because she called after me, 'Do return when the odor has abated!' I hated to pretend I had not heard her, but this was no time to waver, and besides, the smell really was rather overpowering...[21]

The screen, behind which our so unromantic female scholar speaks, is a welcome prop that piques the romantic imagination of the suitor in search of amorous adventure. She might be mad at him for his long absence, he thinks, and the very thought of her jealousy—finally a normal feeling for a normal woman—whets his erotic appetite. But his ray of hope for a normal Heian romance is destroyed by her formal lecture on her condition and on her ingestion of garlic.

The agonizing Chief Equerry makes it clear to his spellbound male companions that he hates academic, Sinicized women and that, if already they are educated, they should hide their abilities to avoid intimidating their male lovers:

> There is nothing at all attractive about having absorbed weighty stuff like the Three Histories and the Five Classics, and besides, why should anyone, just because she is a woman, be completely ignorant of what matters in this world, public or private? A woman with any mind at all is bound to retain many things, even if she does not actually study. So she writes cursive Chinese characters after all and crams her letters more than half full of them, even ones to other women, where they are hopelessly out of place, and you think, Oh no! If only she could be more feminine! She may not have meant it that way, but the letter still ends up

---

[21] Tyler 2001, 34. *Genji monogatari*, "Hahakigi," 87. 「さて、いと久しくまからざりしに、もののたよりに立ち寄りてはべれば、常のうちとけゐたる方にははべらで、心やましき物越しにてなむ逢ひてはべる。ふすぶるにやと、をこがましくも、また、よきふしなりとも思ひたまふるに、このさかし人、はた、軽々しきもの怨じすべきにもあらず、世の道理を思ひ取りて恨みざりけり。声もはやりかにて言ふやう、『月ごろ、風病重きにたへかねて、極熱の草薬を服して、いと臭きによりなむえ対面賜らぬ。目のあたりならずとも、さるべからむ雑事らはうけたまはらむ』といとあはれにむべむべしく言ひはべり。答へに何とかは、ただ、『うけたまはりぬ』とて、立ち出ではべるに、さうざうしくやおぼえけむ、『この香失せなむ時に立ち寄りたまへ』と高やかに言ふを聞きすぐさむもいとほし、しばし休らふべきに、はた、はべらねば、げにそのにほひさへはなやかにた立ち添へるもすべなくて 。

being read to her correspondent in a stiff, formal tone, and it sounds as though that was what she had meant all along. A lot of senior gentlewomen do that sort of thing, you know. The woman out to make poetry becomes so keen on it [i.e., to produce a stiff, formal tone?] that she stuffs her very first line with allusions to great works from the past, until it is a real nuisance to get a poem from her when you have other things on your mind. You cannot very well not reply, and you look bad if circumstances at the moment prevent you from doing so. Take the festivals, for example. Say it is the morning of the Sweet Flag Festival. You are off to the palace in such a rush that everything is a blur, and she presents you with one of her efforts, quivering with incredible wordplays; or it is time for the Chrysanthemum Festival, you are racking your brains to work out a tricky [Sino-Japanese] poem, and here comes a lament from her, full of 'chrysanthemum dew' and, as usual, quite out of place. At other times, too, her way of sending you out of season a poem that afterward you might admit is not actually at all bad, without pausing to think that you may be unable even to give it a glance, can hardly be called very bright. She would do better to refrain from showing off her wit and taste whenever her failure to grasp your circumstances leaves you wondering why she had to do it, or cursing the fix she has put you in. A woman should feign ignorance of what she knows and, when she wants to speak on a subject, leave some things out.[22]

Whom is our female author Murasaki making fun of? Of culturally transgendered, or rather "transculturalized," women who show off their education in courtship as if in a male court setting, or of untalented dull men like the Chief Equerry who are afraid of being outwitted by clever women precisely in those anxious moments before facing an official court celebration? As the erudite woman puts her dull lover "into a fix" the author Murasaki clamps her readers' sympathies between an impenetrable and pathetic Lady Doctor and a self-proclaimed and ridiculous Mister Dunce.

Thus, we see that the *Tale of Genji* is highly ambivalent and pursuing a zigzag strategy in its incursions into the Sino-Japanese male space of academic learning. Although the spokesmen of Confucian education are generally the butt of satire rather than the mouth of reason, Murasaki also acknowledges and reinforces belief in the higher values of that education. In addition, she does not so much assert superiority over the doctors through satire, but experiments with the access to her object of satire. As author she challenges the boundaries between the "public" and "private"

---

[22] Tyler 2001, 34–35. *Genji monogatari*, "Hahakigi," 89–90. 三史五経、道々しき方を明らかに悟り明かさむこそ愛敬なからめ、などかは女といはむからに、世にあることの公私につけて、むげに知らずいたらずしもあらむ。わざと習はまねばねど、すこしもかどあらむ人の耳にも目にもとまること、自然に多かるべし。さるままには真名を走り書きて、さるまじきどちの女文に、なかば過ぎて書きすすめたる、あなうたて、この人のたをやかならましかばと見えたり。心地にはさしも思はざらめど、おのづからこはごはしき声に読みなされなどしつつ、ことさらびたり。上臈の中にも多かることぞかし。歌詠むと思へる人の、やがて歌にまつはれ、をかしき古言をもはじめよりとりこみつつ、すさまじきをりをり詠みかけたるこそ、ものしきことなれ。返しせねば情なし、えせざらむ人ははしたなからむ。さるべき節会など、五月の節に急ぎ参る朝、何のあやめも思ひしづめられぬにえならぬ根を引きかけ、九日の宴にまづ難き詩の心を思ひめぐらし暇なきをりに、菊の露をかこち寄せなどやうの、つきなき営みにあはせ、さならずも、おのづから、げに、後に思へば、をかしくもあはれにもあべかりけることの、そのをりにつきなく目にとまらぬなどを、おしはからず詠み出でたる、なかなか心おくれて見ゆ。よろづのことに、などかはさても、とおぼゆるをりから、時々、思ひ分かぬばかりの心にては、よしばみ情だたざらむなむめやすかるべき。すべて、心に知れらむことをも知らず顔にもてなし、言はまほしからむことをも、一つ二つのふしは過ぐすべくなむあべかりける」

worlds, weaving in and out of them by way of different protagonists such as Yūgiri or the female scholar. As author figure she sweeps on the scene at the last minute and retreats into her female social role before the experiment can backfire and point the satirical edge against her.

Now, the medieval *Sino-Japanese Poems Composed on the Tale of Shining Genji* take Murasaki's seriosatirical inroads into Confucian education a step further. They undertake an inverse transposition of the *Genji* from Japanese to Sino-Japanese, from prose to poetry, and from female author to male interpreter. They were obviously written by somebody with a Confucian education. Although we cannot be sure whether the author was indeed a man because the piece is anonymous, it is unmistakably written in a male voice. To legitimize the female vernacular tale in its new male Sino-Japanese environment, the preface to the *Genji Poems* hails the *Tale of Genji* as a work of official historiography, taking advantage of the path already laid out in the "Fireflies" Chapter of the *Tale of Genji* where vernacular tale literature in general is defended as a better form of Chinese-style historiography. As such, the author makes the *Genji* a text, which—like the three Chinese canonical histories—would be studied in the "History Track" and on which students and doctors would write poems at Academy banquets.

The preface follows the protocol of prefaces written at Academy banquets on the Chinese canonical histories. They usually open on a grand statement of the significance of the canonical text chosen for the occasion and then expound on the origin and main message of the text.[23] In similar fashion the preface to the *Genji Poems* declare the tale in the very opening into a national classic:

> The *Tale of Shining Genji* is a profound text of our nation. If you skim it and know little about it you consider it a playful toy; but if you ponder on it and study it well you will take it as the foundation of devoted learning. It records events since the Divine Age and describes those of the Human Age, just like the illustrious volumes by our courtiers and princes, (the *Chronicles of Japan*); in assembling hundreds of texts into one book, it is like Sima Qian's *Historical Records*. Who would ever call it "a go-between of flowers and birds"? In short, it sums up all of Japanese and Chinese writing.[24]
>
> 夫、光源氏物語者本朝神秘書也。淺見寡聞之者、以之為遊戲之弄、深思好學之者、以之為惇誨之基。載神代之事述人代之事、孰與舍人親王之華篇、惣百家之書編一家之書、其奈司馬子長之實錄。誰謂花鳥之媒、即通和漢之籍。

It is unmistakable what the *Tale of Genji* is supposed to be. First and foremost it is an official history like the venerable *Chronicles of Japan* (*Nihon shoki* 日本書紀, 720). In a second step, which consciously goes against chronology and degree of canonicity, the *Genji* is compared to China's first comprehensive history, the *Historical Records*

---

[23] See in particular the prefaces to poems on the *Later Han History* and on the *Classic of Documents* in *Honchō zoku monzui* Kokushi taikei 29, 130, 132.

[24] Text and translation are based on *Gunsho ruijū* 134, 270–81 and Gotō Akio's commentary on the preface in Gotō 2004. Punctuation adapted by author.

(ca. 90 BCE) by Sima Qian, the first of the canonical Three Histories. And the preface states clearly what the *Genji* is *not* supposed to be. According to the author, the *Genji* is of course not a "go-between of flowers and birds," a derogatory term that the prefaces to the *Kokinshū* (905) had used to describe vernacular poetry abused for trivial love exchanges. Even if the author tries hard to defend the *Genji* against such a prejudice, any reader of the tale knows of course that most of its poetry derives indeed from love exchanges—though not trivial ones.

To claim the *Genji* as official historiography and defend it against prejudices associated with the genre of vernacular poetry was impossible enough. Yet the most grandiose gesture in the opening of the preface is the statement that the *Genji* sums up *all* Japanese and Chinese-style writings. The author thus breaks down the entrenched hierarchy between the "public" and "private" worlds, just to make *Genji*, a text that belongs linguistically into the "private" world, into the ultimate embodiment of textuality beyond that division. Not only is the hierarchy between the "public" and more authoritative and "private" and more intimate inverted, but the *Genji* presumably transcends it completely.

Because there is nothing to add to this leap of faith, the author retreats humbly to his task of proving at least that the *Genji* measures up to Chinese-style historiography. The best strategy to accomplish this was to claim that the *Genji* was not just like official historiography, but was actually recorded by court historians:

> This is the gist of the *Tale of Genji*: As four generations of benevolent sovereigns succeed one another, their magnificent abundant virtue spreads everywhere and their bond with the Three Dukes and Hundred Officials, who admire (their ruler's) transformative moral power, is like fish in water.[25] At one time (Genji) enters the flowery curtains of the female palace quarters and ties the knot in secret (with Fujitsubo[26]), just as the Middle Captain Ariwara (no Narihira) abandoned himself to beautiful ladies. Another time (the Akashi) lady from humble origins becomes his mate[27], just like the girl of (Lieutenant) Katano rising to prosperity. [28] [...] All of this is in keeping with the laws of the sage governance of sage eras and absolutely had to be recorded by the Left and Right Historian.

> 此物語之為體也、仁主四代之繼天祚焉、鴻濡德遍、三公百僚之仰風化矣、鱗水契深。或入深宮之華帳兮結密契、摸在原中將之耽艷色、或出散地之松戶兮為好述、如交野小女顯榮昌。　　［...是皆追聖代聖治之法度、莫不可左史右史之書紀。

---

[25] Like the proverbially close bond between Liu Bei (161–223), the ruler of the Chinese Kingdom of Shu, and his general Zhuge Liang.

[26] Referring to Genji's affair with Fujitsubo, the wife of his father, Emperor Kiritsubo, which resulted in the birth of Genji's illegitimate son, the later Emperor Reizei.

[27] Referring to Genji's marriage with the Lady from Akashi, whom Genji met during his exile away from the capital in the provinces.

[28] Both Ariwara no Narihira and the Lieutenant of Katano are protagonists in earlier romantic tales and considered models for Murasaki Shikibu's Genji figure. Narihira's love affair with the Nijō Consort appears in the *Tales of Ise*. Although the *Katano shojō monogatari* is lost, we understand from allusions to it in the *Genji* that the Katano Lieutenant's beloved rose from humble origins to prominent reputation through marriage, just like the Akashi Lady.

The Confucian classic *Record of Rites* (*Liji* 禮記) assigns the recording of the ruler's acts to the Left, and the recording of the ruler's words to the Right Historian. Synecdochically, both offices stand for the practice of official historiography, which in China from Sima Qian into the twentieth century led to twenty-five voluminous dynastic histories produced by a massive staff of court-employed historians over more than twenty centuries. In contrast, Japanese official historiography flourished briefly between 712 and 901 and produced only six considerably shorter histories. The author claims pretentiously that the *Genji* was produced by a staff of imaginary court historians, who did not exist in Murasaki's time, but were fashioned after their appearance in the Confucian Classics.

The invention of imposing court historians contrasts hilariously with the events they supposedly had to record: Genji's incestuous liaison with his stepmother, his affair with the Lady of Akashi during the boredom of exile in the provinces and other amorous adventures resembling those of his dubious role models, Ariwara no Narihira or the Katano Lieutenant.

After making the *Genji* into the all-encompassing canonical history beyond the division between the "public" and "private" worlds, the author is ready to make the next breath-taking claim, namely that the *Genji* is the best of governance manuals and teaches the truths of the "Three Teachings" of Confucianism, Buddhism, and Shinto.[29] We see here one of the earliest statements of the second major strategy developed by medieval *Genji* critics to defend the value of tale literature, a strategy that went beyond those Murasaki Shikibu had already built into the *Genji* for her own justification.

> What's more, when discussing principles of government, (the *Tale of Genji*) reveres the Confucian way of "Three Relations" and "Five Constants."[30] With the procession to Ōhara at Mount Oshio (in Chapter 29) it describes hunting outings.[31] In discussing the divinations for the High Priestess of Ise it pays its respects to the Gods.[32] And when showing the deep tenants of manifest and secret teachings, it turns to the Buddha.[33]
>
> 況又、論政理、則紀三綱五常之道、述畋遊、亦幸大原小鹽之山、敬靈神、議齋宮齋院之卜定、歸覺王、示顯教密教之奧旨。

After establishing the *Genji* as official historiography—even as crowning synthesis of Japanese and Chinese-style writings beyond the canonical curriculum—and as

---

[29] The preface later introduces another move that was to become standard in defending the low status of fiction in China and Japan, namely the claim that fictional stories are an "expedient means," which convey deeper, otherwise inexpressible truths, just like parables in Buddhist sutras.

[30] "Three Relations": between ruler and subject, father and son, husband and wife. For the "Five Constants" there are different lists, but one includes the Confucian virtues of benevolence, righteousness, ritual, wisdom, and trustworthiness.

[31] In chapter 29 Emperor Reizei makes an excursion to the Ōhara and Oshio Slopes. This excursion is evoked as example of a Confucian ceremony.

[32] This refers to the establishment of the daughter of the Rokujō Haven as Ise Priestess described in Chapter 9.

[33] This reference to Buddhism concludes the three examples for how the *Tale of Genji* addresses the "Three Teachings" of Confucianism, Shintō, and Buddhism.

repository of religious truths, the author jumps to what he considers the essential meaning of the *Genji*. Any reader of the *Genji* will be surprised to hear that the *Genji*'s essence lies in the figure of Genji's son Yūgiri. Certainly, Yūgiri is an important figure among the more than four hundred protagonists in the tale, especially as a contrast to his father and as a channel for the female author into the "public" world of the Academy. But how can Yūgiri be so essential? The blatantly disproportionate attention of the preface's author to Yūgiri reveals his intentions. If he wants to "translate" the *Genji* from the "private" to the "public" space and elevate it to canonical status in that Sino-Japanese world, his best bid is Yūgiri, the most scholarly figure of the *Tale of Genji*:

> How great that there is the beloved heir of the Genji clan, (Yūgiri), a disciple of Apricot Terrace[34] in Locust Tree District.[35] Tirelessly he studied at night, the snow making up for a cantilevered lamp. He reviewed unremittingly, while fireflies shed their light on his five-colored bamboo mat....Meeting with enlightened times, he exercised ministerial powers on behalf of the realm. This clearly is the significance of the saying that "he governed the world through *wen*.[36]"

> 抑、有源氏家督之愛子、列杏壇槐市之生徒。夜學無倦、雪代九枝之灯、時習不懈、螢照五華之筵。　[...]逢明時而底天時之變[37]　理。以文治世、其義云明。

Yūgiri imitates the famously diligent Chinese students Che Yin and Sun Kang, who use ingenious methods to compensate for their lack of money for candle oil when studying day and night for the official exams: Che Yin supposedly caught fireflies during the day that he releases after nightfall and Sun Kang sat close to the reflecting snow so that he could continue his studies at night. Yūgiri's highly successful devotion to his academic studies is praised as an act of filial piety, showing that he takes his Confucian duties as legitimate male heir seriously. The preface closes Yūgiri's case accordingly with heavy-handed Confucian praise. (see Figure 7.1)

Given that the author has taken pains to establish *Genji* as canonical historiography, as a repository the deeper truths of the three teachings, and that he has hailed Yūgiri as the guiding protagonist of that vision, the closure of the preface with its strange mixture of playful self-deprecation and its unexpected celebration of the instincts of vernacular poetry comes as a surprise and yet another turn of tone in the preface.

> But unfortunately, my "Lu-ish" dullness is incorrigible,[38] I am worlds apart from Bo Juyĭ's ancient style, and since it's hard for me to get used to the "Hymns of

---

[34] Name of Confucius's school near Qufu in present-day Shandong Province.

[35] Poetic name for the state academy.

[36] Yūgiri is described in the words the *Record of Rites* uses for the virtuous King Wen (twelfth century BCE) of the Zhou Dynasty. As we explored in Chapter 2 and 3 wen has a broad spectrum of meanings, ranging from pattern and ornament to civilization, cultivation, sophistication, and literature.

[37] In the *Gunsho ruijū* edition this character has a "fire" radical (火).

[38] As a compound 魯昏 just means "dullness." Read in parallel to the "Hymns of Zhou" in the next line the character *ro* 魯 can also refer to the State of Lu, Confucius's home state. Hence the satirical pun on *ro* as both "dull" and "from Lu/Confucian."

FIGURE 7.1 *The nonacademic Yūgiri as he appears in the original* Tale of Genji, *but not in the Genji Poems: His jealous wife Kumoi-no-kari suspects him of reading a letter from his lover*
Scene from Picture Scroll of the *Tale of Genji*. Late Heian Period, 12th century © The Gotoh Museum, Tokyo.

Zhou" (from the *Classic of Poetry*) I am ashamed to play around with the evanescent words of Murasaki Shikibu. That's what (Zhuangzi) means when he says that the wisdom of a frog in the well knows nothing of the turtle in the ocean and the happy quail on the fence does not envy the giant *peng* bird in the clouds. Natural principle makes it thus.[39]

但、魯昏之性不悛、空隔白大保之昔樣、周年之頌難慣、慙翫紫式部之露詞。
是則井蛙之智、不知海鼈、籬鷃之楽、不羨雲鵬之謂也。自然理、又亦
如此。

What on earth does the author want us to make of this closure? His self-deprecating "Lu-ish dullness" discredits Confucianism, the teachings from Confucius's home-state of Lu, alias "Dull Country." His confessions of indulgence into Murasaki's ephemeral dew-like words rather than allegiance to the venerable Zhou hymns or the model of Bo Juyi (772–846), who since the Heian Period had been the most beloved Chinese poet in Japan, betray false humility. Equally, when the author makes himself into a frog and a quail—images of people with petty understanding—rather than into an ocean turtle or enormous Peng bird, he does not apologize for his pettiness. To the contrary, he invests in Daoist fashion the values of

[39] This phrase echoes the Sino-Japanese Preface to the *Kokinshū*, where it describes waka poetry as the product of a natural human instinct to respond to the world. Ironically, though, not waka but kanshi poems, which the *Kokinshū* Preface disdains as an artificial genre introduced from China, follow this closure to the preface of "Sino-Japanese Poems."

the grand and petty and turns his apology for his narrow-mindedness and lack of literary education into a celebration of true grandeur of the vernacular tradition.

This sets the scene for the memorable closure that "natural principle" makes the author into a petty poet with little talent and ephemeral vernacular tastes. With these very words the preface to the *Kokinwakashū* had claimed that vernacular poetry was a natural outburst of human emotions in response to external stirring. And what follows this preface is precisely the author's poetic outburst in response to the *Tale of Genji*, but, ironically, not in the vernacular, but in Sino-Japanese.

Thus, we have a bag of very mixed messages that leaves the reader wondering about what this text actually is. Does it really want to elevate the status of the *Genji* by "translating" it into the authoritative space of Academy learning? Or does it satirize the stilted style of dull academicians? Is it a parody of the Academy's protocol of poetic composition on Chinese canonical works? Or does it want to save the academicians from the scorching ridicule they had been subjected to by Murasaki Shikibu? An argument for canonization, a satire, a parody, or a rescue attempt of the Academy from its own pretentiousness, the *Sino-Japanese Poems on the Tale of Shining Genji* are a living testimony to the indeterminacy of texts that challenge conventions of language choice, gender, genre, and occasion in multiliterate cultures.[40]

4. *Allegorical Satire in Martianus Capella's* Marriage of Philology and Mercury

Martianus's *Marriage* has often been considered a pedagogical schoolbook prefaced by an allegorical sugarcoating designed to sweeten the bitter medicine of academic study administered in the ensuing chapters on each of the Seven Liberal Arts. Against this instrumental reading of the allegorical framing, I propose a reading that places the framing at the heart of Martianus's overall agenda, namely to show the way to "salvation through *paideia* [education]."[41] Inspired by Cicero's claim that the truly educated man combines rhetorical skill with expert knowledge in various philosophical and legal disciplines, Martianus continues Cicero's attack on Greek philosophy in *On the Orator*, in particular on Plato's polemical division of a presumably "treacherous" rhetoric and "true" philosophy.[42] Cicero had outdone Greek *wisdom love* (*philosophia*) by imagining a new Roman philosophy that would join rhetoric and philosophy under the broader concept of *wisdom tout court* (*sapientia/ sophia*). Martianus gives flesh to Cicero's proposed union in the figures of Mercury as rhetoric and Philology representing philosophy. It is revealing that the woman Mercury most desires to marry is Wisdom (in Martianus called by her Greek name, Sophia). But his quest fails, because she has promised her foster sister Athena eternal chastity. Thus, Wisdom remains chaste, but stands for Mercury's desire to unite his human logos with human episteme, embodied in his actual bride Philology. To

[40] For further exploration of the *Genji Poems* in the context of the medieval reception of the *Tale of Genji* see Denecke 2008.
[41] Stahl 1971, 88.
[42] Cicero. *De oratore* III.60-61. Nuchelmans 1957 traces this Ciceronian critique in Martianus and the reception history of the *Marriage*.

flesh out this reading of the *Marriage* that emphasizes Martianus's contribution to late classical discourse about philosophy, let us briefly rehearse the plot.

Young Mercury, inspired by the liaisons of other gods around him, decides to look for an appropriate mate. At first he has bad luck. Wisdom has promised Athena eternal chastity, Prophecy is already Apollo's lover (who is not to be messed with) and Psyche, the daughter of Entelecheia (Aristotelian category of "potentiality") and Sun, is off with Cupid (and celebrates her own marriage in Apuleius's *Golden Ass,* which clearly influenced Martianus's marriage tale). Finally, Philology is proposed as a proper mate, and Mercury prepares for their union by acquiring elegant diction and taking into his household seven servant ladies who will later serve as dowry—the Seven Liberal Arts. Athena first objects, because she wishes Philology to remain a virgin just like herself and Wisdom. But the marriage is approved by a council of the gods under Jupiter's leadership and deliberations begin on the invitee list, which include many good friends of Philology such as "Genius," "Liber" (book), "Nocturnus" (God of the night), and as archival assistants of the heavens, the Three Fates determining an individual's life span, namely Clotho, Lachesis, and Atropos.

At the marriage ceremony, the Muses and Virtues give their blessings. Philology now prepares for her ascent to heaven where the marriage ceremony will take place. Immortality, her handmaid in this, administers to Philology an emetic to rid her of the weight of unnecessary knowledge that would encumber her ascent. She is purified and ascends through the tones of the various celestial spheres to heaven, where she is greeted against the backdrop of a stunningly beautiful Milky Way by Jove, the gods, and an array of great philosophers and immortalized poets. Before proceeding to the wedding night, the couple has to listen to the expositions of the Seven Liberal Arts in seven lengthy books, indeed an irritating postponement of their first union.

Unlike the author of the *Genji Poems,* who targets the polar disjunction between Chinese-style education and vernacular literature, Martianus harmonizes the confusing variety of contending cultural, religious, and philosophical traditions associated with Egyptian, Babylonian, Greco-Roman, Etruscan, and various other Mediterranean traditions into an allegorical marriage tale. The *Genji Poems* "translated" a vernacular tale by a female author into the idiom, generic decorum, and literary canon of male Confucian education. Martianus, in turn, propagates his vision of universal Roman wisdom that combines rhetoric and human ingenuity with philosophy and human knowledge by "translating" it into the allegorical marriage of ingenuous Mercury with erudite Philology.

The choice of Philology and Mercury as bride and groom can be extended into a number of suggestive directions. Hermes/Mercury, the god of inventiveness, master hermeneutist and thus patron of orators, the translator of messages and crafty trickster marries Philology, foster sister of Athena and Wisdom, embodiment of human knowledge and thus mistress of the Seven Liberal Arts. [43] Not Philosophy,

---

[43] For the broad cultural and semantic baggage of Mercury and Philology see Grebe 1999, 841–46. In the *Marriage* Mercury's identification with the Egyptian god Thoth is particularly prominent.

the Greek master science, but Philology, a scion of Cicero's vision of "wisdom," is courted. Wisdom and by extension Philology indeed appeared to be a much more spacious category under which Martianus could unite the highly syncretic thought world of Late Antiquity. This was not as easily possible with Plato's and Aristotle's very assertive ethnic notion of philosophy, which made philosophical *logos* Greek and ambivalently superior to Egyptian or other "oriental" *mythos*. Perfectly consistent with Martianus's vision of wisdom, Discordia, as the notorious enemy of Philology, is the only person who gets officially disinvited from the marriage ceremony. This is a clear sign that syncretic eclecticism should reign over narrowly philosophical sectarianism in Martianus's new vision of wisdom (Stahl, 22).

If my reading of the *Marriage* emphasizes Martianus's contribution to a discourse about philosophy, this is also where Menippean satire comes into play. Menippean satire is the strangest and most promiscuous of all Greco-Roman satirical genres. The most famous examples included Varro's *Menippeae*, Seneca's *Pumpkinification of Emperor Claudius* (*Apocolocyntosis divi Claudii*), and the works of the Greek writer Lucian of Samosata.[44] It was different from the verse satirists such as Horace, Persius, or Juvenal, who were claimed by Quinitilan to be entirely Roman.

For our purposes the most interesting feature of the Menippean satire is that it is *intraphilosophical*. Menippus belonged to the Cynic school and the satirical exposure of other philosophers' ridiculous truth claims and hypocritical manners was precisely part of the philosophical program, not simply an outside view of a pragmatic educated citizen on an outlandish esoteric profession. The Hellenistic school of the Cynics, ancestors of the collusion between philosophical ambition and intellectual derision, was driven both by philosophical inquiry and by the satirical exposure of the occupational disease called "philosophy." At the bottom of this double impulse lay—like with the other "Socratic" schools such as the Cyrenaics[45]—the Socratic irony that exposed its interlocutor's prejudices and helped him or her through the master's "midwifery" (*maieutics*), to recognize the real truth behind hypocritical pretenses.

---

[44] In combining the earnest encyclopedic sweep with the framing of a Menippean satire, Martianus had one crucial predecessor: the antiquarian and polymath Varro Reatinus (116–27 BC), who wrote on almost any conceivable topic. As with most of his other works, his *Nine Book on the Disciplines* (*disciplinarum libri IX*) is lost and of his 150 books of Menippean Satires only six hundred verses survive in fragments. From the fragments we can see that Varro's pieces, like later Menippean satires, included biting exposure of social vices, a relish in eccentric language, including many grecisms, archaisms, and hapax legomena, and the treatment of fantastic celestial themes such as councils of gods and descents to the Underworld. On the genre of Menippean satire see Relihan 1993.

[45] Diogenes Laertius gives us a colorful picture of the Cynics and Cyrenaics: they were mostly of low-born origin and included many slaves and also women. Diogenes's account includes a hilarious story about how one of the female members, Hipparchia, cleverly proves her equality with men through a mock-syllogism. They get famous with their defty and scatological verses, such as the "farter" Metrokles, and their strange outfits and props, such as Diogenes with his barrel or a certain Menedemos, whose potpourri outfit included high-heel theater shoes, an Arkadian felt hat embroidered with the signs of the zodiac, and a beard reaching down to his shoes. It is significant that Diogenes insists on calling these schools philosophical and not just a "way of life" (*enstatis biou*), although they rejected natural philosophy and logic and only accepted ethics, the third subject of Greco-Roman philosophy, as a worthwhile topic of reflection.

This deeply philosophical impulse pervades Lucian's Menippean satires, which exerted profound influence on Martianus's text. Lucian (120–80), a Syrian rhetorician and teacher, wrote in elegant Attic Greek, diametrically opposed to Martianus's baroque Latin larded with semi-scientific Grecisms, solitary neologisms, and tortuous syntax. However, the combination of Socratic midwifery, pedagogics, and satire is characteristic of both authors. In "Hermotimus or about philosophical schools" (*Hermotimos e peri haireseōn*) Lucian attacks the dogmatic self-assertion of philosophical schools, in particular the thriving Stoic school. Hermotimus, who has spent much of his lifetime and money on his philosophical instruction, is set straight on the inefficiency, hypocrisy, arrogance, and impracticality of philosophical school training by Lycinus, a namesake of the author, who appears here as the midwife Socrates to awaken Hermotimus to start a new life sheltered from philosophical stupidities. At the height of Hermotimus's birth as a new person, Lycinus tells the poignant story of the effects of philosophical training told by an angry old man who refused to pay a philosophy teacher because he did not see any educational effects on his nephew.

> As to what you have sold us, you have got it still; your stock of learning is none the less; and in what I really sent the boy to you for, you have not improved him a bit; he has carried off and seduced neighbour Echecrates's daughter, and there would have been an action for assault, only Echecrates is a poor man; but the prank cost me a couple of hundred. And the other day he struck his mother; she had tried to stop him when he was smuggling wine out of the house, for one of his club-dinners, I suppose. As to temper and conceit and impudence and brass and lying, he was not half so bad twelve months ago as he is now. That is where I should have liked him to profit by your teaching.[46]

This well-chosen anecdote leads Hermotimes to his moment of healthy revelation that Lycinus is the true philosopher—although Hermotimes had started out on the proud pretense of generously introducing his friend to the mysteries of philosophy that only he possessed—and that he has wasted more than his money. Hermotimes's realization comes literally along as a new birth, with a baby's cry:

LYCINUS: "Were our original expectations from philosophy at all of a different nature, by the way? Did they contemplate anything beyond a more decent behaviour than the average? Why this obstinate silence?"

---

[46] *Lucian. Hermotimus* 81. Greek text from Kilburn 1959, vol. 6, 408. Translation from Fowler 1905, 87. καίτοι ἃ μὲν ἡμῖν πέπρακας, ἔχεις ἔτι καὶ αὐτὸς καὶ οὐδὲν ἔλαττον γέγονέ σοι τῶν μαθημάτων: τὰ δ' ἄλλα ὧν ἐξ ἀρχῆς ἐπιθυμῶν συνέστησά σοι τὸν νεανίσκον, ὁ δ' οὐδὲν ἀμείνων γεγένηται διὰ σέ, ὃς τοὐμοῦ γείτονος Ἐχεκράτους, τὴν θυγατέρα συναρπάσας παρθένον οὖσαν διέφθειρεν καὶ ὀλίγου δίκην ἔφυγε βιαίων, εἰ μὴ ἐγὼ ταλάντου ὠνησάμην τὸ πλημμέλημα παρὰ πένητος ἀνδρὸς τοῦ Ἐχεκράτους: τὴν μητέρα δὲ πρῴην ἐρράπισεν, ὅτι αὐτοῦ ἐλάβετο ὑπὸ κόλπου ἐκκομίζοντος τὸν κάδον, ὡς ἔχοι συμβολὰς οἶμαι καταθεῖναι. τὰ μὲν γὰρ ἐς ὀργὴν καὶ θυμὸν καὶ ἀναισχυντίαν καὶ ἐς τόλμαν καὶ ψεῦδος μακρῷ τινι ἄμεινον εἶχε πέρυσιν ἢ νῦν. καίτοι ἐβουλόμην ἂν αὐτὸν ἐς ταῦτα ὠφελῆσθαι ὑπὸ σοῦ μᾶλλον ἤπερ ἐκεῖνα εἰδέναι.

HERMOTIMUS: "Oh, why but that I could cry like a baby? It cuts me to the heart, it is all so true; it is too much for me, when I think of my wretched, wasted years—paying all that money for my own labour, too! I am sober again after a debauch, I see what the object of my maudlin affection is like, what it has brought upon me."[47]

The moment of sudden revelation and liberation from darkness and blindness produces an interesting afterbirth: although Hermotimus has been "delivered" by Lycinus, he realizes after his infantile cries that he has been miseducated and wishes for an emetic to get rid of that poison, because only this afterbirth will allow him a new start:

"I only wish there were an emetic that would purge out every doctrine they have instilled into me; I assure you, if I could reverse Chrysippus's plan with the helle-bore, and drink forgetfulness, not of the world but of Stoicism, I would not think twice about it. Well, Lycinus, I owe you a debt indeed... Henceforth, if I meet a philosopher on my walks (and it will not be with my will), I shall turn aside and avoid him as I would a mad dog."[48]

The dialogue ends in true cynic fashion in that Hermotimes promises to avoid phi-losophers like mad dogs (kynos; thus cynic="doggish philosopher"). The amused reader assumed thus that Hermotimes might henceforth seek instruction from the "sane dogs" and true philosophers, the cynics.

Apart from the Socratic combination of irony with midwifery, Martianus shares another very important feature of the Menippean satire. Lucian often reconfigures the world through fleshing out names, ideas, or concepts into real-life actors and enjoys playing through the implications of his newly bred incarnations borrowed from abstract philosophical discourse. In his *Dialogues of the Dead* Lucian has the cynic philosopher Diogenes invite Menippus to the underworld and promises that Menippus will have an even merrier time gossiping and attacking people down there than on earth. Menippus gets into trouble when waiting with many other shades to be ferried over Lethe, the underworld's "River of Oblivion." Not only does Hermes have to pay his passage. More importantly, the shades have too much baggage for the little ferry boat. Everybody is asked to relinquish their prop-erty, which proves particularly difficult in the case of a philosopher:

MENIPPUS: It's a philosopher—I mean a quack full of tricks. Make him strip too. You'll find a lot to give you a laugh hidden under that cloak.

---

[47] *Lucian. Hermotimus* 83. Kilburn 1959, vol. 6, 412. Fowler 1905, 89. Λυκῖνος: ἢ ἐπ᾽ ἄλλαις ἐλπίσιν ἐξ ἀρχῆς φιλοσοφεῖν ἠξιοῦμεν, οὐχ ὡς τῶν ἰδιωτῶν κοσμιώτεροι εἴημεν περινοστοῦντες; τί οὖν οὐκ ἀποκρίνῃ καὶ τοῦτο;Ἑρμότιμος: τί δὲ ἄλλο ἢ ὅτι καὶ δακρῦσαι ὀλίγου δέω; ἐς τοσοῦτό μου καθίκετο ὁ λόγος ἀληθὴς ὤν, καὶ ὀδύρομαι, ὅσον ἄθλιος χρόνον ἀνάλωκα καὶ προσέτι μισθοὺς οὐκ ὀλίγους τελῶν ἀντὶ τῶν πόνων. νυνὶ γὰρ ὥσπερ ἐκ μέθης ἀνανήφων ὁρῶ οἷα μέν ἐστιν ὧν ἤρων, ὁπόσα δὲ πέπονθα διὰ ταῦτα.
[48] *Lucian. Hermotimus* 86. Kilburn 1959, vol. 6, 414. Fowler 1905, 90. ὡς εἴθε γε καὶ ἐξεμέσαι δυνατὸν ἦν ἅπαντα ἐκεῖνα, ὁπόσα ἤκουσα παρ᾽ αὐτῶν, καὶ εὖ ἴσθι, οὐκ ἂν ὤκνησα καὶ ἐλλέβορον πιεῖν διὰ τοῦτο ἐς τὸ ἔμπαλιν ἢ ὁ Χρύσιππος, ὅπως μηδὲν ἔτι νοήσαιμι ὧν φασιν. σοὶ δ᾽ οὖν οὐ μικρὰν χάριν οἶδα, ὦ Λυκῖνε...φιλοσόφῳ δὲ εἰςτὸ λοιπὸν κἂν ἄκων ποτὲ ὁδῷ βαδίζων ἐντύχω, οὕτως ἐκτραπήσομαι καὶ περιστήσομαι ὥσπερ τοὺς λυττῶντας τῶν κυνῶν.

HERMES: Off with your clothes first and all the rest later. My god! What a load of quackery, ignorance, argumentativeness, conceit, useless questions, thorny words, sophistic ideas! Plus plenty of useless effort, quite a bit of nonsense, humbug, and hairsplitting. What do you know about that! He's got money, too, and easy living, shamelessness, bad temper, sloth, and effeteness! You can hide them all you want, I can still see them. And get rid of the falsehood and the delusions and this thinking you're better than everyone else. Even a battleship wouldn't hold you if you got on board with all that![49]

Menippus has Hermes taking further care of the problem of over-freight by suggesting to cut of the philosopher's six pounds of beard and the long eyebrows, and, last of all, the heaviest thing of all, which the philosopher had been hiding under his arm: flattery—"something he's found very useful all his life." The laugh the reader gets out of this passage is not so much the list of vices for which the philosopher is held responsible, but the way he is viciously decorated with the physical allegory of those vices—of which flattery has most pounds. It is the translation of the vices into visual emblems—precisely what we can later really see in Baroque emblems of virtues and vices—that is funny.

In his *Philosophies for Sale*, a delightful account of an auction of famous philosophers, Lucian ridicules and at times physically fleshes out doctrinal tenets of the various schools. Not all philosophers are marketable—who would want a Democritus declaring the world void with some occasional atoms in motion or a Heraclitus whining about the eternal changes in the fleeting universe? Socrates, proudly proclaiming to be a "pederast" and "very knowledgeable in matters of sex" can only be bought on credit. The buyer of the Stoic logician Chrysippus gets to taste the potential lethality of Lucian's allegorizing game:

CHRYSIPPUS: "Being funny, eh? Watch out—I'll shoot you down with my Indemonstrable Syllogism.
SEVENTH BUYER: "Sounds terrible. What happens to the victim?"
CH.: "Bafflement, stopped mouth, and severe dislocation of the brain. My best, though, is this: if I want, I can turn you to stone in this instant.
B.: "Stone? How? You don't look to me like Perseus[50], my friend."
CH.: "This way. Tell me, is a stone a substance?"
B.: "Yes."
CH.: "Something animate is a substance, right?"
B.: "Right."

---

[49] *Lucian. Dialogi mortuorum* 20 (10).8. Translation from Casson 1962, 200–201. Μένιππος: φιλόσοφός τις, ὦ Ἑρμῆ, μᾶλλον δὲ γόης καὶ τερατείας μεστός: ὥστε ἀπόδυσον καὶ τοῦτον: ὄψει γὰρ πολλὰ καὶ γελοῖα ὑπὸ τῷ ἱματίῳ σκεπόμενα. Ἑρμῆς: κατάθου σὺ τὸ σχῆμα πρῶτον, εἶτα καὶ ταυτὶ πάντα. ὦ Ζεῦ, ὅσην μὲν τὴν ἀλαζονείαν κομίζει, ὅσην δὲ ἀμαθίαν καὶ ἔριν καὶ κενοδοξίαν καὶ ἐρωτήσεις ἀπόρους καὶ λόγους ἀκανθώδεις καὶ ἐννοίας πολυπλόκους, ἀλλὰ καὶ ματαιοπονίαν μάλα πολλὴν καὶ λῆρον οὐκ ὀλίγον καὶ ὕθλους καὶ μικρολογίαν, νὴ Δία καὶ χρυσίον γε τουτὶ καὶ ἡδυπάθειαν δὲ καὶ ἀναισχυντίαν καὶ ὀργὴν καὶ τρυφὴν καὶ μαλακίαν: οὐ λέληθεν γάρ με, εἰ καὶ μάλα περικρύπτεις αὐτά. καὶ τὸ ψεῦδος δὲ ἀπόθου καὶ τὸν τῦφον καὶ τὸ οἴεσθαι ἀμείνων εἶναι τῶν ἄλλων: ὡς εἴ γε ταῦτα πάντα ἔχων ἐμβαίης, ποία πεντηκόντορος δέξαιτο ἄν σε;
[50] Perseus possessed for a while the head of Gorgon Medusa, who would turn everybody to stone who saw her.

CH.: "Are you something animate?"

B.: "I should think so."

CH.: "Then you're a substance—which makes you a stone."

B.: "No, no! For god's sake, reverse the logic and turn me back into a man!"[51]

Chrysippus turns his potential buyer back into a man by a similar absurd logic and the buyer is deeply grateful: "Thank you, thank you! My legs were already getting cold and stiff...I'm buying you. Hermes, how much do I have to pay for this fellow?" Lucian's jokes about the various philosophers who are sold are of course always at their expense, as is the reader's laughter. Yet as we see with Chrysippus, the embodiment of the sophistries of Stoic logic, Lucian indirectly also proves the opposite, namely that school philosophy, always decried for her impotent inefficiency, can be effective, in fact lethally effective.

It was this blade of the two-edged sword of allegorical translation that Martianus put to use in his allegorical marriage between Philology and Mercury: In having these two figures (and especially the purely conceptual, non-mythical Philology) putting on allegorical flesh and uniting in marriage, Martianus, at his most serious, chooses a highly effective and, literally, most weighty tool to propagate a Ciceronian vision of Roman philosophy as comprehensive wisdom.

Given that allegorical narration clothes concepts in human form, or visualizes typical attributes of well-known figures, it is obvious that clothing plays a large role in Menippean satire in general and Martianus's *Marriage* in particular. The play with what is hidden and what is displayed, the tuning of inner content to outer (possibly misleading) appearance becomes ultimately a symbol for truth versus fiction, content versus framing tale in the *Marriage*.

The need for clothes is, after all, the trigger of Martianus's whole tale. Pubescent Mercury needs to marry at the very moment when his body becomes too masculine to stay naked:

> His mother [Venus] had encouraged him in [his inclination to marry] when, on his yearly journey through the zodiac, he greeted her in the company of the Pleiades. She was concerned about him, especially because his body, through the exercise of wrestling and constant running, glowed with masculine strength and bore the muscles of a youth perfectly developed. Already with the first beard on his cheeks, he could not continue to go about half naked, clad in nothing but a short cape covering only the top of his shoulders—such a sight caused the Cyprian [Venus] great amusement. With all this in mind he decided to marry.[52]

---

[51] Lucian. *Philosophies for Sale* 24–25. Greek text from Harmon 1960-67, 498–500. Translation from Casson 1962, 328. Χρύσιππος: σκώπτεις, ὦ οὗτος. ἀλλ᾽ ὅρα μή σε ἀποτοξεύσω τῷ ἀναποδείκτῳ συλλογισμῷ.Ἀγοράστης: καὶ τί δεινὸν ἀπὸ τοῦ βέλους;Χρύσιππος: ἀπορία καὶ σιωπὴ καὶ διαστραφῆναι τὴν διάνοιαν. ὃ δὲ μέγιστον, ἢν ἐθέλω, τάχιστά σε ἀποδείξω λίθον. Ἀγοράστης: πῶς λίθον; οὐ γὰρ Περσεὺς σύ, ὦ βέλτιστε, εἶναί μοι δοκεῖς.Χρύσιππος: ὧδέ πως: ὁ λίθος σῶμά ἐστι;Ἀγοράστης: ναί.Χρύσιππος: τί δέ; τὸ ζῷον οὐ σῶμα;Ἀγοράστης: ναί. Χρύσιππος: σὺ δὲ ζῷον;Ἀγοράστης: ἔοικα γοῦν.Χρύσιππος: λίθος ἄρα εἶ σῶμα ὄν.Ἀγοράστης: μηδαμῶς. ἀλλ᾽ ἀνάλυσόν με πρὸς τοῦ Διὸς καὶ ἐξ ὑπαρχῆς ποίησον ἄνθρωπον.

[52] Martianus. *De nuptiis* 5. Translation from Stahl 1977, 6. *in quam sententiam mater illum anxia, cum annua peragratione Zodiactea in Pliadum numero salutaret, impulerat, praesertimque quod palaestra crebisque discursibus exercitum corpus lacertosis in iuvenalis roboris excellentiam toris virile quadam*

To make her daughter ready for the betrothal, Philology's mother chooses the proper diadem and belt and gives her what appears to be a dress of pure silk:

> She gave her a dress and robe white as milk, which seemed made of that fleece from the precious shrub in which, they say, the sages of India and the inhabitants of the mountain of shadow are clothed, and of threads of shining cotton, as much as that country produces.[53]

The choice of pure white silk is deliberate and contrasts favorably with her previous ornate and pompous attire. But it also points to the problem that Philology's inner mind does not yet match her outer dress of pure simplicity. She suffers from worldly overload, which she has to get rid of before her ethereal ascent to heaven with the help of an emetic:

> [Immortality] lightly felt with her right hand Philology's heartbeat and breast; when she found that it was greatly swollen with some inner fullness, she said "Unless you retch violently and void this matter which is choking your breast, you will never attain the throne of immortality at all." The girl strained hard and with great effort vomited up the weight she was carrying in her breast. Then that nausea and labored vomit turned into a stream of writings of all kinds. One could see what books and what great volumes and the works of how many languages flowed from the mouth of the maiden. There were some made of papyrus which had been smeared with cedar oil, other books were woven of rolls of linen, many were of parchment, and a very few were written on linden bark. There were some written with a sacred ink, whose letters were thought to be representations of living creatures; when Immortality saw the writings of these books, she ordered them to be inscribed on certain imposing rocks and placed inside a cave within the sanctuaries of the Egyptians, and she called these stones *stelae* and ordained that they should contain the genealogies of the gods. But while the maiden was bringing up such matter in spasms, several young women, of whom some are called the Arts and others the Disciplines, were straightway collecting whatever the maiden brought forth from her mouth, each one of them taking material for her own essential use and her particular skill...After the maiden had with travail brought forth from deep inside herself all that store of literary reproduction, worn out and pale with exhaustion, she asked help from Immortality, who had witnessed such a great effort.[54] (Stahl, 46–48).

Only after this violent cleansing does the simplicity of Philology's white silk dress finally match her inner purity. She is born anew as an immortal ready to ascend in

---

amplitudine renidebat. ac iam pubentes genae seminudum eum incedere chlamidaque indutum parua invelatum cetera humerorum cacumen obnubere sine magno risu Cypridis non sinebant. rationabili igitur proposito constituit pellere caelibatum.

[53] Martianus. *De nuptiis* 114. Stahl 1977, 39. *itaque vestum peplumque lactis instar fulgidum dedit, quod vel ex illa herbarum felicium lana, qua indusiari perhibent Indicae prudentiae vates accolasque montis umbrati, et, quantum usus eius telluris apportat, ex candentis byssi netibus videbatur.*

[54] Martianus. *De nuptiis* 135–39. Stahl 1977, 46–48. [...] *leniter dextra cordis eius pulsum pectusque pertractat ac nescio qua intima plenitudine distentum magno cum turgore respiciens "ni haec," inquit, "quibus plenum pectus geris, coactissima egestione vomueris forasque diffuderis, immortalitatis sedem nullatenus obtinebis." At illa omni nisu magnaque vi quicquid intra pectus perpenderat evomebat. tunc vero illa nausea ac vomitio elaborata in omnigenum copias convertitur litterarum. cernere erat, qui libri*

the same way as Hermotimus is cleared of his misconceptions about the philosophical life and brought to a new life through his Socratic midwife Lycinius.

Yet, on the level of narrative, "clothing" means wrapping the naked truth in the yarn of myth and fiction. Martianus promises at various points to leave his allegorical framework and get down to the naked truth, but with little sincere conviction. Right before the Seven Arts start to lecture on their disciplines, the author turns to the reader with a promise to put an end to the mythical:

> Reader, we have covered a great part of the story... So now the mythical part is ended; the books which follow set forth the arts. With true intellectual nourishment they put aside all fable and for the most part explain serious studies, without however avoiding entertainment. Now you know what will follow, given the goodwill of the heavenly powers and the Muses and the lyre of Latona's son [Apollo].[55]

But this oath of abstention is broken right away when Grammar comes in and insists on further myths so that Martianus has to give in:

> "But," I cried, "in the previous book notice is given that the myths have been put away and that the precepts in the volumes which follow are a work of those Arts which tell that which is the truth." But with a laugh she joked at this and said: "Let us tell no lies, and yet let the Arts be clothed. Surely you will not give the band of sisters naked to the bridal couple? Surely they will not go like that before the senate of the Thunderer [Jove] and the heavenly gods? To say no more about embellishment, what is to be the program?" "Surely, let them speak on their own teachings, and let them be clothed in incorporeal utterance." "Now you are deceiving me and are not consistent with your promise; why do you not admit that your work cannot be composed except by the use of imagery?" With these words the Muse got the better of me: "Are you running way?" "I am joining in the game."[56]

Clothing is necessary in good society and so the disciplines receive their rhetorical coatings of "incorporeal utterance," despite protestations of the author.

---

quantaque volumina, quot linguarum opera ex ore virginis diffluebant. alia ex papyro, quae cedro perlite fuerat, videbantur, alii carbasinis voluminibus implicati libri, ex ovillis multi quoque tergoribus, rari vero in philyrae cortice subnotati. erantque quidam sacra nigredine colorati, quorum litterae animantum credebantur effigies, quasque librorum notas Athanasia conspiciens quibusdam eminentibus saxis iussit adscribi atque intra specum per Aegyptiorum adyta collocari, eademque saxa stelas appellans deorum stemmata praecepit continere. sed dum talia virgo undanter evomeret, puellae quamplures, quarum Artes aliae, alterae dictae sunt Disciplinae, subinde, quae ex ore virgo effuderat, colligebant in suum unaquaeque illarum necessarium usum facultatemque corripiens...postquam igitur illam bibliothecalem copiam nixa imi[ta]tus uirgo diffudit, exhausto pallore confecta Athanasiae opem, quae tanti laboris conscia fuerat, postulavit.
[55] Martianus. De nuptiis 219–20. Stahl 1977, 63. Transcursa, lector, parte magna fabula...nunc ergo mythos terminator; infiunt / artes libelli qui sequentes asserent. / nam fruge vera omne fictum dimovent / et disciplinas annotabunt sobrias / pro parte multa nec vetabunt ludicra. / habes quid instet, si potestas caelitum / faveantque Musae et chelys Latoia.
[56] Martianus. De nuptiis 222. Stahl 1977, 64. "atquin prioris ille / titulus monet libelli / mythos ab ore pulsos / Artesque vera fantes / voluminum sequentum / praecepta comparare." / at haec iocante rictu / "nil mentiamur" inquit / "et vestiantur Artes. / an tu gregem sororum / nudum dabis iugandis, / et sic petent Tonantis / et caelitum senatum? / aut si tacere cultum / placet, ordo quis probatur?" / "certe loquentur illae, / quicquid erat docendum, / habitusque consequentur / asomato in profatu." / "haec nempe ficta vox est, / et devius promissi es; / cur ergo non fateris / ni figminis figura / nil posse comparari?" / his me Camena vicit: / "fugis?" "iugabo ludum."

In the end the issue of clothing even gives Martianus the chance to satirize Satire. As we learn from the opening of the *Marriage,* the marriage tale we are reading is actually a tale Lady Satire told Martianus on long winter nights. At the end of the book Satire accuses her scribe, Martianus, of being too cheap with her accoutrements:

> Our garrulous Satire has heaped learned doctrines upon unlearned, and crammed sacred matters into secular; she has commingled gods and the Muses, and has had uncouth figures prating in a rustic fiction about the encyclopedic arts. Herself distressed by awareness of the triviality of her composition, and swollen with gall and bile, she said: "I could have come forth in a grand robe, to be admired for my learning and refinement, decorous in appearance, as if just coming from the court of Mars. Instead I have been inspired by Felix Capella— whom ignorant generations have observed ranting as he passed judgment on barking dogs, giving to the high office of proconsul a bumble bee long separated from his blossoms by the sickle, and in his declining years; a man whom the prosperous city of Elissa has seen as a fosterling settled in a neighborhood of slothful herdsmen, barely managing on a small income, drowsy by day and blinking his eyes with effort—when I could fittingly quaff the Pegasean draught." And so, my son, in accordance with the testimony of an old man, show indulgence, as you read, for the trifles which he has produced.[57]

This end of Martianus's long book is a decorous gesture of humility, asking the reader and his son (to whom his book is addressed) indulgence for his trivial composition. Humility and self-deprecation are good defense mechanisms helping him conclude his daunting task of writing an encyclopedic coverage of the Liberal Arts. Menippean satire had helped Martianus to advance his syncretic vision of wisdom and philosophy by giving it rich allegorical clothing. There are moments of naked truth that promise riddance of ornateness, such as the administering of the emetic to Philology or Martianus's promise before the discourses of the Liberal Arts to end his myth-telling.

But overall Martianus is clearly on the side of ornate rhetoric, heavy clothing, and elaborate allegory for pedagogical purposes, but obviously also for his own playful indulgence. Lady Satire, throughout the book a rather morose and pretentious character, disapproves of the author's presumably rustic outfit for her. He thus helps Martianus's self-deprecating bows to the reader and seems to say: *He* could have done better, but here *I* stand. Ultimately, Satire will have to take responsibility for Martianus's eccentric tale, which is not too far from the desire of the author of the odd *Genji Poems* to remain unnamed.

---

[57] Martianus. *De nuptiis* 998–1000. Stahl 1977, 381–82. *haec quippe loquax docta indoctis aggerans / fandis tacenda farcinat, immiscuit / Musas deosque, disciplinas cyclicas / garrire agrestic cruda finxit plasmate. / hac ipsa namque rupta conscientia / turgensque felle ac bili "multa chlamyde / prodire doctis approbanda cultibus / possemque comis utque e Martis curia; / Felicis" inquit "sed Capellae flemine / indocta rabidum quem uidere saecula / iurgis caninos blateratus pendere, / proconsulari vero dantem culmini / ipsosque dudum bombinat ore flosculo / decerptum falce iam canescenti rota, / beata alumnum urbs Elissae quem vidit / iugariorum murcidam viciniam / parvo obsidentem vixque respersum lucro, / nictante cura somnolentum lucibus— / ab hoc creatum Pegaseum gurgitem / decente quando possem haurire poculo?" / testem ergo nostrum quae veternum prodidit / secute nugis, nate, ignosce lectitans.*

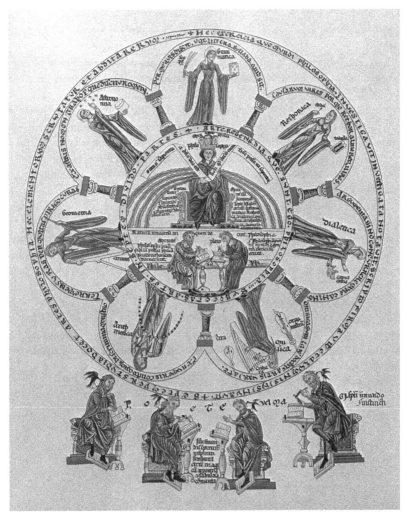

FIGURE 7.2 *With Lady Satire nowhere in sight: Although an important character in Martianus's compendium, serious medieval depictions of the well-robed Ladies of the Seven Liberal Arts are centered instead around Philosophia, Socrates, and Plato*
"The Seven Liberal Arts" from the *Hortus deliciarum* by Herrad von Landsberg (twelfth century, destroyed 1870). From the Metropolitan Museum of Art's copy of Christian Moritz Engelhardt's *Herrad von Landsperg, Hortus Deliciarum* (Stuttgart 1818). Photo: Elizabeth G. C. Menzies (Creative Commons).

5. Outlook

We have looked at two highly ambivalent texts that deal with the borders and "translation" between different worlds—between the "public" and the "private" spaces in the case of the *Genji Poems* and between the invisible world of philosophical concepts and the landscape of allegorical embodiments in Martianus's *Marriage*.

Both texts obviously intend to promote canonization of their body of knowledge, the *Tale of Genji* and the Liberal Arts education. And both employ their comical escapades not just to sugarcoat the bitterness of learning, but to sketch new visions with the help of a translation experiment. The *Genji Poems* try to claim a world beyond the *wa-kan* division. Martianus's *Marriage* experiments with a personified allegory of syncretic encyclopedic knowledge that makes cultural and disciplinary in fights—so much criticized by Lucian—into a thing of the past. Also, moments of comic self-deprecation help to suspend these odd translation experiments beyond their authors.

If the *Genji Poems* have been neglected by the vast community of *Genji* scholars, it is because they are insignificant from the point of view of *Genji* reception. Yet as an experiment with the *wa-kan* dynamics they become a highly interesting document in their own right. Martianus's *Marriage*, though eagerly researched in the medieval context, needs more attention from classicists interested in the rise of the novel and Apuleius's *Golden Ass*, in intraphilosophical satire in the style of Lucian, and from scholars of classical philosophy. If anything, both texts are a powerful testimony that satire as a tool of education, of cultural reconciliation, and empowering self-deprecation thrives in multiliterate cultures and produces pieces that are not always outright funny, but stand out as courageous translation experiments in their complex worlds.

CHAPTER 8 | # The Synoptic Machine
Sino-Japanese and Greco-Roman
Juxtapositions

1. Synoptic Texts

Satire was a versatile mode for writers of younger literatures to relate to their reference culture in a playful, liberating, and ambiguously subversive way. In this last chapter we will explore another strategy of directly relating reference and younger cultures: "synoptic texts." I use the term here not in reference to texts that have survived in multiple versions and are printed in columns side-by-side, as New Testament scholars do when they talk of the "synoptic gospels" of Matthew, Mark, and Luke. In this chapter I call "synoptic" those texts that explicitly juxtapose elements of one culture or language with those of another, arranging them in a virtually visual diptych that urges the reader to compare and contrast the two sides. As examples of this rather peculiar textual arrangement, we will analyze a text that juxtaposes biographies of famous Greeks and Romans and a poetry anthology that matches vernacular waka with Sino-Japanese kanshi poems.

Synoptic texts are of unusual interest as they are philosophical and aesthetic experiments that display cultural difference or similarity in a highly structured scheme by inserting their target units—lives or poems in our case—into what one could call a "synoptic machine." The binary format of juxtaposition prompts the reader to discern similarities or contrasts, recognizing human universals or discovering cultural peculiarities. This "synoptic machine" could reveal fundamental differences, but it could also produce false contrasts, resulting in mutual warping of the vision of what constitutes "Greek" or "Roman," "Chinese," "Sino-Japanese" or "Japanese" identity.

Both in Greco-Roman and Japanese literary cultures, there was no established genre of this kind. What were the motivations for authors or compilers of synoptic texts when they juxtaposed different cultures or traditions in a climate of complex political and cultural hierarchies? What were the deliberate and what were the unintended effects of the synoptic format that folds complex historical patterns of cultural, linguistic, and literary contact zones into memorable miniature diptychs? If many texts written in multiliterate contexts can hide their implicit target of comparison from the readers' immediate sight, what, then, do "synoptic texts," with their overdetermined, drastically magnified power to compare, reveal?

We explore these questions on the example of two texts almost too different to be truly comparable: the poetry collection *Newly Selected Collection of Myriad Leaves* (*Shinsen Man'yōshū* 新撰万葉集, hereafter: *New Myriad Leaves*), which matches vernacular waka with Sino-Japanese kanshi poems and Plutarch's *Parallel Lives* (*Bioi Parallêloi*, after 96 CE), which couples biographies of famous Greeks with fitting Roman counterparts. Our two separate case studies will ultimately allow us to see common patterns of how the polarizing force of the "synoptic machine" adds meaning between the lines and even inscribes itself into the narrative logic of both texts.

2. *First Case Study: Divergent Poetics in the* New Myriad Leaves

The *New Myriad Leaves* is a collection of about 250 waka poems (consisting of 5-7-5-7-7 syllables) that are matched with Sino-Japanese heptasyllabic quatrains (four lines of seven syllables each).[1] We know that 170 of the waka stem from the *Poetry Contest of the Kanpyō era (889–898) for his Majesty (Kanpyō no ōntoki kisainomiya no utaawase* 寛平御時后宮歌合).[2] Between 889 and 893 two parties composed poems in 20 rounds on the topics of "spring," "summer," "fall," "winter," and "love." These five topics became the basic arrangement pattern of later imperial waka anthologies such as the *Kokinshū*, which includes a number of poems from this contest.[3] Although the collection has been attributed to Sugawara no Michizane, many doubts remain as to whether he actually did compile the collection and might have written some of the Sino-Japanese quatrains.

New Myriad Leaves was compiled at a crucial turning point in Japanese history. The late ninth century saw the end of official missions to the Chinese Tang court, not the least precipitated by Michizane's opposition to the missions. It witnessed the rise of the northern branch of the Fujiwara to the regency and the decline of the power of non-Fujiwara nobility, a factor that resulted in Michizane's exile to Dazaifu. And it coincided with the emergence of *kana* literature and of the ascent of waka at court, not the least thanks to poetry matches such as the one that produced *New Myriad Leaves*. Deliberately rendered in the older Man'yōgana script that uses only Chinese characters instead of the recently developing *kana* syllabary, *New Myriad Leaves* both furthered the rise of waka's reputation but also resisted the new *kana* script that came along with it.

In this pivotal moment when the vernacular tradition regained a footing at court after a period of imperial support for Sino-Japanese anthologies in the early ninth century, *New Myriad Leaves* was one of a few bold literary experiments

[1] The exact number of poems differs depending on the manuscript lineage. There is especially large variation with the second of the two books into which the anthology is divided. Some editions omit the quatrains and the preface to the second book completely and only feature the waka. In this chapter I focus exclusively on the first book, which contains quatrains of higher quality. Its preface is dated to 893, while the preface to the second book refers to 913.

[2] This contest was probably celebrated for Hanshi, the mother of the reigning Emperor Uda. The meaning and translation of the title are disputed.

[3] The collection has received surprisingly little scholarly attention despite its great significance for literary history. Helen McCullough has given it its due place as a crucial stepping-stone towards the *Kokinshū* in McCullough 1985. The recent richly annotated multivolume edition *Shinsen Man'yōshū chūshaku* will hopefully lead to more interpretive study.

with the juxtaposition of "Japanese" (*wa* 和) and "Chinese-style" (*kan* 漢) sensibilities. Other synoptic texts compiled during that time included Ōe no Chisato's *Waka on Topic Lines* (*Kudai waka* 句題和歌 or *Chisatoshū* 千里集, 897), which culled Chinese lines from famous poems mostly by the Tang poet Bo Juyi and his friend Yuan Zhen and juxtaposed them with an adaptation of their content into waka poems, and the two prefaces to the *Kokinshū*, one in Japanese and one in Chinese-style.

The *New Myriad Leaves* is unusual among these and later synoptic *wa-kan* collections, because it first gives the waka, which is then followed by a Sino-Japanese quatrain composed in response to the waka. In contrast, Chisato's *Waka on Topic Lines* focuses on the Chinese lines to which the waka are meant to respond. To adopt a format where kanshi are fitted into the framework of preceding waka was a bold move in the late ninth century and we need to understand it as a significant step in the reassertion of vernacular poetry as public court poetry. The use of Man'yōgana script and the very title of the collection emphasized continuity with the tradition of court panegyrics preserved in the *Collection of Myriad Leaves* (*Man'yōshū* 万葉集, ca. 759). The concern with creating pedigree and a long history for vernacular court poetry is further highlighted in the preface, which opens on the phrase: "The *Myriad Leaves* is a strand of the old songs 夫萬葉集者古歌之流也."[4] This is a reformulation of the claim the Han Dynasty historian Ban Gu (32–92) made when he said that the genre of "poetic expositions" or "rhapsodies" (*fu* 賦) popular in his own time was actually a strand of the "Old Poems," that is of the canonical *Classic of Poetry* compiled seven centuries earlier. The compiler of the *New Myriad Leaves* adopts Ban Gu's strategy to legitimize younger genres by linking them historically to older ones. It constructs a three-tier literary history that consists of the most archaic "old songs," followed by the *Myriad Leaves* and succeeded by the *New Myriad Leaves,* the collection at hand. This emphasis on literary pedigree masks the novelty of the poetry included in the collection whose aesthetics sets it apart from the older poetry in the *Myriad Leaves.*

Reading the poems in the *New Myriad Leaves* is a pleasantly disturbing experience. Just when one thinks one has grasped a beautiful poetic turn of phrase in a waka, the corresponding kanshi twists or contradicts the waka, suddenly rendering its poetic message brittle and estranged. It is as if one were to change glasses at frantic speed and had to readjust one's eyes each time anew.

Cosmology

Let us observe this process at close range. Consider the pair of poems that opens the collection:

Waka:

(text in *Man'yōgana*)	(text in *kana* orthography)	(translation)
水之上丹	水の上に	How can the spring rain
文織紊	あや織り乱る	That weaves wild, shifting patterns

---

4 *Shinsen Man'yōshū* Preface. *Shinsen Man'yōshū chūshaku* I, 4.

春之雨哉	春の雨や	On the water's face
山之綠緒	山の緑を	Yet spread a green, unvaried dye
那倍手染濫	なべて染むらむ	Along the mountain slopes? [5]

Kanshi:

春來天氣有何力	When spring comes, what strength has the heavenly *qi* (=vital breath)?
細雨濛濛水面縠	Fine drizzle through mist turns water surfaces into wavy gauze.
忽望遲遲暖日中	Suddenly you see on a slowly warming day:
山河物色染深綠[6]	Over mountain and river all things appear dipped in lush green.

Both poems unroll an early spring scene before our eyes: fine rain that produces delicate textile patterns on still water surfaces and mountain slopes that are dyed in fresh green. But if we look a bit closer, the basic similarity dissolves into fundamental differences: the mystery whispered to us in the waka—the inexplicable translation of the wild patterns on the water surface into a continuous carpet of green on the mountain slopes—is explained away in the quatrain with a cosmological vocabulary that fixes the delicately floating scene in the waka into categories of time, space, and seasonal logic. The *kanshi* infuses the self-contained visual snapshot of the waka with causal terminology: the "strength of heaven's *qi*" causes the days to warm and the rain spreads "wavy gauze" on the water and greenery over the slopes. The quatrain also imposes order by means of temporal progression and spatial orientation. The quatrain's emphasis on temporal progression from the coming of spring, to the onset of rain and the slow warming of the days that leads to a greening of all "things" in the cosmos stands in striking contrast to the waka's atemporality. Similarly, the quatrain's emphasis on a particular perspective—we don't know exactly who is doing the "gazing" in the third line, but the reader sees the scene through the eyes of this unnamed spectator—contrasts with the lack of spatial orientation in the waka, where the scene exists in a mode compellingly independent from human perception.

Considered separately, each of the poems is a fine and consistent treatment of early spring. Read together, the intuitive consistency that the reader feels at first crumbles. We are left wondering whether the waka's blurred coexistence of wild patterning with the smooth lack of patterning is more appealing, or whether the quatrain's explanation of the cosmological mechanics of early spring and its effects on a spectator is more attractive, more poetic, more logical.

Which of these approaches to early spring grants the poem and the poet more power over the cosmos? In the next pair of poems it is clearly the kanshi:

---

[5] Translation from Cranston 2006, vol. 2, 557. All translations of poems from the *New Myriad Leaves* are mine unless indicated otherwise.
[6] *Shinsen Man'yōshū* 1.1-2. *Shinsen Man'yōshū chūshaku* I, 35–36.

Waka:

春霞	春霞	Come, spring mist,
網丹張牢	網にはりこめ	Stretch a net around the tree:
花散者	花ちらば	If the blossoms fall,
可移徒	うつろひぬべき	The warbler will be sure to leave—
鸎將駐	鸎とめむ	Keep him here on the bough![7]

Kanshi:

春嶺霞低繡幕張	Mist hanging from spring peaks: embroidered curtains stretched out.
百花零處似燒香	Places where a hundred flowers fall resemble burnt incense.
艷陽氣若有留術	If there were a method to arrest spring's gentle *yang* energies
無惜鸎聲與暮芳[8]	I would not regret the warbler's voice and the season's last fragrance.

Both poems come up with poetic methods to halt the passing of spring. The waka's proposition to stretch out a net to keep the blossoms from falling and, accordingly, to keep the warbler from leaving at the end of spring, is what doctors would call a mere "symptomatic" treatment of the problem. The quatrain, in contrast, is ambitious enough to want to eradicate the root cause of the evil of passing spring. It proposes doing nothing less than stop the workings of the cosmos: arresting further progression of those *yang* energies would keep the warbler and spring fragrances from disappearing. As in the previous pair of poems, we see a use of cosmological reasoning in the quatrain, where the waka argues by visual appearance only—the fanciful, ineffectual season-stopping net.

Cosmologically inspired poetic arguments in the kanshi of the *New Myriad Leaves* can result in outright parodic poems. Consider this pair of "summer" poems that introduces another seasonal bird, the fickle and adulterous cuckoo:

Waka:

人不識沼	人知れぬ	Are your secret loves
思哉繁杵	思ひや繁き	So incessant a yearning?
郭公鳥	ほととぎす	For you cry, cuckoo,
夏之夜緒霜	夏の夜をしも	All the livelong summer night
鳴明濫	鳴き明かすらむ	Till the sky is bright with dawn.

Kanshi:

三夏鳴禽號郭公	The creature singing throughout the summer months? That's called "cuckoo"!
從來狎媚叫房櫳	You have always played tame and seductive, calling at my bedroom window.

---

[7] Translation from Cranston 2006, vol. 1, 558.
[8] *Shinsen Man'yōshū* 1.9-10. *Shinsen Man'yōshū chūshaku* I, p.72.

| 一聲觸處萬恨苦 | Wherever just one of your cries touches: thousands of hateful sufferings— |
| 造化功尤任汝躬⁹ | The workings of creation were entrusted to you entirely! |

Both poems deal with the question of why the cuckoo is crying relentlessly all night long for three full summer months, and both poems turn directly to the bird for an answer. The waka assumes that the bird must have many secret loves, "unknown by people," which force incessant yearnings with all urgency upon the poor bird and, by implication, upon lovers in the summer. Where the waka asks and speculates, the kanshi answers and boasts its cosmological knowledge: That creature singing all the time in summer? That's of course the "cuckoo"! And, as any good Heian poet consulting standard poetic encyclopedias would know, the cuckoo belongs to the "tame" birds that approach humans like the seagulls in the Daoist Master Text *Liezi* who are "tame" toward people who harbor good intentions. Worse, the cuckoo "seduces" humans, inflicting innumerable sufferings on those who are even briefly exposed to its song. Why, then, would it be singing all the time? It faithfully executes the "workings of creation" with which the heavenly "creator" entrusted it and ensures that humans fall in love, have sex, and procreate.

The contrast between the vulgar business of copulation and the bird's devoted service to the creator reminds us of other Heian texts that parody scholarly cosmological vocabulary in the process of pontificating on sex, such as Ōe no Asatsuna's (886–957) "Rhapsody on the Marriage of Husband and Wife" (*Danjo kon'in fu* 男女婚姻賦). Because it is a long "rhapsody" Asatsuna can go into scholarly detail about how exactly the Yin and Yang forces in the cosmos cause juices in different parts of the body to flow and effect the "workings of creation" that ensure human procreation. But the basic conceit of evoking elevated cosmological vocabulary to talk sex is the same. And in the process it relieves the victims of any responsibility for indulging their lust and sexual desire: it's simply nature.

Cosmological concepts pervade the quatrains, whether they describe seasonal change, devise methods to stop seasonal change, or use technical language to talk about procreation, as we saw in the three examples above. In contrast, the waka are conspicuously lacking in a cosmological framework.

Poetic Logic

The direct, synoptic juxtaposition of a waka with a kanshi poem in the *New Myriad Leaves* also brings to sudden light just how differently poetic logic can work in these two genres. Even if deployed to explain the same seasonal phenomenon, the mechanisms are profoundly different. Consider the following couple of poems:

Waka:

蛻蟬之	空蝉の	What is sad
侘敷物者	侘しきものは	About the "empty locust"
夏草之	夏草の	Is that its body

---

⁹ *Shinsen Man'yōshū* 1.83-84. *Shinsen Man'yōshū chūshaku* I, 363–64.

| 露丹懸禮留 | 露にかかれる | Merely depends on the dew |
| 身丹許曾阿里藝禮 | 身にこそありけれ | Of summer grasses |

Kanshi:

蟬人運命惣相同	The fate of the locust and man—isn't it all the same?
含露殉飡暫養躬	Drinking dew and searching for food keeps them alive for a while.
三夏優遊林樹裏	Throughout the three summer months they frolic among the trees of the woods
四時喘息此寰中[10]	Through all the four seasons: their faint breath in the middle of this vast universe.

Both poems reflect on the transience of life through the image of the locust, but the underlying logic differs. The waka does not directly compare human transience to the transience of the locust, but the tone of lament over the transient "self/body" (*mi* 身) of the locust applies by implication to the frailty of human life. In contrast to the waka's use of hidden metaphor, the quatrain opens on a cumbersome simile: "The fate of the locust and man—isn't it all the same?" The overly explicit analogy injects a comic undertone into the next line: we are asked to imagine humans, like locusts, sucking dew off summer grasses and seeking their food in the fields to satisfy their creaturely needs. The last two lines rely again on the idea that humans and locusts are on equal footing as members of the "myriad things" under heaven, sport alongside each other among the trees in the woods and breathe alongside each other in the vast universe. The quatrain's attempt to explicate the waka by spelling out the logical connection between locust life and human life produces an ambivalent message. Although the quatrain still laments the dew-like transience of human life, its frailty is its charm and beauty: roaming in the woods and living through the seasons is as ravishing as it might be lamentable.

In the next pair of poems the different poetic logic of the two poems in describing the same constellation of seasonal phenomena is even more pronounced:

Waka:

雁之聲丹	かりのねに	Since the night is cold
管子纏於砥之	くだまく音の	When thread-spinning insect sounds
夜緒寒美	夜を寒み	Respond to geese voices
蟲之織服	虫の織りきる	I want to borrow that robe
衣緒曾假	衣をぞ借る	Which these insects weave to wear.

Kanshi:

鳴雁鳴蟲一一清	Cries of geese and cries of insects—each so clear.
秋花秋葉班班聲	Sounds come from the patches of autumn flowers and autumn leaves.
誰知兩興無飽足	Who would have known that I can't get enough of these two "stimuli"—autumn sounds and autumn plants!

<hr />

[10] *Shinsen Man'yōshū* 1.67-68. *Shinsen Man'yōshū chūshaku* I, 305.

山室沈吟獨作情[11]　　Absorbed in chanting alone in my mountain cottage, I make my feelings into poems.

Both poems treat a typical autumn topic, the blending of cricket and geese voices on a cooling autumn night. The quatrain adds a visual cue, "autumn flowers and leaves," to the soundscape of crickets and geese and increases the sensory depth of the autumn mood. However, the difference between the poems lies not in the sensory "more" of autumn in the quatrain, but in the poetic "how" of autumn. The waka uses, again, a metaphor to connect the crickets to the human world, but, unlike in the previous waka the metaphor is made flesh and thread: shivering in autumn's new coolness, the poet wants to borrow the robe that the crickets spin for themselves.

In the waka cricket and human worlds overlap, because the robe that the crickets presumably spin while chirping protects the poet against the cold. But the quatrain is structured around the construction of two parallel worlds that resonate with each other, but do not overlap. Everything, except for the poet's loneliness and his mountain cottage, comes in double number: the cries of geese and of insects; the autumn flowers and autumn leaves, in short the "two stimuli" of which the poet cannot get enough. The concept of "stimulus" here reveals the poetic logic at work: one of the rhetorical devices from the poetics of the *Classic of Poetry*, "stimulus" (Ch. *xing*, J. *kyō* 興) describes the mutual resonance between events in nature and the human realm. In the separate worlds of crickets and humans each spins what befits his species: the crickets spin robes, while humans produce poetry in response to the stimulus from nature.

Poets in *waka* and *kanshi*

If the poetic logic of most waka in the *New Myriad Leaves* eliminates the division between nature and the human world and merges them through metaphors that naturalize the human world just as much as they humanize the natural world, the quatrains in the *New Myriad Leaves* uphold the boundaries between nature and the human world and insist on their different workings, even if they are closely connected through a logic of mutual resonance and analogy. This has profound implications for how the composition of poetry, a distinctly man-made product, can be represented in poems. Many of the quatrains in the *New Myriad Leaves* put the poet into the scene of his own poem and celebrate the chanting and composing of poetry. Waka are obviously poems, but none of the waka in the *New Myriad Leaves* features a poet in the act of producing or reciting poetry. Consider the following example:

Waka:

夏之夜之	夏の夜の	Hardly have you gone to bed
臥歟砥為禮者	臥すかとすれば	On a summer night
郭公	ほととぎす	When brightening dawn comes
鳴人音丹	鳴く一声に	With one cry
明留篠之目	明くるしののめ	Of a singing cuckoo.

---

[11] *Shinsen Man'yōshū* 1.115-16. *Shinsen Man'yōshū chūshaku* II, 117.

Kanshi:

日長夜短懶晨興	When days are long and nights short I'm weary to get up in the morning
夏漏遲明聽郭公	And hear the cuckoo when the summer water clock announces daybreak.
嘯取詞人偷走筆	Whistling along, the poet furtively lets his brush roam:
文章氣味與春同[12]	the flavor of his fine piece becomes one with spring.

Both poems describe an early morning scene in summer and note the paradox of summer: although night and day would still each have six double-hours according to the Japanese system of counting hours relative to the season, not in absolute measure, the nights are short and the days long. The paradox is highlighted in the quatrain, which refers to the time-measurement device of a "water-clock." In the quatrain after the first touch of morning sulkiness the poet comes into his own: "whistling along," he is inspired to take his brush and write and, against all odds, a "fine piece" of writing emerges that is "one with spring," the season considered poetically much more productive. Not only does the poet of the quatrain describe his activity as a poet, which we do not see in any waka of the same collection. What is more, the summer-weary poet writes *against* nature and goes on to happily produce in plain summer a piece with the flavor of "spring."

True, the *Kokinshū* Prefaces will make a bold and successful attempt to naturalize poetry completely, by declaring that waka is a specifically human "song," which, just like the "songs" of birds and other animals, emerges spontaneously in response to changing seasonal beauty. The celebration of the poet as a creator of human culture who even has the power to rewrite the seasons that we see in the kanshi is diametrically opposed to the waka's emphasis on poetry as a natural response in harmony with the seasons.

Let us look at another example of the suggestive contrast between the lack of poetic agency in the waka and the assertion of it in the Sino-Japanese quatrains of the *New Myriad Leaves*:

Waka:

日夕芝丹	ひぐらしに	Because I passed through
秋之野山緒	秋の野山を	Autumn's fields and mountains
別來者	わけくれば	From dawn til dusk
不意沼	心にもあらぬ	I have suddenly dressed in brocade
錦緒曾服	錦をぞきる	Without intending to.

Kanshi:

終日遊人入野山	A traveler, I went through fields and mountains all day:
紛紛葉錦衣戔戔	My robe gleaming with patches of foliage's brocade,

---

[12] *Shinsen Man'yōshū* I.51-52. *Shinsen Man'yōshū chūshaku* I, 243.

登峯望壑回眸切	I climbed peaks, looked closely at ravines below with my wandering eyes
石硯濡毫樂萬端[13]	And then moistened my ink on the stone, delving into myriad modes of pleasure.

The first half of the quatrain roughly covers the content of the waka: the traveler seems clothed in brocade after wandering through the autumn landscape all day and picking up foliage that sticks to his robes along the way. Waka and kanshi coincide in the charm of the spontaneous, the joy over unexpected effects: the waka poet unintentionally gathers a robe of foliage brocade and the kanshi poet ends up with poems. A good number of manuscripts have the character *kyō* 興 instead of the word *tanoshimi* 楽しみ, thus meaning "myriad modes of stimuli" instead of "myriad modes of pleasure." Thus, while the waka poet's heart is empty of intentions, the kanshi poet's heart is too full of them: it's so full that it first drives the poet to let his "eyes wander" over the compelling panorama from above, which is paralleled by a "wandering" of the moistened brush that allows for myriad pleasures.

Again, writing in response to the "stimuli" that present themselves in the gorgeous vista makes the line sound a bit more technical, as it uses the trope from the poetics of the *Classic of Poetry*. The quatrain does not mention the word "intention" (*kokorozashi* 志), which is where poems start according to the psychology of composition described in the "Great Preface" to the classic. But the waka indirectly does, when emphasizing that the traveler "didn't have it in his heart" (*kokoro ni mo aranu*) to get dressed in the brocade of autumn foliage. Although this is the typical place where "intentions" that ultimately result in the composition of kanshi reside, the turn of phrase is rarely used in waka. Curiously, the waka rejects a poetics of intention by mentioning their absence in the heart, whereas in the analogous place the kanshi fails to mention intentions to imply their presence, as the poet pours them into his poems. Once we read the unusual formulation *kokoro ni aranu* in conjunction with the kanshi, the formulation makes a perfect contrastive match with the conventional poetic psychology on which the kanshi relies. This is one of the most suggestive examples of the difference between waka and kanshi in the *New Myriad Leaves*: the first downplays, the later elevates the poet's subjective agency within the poems.

On the example of cosmology, poetic logic, and the agency of the poet in the poem we have shown in three instances how kanshi and waka function differently. We also observed in detail how the juxtaposition of the two poems brings these differences to light in the first place and forces the reader to reconsider her understanding of the two separate poems in mutual illumination and contrast. For now we have seen enough of the "synoptic machine" at work in the *New Myriad Leaves* to proceed to our second case study of a synoptic text.

---

[13] *Shinsen Man'yōshū* I: 111-12. *Shinsen Man'yōshū chūshaku* II, 103.

3. Second Case Study: Synoptic Lives in Plutarch

When Plutarch wrote his *Parallel Lives* (dating from ca. 96–120 CE) Rome had ruled Greece for about two and a half centuries. As a Roman subject of the Greek province of Achaea, he found himself impelled to ask questions such as why Rome's political fortunes had so brilliantly risen and forced Greece under Roman rule. Plutarch was an essayist, historian, philosopher, and local politician from Chaironeia, a little town in Boeotia close to Delphi, at whose sanctuary he seems to have served as a priest. As part of the Greek elite living under Roman imperial rule, he undertook educational travels to Athens, Egypt, and repeatedly to Rome, where he apparently spent his time giving lectures and completing political missions. He was well-connected with the Roman officials ruling Greece and their friends in Rome; in recognition of his services Emperor Hadrian possibly made him procurator of the province of Achaea late in life.[14]

Plutarch was voracious in his reading and writing tastes. The *Lives* are his most famous work together with the *Moralia,* which constitute the most important surviving corpus of philosophical dialogues from antiquity after Plato. The *Lives* include twenty-two pairs (including one double pair) of biographies of prominent Greek and Roman leaders, ranging from the legendary beginnings to the Hellenistic and late Republican Periods and including such varied figures as Theseus, Pericles, and Alexander on the Greek side, and Romulus, Caesar, and Cicero on the Roman side.

The *Lives* are a bewildering project, painting a vast mural of Greek and Roman history through the relentlessly detailed coupled biographies of its heroes.[15] Biographies of famous statesmen, generals, philosophers, or poets were a well-established Hellenistic genre, but nobody before Plutarch had used it as a tool for panoramic historiography through the means of biography. Also, only Plutarch devised his project in synoptic fashion, welding the histories of two countries into sets of paired biographies. Before Plutarch, the Roman Republican author Nepos (ca. 99–24 BCE) had written biographies of Roman politicians and foreign nations, but he did not group them in diptychs as Plutarch did. Plutarch's expansive synoptic project of the *Lives* was unprecedented and was to remain unique.

While not moralistic, Plutarch was fascinated by human moral psychology; he was widely read, though not an antiquarian, and was sensitive to the complex plight of Greeks under Roman rule. These qualities made him a popular writer to whom people turned for moral guidance and edification as well as for entertainment and suspense. Since the nineteenth century, when Plutarch's fortunes as an entertaining classical writer declined, scholars have undertaken extensive source criticism of his work, examining what plot elements he took from which sources and with what degree of reliability. Much less attention has been devoted to questions about

---

[14] For a vibrant treatment of Plutarch's life and work in the context of his time see Lamberton 2001.
[15] For an overview of Plutarch's programmatic statements about his enterprise see Duff 1999, 13–51. On the complex issues of Plutarch's construction of "Greek" and "Roman" identities in the *Lives* see Duff, "The Politics of Parallelism," 287–309. On the relation of Plutarch and his work to Rome more generally see C. P. Jones, *Plutarch and Rome* (Oxford: Clarendon Press, 1971).

his project as a whole, such as why and to what effect he used a synoptic format that transformed what could have become a random string of biographies into a complex historical canvas of the Greco-Roman cultural constellation.

The Rhetoric of Plutarch's *synkriseis*

To most of his diptychs Plutarch appends a short "comparison" (*synkrisis*) that confronts the protagonists in a final fictional showdown, picking up specific thematic strands to compare the two characters. As Christopher Pelling has shown, even the protagonists' deaths are carefully balanced against each other and urge us to understand that Plutarch's "artistic unit is not the individual *Life*, it is the pair."[16]

The synkrisis typically opens on a *caesura*, a moment where Plutarch states that this is what he found in sources about his protagonists and that he will now proceed to compare and contrast their precise points of difference and similarity. The synkrisis of Lycurgus, the Spartan law-giver and king, and Numa Pompilius, Rome's second king, is a good example to show how the syncritic sections are framed:

> Now that we have recounted the lives of Numa and Lycurgus, and both lie clearly before us, we must attempt, even though the task be difficult, to assemble and put together their points of difference. For their points of likeness are obvious from their careers: their wise moderation, their piety, their talent for governing and educating, and their both deriving their laws from a divine source. But each also performed noble deeds peculiar to himself. To begin with, Numa accepted, but Lycurgus resigned a kingdom. One got it without asking for it, the other had it and gave it up.[17]

To garner sympathy from the audience, Plutarch emphasizes the difficulty of his task. He then adopts a very visual approach to comparison: because the biographies "lie clearly before us," the points of likeness are "obvious" to everybody's eyes, as are the points of difference, which Plutarch likes to deliver in the fashion of logical opposites: "Numa accepted, but Lycurgus resigned a kingdom." As the synkrisis proceeds, Plutarch helps each protagonist score points. Plutarch has little interest in any of the candidates winning the day, but places the reader into the role of ultimate judge. The careful musing on issues of moral judgment is more important than easy declarations of victory. Tim Duff makes this point for Plutarch's works in general: "This tendency to use synkrisis to provoke thought and raise questions is particularly and distinctively Plutarchan. He often uses synkrisis not

---

[16] Pelling 1997, 228. See also the excellent article Lamberton 1997. Tim Duff shows through extensive case studies how important it is to read the biographies as pairs. For his reflections on synkrisis in the *Lives* see Duff 1999, 243–286. For more recent scholarship that discusses the dynamic of pairing see ibid., 250, Fn. 25.

[17] Plutarch, *Lycurgus and Numa* 1.1-2. English translations are from Perrin 1928. Perrin I, 383–85. Ἀλλ' ἐπεὶ τὸν Νομᾶ καὶ Λυκούργου διεληλύθαμεν βίον, ἐκκειμένων ἀμφοῖν, εἰ καὶ χαλεπὸν ἔργον, οὐκ ἀποκνητέον συναγαγεῖν τὰς διαφοράς. αἱ μὲν γὰρ κοινότητες ἐπιφαίνονται ταῖς πράξεσιν, οἷον ἡ σωφροσύνη τῶν ἀνδρῶν, ἡ εὐσέβεια, τὸ πολιτικόν, τὸ παιδευτικόν, τὸ μίαν ἀρχὴν παρὰ τῶν θεῶν ἀμφοτέρους λαβεῖν τῆς νομοθεσίας· τῶν δὲ ἰδίᾳ ἑκατέρου καλῶν πρῶτόν ἐστι Νομᾶ μὲν ἡ παράληψις τῆς βασιλείας, Λυκούργῳ δὲ ἡ παράδοσις. ὁ μὲν γὰρ οὐκ αἰτῶν ἔλαβεν, ὁ δὲ ἔχων ἀπέδωκε.

to demonstrate the superiority of one side of the equation over the other, but rather to explore the issues raised as a whole."[18]

The deployment of synkrisis to explore general questions of human character, ethical principle, and pragmatic politics shows us Plutarch the practical thinker, a philosopher in a minor mode. What about synkrisis and Plutarch the biographer and historian? Whereas the syncritic evaluations of each pair are short, the biographies are long, meandering affairs studded with plot detail whose significance is not always apparent. Does Plutarch take the syncritic texts as an opportunity to bring a higher purpose to each life and each diptych of lives, and to satisfy the reader's desire for closure?

Often Plutarch succeeds in retracing each character with broader strokes and highlighting each pair's traits effectively by contrast. But the desire for summary balance can also give way to unexpected distortions. Take for example the synkrisis for Theseus and Romulus. As we will discuss below, Theseus, king of Athens and the slayer of the Minotaur, is matched with Romulus, the founder of Rome. In his biography Theseus performs Herculean tasks for the benefit of the people and frees them from the yoke of Cretan vassalage. But in the synkrisis Plutarch suddenly lashes out against him as a womanizer, even a vile rapist:

> [T]he transgressions of Theseus in his rapes of women admit of no plausible excuse. This is true, first, because there were so many; for he carried off Ariadne, Antiope, Anaxo of Troezen, and last Helen, when he was past his prime and she had not reached her prime, but was an unripe child, while he was already of an age too great for even lawful wedlock. It is true, secondly, because of the reason for them... But one may suspect that these deeds of his were done in lustful wantonness. Romulus, on the other hand, in the first place, although he carried off nearly eight hundred women, took them not all to wife, but only one, as they say, Hersilia, and distributed the rest among the best of the citizens. And in the second place, by the subsequent honour, love, and righteous treatment given to these women, he made it clear that his deed of violence and injustice was a most honourable achievement, and one most adapted to promote political partnership. In this way he intermixed and blended the two peoples with one another, and supplied his state with a flowing fountain of strength and good will for the time to come. And to the modesty, tenderness, and stability which he imparted to the marriage relation time is witness. For in two hundred and thirty years no man ventured to leave his wife, nor any woman her husband.[19]

---

[18] Duff 1999, 245.
[19] Plutarch, *Theseus and Romulus* 6.1-3. Perrin I, 197–99. Καὶ μὴν τὰ περὶ τὰς ἁρπαγὰς τῶν γυναικῶν ἡμαρτημένα Θησεῖ μὲν εὐσχήμονος ἐνδεᾶ προφάσεως γέγονε. πρῶτον μὲν ὅτι πολλάκις· ἥρπασε γὰρ Ἀριάδνην καὶ Ἀντιόπην καὶ Ἀναξὼ τὴν Τροιζηνίαν, ἐπὶ πάσαις δὲ τὴν Ἑλένην, παρηκμακὼς οὐκ ἀκμάζουσαν, ἀλλὰ νηπίαν καὶ ἄωρον αὐτὸς ὥραν ἔχων ἤδη γάμων πεπαῦσθαι καὶ νομίμων· ἔπειτα διὰ τὴν αἰτίαν· ... ἀλλὰ ταῦτα μὲν ὑποψίαν ἔχει πρὸς ὕβριν καὶ καθ᾽ ἡδονὴν πεπρᾶχθαι. Ῥωμύλος δὲ πρῶτον μὲν ὀκτακοσίων ὀλίγον ἀριθμῷ δεούσας ἁρπάσας, οὐ πάσας, ἀλλὰ μίαν, ὥς φασιν, Ἑρσιλίαν ἔλαβε, τὰς δ᾽ ἄλλας διένειμε τοῖς ἀγαθοῖς τῶν πολιτῶν· ἔπειτα τῇ μετὰ ταῦτα τιμῇ καὶ ἀγαπήσει καὶ δικαιοσύνῃ περὶ τὰς γυναῖκας ἀπέδειξε τὴν βίαν ἐκείνην καὶ τὴν ἀδικίαν κάλλιστον ἔργον καὶ πολιτικώτατον εἰς κοινωνίαν γενομένην. οὕτω συνέμιξεν ἀλλήλοις καὶ συνέπηξε τὰ γένη, καὶ παρέσχε πηγὴν τῆς εἰς αὖθις εὐνοίας καὶ δυνάμεως τοῖς πράγμασιν. αἰδοῦς δὲ καὶ φιλίας καὶ βεβαιότητος, ἣν εἰργάσατο περὶ τοὺς γάμους, ὁ χρόνος ἐστὶ μάρτυς. ἐν γὰρ ἔτεσι τριάκοντα καὶ διακοσίοις οὔτ᾽ ἀνὴρ ἐτόλμησε γυναικὸς οὔτε γυνὴ κοινωνίαν ἀνδρὸς ἐγκαταλιπεῖν.

Plutarch pits bad rape against good rape: We should despise Theseus for his promiscuity and sexual transgressions; but we should admire Romulus's "rape of the Sabines," when Romulus and his men—all bachelors in need of wives—abducted women of the indigenous Sabine tribe to secure the survival of the fledgling polity of Rome. This was an act of wise marriage politics, which resulted in the establishment of a Latin-Sabine dual kingship that masked subjugation and resonated with Republican ideas of dual structures of government. Plutarch's defense of the "rape" is so overblown, Romulus's sexual virtue is so disproportionately praised—his rape is virtuously "monogamous" since he only took Hersilia for himself—and Theseus's selfish lust is so overstated that we might wonder whether the entire episode about Theseus's promiscuity is motivated by Plutarch's desire to justify Romulus's rape of the Sabines by contrast. Would Plutarch otherwise have discussed Theseus's romantic escapades at such length and in such a light? Is the odd black-and-white diptych of Theseus's and Romulus's sexual and political ambitions an effect of the "synoptic machine"? There is no way to know for sure, but this example shows that the framework of synkrisis could add complex new brushstrokes to a protagonist's biography and generate more questions about what the juxtaposition of two lives means to say about these two individuals separately and in conjunction.

Entangled Beginnings: Rome and Athens in the Biographies of Romulus and Theseus

Plutarch shows how both Greek and Roman lives are driven by the same forces: virtue and vice, ambition, thirst for honor and reputation, wisdom and righteousness or foolishness and lack of cultivation. This shared moral vocabulary, though ultimately rooted in classical Greek philosophy, applies to all lives, and ethnicity is independent of moral capacity. Sometimes a Roman is more "civilized" and "Greek" than a reckless individual who happens to be ethnically Greek. It is of course not surprising that Plutarch considered moral values universal, just as Plato and other classical Greek philosophers had claimed. However, Plutarch is also aware of a historical dimension of morality and seems at times unsure whether to ascribe it to nature or nurture, innate talent or education.

Despite the shared moral psychology that holds for Greeks and Romans alike, Plutarch sketches a different political cosmology in the lives of the foundational figures he chooses to represent Greece and Rome: Theseus and Romulus. His pride as a historian of events, not a poet of myths, makes him self-conscious about his decision to include the legendary past into the purview of historical biography, as he explains to his Roman friend, the consul Socius Senecio:

> Just as geographers, O Socius Senecio, crowd on to the outer edges of their maps the parts of the earth which elude their knowledge, with explanatory notes that "What lies beyond is sandy desert without water and full of wild beasts," or "blind marsh," or "Scythian cold," or "frozen sea," so in the writing of my *Parallel Lives*, now that I have traversed those periods of time which are accessible to probable reasoning and which afford basis for a history dealing with facts, I might well say of the earlier periods: "What lies beyond is full of marvels and unreality,

and a land of poets and fabulists, of doubt and obscurity." But after publishing my account of Lycurgus the lawgiver and Numa the king, I thought I might not unreasonably go back still farther to Romulus, now that my history had brought me near his times...May I therefore succeed in purifying Fable (*mythôdes*), making her submit to reason (*logos*) and take on the semblance of History (*historia*). But where she obstinately disdains to make herself credible, and refuses to admit any element of probability, I shall pray for kindly readers, and such as receive with indulgence the tales of antiquity.[20]

What could be a safer start for a historian venturing into the dangerous waters of the mythic past than a prayer to the reader promising that all will be fine, if myth only "makes herself credible"? Plutarch promises to draw History out of Myth with the rope of Reason. After writing the biographies of Lycurgus and Numa Pompilius, only slightly less legendary than Romulus, Plutarch felt encouraged to go back all the way to the beginnings of Rome. Romulus was in many ways an ideal starting point for his project: He founded the city that became synonymous with the empire under which Plutarch lived. Plutarch's sprawling ruminations on various etymologies of "Rome" start with the name of "Romulus," and only then head off in various other directions. Intriguingly, Plutarch does not discuss the etymology of "Athens." And here emerges the most interesting paradox in Plutarch's sketch of the different political cosmology of Greece and Rome through the figures of Theseus and Romulus: On the one hand, Plutarch starts his story from Romulus, not Theseus, and shows Rome in possession of a charismatic mandate that began with the rule of Romulus. On the other hand, Rome is portrayed as a belated newcomer to the history of civilizations: Plutarch is careful to highlight Greece's connection to old world civilizations such as Crete.

Let us look in more detail at this ambivalence of cultural destiny. The clearest indication that Plutarch wants to show Rome as the possessor of a charismatic mandate and Athens as a place of factional strife and discontinuity is the radically different portrayal of Theseus's and Romulus's deaths. Theseus dies ignominiously and has to wait until the fifth century BCE to be rehabilitated, while Romulus, in accord with the ideology of the imperial cult of Plutarch's own times, ascends to heaven in a glorious apotheosis. Theseus's trajectory is dubious: he leaves Athens to its own devices for a love conquest, so that Menestheus, another

---

[20] Plutarch, *Theseus* 1.1-3. Perrin I, 3–5. ὥσπερ ἐν ταῖς γεωγραφίαις, ὦ Σόσσιε Σενεκίων, οἱ ἱστορικοὶ τὰ διαφεύγοντα τὴν γνῶσιν αὐτῶν τοῖς ἐσχάτοις μέρεσι τῶν πινάκων πιεζοῦντες, αἰτίας παραγράφουσιν ὅτι "τὰ δ' ἐπέκεινα θῖνες ἄνυδροι καὶ θηριώδεις" ἢ "πηλὸς ἀϊδνὴς" ἢ "Σκυθικὸν κρύος" ἢ "πέλαγος πεπηγός," οὕτως ἐμοὶ περὶ τὴν τῶν βίων τῶν παραλλήλων γραφήν, τὸν ἐφικτὸν εἰκότι λόγῳ καὶ βάσιμον ἱστορίᾳ πραγμάτων ἐχομένῃ χρόνον διελθόντι, περὶ τῶν ἀνωτέρω καλῶς εἶχεν εἰπεῖν· "τὰ δ' ἐπέκεινα τερατώδη καὶ τραγικὰ ποιηταὶ καὶ μυθογράφοι νέμονται, καὶ οὐκέτ' ἔχει πίστιν οὐδὲ σαφήνειαν." ἐπεὶ δὲ τὸν περὶ Λυκούργου τοῦ νομοθέτου καὶ Νομᾶ τοῦ βασιλέως λόγον ἐκδόντες, ἐδοκοῦμεν οὐκ ἂν ἀλόγως τῷ Ῥωμύλῳ προσαναβῆναι, πλησίον τῶν χρόνων αὐτοῦ τῇ ἱστορίᾳ γεγονότες,...εἴη μὲν οὖν ἡμῖν ἐκκαθαιρόμενον λόγῳ τὸ μυθῶδες ὑπακοῦσαι καὶ λαβεῖν ἱστορίας ὄψιν, ὅπου δ' ἂν αὐθαδῶς τοῦ πιθανοῦ περιφρονῇ καὶ μὴ δέχηται τὴν πρὸς τὸ εἰκὸς μῖξιν, εὐγνωμόνων ἀκροατῶν δεησόμεθα καὶ πράως τὴν ἀρχαιολογίαν προσδεχομένων.

descendant of Athens' older king Erechtheus, takes over the kingdom. Later he barely escapes execution with Hercules's help. When he leaves Athens for good he curses the Athenians, who have come to hate him, in a place thereafter called "Araterion" or "Place of Cursing." He dies a refugee on the island of Scyros, where his family had ancestral estates. That it remains unclear whether the king of Scyros pushed Theseus down the cliffs or he fell by chance makes his end only more shameful. Theseus's death goes unnoticed and only after Menestheus's death do Theseus's sons recover rule over Athens.

Plutarch draws a partial parallel to how Romulus because of his increasingly arrogant and autocratic behavior lost popular footing in Rome toward the end of his life. But we need to compare the description of Romulus's death with Theseus's dubious and insignificant end to appreciate the difference between these two heroes. Just at the moment when Romulus has disappeared and evil rumors start spreading that some patricians tried to cover up their murder of Romulus by telling the populace he had risen to heaven, a reliable witness bursts on the scene with happy tidings:

> At this pass, then, it is said that one of the patricians, a man of noblest birth, and of the most reputable character, a trusted and intimate friend also of Romulus himself, and one of the colonists from Alba, Julius Proculus by name, went into the forum and solemnly swore by the most sacred emblems before all the people that, as he was traveling on the road, he had seen Romulus coming to meet him, fair and stately to the eye as never before, and arrayed in bright and shining armour. He himself, then, affrighted at the sight, had said: "O king, what possessed thee, or what purpose hadst thou, that thou hast left us patricians a prey to unjust and wicked accusations, and the whole city sorrowing without end at the loss of its father?" Whereupon Romulus had replied: "It was the pleasure of the gods, O Proculus, from whom I came, that I should be with mankind only a short time, and that after founding a city destined to be the greatest on earth for empire and glory, I should dwell again in heaven. So farewell, and tell the Romans that if they practice self-restraint, and add to it valour, they will reach the utmost heights of human power. And I will be your propitious deity, Quirinus." These things seemed to the Romans worthy of belief, from the character of the man who related them, and from the oath which he had taken; moreover, some influence from heaven also, akin to inspiration, laid hold upon their emotions, for no man contradicted Proculus, but all put aside suspicion and calumny and prayed to Quirinus, and honoured him as a god.[21]

---

[21] Plutarch, *Romulus* 28.1-3. Perrin I, 177–79. Οὕτως οὖν ἄνδρα τῶν πατρικίων γένει πρῶτον, ἤθει τε δοκιμώτατον, αὐτῷ τε Ῥωμύλῳ πιστὸν καὶ συνήθη, τῶν ἀπ᾽ Ἄλβης ἐποίκων, Ἰούλιον Πρόκλον, εἰς ἀγορὰν προελθόντα καὶ τῶν ἁγιωτάτων ἔνορκον ἱερῶν ἁψάμενον εἰπεῖν ἐν πᾶσιν ὡς ὁδὸν αὐτῷ βαδίζοντι Ῥωμύλος ἐξ ἐναντίας προσιὼν φανείη, καλὸς μὲν ὀφθῆναι καὶ μέγας, ὡς οὔποτε πρόσθεν, ὅπλοις δὲ λαμπροῖς καὶ φλέγουσι κεκοσμημένος. αὐτὸς μὲν οὖν ἐκπλαγεὶς πρὸς τὴν ὄψιν "ὦ βασιλεῦ," φάναι, "τί δὴ παθὼν ἢ διανοηθεὶς ἡμᾶς μὲν ἐν αἰτίαις ἀδίκοις καὶ πονηραῖς, πᾶσαν δὲ τὴν πόλιν ὀρφανὴν ἐν μυρίῳ πένθει προλέλοιπας;" ἐκεῖνον δ᾽ ἀποκρίνασθαι. "θεοῖς ἔδοξεν, ὦ Πρόκλε, τοσοῦτον ἡμᾶς γενέσθαι μετ᾽ ἀνθρώπων χρόνον, ἐκεῖθεν ὄντας, καὶ πόλιν ἐπ᾽ ἀρχῇ καὶ δόξῃ μεγίστῃ κτίσαντας αὖθις οἰκεῖν οὐρανόν. καὶ φράζε Ῥωμαίοις ὅτι σωφροσύνην μετ᾽ ἀνδρείας ἀσκοῦντες ἐπὶ πλεῖστον ἀνθρωπίνης ἀφίξονται δυνάμεως. ἐγὼ δὲ ὑμῖν εὐμενὴς ἔσομαι δαίμων Κυρῖνος. " ταῦτα πιστὰ μὲν εἶναι τοῖς Ῥωμαίοις ἐδόκει διὰ τὸν τρόπον τοῦ λέγοντος καὶ διὰ τὸν ὅρκον· οὐ μὴν ἀλλὰ καὶ δαιμόνιόν τι συνεφάψασθαι πάθος ὅμοιον ἐνθουσιασμῷ· μηδένα γὰρ ἀντειπεῖν, ἀλλὰ πᾶσαν ὑπόνοιαν καὶ διαβολὴν ἀφέντας εὔχεσθαι Κυρίνῳ καὶ θεοκλυτεῖν ἐκεῖνον.

Plutarch goes on to ridicule other tales of miraculous disappearances of people. Yet, as with his play in the opening of Theseus's biography with truth and fiction, history and myth, maps and their wondrous peripheries, Plutarch wants us to both believe and doubt that Romulus became the god Quirinus.

Although Theseus's ignominious death contrasts with Romulus's imperial apotheosis, Plutarch later introduces an interesting parallel to Romulus's miraculous transformation into Quirinus, which explains a bit better why Plutarch paired Romulus with Theseus: in a vision Theseus appears to the Greek soldiers fighting the Persians at Marathon in 490 BCE and urges them on to victory. When the oracle of Delphi advises the Athenians to search for Theseus's gravesite, they indeed find "a coffin of a man of extraordinary size, a bronze spear lying by its side, and a sword" (*Theseus* 36.2. Perrin I, 85). In the 470s BCE Theseus's remains are brought to Athens and enshrined amid solemn processions and sacrifices. The physical installment of Theseus's body in fifth-century Athens constitutes a partial parallel to Romulus's death and apotheosis with the difference that Romulus's body disappears whereas Theseus's finally reappears. Plutarch's account of Theseus's rehabilitation holds an important key to why Plutarch chose Theseus to match his biography of Romulus. In this way Theseus becomes a hero not of mythical, but classical Athens, of the Athens that was to become the center of Greek civilization and democracy. That Plutarch refers to the concept of "democracy" to describe Theseus's rule makes it all the clearer that it was the future of Rome and Athens that made Romulus and Theseus into a fitting pair for Plutarch.

Although Plutarch celebrates Rome and the Roman mandate to rule the world, he also shows it as a newcomer to the history of civilizations, emphasizing by contrast Greece's mythical and historical depth. This is evident, first, in the family pedigree of our heroes: both Theseus and Romulus are of divine parentage— offsprings of Poseidon and Venus, respectively—but Romulus is a nobody who rises to extraordinary heights, while, as a blood relative of Hercules, Theseus is a younger member of the world of Greek gods and demigods.

Second, we see it play out in the history of their respective cities. As Plutarch observes, "of the world's two most illustrious cities…Rome and Athens, Romulus founded the one, and Theseus made a metropolis of the other." (*Theseus* 2.1. Perrin I, 5). Theseus's mortal father Aegeus, who by chance impregnates Aethra, the daughter of the king of Troezen, on his way to Athens, stood in a longer line of kings of Athens, which had been ruled by descendants of Cecrops and Erechtheus. When Theseus hears from his mother that the king of Athens is his father, he goes to claim the throne. He does not need to found a city as did Romulus. Pairing Theseus with Romulus thus gave Greece, represented by Athens, a much greater, even if tumultuous, historical depth than Rome.

Third, Plutarch's choice of role model for our protagonists allows Greece to participate in a political cosmology of mythical charisma that Rome simply lacks. Plutarch shows at excessive length how Theseus's actions are driven by the example of Hercules.[22] Theseus chooses the dangerous land road to Athens when claiming

---

[22] David Larmour notes in "Plutarch's Compositional Methods in the Theseus and Romulus," that "[t]he role of Heracles in the *Theseus* is large and important, so much so that it almost causes

the throne, which gives him the opportunity to prove himself in overcoming great challenges in the fashion of his admired hero:

> [He], as it would seem, had long since been secretly fired by the glorious valour of Heracles, and made the greatest account of that hero, and was a most eager listener to those who told what manner of man he was, and above all to those who had seen him and been present at some deed or speech of his…Theseus admired the valour of Heracles, until by night his dreams were of the hero's achievements, and by day his ardour led him along and spurred him on in his purpose to achieve the like.[23]

It is not so much that with his portrayal of Theseus as a second Hercules Plutarch leaves the safe haven of history for myth. Rather, the connection with Hercules allows Plutarch to show Theseus as a participant in an older, semi-divine political cosmology that adds to his charisma as a political leader.

A last example of how eager Plutarch is to endow Greece with historical age and mythical charisma is the account of Theseus's liberation of Athens from vassalage to Crete. When tribute collectors from Crete come to collect the seven young men and girls whom the Athenians had been sending to Crete to atone for the killing of a Cretan envoy, Theseus decides to go himself and ends up killing the Minotaur with the help of Minos's daughter Ariadne, who lends him the famed thread to navigate the treacherous labyrinth. Plutarch gives various accounts of this famous episode, but one point is clear: Plutarch defends the older civilization of Crete against the poets of Athens who have represented it merely as an Oriental oppressor; Athens should be proud to have been subservient to an older civilization with a "language and literature":

> And verily it seems to be a grievous thing for a man to be at enmity with a city which has a language and a literature. For Minos was always abused and reviled in the Attic theatres, and it did not avail him either that Hesiod called him "most royal," or that Homer styled him "a confidant of Zeus," but the tragic poets prevailed, and from platform and stage showered obloquy down upon him, as a man of cruelty and violence. And yet they say that Minos was a king and lawgiver, and that Rhadamanthus was a judge under him, and a guardian of the principles of justice defined by him.[24]

Whether in enmity or peace, Greece is woven into a fabric of older civilizations that had literature, laws, and judges long before Rome. To add a last layer of

---

an artistic imbalance" (p. 363). He shows how Plutarch tries to counterbalance this asymmetry by bringing in references to Hercules in Romulus's biography, for example the tradition that Roma was the daughter of Telephus, the son of Hercules. I would argue that, despite these sparse attempts to redress the balance between the two protagonists, Plutarch uses Hercules also to distinguish Theseus from Romulus, Greece from Rome and to show Theseus as member of an old world of mythical rule, in contrast to Romulus's and Rome's entrance on the stage of the *realpolitik* of history.

[23] Plutarch, *Theseus* 6.6-7. Perrin I, 15–17. τὸν δὲ πάλαι μέν, ὡς ἔοικε, λεληθότως διέκαιεν ἡ δόξα τῆς Ἡρακλέους ἀρετῆς, καὶ πλεῖστον ἐκείνου λόγον εἶχε, καὶ προθυμότατος ἀκροατὴς ἐγίνετο τῶν διηγουμένων ἐκεῖνον οἷος εἴη, μάλιστα δὲ τῶν αὐτὸν ἑωρακότων καὶ πράττοντι καὶ λέγοντι προστετυχηκότων … τοῦ Ἡρακλέους θαυμάζοντι τὴν ἀρετήν, καὶ νύκτωρ ὄνειρος ἦσαν αἱ πράξεις, καὶ μεθ᾽ ἡμέραν ἐξῆγεν αὐτὸν ὁ ζῆλος καὶ ἀνηρέθιζε ταὐτὰ πράττειν διανοούμενον.

[24] Plutarch, *Theseus* 16.2-3. Perrin I, 31–33. ἔοικε γὰρ ὄντως χαλεπὸν εἶναι φωνὴν ἐχούσῃ πόλει καὶ μοῦσαν ἀπεχθάνεσθαι. καὶ γὰρ ὁ Μίνως ἀεὶ διετέλει κακῶς ἀκούων καὶ λοιδορούμενος ἐν τοῖς Ἀττικοῖς θεάτροις, καὶ οὔτε Ἡσίοδος αὐτὸν ὤνησε "βασιλεύτατον" οὔτε Ὅμηρος "ὀαριστὴν"

complexity, we should note that Crete, from a synchronic perspective, could also be seen as a remote precedent for the contemporary Roman domination of Greece Plutarch was witnessing in his own times.

Our discussion of the pairing of Romulus and Theseus has highlighted only a few of the ambivalent parallels and contrasts around which Plutarch builds the lives of his two heroes. Things get yet more complicated when we take into account that Plutarch wrote his diptych of Romulus and Theseus after completing the paired biographies of Numa Pompilius, successor of Romulus and the second of the seven kings who ruled Rome before the foundation of the Republic in 509 BCE, and Lycurgus, the notorious Spartan lawgiver and founder of Spartan political institutions.

Double Beginnings: Romulus and Theseus in the Light of Numa Pompilius and Lycurgus

Embarking on reading two pairs of two heroes as a set of two diptychs takes us into a higher gear of the "synoptic machine" and closer to the limits of what the device of synoptic juxtaposition can meaningfully say about both constituent parts. Again, Plutarch's pairing was motivated through the Roman side. From Numa Pompilius, the second king of Rome, it was logical to proceed to Romulus, its founder and first king. But moving from Lycurgus to Theseus constituted a quantum leap. Certainly, Lycurgus, first mentioned as late as Herodotus, is a shadowy figure who might have lived between the ninth to seventh centuries BCE, if he lived at all. But his historical elusiveness is of a different quality than that of Theseus. Theseus was Heracles's cousin, whereas Lycurgus might have been his descendant in the eleventh generation, but inhabited a very different, more distinctly human and postheroic world.

Let us first look at some of the broader patterns that connect the two biographical diptychs. The choice of the Athenian hero Theseus and the Spartan lawgiver Lycurgus highlights the competitive axis of Athens-Sparta, so constitutive of Greek cultural consciousness. On the Greek side the logic of cultural complementarity is more decisive than genealogy. In the Roman case, instead, royal succession and the logic of cultural complementarity overlap: Romulus founded Rome in military and political terms and Numa Pompilius gave the city its religious institutions. More intriguingly, the cultural profile of Rome and Greece as embodied by founding figures of the first and second generation is suddenly inverted: Romulus was the charismatic newcomer set against a historically and mythically well-connected Theseus in a civilized Athens dominated at first by a yet more civilized and old Crete. But with his notorious measures to discourage wealth, luxury, and excess and to "banish the unnecessary and superfluous arts," (*Lycurgus* 9.3. Perrin I, 231) Lycurgus represents a cultural reversal, a conscious relapse into a kind of secondary primitivism, where children are only taught basic literacy, "enough to serve their turn; all the rest of their training was calculated to make them obey commands well, endure hardships, and conquer in battle" (*Lycurgus* 16.6. Perrin I, 257); even laws are to be inculcated and were not permitted to be written down. This stands in suggestive contrast to Plutarch's all-too-educated Roman king Numa who not just reads but presumably writes books.

To capture how Lycurgus and Numa function as contrastive, mutually illuminating foils, Plutarch uses a musical metaphor: "Just as musicians tune their lyres, so Lycurgus tightened the strings at Sparta, which he found relaxed with luxury, and Numa loosened the strings at Rome, where the tones were sharp and high" (*Lycurgus and Numa* 1.3. Perrin I, 385). By juxtaposing the secondary primitivist utopia of Lycurgus's Sparta with the gradual refinement of Rome's primary primitivism after the age of Romulus, Plutarch draws again attention to the civilizational gap between Greece and Rome.

But the most interesting point of contrast between the two kings is their legacy: Sparta loses supremacy over the Greek states after abandoning the precepts of Lycurgus and, similarly, Rome falls into a phase of bloody wars after Numa's death. Despite some opposite political measures, they are both effective leaders whose polities descend into chaos after their passing. However, whatever Plutarch might say about the wars after Numa's death, he had to acknowledge that, while there was never a world-spanning Spartan empire, the Roman Empire eventually did dominate the world through war:

> Thus not even for a little time did the beautiful edifice of justice which he [Numa] had reared remain standing, because it lacked the cement of education. "What, then!" someone will say, "was not Rome advanced and bettered by her wars?" That is a question which will need a long answer, if I am to satisfy men who hold that betterment consists in wealth, luxury and empire, rather than in safety, gentleness, and that independence which is attended by righteousness. However, it will be thought, I suppose, to favour the superior claims of Lycurgus, that, whereas the Romans increased in power as they did after abandoning the institutions of Numa's time, the Lacedaemonians, on the other hand, just as soon as they forsook the precepts of Lycurgus, sank from the highest to the lowest place, lost their supremacy over the Greeks, and were in danger of utter destruction. Nevertheless, this remains a great feature in Numa's career, and one really divine, that he was a stranger, and yet was summoned to the throne, where he changed the whole nature of the state by force of persuasion alone, and mastered a city which was not yet in sympathy with his views; and that he accomplished this without appeal to arms or any violence (unlike Lycurgus, who led the nobles in arms against the commons), but by his wisdom and justice won the hearts of all the citizens and brought them into harmony.[25]

Διὸς" προσαγορεύσας, ἀλλ᾽ ἐπικρατήσαντες οἱ τραγικοὶ πολλὴν ἀπὸ τοῦ λογείου καὶ τῆς σκηνῆς ἀδοξίαν αὐτοῦ κατεσκέδασαν ὡς χαλεποῦ καὶ βιαίου γενομένου. καίτοι φασὶ τὸν μὲν Μίνω βασιλέα καὶ νομοθέτην, δικαστὴν δὲ τὸν Ῥαδάμανθυν εἶναι καὶ φύλακα τῶν ὡρισμένων ὑπ᾽ ἐκείνου δικαίων.

[25] Plutarch, *Lycurgus and Numa* 4.6-8. Perrin I, 399–401. καὶ οὐδὲ ὀλίγον χρόνον ἡ καλλίστη καὶ δικαιοτάτη κατάστασις ἔμεινεν, ἅτε δὴ καὶ τὸ συνδετικὸν ἐν αὐτῇ, τὴν παιδείαν, οὐκ ἔχουσα. "Τί οὖν," φήσει τις, "οὐκ ἐπὶ τὸ βέλτιον ἡ Ῥώμη προῆλθε τοῖς πολεμικοῖς;" ἐρωτῶν ἐρώτημα μακρᾶς ἀποκρίσεως δεόμενον πρὸς ἀνθρώπους τὸ βέλτιον ἐν πλούτῳ καὶ τρυφῇ καὶ ἡγεμονίᾳ μᾶλλον ἢ σωτηρίᾳ καὶ πρᾳότητι καὶ τῇ μετὰ δικαιοσύνης αὐταρκείᾳ τιθεμένους. οὐ μὴν ἀλλὰ καὶ τοῦτο Λυκούργῳ που δόξει βοηθεῖν, τὸ Ῥωμαίους μὲν τὴν ἐπὶ Νομᾶ κατάστασιν ἐξαλλάξαντας ἐπιδοῦναι τοῖς πράγμασι τοσοῦτον, Λακεδαιμονίους δὲ ἅμα τῷ πρῶτον ἐκβῆναι τὴν Λυκούργου διάταξιν, ἐκ μεγίστων ταπεινοτάτους γενέσθαι καὶ τὴν τῶν Ἑλλήνων ἡγεμονίαν

Plutarch makes at least four complicated moves at once. First, Rome sunk into a period of war because, unlike Lycurgus, Numa did not put enough weight on *paideia*, the public education of his citizens. Second, Sparta lost hegemony because it abandoned Lycurgus's legacy, whereas Rome gained hegemony despite Numa's lack of educational policies. Third, some people might be proud of how wars made Rome great and enabled its wealth, luxury, and imperial tastes, but Plutarch would favor "safety, gentleness, and that independence which is attended by righteousness" (*Lycurgus and Numa* 4.7. Perrin I, 399). And fourth, Numa, standing on the side of civilization rather than uncultivated raw force, is to be congratulated on his skills as persuader and orator that gained him the people's sympathy and support.

This is a complex scheme of praise and blame. It becomes yet more puzzling when we consider how much Plutarch emphasizes Numa's thirst for self-cultivation: Plutarch explains that Numa was called to the throne after Romulus's miraculous disappearance and a short interregnum of factional strife between Romans and Sabines. Numa was chosen for his virtue (*aretê*), acquired through discipline (*paideia*), hardships (*kakopatheia*), and the study of wisdom or "philosophia." (*Numa* 3.3,5). In his process of self-cultivation Numa applies reason (*logos*) to the unbridled passions (*epithymioi*) and renounces the romance with violence that is typical for primitive barbarians:

> He had thus put away from himself not only the infamous passions of the soul, but also that violence and rapacity which are in such high repute among Barbarians, believing that true bravery consisted in the subjugation of one's passions by reason. On this account he banished from his house all luxury and extravagance, and while citizen and stranger alike found in him a faultless judge and counselor, he devoted his hours of privacy and leisure, not to enjoyments and money-making, but to the service of the gods, and the rational contemplation of their nature and power.[26]

Plutarch presents Numa here as a natural philosopher who devotes his time to contemplating secrets of nature, and as a chief priest who founds the religious institutions of Rome and inspires his people to develop sentiments of piety toward the gods. Plutarch mentions that it is unclear whether Numa studied Pythagorean writings, but he seems inclined to not reject the idea outright, saying that "(t)his was the chief reason why Numa's wisdom and culture were said to have been due to his intimacy with Pythagoras; for in the philosophy of the one, and in the

---

ἀποβαλόντας κινδυνεῦσαι περὶ ἀναστάσεως. ἐκεῖνο μέντοι τῷ Νομᾷ μέγα καὶ θεῖον ὡς ἀληθῶς ὑπάρχει, τὸ ξένῳ τε μεταπέμπτῳ γενέσθαι καὶ πάντα πειθοῖ μεταβαλεῖν, καὶ κρατῆσαι πόλεως οὔπω συμπεπνευκυίας, μήτε ὅπλων δεηθέντα μήτε βίας τινός, ὡς Λυκοῦργος ἐπὶ τὸν δῆμον ἦγε τοὺς ἀρίστους, ἀλλὰ σοφίᾳ καὶ δικαιοσύνῃ πάντας προσαγαγόμενον καὶ συναρμόσαντα.
[26] Plutarch, *Numa* 3.5-6. Perrin I, 315. οὐ μόνον τὰ λοιδορούμενα πάθη τῆς ψυχῆς, ἀλλὰ καὶ τὴν εὐδοκιμοῦσαν ἐν τοῖς βαρβάροις βίαν καὶ πλεονεξίαν ἐκποδὼν ποιησάμενος, ἀνδρείαν δὲ ἀληθῆ τὴν ὑπὸ λόγου τῶν ἐπιθυμιῶν ἐν αὐτῷ κάθειρξιν ἡγούμενος. ἐκ δὲ τούτου πᾶσαν οἴκοθεν ἅμα τρυφὴν καὶ πολυτέλειαν ἐξελαύνων, παντὶ δὲ πολίτῃ καὶ ξένῳ χρῆσθαι παρέχων ἑαυτὸν ἄμεμπτον δικαστὴν καὶ σύμβουλον, αὐτὸς δ' ἑαυτῷ σχολάζοντι χρώμενος οὐδὲν πρὸς ἡδυπαθείας καὶ πορισμούς, ἀλλὰ θεραπείαν θεῶν καὶ θεωρίαν διὰ λόγου φύσεώς τε αὐτῶν καὶ δυνάμεως.

civil polity of the other, religious services and occupations have a large place."
(*Numa* 8.4. Perrin I, 333). Plutarch quotes sources that state that twelve pontifical
books, and twelve others of Greek philosophy, were placed in a coffin upon his
death. When the coffins came to light four hundred years later after heavy rainfall,
one coffin was found empty, without a trace of a body, while the other contained
Pythagorean writings (*Numa* 22.5). They were then solemnly burned at the comi-
tium, perhaps in keeping with the Pythagorean precept of keeping the teachings
secret.

Undeniably, Numa is a *rex doctus*, erudite, virtuous, and pious; the only criticism Plutarch advances against him on the subject of education is that he didn't
make it into a public matter, but left education uncontrolled in the hands of the
parents, unlike Lycurgus, who separated children from their families at an early
age and subjected them to heavy doses of public education in physical prowess,
warfare, and basic literacy.

Reading the pair of Lycurgus and Numa in conjunction with the closely related
pair of Theseus and Romulus, we can see Plutarch spin out his thoughts on
the beginnings of cultures and polities through the lens of two generations of
founding figures. Romulus has proleptic imperial charisma, but lacks illustrious
pedigree and land. Theseus lacks moral charisma, but has the family tree and
a city. Numa, the second king, adds to Romulus's charisma erudition and piety.
Lycurgus, the leader of Sparta, the other, non-Athenian Greece, adds to Athenian
exuberance the insight that in the face of the experience of luxury, a conscious
"retrovolution" to primitive simplicity is the best way to hegemony.

Let us return once more to the complex scheme of praise and blame that closes
the synkrisis of Lycurgus and Numa. Plutarch's sympathy for Lycurgus and his
relative lack of sympathy for Numa is striking and puzzling. Does Numa symbol-
ize how important the injection of Greek wisdom (and persuasion and oratory)
into the earliest history of Rome was? Or, in contrast, does Lycurgus illustrate
how a Greek who understood the value to resist civilization and opt for simplicity
could have stopped the decline that comes with wealth and overrefinement—a
criticism often expressed by Romans who saw their pristine values corroded by
Greek influence? Do we have here a Roman king who is Greek enough to be wise
and erudite (although it does not help his kingdom) and a Greek/Spartan king
who restores Roman values of rustic simplicity and martial prowess (although his
vision implies a secondary, not pristine primitivism)?

Cultural values and cultural belonging of our Greek and Roman kings seem to
switch sides in *Lycurgus* and *Numa*. What does this mean? Given Plutarch's enthusiasm for all four protagonists at one point or the other, we might speculate that
Plutarch envisioned the ideal founding figure, who founds, launches, and keeps
his polity on the right track, like the qualities of Theseus, Romulus, Lycurgus, and
Numa rolled into one: perhaps a king living in close physical bond with the ideals of the heroic age, but also someone whose charisma allows him to suddenly
rise from nowhere, who knows how to resist the temptations of refinement and
laxity, but who is at the same time erudite, wise, pious, and well supplied with
Greek books?

4. The Synoptic Machine

Incomparable as our two case studies may be in genre, linguistic constellation, authorship, scope, motivation, and reception, it is meaningful to place them side by side—juxtapose them as a diptych of "case studies"—and use them to reflect more generally on the nature of synoptic texts. We showed in close detail how their synoptic format brought to light broader arguments about the relationship of Greek to Roman culture, and Japanese to Chinese-style poetics and exerted pressures of contrast and balance on both sides that we described with the term "synoptic machine." The form of these texts exceeds their content, and rather than declaring Greek or Japanese victors for patriotic purposes, both the *Lives* and the *New Myriad Leaves* seem absorbed in working out the warps and wefts that their suggestive juxtapositions force upon them.

The two case studies also showed how stunningly indeterminate synoptic texts tend to be. The excess of meaning that the synoptic format generates takes the shape of a persistent question, an open-ended experiment. The compiler of the *New Myriad Leaves* seems to ask: what happens to our perception of the world and to poetry if we directly confront Chinese-style and Japanese diction, rhetoric, and topic conventions, which are so incommensurable? Plutarch, in turn, asks: What happens if we confront the driving forces that have shaped lives of great Greeks and Romans and compare their moral values, actions, and outcomes? What happens if we view the actions of great Greeks and Romans alike through the screen of Greek philosophical vocabulary? Plutarch's dominant conceptual vocabulary of democracy versus tyranny, fate (*tychê*) versus virtue (*aretê*), prudence (*sôphrosynê*), self-control (*enkrateia*) and ambition (*philotimia*) derive mostly from Platonic and Hellenistic philosophy. The texts' strongest and most interesting claims do not lie in the surface content, but in the implications that arise from the juxtaposition. The degree of ambivalence and open-endedness of this "metatext" is what makes the *Lives* so fascinating and puzzling. In that sense Plutarch's *Lives*, despite appearances, are not just historical explorations, but exercises in Socratic midwifery, which have strayed from their place in the dialogue form and dressed up in the genre of biography.[27]

Moreover, both of our case studies emerged from a cultural milieu of agonistic comparison that provides a milieu for synoptic texts to thrive. *New Myriad Leaves* was produced in the very period when, after strong imperial sponsorship in the early ninth century for Sino-Japanese poetry, vernacular poetry was gaining ground as a public genre. Until the mid-eighth century vernacular poetry, especially in the long-verse form, had held a prominent function as a canvas

---

[27] Duff 1999 shows how exploratory and thought-provoking rather than descriptive and antiquarian Plutarch's *Lives* really are. Translated into genre terms, Plutarch's oscillation between biography and philosophical dialogue might be more interesting than the often-discussed oscillation between historiography and biography. Given that Plutarch was a copious writer of dialogues, and the only two surviving corpora of Greek philosophical dialogues are indeed Plato's and Plutarch's, Plutarch's inclination to generate questions rather than produce answers in the *Lives* is close in intent, if not in form, to the dialogue genre. On Plutarch as a philosopher and on his dialogues see Lamberton 2001, 26–44 and 146–87.

on which to display imperial grandeur, but the late ninth century propagation of the short thirty-one-syllable waka form at court was a new phenomenon that radically reshaped the early Japanese literary landscape. This competition between the Sino-Japanese and vernacular traditions culminated in the production of the *Kokinshū*, which as we saw in Chapter 1 invented ingenious strategies to outdo Sino-Japanese poetry by claiming that waka originated in the age of the gods and the depths of the human heart rather than, like Sino-Japanese poetry, in historical time and through the imitation of previous pattern and models.

In the case of Plutarch, Hellenistic culture was ripe with practices built on agonistic comparison.[28] The standard education included rhetorical exercises like the "encomium," fictional eulogies that praised well-known historical figures through contrast and comparison and relied on a highly polarized moral vocabulary. Students also had to produce, in true sophistical fashion, paired speeches that would argue for both sides of a question. Many of Plutarch's essays bear titles that smack of the rhetorical culture of agonistic comparison and contrast, such as "Did Rome gain hegemony thanks to fate or virtue?" Even if Plutarch most often comes down in between the two options, his style of argument is driven by an agonistic rhetoric that gives the illusion that there could be a simple solution.

If one looks too closely at synoptic texts, one quickly finds one's head spinning. The simple device of juxtaposition creates a *perpetuum mobile* where the reader is plunged into distinguishing significant from insignificant contrasts and constitutive from coincidental similarities of the juxtaposed entities. We are sometimes forced to change perspective at each new turn of phrase. As readers we can compensate for the overdetermination inherent in the synoptic form only by overinterpretation of the author's intentions. Like eyes that grow weary from gliding back and forth between close and distant objects, our moving between the elliptical, underdetermined synoptic text and our systematic overreading of it is as exciting as disturbing. I think it has yet to be fully recognized just how vertiginous both the *New Myriad Leaves* and the *Parallel Lives* are by virtue of their synoptic format, and how much we can learn from synoptic texts about the gradual and often coincidental process of shaping cultural identities through juxtaposition and contrast.

---

[28] See Pelling 2000 and 2002 and Duff 1999, 243–47.

| Beyond the Comforts of Influence:
Deep Comparisons

1. The Comparative Imperative, Revisited

Over the past decade, "World Literature" has advanced to become a candidate for the most recent paradigm in the field of comparative literature and a literary correlate to other "world" paradigms, such as world history/global history, that have made themselves felt in agendas for teaching, research, and hiring. I dare say that the new excitement over the significance, methodology, and pedagogy of "World Literature" is rather unlike any other paradigm that has swept over the stage of literature departments in North America over the past half century—including heavyweights such as New Criticism, Deconstruction, Postmodernism, Gender Studies, or Postcolonialism. "World Literature" is a new movement with an old name that dispenses with some of the iconoclastic clamor that has surrounded previous paradigms in comparative literature. Some of its most prominent proponents at times even make a point of picking up a job left unfinished ever since Johann Wolfgang Goethe brought the concept of *Weltliteratur* into circulation in his conversations with his confidant Johann Peter Eckermann in 1827. Mindful of Goethe's use of the concept, David Damrosch emphasizes that *Weltliteratur* is a state of mind and a method, not a corpus of texts:

> World literature is fully in play once several foreign works begin to resonate together in our mind. This provides a further solution to the comparatist's lurking panic: world literature is not an immense body of material that must somehow, impossibly, be mastered; it is a mode of reading that can be experienced intensively with a few works just as effectively as it can be explored extensively with a large number.[1]

And despite their otherwise diverging vision and practice of "World Literature," Franco Moretti makes a related point in his "Conjectures on World Literature":

> World literature is not an object, it's a problem, and a problem that asks for a new critical method; and no-one has ever found a method by just reading more texts.

---

[1] Damrosch 2003, 298–99.

That's not how theories come into being: they need a leap, a wager—a hypothesis—to get started.[2]

After quoting Goethe and Karl Marx on *Weltliteratur* Moretti laments that we have failed to live up to their vision and urges us to try again:

> Well, let me put it very simply, we have not lived up to these beginnings: the study of comparative or international literature has been a much more modest intellectual enterprise, fundamentally limited to Western Europe, and mostly revolving around the river Rhine (German philologists working on French literature). Not much more.... I think it's time we return to that old ambition of *Weltliteratur*: after all, the literature around us is now unmistakably a planetary system. The question is not really *what* we should do—the question is *how*.[3]

Just as the proponents of *Weltliteratur* make a connection between an old concept and their novel endeavor current world literature pedagogy is both novel and conscious of its twentieth century precedents. With his *World Literature and Its Place in General Culture* of 1911, Richard G. Moulton of the University of Chicago laid an important foundation for the introduction of world literature courses and "Great Books" courses into general college education in North America during the twentieth century. The idea that reading masterpieces of literature from around the world in translation would counteract the progressive specialization in the humanities and would give students *Herzensbildung*—moral judgment, aesthetic appreciation, and civic competency—led to a unique expansion of world literature pedagogy over the past century. As John Pizer reminds us, this has indeed been an American phenomenon, despite *Weltliteratur*'s roots on the old continent.[4]

Philo Buck of the University of Wisconsin compiled one of the earliest anthologies of World Literature for college use in the 1930s. It contained about 90 percent of European literature, with the slight rest split between Sanskrit, Persian, and Arabic, all traditions that have influenced European writers. Subsequent anthology projects would occasionally aim to include a bit more of the world, but it was not until the 1990s that more forceful efforts were made to produce truly global anthologies. According to recent estimates by the college book publisher Norton, about 1,200 institutions in North America currently offer World Literature courses in their general education program and enroll somewhere between 100,000 and 120,000 students each year. These courses rely on the major anthologies currently on the market produced by Norton, Longman, and Bedford: all in six hefty volumes, largely arranged chronologically, and spanning texts from Ancient Egypt to postcolonial Trinidad and India. Whereas Norton's tradition of publishing anthologies of *World Masterpieces* goes back to the 1950s, the first editions of the *Longman Anthology of World Literature* and the *Bedford Anthology of World Literature* date to the last decade and testify to the ascent of the new World Literature paradigm in college pedagogy.

---

[2] Moretti 2004 149.
[3] Ibid., 148.
[4] On the history of the development of world literature courses in America see Chapter 5 of Pizer 2006.

It is the complex nexus between World Literature theory and pedagogy that makes the paradigm in America so promising and unprecedented. First, in terms of sheer numbers the dynamic of its future development is bottom-up, driven by mass education and urged on by anthology editors and new visions of liberal arts education. Unlike deconstruction and postmodernism, let's say, it is not only being designed by a few rarified bright theorists whose work will eventually trickle down into the catacombs of academe—undergraduate education—and become canonized in "theory courses" that are already somewhat dated when they make it into the curriculum of literature departments. This time theory has a hard time catching up with pedagogy.[5]

This inverse and synchronic nexus between *Weltliteratur* theory and practice also challenges cherished myths about the origins and spirit of comparative literature as an academic discipline. Still today, the patina of an "old world" myth coats the self-understanding of American comparatists. Didn't the nineteenth-century founding fathers of the discipline, such as the Hungarian-speaking Transylvanian Hugo Meltzl and the Dane Georg Brandes, come from multilingual peripheries that predisposed them to become comparatists in the first place? Weren't Erich Auerbach and Leo Spitzer, towering twentieth-century comparatists, who founded the discipline in North America, erudite Europeans whose traumatic escape from the terror of Nazism and the horrors of wars on the Old Continent brought aesthetic sophistication and a higher, authenticating wisdom to the discipline? And isn't comparative literature predicated on the tantalizingly effortless multilinguality—in high literary European languages, that is, not the pidgin languages and dialects of non-Western immigrants—that Europeans seem to imbibe with their mothers' milk?

Undoubtedly there are renowned comparatists and programs of Comparative Literature in Europe, but their number and scope hardly bears comparison to the prominence of the discipline in North America. And unlike in America, where the discipline is increasingly transformed by scholars working in Asian, Middle Eastern, and African languages, the number of Europe's comparatists who work beyond the major European languages is minimal. Again, large-scale publication projects like the new, global third edition of *Kindlers Literatur Lexikon* in nineteen volumes (Berlin: J. B. Metzler, 2009) show that *Weltliteratur* still holds its place in scholarly agendas. But one could only wish—in vain—that the currently all-too-frantic reformers of German higher education realized that *Weltliteratur* should be read extensively by entering university students, that universities should establish and staff centers and departments to teach it. Such a program could revolutionize the German academic landscape by bringing a true, solid global edge to the education of future generations and help integrate a society that for all too long has neglected its ethnic diversity; *Weltliteratur* in the country of Goethe should not just languish in dusty reference works on dark library shelves.

---

[5] Recent pedagogical guides and reference works include Damrosch 2009a and 2009b and D'Haen, Damrosch, and Kadir 2012.

The new American paradigm thrives on the tension between world literature as method and theory and world literature as canon and general education pedagogy. While a large amount of world literature theory develops in the context of the analysis of modern literatures, the world literature canon as featured in the college anthologies leans heavily toward premodern traditions, the first few millennia of world literature that preceded the past century. Considering that most literary traditions in Asia, Africa, and the Middle East only fully connected with Western modernity late in the nineteenth century, nearly five out of the six volumes of the above-mentioned world literature anthologies consist of works that precede the modern period. This creates formidable challenges for the instructors of American world literature courses, most often trained in English or another European literature. Reading Salman Rushdie and V. S. Naipaul will allow students and instructors alike to stay close to their comfort zone of cultural difference, but an instructor teaching the Indian epic Mahabharata alongside the Japanese warrior tale *The Tales of the Heike* and Homer's *Iliad* will have to face pressing questions in an introductory level undergraduate course, that no scholar so far—to my knowledge—has had the expertise and courage to tackle comparatively in her research.

This paradoxical nexus between modern-oriented theory and an overwhelming premodern canon offers a fantastic opportunity and has the potential to become a truly creative site for developing theories of premodern comparative studies. How should we face independent cultural development, and compare distinctive, largely self-contained traditions such as Chinese, Indian, and Arabic literature before the advent of global modernity? Making the best out of this opportunity will to some degree go against much of the recent excitement about the "world" and the "global" in other disciplines such as history, religion, or archeology. "Travel," "migration," and "diffusion" have been key terms and central assumptions and have opened fascinating vistas on the vivid interconnections among cultures and worlds ever since at least the Neolithic Period. But textual traditions, in particular the elite traditions that became the foundation of classical civilizations, do not travel like guns, germs, and steel; not even like coins, miniature paintings, or religious statuettes. The Roman senate did at some point ban Chinese silk for its suggestive eroticism and its ability to drain the empire's silver reserves when it became fashionable among the capital's rich, but not one of the most erudite and cosmopolitan members of the Roman elite ever had the faintest inkling of the metrics of classical Chinese poetry, a single concept of Confucian ethics, or the most basic conventions of Chinese historiography. In short, in the larger context of comparative studies, comparative literature faces particular challenges because of the exceptional patterns of circulation (or lack thereof) of its object of study, literary texts. This problem might yield a more thought-provoking criterion to define the discipline in the future than the well-worn "literariness" of texts that the last report about the state of the field has brought up again to define the distinctiveness of comparative literature.[6]

---

[6] Saussy 2006, 17.

The fact that literary texts are among the cultural products most resistant to travel and to successful diffusion should make us think more about the relative proportion of studies of cultural diffusion versus studies of genetic difference in comparative literature. Particularly in its traditional Euro-centripetal approach, but also in its global incarnation with a modern and postmodern focus, much of the work done in comparative literature is a variant of "reception studies." Studying the reception of Greco-Roman antiquity in European vernaculars, the mutual reception processes between European vernaculars, or even the assertive responses of non-Western writers to the impact of colonization and Western modernity, builds on one and the same assumption: historical influence and reception are what matters. Comparisons across historically nonrelated cultures have been, and still are, vastly outnumbered by studies of influence and reception. Courageous comparatists working between East Asian and Western traditions, such as Zhang Longxi, Earl Miner, Anthony Yu, Eugene Eoyang, Pauline Yu, Stephen Owen, and, more recently, Alexander Beecroft have made great contributions to the methodology of comparisons of historically unrelated literary traditions. But based on a logic of sheer numbers, reception and influence studies have developed a much richer and more sophisticated methodological repertoire than comparisons that are facing the challenges of engaging historically unmediated cultural difference.

This book interweaves two cases of reception—Sino-Japanese and Greco-Roman—and has compared these historically unrelated processes, making for three storylines with a radically different research history. Greco-Roman "reception studies" in the broadest sense have the longest and richest pedigree and the most sophisticated repertoire of methodological tools. Confronting the wealth and depth of that scholarship is a daunting enterprise. In contrast, the academic study of Sino-Japanese cultural exchange and reception is underdeveloped. Traditional Sinology in Japan goes back to the early period, but it was largely limited to the production of philological reference works, commentaries, and textual editions. For centuries Sino-Japanese reception processes were the underlying, unquestioned assumption, not a dynamic requiring investigation and interpretation, let alone explanation. Although the formation of the modern discipline of literary studies since the Meiji Period opened scholarship to questions of interpretation and criticism, it also enshrined "national literature" (*kokubungaku* 国文学)—with a focus on vernacular works such as the *Man'yōshū* and the *Tale of Genji* as the canon of Japanese literature—and marginalized the grand old Sino-Japanese literary tradition. The twentieth century can boast a good number of groundbreaking *kanbun* scholars who have investigated Sino-Japanese reception processes; and since the 1980s the *Wakan hikaku bungakkai* 和漢比較文学会 (Wa-kan/Sino-Japanese Comparative Literature Association), which also edits a high-quality journal, has proven a lively platform for scholars researching Japanese literature from Chinese and Sino-Japanese perspectives. But Sino-Japanese studies constitute a small minority in literary studies in Japan and the West. And we cannot emphasize enough that the "Sino-Japanese Comparative Literature Association" consists of scholars of Japanese literature who are largely out of touch with Japan's academic discipline of "Comparative Literature," which has focused largely on Japan's reception of Western literatures in the modern period. This discipline developed on the Eurocentric Western model, with the addition of a Japanese point of reference, but it has so far failed to produce a "Comparative Literature" of the first order that we should expect in Japan: a field that studies Japanese literature comparatively in relation to the other East Asian traditions of China, Korea, and Vietnam, and more broadly to South and Southeast Asia. Whereas we are striving to overcome the Euro-centripetal legacy of comparative literature, we could wish that a more "Asia-centric" comparative literature model takes hold in future literary studies in Japan.

A major motivation for writing this book has been a desire to reflect more methodically on the processes of Sino-Japanese reception, taking inspiration from the far more developed and mature studies of reception in the Greco-Roman context. But the ultimate challenge has been the third storyline, the one that connects our two stories of Greco-Roman and Sino-Japanese reception. To my knowledge nobody to date has ever undertaken a book-length study in any language that compares these two historically unrelated reception processes. Developing that storyline without any precedent to go by has been the most enticing and daunting challenge of this project. In phases of doubt I was in turns urged on and taken aback by Erich Auerbach's apt words on the conditions for bold synthesis:

> But how is the problem of synthesis to be solved? A single lifetime seems too short to create even the preliminaries. The organized work of a group is no answer, even if a group has high uses otherwise. The historical synthesis of which I am speaking, although it has significance only when it is based on a scholarly penetration of the material, is a product of personal intuition and hence can only be expected from an individual.[7]

Although collaboration is often the most practical and therapeutic answer to the formidable challenges of bold comparative projects, they can ultimately only cohere intellectually in individual minds, even if inspired and enhanced by a group effort. What can the intuition of an individual hold on to for discerning relevant connections and producing bold syntheses?

For historically unrelated comparisons, the dominant answers have involved versions of formalism and the belief that comparability requires abstraction, reduction, typologization, or formal equation. For Japanese literature Earl Miner's study *Comparative Poetics* has been a groundbreaking effort in this direction. Analyzing Asian and Western literatures through the prism of the Western genre categories of drama, lyric, and narrative while being aware of their relativity and cultural inflection, Miner strongly believed that poetics—meta-discourses about literature—provided the most accessible avenue to bold comparisons. This posits comparability on the level of a set of shared concepts of a higher order.

---

[7] Auerbach 1969, 11 (originally published in German in 1952).

2. Comparing Literary Cultures

In this study I decided to renounce this scheme of a shared formal typology. Instead I tried to show how comparability arises from a complex translation process of incommensurate concepts, not from a higher order of abstraction or reduction. In several chapters I have undertaken this translation with the help of the notion of "literary culture." For a genre formalist the *Iliad* is mainly an epic. For the student of literary cultures it is that and much more: the most important schoolbook text in the Hellenistic world, which was read with the Alexandrian apparatus of philological and commentarial scholarship, and which has thus left a massive record in material culture as young children in Egypt, Rome, or Gaul used it as writing practice; and the top text on top of the genre hierarchy that invited veneration, memorization, allegorical interpretation, parody, recitation, recreation, quotation, allusion. With our comparison of literary cultures rather than literary works, we move from single, surface equivalences of concepts and literary texts to what I would like to call a "deep comparison" that approximates and counter-highlights literary cultures.

Studies of "literary culture" have enjoyed great popularity over the past decade. Suddenly every period and era, place and tradition has gained its own characteristic "literary culture" worthy of scholarly elaboration. This loosely intuitive, yet capacious and suggestive concept has opened literary studies to a rich array of new horizons: suddenly the material culture of reading and writing, producing and circulating, copying and printing, compiling, rearranging and disseminating of texts has become as important as their content, which for so long had monopolized scholarly attention; the social contexts, audiences, users, patrons and performers of literary texts have entered the stage; and the connections between literary production and political culture, religious practice, and economic development now create a matrix around literary texts that has become constitutive of, not just collateral, to their meaning.

The comparison of Roman and Early Japanese literature in this book has focused on four particular aspects of literary culture that have enabled us to go beyond surface appearances and undertake focused "deep comparisons": education, literacy, genre hierarchies, and genre translations. In setting the stage for our comparison I emphasized the importance of the canon and process of education: Greece and China were only "reference cultures" in the full sense of all meanings spelled out in the first chapter because Roman and Japanese elites were trained from childhood in the Hellenistic or Chinese canon, aided by the relevant scholarship, commentaries, and philological reference works. The focus on education allowed us to contrastively develop a nuanced picture of different forms of literacy—a definition of "literacy" that accounts not just for basic reading and writing, as the term is generally understood, but for cultural, political, religious, and literary practices associated with the reading and writing of texts. I have characterized Japanese literary culture as predominantly monolingual, biliterate, and tricanonical, and contrasted it with Roman literary culture that functioned mainly in a bilingual, monoliterate, and bicanonical fashion. This threefold scheme of literacy allowed us also to explore the radical differences between literatures written in characters and those recorded in alphabetic systems: while Roman literature started as a "translation literature" that required translation for the study and absorption of Greek literature, Japanese literature launched unto a bifurcated path, with Chinese-style literature accessible without translation and vernacular literature as a separate, independent tradition heavily influenced by the Chinese tradition but without direct Chinese precedent.

The third aspect of "literary cultures" that we encountered repeatedly also relates to questions of education: the importance of genre hierarchies, which determine the relative status and significance of certain genres within a culture and which engendered rhetorical forms such as recusatio and satire, expressing competition over the relative status of genres. Deep comparison is particularly crucial when it comes to thinking through genres across cultures. Formalist criticism most easily succumbs to the "comparative fallacy" of equating genre labels across cultures without any regard to their status in the genre hierarchy. Yet while the two genres of highest standing in Greco-Roman and European literatures—epic and drama—did not exist in early Japan, the two literary genres of highest standing in early and medieval Japan—short lyrical genres such as kanshi and waka (excluding here the Chinese Confucian Classics and Official Histories)—were absent from the influential poetological schemes of Plato and Aristotle.

Shifting our comparisons from genres to genre hierarchies produces a set of fascinating questions: what does it mean for a literary tradition if lyrical poetry—with its highly metaphorical imagery and its potentially intimate voice—stands at the top of the genre hierarchy and becomes the venue for articulating "epic" themes of governance, court culture, public life? Don't we need a different vocabulary to talk about the imagery and rhetorical repertoire in Japanese poetry? If we take the comparison between early Japanese and Latin literature seriously, would we not need to read official kanshi and waka as the functional equivalent to Western epic poetry, and read it as we would read Homer or Virgil? How can we compare functional *topologies* (location of genres within genre hierarchies) rather than formalistic *typologies* of genre?

Things can get still more difficult, even if "false friends" or fallacious equivalences are absent, which brings us to our fourth insight about literary cultures. Deep comparison requires transposition, the functional and symbolic translation of disciplines and genres that only one of the cultures in comparison might possess. Several of the preceding chapters developed strategies to "translate" the central importance of rhetoric and oratory in Greco-Roman education and political culture into comparable practices in Early Japan. In Chapter 2 we compared Cicero's account of the history of Roman oratory to Japanese prefaces of poetry anthologies that related poetry to the origin of the cosmos, civilization, and political development. And in Chapter 6 we compared Ovid's oratorical panache in his exile poetry to Michizane's reliance on plant imagery in lyric poetry. On a general level, poetry training in China and Japan held a similar role in elite education, as it was considered the road to polished speech and writing, competent citizenship and, for some time in China, civil service. Again, only a functional topology of certain practices rooted in a certain literary culture can lead us to a meaningful deep comparison that brings to light what appeared untranslatable in the first place.

3. Disciplinarity and Layered Comparison

The ubiquitous praise of "interdisciplinarity" that has been with us for a while can make us forget what we can gain from observing standards and practices in other disciplines and applying them to our own. In this book I have consciously taken the role of the Japanologist and Sinologist who uses the Greco-Roman literary tradition and its academic discipline, Classics, as a theoretical and critical framing device to better understand early East Asia. I did so with the hope that scholars of Classics might conversely benefit from using East Asian studies as a framing device that could inspire new questions, answers, or methods in Classics. This is a form of comparison that newly values disciplinarity, not to resist the synthesizing, visionary forms of interdisciplinarity, but to benefit from the depth and precision of disciplines by making them into comparative tools. This approach connects scholars' minds more strongly through the philological study, interpretation, and mutual illumination of the literary canons of the cultures under scrutiny, and less through the handier shortcuts of a limited, reductive critical vocabulary that always somehow predetermines the convergence of the results. Ultimately, it strives to bring into dialogue various layers of comparison: of artifacts (such as texts), of cultural systems (like literary cultures), of critical concepts extracted from case studies within a tradition; and lastly, of academic disciplines with their specific histories, practices, and current agendas.

In the introduction I touched on the many ways in which studies of East Asian literatures, as young academic disciplines in the West, could benefit from the venerable field of Classics, and I postponed remarks on how Classics could benefit from East Asian studies to the end of the book. I will limit myself here to a few points. First, the natural connection between the premodern and modern, which is the result of the long, continuous literary histories of China and Japan, gives the study of ancient East Asia a relevance and multifaceted vibrancy that Classics has been struggling to maintain. One of the recent attempts to recover relevancy in Classics has been the new subfield of "reception studies" (in a more specialized sense than I used the term above), which explores the afterlife of Ancient Greece and Rome in Western cultural history up to the present. However, this hardly compares to the powerful intellectual, cultural, and economic motivation behind the study of the living literary histories of East Asia. Fascination with modern East Asia is a strong driving factor behind increasing student enrollments, departmental growth, and funding opportunities in the United States, and the study of premodern East Asia has been benefiting as well from the current trend of swift expansion, which stands in contrast to the anxieties surrounding the shrinkage in Classics.

Thus, although the denationalized nature of Classics discussed in the introduction has more successfully avoided imposing nineteenth-century concepts of the nation-state on the ancient world, the political and academic institutionalization of Chinese and Japanese national literary studies has merits of its own: the vitality and high quality of source-criticism scholarship produced in particular by Japanese and Chinese scholars working on their native tradition provides a fundamental basis for Western studies of China and Japan. And a crucial part of the academic life of today's scholars of East Asia is the collaboration among Asian, Asian-heritage, and non-Asian scholars working and living in between various countries as well as the negotiation between a "self-reflective" native approach and "heteroscopic" outsider perspective. It is this constant negotiation of the ever shrinking difference between a "self," which is heavily inflected by close familiarity with the other tradition, and the "other tradition" that has become more own than other, which provides a powerful intellectual stimulus for creative thinking for East Asianists, Eastern and Western, as well as everybody in-between. The very fact that still today great numbers of cultivated Japanese aficionados write in the ancient genres of waka poetry and haiku practice traditional forms of poetry chanting, makes ancient Japanese poetry accessible from angles that have been completely occluded for Classicists.

The natural institutional and intellectual connection between the premodern and the modern in East Asian Studies also stimulates a more variegated market of approaches and methods. If Classics has hardly been known for theoretical panache or visionary methodological experimentation, scholarship on East Asia can boast a wide spectrum of intellectual styles ranging from heavily philological to highly theoretical scholarship depending on period, project, scholar, and materials. Although many scholars might stick to the same period and materials, the most innovative scholarship has often come from scholars who have combined premodern with modern, and philological with theoretical concerns.

Overall, it is most pleasant to imagine how a fuller engagement with other antiquities—in particular Near Eastern, Indian, Chinese—with their own distinctive shapes of historical, intellectual, and literary traditions, could give new questions, even new answers, and certainly a new conceptual vocabulary and a new global edge to the discipline of Classics.

More concretely, I hope that this book has thrown new light on specific questions and texts of the Latin and Japanese traditions. Sometimes I have attempted to offer new answers to old, impossible inquiries that seemed to beg the question: just as Japan scholars should be more actively grateful for the preservation of scores of texts from the first two centuries of full-fledged literacy, should not Latinists take the loss of early Latin literature less for granted? Instead, the connection between the nature of its tradition as a "translation literature" and the language complex vis-à-vis Greece that came with it will hopefully inspire further exploration. In addition, with the concept of a "Roman Atticism" promoted by Cicero in his *Brutus* I aimed to add a new perspective to discussions of the Atticism-Asianism debate and Rome's seminal role in it.

At other times, this comparative project has generated new questions and perspectives on some of the most canonical and heavily researched texts: for example we asked why the *Aeneid*'s portrayal of Aeneas as a not quite illiterate but an "a-literate" figure has bothered so few readers and modern scholars, but how poor a figure, despite his city building skills, he would have made in Early Japan, where literacy and the manipulation of wen in all its meanings embodied the highest ornament of cultivation and moral exemplarity.

At yet other times, we drew into the limelight texts that have received little attention in their own literary cultures but that use strategies that resemble those from another literary culture where they were extremely successful. Velleius Paterculus has been considered a minor writer, but he proposed theories of literary production similar to the highly successful *Kokinshū* Prefaces in Japan. In turn, while Martianus Capella's *Marriage of Mercury and Philology* became a standard work of medieval education, the *Genji Poems* remained odd, erratic, and have received almost no scholarly attention.

Lastly, we can identify strategies that Rome and early Japan either shared in positioning themselves vis-à-vis Greek and Roman literary precedents or that are distinctive of either of them. We analyzed texts that tried to "outpast" the older reference culture and we saw that both in eighth- and ninth-century Japan and, probably, in early Rome, the intuitive attraction of sophistication and rhetorical ornament preceded the rise of a discourse of simplicity and austerity that was claimed as emblematic of the younger, less "corrupted" culture. Both Roman and early Japanese authors were aware of the "historical flatness" of their literary culture and had a strong consciousness of the age difference that separated them from their reference culture. Both tried to devise ways to lay claim to a purity and pristineness that would give their tradition older age, dignity, and independence. On the other hand, Early Japanese and Roman literary cultures developed a different repertoire of tropes to negotiate the problem of cultural influence and competition. The "inventor discourse" so prominent in Roman culture, which gave Roman writers a more aggressive agency in the face of the Greek originators of certain genres and cultural practices, was not significant in early Japan. And the prominent trope of recusatio, of writing in a lesser genre or lesser tradition, could take opposite shape in Japan, where vernacular texts such as the *Tale of Genji* engaged in an *anti-recusatio* of sorts, attempting to claim that their status exceeded that of the venerable Confucian Classics.

***

On various levels of the layered comparisons proposed in this book, I have promoted one trope of comparison in particular: catachresis. It is not one of the darling master tropes of European cultural history, such as metaphor, metonymy, or allegory. To the contrary, it has often been considered a rhetorical vice and has accrued unsavory associations with linguistic incompetence: the misapplication of a word for lack of linguistic correctness the sloppiness of mixed metaphors for lack of stylistic soundness. In short, catachresis has come to mean an "abuse" of the linguistic repertoire of competent speakers. The Latin equivalent of the Greek term is indeed *abusio*. And the reputation of catachresis as the bastard brother of metaphor, as a botched, deviant metaphor has only slightly improved its standing now and then: the eighteenth-century grammarian and philosopher César Chesneau Dumarsais promoted catachresis to the venerable position of metaphor in his treatise *Des Tropes* (1730), and some deconstructionist and postcolonial critics have attempted to mine the subversive potential of the concept for their purposes.[8] Already its earliest theorists had mixed feelings about this ambivalent

---

[8] On the debates over the relation between the two tropes and on Dumarsais see Parker 1990.

trope, as we can see in Quintilian's large work on the pedagogy of oratory, but he credited it with two positive functions: he emphasized that it could serve as a stand-in to refer to something for which a proper word is missing (like a table's "legs") and, by extension, that it can be a therapeutic trope in situations where one language's poverty can be mended by another language's bounty, in particular Latin by Greek (*Quintilian* 8.6.34).[9]

In an imaginary *Tropology of Comparison*, which has yet to be written, catachresis would be the master trope of deep comparison. It is the inverse of ellipsis, which diagnoses the absence of a defining phenomenon in another culture by comparison and sidesteps unproductive but popular questions such as: Can a civilization without epic, tragedy, or philosophy truly be civilized? Catachresis, in contrast, allows us to profit from the asymmetries of the comparison of historically unrelated cultures. It turns asymmetry and incommensurability into a key heuristic device to make the comparison productive, to imagine scenarios of mutual virtual history that let actual history appear with greater clarity and genuine significance. As a trope of relative enrichment under messy circumstances, catchresis well befits a study of the relative age of literary cultures and of academic disciplines. And in the end, it is a perfect cipher for a methodology of deep comparison.

---

[9] For definitions of catachresis in Greek and Roman texts see Lausberg 1960 221, 282, 289.

BIBLIOGRAPHY

Throughout this book I follow the Chinese and Japanese naming conventions of providing the family name first, followed by the given name. Translations from any language are mine, unless otherwise noted.

Source Texts

Note: For the curious reader I include basic editions of Chinese, Japanese, Greek, and Latin source texts central to this book at the beginning of this bibliography, accompanied by prominent translations into English or other Western languages (sometimes partial translations if no complete translations are available). Translations of the source texts are set in smaller font. For the Greek and Latin source texts I rely on the Loeb Classical Library editions unless otherwise indicated.

Abbreviations:

BMFEA	*Bulletin of the Museum of Far Eastern Antiquities*
CQ	*Classical Quarterly*
HJAS	*Harvard Journal of Asiatic Studies*
JATJ	*The Journal of the Association of Teachers of Japanese*
JJS	*Journal of Japanese Studies*
JRS	*Journal of Roman Studies*
KST	*Shintei zōho Kokushi taikei*
MN	*Monumenta Nipponica*
NKBT	*Nihon koten bungaku taikei*
NKBZ	*Nihon koten bungaku zenshū*
SKT	*Shinshaku kanbun taikei*
SNKBT	*Shin Nihon koten bungaku taikei*
SNKBZ	*Shinpen Nihon koten bungaku zenshū*
TAPA	*Transactions of the American Philological Association*

TLS   *Time Literary Supplement*
WBT   *Waka bungaku taikei*
WHB   *Wakan hikaku bungaku*

I. Chinese and Japanese Source Texts and Selected Translations

Akazome Emon et al. *Eiga monogatari (Tale of Flowering Fortunes)*. Yamanaka Yutaka et al., eds. *Eiga monogatari*. 1995–98. NKBZ 31–33. Tokyo: Shōgakkan.

McCullough, Helen Craig and William H. McCullough, trans. 1980. *A Tale of Flowering Fortunes: Annals of Japanese Aristocratic Life in the Heian Period*. 2 vols. Stanford: Stanford University Press.

Bo Juyi's Collected Works. 1988. Zhu Jincheng, ed. *Bo Juyi ji jian jiao*. 6 vols. Shanghai: Shanghai guji chubanshe.

Chōya gunsai (Compendium of Texts for Court and Provinces). Kuroita Katsumi et al., eds. 1964–67. *Chōya gunsai*. KST, Vol. 29. Tokyo: Yoshikawa Kōbunkan.

Chuci (Songs of Chu). Wang Yi, comp. 1989. *Chuci buzhu*. Annot. Hong Xingzu. Taibei: Tiangong shuju.

Hawkes, David, trans. 1985. *The Songs of the South: an Ancient Chinese Anthology of Poems by Qu Yuan and Other Poets*. Harmondsworth and New York: Penguin Books.

Ennin. *Nittō guhō junrei kōki (Record of a Pilgrimage to Tang China in Search of the Law)*. Ono Katsutoshi, ed. 1992. *Ru Tang qiufa xunli xingji jiaozhu*. Shijiazhuang: Huashan wenyi chubanshe.

Reischauer, Edwin, trans. 1955. *Ennin's Diary: The Record of a Pilgrimage to China in Search of the Law*. New York: The Ronald Press Company.

Fujiwara no Akihira. *Shin sarugaku ki (Record of New Monkey Music)*. Kawaguchi Hisao, ed. 1983. *Shin sarugaku ki*. Tokyo: Heibonsha.

Gunsho ruijū (Classified Series of Various Books). Hanawa Hokinoichi, comp. 1959–60. *Gunsho ruijū*. 29 vols. Tokyo: Zoku Gunsho Ruijū Kanseikai.

Han shu (Book of the Han). Ban Gu, comp. *Han shu*. 1986. *Er shi wu shi*. Shanghai: Shanghai guji chubanshe.

Dubs, Homer, trans. 1938. *The History of the Former Han Dynasty by Pan Ku. A Critical Translation, with Annotations*. 3 vols. London: Kegan Paul, Trench, Trubner.

Honchō monzui (Literary Essence of Our Court). Comp. Fujiwara no Akihira. Gotō Akio et al., eds. 1992. *Honchō monzui*. SNKBT 27. Tokyo: Iwanami shoten.

Rabinovitch, Judith and Timothy Bradstock, trans. 2005. *Dance of the Butterflies. Chinese Poetry from the Japanese Court Tradition*. Ithaca: East Asia Program, Cornell University.

Kaifūsō (Florilegium of Cherished Airs). 1964. Kojima Noriyuki, ed., *Kaifūsō, Bunka shūreishū, Honchō monzui*. NKBT 69. Tokyo: Iwanami Shoten.

Rabinovitch, Judith and Timothy Bradstock, trans. 2005. *Dance of the Butterflies. Chinese Poetry from the Japanese Court Tradition*. Ithaca: East Asia Program, Cornell University.

Maurizi, Andrea, trans. 2002. *Il più antico testo poetico del Giappone: il Kaifūsō (Raccolta in onore di antichi poeti)*. Pisa: Istituti Editoriali e Poligrafici Internazionali.

Ki no Tsurayuki. *Tosa nikki (Tosa Diary)*. Kikuchi Yasuhiko et al., eds. 1995. *Tosa nikki. Kagerō nikki*. NKBZ 13. Tokyo: Shōgakkan.

McCullough, Helen, trans. 1990. *Classical Japanese Prose. An Anthology*. Stanford: Stanford University Press, 73-102.

Kojiki (Records of Ancient Matters). Kōnoshi Takamitsu et al. 2007. *Kojiki*. SNKBZ 1. Tokyo: Shōgakkan.

Philippi, Donald L., trans. 1968. *Kojiki*. Tokyo: University of Tokyo Press.

Kokinshū (Collection of Ancient and Modern Poetry). Comp. Ki no Tsurayuki et al. Kojima Noriyuki and Arai Eizō, eds. 1989. *Kokin wakashū*. SNKBT 5. Tokyo: Iwanami shoten, and Katagiri Yōichi. 1998. *Kokinwakashū zenhyōshaku*. Tokyo: Kōdansha.

Cranston, Edwin, trans. 2006. *A Waka Anthology. Volume Two: Grasses of Remembrance.* Stanford: Stanford University Press.

Rodd, Laurel Rasplica, trans. 1984. *Kokinshū. A Collection of Poems Ancient and Modern.* Princeton: Princeton University Press.

Li Han. *Mengqiu*. Hayakawa Mitsusaburō, ed. 1973. *Mōgyū*. SKT 58-59. 2 vols. Tokyo: Meiji Shoin.

Watson, Burton, trans. 1979. *Meng ch'iu: Famous Episodes from Chinese History and Legend*. Tokyo, New York: Kōdansha.

Man'yōshū (Collection of Myriad Leaves). Annot. Kojima Noriyuki et al. 1994–96. SNKBZ 9. Tokyo: Shōgakkan.

Cranston, Edwin, trans. 1993. *A Waka Anthology. Volume I: The Gem-Glistening Cup*. Stanford: Stanford University Press.

Michitsuna's Mother. *Kagerō nikki (Gossamer Diary)*. Kikuchi Yasuhiko et al., eds. 1995. *Tosa nikki. Kagerō nikki*. NKBZ 13. Tokyo: Shōgakkan.

Arntzen, Sonja, trans. 1997. *The Kagerō Diary. A Woman's Autobiographical Text from Ancient Japan.* Ann Arbor: Center for Japanese Studies, University of Michigan.

Murasaki Shikibu. *Genji monogatari (The Tale of Genji)*. Abe Akio et al., ed. 1994- *Genji monogatari*. SNKBZ 20–25. Tokyo: Shōgakkan.

Seidensticker, Edward, trans. 1976. *The Tale of Genji*. 2 vols. New York: Knopf.

Tyler, Royall, trans. 2001. *The Tale of Genji*. 2 vols. New York: Viking.

Nara ibun (Documents Remaining from the Nara Period). Takeuchi Rizō et al., eds. 1943–44. *Nara ibun*. Tokyo: Yagi shoten.

Nihon kiryaku (Abbreviated Record of Japan). Kuroita Katsumi, ed. 1929. *Nihon kiryaku*. 2 vols. KST, vols. 10–11. Tokyo: Kokushi Taikei Kankōkai.

Nihon shoki (Chronicles of Japan). Kojima Noriyuki et al., eds. 1994- *Nihon shoki*. 3 vols. Tokyo: Shōgakkan.

Aston, W. G., trans. 1956. *Nihongi: Chronicles of Japan from the Earliest Times to A. C. 697*. London: Allen & Unwin.

Quan Tang shi (Complete Tang Poetry). 1960. Beijing: Zhonghua shuju.

Sei Shōnagon. *Makura no sōshi (The Pillow Book)*. Matsuo Satoshi and Nagai Kazuko, eds. 1997. *Makura no sōshi*. SNKBZ 18. Tokyo: Shōgakkan.

McKinney, Meredith, trans. 2006. *Sei Shōnagon. The Pillow Book*. Penguin, 2006.

Morris, Ivan, trans. *The Pillow Book of Sei Shōnagon*. 2 vols. New York: Columbia University Press.

Shijing (Classic of Poetry). Kong Yingda, annot. 1999. *Shisanjing zhushu. Maoshi zhengyi*. 3 vols. Beijing: Beijing daxue chubanshe.

Legge, James, trans. 1893-95. *The Chinese Classics*, Vol. 4, Part I, II. 2nd rev. ed. Oxford: Clarendon Press.

Shinsen Man'yōshū (Newly Selected Collection of Myriad Leaves). Shinsen Man'yōshū kenkyūkai, ed. 2005. *Shinsen Man'yōshū chūshaku*. 2 vols. Osaka: Izumi shoin.

Shōtoku taishi denryaku (Abridged Biography of Prince Shōtoku). Suzuki Gakujutsu Zaidan, ed. 1970–73. *Dai Nihon Bukkyō zensho*. Tokyo: Kankō Suzuiki Gakujutsu Zaidan: Hatsubai Kōdansha.

Shūi wakashū (Collection of Waka Gleanings). Komachiya Teruhiko et al., eds. 1990. *Shūi wakashū*. SNKBT 7. Tokyo: Iwanami shoten.

Cranston, Edwin, trans. 2006. *A Waka Anthology. Volume Two: Grasses of Remembrance.* Stanford: Stanford University Press.

Richardson, Donald M, trans. 2002. *A Collection of Rescued Japanese Poetry. Shūi wakashū.* 2 vols. Winchester, VA: D. M. Richardson.

Sugawara no Michizane. *Kanke bunsō (Literary Flourish of the Sugawara Family).* Kawaguchi Hisao, ed. 1966. *Kanke bunsō, Kanke kōshū.* NKBT 72. Tokyo: Iwanami shoten.

Rabinovitch, Judith and Timothy Bradstock, trans. 2005. *Dance of the Butterflies. Chinese Poetry from the Japanese Court Tradition.* Ithaca: East Asia Program, Cornell University.

Borgen, Robert, 1986. *Sugawara no Michizane and the Early Heian Court.* Cambridge, Mass.: Harvard University Press.

Wakan rōeishū (Collection of Japanese and Chinese Texts for Recitation). Comp. Fujiwara Kintō. Satō Michio et al., eds. 2011. *Wakan rōeishū. Shinsen rōeishū.* WBT 47. Tokyo: Meiji Shoin. And Ōsone Shōsuke et al., eds. 1983. *Wakan rōeishū.* Shinchō Nihon koten shūsei. Tokyo: Shinchōsha.

Rimer, J. Thomas and Jonathan Chaves, trans. 1997. *Japanese and Chinese Poems to Sing: the Wakan rōeishū.* New York: Columbia University Press.

Wenxuan (Literary Selections). Xiao Tong, comp. 1986. *Wenxuan.* Annot. Li Shan. 6 vols. Shanghai: Shanghai guji chubanshe.

Knechtges, David, trans. 1982-1996. *Wen xuan or Selections of Refined Literature.* 3 vols. Princeton: Princeton University Press.

Wenyuan yinghua (Flowers from the Garden of Literature). 1979. Li Fang, comp. Taibei: Xinwenfeng chubanshe.

Yang Xiong. *Fayan (Model Words).* 1987. *Fayan yishu.* Annot Wang Rongbao. Beijing: Zhonghua shuju.

Yijing (Classic of Changes). Kong Yingda, annot. 1999. *Shisanjing zhushu. Zhouyi zhengyi.* Beijing: Beijing daxue chubanshe.

Lynn, Richard John, trans. 1994. *The Classic of Changes: A New Translation of the I Ching as Interpreted by Wang Bi.* New York: Columbia University Press.

Yiwen leiju (Compendium of Letters Arranged by Category). Ouyang Xun, comp. 1974. *Yiwen leiju.* Taibei: Wenguang chubanshe.

Yutai xinyong (New Songs from a Jade Terrace). Xu Ling, comp. 1985. Wu Zhaoyi and Cheng Yan, eds. *Yutai xinyong jianzhu.* 2 vols. Beijing: Zhonghua shuju.

Birrell, Anne, trans. 1995. *Chinese Love Poetry: New Songs from a Jade Terrace: a Medieval Anthology.* 2nd ed. London and New York: Penguin.

Zhou li (Rituals of the Zhou). 1999. *Zhou li zhushu. Shisanjing zhushu.* 2 vols. Beijing: Beijing daxue chubanshe.

Zoku honchō monzui (Sequel to Literary Essence of Our Court). Kuroita Katsumi et al., eds. 1965. *Honchō monzui. Honchō zoku monzui.* KST vols. 29.2. Tokyo: Yoshikawa Kōbunkan.

II. Greek and Latin Source Texts and Selected Translations

Aulus Gellius. *Noctes Atticae (The Attic Nights).* Rolfe, John C., trans. 1967. *The Attic Nights of Aulus Gellius.* Loeb Classical Library. Cambridge, Mass.: Harvard University Press.

Cassius Dio. *History Romana (Roman History).* Cary, Earnest, trans. 1970-1987. *Cassius Dio. Roman History.* 9 vols. Loeb Classical Library. Cambridge, Mass.: Harvard University Press.

Veh, Otto, trans. 1985. *Cassius Dio. Römische Geschichte.* 5 vols. Zürich: Artemis.

Cicero. *Academica*. Rackham, H., trans. 1967. *De natura deorum: Academica*. Loeb Classical Library. Cambridge, Mass.: Harvard University Press.

Cicero. *Brutus*. Hendrickson, G. L., trans. 1936. *Cicero. Brutus*. Loeb Classical Library. Cambridge, Mass.: Harvard University Press.

Cicero. *De fato (On Fate)*. Sutton, E. W. and H. Rackham, trans. 1948. *De oratore, together with De fato, Paradoxa stoicorum, De partitione oratoria*. Loeb Classical Series. Cambridge, Mass.: Harvard University Press.

Cicero. *De finibus bonorum et malorum (On the Ends of Good and Evil)*. Rackham, H., trans. 1931. *De finibus bonorum et malorum*. Loeb Classical Library. Cambridge, Mass.: Harvard University Press.

Annas, Julia, ed. 2001. *Cicero. De finibus bonorum. On Moral Ends*, trans. Raphael Woolf. Cambridge and New York: Cambridge University Press.

Cicero. *De oratore (On the Orator)*. Sutton, E. W. and H. Rackham, trans. 1948. *De oratore, together with De fato, Paradoxa stoicorum, De partitione oratoria*. Loeb Classical Series. Cambridge, Mass.: Harvard University Press.

May, James M. and Wisse, Jakob, trans. 2001. *Cicero on the Ideal Orator. De oratore*. New York and Oxford: Oxford University Press.

Cicero. *De re publica (On the Commonwealth)*. Keyes, Clinton Walker, trans. 1977. *Cicero. De re publica, De legibus*. Loeb Classical Library. Cambridge, Mass.: Harvard University Press.

Zetzel, James E. G., trans. 1999. *Cicero. On the Commonwealth and On the Laws*. Cambridge, New York: Cambridge University Press.

Ennius. *Annals*. Warmington, E. H., trans. 1935-40. *Remains of Old Latin*. Vol. 1. Loeb Classical Library. Cambridge, Mass.: Harvard University Press.

Dionysius of Halicarnassus. Earnest Cary, trans. 1937-50. *The Roman Antiquities of Dionysius of Halicarnassus*. Loeb Classical Literary. 7 vols. Cambridge, Mass.: Harvard University Press.

Fragmenta Poetarum Latinorum. Jürgen Blänsdorf et al., eds. 1995. 3rd ed. Stuttgart: Teubner.

Die Fragmente der griechischen Historiker. Jacoby, Felix, ed. 1923–58. Berlin: Weidman.

Horace. *Carmina (Odes)*. Niall Rudd, trans. 2004. *Horace. Odes and Epodes*. Loeb Classical Library. Cambridge, Mass.: Harvard University Press.

Shepherd, W. G., trans. 1983. *The Complete Odes and Epodes: With the Centennial Hymn*. Penguin.

Livius Andronicus. Warmington, H., trans. 1982. *Remains of Old Latin*. Vol. 2. Loeb Classical Library. Cambridge, Mass: Harvard University Press.

Livy. *Ab urbe condita libri (History Since the Foundation of the City of Rome)*. Foster, B. O., trans. 1967–84. *Livy*. Loeb Classical Library. 14 vols. Cambridge, Mass.: Harvard University Press.

Lucian. *Dialogi mortuorum. Hermotimus. Vitarum auctio* (Dialogues of the Dead; Hermotimus; Philosophies for Sale). Harmon, A. M., K. Kilburn and M. D. Macleod, trans. 1960–67. *Lucian*. 8 vols. Loeb Classical Library. Cambridge, Mass.: Harvard University Press.

Fowler, H. W. and Fowler, F. G., trans. 1905. *The Works of Lucian of Samosata*. 4 vols. Oxford: Clarendon Press.

Casson, Lionel, trans. 1962. *Selected Satires of Lucian*. New York: Norton.

Martianus Capella. *De nuptiis Philologiae et Mercurii (On the Marriage of Philology and Mercury)*. Dick, Adolf, ed. 1969. *Martianus Capella. De nuptiis Philologiae et Mercurii*. Stuttgart: Teubner.

Stahl, William Harris, trans. 1977. *The Marriage of Philology and Mercury*. New York: Columbia University Press.

Plato. *Timaeus*. Bury, R. G., trans. 1929. *Plato. Timaeus; Critias; Cleitophon; Menexenus; Epistles*. Loeb Classical Library. London: W. Heinemann.

Waterfield, Robin, trans. 2008. *Plato, Timaeus and Critias*. Oxford and New York: Oxford University Press.

Plutarch. Perrin, Bernadotte, trans. 1928. *Plutarch's Lives*. 11 vols. Loeb Classical Library. London: William Heinemann.

Polybius. *Histories*. Paton, W. R. 1922–1927. *Polybius*. Loeb Classical Library. Cambridge, Mass.: Harvard University Press.

Scott-Kilvert, Ian, trans. 1979. *The Rise of the Roman Empire*. Penguin.

Ovid. *Fasti*. Frazer, Sir James George and Goold, G.P., trans. 1989. *Ovid. Fasti*. Loeb Classical Library. Cambridge, Mass.: Harvard University Press.

Wiseman, Peter and Anne Wiseman, trans. 2011. *Ovid: Times and Reasons. A New Translation of Fasti*. Oxford: Oxford University Press.

Ovid. *Tristia. Epistulae ex Ponto (Tristia. Letters from the Black Sea)*. Goold, G. P. and Wheeler. A. L., trans. 1988. *Ovid. Tristia. Ex Ponto*. Loeb Classical Library. Cambridge, Mass.: Harvard University Press.

Green, Peter, trans. 2005. *Ovid. The Poems of Exile. Tristia and the Black Sea Letters*. Berkeley: University of California Press.

Pliny. *Naturalis historia (Natural History)*. Rackham, Harris, trans. 1967–75. *Pliny. Natural History* Loeb Classical Library. Cambridge, Mass.: Harvard University Press. Vol. 8 trans.W. H. S. Jones, 1968.

Healy, John F., trans. 1991. *Pliny. Natural History*. Penguin.

Propertius. *Elegies*. Goold, G. P., trans. 1990. *Propertius. Elegies*. Loeb Classical Library. Cambridge, Mass.: Harvard University Press.

Katz, Vincent, trans. 2004. *The Complete Elegies of Sextus Propertius*. Princeton: Princeton University Press.

Quintilian. *Institutio oratoria (The Orator's Education)*. Russell, Donald A., trans. 2001. *Quintilian. The Orator's Education*. 5 vols. Loeb Classical Library. Cambridge, Mass.: Harvard University Press.

Suetonius De Grammaticis et Rhetoribus (On Grammarians and Rhetors). Rolfe, J. C., trans. 1997–98. *Suetonius. Works*. 2 vols. Cambridge, Mass.: Harvard University Press.

Kaster, Robert, trans. 1995. *C. Suetonius Tranquillus. De Grammaticis et Rhetoribus*. Oxford: Clarendon Press.

Tacitus. *Dialogus de oratoribus (Dialogue on Orators)*. Peterson, William, trans. 1939 *Tacitus. Dialogue, Agricola, Germania*. Loeb Classical Library: Cambridge, Mass.: Harvard University Press.

Benario, Herbert W., trans. 1991. *Tacitus' Agricola, Germany, and Dialogue on Orators*. Revised edition. Norman and London: University of Oklahoma Press.

Volkmer, Hans, trans. 1979. *Dialogus de oratoribus. Das Gespräch über den Redner: lateinisch-deutsch*. München: Heimeran.

Valerius Maximus. *Factorum et dictorum memorabilium (Memorable Doings and Sayings)*. Shackleton Bailey, D. R., trans. 2000. *Memorable Doings and Sayings*. 2 vols. Loeb Classical Library. Cambridge, Mass.: Harvard University Press.

Velleius Paterculus. *Historiae Romanae (Roman History)*. Shipley, Frederick W., trans. 1979. *Velleius Paterculus, Historiae Romanae*. Loeb Classical Library. Cambridge, Mass.: Harvard University Press.

Virgil. *Aeneid*. Fairclough, H. R. and Goold, G.P. 1998-1999. *Virgil*. 2 vols. Loeb Classical Library. Cambridge, Mass. and London: Harvard University Press.

Fagles, Robert. 2006. *The Aeneid. Vergil*. Viking, 2006. Ruden, Sarah, trans. 2008. *The Aeneid. Vergil*. New Haven and London: Yale University Press.

Lombardo, Stanley, trans. 2005. *Aeneid. Vergil*. Indianapolis: Hackett Publishing.

III. Secondary Sources

Abramson, Marc S. 2008. *Ethnic Identity in Tang China*. Philadelphia: University of Pennsylvania Press.

Alcock, S. E. 1993. *Graecia Capta. The Landscapes of Roman Greece*. Cambridge: Cambridge University Press.

——— ed. 1997. *The Early Roman Empire in the East*. Oxford: Oxbow Books.

Amagai Hiroshi et al., eds. 2001. *Makura no sōshi daijiten*. Tokyo: Benseisha.

Anderson, Graham. 1993. *The Second Sophistic: a Cultural Phenomenon in the Roman Empire*. London and New York: Routledge.

Anderson, Michael J. 1997. *The Fall of Troy in Early Greek Poetry and Art*. Oxford and New York: Oxford University Press.

Annas, Julia, ed. 2001. *Cicero. De finibus bonorum. On Moral Ends*, trans. Raphael Woolf. Cambridge and New York: Cambridge University Press.

Arnold, Heinz Ludwig, ed. 2009. *Kindlers Literatur Lexikon*. 19 vols. Berlin: J. B. Metzler.

Arntzen, Sonja. 1997. *The Kagerō Diary. A Woman's Autobiographical Text from Ancient Japan*. Ann Arbor: Center for Japanese Studies, University of Michigan,

Assmann, Jan. 2002. *The Mind of Egypt: History and Meaning in the Time of the Pharaohs*. New York: Metropolitan Books.

———.2005. "Periergia: Egyptian Reactions to Greek Curiosity." In *Cultural Borrowings and Ethnic Appropriations in Antiquity*, ed. Erich Gruen. Wiesbaden: Franz Steiner Verlag, 37–49.

Auerbach, Erich. 1969. "Philology and Weltliteratur." Trans. Maire and Edward Said. In *The Centennial Review* 13.1, 1–17.

Ax, Wolfram. 2006. "*Quattuor Linguae Latinae Aetates*. Neue Forschungen zur Geschichte der Begriffe Goldene und Silberne Latinität." In *Text und Stil. Studien zur antiken Literatur und deren Rezeption*, ed. Christian Schwarz. Stuttgart: Franz Steiner Verlag, 111–30.

Bakhtin, Mikhail. 1986. *Speech Genres and Other Late Essays*, ed. Michael Holquist. Austin: University of Texas Press.

Barchiesi, Alessandro and Walter Scheidel. 2010. *The Oxford Handbook of Roman Studies*. Oxford and New York: Oxford University Press.

Barnes, Gina. 1993. *China, Korea, and Japan. The Rise of Civilization in East Asia*. London: Thames and Hudson.

———. 2007. *State Formation in Japan. Emergence of a Fourth-century Ruling Elite*. New York: Routledge.

Batten, Bruce. 2006. *Gateway to Japan. Hakata in War and Peace, 500–1300*. Honolulu: University of Hawai'i Press.

Beecroft, Alexander. 2010. *Authorship and Cultural Identity in Early Greece and China: Patterns of Literary Circulation*. Cambridge: Cambridge University Press.

Bennett, C. E. 1968. *Horace. Odes and Epodes*. Loeb Classical Library. Cambridge, Mass.: Harvard University Press.

Binder, Gerhard. 1971. *Aeneas and Augustus. Interpretationen zum 8. Buch der Aeneis*. Meisenheim am Glan: Verlag Anton Hain.

Birrell, Anne. 2004. *Games Poets Play. Readings in Medieval Chinese Poetry*. Cambridge: McGuinness China Monographs.

Bloomer, M. Martin. 1997. *Latinity and Literary Society at Rome*. Philadelphia: University of Pennsylvania Press.

Boardman, John. 1980. *The Greeks Overseas. Their Early Colonies and Trade*. London: Thames and Hudson.

Bol, Peter. 1992. *"This Culture of Ours": Intellectual Transitions in T'ang and Sung China*. Stanford: Stanford University Press.

Bonner, Stanley F. 1977. *Education in Ancient Rome*. Berkeley and Los Angeles: University of California Press.

Borgen, Robert. 1986. *Sugawara no Michizane and the Early Heian Court*. Cambridge, Mass.: Harvard University Press.

———. May 2004. "Love in Heian Japan. Domestic and Imported." Unpublished paper at the workshop "New Approaches to Early Japanese Textuality: Boundaries, Genres, and Contexts of Sino-Japanese Literature." Harvard University.

Boyd, Barbara Weiden, ed. 2002. *Brill's Companion to Ovid*. Leiden, Boston, Köln: Brill.

Bungaku 2010. "Zadankai: Waka to Girisha, Rōma no shi." 11.4, 116–52; and "Zadankai: Waka to Girisha, Rōma no shi." 11.6, 160–94.

Cai Zongqi. 2001. *A Chinese Literary Mind. Culture, Creativity, and Rhetoric in* Wenxin Diaolong. Stanford: Stanford University Press.

Cairns, Francis. 2006. "Propertius and the Origins of Latin Love Elegy," in *Brill's Companion to Propertius*, ed. Hans-Christian Günther. Leiden and Boston: Brill, 67–95.

Cameron, Alan. 2004. *Greek Mythography in the Roman World*. Oxford and New York: Oxford University Press.

Cary, Earnest, trans. 1937-50. *Dionysius of Halicarnassus. Roman Antiquities*. Loeb Classical Library. 7 vols. Cambridge, Mass.: Harvard University Press.

———, trans. 1970-1987. *Cassius Dio. Roman History*. Loeb Classical Library. 9 vols. Cambridge, Mass.: Harvard University Press.

Casali, Sergio. 2010. "The Development of the Aeneas Legend." In *A Companion to Vergil's* Aeneid *and Its Tradition*, ed. Joseph Farrell and Michael C. J. Putnam. Malden, Mass.: Wiley-Blackwell, 37–51.

Casson, Lionel, 1962. trans. *Selected Satires of Lucian*. New York: Norton.

Ceugniet, Atsuko. 2000. *L'office des études supérieures au Japon du VIIIe au XIIe siècle et les dissertations de fin d'études*. Genève: Librairie Droz.

Champion, Craige B., ed. 2004. *Roman Imperialism. Readings and Sources*. Malden: Blackwell Publishing.

Chiappinelli, Francesco. 2007. *Impius Aeneas*. Acireale: Bonanno.

Christes, Johannes. 1979. *Sklaven und Freigelassene als Grammatiker und Philologen im antiken Rom*. Wiesbaden: Franz Steiner Verlag.

Claassen, Jo-Marie. 1999. *Displaced Persons. The Literature of Exile from Cicero to Boethius*. Madison: University of Wisconsin Press.

Como, Michael. 2008. *Shōtoku. Ethnicity, Ritual, and Violence in the Japanese Buddhist Tradition*. Oxford and New York: Oxford University Press.

Conte, Gian Biagio. 1994a. *Genre and Readers. Lucretius, Love Elegy, Pliny's Encyclopedia*. Baltimore and London: The Johns Hopkins University Press.

———. 1994b. *Latin Literature. A History*. Baltimore and London: The Johns Hopkins University Press.

———. 2007. *The Poetry of Pathos. Studies in Virgilian Epic*, ed. Stephen Harrison. Oxford and New York: Oxford University Press.

Copenhaver, Brian. 1992. *The Greek Corpus Hermeticum and the Latin Asclepius*. Cambridge: Cambridge University Press.

Cornell, T. J. 1995. *The Beginnings of Rome. Italy and Rome from the Bronze Age to the Punic Wars (c. 1000–264 bc)*. London: Routledge.

Cranston, Edwin. 1993. *A Waka Anthology. Volume I: The Gem-Glistening Cup*. Stanford: Stanford University Press.

———. 2006. *A Waka Anthology. Volume 2.* 2 vols. *Grasses of Remembrance*. Stanford: Stanford University Press.

Cribiore, Rafaella. 2001. *Gymnastics of the Mind. Greek Education in Hellenistic and Roman Egypt*. Princeton: Princeton University Press.

Cristofani, Mauro. "Litterazione e processi di autoidentificazione etnica fra le genti dell'Italia arcaica." In *La colonisation grecque en Méditerranée occidentale: Actes de la rencontre scientifique en hommage à Georges Vallet organisée par le Centre Jean-Bérard, l'Ecole française de Rome, l'Istituto universitario orientale et l'Università degli studi di Napoli Federico II, Rome, Naples, 15-18 novembre 1995*. Rome: Ecole française de Rome, 1999, 345–60.

Dale, Peter N. 1986. *The Myth of Japanese Uniqueness*. London: Croom Helm.

Damrosch, David. 2003. *What Is World Literature?*. Princeton: Princeton University Press.

———, ed. 2009a. *Teaching World Literature*. New York: MLA.

———. 2009b. *How to Read World Literature*. Malden, Mass.: Wiley-Blackwell.

David Sedley, ed. 2003. *The Cambridge Companion to Greek and Roman Philosophy*. Cambridge: Cambridge University Press.

Dearden, C. W. 1990. "Fourth-Century Tragedy in Sicily: Athenian or Sicilian?" In *Greek Colonists and Native Populations*, ed. Jean-Paul Descoeudres. Oxford: Clarendon Press, 221–42.

DeBlasi, Anthony. 2002. *Reform in the Balance. The Defense of Literary Culture in Mid-Tang China*. Albany: SUNY Press.

Dench, Emma. 2010. "Roman Identity." In *Oxford Handbook of Roman Studies*, ed. Alessandro Barchiesi and Walter Scheidel. Oxford and New York: Oxford University Press, 266–80.

Denecke, Wiebke. 2004 issue, 2006. "Writing History in the Face of the Other: Early Japanese Anthologies and the Beginnings of Literature." In *BMFEA* 76, 71–114.

————. 2005. "Bilingual Landscapes: Divided Pleasures at Yoshino Palace in Early Japanese and Sino-Japanese Poetry." In *Minds of the Past. Representations of Mentality in Literary and Historical Documents of Japan and Europe*, ed. Takami Matsuda and Michio Satō. Tokyo: Keiō University Press, 165–89.

————. 2007. "'Topic Poetry is All Ours'—Poetic Composition on Chinese Lines in Early Heian Japan." In *HJAS* 67.1, 1–49.

————. 2008 . *"Seitenkasaseru Parodi—shoki Genji monogatari juyō toshite no Fu Hikaru Genji monogatari shi ni tsuite."* In *Kōza Genji monogatari kenkyū*. Vol. 11. "Kaigai ni okeru Genji monogatari," ed. Ii Haruki and Haruo Shirane. Tokyo: Ōfūsha, 164–90.

————. 2010. *The Dynamics of Masters Literature: Early Chinese Thought from Confucius to Han Feizi*. Cambridge, Mass.: Harvard University Press.

————. 2012. "Japan's Vernacular and Sino-Japanese Poetry: a Bird's Eye View from Rome." In *Sekai no naka no waka bungaku*, eds. Haruo Shirane et al. Tokyo: Bensey Publishing, 19–32 and 203–15.

————. 2014. "Worlds Without Translation. Traditional East Asia and the Power of Character Languages." In *A Companion to Translation Studies*, ed. Sandra Bermann and Catherine Porter. Malden, Mass., and Oxford: Blackwell Publishers.

Denecke, Wiebke and Kōno Kimiko. 2013. *Nihon ni okeru bun to bungaku. Ajia yūgaku* 162. Tokyo: Benseisha.

Denoon, Donald, Mark Hudson, Gavan McCormack, and Tessa Morris-Suzuki, eds. 1996. *Multicultural Japan. Palaeolithic to Postmodern*. Cambridge: Cambridge University Press.

Dewar, Michael 2002. "Siquid habent ueri uatum praesagia: Ovid in the 1st–5th Centuries A.D." In *Brill's Companion to Ovid*, ed. Barbara Weiden Boyd. Leiden, Boston, Köln: Brill, 383–412.

D'Haen, Theo, David Damrosch, and Djelal Kadir, eds. 2012. *The Routledge Companion to World Literature*. New York: Routledge.

Dick, Adolf. 1969. *Martianus Capella. De nuptiis Philologiae et Mercurii*. Stuttgart: Teubner.

Dickey, Eleanor. 2007. *Ancient Greek Scholarship. A Guide to Finding, Reading, and Understanding Scholia, Commentaries, Lexica, and Grammatical Treatises, From Their Beginnings to the Byzantine Period*. Oxford: Oxford University Press.

Duff, Tim. 1999. *Plutarch's Lives. Exploring Virtue and Vice*. Oxford: Oxford University Press.

Eckstein, Arthur M. 2008. *Rome Enters the Greek East: From Anarchy to Hierarchy in the Hellenistic Mediterranean, 230–170 BC*. Malden, Mass. and Oxford: Blackwell Publishers.

Edwards, Catherine. 1996. *Writing Rome. Textual Approaches to the City*. Cambridge: Cambridge University Press.

Edwards, Catherine. 2003b. "Incorporating the Alien: the Art of Conquest." In *Rome the Cosmopolis*, ed. Catharine Edwards and Greg Woolf. Cambridge: Cambridge University Press, 44–70.

Edwards, Catherine and Greg Woolf. 2003a. *Rome the Cosmopolis*. Cambridge: Cambridge University Press.

Eliot, T. S. 1957. *On Poetry and Poets*. London: Faber and Faber.

Elman, Benjamin. 2000. *A Cultural History of Civil Examination in Late Imperial China*. Berkeley: University of California Press.

Fagles, Robert. 2006. *The Aeneid. Vergil*. New York: Viking.

Fairclough, H. R. *Horace*. 1929. *Satires, Epistles, Ars Poetica*. Loeb Classical Library. Cambridge, Mass.: Harvard University Press.

Fairclough, H. R. and Goold, G.P. 1998-1999. *Virgil*. 2 vols. Loeb Classical Library. Cambridge, Mass.: Harvard University Press.

Fairweather, J. 1987. "Ovid's autobiographical poem, *Tristia* 4.10." In *CQ* 37, 181–96.

Fantham, Elaine. 1996. *Roman Literary Culture from Cicero to Apuleius*. Baltimore: Johns Hopkins University Press.

———. 2004. *The Roman World of Cicero's* De oratore. Oxford: Oxford University Press.

Farrell, Joseph. 2001. *Latin Language and Latin Culture. From Ancient to Modern Times*. Cambridge and New York: Cambridge University Press.

Farrell, Joseph and Michael C. J. Putnam, eds. 2010. *A Companion to Vergil's Aeneid and Its Tradition*, Malden, Mass.: Wiley-Blackwell.

Farris, William Wayne. 1998. *Sacred Texts and Buried Treasures. Issues in the Historical Archaeology of Ancient Japan*. Honolulu: University of Hawai'i Press.

———. 2009. *Japan to 1600. A Social and Economic History*. Honolulu: University of Hawai'i Press.

Feeney, Denis. 1991. *The Gods in Epic. Poets and Critics of the Classical Tradition*. Oxford: Clarendon Press.

———. 2000. Review of English translation of Dupont, *L'invention de la littérature: de l'ivresse grecque au livre latin*. Paris, *TLS* 28. April, p. 9.

———. 2005. "The Beginnings of a Literature in Latin." (Review of W. Suerbaum's *Handbuch der lateinischen Literatur der Antike. Erster Band*). In *JRS*, vol. 95, 226–40.

———. 2007. *Caesar's Calendar. Ancient Time and the Beginnings of History*. Berkeley: University of California Press.

———. 2009. "Time." In *The Cambridge Companion to the Roman Historians*, ed. Andrew Feldherr, 139–51.

Feldherr, Andrew, ed. 2009. *The Cambridge Companion to the Roman Historians*. Cambridge: Cambridge University Press.

Ferguson, Niall, ed. 1997. *Virtual History: Alternatives and Counterfactuals*. London: Picador.

Fiévé, Nicolas, ed. 2008. *Atlas historique de Kyoto: analyse spatiale des systèmes de mémoire d'une ville, de son architecture et de son paysage urbain*. Paris: Editions de l'Amateur.

Fiske, George Converse. 1920. *Lucilius and Horace. A Study in the Classical Theory of Imitation*. Madison, Wis.: University of Wisconsin Press.

Foegen, Thorsten. 2000. *Patrii sermonis egestas. Einstellungen lateinischer Autoren zu ihrer Muttersprache. Ein Beitrag zum Sprachbewußtsein in der römischen Antike*. München, Leipzig: K. G. Saur.

Fogel, Joshua. 1996. *The Literature of Travel in the Japanese Rediscovery of China. 1862-1945*. Stanford: Stanford University Press.

———. 2009. *Articulating the Sinosphere. Sino-Japanese Relations in Space and Time.* Cambridge, Mass.: Harvard University Press.

Foster, B. O., trans. 1967-84. *Livy.* 14 vols. Loeb Classical Library. Cambridge, Mass.: Harvard University Press.

Fowden, Garth. 1986. *The Egyptian Hermes. A Historical Approach to the Late Pagan Mind.* Cambridge: Cambridge University Press.

Fowler, H. W. and Fowler, F. G., trans. 1905. *The Works of Lucian of Samosata.* 4 vols. Oxford: Clarendon Press.

Frazer, Sir James George and Goold, G. P., trans. 1989. *Ovid. Fasti.* Loeb Classical Library. Cambridge, Mass.: Harvard University Press.

Freudenburg, Kirk. 1993. *The Walking Muse. Horace on the Theory of Satire.* Princeton: Princeton University Press.

———, ed. 2005. *Cambridge Companion to Roman Satire.* Cambridge: Cambridge University Press.

Froesch, Hartmut. 1976. *Ovid als Dichter des Exils.* Bonn: Bouvier Verlag.

Fuhrmann, Manfred. 2005. *Geschichte der römischen Literatur.* Stuttgart: Reclam.

Fujiwara Katsumi. 2001. *Sugawara no Michizane to Heianchō kanbungaku.* Tokyo: Tōkyō daigaku shuppankai.

———. 2002. *Sugawara no Michizane. Shijin no unmei.* Tokyo: Wedji.

Fukumori, Naomi. 1997. "Sei Shonagon's Makura no sōshi: A Re-Visionary History." In *JATJ*, Vol. 31.1. Apr., 1–44.

Furuse Natsuko. 2003. *Kentōshi no mita Chūgoku.* Tokyo: Yoshikawa kōbunkan.

Garrison, James D. 1992. *Pietas from Vergil to Dryden.* University Park, Pa.: The Pennsylvania State University Press.

Gee, Emma. 2000. *Ovid, Aratus, and Augustus. Astronomy in Ovid's* Fasti. Cambridge: Cambridge University Press.

Gibson, Roy. "Love Elegy." In *Companion to Latin Literature*, ed. Stephen Harrison. Malden, Mass.: Blackwell, 159–73.

Goethe, Johann Wolfgang von. 1805. *Winckelmann und sein Jahrhundert. In Briefen und Aufsätzen herausgegeben.* Tübingen: Cotta.

Goldberg, Sander. 2005. *Constructing Literature in the Roman Republic.* Cambridge: Cambridge University Press.

Goldhill, Simon, ed. 2001. *Being Greek Under Rome: Cultural Identity, the Second Sophistic, and the Development of Empire.* Cambridge: Cambridge University Press.

Goold, G. P. 1990. *Propertius. Elegies.* Loeb Classical Library. Cambridge, Mass.: Harvard University Press.

Goold, G. P. and Wheeler. A. L. 1988. *Ovid. Tristia. Ex Ponto.* Loeb Classical Library. Cambridge, Mass.: Harvard University Press.

Gotō Akio. 1986-87. "Ōe no Masafusa 'Shikyōki shichū." In *Chūko bungaku to kanbungaku II.* Tokyo: Kyūko shoin, 303–26.

———. 1993a. "Sugawara no Michizane no eichikushi." In Gotō, *Heianchō Bunjinshi.* Tokyo: Yoshikawa Kōbunkan, 102–34.

———. 1993b. "Sugawara no Michizane to Haku Kyoi—shi no chūki to *Kanke bunsō* no hensan." In *Haku Kyoi kenkyū kōza.* Vol. 3, ed. Ōta Tsugio et al. Tokyo: Benseisha, 75–94.

————. 2004. "Fu Hikaru Genji monogatari shijo ni tsuite." In *Gobun* 80.81, 3–12.

Gowers, Emily. 2005. "The Restless Companion: Horace, *Satires* 1 and 2." In *The Cambridge Companion to Roman Satire*, ed. Kirk Freudenburg. Cambridge: Cambridge University Press, 48–61.

Gransden, K. W. 1976. *Vergil. Aeneid. Book VIII*. Cambridge: Cambridge University Press.

Grebe, Sabine. 1999. *Martianus Capella, "De nuptiis Philologiae et Mercurii": Darstellung der sieben freien Kuenste und ihrer Beziehungen zueinander*. Stuttgart: Teubner.

Green, Peter. 2005. *Ovid. The Poems of Exile. Tristia and the Black Sea Letters*. Berkeley: University of California Press.

Griffin, Miriam and Jonathan Barnes, eds. 1989, 1997. *Philosophia Togata. Essays on Philosophy and Roman Society I+II*. Oxford: Clarendon Press.

Groner, Paul. 2007. *Ryōgen and Mount Hiei: Japanese Tendai in the Tenth Century*. University of Hawai'i Press.

Gruen, Erich S. 1984. *The Hellenistic World and the Coming of Rome*. 2 vols. Berkeley: University of California Press.

————. 1992a. *Culture and National Identity in Republican Rome*. Ithaca: Cornell University Press.

————. 1992b. "The Making of the Trojan Legend." In Gruen, Erich S. *Culture and National Identity in Republican Rome*. Ithaca: Cornell University Press, 6–51.

Gunsho ruijū. 1959-1960. 29 vols. Zoku Gunsho Ruijū Kanseikai.

Günther, Hans-Christian, ed. 2006. *Brill's Companion to Propertius*. Leiden and Boston: Brill.

Gutzwiller, Kathryn. 1998. *Poetic Garlands: Hellenistic Epigrams in Context*. Berkeley, Los Angeles, London: University of California Press.

————. 2007. *A Guide to Hellenistic Literature*. Malden, Mass.: Blackwell Publishers.

Hall, John W. 1974. "Kyoto as Historical Background." In *Medieval Japan. Essays in Institutional History*, ed. Hall and Jeffrey P. Mass. New Haven: Yale University Press, 3–38.

Hansen, Inge Lyse. 2011. "Between Atticus and Aeneas: the Making of a Colonial Elite at Roman Butrint." In *Roman Colonies in the First Century of Their Foundation*, ed. Rebecca J. Sweetman. Oxford and Oakville: Oxbow Books, 85–100.

Hardie, Philip. 1993. *The Epic Successors of Virgil. A Study in the Dynamics of a Tradition*. Cambridge: Cambridge University Press.

————. 1998. *Vergil*. Greece & Rome. New Surveys in the Classics No. 28. Oxford and New York: Oxford University Press.

Harmon, A. M., K. Kilburn and M. D. Macleod, trans. 1960-67. *Lucian*. 8 vols. Loeb Classical Library. Cambridge, Mass.: Harvard University Press.

Harris, William V. 1989. *Ancient Literacy*. Cambridge, Mass.: Harvard University Press.

Harrison, Stephen, ed. 2005. *A Companion to Latin Literature*. Malden, Mass.: Blackwell.

————. 2007. *Generic Enrichments in Vergil and Horace*. Oxford and New York: Oxford University Press.

Hatooka Akira. 2005. *Kyūtei shijin Sugawara no Michizane*. Kanke bunsō, Kanke kōshū *no sekai*. Tokyo: Kasama shoin.

Hawthorne, Geoffrey. 1991. *Plausible Worlds: Possibility and Understanding in History and the Social Sciences*. Cambridge University Press.

Hayakawa Mitsusaburō, ed. 1973. *Mōgyū (Ch. Mengqiu)*. SKT, vol. 58-59. Tokyo: Meiji shoin.

Haynes, Kenneth. 2010. "Classic Virgil." In *A Companion to Vergil's Aeneid and Its Tradition*, ed. Joseph Farrell and Michael C. J. Putnam. Malden, Mass.: Wiley-Blackwell, 421–34.

Hayot, Eric, Haun Saussy, and Steven G. Yao, eds. 2008. *Sinographies. Writing China*. Minneapolis: University of Minnesota Press.

Hendrickson, G. L. 1936. *Cicero. Brutus*. Loeb Classical Library. Cambridge, Mass.: Harvard University Press.

Henry, Elizabeth. 1989. *The Vigour of Prophecy. A Study of Vergil's* Aeneid. Bristol: Bristol Classical Press.

Hérail, Francine. 1995. *La cour du Japon à l'époque de Heian aus Xe et XIe siècles*. Paris: Hachette.

Herzfeld, Michael. 1987. *Anthropology through the Looking-Glass: Critical Ethnography in the Margins of Europe*. Cambridge: Cambridge University Press.

———. 2002. "The Absent Presence: Discourses of Crypto-Colonialism." In *South Atlantic Quarterly* 101.4, 899–926.

Herzog, Reinhart and Peter Lebrecht Schmidt. 1989-. *Handbuch der lateinischen Literatur der Antike*. 5 Vols. München: C. H. Beck.

Hexter, Ralph. 2002. "Ovid in the Middle Ages: Exile, Mythographer, Lover." In *Brill's Companion to Ovid*, ed. Barbara Weiden Boyd. Leiden, Boston, Köln: Brill, 413–42.

Hibbert, Christopher. 1985. *Rome. The Biography of a City*. Hammondsworth: Penguin.

Hillen, Hans Jürgen. 2003. *Von Aeneas zu Romulus. Die Legenden von der Gründung Roms. Mit einer lateinisch-deutschen Ausgabe der* Origo gentis Romanae. Düsseldorf: Artemis & Winkler.

Hinds, Stephen. 1998. *Allusion and Intertext. Dynamics of Appropriation in Roman Poetry*. Cambridge: Cambridge University Press.

Hisaki Yukio. 1990. *Nihon kodai gakkō no kenkyū*. Tokyo and Machida: Tamagawa Daigaku Shuppanbun.

Hoff, Michael C. and Susan I. Rotroff, eds. 1997. *The Romanization of Athens*. Oxford: Oxbow Books.

Holcombe, Charles. 2001. *The Genesis of East Asia. 221 B.C.–A.D. 907*. Honolulu: University of Hawai'i Press.

Hollis, Adrian. 2006. "Propertius and Hellenistic Poetry." In *Brill's Companion to Propertius*, ed. Hans-Christian Günther. Leiden and Boston: Brill, 97–125.

Hu Zhi'ang. J. Ko Shikō. 1998. *Nara Man'yō to Chūgoku bungaku*. Tokyo: Kasama shoin.

Hubbard, Margaret. 1974. *Propertius*. London: Duckworth.

Hudson, Mark J. 1999. *Ruins of Identity. Ethnogenesis in the Japanese Islands*. Honolulu: University of Hawai'i Press.

Hutcheon, Linda. 2000. *A Theory of Parody. The Teachings of Twentieth-Century Art Forms*. 2nd ed. Urbana and Chicago: University of Illinois Press.

Iida Mizuho. 2000. *Shōtoku Taishi den no kenkyū*. Tokyo: Yoshikawa kōbunkan.

Inaga Keiji. 2008. *Nikki bungaku to Makura no sōshi no tankyū*, ed. Senō Yoshinobu. Tokyo: Kasama Shoin.

Jacoby, Felix. 1923-58. *Die Fragmente der griechischen Historiker*. Berlin: Weidman.

James, Sharon L. 2003. *Learned Girls and Male Persuasion. Gender and Reading in Roman Love Elegy*. Berkeley, Los Angeles, London: University of California Press.

Johnson, W. R. 2009. *A Latin Lover in Ancient Rome. Readings in Propertius and His Genre*. Columbus: The Ohio State University Press.

Jones, C. P. 1971. *Plutarch and Rome*. Oxford: Clarendon Press.

Jongman, Willem. 2003. "Slavery and the Growth of Rome. The Transformation of Italy in the Second and First Centuries BCE." In *Rome the Cosmopolis*, ed. Catharine Edwards and Greg Woolf. Cambridge: Cambridge University Press, 100–22.

Joyal, Mark, Iain McDougall, and J. C. Yardley. 2009. *Greek and Roman Education. A Sourcebook*. London and New York: Routledge.

Kamens, Edward. 1997. *Utamakura, Allusion, and Intertextuality in Traditional Japanese Poetry*. New Haven: Yale University Press.

———. 2007. "Terrains of Text in Mid-Heian Court Culture." In *Heian Japan, Centers and Peripheries*, ed. Mikael Adolphson, Edward Kamens, and Stacie Matsumoto. Honolulu: University of Hawaiʻi Press, 129–52.

Kaster, Robert A. 1988. *Guardians of Language: The Grammarian and Society in Late Antiquity*. Berkeley, Los Angeles: University of California Press.

———. 1995. *C. Suetonius Tranquillus. De Grammaticis et Rhetoribus*. Oxford: Clarendon Press.

Katagiri Yōichi. 1998. *Kokinwakashū zenhyōshaku*. Tokyo: Kōdansha.

Kawaguchi Hisao. 1966. *Kanke bunsō, Kanke kōshū*. NKBT 72. Tokyo: Iwanami shoten.

Keyes, Clinton Walker, trans. 1977. *Cicero. De re publica, De legibus*. Loeb Classical Library. Cambridge, Mass.: Harvard University Press.

Kilburn, K. 1959. *Lucian*. 8 vols. Cambridge, Mass.: Harvard University Press.

Kimiya Yasuhiko. 1965. *Nikka bunka kōryūshi*. Tokyo: Fuzanbō.

Kin Bunkyō. 2010. *Kanbun to Higashi Ajia: kundoku no bunkaken*. Tokyo: Iwanami shoten.

Kojima Noriyuki, ed. 1964. *Kaifūsō, Bunka shūreishū, Honchō monzui*. NKBT 69. Tokyo: Iwanami shoten.

Kojima Noriyuki and Arai Eizō, eds. 1989. *Kokin wakashū*. SNKBT 5. Tokyo: Iwanami shoten.

Kojima Noriyuki et al., eds. 1994-. *Nihon shoki*. SNKBZ. 3 vols. Tokyo: Shōgakkan.

———. et al., eds. 1994-96. *Man'yōshū* SNKBZ. 4 vols. Tokyo: Shōgakkan.

Kojima Noriyuki and Yamamoto Tokuro. 1998. *Sugawara no Michizane*. Tokyo: Kenbun shuppansha.

Komachiya Teruhiko, ed. 1990. *Shūiwakashū*. SNKBT. Tokyo: Iwanami shoten.

Kōnoshi Takamitsu and Sakamoto Nobuyuki, eds. 1999-. *Seminā Man'yō no kajin to sakuhin*. Osaka: Izumi shoin.

Kornicki, Peter. 1998. *The Book in Japan. A Cultural History from the Beginnings to the Nineteenth Century.* Leiden: Brill.

——. 2008. *Having Difficulty with Chinese? The Rise of the Vernacular Book in Japan, Korea and Vietnam.* Sandars Lectures.

——. 2010. "A Note on Sino-Japanese: A Question of Terminology." In *Sino-Japanese Studies* 17, 29–44.

Kroll, Wilhelm. 1924. *Studien zum Verständnis der römischen Literatur.* Stuttgart: J. B. Metzler.

Kudo Shigenori. 1993. *Heianchō ritsuryō shakai no bungaku.* Tokyo: Perikansha.

Kuriyama, Shigehisa. 1999. *The Expressiveness of the Body and the Divergence of Greek and Chinese Medicine.* New York: Zone Books.

Kuroita Katsumi and Kokushi Taikei Henshūkai, eds. 1965a. *Honchō zoku monzui.* KST 29.2. Tokyo: Yoshikawa Kōbunkan.

——, eds. 1965b. *Nihon kiryaku.* KST 10-11. Tokyo: Yoshikawa Kōbunkan.

LaMarre, Thomas. 2000. *Uncovering Heian Japan. An Archaeology of Sensation and Inscription.* Duke University Press.

Lamberton, Robert. 1997. "Plutarch and the Romanization of Athens." In *The Romanization of Athens*, ed. Michael C. Hoff and Susan I. Rotroff. Oxford: Oxbow Books, 150–60.

——. 2001. *Plutarch.* New Haven and London: Yale University Press.

Larmour, David. 1988. "Plutarch's Compositional Methods in the Theseus and Romulus." In *TAPA* 118, 361–75.

Lausberg, Heinrich. 1960. *Handbuch der literarischen Rhetorik. Eine Grundlegung der Literaturwissenschaft.* München: M. Hueber.

Lee, Thomas H. C. 2000. *Education in Traditional China. A History.* Leiden: Brill.

Legge, James. 1994. *The Chinese Classics. The She King* rpt. Taipei: SMC Publishing.

Lewis, Mark. 1999. *Writing and Authority in Early China.* Albany: State University of New York Press.

——. 2006. *The Construction of Space in Early China.* Albany: State University of New York Press.

Li, Fang. 2006. *Wenyuan yinghua.* Beijing: Beijing tushuguan chubanshe.

Li, Wai-yee. 2001. "Between 'Literary Mind' and 'Carving Dragons': Order and Excess in *Wenxin dialong.*" In *A Chinese Literary Mind. Culture, Creativity, and Rhetoric in Wenxin Diaolong*, ed. Cai Zongqi. Stanford: Stanford University Press, 193–225.

Lloyd, Geoffrey E. R. 2005. *The Delusions of Invulnerability: Wisdom and Morality in Ancient Greece, China and Today.* London: Duckworth.

Lowenstein, Susan Fleiss. 1965. "Urban Images of Roman Authors." In *Comparative Studies in Society and History*, Vol. **8**.1, 110–23.

Lowrie, Michèle. 2009. *Writing, Performance, and Authority in Augustan Rome.* Oxford and New York: Oxford University Press.

Lu, Yan. 2004. *Re-understanding Japan. Chinese Perspectives 1895-1945.* Honolulu: University of Hawai'i Press.

Lu, Xing. 1998. *Rhetoric in Ancient China, Fifth to Third Century BCE: a Comparison With Classical Greek Rhetoric.* Columbia, SC: University of South Carolina Press.

Lurie, David. 2007. "The Subterranean Archives of Early Japan: Recently Discovered Sources for the Study of Writing and Literacy." In *Books in Numbers*, ed. Wilt L. Idema. Cambridge, Mass.: Harvard-Yenching Library, 91–112.

———. 2011. *Realms of Literacy: Early Japan and the History of Writing*. Cambridge, Mass.: Harvard University Press.

———. "The Author Formerly Known as Prince Shōtoku: Royal Authority and Narratives of Literacy in Early Japan." Unpublished Paper.

Ma Maoyuan, ed. 1993. *Chuci zhushi*. Taibei: Wenjin chubanshe.

Macmullen, Ramsay. 2000. *Romanization in the Time of Augustus*. New Haven & London: Yale University Press.

Marrou, Henri Irénée. 1971. *Histoire de l'éducation dans l'antiquité*. Paris: Éditions du Seuil.

Martindale, Charles and Richard F. Thomas, eds. 2006. *Classics and the Uses of Reception*. Malden, MA: Wiley-Blackwell.

Matsumoto Shinsuke. 2007. *Shōtoku Taishi den to kassentan*. Tokyo: Benseisha.

Matsuo Satoshi and Nagai Kazuko, eds. 1997. *Makura no sōshi*. SNKBZ 18. Tokyo: Shōgakkan.

May, James M., ed. 2002. *Brill's Companion to Cicero. Oratory and Rhetoric*. Leiden, Boston, Köln: Brill.

May, James M. and Wisse, Jakob, trans. 2001. *Cicero on the Ideal Orator. De oratore*. New York and Oxford: Oxford University Press.

McCullough, Helen Craig. 1985. *Brocade by Night. Kokin wakashū and the Court Style in Japanese Classical Poetry*. Stanford: Stanford University Press.

McCullough, Helen Craig. 1990. *Classical Japanese Prose. An Anthology*. Stanford: Stanford University Press.

McCullough, William. 1999. "The Capital and Its Society." In *Cambridge History of Japan. The Heian Period*, ed. John W. Hall. Cambridge and New York: Cambridge University Press, 97–182.

McCullough, William H. and Helen Craig McCullough. 1980. *A Tale of Flowering Fortunes. Annals of Japanese Aristocratic Life in the Heian Period*. Stanford: Stanford University Press.

McGinn, Thomas. 1998. *Prostitution, Sexuality, and the Law in Ancient Rome*. Oxford and New York: Oxford University Press.

McKinney, Meredith. 2006. *Sei Shōnagon. The Pillow Book*. Penguin.

Miner, Earl. 1990. *Comparative Poetics. An Intercultural Essay on Theories of Literature*. Princeton: Princeton University Press.

Mitamura Masako. 1994. *Makura no sōshi. Hyōgen to kōzō*. Tokyo: Yūseidō.

Miyazaki, Ichisada. 1976. *China's Examination Hell. The Civil Service Examination of Imperial China*. Trans. Conrad Schirokauer. New York: Weatherhill.

Momo Hiroyuki. 1994. *Jōdai gakusei no kenkyū*. Rev. ed. Kyoto: Shibunkaku Shuppan.

Moreno, Miryam Librán. 2007. "Odiseo, Eneas y la fundación de Roma en las Fuentes griegas." In *De Grecia a Roma y de Roma a Grecia. Un camino de ida y vuelta*, ed. Á. Sánchez-Ostiz et al. Pamplona: Ediciones Universidad de Navarra, 167–85.

Moretti, Franco. 2004. "Conjectures on World Literature." In *Debating World Literature*, ed. Christopher Prendergast. London and New York: Verso, 148–62.

Morford, Mark. 2002. *The Roman Philosophers. From the Time of Cato the Censor to the Death of Marcus Aurelius*. London and New York: Routledge.

Morgan, Teresa. 1998. *Literate Education in the Hellenistic and Roman Worlds*. Cambridge: Cambridge University Press.

Morris, Ivan. 1994. *The World of the Shining Prince. Court Life in Ancient Japan*. Kodansha. Rpt.

Morwood, James. 1991. "Aeneas, Augustus, and the Theme of the City." In *Greece & Rome*. Second Series. Vol.38.2. Oct., 218–21.

Mostow, Joshua. 2004. *At the House of Gathered Leaves*. Honolulu: University of Hawaiʻi Press.

Murray, A. T. and George E. Dimock, trans. 1995. *Homer. The Odyssey*. Loeb Classical Library. Cambridge, Mass.: Harvard University Press.

Mutschler, Fritz-Heiner and Achim Mittag, eds. 2008. *Conceiving the Empire: China and Rome Compared*. Oxford and New York: Oxford University Press.

Nagle, Betty Rose. 1980. *The Poetics of Exile. Program and Polemic in the Tristia and Epistulae ex Ponto of Ovid*. Bruxelles: Latomus.

Nakamura Hajime. 1992. *Shōtoku taishi. Chikyū shikōteki shiten kara*. Tokyo: Tokyo shoseki.

Narducci, Emanuele. 1997. *Cicerone e l'eloquenza romana: retorica e progetto culturale*. Roma-Bari: Editori Laterza.

———. 2002. "Brutus: The History of Roman Eloquence." In *Brill's Companion to Cicero: Oratory and Rhetoric*, ed. James M. May. Leiden and Boston, Brill, 401–25.

Nishimura Satomi. 2005. *Heiankyō no kūkan to bungaku*. Tokyo: Yoshikawa kōbunkan.

Nishiyama Ryōhei. 2004. *Toshi Heiankyō*. Kyoto: Kyoto daigaku gakujutsu shuppankai.

Noy, David. 2000. *Foreigners at Rome. Citizens and Strangers*. London: Duckworth.

Nuchelmans, G. 1957. "Philologia et son marriage avec Mercure jusqu'à la fin du XIIe siècle." In *Latomus* 16, 84–107.

O'Hara, James. 1990. *Death and the Optimistic Prophecy in Vergil's* Aeneid. Princeton: Princeton University Press.

———. 1996. *True Names. Vergil and the Alexandrian Tradition of Etymological Wordplay*. Ann Arbor: The University of Michigan Press.

Okada, Richard. 1991. *Figures of Resistance: Language, Poetry, and Narrating in The Tale of Genji and Other Mid-Heian Texts*. Durham: Duke University Press.

Okimori Takuya et al. 1993. *Kakyō hyōshiki: chūshaku to kenkyū*. Tokyo: Ōfūsha.

Ono Katsutoshi. 1992. *Ru Tang qiufa xunli xingji jiaozhu*. Shijiazhuang: Huashan wenyi chubanshe.

Ōsone Shōsuke. ed. 1965. *Wakan rōeishū*. Shinchō Nihon koten shūsei. Tokyo: Shinchōsha, 1983.

———. 1998a. "Sugawara no Michizane—shijin to kōju." In *Ōsone Shōsuke Nihon kanbungaku ronshū*. Tokyo: Kyūko shoin.

———. 1998b. *Ōsone Shōsuke Nihon kanshibungaku ronshū*. 3 vols.Tokyo: Kyūko shoin.

Owen, Stephen. 1975. *The Poetry of Meng Chiao and Han Yü*. New Haven and London: Yale University Press.

———. 1996a. *Anthology of Chinese Literature. Beginnings to 1911*. New York: W. W. Norton & Company.

————. 1996b. *The End of the Chinese 'Middle Ages': Essays in Mid-Tang Literary Culture*. Stanford: Stanford University Press.

Parker, Patricia. 1990. "Metaphor and Catachresis." In *The Ends of Rhetoric: History, Theory, Practice*, ed. John B. Bender and David E. Wellbery. Stanford: Stanford University Press, 60–76.

Paschalis, Michael. 1997. *Virgil's Aeneid. Semantic Relations and Proper Names*. Oxford: Clarendon Press; New York: Oxford University Press.

Paton, W. R. 1922-1927. *Polybius*. Loeb Classical Library. Cambridge, Mass.: Harvard University Press.

Pelling, C. B. R. 1997. "Is Death the End? Closure in Plutarch's *Lives*." In *Classical Closure. Reading the End in Greek and Latin Literature*, ed. Deborah H. Roberts, Francis M. Dunn, and Don Fowler. Princeton, Princeton University Press, 228–50.

————. 2000. "Rhetoric, Paideia, and Psychology in Plutarch's Lives." In *Rhetorical Theory and Praxis in Plutarch*, ed. L. van der Stockt. Leuven: Peeters. Namur: Société des Etudes Classiques 331–39.

————. 2002. *Plutarch and History. Eighteen Studies*. Swansea: Classical Press of Wales.

Pernot, Laurent. 2005. *Rhetoric in Antiquity*, trans. W. E. Higgins. The Catholic University of America Press.

Perrin, Bernadotte. 1928. trans. *Plutarch's Lives*. 11 vols. Loeb Classical Library. London: William Heinemann.

Persson, Sebastian and Thomas Eske Rasmussen. 2010. trans. *Velleius Paterculus: en kortfattet romersk verdenshistorie*. Copenhagen: Museum Tusculanums forlag, Københavns universitet.

Piggott, Joan. 1997. *The Emergence of Japanese Kingship*. Stanford: Stanford University Press.

Pizer, John. 2006. *The Idea of World Literature. History and Pedagogical Practice*. Baton Rouge: Louisiana State University Press.

Pollack, David. 1986. *The Fracture of Meaning: Japan's Synthesis of China from the Eighth Through the Eighteenth Centuries*. Princeton, N.J.: Princeton University Press.

Ponsonby-Fane, Richard A. 1979. *Imperial Cities: The Capitals of Japan from the Oldest Times until 1229*. Rpt. Washington: University Publications of America.

Powell, Barry B. 2002. *Writing and the Origins of Greek Literature*. Cambridge: Cambridge University Press.

Prendergast, Christopher, ed. 2004. *Debating World Literature*. London, New York: Verso.

Quan Tang shi. 1999. Beijing: Zhonghua shuju.

Quan Tang shiyi. Vol. 13 of *Quan Tang shi*. 1999. Beijing: Zhonghua shuju.

Quint, David. 1993. *Epic and Empire. Politics and Generic Form from Virgil to Milton*. Princeton: Princeton University Press.

Rabinovitch, Judith. 1991. "Wasp Waists and Monkey Tails: A Study and Translation of Hamanari's *Uta no Shiki*. The Code of Poetry, 772, Also Known as *Kakyō Hyōshiki*. A Formulary for Verse Based on The Canons of Poetry." In *HJAS* Vol. 51. 2. Dec., 471–523.

Rabinovitch, Judith and Timothy Bradstock, trans. 2005. *Dance of the Butterflies. Chinese Poetry from the Japanese Court Tradition*. Ithaca: East Asia Program, Cornell University.

Raphals, Lisa A. 1992. *Knowing Words: Wisdom and Cunning in the Classical Traditions of China and Greece*. Ithaca: Cornell University Press.

Reding, Jean-Paul. 1985. *Les fondements philosophiques de la rhétorique chez les sophistes grecs et chez les sophistes chinois*. Bern and New York: Peter Lang.

Reed, J. D. 2007. *Virgil's Gaze. Nation and Poetry in the Aeneid*. Princeton: Princeton University Press.

Reischauer, Edwin O. 1955a. *Ennin's Travels in Tang China*. New York: The Ronald Press Company.

———. 1955b. *Ennin's Diary: The Record of a Pilgrimage to China in Search of the Law*. New York: The Ronald Press Company.

Relihan, Joel. 1993. *Ancient Menippean Satire*. Baltimore and London: Johns Hopkins University Press.

Rimer, J. Thomas and Jonathan Chaves, trans. 1997. *Japanese and Chinese Poems to Sing: the Wakan rōeishū*. New York: Columbia University Press.

Rodd, Laurel Rasplica, trans. 1984. *Kokinshū. A Collection of Poems Ancient and Modern*. Princeton: Princeton University Press.

Rolfe, John C, trans. 1967. *The Attic Nights* of *Aulus Gellius*. Loeb Classical Library. Cambridge, Mass.: Harvard University Press.

Roman, Luke. 2001. "The Representation of Literary Materiality in Martial's 'Epigrams.'" In *JRS*, Vol. 91, 113–45.

Rose, Herbert Jennings. 1936. *A Handbook of Latin Literature from the Earliest Times to the Death of St. Augustine*. London: Methuen & Co.

Rudd, Niall. 1966. *The Satires of Horace*. Cambridge: Cambridge University Press.

Ruden, Sarah. 2008. *The Aeneid. Vergil*. New Haven and London: Yale University Press.

Russell, Donald A., trans. 2001. *Quintilian. The Orator's Education*. 5 vols. Loeb Classical Library. Cambridge, Mass.: Harvard University Press.

Sakaki, Atsuko. 2006. *Obsessions with the Sino-Japanese Polarity in Japanese Literature*. Honolulu: University of Hawaiʻi Press.

Sallis, John. 1999. *Chorology. On Beginning in Plato's Timaeus*. Bloomington and Indianapolis: Indiana University Press.

Sánchez-Ostiz, Á., J. B. Torres Guerra.and R. Martínez, eds. 2007. *De Grecia a Roma y de Roma a Grecia. Un camino de ida y vuelta*. Pamplona: Ediciones Universidad de Navarra.

Satō Michio. 2006. "*Wakan rōeishū*, yōgakusho e no michi." In *WHB* 36, 35–48.

———. ed. 2007. *Kudaishi kenkyū*. Tokyo: Keiō University Press.

Satō Taketoshi. 1974. *Chōan. Kodai Chūgoku to Nihon*. Kyoto: Hōyū shoten.

Saussy, Haun. 1997. "The Prestige of Writing: *Wen*, Letter, Picture, Image, Ideography." In *Sino-Platonic Papers* 75.

———. ed. 2006. *Comparative Literature in an Age of Globalization*. Baltimore: Johns Hopkins University Press.

Scheidel, Walter, ed. 2009. *Rome and China: Comparative Perspectives on Ancient World Empires*. Oxford and New York: Oxford University Press.

Scheidel, Walter, Ian Morris, and Richard P. Saller, eds. 2008. *The Cambridge Economic History of the Greco-Roman World*. Cambridge: Cambridge University Press.

Schmitzer, Ulrich. 2000. *Velleius Paterculus und das Interesse an der Geschichte im Zeitalter des Tiberius*. Heidelberg: Universitätsverlag Winter.

Schwindt, Jürgen Paul. 2000. *Prolegomena zu einer „Phänomenologie" der römischen Literaturgeschichtsschreibung*. Göttingen: Vandenhoeck & Ruprecht.

Selden, Daniel L. and Phiroze Vasunia. *The Oxford Handbook of Literatures of the Roman Empire*. Oxford and New York: Oxford University Press (in preparation).

Shackleton Bailey, D.R. 2000. *Valerius Maximus. Memorable Doings and Sayings*. Cambridge, Mass.: Harvard University Press.

Shankman, Steven. 2000. *The Siren and the Sage: Knowledge and Wisdom in Ancient Greece and China*. London and New York: Cassell.

Shankman, Steven and Stephen W. Durrant, eds. 2002. *Early China/Ancient Greece: Thinking Through Comparisons*. Albany: State University of New York Press.

Shanza, Danuta. 1986. *A Philosophical and Literary Commentary on Martianus Capella's De Nuptiis Philologiae et Mercurii, Book I*. Berkeley: Berkeley University Press.

Shinma Kazuyoshi. 2003. *Genji monogatari to Haku Kyoi no bungaku*. Osaka: Izumi shoin.

———. 2009. *Genji monogatari no kōsō to kanshibun*. Osaka: Izumi shoin.

Shinsen Man'yōshū kenkyūkai, ed. 2005-. *Shinsen Man'yōshū chūshaku*. Osaka: Izumi shoin.

Shipley, Frederick W., trans. 1979. *Velleius Paterculus, Historiae Romanae*. Loeb Classical Library. Cambridge, Mass.: Harvard University Press.

Shirane, Haruo. 1987. *The Bridge of Dreams: a Poetics of the Tale of Genji*. Stanford: Stanford University Press.

———. 2000b. "Curriculum and Competing Canons." In *Inventing the Classics: Modernity, National identity, and Japanese Literature*, ed. Haruo Shirane and Tomi Suzuki. Stanford: Stanford University Press, 220–49.

Shirane, Haruo and Tomi Suzuki, eds. 2000a. *Inventing the Classics: Modernity, National Identity, and Japanese Literature*. Stanford: Stanford University Press.

Smith, Henry. "Tokyo as an Idea: An Exploration of Japanese Urban Thought until 1945." In *JJS*, Vol. 4.1, Winter, 1978, 45–80.

Smits, Ivo. 2000a. "Song as Cultural History: Reading *Wakan Rōeishū*. Texts." In MN 55.2, 225–56.

———. 2000b. "Song as Cultural History: Reading *Wakan Rōeishū*. Interpretations." In *MN* 55.3, 399–427.

———. 2007. "The Way of the Literati: Chinese Learning and Literary Practice in Mid-Heian Japan." In *Heian Japan, Centers and Peripheries*, ed. Mikael Adolphson, Edward Kamens, and Stacie Matsumoto. Honolulu: University of Hawai'i Press, 105–28.

Snodgrass, A. M. 1994. "The Growth and Standing of the Early Western Colonies." In *The Archaeology of Greek Colonisation. Essays Dedicated to Sir John Boardman*, ed. Tsetskhladze, and F. de Angelis. Oxford: Oxford University Committee for Archaeology, 1–10.

Stahl, William Harris. 1971, 1977. *Martianus Capella and the Seven Liberal Arts*. 2 vols. New York: Columbia University Press.

———. 1977. *The Marriage of Philology and Mercury*. New York: Columbia University Press.

Stambaugh, John E. 1988. *The Ancient Roman City*. Baltimore: Johns Hopkins University Press.

Steel, Catherine. 2007. "Lost Orators of Rome." In *A Companion to Roman Rhetoric*, ed.William Dominik and Jon Hall. Malden, Mass.: Blackwell, 237–49.

Steiner, Deborah. 1994. *The Tyrant's Wit. Myths and Images of Writing in Ancient Greece*. Princeton: Princeton University Press.

Steinhardt, Nancy S. 1990. *Chinese Imperial City Planning*. Honolulu: University of Hawai'i Press.

Steininger, Brian. 2010. "Poetic Ministers: Literacy and Bureaucracy in the Tenth-Century State Academy." PhD Dissertation. Yale University.

Suerbaum, Werner. 1968. *Untersuchungen zur Selbstdarstellung älterer römischer Dichter*. Hildesheim: Georg Olms Verlagsbuchhandlung.

Suerbaum, Werner et al., eds. 2002. *Handbuch der lateinischen Literatur der Antike. Erster Band: Die archaische Literatur. Von den Anfängen bis zu Sullas Tod. Die vorliterarische Periode und die Zeit von 240 bis 78 v. Chr.* München: Beck.

Sugano Hiroyuki, ed. 1999. *Wakan rōeishū*. SNKBZ 19. Tokyo: Shōgakukan.

Sun Changwu. 1984. *Tangdai guwen yundong tonglun*. Tianin: Baihua wenyi chubanshe.

Sutton, E. W. and H. Rackham, 1948. trans. *De oratore, together with De fato, Paradoxa stoicorum, De partitione oratoria*. Loeb Classical Series. Cambridge, Mass.: Harvard University Press.

Suzuki Gakujutsu Zaidan, ed. 1970-1973. *Dai Nihon Bukkyō zensho*. 100 vols. Tokyo: Kankō Suzuki Gakujutsu Zaidan, Kōdansha.

Swain, S. C. R. 1989. "Plutarch's *De Fortuna Romanorum*." In *CQ* 39.2, 504–16.

———. 1996. *Hellenism and Empire: Language, Classicism, and Power in the Greek World*, AD 50–250. Oxford: Clarendon Press.

Takahashi Tomio. 1963. *Ezo*. Tokyo: Yoshikawa kōbunkan.

Takeuchi Rizō et al., eds. 1943–44. *Nara ibun*. Tokyo: Yagi shoten.

Tanaka Mikiko. 2006. *Wakan rōeishū to sono juyō*. Ōsaka: Izumi shoin.

Tatsumi Masaaki. 1997. *Man'yōshū to hikaku shigaku*. Tokyo: Ōfūsha.

Thomas, Richard A. 2001. *Virgil and the Augustan Reception*. Cambridge: Cambridge University Press.

Tian, Xiaofei. 2007. *Beacon Fire and Shooting Star: the Literary Culture of the Liang*. 502–57. Cambridge, Mass.: Harvard University Press.

Toby, Ronald P. 1985. "Why Leave Nara? Kammu and the Transfer of the Capital." In *MN*, Vol. 40.3. Autumn, 331–47.

Tōkyō daigaku kyōyō gakubu, ed. 2007. *Koten Nihongo no sekai. Kanji ga tsukuru Nihon*. Tokyo: University of Tokyo Press.

Tōno Haruyuki. 1977. "Rongo Senjimon to Fujiwara no miya Mokkan" In Tōno Haruyuki, *Shōsōin monjo to Mokkan kenkyū*. Tokyo: Hanawa Shobō.

———. 1999. *Kentōshisen. Higashi Ajia no naka de*. Tokyo: Asahi Shinbunsha.

Tsuboi Kiyotari and Tanaka Migaku. 1991. *The Historic City of Nara. An Archeological Approach*, trans. David H. Hughes and Gina L. Barnes. Tokyo, Centre for East Asian Cultural Studies/UNESCO.

Tyler, Royal. 2001. *The Tale of Genji*. New York: Viking.

Ury, Marian. 1999. "Chinese Learning and Intellectual Life." In *The Cambridge History of Japan. Heian Japan*, ed. Donald H. Shively and William H. McCullough. Cambridge: Cambridge University Press, 341–89.

van Goethem, Ellen. 2008. *Nagaoka. Japan's Forgotten Capital*. Leiden and Boston: Brill.

von Verschuer, Charlotte. 1985. *Les relations officielles du Japon avec la China du VIIIe au IX siècles*. Genève, Droz.

———. 2006. *Across the Perilous Sea: Japanese Trade with China and Korea from the Seventh to the Sixteenth Centuries*. Ithaca: East Asia Program, Cornell University.

Verrusio, Maria. 1977. *Livio Andronico e la sua traduzione dell' Odissea Omerica*. Rome: Giorgio Bretschneider.

von Albrecht, Michael. 2003. *Ovid. Eine Einführung*. Stuttgart: Reclam.

Wakan hikaku bungakkai, ed. 1986-87. *Chūko bungaku to kanbungaku*. 2 vols. Tokyo: Kyūko shoin.

Walker, Susan. 1997. "Athens under Augustus." In *The Romanization of Athens*, ed. Michael C. Hoff and Susan I. Rotroff. Oxford: Oxbow Books, 67–80.

Wallace-Hadrill, Andrew. 2008. *Rome's Cultural Revolution*. Cambridge and New York: Cambridge University Press.

Wang Yong. 1994. *Shōtoku Taishi jikū chōetsu: rekishi o ugokashita Eshi kōshinsetsu*. Tokyo: Taishūkan shoten.

———. 1998. *Tō kara mita kentōshi. Konketsujitachi no Dai Tō teikoku*. Tokyo: Kōdansha.

Wang Zhenping. 2005. *Ambassadors from the Islands of Immortals. China-Japan Relations in the Han-Tang Period*. Honolulu: University of Hawai'i Press.

Warmington, E. H. 1982. *Remains of Old Latin II*. Loeb Classical Library. Cambridge, Mass.: Harvard University Press.

Waterfield, Robin. 2008. *Plato. Timaeus and Critias*. Oxford and New York: Oxford University Press.

Weinbrot, Howard D. 2005. *Menippean Satire Reconsidered. From Antiquity to the Eighteenth Century*. Baltimore: John Hopkins University Press.

Welch, Tara. 2005. *The Elegiac Cityscape: Propertius and the Meaning of Roman Monuments*. Columbus: Ohio State University Press.

West, David. 1997. *Horace. The Complete Odes and Epodes*. Oxford and New York: Oxford University Press.

Wheatley, Paul and Thomas See. 1978. *From Court to Capital. A Tentative Interpretation of the Origins of the Japanese Urban Tradition*. Chicago: The University of Chicago Press.

White, Peter. 1993. *Promised Verse. Poets in the Society of Augustan Rome*. Cambridge, Mass.: Harvard University Press.

———. 2002. "Ovid and the Augustan Milieu." In *Brill's Companion to Ovid*, ed. Barbara Weiden Boyd. Leiden, Boston, Köln: Brill, 1–25.

Whitmarsh, Tim. 2005. *The Second Sophistic*. Oxford: Oxford University Press.

Williams, Gareth. 2002. "Ovid's Exilic Poetry: Worlds Apart." In *Brill's Companion to Ovid*, ed. Barbara Weiden Boyd. Leiden, Boston, Köln: Brill, 337–81.

———. 1994. *Banished Voices: Readings in Ovid's Exile Poetry*. Cambridge: Cambridge University Press.

Wiseman, Peter and Anne Wiseman, trans. 2011. *Ovid: Times and Reasons. A New Translation of* Fasti. Oxford: Oxford University Press.

Wisse, Jakob. 1995. "Greeks, Romans, and the Rise of Atticism." In *Greek Literary Theory after Aristotle*, Festschrift D.M. Schenkeveld. Amsterdam: VU University press, 65–82.

———. 2002a. "The Intellectual Background of Cicero's Rhetorical Works." In *Brill's Companion to Cicero: Oratory and Rhetoric*, ed. James M. May. Leiden and Boston: Brill, 331–74.

———. 2002b. "*De oratore*: The Orator, Rhetoric, and Philosophy." In *Brill's Companion to Cicero: Oratory and Rhetoric*, ed. James M. May. Leiden and Boston: Brill, 375–400.

Wixted, John Timothy. 1983. "The Kokinshū Prefaces: Another Perspective." *HJAS* 43.1, 215–38.

———. 1998. "*Kanbun*, Histories of Japanese literature, and Japanologists." In *Sino-Japanese Studies* 10.2, 23–31.

Woodman, A. J. 1975. "Velleius Paterculus." In *Empire and Aftermath. Silver Latin II*, ed. T. A. Dorey. London: Routledge, 1–25.

Woolf, G. D. 1994. "Becoming Roman, Staying Greek. Culture, Identity and the Civilizing Process in the Roman East." In *Proceedings of the Cambridge Philological Society* 40, 116–43.

———. 1998. *Becoming Roman. The Origins of Provincial Civilization in Gaul.* Cambridge: Cambridge University Press.

Woolf, Greg. 2003. "The City of Letters." In *Rome the Cosmopolis*, ed. Catharine Edwards and Greg Woolf. Cambridge: Cambridge University Press, 203–21.

Wright, W. C., trans. 1952. *Philostratus and Eunapius. Lives of the Sophists*. Loeb Classical Library. Cambridge, Mass.: Harvard University Press.

Wu, Fusheng. 1998. *The Poetics of Decadence. Chinese Poetry of the Southern Dynasties and Late Tang Periods*. Albany: SUNY Press.

Wyke, Maria. 1987. "Written Women: Propertius' Scripta Puella" In *JRS*, Vol. 77, 47–61.

Yamada Yoshio. 1942. *Sakura shi*. Tokyo: Sakura Shobō.

Yamaguchi Yoshinori and Kōnoshi Takamitsu. 2007. *Kojiki*. SNKZ. Tokyo: Shōgakukan.

Yang, Guobin, trans. 2003. *Wenxin diaolong*. 2 vols. Beijing: Waiyu jiaoxue yu yanjiu chubanshe.

Yang Xiong. 1987. *Fayan yishu*. Beijing: Zhonghua shuju.

Yoshida Eitetsu and Okuda Kiyoaki. 1995. *Kakikudashi Shōtoku taishi denryaku*. Tokyo: Sekai seiten kankō kyōkai.

Yoshikawa Shinji. 2002. *Heiankyō. Nihon no jidaishi* 5. Tokyo: Yoshikawa kōbunkan.

Zetzel, James. 2002. "Dreaming About Quirinus: Horace's *Satires* and the Development of Augustan Poetry." In *Traditions and Contexts in the Poetry of Horace,* ed. Denis Feeney and Tony Woodman. Cambridge University Press, 38–52.

———. 2003. "Plato with Pillows: Cicero on the Uses of Greek Culture." In *Myth, History and Culture in Republican Rome. Studies in Honour of T. P. Wiseman.* Exeter: University of Exeter Press, 119–38.

———. 2005. Review of Elaine Fantham. *The Roman World of Cicero's* De Oratore. New York and Oxford: Oxford University Press, 2004 in *Bryn Mawr Classical Review* 09.05.

Zhang Buyun. 1984. *Tangdai Zhong Ri wanglai shi jizhu.* Xi'an: Shanxi renmin chubanshe.

Zhang Longxi. 1998. *Mighty Opposites: From Dichotomies to Differences in the Comparative Study of China.* Stanford: Stanford University Press.

———. 2007. *Unexpected Affinities: Reading Across Cultures.* Toronto, Buffalo, London: University of Toronto Press.

Zhang Xihou. 1995. *Wang Ji yanjiu.* Taibei: Xin wen feng chuban gufen youxian gongsi.

Abe clan, 126

Abridged Biography of Prince Shōtoku. See Shōtoku taishi denryaku

Academics (Platonic Academy), 38, 234

Accius, 72, 115

Account of the Eastern Expedition of the Great Tang Priest (Tō daiwajō tōseiden) (Mifune), 125

Achaean League, 36, 83

Actio, 88

Actium, battle of, 33–34

Aeneas, 16, 17, 18–19, 120–24, 127–34, 139–46, 147, 151–53, 154, 172–74, 298

    foreign edge of, 120–21, 127–28

    pietas of, 121, 139

    popularity of, 123

    Shōtoku compared with, 124, 135, 138, 153

Aeneas and the Building of Carthage (Vergilius Vaticanus), 145(figure)

Aeneid (Virgil), 17, 18–19, 113, 121, 122–24, 127–28

    city-building motif, 139–46, 147, 153

    described, 122

    as a double text, 123

    literacy theme absent in, 151–53, 298

    prophecy motif, 127, 128–34, 135, 138–39

    Rome envisioned in, 160, 172–74, 186–200

    Shōtoku taishi denryaku compared with, 123, 124, 138–39

    twists added to myth in, 128

Aeschylus, 35

Age of the Masters, 82

Agglutinative languages, 46

Akahito, Yamabe no, 81, 99

Akazome Emon, 190

Akihira, Fujiwara no, 167, 236

Akihito, Emperor of Japan, 159

Alaric, 238

Alcaeus, 113

Alexander the Great, 8, 34, 36, 37, 84, 275

Alkimos, 127

Allegorical satire. *See De Nuptiis Philologiae et Mercurii*

Alphabetic languages, 46–47, 296

Altar of Peace *(Ara pacis),* 120

Amaterasu, 66, 161, 164

American paradigm of world literature, 291–92

Amores (Ovid), 219

Analects, 21, 29, 30–31, 47, 66, 71, 99, 100, 241

    described, 23

    opening text of, 31(figure)

Ancus Marcius, 166

Anecdotal literature *(setsuwa),* 61

Ankō, Emperor of Japan, 185

Annals (Ennius), 45, 58, 113

Anthologia Palatina, 179n46

Antiochus III of Seleucid Empire, 36

Antonius Pius, 53

Apion, 9

Apocolocyntosis divi Claudii (Pumpkinification of Emperor Claudius) (Seneca), 255

Apologus, 28

Apostrophe, 224
Aptum, 88
Apuleius, 254, 264
Ara pacis (Altar of Peace), 120
Aratus, 223
Archilochus, 113
Aretê, 171
Aristarchus of Alexandria, 22, 29
Aristophanes, 114
Aristotle, 57, 88, 105, 106, 255, 296
Ars amatoria (Art of Love) (Ovid), 204, 222
"Asiatic" style, 86, 89, 108–9, 111, 118
"Asking the Autumn Moon"
    (Michizane), 227–28
Assmann, Jan, 9
Asuka, 154, 175
Atlantis, 2, 3
Attalus, 22
Atticism, 86, 89, 103, 107–13, 117, 118
    Roman, 111–12, 298
Attic Nights (Aulus), 53
Atticus, 72, 73, 74–76, 80, 108, 112
Auerbach, Erich, 291, 294
Augustan Period, 17, 18, 115, 116, 160, 161,
    170, 177
Augustus, 33–34, 60, 76, 120, 157, 164,
    170, 192–93
    Aeneid on, 122, 123, 124, 128, 140, 142,
        153, 173
    Ovid exiled by, 17, 203, 204, 207,
        209–10, 219, 222, 223, 224
    Varro Reatinus and, 72
Aulus Gellius, 53, 54, 55
Authorized transgression, 240–41
Auto-apology, 224, 225
Auto-apotheosis, 224, 225
"Autumn Thoughts" (poetry theme),
    210–12
Ax, Wolfram, 82n3
Axial Age paradigm, 10

Bakhtin, Mikhail, 218
Ban Gu, 267
Barbarianism, 5, 6, 17, 50, 55
Bedford Anthology of World Literature,
    290

Beecroft, Alexander, 293
Bi (comparison), 94
Bicanonical education, 46, 295
Bidatsu, Emperor of Japan, 121, 136
Bilingual literary cultures, 46, 49, 56,
    295
Biliterate literary cultures, 46, 48, 56,
    295
Binary comparative approach, 12–13
"Biography of the Iron Hammer"
    (Ratai), 236
Bioi parallêloi (Parallel Lives) (Plutarch),
    18, 266, 275–86
    double beginnings in, 283–86
    Rome and Athens in, 278–83
    Shinsen Man'yôshû compared with,
        287–88
    synkrisis in, 276–78, 286
Black Sea Letters (Ovid). *See Epistulae ex
    Ponto*
Boethius, 219
Bo Juyi, 180, 181, 252, 267
    Makura no sôshi allusions to, 196–97,
        200
    Michizane influenced by, 208,
        209, 211, 214, 216, 217, 218, 227,
        228–29, 230, 233
Book of the Han Dynasty, 26
Book of the Later Han Dynasty, 26
Brandes, Georg, 291
Brush talk, 48, 151
Brutus (Cicero), 16, 72–76, 298
    autobiographical history of oratory
        in, 74
    described, 72
    home-coming image in, 72, 74
    natural history of oratory in, 73–74,
        75, 76, 79, 108
    reception history of oratory in, 74, 76
    simplicity in, 86, 103, 107–13, 119
Brutus, Decimus Junius, 222. *See also
    Brutus* (Cicero)
Brutus, Lucius Junius, 120
Buck, Philo, 290
Buddhism, 12, 41, 44–45, 83, 94
    arrival in China, 134

language and, 48
Michizane on, 228
persecution of followers, 33, 44
Shōtoku's role in introducing, 121,
    124–27, 135–39, 148, 150, 151
textual canon of, 26
Tiantai (Tendai) school of, 124,
    125, 148
Bun. See Wen
Büring, Johann Gottfried, 7
Byōdōin, 155

Caesar, 57, 72, 103, 123, 275
*Caesar's Calendar: Ancient Time
    and the Beginnings of History*
    (Feeney), 3–4
Caesura, 276
Callimachus, 21, 84, 113, 114
Calvus, 107, 109, 111
Camena, 50, 58, 59
Camillus, 208
Cang Jie, 67, 68, 151
Cao Pi, Emperor of China, 99
Cao Zhi, 99
Capella, Martianus, 18, 238–39,
    253–62, 264, 299. *See also De Nuptiis
    Philologiae et Mercurii*
Capital laments, 175–76, 185
Capitals, 16–17, 154–202. *See also* Kyôto;
    Rome (capital)
    romance vectors in, 17, 160–61,
        186–202
    time vectors in, 17, 160, 169–86
    unequal, 161–69
Carneades of Cyrene, 38
Cassius Salanus, 223–24
Catachresis, 13, 202, 299–300
Catiline conspiracy, 219
Cato the Elder, 5, 38, 53, 57, 102
    in *Brutus*, 72, 73–76, 79, 108, 111–12
    decline narratives of, 81–82, 83, 87
Cato the Younger, 208
Catullus, 187, 194
Cento, 179
Chantefable tradition, 238
Chen Dynasty, 137

Cherry Tree, 156(figure), 159, 242
*Cherry Tree in the Inner Imperial Palace,
    The* (Yoshiiku), 156(figure)
Chest-Tail defect, 94n19
Che Yin, 251
China
    age of culture in, 1–2
    centralized rule in, 7
    conquest by Japan, 33, 36
    marginality of Japan to, 44–45
    missions from Japan to, 42–44
Chinese canon, 26, 46, 48
Chinese language, 46–49
Chinoiseries, 7
Chisatoshû (Chisato Collection) (Chisato),
    240–41, 267
Chōka ("long poems"), 96
Chreia, 28
Chronicles of Japan. See Nihon shoki
Chrysippus, 258–59
Cicero, 16, 18, 21, 38, 49, 53, 72–76, 79,
    80, 102, 103–13, 117, 118, 119, 208, 275,
    296, 298. *See also* specific works of
    Capella influenced by, 253, 255
    importance as a literary mediator, 86
    on language enrichment, 54–55
    Ovid compared with, 219
    as self-proclaimed oratory
        champion, 74
City-building, 139–46, 147, 153
Claassen, Jo-Marie, 219
Classic of Changes, 67, 147
Classic of Poetry. See Shijing
Classics, 13–15
Code of Waka Poetry (Fujiwara no
    Hamanari). *See Uta no Shiki*
*Collection of Ancient and Modern Poems.
    See Kokinshū*
*Collection of Japanese and Chinese-style
    Poems for Recitation. See Wakan
    rôeishû*
*Collection of Myriad Leaves. See
    Man'yôshû*
Comedy, 60, 84
    New, 60
    Old, 60, 114, 116, 235

Como, Michael, 124n8, 125, 126

Comparative approaches
  binary, 12–13
  deep, 295–96, 300
  layered, 297–99
  ontological, 12–13

Comparative fallacy, 296

Comparative imperative
  overview, 10–19
  revisited, 289–94

Comparative Poetics (Miner), 294

*Compendium of Roman History
  (Historiae Romanae)* (Velleius),
  76–80

Competitive imitation, 77, 79

"Composed to Myself" (Michizane),
  208, 209, 218

Confucian Classics, 20, 22, 27, 51, 69,
  82, 84, 299
  Fu Hikaru Genji monogatari shi on,
    250
  reasons for studying, 8
  track of study devoted to, 26

Confucianism, 6, 24, 28, 82, 188
  Fu Hikaru Genji monogatari shi on,
    252
  Genji monogatari on, 241
  satire and, 234
  wen in, 66–67

Confucius, 84
  death of, 82
  Kokinshū on, 71
  on ornament and substance, 87
  ritual observances to, 24, 216

"Conjectures on World Literature"
  (Moretti), 289–90

Consolations (Seneca), 219

Consolations of Philosophy (Boethius),
  219

Consolatory letters, 219

Constantinople, 155

Contaminatio, 60

Conte, Gian Biagio, 134

Continuity, 14, 50, 56, 113, 176, 177, 267

Controversiae, 28

Copia, 88, 109

Core/periphery model of education, 28

Coriolanus, 208

Cornelius Severus, 222

Corpus Hermeticum, 9

Cosmogony, 69–70, 71–72

Cosmology, 267–70

Cotta Maximus, 222

Couplet culture, 178

Crassus, Lucius Licinius, 38, 103–4,
  105–7

Crates of Mallos, 22, 24, 29

Critias, 2–4

Critical marks, 29, 30, 31

Crypto-colonialism, 34

Cultural capital, 1, 16, 37, 98

Cultures
  daughter, 4, 5
  host, 5
  literary (*see* Literary cultures)
  mother, 4, 5
  reference (*see* Reference cultures)
  relative age of, 1–4
  source, 5
  target, 5

Cursus honorum, 161

Cynics, 105, 255, 257

Cyrenaics, 105, 255

Daigakuryō (State Academy), 22, 26, 27,
  51, 162, 182
  importance of, 24–25
  Michizane's service in, 205
  satire and, 234, 237, 242, 244,
    245, 253

Daigo, Emperor of Japan, 69, 71,
  184, 206, 209, 210–11, 226, 228, 231

Daijōkan, 162

Damrosch, David, 289

Danjo kon'in fu ("Rhapsody on the
  Marriage of Husband and Wife")
  (Asatsuna), 270

Dao (*michi*; the Way)
  in *Kokinshū*, 69–72, 79, 80
  Yakamochi-Ikenushi correspondence
    on, 98, 99

Daoists, 234

Dardanus, 127, 128, 133, 134

Daughter cultures, 4, 5

Dazaifu, 17, 203, 206, 214, 215–17, 232, 266

Decline narratives, 81–83, 85–86, 87, 95, 103–7, 116, 117, 119. See also specific works

Deep comparison, 295–96, 300

Demosthenes, 106, 110

De Nuptiis Philologiae et Mercurii (The Marriage of Philology and Mercury) (Capella), 18, 238–39, 253–62, 264, 299
  historical context of, 238
  plot of, 254
  role of clothing in, 259–62

De oratore (On the Orator) (Cicero), 16, 38, 73, 85, 86, 112, 117
  De Nuptiis Philologiae et Mercurii compared with, 253
  on rhetoric vs. philosophy, 104, 105–7, 118
  on sapientia, 103, 104–5, 107, 112, 117

De re publica (On the Republic) (Cicero), 73, 104

Des Tropes (Dumarsais), 299

Detached Palace, 175

Dialogues of the Dead (Lucian), 257–58

Dialogus de oratoribus (Dialogue on Orators) (Tacitus), 85–86

Diaochonglun (Discussion of Insect Carving) (Pei), 100n30

Diaries. See Nikki

"Did Rome gain hegemony thanks to fate or virtue?" (Plutarch), 288

Diodorus Diculus, 8

Diogenes Laertius, 255n46, 257

Dionysius of Halicarnassus, 55, 111n52, 127, 128, 133, 157–59

Dionysius I of Syracuse, 35

Disciplinarity, 297–99

Discussion of Insect Carving (Diaochonglun) (Pei Ziye), 100n30

Dispositio, 88

Double-Ninth Festival, 150, 210–12

Douglas, Gavin, 122

"Dragon carving," 98–100

Dragon texts, 68

Drama and theater, 7, 16
  literary cultures lacking, 59
  Noh, 11, 56, 167, 235
  standing in genre hierarchy, 56, 57, 58, 59–60, 296

Drama of continuity, 50

Drama of translation, 50, 56, 58–59

Dream of the Red Chamber (Story of the Stone), 134–35

Dryden, John, 122

Dual-structure hypothesis, 40

Duff, Tim, 276–77

Dumarsais, César Chesneau, 299

Du Xunhe, 180

Eckermann, Johann Peter, 289

Eckstein, Arthur, 35–36, 40

Eclogues (Virgil), 113

Edo (city), 155

Edo (period), 235

Education, 15–16, 83
  bicanonical, 46, 295
  canonical hierarchy in, 26
  canons adopted and adapted in, 22–23
  core/periphery model of, 28
  deep comparisons of, 295–96
  satire on (see De Nuptiis Philologiae et Mercurii; Fu Hikaru Genji monogatari shi; Genji monogatari)
  state involvement in, 24–26, 32
  tracks of study in, 26–27
  tricanonical, 46, 48, 56, 295

Egypt, 36, 40
  archeological excavations in, 28, 29–30
  failure to become a reference culture, 8–10
  relative age of culture, 2–4

Eibutsushi (Poems on Things), 229

Eiga monogatari (Tale of Flowering Fortunes) (Michinaga), 177

Elegies, 84
    epistolary, 218–19, 233
    love, 160–61, 187–94, 219
    praise, 201
    standing in genre hierarchy, 57
Elegies (Propertius), 17, 154, 190, 191–94
    Makura no sōshi compared with,
        198–202
    recusatio in, 192–94, 199–201, 202
Eliot, T. S., 122n2
Ellipsis, 13, 202
Elocutio, 88
Emishi tribes, 163
Enchō Tamura, 125
Encomia/encomium, 28, 288
"Encountering Sorrow" (Qu Yuan). *See*
    Lisao
Engi Era, 226
Enkyklios paideia, 27
Ennin, 33, 44–45, 63n3
Ennius, 22, 23, 24, 45, 50, 58, 103, 113,
    114, 115, 127
Ensai, 150
Entire Body defect, 94n19
Envy theme, 77, 79, 80
En'yū, Emperor of Japan, 181
Eoyang, Eugene, 293
Epic of Gilgamesh, 139
Epics, 16, 84
    on city-building, 139–40
    literary cultures lacking, 56, 59
    love elegies compared with, 187, 188,
        189, 201
    standing in genre hierarchy, 56, 57,
        58–59, 296
Epicureans, 105, 234
Epigram tradition, 57, 187
Epistolary elegies, 218–19, 233
Epistulae ex Ponto (Black Sea Letters)
    (Ovid), 205, 219
Epodes (Horace), 113, 115
Eshi. *See* Huisi
Essays *(zuihitsu),* 190–91
*Essential History of the Song Dynasty
    (Song lüe)* (Pei Ziye), 100n30
Etruscan (language), 45

Etruscans, 35, 41
Euripides, 28, 35, 215
Eusebius, 4n3
Examination system (Japanese), 26, 27,
    32, 57, 182, 236, 242
Exile poetry, 17, 203–33, 296. *See also*
    Sugawara no Michizane; Ovid;
    specific works

Fabii family, 57, 205
Fabius Pictor, 46, 57, 127, 164
Fabula, 28
Fachprosa, 57
Fagles, Robert, 122
Farrell, Joseph, 54n71
Farris, William Wayne, 41
Fasti (Ovid), 166, 204, 223
Favorinus, 25
Feeney, Denis, 3–4, 46n55, 73, 152
Feng ("Airs"), 94
Ficus ruminalis, 157
Fitzgerald, Robert, 122
"Five Constants," 250n31
Five Dynasties Period, 43
Florilegium of Cherished Airs. See Kaifūsō
Flourish, 94, 101–2, 105
Foreign edge of founding figures,
    120–21, 124–28
"Four tones and eight faults" rule
    (sisheng babing), 92
Frederick the Great, 7
Freudenburg, Kirk, 113–14n55
Fu (enumeration), 60, 94, 174, 267
Fūdoki (Records of Wind and Earth), 66
Fugu ("Returning to Antiquity"), 82
*Fu Hikaru Genji monogatari shi (Genji
    Poems),* 18, 59, 237–38, 239, 248–53
    confusing closure in, 251–53
    De Nuptiis Philologiae et Mercurii
        compared with, 254, 262, 299
    historical context of, 237
    lack of scholarly attention to, 299
    male voice in, 248
    on public *vs.* private space, 249, 250,
        251, 264
Fujiwara (city), 164, 166

Fujiwara (family), 24, 26, 162, 182, 189, 237
    Michizane and, 205, 207, 211, 266
    women of, 186
Fujiwara Katsumi, 229
Fujiwara no Fuhito, 90
Fujiwara no Kintō, 177–86. *See also*
    Wakan rōeishū
Fujiwara no Michinaga, 177
Fujiwara no Muchimaro, 92
Fujiwara no Nobuomu, 184
Fujiwara no Tadanobu, 194–200
Fujiwara no Tanetsugu, 168
Fujiwara no Tokihira, 205–6, 209, 231
Fujiwara no Kintō, 177–86. See also
    Wakan rōeishō
Fukuhara, 169
Fulvius Nobilior, 58
Fumi no Obito, (lineage of scribes), 21
Fu Xi, 67, 68, 151

Ganjin (Jianzhen), 124–25
Gender. *See also* Women
    Genji monogatari on, 240–41
    language and, 48
    romance vectors and, 189, 190
Genji monogatari (Tale of Genji)
    (Murasaki Shikibu), 18, 61, 160, 174, 186, 187, 237, 239–53, 264, 293
    anti-*recusatio* in, 299
    as authorized transgression, 240–41
    as historiography, 248–51
    Michizane evoked in, 230
    picture scroll of, 252(figure)
    on public *vs.* private space, 239–40, 241, 242, 245, 247–48
Genji Poems. See Fu Hikaru Genji monogatari shi
Genre hierarchies, 14, 56–61
    deep comparisons of, 295, 296
    of Kyoto, 174–76
    romance vectors in, 187, 188
Geopolitics, 32–45
    conquest and, 33–39
    major differences in, 39–44

Georgics (Virgil), 215
Germanicus, 223–24
Gloss-reading. *See Kundoku*
Goethe, Johann Wolfgang, 77, 289–91
Golden Ass (Apuleius), 254, 264
Golden Latinity, 82
Golden Pavilion, 156
Gossamer Diary (Kagerō nikki) (Mother of Michitsuna), 189
Gotō Akio, 229
Grammar, 21–22, 23, 24, 29
Grand Palace of Kadono, 168
Greece
    age of culture, 1–4
    Bioi parallêloi on, 278–83
    conquest by Alexander the Great, 8
    conquest by Rome, 33, 34, 35, 36–39, 83
    conquest of Western Mediterranean, 34–35, 83, 139
    Hellenic connection to founding of Rome, 127
    as Magna Graecia, 34, 35, 41, 127
Greek language, 45–47, 57
Green, Peter, 213
Gruen, Erich, 74n26
Guangwu, Emperor of China, 42
Gunki monogatari (War Tales), 58

Habinek, Thomas, 76
Hadrian, 23, 53, 275
Haikai (haiku), 235, 240, 298
Hamamatsu Chūnagon monogatari (Tale of Middle Councilor Hamamatsu), 139
Hamanari, Fujiwara no, 16, 92–96, 105, 117, 118. *See also Uta no Shiki*
Handbook of Latin Literature (Rose), 238
Han Dynasty, 26, 28, 29, 41, 42, 84, 151, 174
Han History, 82
Hanihara, Kazurô, 40
Hardie, Philip, 123
Hare ("formal"), 69
Hartley, L. P., 105
Hata clan, 126, 168
Hatooka Akira, 214

Head-Tail defect, 94n19
Heian-kyō (Kyoto), 154, 157, 168
Heian Period, 2, 33, 48, 57, 58, 65, 69, 154, 202
    education during, 24, 26, 28, 29
    Kyôto during, 155, 157, 161, 162, 163, 169
    satire during, 235, 237
Heijō, 164
Hellenism, self-reflexive, 113–16
Hellenismos, 88
Hellenistic literature, 84
Hellenistic Period, 21
"Hellenistic Six Dynasties Period," 21
Hermotimos e peri haireseôn
    ("Hermotimus or about philosophical schools") (Lucian), 256–57
Herodotus, 8, 152, 204
Heroides (Ovid), 219, 233
Herzenbildung, 290
Herzfeld, Michael, 34, 37
Hesiod, 3
Heteroscopic approach to studies, 298
Herodotus, 132
Hexagrammatic literacy, 68, 69, 75, 79, 151
He Yan, 29
Himiko, Queen of Japan, 120
Hinds, Stephen, 58, 113
Historiae Romanae (Compendium of Roman History) (Velleius Paterculus), 76–80
Historical flatness, 4, 13, 16, 61, 65, 83, 299
Historical Records (Sima Qian). *See Shiji*
Histories (Polybius), 170
Historiography, 57, 84, 248–51
Kakinomoto no Hitomaro, 71, 81, 99, 175, 178
Homer, 3, 8, 21, 28, 29, 49, 58, 83, 84, 128, 172, 179, 292, 296. *See also* specific works of
    Ennius on, 113
    Horace on, 115

literacy theme absent in works of, 152–53
    Ovid on, 210
    Virgil influenced by, 122, 123, 132, 133
Homophone Rhyme defect, 94n19
Honchō monzui (Literary Essence of Our Court) (Akhira), 236
Horace, 16, 60, 86, 102, 103, 112–16, 117, 118, 119, 190, 194, 207, 235. *See also* specific works of
    Capella compared with, 255
    Rome envisioned by, 171–72
"Horace moment," 103, 113–16, 118
Horapollon Nilotes, 9
Horikawa, Emperor of Japan, 157
Hortensius, 111
Host cultures, 5
Huang niao ("Yellow Bird"), 208–9
Huisi (Eshi), 17, 120, 124–25, 126, 135, 136–37, 149, 150
Hutcheon, Linda, 236
Hut of Romulus, 157–59, 170

Iamblichus, 8
Ibis (Ovid), 219
Iccius, 171–72
Iconization, 7, 10, 18
Iliad (Homer), 29, 30(figure), 122, 123, 127, 133, 292, 295
Imperial Palaces (Japan), 155, 159, 162, 181, 182
Index locorum, 14
Influence studies, 293
"Insect carving," 90, 98–100
Institutio (Quintilian), 28
Inventio, 88
Inventor trope, 58, 113–16, 118, 299
Ise Shrines, 164
Isokola, 88–89
Isolating languages, 46
Izumi Shikibu, 190

Jakobson, Roman, 88
Japan
    age of culture, 1–2
    centralized rule in, 7, 66

claims to uniqueness in, 4
conquest and colonization by, 33,
   34, 36
female emperors of, 120
foundation of empire, 120
marginality to China, 44–45
missions to China, 42–44
origins of, 39–40
Japanese language, 46–48
Japanese Preface to *Kokinshū* (Ki no
   Tsurayuki), 69, 101–2
Jaspers, Karl, 10
Jerome, 4n3
Jianzhen (Ganjin), 124–25
Jin Dynasty, 137
Jingū, Empress of Japan, 68
Jinmu, Emperor of Japan (legendary),
   67n9, 120, 124, 161, 176
Jinshin War, 92
Jitō, Empress of Japan, 175
Jōmon Period, 40
Journey to the West, 134
Jukkaishi (Poems on "Expressing One's
   Inner Feelings"), 229
Jusha (Confucian Scholars), 242
Jūshichijō kenpō ("Seventeen
   Article Code of Conduct")
   (Shōtoku), 148
Juvenal, 235, 255

Kagerō nikki (Gossamer Diary) (Mother
   of Michitsuna), 189
Kaifūsō (Florilegium of Cherished Airs),
   16, 51, 53, 66–69, 79, 80
   Brutus compared with, 75
   described, 66
   ornament and, 85, 89–92
   on Shōtoku, 150–51
Kakinomoto no Hitomaro, 71, 81, 99,
   175, 178
Kakyō hyōshiki (Model Forms for the
   Canon of *Waka* Poetry), 92
Kamakura Period, 237
Kamakura shogunate, 154–55, 237
Kamatari, Nakatomi no, 92
Kamen, Edward, 202n78

Kan (Chinese-style), 267. *See also*
   Wa-kan division
Kana, 160, 186, 196, 266
Kanbun (Sino-Japanese literature),
   47–48, 60, 121, 293. *See also* specific
   works
Kaneie, Fujiwara no, 189
Kanemichi, Fujiwara no, 181
Kanezane, Fujiwara no, 169
*Kanke kōshū (Later Collection of the
   Sugawara Family)* (Michizane), 214,
   218
Kanmu, Emperor of Japan, 154, 157,
   168–69, 175
Kanpyō no ōntoki kisainomiya
   no utaawase *(Poetry Contest
   of the Kanpyō era for his
   Majesty)*, 266
Kanshi (Sino-Japanese poetry), 16, 51,
   56, 57, 92, 118, 139, 185, 265. *See also*
   specific works
   romance vectors and, 186
   in *Shinsen Man'yôshû*, 266–74
   Yakamoch-Ikenushi correspondence
   and, 97
Kantō, 154
Katai, 92
Ke ("informal"), 69
Kenkei (riddle type of poetry), 95
Kidendō (literature and history track),
   26, 242
Ki no Haseo, 214
Ki no Tsurayuki, 101–2, 105, 118
Ki no Yoshimochi, 81, 83, 87, 101, 102,
   105
Kinai rulers, 164
Kindlers Literatur Lexikon, 291
Kishi clan, 126
Kitano Tenmangu Shrine, 212, 231
Koguryo, 41, 42, 83, 126
Koizumi, Junichiro, 120
Kojiki (Record of Ancient Matters), 21, 23,
   24, 29, 41, 57, 66, 161
*Kokinshū (Collection of Ancient and
   Modern Poems; Kokinwakashū)*, 16,
   61, 67, 93, 94, 249, 253

Kokinshū (Cont.)
  Cicero's work compared with, 104,
    112, 117, 118
  dao in, 69–72, 79, 80
  described, 69
  reverse view from, 100–102
  romance works and, 186
  Shinsen Man'yōshū compared with,
    266, 267, 288
  simplicity and, 85, 86, 117
  Velleius Paterculus's work compared
    with, 299
"Kokinshū moment," 86, 103, 112, 117
Kokinwakashū. See Kokinshū
Kokubungaku (national literary studies),
    4, 293
Kōnin, Emperor of Japan, 92
Kōnin Period, 65
Korea, 14, 36, 174
  conquest by Japan, 33
  education influenced by, 24, 25
  geopolitics influenced by, 39, 40,
    41, 44
  immigrant lineages from, 83,
    125–27
  literary culture of, 48
  writing system and, 67, 68–69
Kōtoku, Empress of Japan, 121
Kudaishi (Topic Poetry), 60–61, 178
Kudai waka (Waka on Topic Lines)
    (Chisato), 267
Kundoku (gloss-reading), 30–31, 47
Kuni, 164, 175
Kyō (stimulus), 272, 274
Kyōgen, 235
Kyoto, 7, 42, 43, 154–69
  as "Capital of Peace," 154, 163
  cityscape of, 155–59
  founding of, 154
  government of, 161–62
  ideological significance of, 164
  literacy of, 167–68
  map of, 165(figure)
  romance vector and, 17, 186–91,
    194–202
  social life in, 167

as a symbolic capital, 155
time vector and, 17, 174–86
topography of, 164–66

LaMarre, Thomas, 69
"Lamplight Gone" (Michizane), 212–13
Language, 45–56. See also Literacy
  agglutinative, 46
  alphabetic, 46–47, 296
  isolating, 46
  logographic, 47
  preservation patterns and, 53–54
  SOP, 46
  source, 5
  SPO, 46
  target, 5
Latecomers, 16, 20, 84–85. See also
    Decline narratives; Ornament;
    Simplicity
Later Collection of the Sugawara Family
    (Michizane). See Kanke kōshū
Late Republican Period, 53, 57, 60
  oratory during, 74, 79
  simplicity during, 85, 86, 89, 102–16
Latin (language), 45, 46, 47, 48,
    54–55, 57
Latinitas, 88
Latium, 2, 5, 130, 132, 133–34, 142, 146,
    154, 162
Lavinium, 121, 122, 123, 131, 139, 154
Layered comparison, 297–99
Legalists, 234
Lesser genres, 57, 59
Letters from Pontus (Ovid), 17
Liang Dynasty, 137
Liber Annalis (Atticus), 73
Liezi, 270
Liji (Record of Rites), 204, 249
Lingering Fragrance Festival
    (yōkosai), 212
Linked poems (renku), 182–83
Lion's Roar Sutra, 148
Lisao ("Encountering Sorrow")
    (Qu Yuan), 208, 228
Literacy, 147–53. See also Language;
    Writing

absence of theme in *Aeneid,* 151–53, 298
deep comparisons of, 295
differences in patterns, 46
hexagrammatic, 68, 69, 75, 79, 151
of Kyoto, 167–68
Shōtoku taishi denryaku on, 147–51
Literary cultures, 4, 10–11, 12, 13, 15–16
Cicero's contributions to, 76
deep comparisons of, 295–96
dissimilitudes in, 32–61
education in (*see* Education)
genres in (*see* Genre hierarchies)
geopolitics in (*see* Geopolitics)
increased popularity of studies, 295
language and (*see* Language)
latecomer status and (*see* Latecomers)
refinement in, 20–21
similarities in, 20–32
Literary density, 83
Literary Essence of Our Court (Honchō monzui) (Akhira), 236
Literary history, 62–65
Literary Mind and the Carving of Dragons, The (Wenxin diaolong) (Liu Xie), 87n6
Literary Selections. See Wenxuan
Literati, 242n13
Liu Xie, 87, 89
Liu Yuxi, 211
Livia, 204, 223
Livius Andronicus, 58, 59, 84, 102
as a teacher, 21, 22, 23, 24, 25
translations by, 49–50, 52–53
Livy, 57, 77, 161, 164, 166, 170, 174
Logicians, 234
Logographic languages, 47
Lombardo, Stanley, 122
"Longing for my bamboo at home on a snowy night" (Michizane), 229
Longman Anthology of World Literature, 290
Lotus Sutra, 125, 148, 149–50
Love elegies, 160–61, 187–94, 219
Lowrie, Michèle, 153

Lucian of Samosata, 255, 256–59
Lucilius, 86, 113–16, 117, 118, 119
Lucretius, 54
Ludi Romani, 59
Ludi scenici, 59
Lu Ji, 99
Luoyang, 166
Lupercal Cave, 159
Lüshi (regulated poetry), 20, 92
Lycurgus, 276, 279, 283–86
Lysias, 75, 111

Macedonian Wars, 36
Macer, 222
Maecenas, 115, 190, 191, 192–94, 199, 201
Magna Graecia, 34, 35, 41, 127
Mahabharata, 292
Makura no sōshi (Pillow Book) (Sei Shōnagon), 17, 154, 161, 186, 194–202
Elegies compared with, 198–202
plot of, 194–98
subtlety in, 194–95
unusual format of, 190–91
Manetho, 9
Man'yōgana script, 266, 267
Man'yōshū (Collection of Myriad Leaves), 16, 51, 53–54, 61, 71, 85, 118, 157, 215, 293
on capitals, 174, 175
on ornament *vs.* simplicity, 96–100
Marc Aurel, 53
Marcus Aper, 86
Mark Antony (Marcus Antonius), 34, 72, 104
Marriage of Philology and Mercury, The (Martianus Capella). *See De Nuptiis Philologiae et Mercurii*
Martianus Capella. *See* Capella, Martianus
Martindale, Charles, 14–15
Marx, Karl, 290
Master Texts, 134, 147, 270
Maternus, 86
Meltzl, Hugo, 291
Memorable Doings and Sayings (Valerius Maximus), 32, 37

Memoria, 88
Menander, 28, 60
Menippeae (Varro), 255
Menippean satire, 235, 239, 255–59, 262
Menippus of Gadara, 235
Messalinus, 222
Messalla Corvinus, 115, 204, 222
Metamorphoses (Ovid), 204, 215
Michi. See Dao
Michizane Bidding Farewell to his Red
    Plum Tree in Kyoto When
    Departing for Exile (picture scroll),
    232(figure)
Middle Republic Period, 2
Mighty Opposites: From Dichotomies to
    Differences in the Comparative Study of
    China (Zhang Longxi), 12
Minamoto no Nobukata, 197
Minamoto no Yoritomo, 169
Miyako no Yoshika , 182
Miner, Earl, 293, 294
Model Forms for the Canon of Waka
    Poetry (Kakyō hyōshiki), 92
Mohists, 234
Mokkan (wooden tablets), 30
Mole defect, 94n19
"Monkey Music," 236
Monmu, Emperor of Japan, 90–92
Monobiblos, 191
Monogatari (tale literature), 61, 160, 174,
    186–91, 195. See also specific works
Monolingual literary cultures, 45, 46,
    48, 295
Monoliterate literary cultures, 46, 56,
    295
Mononobe clan, 126, 135, 137
Moralia (Plutarch), 275
Moretti, Franco, 289–90
Morgan, Teresa, 28
Morris, Ivan, 174
Morwood, James, 140
Mos maiorum, 157
Mother cultures, 4, 5
Mother of Michitsuna, 189
Moulton, Richard G., 290
Murakami, Emperor of Japan, 157

Murasaki Shikibu, 18, 61, 160, 174, 186,
    187, 190, 196, 230, 237, 239–53. See
    also Genji monogatari
Muromachi Period, 155
Mussolini, Benito, 120
Mutual virtual history, 102–3, 117–18, 119
Myōbōdō (Law track), 26, 242
Myōgyōdō (Classics track), 26, 242
Monjōdō (Literature track), 26
Mystery cults, 9
Myth of exile, 219

Naevius, 103, 127
Nagaoka, 164, 168
Nagaya, Prince, 92
Nagle, Betty Rose, 219
Naipaul, V. S., 292
Nakatomi family, 126, 135, 137
Naniwa, 164, 175
Nanyue Peak, 125
Nara (city), 7, 42, 43, 177, 184–85
    capital lament on, 175
    founding of, 164
Nara (period), 2, 57, 118
    education during, 28, 29
    government during, 161, 162
    ornament during, 88
Narratio, 28
National literary studies. See
    Kokubungaku
Neoteric poetry, 187
Nepos, 275
Nero, 207
New Comedy, 60
Newly Selected Collection of Myriad
    Leaves. See Shinsen Man'yōshū
New Monkey Music (Shin sarugaku ki)
    (Fujiwara no Akihira), 167
Niebuhr, Barthold Georg, 76
Nihon (Japan), 6
Nihonjinron, 39–40
Nihon shoki (Chronicles of Japan), 41, 57,
    66, 71, 72, 126, 150, 161, 248
Nikki (diaries), 61, 160, 186–91. See also
    specific works
Ninken, Emperor of Japan, 185

Nittō guhō junrei kōki (*Record of a Pilgrimage to Tang China in Search of the Law*) (Ennin), 33
Noh theater, 11, 56, 167, 235
Nukata, Princess, 51–53
Numa Pompilius, 157, 276, 279, 283–86

Obelos, 29
Object reference, 7, 10
Octavian. *See* Augustus
Odes (Horace), 113, 115, 172
Odoacer, 155
Odusia (Livius), 49–50, 52–53
Odyssey (Homer), 29, 49, 84, 128
Ōe clan, 24, 182, 242
Ōe no Asatsuna, 181, 270
Ōe no Chisato, 240–41, 267
Ōe no Masafusa, 62–65, 69, 72. *See also* specific works of
Ōe no Masahira, 121
O'Hara, James, 129
Ōjin, Emperor of Japan, 68
Old Comedy, 60, 114, 116, 235
Old Poems, 267
Ōmi, 168, 175–77
Ōmi no Mifune, 124–25
Ōmiwa no Takechimaro, 90
"On a bamboo armchair" (Michizane), 216–17
On Agriculture (Cato), 53, 72
Ondoku, 47n59
On Grammarians and Rhetors (Suetonius), 22, 23
Onmyōdō, 94
"On Reading the Imperial Edict Announcing the Beginning of the New Era" (Michizane), 226–27
On the Ends of Good and Evil (Cicero), 54
On the Orator (Cicero). *See De oratore*
On the Republic (Cicero). *See De re publica*
Ono no Imoko, 149–50
Ontological comparative approach, 12–13
Opici tribe, 82
Orange Tree. *See* Tachibana Orange Tree
Oratory, 84

Brutus on, 72–76, 79, 108
decline of, 86
of Ovid, 222–26
"Organ Extraordinary" (Ratai), 236
Ornament, 82, 85, 86, 87–119
debates on simplicity *vs.*, 96–100, 102–16
elusiveness of, 87–89
embracing, 89–102
Ornatus, 87, 88
Oscan (language), 45
Ōsone Shōsuke, 229
Ōtomo no Ikenushi, 96–100, 118
Ōtomo no Tabito, 215
Ōtomo no Yakamochi, 96–100, 117, 118
Ōtomo, Prince, 51, 52–53, 90
Ōtsu, Prince, 81, 85, 90–91, 92, 101, 102, 105, 112
Out-pasting, 3–4, 299
Ovid, 17, 166, 187, 190, 206–15, 218–26, 230–33, 296. *See also* specific works of
addressivity of, 218–22, 227, 231
impact of exile on, 203–5, 206
letters to wife, 219, 220–22
life and works of, 204
pleas of, 222–26
as poet-provocateur, 207–13
realism in works of, 213–15
reason for exile of, 204, 207
Ovid Among the Scythians (Delacroix), 216(figure)
Owen, Stephen, 293

Paekche, 21, 23, 41, 42, 83, 126, 148
Palatine, 157, 159, 166
Pallanteum, 128, 133, 135, 144
Palliatae, 60
Panaetius, 114, 172
Panathenaic Games, 3
Pan Yue, 88, 99
Parallelism, 51, 52, 88–89, 94
Parallel Lives (Plutarch). *See Bioi paralléloi*
Parhae, 163
Paullus, L. Aemilus, 114

Paullus Fabius Maximus, 222
Pedagogy, 290–91
Pei Ziye, 100n30
Pelling, Christopher, 276
Pericles, 275
Perilla, 219, 222
Peripatetics, 38, 234
Peripatos, 105
Persians (Aeschylus), 35
Persius, 235, 255
Perspicuitas, 88
Persuasive speeches, 88
Phaedrus (Plato), 152
Phaenomena (Aratus), 223
Philip V of Macedon, 36
Philo of Larissa, 107
Philosophies for Sale (Lucian), 258–59
Philosophy
    rhetoric *vs.*, 104, 105–7, 118
    satire and, 234–37 (*see also De Nuptiis
        Philologiae et Mercurii*)
Philoxenos, 55
Phoenix Hall, 155
Pietas, 121, 139
Pillow Book (Sei Shōnagon). *See Makura
    no sōshi*
Pillow words, 176, 185
Pizer, John, 290
"Planting Chrysanthemums"
    (Michizane), 229–30
Plato, 2–4, 72, 152, 253, 255, 278, 296.
    See also specific works of
Platonic Academy, 38, 105, 106, 107, 114
Plautus, 50, 53, 55, 60, 102
Pliny, 82
Plutarch, 8, 18, 170–71, 266, 275–86,
    288. *See also* specific works of
Poetic banquets, 52, 150, 241, 242,
    243n15
Poetic elaboration, 241
Poetic expositions (*fu*), 267
Poetic faults, 92, 93, 94
Poetics (Aristotle), 57
Poetogony, 71–72, 79
Poetry. *See also* specific works
    development of, 84

epic (*see* Epics)
exile (*see* Exile poetry)
haikai (haiku), 235, 240, 298
kanshi (*see* Kanshi)
kenkei, 95
kudaishi, 60–61, 178
lüshi, 20, 92
neoteric, 187
praise, 174–75
renku, 182–83
rhyme in, 92, 93
standing in genre hierarchy, 57–58
uta, 51–53
waka (*see* Waka)
*Poetry Contest of the Kanpyō era for
    his Majesty* (*Kanpyō no ōntoki
    kisainomiya no utaawase*), 266
Political capital, 1, 16, 37
Politum, 74
Pollio, 115
Polybius, 114, 170, 174
Pompey the Great, 103, 208
Ponsonby-Fane, Richard A., 164
Pontifices, 157
Porcius Licinius, 72
Powell, Barry, 152
Praise elegies, 201
Praise poems, 174–75
Praise speeches. *See Encomia/
    encomium*
Prefaces
    development of genre, 60
    to *Fu Hikaru Genji monogatari shi*,
        248–53
    to *Kaifūsō* (*see Kaifūsō*)
    to *Kokinshū* (*see* Japanese Preface
        to *Kokinshū*; *Kokinshū*; Sino-
        Japanese Preface to *Kokinshū*)
    to *Shijing*, 63–64, 69, 70, 94, 235,
        274
Prince Shōtoku Lecturing on the Lion's
    Roar Sutra, 148(figure)
Progymnasmata, 28
Propertius, 17, 113, 123, 154, 161, 187,
    190, 191–94, 198–202. *See
    also Elegies*

Prophecy, 127, 128–34, 135, 138–39
Prosopopoeia, 28, 224
Ptolemy II Philadelphus, 21
Public *vs.* private space, 239–40, 241,
    242, 245, 247–48, 249, 250, 251,
    263–64
*Pumpkinification of Emperor Claudius
    (Apocolocyntosis divi Claudii)*
    (Seneca), 255
Punic Wars, 22
Pyrrhus, King of Epirus, 35
Pythagorean philosophy, 35

Qi Dynasty, 137
Qin Dynasty, First Emperor of, 45
Qing Dynasty, 26
Quadrivium, 27, 238
Quintilian, 27, 28, 30, 54, 60, 61, 114,
    187, 235, 300
Qu Yuan, 207–8, 217, 228, 230

Ransom of Hector (Dionysius I), 35
Ratai ("Organ Extraordinary"), 236
Realism, 213–18
Reception studies, 8, 15, 293–94, 297
Record of Ancient Matters. See Kojiki
*Record of a Pilgrimage to Tang China in
    Search of the Law (Nittō guhō junrei
    kōki)* (Ennin), 33
Record of Rites. See Liji
"Record on the Land of Drunkenness"
    (Wang Ji). *See Zuixiangji*
"Record on the Land of Stillness and
    Enlightenment" (Ennin), 63n3
"Record on the Realm of Poetry"
    (Masafusa). *See Shikyōki*
Records of the Grand Historian, 26
Records of Wind and Earth (Fūdoki), 66
Recusatio, 59, 60, 188, 296, 299
    in *Elegies*, 192–94, 199–201, 202
    in *Makura no sōshi*, 199–201, 202
Reference cultures, 1, 4–10, 21, 61, 84,
    116, 128, 295, 299
    allusions to, 8
    bibliographical dimension, 8
    conquest and, 33

defined, 4
education and, 16, 22, 24, 32, 83
ethical dimension, 6
language and, 45
legal meaning, 6
linguistic sense, 7
literary history and, 65
manifold perspectives on, 2
material dimension, 6–7
romance vectors and, 200
satire and, 17, 18, 234–35
synoptic texts and, 265
Refinement, literary, 20–21
Reform movements, 82–83, 89
Refusal trope. *See Recusatio*
Regulated poetry. *See Lüshi*
Reincarnation, 134–39
    popularity as narrative device,
        134–35
    prophecy compared with, 134, 135,
        138–39
    as *Shōtoku* theme, 120, 124–25,
        128–29, 135–39
Remus, 157
Renku (linked poems), 182–83
Republic (Plato), 3
Rerum rusticarum libri tres (Varro), 72
Returning to antiquity *(fugu)*
    movements, 82
Reverse *kundoku*, 47
Rhapsodies *(fu)*, 60, 84, 98, 174, 267,
    270
"Rhapsody on daybreak" (Xie Guan), 180
"Rhapsody on the Marriage of Husband
    and Wife" *(Danjo kon'in fu)* (Ōe no
    Asatsuna), 270
Rhetoric
    Brutus on, 72
    De oratore on, 104, 105–7, 118
    standing in genre hierarchy, 57–58
    study of, 23, 28
    of *synkrisis* in Plutarch, 276–78
Rhyme, 92, 93
Riddle type of poetry *(kenkei)*, 95
Ritsuryō (statutory law) *system*, 161
Rituals of the Zhou (Zhou li), 182

Roaming Wind defect, 94n19
Roman Atticism, 111–12, 298
Romance vectors, 186–200
    of Kyoto, 17, 186–91, 194–202
    of Rome, 17, 160–61, 186–94,
        198–202
Rome (capital), 16–17, 154–67
    cityscape of, 155–59
    current status as capital, 155
    founding of, 155
    government of, 161
    ideological significance of, 164
    imaginary plan of, 167(figure)
    romance vector and, 17, 160–61,
        186–94, 198–202
    social impact of military expansion,
        162–63
    sophistication of, 166–67
    time vector and, 17, 169–74
    topography of, 166
Rome (empire)
    age of culture in, 1–2
    Bioi parallêloi on, 278–83
    conquest of Greece, 33, 34, 35,
        36–39, 83
    expulsion of Greeks from, 38
    founding of republic, 120
Romulus, 120, 122, 140, 173, 191, 275,
    277–86
    as Aeneas's grandson, 127
    death of, 279
    Hut of, 157–59, 170
    in light of Numa Pompilius, 283–86
    Rome in the biography of, 278–83
    synkrisis for, 277–78, 286
Romulus Agustulus, 155
Rose, H. J., 238
Rudd, Niall, 114n55
Ruden, Sarah, 122
Rulin waishi (The Scholars) (Wu Jingzi),
    235
Rushdie, Salman, 292
Ryōshi (bureau exam), 27

Saichō, 125
Saimon, 212

Sainte-Beuve, Charles Augustin, 76
Sallust, 57
Sandō (mathematical track) 26, 242
Sangyōgisho ("The Three Sutra
    Commentaries") (Shōtoku), 148–49
Sanshi (Three Histories), 236
Sapientia, 103, 104–5, 107, 112, 117
Sappho, 84, 113
Satire, 17–18, 234–36, 265. See also
    specific works
    Menippean, 235, 239, 255–59, 262
    standing in genre hierarchy, 57, 60,
        296
Satires (Horace), 16, 86, 103, 112–16
Sawara, Prince, 168
Scaevola, Quintus Mucius, 104
Scholars, The (Rulin waishi) (Wu Jingzi),
    235
Schwindt, Jürgen Paul, 74n27, 79
Scipio Aemilinus, 114, 208
Sei Shônagon, 17, 154, 161, 186, 194–202.
    See also Makura no sōshi
Sekiten, 24, 216
Selections of Refined Literature. See
    Wenxuan
Seleucid Empire, 36, 40
Self-colonization, 1, 34, 39
Self-reflective approach to studies, 298
Self-reflexive Hellenism, 113–16
Seneca, 208, 219, 255
Sententia, 28
Servius Tullius, 132, 164
Setsuwa (anecdotal literature), 61
Seven Hills, 166
Seven Liberal Arts, 18, 238, 253, 254,
    261, 263(figure)
"Seven Sages of the Bamboo Grove,"
    229
"Seventeen Article Code of
    Conduct" (Jūshichjiō kenpō)
    (Shōtoku), 148
Sextus Pompeius, 222
Shiji (Historical Records) (Sima Qian),
    151, 214, 248
Shijing (Classic of Poetry), 20, 84, 92,
    208–9

date of compilation, 65
Great Preface to, 63–64, 69, 94,
    235, 274
Shinsen Man'yōshū compared with,
    267, 272, 274
Shikyōki ("A Record on the Realm of
    Poetry") (Masafusa), 62–65
Shimada no Tadaomi, 229
Shin sarugaku ki (New Monkey Music)
    (Fujiwara no Akihira), 167
*Shinsen Man'yōshū (Newly Selected
    Collection of Myriad Leaves)*, 18,
    266–74
    Bioi parallêloi compared with,
        287–88
    cosmology in, 267–70
    described, 266
    poetic agency in, 272–74
    poetic logic in, 270–72
Shitennōji temple, 121, 126
Shōshi (ministry exam), 27
Shōtoku, Prince, 16, 17, 18–19, 123,
    135–39, 147–51, 153, 154
    Aeneas compared with, 124, 135, 138,
        153
    birth of, 135–36
    cult of, 121
    as first author in Japanese history,
        148–49
    foreign edge of, 120–21, 124–27
*Shōtoku taishi denryaku (Abridged
    Biography of Prince Shōtoku)*,
    123–27, 153
    Aeneid compared with, 123, 124,
        138–39
    described, 121
    literacy motif, 147–51
    reincarnation motif, 120, 124–25,
        128–29, 135–39
Shun, Emperor of China, 217
Signatures, 59
Silk Road, 163, 235
Silla, 41, 42, 83, 126, 135, 163
Silver Latinity, 82
Sima Qian, 151, 214, 248, 250
Simplicity, 82, 85, 86, 94, 102–19

Attic (*see* Atticism)
    in decline narrative, 103–7
    Hellenism and, 113–16
    wa-kan game and, 96–100
Sinographic sphere, 48–49, 151
Sino-Japanese canon, 46
Sino-Japanese literature. *See* Kanbun
*Sino-Japanese Poems Composed on the
    Tale of Shining Genji (Genji Poems)*.
    See Fu Hikaru Genji monogatari shi
Sino-Japanese poetry. *See* Kanshi
Sino-Japanese Preface to *Kokinshū*
    (Ki no Yoshimochi), 69, 81, 85, 94,
    101, 103
    Cicero's work compared with, 105,
        112, 118
    excerpts from, 70–72
Sino-Japanese War, 33
Sisheng babing ("four tones and eight
    faults" rule), 92
Six Dynasties Period, 5, 15, 20, 23, 36, 52
    development of poetry during, 84
Six Dynasties Period
    ornament during, 82, 87, 88, 89,
        92, 117
Six Poetic Modes, 93, 94
Socius Senecio, 278–79
Socrates, 3
    De Nuptiis Philologiae et Mercurii on,
        255, 256, 258
    De oratore on, 85, 103–7, 112
Soga clan, 126, 137
Solon, 2–3
Sone no Yoshitada, 181
Song ("Hymns"), 94
Song Dynasty, 26, 182
*Song lüe (Essential History of the Song
    Dynasty)* (Pei Ziye), 100n30
SOP languages, 46
Sōshi, Empress of Japan, 190
Source cultures, 5
Source language, 5
Spitzer, Leo, 291
SPO languages, 46
Stahl, William, 238
State Academy (Japan). *See Daigakuryō*

"Stating my Feelings" (Prince Ōtsu), 91
Steiner, Deborah, 152
Stesichoros, 132
Stimulus. See Kyō
Stoics, 38, 105, 234, 256, 259
Story of the Stone (Dream of the Red Chamber), 134–35
Strabo, 8, 127
Suasoria, 28, 225, 226
Substance, 87, 88, 89, 94, 101–2, 105
Suetonius Tranquillus, 22, 23, 24, 29, 45, 49
Sugawara family, 24, 182, 242
Sugawara no Fumitoki, 121, 184–85
Sugawara no Michizane, 17, 18, 181, 184, 205–18, 226–33, 296. See also specific works of
    addressivity of, 218, 220–21
    first banishment of, 205
    impact of exile on, 203–4, 206
    letters to wife, 220–21
    life of, 205
    pleas of, 226–30
    as poet-official, 207–13
    realism in works of, 213–18
    reason for exile of, 206, 207
    rehabilitation of, 212, 231
    Shinsen Man'yōshū attributed to, 266
Sui Dynasty, 42
Suiko, Empress of Japan, 124, 148
Sulla, 103, 104
Sulpicia, 189
Sun Kang, 251
Suzaku Avenue, 163
Synchronizing, 4n3
Synkrisis, 276–78, 286
Synoptic machine, 265, 266, 274, 278, 283, 287–88
Synoptic texts, 17, 18, 265–88. See also specific works

Tachibana Orange Tree, 157, 159
Tachibana no Norimitsu, 194, 197
Tacitus, 57, 85–86
Taihō legal code, 90

Taira clan, 121, 169
Taira no Kiyomori, 169
Tale literature. See Monogatari
Tale of Flowering Fortunes (Eiga monogatari) (Michinaga), 177
Tale of Genji (Murasaki). See Genji monogatari
Tale of Middle Councilor Hamamatsu (Hamamatsu Chūnagon monogatari), 139
Tales of the Heike, The, 58, 292
Tales of Ise, 187, 188
Tang Dynasty, 5, 20, 26, 28, 36, 42, 43, 44, 57, 137, 182
    decline narratives during, 82
    development of poetry during, 84
    ornament during, 87, 88, 117
Tanka ("short poems"), 96. See also Waka
Tao Qian, 230
Tao Yuanming, 230
Tarentum, 35
Target cultures, 5
Target language, 5
Tarquinius Superbus, 120
Tebtunis Papyrus, 29, 30(figure)
Teishi, Empress of Japan, 190, 191, 195, 196
Telos, 129, 130, 132, 133, 138, 145–46, 161, 172
Temmu, Emperor of Japan, 92
Temple of Vesta, 155
Tendai school of Buddhism. See Tiantai school of Buddhism
Tenji, Emperor of Japan, 50–52, 90, 92, 168, 175, 176–77
Tenjin, 231, 232
Tenmu, Emperor of Japan, 51, 90, 168
Terence, 53, 60, 102
"Terrains of Text in Mid-Heian Court Culture" (Kamens), 202n78
Theater. See Drama and theater
Theocritus, 113, 215
Theodosius, 155
Theophrastus, 88

Theseus, 275, 277–86
  Athens in the biography of, 278–83
  death of, 279–80
  in light of Lycurgus, 283–86
  synkrisis for, 277–78, 286
Thousand Character Classic, 21, 23, 29
Three Histories (Sanshi), 236
Three Kingdoms Period, 41, 83, 126
"Three Relations," 250n31
"Three Sutra Commentaries, The"
  (Sangyōgisho) (Shōtoku), 148–49
"Three Teachings," 250
Thucydides, 109–10
Tiantai (Tendai) school of Buddhism,
  124, 125, 148
Tiberius, 76, 204, 223
Tibullus, 187, 188, 207
Timaeus (Plato), 2–4, 8
Time vectors, 17, 160, 169–86
  of Kyoto, 17, 174–86
  of Rome, 17, 169–74
*Tō daiwajō tōseiden (Account of the
  Eastern Expedition of the Great Tang
  Priest)* (Ōmi no Mifune), 125
Tokugawa shogunate, 155
Tokyo, 155
Tomb Period, 41
Tomis, 203, 204–5, 215, 216
Topic Poetry. *See Kudaishi*
Tosa nikki (Tosa Diary), 189
Tragedy, 58, 59, 60, 84
Trajan, 23
Translatio, 5, 13, 34, 41, 43
Translation, 16, 47, 49–50, 52–56, 298
  deep comparisons of, 295, 296
  drama of, 50, 56, 58–59
  from source to target language, 5
Transposition, 296
Tricanonical education, 46, 48, 56, 295
Tristia (Ovid), 17, 205, 209–10, 211, 212
  addressivity in, 218–19, 220–22
Trivium, 27, 238
Trojan War, 123, 139, 140–41, 142, 144
Tullia, 219
Tusculan Disputations (Cicero), 219
Tychê, 171

Uda, Emperor of Japan, 180, 205, 206, 211
Umbrian (language), 45
Universal way. *See Dao*
Uta ("song, poetry"), 51–53
Uta no Shiki (Code of Waka Poetry)
  (Fujiwara no Hamanari), 16, 85, 92–96

Valerius Maximus, 32, 37
Valerius Soranus, 72
Varro Reatinus, 72, 157, 255
Velleius Paterculus, 16, 18, 76–80, 299
Vernacular Japanese canon, 26, 46
Vernacular Japanese poetry. *See Waka*
Verres, 111
Vietnam, 14, 36, 48, 174
Vimalakirti Sutra, 149
Vipstanus Messalla, 86
Virgil, 17, 18, 28, 113, 115, 179, 190, 204,
  215, 296. *See also* specific works of
Volcacius Sedigitus, 72
Vulture Peak, 125

Wa ("Japanese"), 6, 40, 42, 267
Wabun, 48
Wadô Era, 92
Waist-Tail defect, 94n19
Waka on Topic Lines (Kudai waka)
  (Chisato), 267
Waka (vernacular poetry), 16, 105, 117,
  118, 139, 185, 265. *See also* specific
  works
  current writing in form of, 298
  earliest treatise on, 85
  elegance and literary knowledge in,
    92–96
  Kokinshū importance to, 69, 70, 71,
    79
  in *Makura no sōshi*, 197, 199, 200
  public and private, 240
  romance vectors and, 186
  in *Shinsen Man'yōshū*, 266–74,
    287–88
  standing in genre hierarchy, 56–57, 61
  women writing in, 196
  Yakamoch-Ikenushi correspondence,
    96–100

Wakan hikaku bungakkai (Wa-kan/Sino-Japanese Comparative Literature Association), 293

Wa-kan polarity, 118
  beginnings of, 96–100
  Fu Hikaru Genji monogatari shi and, 264

Wakan rōeishū (Collection of Japanese and Chinese-style Poems for Recitation), 17, 56, 160, 177–86
  as authorized transgression, 241
  "Forbidden City," 178, 179, 181–84
  "Mountain and Water," 179
  "Old Capitals," 178, 179, 184–85
  "Old Palaces," 178
  "Water, with Fishermen," 178, 179–81

Wa-kan/Sino-Japanese Comparative Literature Association *(Wakan hikaku bungakkai)*, 293

Walking Muse, The: Horace on the Theory of Satire (Freudenburg), 113–14

Wang Ji, 63

Wang Xizhi, 147

Wani-kishi, 21, 23, 25, 29

Warring States Period, 147

War Tales (gunki monogatari), 58

Wei Dynasty, 99, 166

Weltliteratur, 77, 289–91

Wen (bun)
  defined, 66
  in *Kaifūsō*, 66–67, 69, 79, 89–90
  Kokinshū on, 69–70, 71, 79
  ornament and, 87, 88, 89–90, 95
  in *Shōtoku taishi denryaku*, 123–27

Wen, King of China, 66–67, 71, 137

Wenxin diaolong (The Literary Mind and the Carving of Dragons) (Liu Xie), 87n6

Wenxuan (Literary Selections; Selections of Refined Literature), 26, 27, 174, 235–36

Western Han Dynasty, 178

Western Zhou Dynasty, 20

"What Is a Classic?" (Eliot), 122n2

Winding Stream Banquet, 96, 150

Wisse, Jakob, 107

Wixted, John Timothy, 69

Women. *See also* Gender; individual women
  education of, 48
  Genji monogatari on, 245–48
  romance written by, 186, 189, 190, 196, 201
  of Rome, 167

Women of Aetna (Aeschylus), 35

World Literature, 289–94

World Literature and Its Place in General Culture (Moulton), 290

World Masterpieces, 290

World Republic of Letters (Masafusa's vision of), 62, 64

Writing, 67–69, 79. *See also* Literacy
  earliest introduction to Japan, 23
  naturalization of, 67–68

Wu (martial), 89–90

Wu, Emperor of China, 26, 28

Wu, Empress of China, 137

Wu, Fusheng, 87n7

Wu Jingzi, 235

Wuzong, Emperor of China, 33, 44, 45

Xie Guan, 180

Xing ("evocative image"), 94

Xuanzong, Emperor of China, 6

Ya, 94

Yamanoue no Okura, 215

Yamato, 42, 66, 163, 164, 177

Yang strokes, 68

Yang Xiong, 98, 117

Yayoi Period, 40

"Yellow Bird" *(Huang niao)*, 208–9

Yellow Emperor, 151

Yin strokes, 68

Yin-Yang learning, 94, 234

Yōkosai (Lingering Fragrance Festival), 212

Yoshino, 175

"You Dark Heaven" (Michizane), 208–9

Yu, Anthony, 293

Yu, Pauline, 293

Yuan Zhen, 211, 267

Zai Yu, 100

Zerubavel, Eviatar, 3

Zetzel, James, 104n36

Zhang Longxi, 12, 293

Zheng Xuan, 29

Zuihitsu (essays), 190–91

Zhou Dynasty, 66, 137

Zhou li (Rituals of the Zhou), 182

Zhuangzi, 134

Zuixiangji ("A Record on the
  Land of Drunkenness") (Wang Ji),
  63, 65